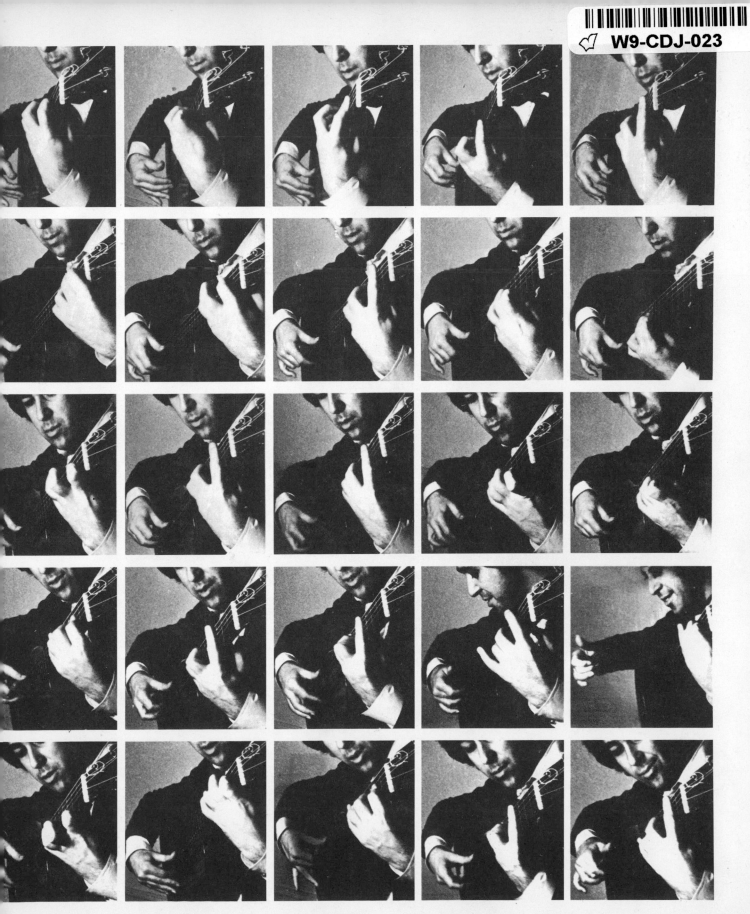

GUITARS
From the Renaissance to Rock

To Stella

from Bruce

11/80

Tom and Mary Anne Evans

GUITARS

Music, History, Construction and Players
From the Renaissance to Rock

Facts On File
119 West 57th Street, New York, N.Y. 10019

Library of Congress Cataloging in Publication Data

Evans, Tom, 1949–
   Guitars: music, history, construction and players
from the Renaissance to rock.

   Bibliography: p.
   Includes index.
   1. Guitar. I. Evans, Mary Anne, joint author.
II. Title.
ML 1015.G9 E9   787'.61   77-4461
ISBN 0-87196-321-3
Previously 0-448-22240-X

TABLE OF CONTENTS

ACKNOWLEDGMENTS   8

INTRODUCTION: The family of the guitar   10

THE CLASSICAL GUITAR   14
THE INSTRUMENTS
The vihuela and the four-course guitar   16
Introduction   16
Gallery   19
The five-course guitar   24
Introduction   24
Gallery   27
The transitional guitar   40
Introduction   40
Gallery   43

The modern classical guitar   56
Introduction   56
Gallery   60
Construction   75

MUSIC FOR THE CLASSICAL GUITAR
Music for the vihuela   101
Four-course guitar music   107
Five-course guitar music   110
Music for the transitional guitar
   *Six courses and the pre-modern six
      single-string guitar*   117
Modern guitar music   122

SOCIAL HISTORY OF THE CLASSICAL GUITAR
Prince and peasant   129
Baroque glory   136
Fashion and sentiment   144
Virtuosi and enthusiasts   152
The widening audience   161

THE FLAMENCO GUITAR   168

    The Origins and Development of Flamenco   170

    The Modern Flamenco Guitar   181

        Introduction   181

        Gallery   184

    The Guitar in Flamenco   191

    Introduction to the *Toques*   202

THE GUITAR IN LATIN AMERICA   208

THE STEEL-STRING ACOUSTIC GUITAR   218

THE INSTRUMENTS   220

  Introduction   220
    Gallery: Arch-top guitars   225
    Gallery: Flat-top guitars   235
    Gallery: Resonator guitars   258
    Gallery: Twelve-string guitars   258
  Construction   260

MUSIC AND PLAYERS   286
  The birth of the American guitar   286
  "There's a lot of things that give you the
    blues . . ."   289
  "My home is in the Delta"   293
  Walking the basses   298
  Ragging the blues   302
  "Train time"   305
  The Depression and after   306
  Country music   311
  "Walking down the big road"   322

THE ELECTRIC GUITAR   336

THE INSTRUMENTS   338
  Introduction   338
    Gallery   344
  Construction   368

MUSIC AND PLAYERS   388
  The birth of a new sound   388
  Rock 'n' roll   398
  Scream power   406
  "There's one in every crowd . . ."   423

APPENDIX   436

GLOSSARY   437

FOOTNOTES   443

BIBLIOGRAPHY   452

INDEX   462

ACKNOWLEDGMENTS

In creating this book we have received generous assistance from many musicians, instrument makers, museum curators and guitar enthusiasts. We owe special debts of gratitude to Nick Cousins, Juan Martín and John Pearse for their constant advice on numerous aspects of the guitar's music and history, and to our editor, Richard Ehrlich. We would also like particularly to thank the following:

Ken Achard; G. L. Taylor of the Ashmolean Museum; J. Ricart Matas of the Instrument Museum of the Barcelona Conservatory; David Bedford; Julius Bellson; Paulino Bernabe; Bob Bianco; I. C. Bishop; Bill Bogel; Kati Boland; Robert Bouchet; Christopher Burgon of the British Library Music Division; Michael Cameron; Agustin Castellón ("Sabicas"); John Honeysett of CBS/Arbiter; Valerie Cloake; John Cook; Diana Johnson of the Country Music Foundation; Celestine Dars; the Dolmetsch family; Ted Dunbar; Daniel Friedrich; Fred Frith; Walter Fuller; Patrick Aldworth, Gary Aumagher, Jim Beales, Kenneth Killman and Randal Wall of the Gibson company; John Gréven; Stefan Grossman; George Gruhn; Roland Harker; Harvey Hope; Keith Johns; Victoria Kingsley; Hubert Henkel of the Instrument Museum of Karl Marx University, Leipzig; Terry Lewis; David Lubell; Mario Maccaferri; F. H. Martin, Bud Hower, Mike Longworth and Donald Thompson of the C.F. Martin Company; Roy Mickleburgh; Simon Munting; David Roberts and David Seville of Norlin (London); Paul Oliver; Orange (London); Mme J. Bran-Ricci and Mme Florence Abondance of the Instrument Museum of the Paris Conservatory; Les Paul; Paco Peña; Robert Pliskin; José Ramírez III; John Roberts; José Romanillos; Elizabeth Wells of the Instrument Museum of the Royal College of Music, London; Richard Schneider; Peter Sensier; Martin Simpson; Helen Hollis of the Smithsonian Institution; the Spanish Guitar Centre, Bristol; the Spanish Guitar Centre, London; Maurice Summerfield; A. G. Grant of Top Gear (Shoreham); James Tyler; Julia Raynsford of the Department of Furniture and Woodwork, Victoria and Albert Museum; Timothy Walker; Abraham Wechter; Malcolm Weller.

In addition, we are grateful to the following record companies for their help:

ABC; Arhoolie; Biograph; Capitol; CBS/Columbia; Decca; Delmark; Deutsche Gramophon Gesellschaft; Folkways; Fonogram; Hispavox; Island; Polydor; Pye; RCA; Morningstar; Transatlantic; Universal Music Service Corporation; Vanguard; Virgin; WEA.

All photographs not otherwise credited were taken by Tom Evans.

The Ancients were satisfied with such instruments as the guitar . . . .

SIMON GORLIER, 1551

. . . methinks it is but a bauble.

SAMUEL PEPYS

For the guitar is the most unpredictable and least reliable musical instrument in existence—and also the sweetest, the warmest, the most delicate, whose melancholic voice awakes in our soul exquisite reveries.

ANDRÉS SEGOVIA

He was all through the Delta back then, and I used to love to hear him play guitar. He had that bottleneck thing, and he could make the guitar real whiny.

MUDDY WATERS, speaking of SON HOUSE

This Machine Kills Fascists.

Written on WOODY GUTHRIE's guitar

You could go out and eat and come back and the note would still be sounding. It didn't sound like a banjo or a mandolin, but like a guitar, an electric *guitar. That was the sound I was after.*

LES PAUL

I don't have a love affair with a guitar, I don't polish it after every performance; I play *the fucking thing.*

PETE TOWNSHEND of THE WHO

INTRODUCTION

Musical bows from Africa (1–3), North America (4), and Mexico (5). Drawings by the Diagram Group.

The family of the guitar

Anyone concerned with the guitar must often feel that there are several different instruments sharing a single name. The modern classical, flamenco, steel-string and electric guitars seem to be separated by their physical forms, the sounds they make, and the musical attitudes of their players. Each type even has its own vocabulary and technical terms: "apoyando" means as little to a steel-string guitarist as "phase switch" does to a flamenco player.

The differences between various types of guitar have been reflected in the books written about them. The classical guitar has often been taken as the only legitimate form of the instrument, and steel-string and electric guitars dismissed as adjuncts of an ephemeral popular culture. The flamenco guitar has been treated as part of an obscure, purely regional folk music, and the Latin American guitar ignored completely.

But in recent years, guitars of all kinds have been crossing the accepted musical boundaries. The nylon-string instrument has lost its exclusively classical connotations through appearances in jazz and popular music, and the steel-string guitar is played on the concert platform by virtuoso soloists. The electric guitar is beginning to overcome the prejudice of classical musicians, and has been accepted by several leading composers and players, while remaining the essential instrument in rock music. Flamenco's popularity has spread far beyond its native Andalucia, and the flamenco guitar finds listeners and players all over the world. The Latin American guitar has been heard internationally in the works of such composers as Villa-Lobos, Ponce and Barrios, and in the popular rhythms of the samba and bossa nova.

The present pattern of the guitar's musical use makes it impossible to treat the different types in isolation. And

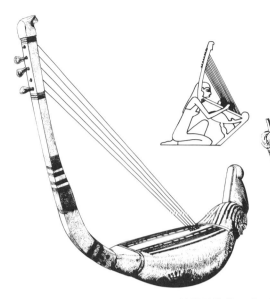

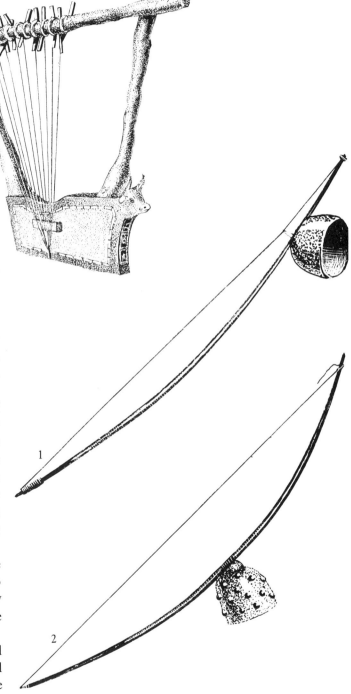

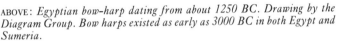

ABOVE: *Egyptian bow-harp dating from about 1250 BC. Drawing by the Diagram Group. Bow harps existed as early as 3000 BC in both Egypt and Sumeria.*

ABOVE RIGHT: *Sumerian silver lyre, from a reconstruction in the British Museum. Drawing by the Diagram Group.*
Sumerian lyres are known to have existed from at least 2800 BC, and had up to eleven strings tuned by levers on the crossbar.

when the various kinds of guitar are examined together, their similarities become more noticeable than their differences. Not only are there musical overlaps between them, but they have a shared ancestry and closely related histories.

All guitars are members of the large group of instruments called chordophones, which are sounded by vibrating strings. The forebear of all other chordophones is believed to be the musical bow, which produces music from a string in the simplest possible way. The twang of the plucked string is amplified by holding one end of the bow to the mouth or, alternatively, a simple permanent resonator can be formed from a gourd attached to the stave of the bow.

The limited musical properties of the bow were extended by the addition of strings of different lengths to give notes of different pitches. The combination of a bow with multiple strings and a permanent resonator box at one end produced the bow-harp.

A slightly different set of physical principles appeared with the lyre, whose strings were of similar or identical length. The pitch differences between strings were controlled by altering their tension, and the vibrations transmitted to the resonator box via a bridge. The Greeks

Musical bows with resonators from Tanzania (1) and South Africa (2). Drawings by the Diagram Group.

had two forms of lyre, the *lyra* and the *kithara*; the *kithara* was adopted by the Romans and its name provided the origin of the modern word *guitar*.

The principle of changing the pitch of the strings by fingering them against a neck was not developed until after lyres and harps were well established. Instruments with long necks and small bodies in the shape of a rounded-off rectangle existed in Mesopotamia in 2000 BC and in Egypt in 1500 BC. The Egyptian type known as the *nefer* had a skin top stretched over a bowl-shaped back, and a long straight neck which extended the length of the body, passing through slits in the skin diaphragm.

The combination of an amplifying device, in the form of a resonating body covered by a diaphragm, with a pitch-changing device in the form of a fingerboard, has been the essential principle of many stringed instruments since the *nefer*. Among these are the Greek and Roman *pandura*; the Indian *sitar*, *surbahar* and *tanpura*; the Japanese *samisen* and Chinese *p'i p'a*; the European lute, the mandolin and the guitar.

Chordophones were spread throughout Europe by the Romans, who played the *cithara*, *pandura* and *fidicula* (a type of small "lute" from whose name the words *violin*, *vihuela* and *viola* were derived). In the eighth century, the Moorish invasion introduced to Spain a number of lute-like instruments, including the *oud*, *rebab* and *quitara*. Outside Spain, a variety of more-or-less primitive chordophones was being played. Manuscript illustrations from the ninth century show that some had necks and others were harps or lyres. The most widely pictured necked type had a long, narrow body with no waist, and three strings passing over the bridge. This instrument confusingly took the name of the Roman lyre, the *cithara*.

Necked chordophones became widely popular in Europe during the succeeding four centuries, and were built in many different shapes and sizes. Some had bodies with concave curves and sharp points, like a holly leaf, and others had a rounded lower bout with projecting "horns" in the region of the upper.

The first true guitars appeared early in the Renaissance. They were distinguished from the other fingerboard instruments of the period, and from their predecessors, by their waisted body shape and smoothly rounded bouts. Since then the guitar has grown larger, its

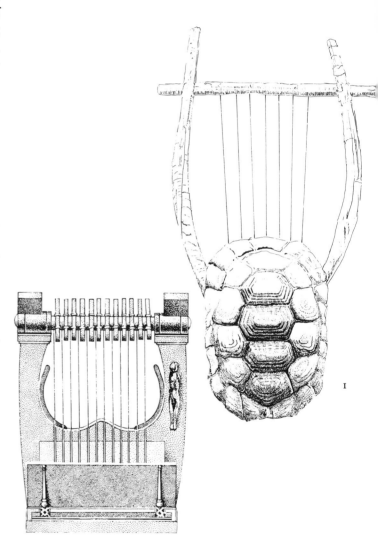

Greek lyra *(1) and* kithara*(2).*
Drawings by the Diagram Group.
The lyra *was said to have been invented by Hermes, messenger of the gods, who used a tortoiseshell as a resonator: throughout history, many chordophones have been built from the carapaces of tortoises, turtles and armadillos. The* lyra *was a popular instrument for amateurs in ancient Greece, while the more complex* kithara *(which had a wooden soundbox) was favored by professional musicians.*

body has become wider and has taken a more sharply waisted shape; there have been changes in the number and tuning of the strings. But through every change of design and construction, a smooth-curved, waisted body with vertical sides remained essential to the guitar. Occasionally, instruments derived from the guitar abandoned the waisted body shape, but these almost always proved to be short-lived freaks of no lasting significance.

The modern classical, flamenco, steel-string and electric guitars are all quite recent developments. Until the mid-nineteenth century there was no division between classical and flamenco guitars, both of which grew out of the general-purpose Spanish guitars of the early part of the century. The steel-string American folk guitar did not make its appearance until fifty years later, around 1900. It too developed from earlier types—from the gut-strung guitars that immigrants had originally brought from Europe, and from guitars coming over the border from Mexico, where the instrument had been established since the Spanish conquest in the sixteenth century. The steel-string guitar was in turn the parent of the electric guitar: the first electric-acoustic guitars of the 1920s and 1930s were virtually identical to the steel-string guitars of the day, save for the addition of a pickup.

Solid-body electric guitars, which appeared after the Second World War, differed so much from other guitars that their very classification as guitars was questioned. But although solid-body guitars sound different, and depend solely on electronic amplification of string vibration, they remain very close to the electric-acoustic guitars from which they evolved. Solid-body and electric-acoustic instruments have similar pickups, necks, fittings and strings; they are played in similar ways, and used in the same musical and cultural contexts. As long as this remains so, it will be impossible to classify them separately.

There are several key questions which can be asked of any guitar. What is its place in the historical development of the instrument? How was it built? What music was played on it? What was its role in society? Although the answers are related, the questions can only be asked separately. This consideration has determined our subdivisions within the major sections on classical, flamenco, steel-string acoustic and electric guitars. The physical development of the guitar is traced in a series of guitar

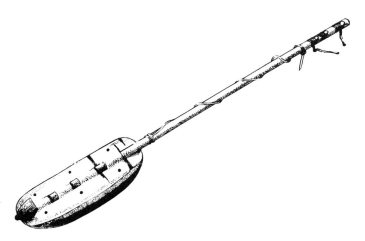

Egyptian nefer.
Drawing by the Diagram Group.

galleries, which give details and specifications of historically important instruments and information about their makers, and other chapters describe current methods of construction. (In deference to the guitar's international status, all measurements are given in centimeters; for conversion, 1″ is exactly 2.54cm and 10cm is approximately 4″.) The history of the guitar's music, and of its status in different societies, is treated separately.

There is naturally some variation in the treatment of the different guitar types, following differences in their form and use. For instance, there is no separate chapter on flamenco guitar construction (which follows essentially the same methods as classical) and it is only in the classical guitar section that we have clearly distinguished between the social and musical uses of the instrument. This is not because the musics of the other types of guitar are any less important, but because their folk elements make it impossible to separate their histories.

The guitar has undergone more changes than any other major type of instrument, and has acquired an extraordinarily rich and diverse history. This history is still unfolding as the guitar's design, construction and musical use continue to change. Surveying its chequered progress, one can only hope that the guitar will never again be plunged into obscurity, but will continue to delight both listeners and players with the qualities which, in the last fifty years, have made it the most popular instrument in the world.

THE CLASSICAL GUITAR

THE INSTRUMENTS

The vihuela and the four-course guitar

The early history of the guitar is confused by the lack of standardized terminology; the same name could be applied to several instruments, or one type of instrument could be known by several names. Our knowledge of the instruments themselves depends on scraps of documentary evidence, and drawings and carvings which are often imprecise or self-contradictory. Thus, the precise manner in which the guitar evolved out of the great variety of plucked string instruments played in medieval Europe is largely a matter for speculation.

In thirteenth- and fourteenth-century Spain, at least two sorts of instrument were known as "guitars," the *guitarra latina* and *guitarra moresca*. The fourteenth-century poet Juan Ruiz, archpriest of Hita, writes of both types in his poem the *Libro del Buen Amor*:

> There's the *guitarra moresca* shouting and wailing,
> With high-pitched voice and sound all whining,
> The fat-bodied lute with its notes a-tripping
> The *guitarra latina* the other two joining.

Juan Ruiz gives us no details of these instruments, but manuscripts and sculptures show the *guitarra moresca* to be shaped like a lute rather than a guitar. The *guitarra latina* is more guitar-like, but still appears to be very close to earlier types of chordophone.

Gradually during the fourteenth and fifteenth centuries the qualifying terms *moresca* and *latina* dropped out of use. Instruments of the guitar family began to be referred to throughout Europe by names such as *guitarra*, *guiterne*, *gittern* and *chitarra*.

At the same time, the terms *vihuela* (in Spain) and *viola* (in Italy) were being used to denote a wide variety of chordophones.[1] Some were played with a bow (*de arco*) and others with a plectrum (*de peñola*) or the fingers (*de mano*); of these three, the vihuela *de mano* developed into a type of guitar.

During the fourteenth and fifteenth centuries the shape of the guitar and vihuela *de mano* underwent considerable modification. Gradually the bouts became more rounded, and a gently incurving waist was adopted. By the beginning of the sixteenth century, both instruments had adopted a shape which is recognizably that of a guitar, although sizes, exact proportions, and details such as peg box construction were far from standardized.

In the sixteenth century, Spain was the leading country for both the guitar and the vihuela (by this time the plucked form was so popular that the *de mano* was dropped from the Spanish name). In Spain the vihuela was an aristocratic version of the guitar, being granted the status accorded to the lute in the rest of Europe. Outside Spain, it was played only in Italy (a country with strong political and social links to Spain) and even in Italy it was overshadowed by the lute.

Accordingly, it is not surprising that Spanish sources provide most of the historical evidence of the vihuela's form, construction and use. The construction of vihuelas was supervised by craft guilds, which could only be entered by apprenticeship and examination. Surviving guild records show that the applicant for membership had to be proficient in the construction of a variety of instruments, including several sorts of vihuela, the harp and clavichord. He must pass an exam, supervised by a master *violero*, and anyone setting up shop as an instrument maker without obtaining his formal qualifications was subject to a severe fine.

The regulations for the *Examen de Violeros* of Seville in 1502 emphasize the importance of the construction of a *vihuela grande de piezas,*[2] presumably a large instrument with extensive marquetry decoration. Elaborate vihuelas apparently made use of exotic woods, such as ebony, walnut and cedar of Lebanon, while ordinary vihuelas used more readily available timbers. Spruce was preferred to common pine for the soundboard, for its straightness of grain and freedom from knots.

A little more precise information on the Spanish vihuela is to be found in Luis Milán's *El Maestro* of 1535, which was the first published book of vihuela music. Milán shows us that the vihuela was shaped like a guitar, and had six courses of strings tuned like those of the lute with intervals 4-4-3-4-4. But the most detailed writings on the vihuela are to be found in a slightly later book, the *Declaración de Instrumentos Musicales* by Juan Bermudo, published in 1555. Bermudo was a friar of the Franciscan order and a keen musical theoretician. Some care is necessary when interpreting his various pronouncements: unwilling to content himself with describing the instruments and musical practices of the day, he suggests various improvements of his own invention.

Bermudo confirms that the ordinary vihuela was strung with six courses of strings. He also mentions a smaller descant vihuela, which he describes as being like a large guitar but with six courses, and various types of seven-course vihuela, some of which appear to have existed only in theory. Although only one small fragment of music for seven-course vihuela survives, Antonio de Cabeçón mentions the seven-course vihuela in his *Obras de Música para Tecla Arpa y Vihuela*, Madrid 1578.

Bermudo says little about the vihuela's construction, but does provide information about its stringing, tuning and fretting. The vihuela, we learn, was fitted with gut frets wound around the fingerboard and tied at the back of the neck. Ten frets were usually considered sufficient, although eleven or twelve were sometimes used.[3] Tied frets were a constant source of trouble: Bermudo states that "The main reason why some vihuelas play badly is the frets" and "One of the things which have not been worked out well on the vihuela is the placing of the frets. This instrument is almost never fretted properly."[4]

The player had to tie the frets himself, and more often than not he would go by eye and ear alone. But "There is a great difference between placing the frets by ear alone and by a conjunction of the ear with art. . . . Not all ears are capable of the work, nor are they ultimately accurate enough."[5]

To overcome the ear's weakness, Bermudo gives several mathematical rules for placing the frets, several of which are of his own devising. The simplest method, which was obviously in general use, uses simple whole number ratios to locate the second, fourth, fifth, seventh, ninth and tenth frets.[6] These do not fall exactly as they would on the modern guitar, fretted for the even-tempered scale, but are placed to give the diatonic tones of the Pythagorean scale. The remaining frets for the semitones had to be placed by ear.

Now the Pythagorean scale contains semitones of two different sizes, and, as Bermudo was well aware, the presence of different-sized semitones within a scale causes considerable problems on fingerboard instruments whose frets span all the strings. If the Pythagorean scale is strictly kept to, some positions on some strings will not yield the correct notes. The performer may overcome the problem by playing the note or chord in a different position, but this could obviously present difficulties. Bermudo suggests as an alternative that two frets could be placed for some positions, one behind the other, so that both the smaller and the larger semitones might be played. For this system to work, it was necessary that the rear fret of the two, which would be very close together, should be "thicker than the first; so that in fretting the note, the other does not touch the string."[7]

Whatever the theory, it is clear that in practice sixteenth-century vihuelists, guitarists and lutenists were moving away from the ancient Pythagorean scale toward the modern even-tempered scale, which has equal semitones. Bermudo admits that "Really, in the common vihuela today there is not a major and minor semitone,"[8] and the fingerings of vihuela tablature suggest that no notice was taken of the theoretical difference between larger and smaller semitones. By the late sixteenth century, the problem was largely solved by the dissemination of a simple formula for fretting fingerboards to give an almost perfect approximation of equal temperament.[9]

Tied gut frets allowed the musician to carry out his own adjustment for correct intonation, and reduced wear on gut strings, but they had their disadvantages. Bermudo commented: "I am persuaded that frets of steel or ivory would make better music. Humidity in the frets, particularly in damp weather, causes serious imperfections on the music which would be avoided by the aforesaid frets."[10] But as far as we know, fixed frets were never actually used.

Although Bermudo's book contains several diagrammatic sketches, he is nowhere explicit about the overall size of the vihuela, its exact proportions, or the materials used in its construction. Most other sources are equally unhelpful. Pablo Nassare, in his *Escuela Música* of 1724, gives typical body proportions; unfortunately, he was writing over a century after the vihuela had gone out of general use, and cannot therefore be taken as a reliable guide. One instrument survives which is generally accepted as being a type of vihuela (see page 21), but this has several features which suggest it is not typical of the sixteenth-century common vihuela. Now that there is a great revival of interest in vihuela music, and a desire to play it on authentic replicas of sixteenth-century instruments, the lack of hard information on the vihuela's exact form has become a source of concern to musicians, musicologists and instrument builders alike.

Although the terms *vihuela* and *guitarra* were sometimes used interchangeably, most sources suggest that, for all their similarities, the sixteenth-century guitar and vihuela were regarded as different instruments. The guitar was a comparatively humble instrument (although it had a vogue in court circles in mid-sixteenth-century France), and was smaller than the vihuela. Early sixteenth-century illustrations show the guitar strung with only four courses of strings. Once again, Bermudo is our best source of documentary information on the instrument. He states that the four-course guitar was very like a small vihuela, a statement which was corroborated later by Sebastián de Covarrubias, who wrote that the guitar was "a small vihuela in size, and also in the [number of] strings."[11] The guitar was fretted like the vihuela, usually with ten frets, though sometimes with as few as five or six for the playing of simple music.

Both the four-course guitar and the vihuela became obsolete in Europe around the beginning of the seventeenth century, by which time they had been overtaken in popularity by the five-course guitar. Both instruments had,

however, been transported to the New World by the conquistadores. As early as 1526 a certain Ortiz, a companion of Cortés, is recorded as being a player of the vihuela and teacher of dancing in Mexico City. The term *vihuela* (or *biguela*, as it was sometimes spelled) passed into the vocabulary of Latin America and from the vihuela and the four-course guitar ultimately developed a whole variety of double-strung South American guitar-type instruments, many of which still survive.

Engraving by Marcantonio Raimondi, 1510, showing the poet Philotes (Giovanni Filoteo Achillini) playing an arched-back viola da mano.

Illustrations from the Cantigas de Santa María: thirteenth century, SPANISH.

Photographs by courtesy of the Library of the Escorial.

(1)  (2)

In (1) a Moor and a European are shown playing the *guitarra moresca*.

In (2) the figure on the left is playing a *guitarra latina*, the one on the right a type of lute which appears to have a hide soundboard attached to the body by laces.

The *guitarra moresca*, with its oval body, long neck and round head, is clearly much closer to the lute than to the guitar.

The *guitarra latina* is shown as having a rounded lower bout, incurved waist, and slight points on the upper bout. Pointed bouts are shown on many representations of medieval plucked string instruments, some of which had a shape rather like a holly leaf.

The strings pass over the bridge to fasten at the base of the body, and the peg box slants back from the head in a shallow curve. From surviving illustrations it appears that curved peg boxes predated both the flat, slightly inclined guitar head and the sharply bent-back straight peg box of the lute. The guitarist is here shown playing with a plectrum.

Crowned musician playing a guitarra latina: from a stone carving, fourteenth century, IN THE WEST PORTAL OF LEON CATHEDRAL.
Photograph by courtesy of Archivo Mas.

This sculpture shows an instrument very similar to that illustrated in the *Cantigas de Santa María*. The body shapes are the same, and there is the same backward-curved peg box. Once again, the *guitarra latina* is being played with a plectrum.

Angel playing a guitar: from a mural painting by Antón Sánchez, fourteenth century, IN THE OLD CATHEDRAL, SALAMANCA.
Photograph by courtesy of Archivo Mas.

This painting shows an intermediate stage in the development of the instrument from the thirteenth-century *guitarra latina* to the late fifteenth-century four-course guitar.

Although the drawing is somewhat schematic, it is clear that the instrument had an elongated body, rounded at each end. All traces of points have disappeared from the bouts, and the waist is sharply defined by a concave indentation. The drawing of the head suggests a backward-curved peg box, and four courses of strings are indicated.

19

Angel musician playing a vihuela de mano: detail from the fifteenth-century retable, attributed to Maestro Perea, IN THE HERMITAGE OF ST. ANNE, JATIVA, VALENCIA. *Photograph by courtesy of Archivo Mas.*

The sharp-cornered semicircular waist indentation survived on Spanish guitar-family instruments into the fifteenth century. The body size, and the size of the peg box, which is bent back as on a lute, suggest that this instrument is a vihuela rather than a guitar.

Angel musician playing a six-course viola da mano: detail from the painting *Madonna and Child with St. Anne* by Gerolamo dai Libri (*c.* 1474–1555).
Photograph by courtesy of the National Gallery London.

This detail shows a typical Italian *viola da mano* of the early sixteenth century. It has six courses of strings, arranged in pairs with the exception of the top course which is a single string. The strings are tied to the bridge, the backward-curved peg box ends in a scroll, and the fingerboard carries tied gut frets.

The *viola's* sides are shown to be of constant depth, indicating that it had a flat back. There is a single central rose to the soundboard.

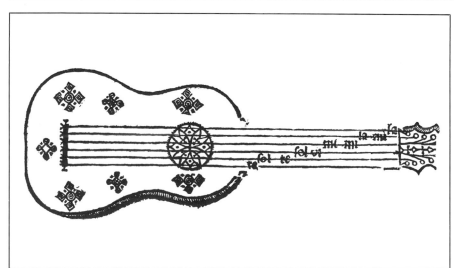

Engraving of a six-course vihuela de mano from Luis Milán's *El Maestro*, 1535. *Photograph by courtesy of the British Library.*

Diagrammatic though it is, this engraving from the first and most famous of the published books of vihuela music is one of the clearest illustrations of the sixteenth-century Spanish vihuela.

It shows a six-course instrument with a flat head, tuned by pegs inserted from the rear, a tied bridge, and a single center soundhole fitted with a fretted rose. The body is unmistakably guitar-shaped, with well-rounded bouts and a smoothly incurving waist.

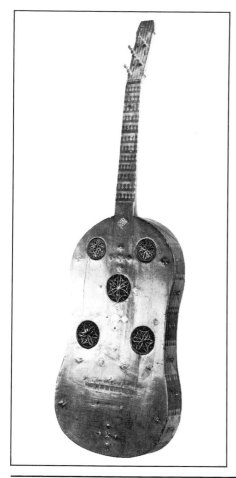

Six-course vihuela de mano, SPANISH, first half of the sixteenth century. *From the Jacquemart André Museum, Paris. Photograph by courtesy of Bulloz.*

Overall length: 109.4cm
Scale length uncertain
Body length: 58.4cm
Body width: upper bout 29.8cm
      waist 25.7cm
      lower bout 32.8cm
Body depth: 7.2cm

This is the only surviving instrument to be generally recognized as an authentic sixteenth-century vihuela. The pine top carries decorations very similar to those shown in Milán's *El Maestro*, but surprisingly has five rosettes instead of one. The sides and back are built of a heavy marquetry of alternate pieces of dark and light wood. The marquetry pieces of the side interlock like the pieces of a jigsaw, while those on the back make up two patterns of rays, with foci in the region of the waist. Both the fingerboard and neck are also covered with marquetry.

Although the bridge is missing, marks on the table show where it was glued. There are two sets of marks, one of which would give a scale length of 80cm, the other (more recent) a scale length of 76cm. The head has holes for twelve pegs, i.e. two pegs per course. (The pegs would have been inserted from the rear,

not from the front as they are shown in the photograph.) The nut, however, has notches for five courses, indicating that this instrument was converted for playing as a five-course guitar at some time after the vihuela went out of fashion.

Ever since it was first identified by Emilio Pujol, this vihuela has been the subject of debate and controversy. On the one hand, its size and marquetry construction suggest that it is a vihuela *grande de piezas* as mentioned in the Seville *Examen de Violeros* of 1502. But several features make it atypical of the generality of sixteenth-century vihuelas as we know them from contemporary illustrations. These illustrations show the vihuela with only one rosette instead of five. More important, the enormously long scale length would make it impossible to play some of the repertoire on this instrument. Finally, the thickness of the timbers suggest that this vihuela was acoustically dead.

We know that vihuelas could be of different sizes, and it is likely that this was a larger instrument than normal. The scale length suggests that it was built as a bass vihuela, and it may well have formed part of a consort. The apparently unusual features of its design, such as the five rosettes, may be a result of its having been built by a provincial *violero* working away from the main centers of Spanish lutherie.

Six-course vihuela by Peter Sensier LONDON, 1975.

Overall length: 99.7cm
Scale length: 60.4cm
Body length: 48.9cm
Body width: upper bout 28.6cm
      waist 24.7cm
      lower bout 34.2cm
Body depth: 8.9cm

Modern luthiers trying to build replicas of the vihuela are faced with enormous problems. A number of copies of the Jacquemart André vihuela have been built, but these have proved to be awkwardly large for the player and acoustically unsatisfactory. Many luthiers are making experiments to arrive at an instrument which appears and sounds "authentic"—but as yet there is no consensus

as to what constitutes authenticity in a vihuela.

This is the eighth vihuela that Peter Sensier has built. Its short scale length is designed for the convenience of the player. The body shape is quite full, and reminiscent of that shown in Gerolamo dai Libri's painting (page 20). The sides and back are built of Spanish cypress, a timber with a long history of use in Spanish guitar construction.

The rosewood fingerboard, which is flush with the table, is fitted with fixed rather than tied frets. Although the sixteenth-century vihuela had tied frets, Sensier feels that fixed frets not only work better but are justified on the vihuela by Bermudo's recommendation that their use would improve the instrument. The most radical departure from sixteenth-century construction practices lies concealed under the soundboard, which is fitted with a simple form of fan strutting. While fan strutting was a Spanish invention, it is not known to have been used before the latter part of the eighteenth century. Peter Sensier feels, however, that the use of fan struts on an instrument of this type, although anachronistic, is justified by the improvement it gives in tone.

A lady playing a four-course guitar: from an engraving attributed to Tobias Stimmer (1539–84).
Photograph by courtesy of the New York Public Library.

The artist refers to this instrument in the accompanying verse as a *quintern*, but it is clearly what we could term a four-course guitar, with three double courses and a single top string. There are six tied frets and a scroll head. The variation in depth of the sides indicates that the back was vaulted; there exist other illustrations that show similar instruments of the latter sixteenth century with flat backs and parallel sides.

Four-course Guitar by Giovanni Smit MILAN, 1646.
Photographs by courtesy of the Kunsthistorisches Museum, Vienna.

Overall length: 56.5cm
Scale length: 37cm
Body length: 26cm
Body width: upper bout 12.1cm
            waist 11.3cm
            lower bout 14.2cm
Body depth: depth of sides 5.5cm

No sixteenth-century four-course guitar is known to survive; by the time this instrument was built, the four-course guitar had been displaced from general use by the five-course guitar.

The sides and vaulted back are built of strips of wood separated by fillets of ivory. The table is decorated with black mastic inlay, in typical eighteenth-century Italian style, and the ivory fingerboard is engraved with hunting scenes. There are six tied gut frets.

This guitar (which was made as a pair with an equally diminutive five-course *chitarra battente*) was intended as a *chitarrino* or *terz* guitar, tuned higher than normal. Its small size cannot therefore be taken as typical of four-course instruments.

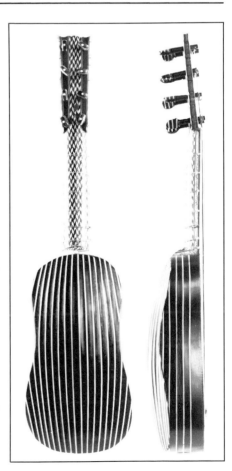

Four-course guitar by Claude Boivin
PARIS, 1749.
Photographs by courtesy of the Instrument Museum of the Paris Conservatory.

Overall length: 94cm
String length: 64cm
Body length: 46cm
Body width: upper bout 21.2cm
            waist 18.5cm
            lower bout 21.8cm
Body depth: increasing from 8 to 9.4cm

Claude Boivin was active from 1730 to 1754, and was the leading French guitar maker of his day. In 1752 he became the head of the Paris luthier's guild. He identified himself on this guitar with the inscription "BOIVIN LUTHIER RUE TICQUETONNE A LA GUITARRE ROYALE A PARIS 1749" engraved on a mother-of-pearl plaque on the base of the body.

It is puzzling that a highly decorated four-course guitar should be built as late as 1749. We know of no new music published for the instrument after 1652, although four-course guitar music continued to be included in reprints of Amat's work for five-course guitar (see page 110), which was first published in 1596. Two possibilities must be considered. One is that this guitar has been modified to its present form. The other is that the four-course guitar continued to be used for more than a hundred years after it became obsolete as a serious instrument, in the early seventeenth century.

This instrument provides evidence to support both hypotheses. The head and bridge (which combines a primitive form of tied bridge with a mother-of-pearl saddle) are not original. The mother-of-pearl inlays to the head, bridge and pegs are by a different hand from those on the sides and back. Although pains have been taken to match the original design, the style of the engraving and pegs suggests nineteenth-century work. However,

it is hard to see why a modification to the number of courses of the guitar should have been made and we conclude on balance that the Boivin guitar could have been built for four courses.

In any case, this instrument is a fine example of French craftsmanship, and shows the typical body shape of the mid-eighteenth-century guitar. The sides and back are built of pine and covered with diamond-shaped lozenges of dark tortoiseshell, separated by inlays of ivory. The inlays of flowers and heraldic fleurs-de-lys within the lozenges are made of mother-of-pearl.

The five-course guitar

The early history of the development of the five-course guitar is hazy. As with the vihuela and four-course guitar, pictorial, literary and musical evidence predate the earliest surviving instruments, and early references are often frustratingly confused and obscure. Pictorial representations of early instruments are particularly unreliable as evidence, and can often be interpreted in a number of different ways. Marcantonio Raimondi's famous engraving of 1510, which shows the poet Philotes playing a guitar-family instrument with ten pegs and seven courses of strings, has been cited variously as evidence of the *viola da mano* and of the early use of five-course guitars!

The five-course guitar probably originated in Spain, and came into use at some time around the middle of the sixteenth century. The first incontrovertible evidence of five-course instruments can be found in Miguel Fuenllana's *Orphenica Lyra* of 1554, which contains some music for a *vihuela de cinco órdenes*. In the following year, Juan Bermudo wrote in his *Declaración de Instrumentos Musicales*: "We have seen a guitar in Spain with five courses of strings."[1] Bermudo mentions later in the same book that "Guitars usually have four courses of strings,"[2] which implies that the five-course guitar was of comparatively recent origin, and still something of an oddity.

The question arises whether Fuenllana and Bermudo were referring to the same instrument. The terms *guitarra* and *vihuela* were, as we have seen, sometimes used synonymously, although the vihuela was often taken to be a larger and grander type of instrument.

Fuenllana's music for the *vihuela de cinco órdenes* suggests an instrument tuned like the normal six-course vihuela with the top course omitted. Bermudo, on the other hand, describes the five-course guitar as being tuned like the four-course guitar, with the addition of a top course of strings tuned a fourth higher.[3] This produces an interval pattern like that of the vihuela with the bottom course omitted.

The combined evidence provided by Bermudo and Fuenllana does no more than establish two types of tuning for five-course instruments. It tells us nothing of the instrument's size or construction, nor can we deduce whether the different tunings indicate five-course instruments of different size and status.

The popularity of the five-course guitar grew considerably in the latter part of the sixteenth century, however, and instruments dating from the early seventeenth century still exist in large numbers.

We know from literary sources that the five-course guitar was immensely popular in Spain in the early seventeenth century, and was also widely played in France and Italy. Yet almost all the surviving guitars from the period 1600 to 1630 were built in Italy, many of them by German craftsmen. We do not know of any surviving Spanish guitars of this period, nor do we know of any outstanding French guitar makers early in the century. This apparent disparity between documentary and instrumental evidence can be explained by the fact that, in general, only the more expensively made guitars have been kept as collector's pieces. During the early seventeenth century, the guitar was an instrument of the people of Spain, but was widely played by the Italian aristocracy.

Italian five-course guitars of the period 1600 to 1630 are generally similar in body shape, with narrow bouts and little indentation at the waist. Both flat and arched-back guitars are common, and the bridge is usually set far down the lower bout. There is, however, considerable variation from instrument to instrument in overall size and in scale length.

Most of the surviving Italian guitars make extensive use of exotic materials such as ebony, ivory and tortoiseshell. Complex inlays, marquetries and engravings were used on five-course guitars throughout the seventeenth century. Italian-based luthiers had a particular fondness for decorating the soundboards with delicate inlay patterns, set with a black mastic compound made with charred ivory powder. Soundholes were filled with rosettes, which were usually cut from parchment and descended into the guitar body in a series of layers. The rosettes were usually painted or gilded.

Guitar fingerboards were set flush with the soundboard, which extended a short way over the neck, adding strength to the joint between neck and body. The frets were of gut and tied in place, as on the four-course guitar and vihuela, and varied in number according to the proficiency of the player and the complexity of the music.

Many five-course guitars were of a type known as the *chitarra battente*, which was particularly popular in Italy.

The *chitarra battente* was designed to be played with a plectrum, and had wire strings. Its five courses were occasionally triple-strung.

The strings of the *chitarra battente* passed over the bridge, and were secured to hitch pins at the base of the body. The rear part of the soundboard was usually tilted down toward the base of the instrument to increase the vertical pressure of the strings on the bridge, which pressure stopped the strings from slipping and produced a greater volume. Fixed frets of some hard material were used in place of tied gut frets, to resist the abrasion of metal strings.

The *chitarra battente* was always built with an arched back. In the past, some confusion has been caused by an incorrect supposition that every arched-back five-course guitar was a *chitarra battente*. As we have stated, many true guitars also had arched backs: the *chitarra battente* is essentially defined by its use of metal strings passing over the bridge.

The Italians' supremacy as makers of the five-course guitar lasted until the end of the 1630s. The Parisian school of luthiers came to the fore during the 1640s, and flourished until the early 1700s under the patronage of the court of Louis XIV. French-built guitars were usually flat-backed, and less heavily ornamented than Italian instruments. Where the Italians delighted in complex marquetry and scrollwork decoration, the French preferred simpler, more geometric patterns. A notable feature of the most lavish guitars of the Parisian school is the use of tortoiseshell as a veneer to the sides, back and neck.

The building of five-course guitars was widespread throughout Europe in the second half of the seventeenth century. A guitar of 1650 in the Stearns Collection in Ann Arbor, Michigan, proves Andreas Ott of Prague to have been a fine craftsman, and toward the end of the century the Hamburg school of luthiers achieved international fame.

The five-course guitar continued to be built in the first half of the eighteenth century, albeit in decreasing numbers. Early eighteenth-century guitars differ little from those of the seventeenth century in design, although they show changes in decorative pattern. The five-course guitar had a brief revival in the third quarter of the century, most notably in France and the Low Countries. The body shape became more waisted at this period, foreshadowing design trends in the nineteenth-century single-string guitar. The five-course guitar was displaced in the 1770s and 1780s by the six-course guitar in Spain and the single-string guitar in France and Italy. By 1800, the five-course double-strung instrument had become obsolete.

The growth of interest in Renaissance and baroque music in recent years has brought with it a new interest in the five-course guitar. Particular attention has been paid to questions of tuning and stringing. Research into the musical and literary sources has shown that, although all the surviving instruments have pegs for five double-strung courses, the top string was usually only fitted with a single string. Obtaining matched pairs of thin gut strings which would play in tune together was obviously a major problem. Seventeenth-century paintings (see pages 138–40) confirm the practice of omitting one of the strings from the top course.

Research has also proven that the tuning of the five-course guitar never became fully standardized, but varied according to the type of music being played. The normal interval pattern was 4-4-3-4, but *scordatura* was also used. Both strings of the second and third courses were tuned in unison, but the relations of the strings of the two lowest courses could vary. The instructions on tuning in the main seventeenth-century guitar books are often imprecise. Although much can be deduced from the music itself, the composer's intentions are not always entirely clear, and considerable modern controversy has resulted.

One of the clearest statements on stringing can be found in Gaspar Sanz's *Instrucción de Música sobre la Guitarra Española* of 1674, in which he states:

There are many ways of stringing, because those Masters in Rome only string the guitar with thin strings, without putting any bourdon [a heavy bass string] on the fourth or fifth. In Spain it is the contrary, because some use two bourdons on the fourth, and others two on the fifth, and at the least, for ordinary use, one on each course. These two methods of stringing are good, but for different effects, for he who wishes to play the guitar to make noisy music, or to play the bass with some *tomo* or *sonada,* the guitar is better with bourdons than without. But if anyone wishes to play separate notes with grace and sweetness, and use *campanellas* which is the modern method of composing, the bourdons do not come out well, but only the thin strings, both on the fourths and fifths, as I have experienced.[4]

So the tuning used in Spain and Italy for contrapuntal music was a re-entrant tuning without bourdons and went aa d'd' gg bb e'. For "noisy music," played in the common *rasgueado* style, tunings varied: both AA dd gg bb e' and Aa dd' gg bb e' being common. The added bourdons, particularly on the fifth course, were necessary to provide the power and sustain needed for dance music accompaniment. A further tuning is given by Robert de Visée and Francesco Corbetta (who are both unfortunately imprecise in their instructions) as aa dd' gg bb e', with a bourdon only on the fourth course.

Now that a small number of five-course guitars have been restored to playing condition and a considerably larger number of replicas built, it is becoming possible to assess the properties of the instrument. As we would expect, the small-bodied early guitar lacks both the power and the variety of tonal shadings of the modern concert instrument. It does possess an attractive voice, however, with a sound somewhat closer to the lute than to the modern guitar. The double stringing produces a rich tonal texture, which is essential to much seventeenth-century guitar music. Consequently, there is a growing move toward playing this music on original or reproduction instruments, rather than on the concert guitar, which requires transcription and inevitably causes a change in musical character.

This five-course guitar is popularly known as the "Rizzio guitar," tradition having decreed that it was given by Mary Queen of Scots to David Rizzio, who was her secretary from 1564 until his murder in 1566. In fact, it was built in France in the seventeenth century, probably by Jean Voboam in about 1680.

Five-course guitar by Belchior Dias
LISBON, 1581.
Photographs by courtesy of the Royal College of Music, London.

Overall length: 76.5cm
String length: 55.4cm
Body length: 36.6cm
Body width: upper bout 16.5cm
waist 14.5cm
lower bout 20cm
Body depth: depth of sides at upper bout, waist and lower bout respectively is 4, 6.5 and 5cm

The label of this guitar reads "Belchior dias a fez em./ 1xª nomes de dez.ro 1581," which translates as "Belchior Dias made me./Lisbon month of December 1581."

Virtually everything on this guitar appears to be original, with the exception of the pegs. There would originally have been a rose in the soundhole.

Particular points of interest about this

guitar are its small size, plain decoration, and vaulted scalloped back. In all of its significant dimensions, it is appreciably smaller than the surviving five-course guitars of the early seventeenth century, and closer in size to the four-course guitars depicted in sixteenth-century illustrations.

The plain decoration has been taken as evidence that early guitars were generally unadorned. This is a dangerous assumption, however. Even during the great age of lavish guitar adornment, the late seventeenth century, many comparatively simple instruments were made.

The arched back is carved from a single piece of wood, and not made from separate strips as were the arched backs of seventeenth-century guitars, making the instrument very heavy for its size. The sides slot into the heel, which continues internally in the form of a slipper foot. This method of joining the neck and body is used on modern classical guitars, and is particularly associated with Iberian construction.

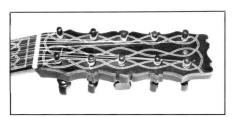

Five-course guitar PORTUGUESE, *c.* 1590.
From the collection of Robert Spencer.

Body length: 45.4cm
Body width: upper bout 20.5cm
waist 17.6cm
lower bout 25.7cm
Body depth: increasing from 8.4 to 9.2cm

Very heavy restoration work has been carried out on this guitar, which at some stage has been converted to a *chitarra battente* with a cranked table, and fitted with frets. The restoration work included the lengthening of the neck (which had been shortened), building up the sides where they had been cut down, and fitting a completely new table and bridge.

Despite these modifications, enough original features remain to give this guitar exceptional historical interest. The inlays to the fingerboard and head are virtually identical to the Dias guitar, and it has the same wedge section to the head. Although the body of this instrument is slightly larger, it has the same type of curvature, and is similarly heavy for its size.

We have no doubt that this is an authentic sixteenth-century guitar, and feel that there is a strong possibility that it too was built by Belchior Dias of Lisbon. The slightly larger size may be an indication of a later date of construction, although it seems unlikely that more than ten years elapsed between the building of the two instruments.

27

Five-course guitar by Christopho Cocko
VENICE, 1602.
*From the Instrument Museum of the Paris
Conservatory.*

Overall length: 91cm
String length: 64cm
Body length: 43.7cm
Body width: upper bout 18.8cm
       waist 15.3cm
       lower bout 24cm
Body depth: increasing from 7.4 to 9.2cm

The label is hidden, but was revealed during the restoration of the guitar and recorded as reading "Christopho Cocko d'Aquila Venetia 1602." There is confusion about the true dates of Christopho Cocko (or Koch, Hoch, Choc or Cocho, as it is variously spelled). Most of his instruments are assigned to the mid-seventeenth century (assuming that the variations of the name refer to the same maker) and there is a *chitarrone* by "Christoff Koch" dated 1650 in the Musical Instrument Museum, Berlin.

This guitar is, however, smaller than the typical surviving Italian instruments of the period 1620 to 1650, and in view of the guitar's

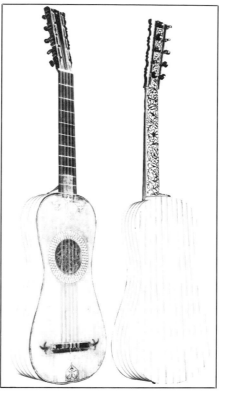

tendency to grow in size, we are happy to accept the date of 1602 as correct. This suggests that there was a family of instrument makers called Koch or Cocko who continued to the mid-century — or that Cocko enjoyed an exceptionally long career!

The sides and back of the guitar are made of ivory strips, connected by small slivers of a dark brown wood. The back of the neck is veneered with ivory with decorative rosewood inlay in a pattern typical of early sixteenth-century Venetian workmanship.

The spruce or pine of the table has a very fine grain, and the decorative inlay on the table is more restrained than on most high-class Italian guitars of the sixteenth century (although the patterns used are typical). The table extends into the fingerboard in the normal fashion, but the fingerboard itself has been widened at some later date.

Much of the attractiveness of this guitar comes from its simple use of a precious material, ivory. There is no attempt to "gild the lily" with unnecessary decoration, and the table (so important to the sound of the guitar) has not been interfered with by excessive inlay.

Five-course guitar by Giovanni Tessler
ANCONA, *c.* 1620.
Photographs by courtesy of the Royal College of Music, London.

Overall length: 88.5cm
String length: 61.5cm
Body length: 45cm
Body width: upper bout 19.8cm
       waist 17.2cm
       lower bout 25cm
Body depth: increasing from 6 to 7cm

Although it has no label, this flat-backed guitar can be positively identified as the work of Giovanni Tessler of Ancona by the presence of his stamp ("GT" surmounting a device like an anchor) at the top end of the table. This guitar has been modified to take six strings at some time in either the late eighteenth or early nineteenth century. Such alterations of seventeenth-century guitars to take six single strings are common. They indicate that the guitars must have been highly prized, and had exceptionally long playing

lives by modern standards despite the delicacy of their construction.

The body is built of strips of a dark hardwood, connected by fillets of ivory. Internally, the back is lined with veneer whose grain runs perpendicular to that of the external strips. The sides are lined with paper.

The spruce top has a very fine grain, and is extensively inlaid with mother-of-pearl and black mastic. The fingerboard is built of a marquetry of mother-of-pearl and ebony, and bound in ivory. (The present frets are later additions, probably put on when the guitar was converted to six single strings.) The back of the neck is covered with a marquetry of alternating timber and ivory rectangles.

Chitarra battente, maker unknown,
ITALIAN *c.* 1620.
*From the Instrument Museum of the Paris
Conservatory.*

Overall length: 92cm
String length: 66cm
Body length: 43cm
Body width: upper bout 19.5cm
          waist 17.2cm
          lower bout 23.4cm
Body depth: the maximum depth of the vault
          is 13cm

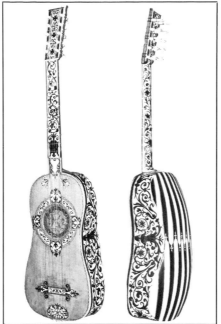

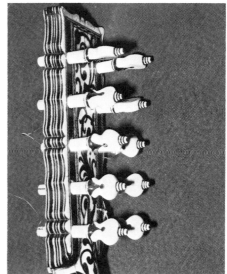

There is no visible maker's mark or label
to this fine *chitarra battente,* but the style of
decoration (particularly that of the neck and
fingerboard) suggests that it is an Italian
instrument of the 1620s.

The marquetry throughout, and the inlay
on the table, is made of ebony and bone. The
pegs are of bone also, finely carved and neatly
decorated. The photograph of the head shows
the typical construction pattern used throughout the seventeenth century. The central
portion of the head is made from a solid block
(covered with marquetry front and back),
surrounded by a decorative edging made of
alternating layers of contrasting material—in
this case, bone and ebony. The head-to-neck
junction is made by a short, stubby V joint.

The parchment rosette of this guitar is an
exceptionally fine one made of five layers with
a Star of David design.

Five-course guitar, ITALIAN, early seventeenth century.
*Photographs by courtesy of the Paris Con-
servatory.*

Overall length: 99cm
String length: 72.5cm
Body length: 48cm
Body width: upper bout 22cm
          waist 19.6cm
          lower bout 26.5cm
Body depth: the maximum overall depth of
          the vault is 13cm

This fine guitar has been extensively
restored by Pierre Abondance, with great
attention to authenticity.

During the restoration it became clear that
the guitar had started life as a *chitarra battente*
(holes for hitch pins were found in the end
block, beneath the ivory engraved panel which
now covers it), but had been converted shortly
after it was made. In the course of conversion,
the canted table of the original instrument was
replaced by the present flat table, and a longer
neck was probably fitted. From the restrained,
stylish table decoration, it seems likely that
this conversion was made around 1620.

Examination of the interior revealed the
junction block used to connect the neck and
body (see detail photograph). The sides are
slotted into the end block, and held in place by
wedges. The foot of the block is nailed down
to a timber member which also helps give
shape to the vault of the back. This type of
construction can be seen on a number of guitars
of the period, and reveals a similarity of
principle to modern methods of construction.

The decoration is restrained, but of high quality. The spherical-ended engraved ivory tuning pegs are particularly attractive. The vaulted back of the body is constructed of alternate strips of ebony and ivory, while the sides are of ebony with an engraved ivory band inset. The character of the engravings, which show hunting scenes, suggests that they were carried out by a German craftsman resident in Italy. At the base of the guitar is an ivory panel

engraved with a picture of Diana. This is the work of a different artist, as are the engravings on the ivory panels on the fingerboard—which are Italian in style. One of the panels on the neck is inscribed "G. C. Fecit." These initials could be those either of the luthier who built the instrument, or the man who modified it, or the engraver. While it is not possible to identify the man from the initials alone, it is worth noting that a luthier named Gironimo

Campi was active in Italy at the start of the seventeenth century.

Thanks to the skill of the restoration, it has proved possible to string and play this guitar, and to assess its tone. The sound proves to be soft, sweet, and very pleasant. In some ways it is closer to that of the lute than to that of the modern guitar, but the tone still has that golden quality common to the guitar family, as distinct from the silvery sound of the true lute.

Five-course guitar converted to a chitarra battente by Matteo Sellas VENICE, 1623. *From the Victoria and Albert Museum, London.*

Overall length : 86.5cm
Body length : 46.5cm
Body width : upper bout 21.7cm
           waist 18.8cm
           lower bout 26.6cm
Body depth : the maximum depth of the vault
           is 14cm

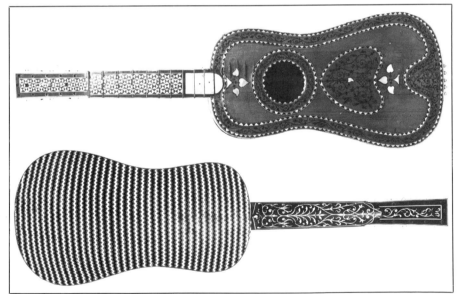

Matteo Sellas was active in Venice during the first half of the seventeenth century. He used a trademark consisting of the initials "MS" and a crown, and often signed himself "Matteo Sellas alla Corona in Venetia." He was considered a rival to Tieffenbrucker as a lute builder in his day, and built many fine guitars. The label on this guitar, on the underside of the table, is difficult to read (although the name of Sellas and the date are clear). It appears to say "Io Mateo Selas/ in 1623/per sua altezza Firenzi." This would indicate that the guitar was made for "His Highness in Florence," who in 1623 was the Grand Duke Ferdinand of Tuscany.

In the conversion to a *chitarra battente*, the table (which is original) has been bent along a line across the middle of the lower bout, and tilted down toward the base. Extra holes have

been drilled in the head to make provision for five more strings, so that as a *chitarra battente* it would have been played with triple-strung courses. Five ivory hitch pins have been added at the base. The neck has also been shortened.

The domed back is built of a marquetry of very fine pieces of ebony and ivory, and is an almost miraculous piece of craftsmanship. The back of the neck is veneered in ebony, with ivory inlay. The style of inlay is typical of

Italian workmanship. Virtually identical neck inlays are found on instruments by different makers, which suggests that they were produced by specialist sub-contractors. The decoration on the table is made up of inlays of mother-of-pearl and black mastic. These inlays are rather more ornate than usual—probably to please the noble patron—but embody the familiar motifs common to many Italian guitars.

Five-course guitar by Giorgio Sellas
VENICE, 1627.
Photographs by courtesy of the Ashmolean Museum, Oxford.

Overall length: 94.2cm
String length: 65.1cm
Body length: 44.5cm
Body width: upper bout 20.9cm
           waist 19cm
           lower bout 25.4cm
Body depth: the instrument depth from front
           to back of the vault is 13.3cm

The instrument is inscribed on the mother-of-pearl facing to the head "Giorgio Sellas/alla Stella/ in Venetia/1627/fecit." Giorgio Sellas came from the same Tyrolean family as Matteo, and was active in Venice *c*. 1620–40. His identifying mark was a star.

This is one of the most exquisitely decorated of all surviving Italian guitars. The vaulted back is made of ebony strips with ivory scrollwork inlays. The sides too are ebony, with extensive ivory inlays of nymphs singing,

satyrs with musical instruments, and floral scrollwork. The fingerboard is inlaid with engraved mother-of-pearl plaques, and the table is decorated with mother-of-pearl and black mastic.

The lavish decoration suggests this instru-ment must have been commissioned by an aristocratic amateur, or as a princely diplo-matic gift. It has, in modern times, been strung as a *chitarra battente*, although its flat table and lack of frets show clearly that it is a true guitar.

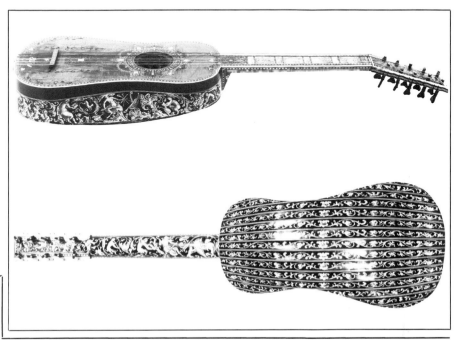

Five-course guitar, GERMAN or ITALIAN, *c*. 1620s.
Photographs by courtesy of the Instrument Museum of the Royal College of Music, London.

Dimensions of this guitar are not available, as its fragile condition precludes handling and measurement.

The origins of this guitar are uncertain. The style and subject matter of the engrav-ings, on the ivory panels of fingerboard, sides and back suggest German workmanship in general and that of Jacob Stadler in particular. The table inlay is more Italianate in character however, and is quite similar to that on a four-course guitar built by Giovanni Smit in Milan in 1646. Most of the guitar makers active in Italy in the sixteenth and seventeenth cen-turies were of German origin, and it is not surprising to find a number of guitars which combine German and Italian features.

There are holes for two extra pegs on the head, which look to be later additions. Five-course guitars with extra strings on the bottom courses are described by M. Corrette in *Les Dons d'Apollon* (*c*. 1763) as "Guitarres à la Rodrigo," tuned AAa ddd' gg bb e'.

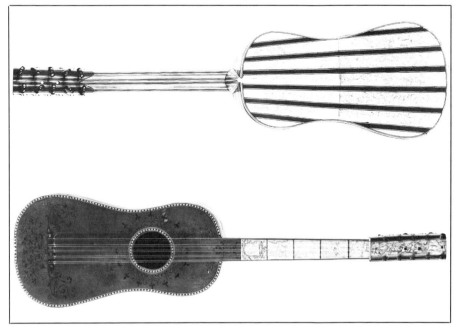

Five-course guitar by René Voboam
PARIS, 1641.
Photographs by courtesy of the Ashmolean Museum, Oxford.

Overall length: 94cm
String length: 69.4cm
Body length: 46.2cm
Body width: upper bout 20.5cm
       waist 18.3cm
       lower bout 24.6cm
Body depth: increasing from 8.3 to 9.3cm

The maker is identified by a small mother-of-pearl plaque on the front of the head which reads "René Voboam 1641." The three famous members of the Voboam family, René, Alexandre and Jean, dominated French guitar making in the seventeenth century. All three worked in Paris. René was the earliest, and Jean was the son of Alexandre. There is a close family resemblance between the instruments of all three.

The spruce of the top has an exceptionally fine grain. It is noticeable that the Voboam family avoided decorative inlays on the functional area of the soundboard on even their most highly embellished guitars. The binding to the top and back, soundhole and fingerboard edges, and the inlay to the bridge, is made of ivory and ebony. All the Voboams used a similar diagonal binding pattern, which was copied by almost every other French luthier of the seventeenth century.

The sides and back are covered in panels of tortoiseshell, divided by narrow strips of ebony and ivory. The small quatrefoil inlays to the back are made of mother-of-pearl.

The decorative pattern of the back is echoed on the rear of the headstock, which is similarly veneered. Tortoiseshell is also used as a veneer to the back of the neck, in a houndstooth pattern with ebony and ivory dividing strips.

Overall, the guitar shows the combination of refined design and proportions with consummate craftsmanship and a lavish use of rare materials which characterizes much of the work of the Voboam family. Both Jean and René (possibly Alexandre as well) favored tortoiseshell-veneered bodies for guitars built for courtly patrons, many of whom treated them more as *objets d'art* than as musical instruments.

Five-course guitar by Du Mesnil
FRANCE, 1648.
Photographs by courtesy of the Instrument Museum of the Paris Conservatory.

Overall length: 96cm
String length: 67cm
Body length: 45cm
Body width: upper bout 21cm
       waist 19.6cm
       lower bout 25.5cm
Body depth: the maximum overall depth of the body is 10.5cm

There is no visible etiquette on this guitar, but a label giving the maker and date was discovered during restoration.

The guitar's general proportions conform to mid-seventeenth-century French standards. The arched back is built of strips of dark brown wood, divided by narrow inlays of ebony and ivory, and the sides are made of ebony.

The most interesting feature of this guitar is the extraordinary carved ivory decoration to the head. The standard of workmanship and design is unusually high, and carries through to the carved ivory "moustaches" at the bridge ends, and the complex ivory inlays. The inlay on the fingerboard contains the initials "J.L."

Five-course guitar converted to a chitarra battente, by Giovanni and Michael Sellas VENICE, 1652.
From the collection of J. & A. Beare Ltd, London.

Overall length: 90.3cm
Scale length: 57.5cm
Body length: 46cm
Body width: upper bout 20.5cm
           waist 17.6cm
           lower bout 25cm
Body depth: the depth of the sides is 6.5cm at the head, 6.3cm at the waist, a maximum of 11cm at the waist, 7.2cm at the lower bout, and 7.6cm at the base

Giorgio and Matteo were not the only luthiers in the Sellas family. There was a third Sellas workshop in Venice, and city records show the family flourished as successful instrument builders as late as the 1740s.

Giovanni and Michael Sellas succeed Giorgio "alla Stella," and their handwritten label reads "Gioane et Michiel Sellas/Littavi alla Stella in Venetia/fecit 1652." There is also an identifying inlay, on the neck below the fingerboard, of a star with the initials "GS."

Giovanni and Michael may not have been entirely literate, but they were craftsmen worthy to follow in Giorgio's footsteps. This is one of the most beautifully built of all Venetian guitars. The body is made of an intricate marquetry of ebony and ivory, which extends as a veneer over the back of the head and neck, and the fingerboard is made of plaques of mother-of-pearl.

A conversion has been made at some date to turn the guitar into a *chitarra battente*. The table has been cranked, and the bridge moved some five or six centimeters up the table to the line of the bend. A new bridge has been added, the soundboard decoration modified and the neck shortened.

Five-course guitar by Alexandre Voboam PARIS, 1676.
Photographs by courtesy of the Instrument Museum of the Paris Conservatory.

Overall length: 94cm
String length: 69.5cm
Body length: 44.7cm
Body width: upper bout 20.7cm
           waist 18.5cm
           lower bout 24.7cm
Body depth: increasing from 8.3 to 10cm

On the head there is a small ivory plaque reading "Alexandre Voboam Le Jeune 1676."

The top of the guitar shows the familiar Voboam diagonal-pattern ebony and ivory inlay, and is otherwise completely devoid of ornament. Ebony is used for the sides, which are made of three strips separated by ivory inlay. The back is of a brown hardwood, divided by inlays consisting of a strip of ivory sandwiched between two thin strips of ebony. The inlays to the back of the head and neck are single strips of ivory.

While this guitar was obviously made for a well-to-do patron, it was designed to be played rather than to be admired. Surviving evidence suggests that the Voboam family had a standard pattern for their "working" guitars. There are two guitars by Jean Voboam, also in the Paris Conservatory, one dated 1676, the other 1690, which are almost identical in their body proportions, materials and decoration. Watteau's guitar drawings and paintings show many similar guitars which can be taken as further evidence of the influence of the Voboams as guitar makers. Interestingly, many of the paintings show the guitar being strummed with the right hand high up the instrument—often over the end of the fingerboard. This is, in fact, the most comfortable way to hold the slim-bodied guitars of the seventeenth century, because of the smallness of the lower bout.

Five-course guitar by Jean Voboam
PARIS, 1687.
*Photographs by courtesy of the Instrument
Museum of the Paris Conservatory.*

Overall length: 95cm
Scale length: 66.5cm
Body length: 45.5cm
Body width: upper bout 21.5cm
             waist 19cm
             lower bout 25.5cm
Body depth: increasing from 8.2 to 10cm

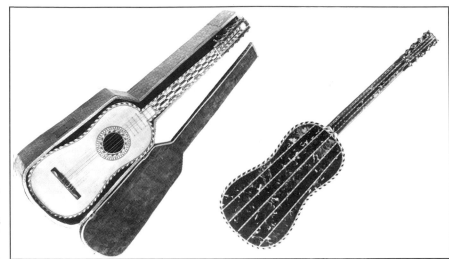

The Voboams enjoyed the extensive patronage of Louis XIV's guitar-mad court. This instrument was built for Mlle. de Nantes, Duchesse de Bourbon, the daughter of *Le Roi Soleil* and Mme. De Montespan.

The spruce of the top has a much coarser grain than is usual on Jean Voboam's instruments, but the decoration is fabulous. The standard Voboam edge inlay is here extended by an extra strip of ivory and ebony inlay, of the same design as is used to divide the tortoiseshell panels covering the sides, back and neck. The soundhole surround also has additional decoration, in the form of alternating squares and circles of mother-of-pearl set in black mastic.

The guitar was converted for use with six single strings at some time around the 1840s. The bridge, and fixed brass frets, date from this time; the tuning pegs also are not original.

One of the most interesting features of the instrument is the case—which *is* original. It is covered in dark red leather, stamped all over with the regal fleur-de-lys in gold.

Five-course guitar by Antonio Stradivari
CREMONA, 1688.
*Photographs by courtesy of the Ashmolean
Museum, Oxford.*

Overall length: 100cm
String length: 74cm
Body length: 47cm
Body width: upper bout 21.5cm
             waist 17.3cm
             lower bout 26.5cm
Body depth: increasing from 10 to 10.9cm

While the reputation of Stradivari, who lived from 1644 to 1737, is founded on his genius as a maker of violin-family instruments, he is known to have made a small number of guitars. However, almost all of the guitars attributed to him at various times have proved to be forgeries. Only one other authentic Stradivari guitar is known; this was built in 1700 to a similar pattern, and is now in a private collection in America.

The Ashmolean Stradivari is, as one would expect, beautifully built and almost entirely unadorned. Its beauty lies in its proportions and the quality of the timbers. The table is spruce; the sides, back, neck and

head are maple. (The tree commonly called *sycamore* in England is actually the Great Maple.) Ebony is used for the headstock veneers both front and back, for the flush fingerboard and frets, and for the inlays to the back of the body and neck. The rosette is fretted from wood, and the surround is decorated with mother-of-pearl lozenges set in black mastic. Where the table extends over the neck, it is lightly engraved with a device of putti holding a crown above a heart that contains an inscription, which time and wear have eaten away. The etiquette on the back of the head is inlaid with black mastic. There is

some disagreement whether the date should be read as 1680 or 1688.

The scale length of 74cm is extraordinarily long, and must have limited the musical use of this guitar. It is possible that it was made as a continuo instrument, or that Stradivari was experimenting to try to obtain greater volume from the guitar. Whatever the case, marks of wear on the fingerboard and table show that it has been much played. Unfortunately, the age and fragility of this wonderful guitar rule out any attempt to tune it to pitch and make an assessment of its tone.

Five-course guitar by Hans Christoph Fleischer HAMBURG, 1684.
From the Instrument Museum of the Paris Conservatory.

Overall length: 91cm
String length: 66cm
Body length: 42.5cm
Body width: upper bout 19cm
      waist 16.1cm
      lower bout 23.3cm
Body depth: the maximum overall depth of the guitar is 11.5cm

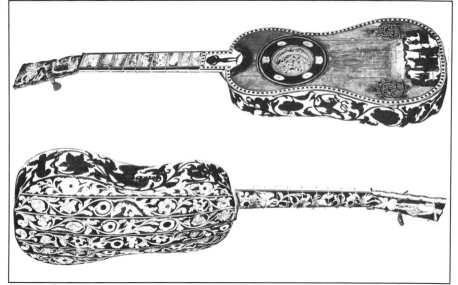

Hans Christoph Fleischer was one of the most successful instrument builders of the late seventeenth century, and was effectively the founder of the Hamburg school of guitar makers.

This arched-back guitar shows the extreme limits of the trend to decoration on seventeenth-century guitars. Wherever possible, timber is replaced by more precious materials—ivory, tortoiseshell and mother of pearl. There is lavish use of decorative engraving, and paste brilliants are pressed into service to highlight certain details. The intricate labor involved in the construction of the ivory and tortoiseshell marquetry of which the sides and back are built, and with which the neck and head are veneered, is staggering.

The various decorative engravings and inlays present a dissertation on the nature of love. Both the engraved figures and the inscriptions which accompany them refer, often in a veiled and allusive manner, to physical love between the sexes and the harmony of the universe in love.

The major burden of the theme is set out

on the nine mother-of-pearl plaques that make up the fingerboard. These show allegorical scenes, with accompanying texts in German. Exact interpretation is complicated by the obscurity of some of the engravings, and by

errors of spelling in some of the texts which suggest that the engraver was not entirely literate, or was not a native-born German. Other, more general engravings and inscriptions on the sides and back, head and neck, build on the central idea.

Finally, there is a tortoiseshell and ivory plaque on the lower part of the table, showing a kneeling youth being crowned by a female figure seated between pillars inscribed *Labor* and *Honor*, and a tortoiseshell band around the soundhole, engraved with cupids carrying mother-of-pearl plaques.

Connections between the guitar, harmony and love have often been drawn in the instrument's long history. Gaspar Sanz, for example, used a comparison between the delights of the guitar and the delights of women as an introductory theme to his *Instrucción de Música sobre la Guitarra Española,* which was first published in 1674. Fleischer's guitar is unique, however, in the extent and complexity of the allegories employed.

Guitar by Joachim Tielke HAMBURG, 1693.
Photographs by courtesy of the Victoria and Albert Museum, London.

Overall length: 102cm
String length: 72.5cm
Body length: 50cm
Body width: upper bout 25cm
            waist 21.2cm
            lower bout 29.8cm
Body depth: the maximum overall depth is
            14.5cm

This guitar carries a label reading "Ioachim Tielke in Hamburg, An. 1693." Tielke (1641–1719) is one of the most famous of all luthiers to have built guitars. He was the second son of Gottfried Tielke, Judge and Chairman of the inner suburb of Konigsberg. In the mid-1660s, he moved to Hamburg, and in 1667 married a daughter of Hans Christoph Fleischer. He had a long and successful career in Hamburg, enjoying the friendship of the leading musicians (including the great or-

ganist and composer Buxtehude) and the patronage of royalty.

Tielke built a wide range of instruments. From the many survivors, which include fifteen guitars, it is clear that he was a craftsman of genius, and it would be fair to say that the delicacy of his workmanship has never been surpassed by a guitar maker.

There are many similarities in construction and decoration between this guitar and the preceding example by Fleischer, but Tielke far surpassed his father-in-law. For all

their complex marquetry and decoration, Tielke's instruments have a lightness and vibrancy which is unique among seventeenth-century decorative guitars. Although this guitar looks like an object made for display, it handles like a truly musical instrument.

The sides and the arched back are constructed from a marquetry of engraved tortoiseshell and ivory inlaid with pewter. This is a true marquetry, not a veneer on a wooden backing, and the materials are so thin as to be translucent. The back of the neck carries a veneer similar to the marquetry of the back.

The soundboard is decorated with a scalloped-sided hexagonal inlay around the soundhole, made of tortoiseshell and ebony set in ivory. Where the table joins the fingerboard there is an inlaid square of mother-of-pearl, from which a leaf pattern inlay of mother-of-pearl, with ebony and pewter embellishment, extends onto the table. The "moustaches" to the bridge are fretted from tortoiseshell.

The construction of the head is one of the most extraordinary features of this instrument. Instead of being built of a solid plate of wood, it is made of three strips which leave an open center. This contains a fretted panel of ivory, delicately carved, showing a putto surrounded by foliage. The top of the head is veneered in ivory, with an inlaid pattern of tortoiseshell and silver. The back of the head carries a similar pattern in negative, with the uses of ivory and tortoiseshell reversed.

The principal decorative device is a sunflower design. This had been used earlier by Fleischer, but became almost a trademark of Tielke's work. There are also several inscribed pictorial panels on the sides, which allude to the power of love and of music. The two most important panels occupy the waist areas. One shows Orpheus playing to an assembly of animals, with the comment *la musique d'Orphée tire tout a soy*. The other is titled *l'injustice de Midée*. It shows the musical contest between Pan and Apollo, who is playing a guitar, in which King Midas was appointed judge.

The guitar is now strung for six courses — five double and one single. While six-course guitars were mentioned in a treatise published in 1741, it is likely that the Tielke guitar was built for five courses. The sixth single string is probably an error of restoration, in which a peg has been fitted to a central hanging hole.

Five-course guitar by Joachim Tielke
HAMBURG, *c*. 1700.

*Photographs by courtesy of the Instrument
Museum of the Royal College of Music, London.*

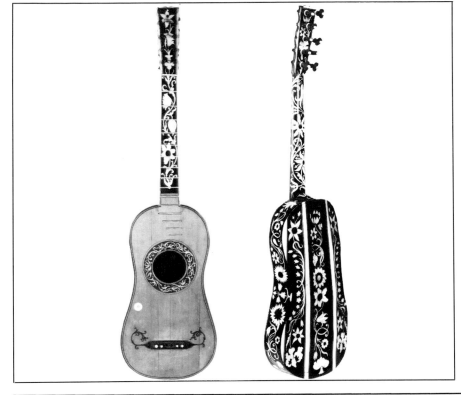

Overall length: 89cm
Scale length: 63cm
Body length: 42.5cm
Body width: upper bout 19.3cm
             waist 16.7cm
             lower bout 23.5cm
Body depth: the greatest overall depth of the
             vault is approximately 9.4cm

Only a fragment of a handwritten label survives, reading "IO...17...", but this guitar is unmistakably the work of Joachim Tielke. It was modified in the nineteenth century by the addition of a pin bridge for six single strings; the pegs and ivory frets also probably date from this period. The rose is missing.

This is a most attractive small guitar, and carries less ornamentation than many surviving examples of Tielke's work. The body is built of ebony and ivory marquetry; the veneer on the neck, head and fingerboard is similar. Tielke's familiar "sunflower" motif predominates throughout.

The body construction is somewhat unusual. The arched back is built of three vaults, with concave cross-sections. Each panel is separated by flat ivory strips. Inside there is a timber plate which braces the back, extending 13cm down from the end block.

Five-course guitar, SPANISH, *c*. 1700.
*From the Instrument Museum of the Barcelona
Conservatory.*

Overall length: 94cm
String length: 67.5cm
Body length: 48.5cm
Body width: upper bout 23.6cm
             waist 18.5cm
             lower bout 27cm
Body depth: increasing from 11 to 13.7cm

The instrument carries no label or maker's identification, but its Spanish origin is confirmed by the shape of the head, the presence of a rudimentary slipper foot, and the use of cypress (in alternation with bands of pale rosewood) for the back and sides. Few Spanish-built five-course guitars survive, and the lack of comparable instruments makes precise dating difficult; but the body shape suggests that the guitar was built around 1700.

By comparison with guitars by the leading French, German, and Italian luthiers the design and craftsmanship of this instrument are lacking in refinement. It is an attractive instrument nevertheless, soundly put together and without pretensions, and has the feel of being a working musician's guitar.

Five-course guitar by Diego Costa, 1715.
Photograph by courtesy of the Instrument Museum of the Karl Marx University, Leipzig.

Overall length: 103cm
String length: 69.3cm
Body length: 49cm
Body width: upper bout 24.2cm
          waist 20.4cm
          lower bout 29cm
Body depth: 12.5cm

The label gives the maker's name, the date, and his address at 21 calle de Cabon, Cadiz.

The top of the guitar is spruce, and the sides and back are maple. The rosette is fretted out of wood, as is the decoration at the base of the soundboard. The fixed frets on the flush fingerboard and table appear to be original.

Five-course guitar by Preston
LONDON, *c*. 1760.
From the collection of James Tyler.

Overall length: 93.2cm
Scale length: 58.7cm
Body length: 46.5cm
Body width: upper bout 23.5cm
          waist 19.5cm
          lower bout 28.7cm
Body depth: increasing from 9.6 to 10cm

Five-course guitar, probably FRENCH and of the first quarter of the eighteenth century. *From the Dolmetsch Collection.*

Overall length: 91.7cm
String length: 66cm
Body length: 44cm
Body width: upper bout 23cm
          waist 17.8cm
          lower bout 25cm
Body depth: increasing from 8.8 to 10cm

The pattern of the ebony and ivory inlay to the top edge and around the soundhole suggests strongly that this guitar was built in

France, and its body shape is consistent with a date early in the eighteenth century. The sides and back are built of maple, and ebony has been used for the flush fingerboard and the head veneer. The lute-style bridge is a modern replacement; marks on the table indicate that the original bridge had the usual "moustaches."

The ostentatious instruments which survive on display in museums today are not entirely typical examples of five-course guitar construction. This neatly made instrument serves as a reminder that the large majority of guitars carried very little decoration.

While the *chitarra battente* was often triple strung, it is most unusual to find a flat-backed gut-strung guitar with three strings to a course. The presence of triple stringing indicates that this guitar was made to be strummed, and used for song and dance accompaniment. This does not mean that it was built as a folk instrument. The popular dances and songs of eighteenth-century southern Spain were taken up by polite society, and this is, by Spanish standards, an expensively made guitar.

English built five-course guitars are extremely rare; during the period when the instrument enjoyed great popularity, in the seventeenth century, the aristocracy usually imported their guitars from France or Italy. This instrument was made at a time when the guitar was out of favor in England, eclipsed by the "English Guitar"—which was not a guitar at all, but a type of large cittern with wire strings and a flat-backed, pear-shaped body.

Preston was the most renowned maker of "English Guitars," and this true guitar is an instrument of quality. It has a darkly var-

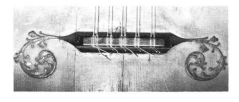

nished spruce top, and maple sides and back. The neck is exceptionally wide for the period, but very flat and shallow. The flush ebony fingerboard extends right up to the body, and is fitted with tied gut frets, although metal frets have been fitted at some time in the past.

The arrangement of the pegs is unusual,

and it is possible that one of the two pegs in the center is a later addition. The "moustaches" at the ends of the bridge turn down, instead of up. While this is an uncommon design, it is by no means unique, and several paintings of the late eighteenth and early nineteenth centuries show bridges of this type.

Five-course guitar by Francisco Perez CADIZ, 1763.
Photograph by courtesy of Peter Sensier.

Overall length: 96.3cm
String length: 63cm
Body length: 45cm
Body width: upper bout 25.8cm
waist 21.5cm
lower bout 30.3cm
Body depth: increasing from 9.3 to 10cm

This guitar raises important questions about the development of the instrument in late eighteenth-century Spain, despite having undergone modifications. Neither the scroll-

work to the ends of the bridge nor the fingerboard is original and the style of the fingerboard indicates that it was added by Louis Panormo of London at some time around the 1830s.

The sides and back are made of cypress, and the neck is joined to the body by a typically Spanish heel and slipper foot. The shape of the body is most unusual; we have seen no other guitar with a similar profile.

The most surprising feature of this guitar, however, is the presence of five fan struts bracing the soundboard. Fan strutting, which improves both the stability and sound qualities of the guitar, was a Spanish invention. But to find it in a guitar built before the 1780s, and in such a sophisticated form, is most surprising. The strutting may be a later addition, possibly by Louis Panormo (who used fan strutting on his own instruments). However, Peter Sensier, who has had the opportunity to give the guitar a thorough examination, believes that the struts are original. If he is correct, this is the earliest known guitar with a fan-strutted table, and predates other surviving examples by some twenty years.

Five-course guitar by Colin PARIS, *c.* 1770s.
Photograph by courtesy of the Instrument Museum of the Royal College of Music, London.

Overall length: 90.5cm
Body length: 42.5cm
Body width: upper bout 19.7cm
waist 15.8cm
lower bout 25.8cm
Body depth: increasing from 8.5 to 9.5cm

This instrument shows the typical features of the late five-course guitar, and was made just at the time when the six single-string guitar was first being introduced.

The body of the guitar is still narrow, but the waist is beginning to become more defined

as the first step toward the familiar nineteenth-century guitar shape. Sides and back are built of maple, with inlaid bands of red lacquered or stained timber. The long V-shaped head was common on late five-course guitars, and this instrument has the typical French type of diagonal pattern inlay to the top edge (here made of alternating strips of tortoiseshell and mother-of-pearl). This inlay pattern virtually disappeared with the five-course guitar.

The bridge and present frets date from a later conversion for use with six single strings. From the marks on the fingerboard left by earlier frets, it is clear that the scale length has also been changed.

The transitional guitar

Up until the last quarter of the eighteenth century, the guitar was still predominantly a five-course instrument; its form, construction and tuning had remained essentially unchanged for centuries. Yet only seventy-five years later, the modern form of six-string classical guitar appeared. The guitar underwent enormous changes in the intervening years, and many experiments in guitar building were carried out between the 1770s and 1850s. Although many of these experiments had no lasting results, the eventual outcome was the modern guitar.

The late eighteenth and early nineteenth centuries thus constitute a period of transition for the instrument. During this time, the changes from five to six courses, from double to single strings, to modern tuning and modern construction techniques, occurred differently in different parts of Europe.

The French and Italians were the first to adopt the six single-string guitar with the modern pattern of tuning. In Spain, the transition to six single strings occurred via the intermediary step of a double-strung six-course guitar, and it was the Spanish who made the most significant advances in construction techniques.

Very little is known of the Spanish construction of the five-course guitar in the eighteenth century—or at any other period, for that matter. But we do know that the six-course guitar was introduced at some date before 1780, and that during the 1780s it became widely popular. The earliest documentary evidence of the six-course guitar in Spain is provided by Antonio Ballesteros' *Obra para guitarra de seis órdenes*, published in 1780. The pitch and interval pattern were those of the modern instrument, and according to Fernando Ferrandière's *Arte de tocar la guitarra española*, published in Madrid in 1799, the strings were tuned in unison with the exception of the lowest pair, which were an octave apart.

Most Spanish six-course guitars come from the south of the country. Cadiz was the main center of lutherie, closely followed by Seville, and surviving six-course guitars made between 1780 and 1810 are fairly numerous. The survival of a reasonably large sample from a restricted geographical area allows us to examine in some detail the development of instrument construction at a critical period.

Guitars by the major luthiers of southern Spain have several features in common. The body shapes are elegant; although still narrow by the standards of today, the bouts are wider and the curvature more pronounced than on the earlier five-course guitars. The bodies are plainly made of either rosewood or spanish cypress, or occasionally of alternating strips of the two. At this period there is no difference in the construction of rosewood- and cypress-bodied guitars. The distinction between rosewood and classical guitars and cypress flamenco guitars was not made until the mid-nineteenth century.

Decoration is restrained, particularly on guitars from Cadiz and Seville. Ornament is often confined to simple inlays of black mastic with small mother-of-pearl inserts, placed around the sound hole and on the lower bout below the bridge. Neither parchment nor fretted wood rosettes were used, and we do not find wood mosaic soundhole inlays until well into the nineteenth century.

Six-course guitars were fitted with tied bridges, whose design changed little from that of late five-course guitar bridges, and simple but elegant "moustaches" continued to be used to decorate the table at the bridge ends. Most Spanish luthiers of the period favored large, unadorned peg heads fitted with plain wooden pegs. At the other end of the neck, the junction to the body is made by an internal slipper foot, and an external heel which by the 1800s had developed into a form very similar to that used on modern guitars.

The fingerboard of the six-course guitar normally stopped at either the sixth or eighth fret, and was set flush with the table. The frets, usually of thin, rectangular metal sections, extend down over the neck on to the table. In instruments that have a fingerboard extending to the soundhole, one suspects a later modification—evidence of which is usually revealed by close examination.

The most important feature of many six-course guitars becomes apparent only when one examines the interior. Many were built with fan-strutted tables, and it is likely that the luthiers building six-course guitars in southern Spain were the first to develop this method of construction. Previously, the lower bout of the guitar was strengthened simply by lateral bars, to resist the pull of the strings, but such cross bracing also inhibits the vibration of the table. Fan strutting, in which the bars run more-or-less longitudinally, at a slight angle to the grain of the table, eliminates the need for transverse struts in the lower bout. The table is given the necessary strength to resist the pull of the strings, and its vibrational efficiency is improved. In one form or another, fan struts are used on almost all modern classical guitars.

The six-course guitars made by Josef Benedit in Cadiz in the 1780s use a simple system of three fan bars. During the 1790s, Juan Pagés (also of Cadiz) developed systems of first five and then seven fans. José Pagés, of the same family, started by using a simple system of three struts in the 1790s, but he too went on to employ more complex strutting as his career progressed. Such a pattern of development suggests that the leading Cadiz luthiers were well aware of the importance of fan strutting to the sound of their guitars. However, very few makers outside Cadiz followed this lead, and there are good-quality southern Spanish guitars of the 1800s that still use only transverse bracing.

The Portuguese followed the Spanish lead in building the six-course instrument. Their guitars, however, show less constructional sophistication and a greater concern for decoration.

Both Spanish and Portuguese persisted in their preference for the six-course guitar long after the six single-string instrument had become common in the rest of Europe. This predilection was not the result of ignorance on their part. Spanish awareness of progress in the rest of Europe is proved by Federico Moretti's *Principios para tocar la guitarra de seis órdenes* (Madrid 1799), which mentions that the French and Italians play the guitar with single strings. The Spanish probably persisted with the double-strung guitar because they found its greater power an advantage in the accompaniment of Andalucian song and dance forms.

It is not known for certain when the six single-string guitar was adopted in Spain. There is a José Pagés guitar with six single strings and machine tuners in the Royal College of Music, London, but this has almost certainly been modified, and was originally double strung. It is most probable that the six single-string guitar came into use in Spain around 1820: Dionisio Aguado's *Escuela de Música* was published in Madrid in 1825 as an instruction book for the single-strung instrument.

Even so, the six-course guitar still retained considerable popularity, and the Englishman George Hogarth described it as late as 1836 as the typical Spanish instrument.[1]

In the rest of Europe, the six single-string guitar with modern tuning was adopted without the intermediary step of the six-course guitar. Nevertheless, the exact stages of this development from the five-course instrument are not entirely clear.

Some authorities hold that the first change from the five-course guitar was to a five single-string instrument, and that the six-string guitar was developed from the five-string guitar by the simple addition of a bass string a fourth below the previous lowest. This theory is attractive, presenting as it does a logical pattern of development, but a careful sifting of evidence is needed before any firm conclusions can be reached. It is certain that five-string guitars existed during the transitional period, but it is difficult to produce watertight evidence that they predate the earliest six-string guitars.

Doisy's *Principes Généraux de la Guitarre à cinq et à six Cordes,* published in Paris in 1801, does no more than establish the simultaneous existence of both types. A five-string guitar made by Gagliano of Naples in 1774 (formerly in the possession of the Cologne Museum, now lost) seems to support the contention that the five-string instrument represents a real intermediary stage. However, while this instrument predates the earliest surviving Italian six-string guitars (which date from the 1780s), it is actually later than a French six-string guitar made by François Lupot in Orleans.

The best conclusion seems to be that, while the five-string guitar was made in small numbers during the period of change from five courses to six single strings, it was not of major significance in the instrument's development. Indeed, it is hard to see how it could have been: the five-string guitar offered neither the extended range of the six-string instrument nor the harmonic sonorities of the five-course. The easier tuning of single strings, and the elimination of the problem of obtaining matched pairs of gut trebles, was equally present on the six single-string guitar.

Although the evidence is inconclusive, it seems most likely that the six single-string guitar first appeared in

France in the early 1770s, and became established in France, Italy, Germany and Austria during the 1780s.

Surviving early six-string guitars include the Lupot guitar of 1773, another French guitar by Montron (1785), one by Antonio Vinaccia of Naples (1785) and one by Stadlman of Vienna (1787). There is also a guitar in Prague, made by Thomas Hulinzky, whose date is given as 1754 (by Alexander Buchner in *Musical Instruments through the Ages,* 1964), which has a head for six strings. The date of this guitar is so far removed from that of any other authentic six-string example, and from any literary and musical references, that we must doubt either the originality of the head or the accuracy of the date.

During the last years of the eighteenth century and the first decades of the nineteenth, the six-string guitar took on a fairly standard pattern. The typical body shape was sharply waisted, with pronounced curvature of the upper and lower bouts. With the introduction of single strings, pin bridges (in which the strings were fixed by a series of wooden pegs passing through the bridge and table) came into favor and replaced the earlier pattern of tied bridge. During the early decades of the nineteenth century, independent bone or ivory saddles started to be used.

The six-string guitar saw the introduction, in rudimentary form, of the modern pattern of fingerboard which extends over the table to the soundhole. The exact date of the first use of this design is uncertain, but it has been credited to the German luthier Georg Staufer, who was granted a license in 1822 to improve guitar construction techniques, in collaboration with Joseph Estel. Staufer is best remembered as the teacher of Christian Friedrich Martin, who emigrated to New York in the 1830s and founded the C. F. Martin company.

C. F. Martin became the most famous of American luthiers, and did much to foster the development of the American guitar. Many other European luthiers emigrated in the nineteenth century, and through them the American steel-strung guitar developed out of the European gut-strung instrument.

Non-Spanish European luthiers usually made the neck-to-body junction via a small triangular heel, which was little different from that on five-course guitars, and a plan end block. The neck was often joined to the heel by a simple sloping miter.

The European six-string guitar was originally tuned by pegs, which were usually fitted to a figure-eight-shaped head which mirrored the shape of the body. Tuning machines, with the familiar worm gear, were used with increasing frequency from the 1820s.

Despite early Spanish experiments with fan strutting, almost all other European guitars continued to be made with transverse table bracing. Louis Panormo of London (active from the 1820s through 1840s) was the only major maker outside Spain to use the system. Panormo was greatly influenced by the guitars of José Pagés, and advertised himself as a "Maker of Guitars in the Spanish style."

Many unusual guitars were made in the nineteenth century: some had movable frets, for experiments with the tuning and temperament, others had unusual body shapes, or scalloped fingerboards. Harp guitars, lyre guitars and lute guitars all had their moments of popularity. Attempts were also made to extend the instrument's range by the addition of extra bass or treble strings, either on or off the fingerboard. Guitars of different pitches were made such as the Terz, Quarte and Quinte-basse guitars, which were tuned respectively a third higher, a fourth higher, and a fifth below the normal. There was also an Octavine, a miniature guitar tuned, as the name suggests, an octave above the ordinary instrument.

None of these oddities has made any lasting impression on the guitar's development, and most north European construction practice was rendered obsolete by Antonio de Torres' introduction of the modern classical instrument in the 1850s. Knowledge of his work took time to be disseminated, however, and comparatively primitive instruments continued to be built throughout the nineteenth century.

Six-course guitar by Josef Benedit
CADIZ, 1783.
*From the Instrument Museum of the Barcelona
Conservatory.*

Overall length: 98.5cm
Scale length: 65.6cm
Body length: 46cm
Body width: upper bout 22.2cm
        waist 17cm
        lower bout 28.5cm
Body depth: increasing from 10 to 11cm

Although this guitar has been played with six single strings at a later date, no structural modifications have been made, and it is a fine example of early Spanish six-course guitar design. Benedit (also spelled Benedid) was one of the most important guitar makers of the Cadiz school, and his instruments are now rare.

The back and sides of the guitar are made of rosewood, which indicates that this was a comparatively expensive instrument. Spanish cypress was used for cheaper models. The rosette patterning, of small squares of mother-of-pearl set diagonally in black mastic, is typical of Spanish work of the period: almost identical designs can be found on the instruments of numerous other makers.

Inside, the guitar has a large, typically Spanish slipper foot of nearly modern design, and the table has three fan struts. Although the exact date of the introduction of fan struts is uncertain, Benedit is one of the first luthiers known to use them consistently.

In its plainness, use of fan strutting, and slipper foot, this guitar anticipates several of the characteristics of the modern instrument.

Six-course guitar by Dionisio Guerra
CADIZ, 1784.
From the José Ramírez instrument collection.

Overall length: 94cm
String length: 59.3cm
Body length: 43.7cm
Body width: upper bout 20.5cm
        waist 16.5cm
        lower bout 27cm
Body depth: increasing from 8.5 to 9.5cm

The pine table of this guitar has no fan strutting, and the back and sides are built of cypress.

This guitar is well built and finely decorated, but does not exhibit the same degree of musical awareness as the previous instrument by Benedit. The absence of fan strutting suggests that in the 1780s the technique was recently discovered and knowledge of it was still restricted.

Seven-course guitar by Francisco Sanguino
SEVILLE, *c.* 1780s.
*From the Instrument Museum of the Barcelona
Conservatory.*

Overall length: 99.5cm
Scale length: 66cm
Body length: 52cm
Body width: upper bout 26.2cm
        waist 22cm
        lower bout 31.5cm
Body depth: increasing from 15.5 to 17.5cm

It is a great pity that there is no legible date

on the label of this extraordinary instrument, which contains so many unusual features.

The first oddity is the use of seven double-strung courses, in place of the normal six. Juan Bermudo had mentioned a seven-course instrument in his book of 1555, but there is no written or musical evidence that a seven-course guitar was used in eighteenth-century Spain. The body of the guitar is unusually wide for the period, and exceptionally long and deep by any standards. The length of the body allows for only nine frets on the neck (eleven was the norm at this date), despite the scale length of 66cm. The table is braced with three fan struts in the lower bout.

There are two possible explanations for the large body. One is that Sanguino was trying to make a louder guitar. The other, more probable, is that this was built as a bass guitar, with an extra course of strings below the normal lowest. As a general rule, the larger the body cavity of the guitar, the more it emphasizes low-frequency vibrations.

The presence of fan strutting makes the illegibility of the date especially unfortunate. Other Sanguino guitars are known, from the period 1750 to 80, and we have seen a six-course guitar of his of 1770 which shows no signs of fan strutting. We are inclined to place this instrument in the early to mid-1780s.

Six-course guitar by Juan Pagés
CADIZ, 1792.
From the Instrument Museum of the Barcelona Conservatory.

Overall length: 100cm
Scale length: 65.5cm
Body length: 47cm
Body width: upper bout 23cm
        waist 18.6cm
        lower bout 29.4cm
Body depth: increasing from 10.5 to 11cm

The sides and back of this guitar are made of rosewood, and in its decoration it lies halfway between the last two examples. The strutting of the table shows a definite advance, however. There are five fan bars in the lower bout. The three center bars are fairly heavy and only slightly splayed, extending well back toward the base of the instrument. The outer two are much lighter, shorter and more widely splayed.

Juan Pagés was obviously aware of the importance of strutting, and developed more sophisticated forms as his career progressed. Another guitar of his dated 1797 (also in the Museum at Barcelona) uses seven fan struts with a similar arrangement: the center five are almost parallel while the two outermost are widely splayed. These two examples show how rapidly Juan Pagés was moving toward a modern strutting pattern.

The body of this guitar is broader than that of the Benedit guitar, showing the start of a move toward modern proportions. Spanish guitars of the late eighteenth century prove that Torres did not conjure the modern classic guitar out of thin air: his work was, rather, the culmination of a long process of development.

Six-course guitar by Pedro Ferreira Oliveira
LISBON, *c.* 1790s.
From the Dolmetsch Collection.

Overall length: 89.6cm
Scale length: 61cm
Body length: 41.8cm
Body width: upper bout 20.3cm
        waist 15.7cm
        lower bout 27.3cm
Body depth: increasing from 7.5 to 9.5cm

The six-course guitar existed in Portugal at much the same time as in Spain. On the

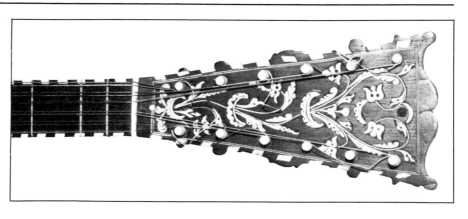

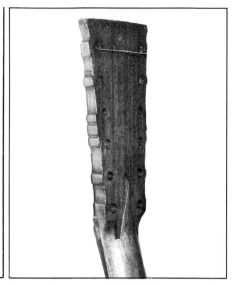

label of this instrument, the numerals "17" are printed, but the luthier has not filled in the last two figures of the date.

The construction is similar to that of equivalent Spanish instruments, although there is no fan strutting.

Portuguese six-course guitars differed from the Spanish mainly in their proportions and degree of decoration. The body shape of this instrument shows less development from that of the later five-course guitars than do the Spanish models, and the wide splay to the head is typical of Portuguese instruments.

The scrollwork inlay to the head and the soundhole is typically Portuguese in style, and more ornate than that commonly found on equivalent Spanish instruments. Six-course guitars have continued in popular use in Portugal to the present century.

Six-course guitar by José Pagés CADIZ, 1798.
From the Victoria and Albert Museum, London.

Overall length: 97.6cm
Scale length: not available
Body length: 45.2cm
Body width: upper bout 21.8cm
           waist 17.3cm
           lower bout 28cm
Body depth: increasing from 9.1 to 10.6cm

José Pagés makes up, with Juan Pagés and Josef Benedit, the trio of leading Cadiz instrument builders of the late eighteenth and early nineteenth centuries.

This guitar was modified in the nineteenth century by the addition of a new fingerboard and bridge, in place of the old flush finger-

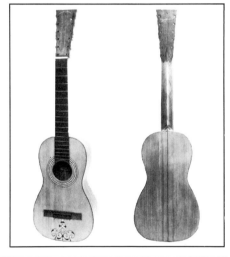

board to the sixth fret and tied bridge, but is still a good example of José Pagés' early work.

The table has three fan struts (not four, as has often been stated). José Pagés was another maker who increased the sophistication of his strutting as his career developed: an instrument of his dated 1806 (in the Barcelona Conservatory) has five well-shaped symmetrical fan bars.

The body is made of cypress, and is smaller than bodies of guitars of similar date by Juan Pagés. Its curvature is surprisingly modern. The body shape should be compared with that of Panormo's six-string guitars of the 1830s (see page 48), which reflect José Pagés' influence. The junction of head to neck, by an extended V joint, is typical of Spanish and Portuguese six-course guitars.

Six-course guitar by Ignacio de los Santos SEVILLE, 1796.
From the Instrument Museum of the Barcelona Conservatory.

Overall length: 89.3cm
Scale length: 61cm
Body length: 40.3cm
Body width: upper bout 19.4cm
           waist 15.2cm
           lower bout 24.2cm
Body depth: increasing from 9 to 10.2cm

Cadiz may have been the main center of guitar building in the late eighteenth century,

but it was not the only important one.

This guitar from Seville is a delicate instrument, with a short scale length and narrow body, but deep sides. Its decoration is very similar to that of guitars built in Cadiz, but there is no sign of any form of fan strutting.

Six-course guitar by Josef Alcañiz
MURCIA, 1804.
*From the Instrument Museum of the Barcelona
Conservatory.*

Overall length: 96.5cm
Scale length: 64cm
Body length: 43.5cm
Body width: upper bout 23cm
          waist 16.1cm
          lower bout 27.5cm
Body depth: increasing from 9.4 to 11.8cm

Murcia is in the southeast of Spain, a little inland from the Mediterranean coast. This instrument shows several features which differ from those of the guitars made in Cadiz and Seville in the southwest.

The curvature of the upper and lower bouts is greater and the waist more pronounced, giving a body shape which is a little closer to that used by French and Italian luthiers of the time. The mother-of-pearl and black mastic inlay of the table and rosette is more ornate than that of the guitars from Seville and Cadiz. Concern with ornamentation is also seen in the black lacquer pattern on the cypress back, the marquetry on the back of the neck and head, and the ivory finials to the tuning pegs. The fingerboard appears to be a later addition, but it has been executed very neatly and with attention to the overall style of the guitar. The table shows no sign of fan strutting, despite the comparatively late date. This again can be taken as further support for the contention that fan bars were first introduced by luthiers in Cadiz, and only slowly became general among the luthiers of the rest of southern Spain.

Six single-string guitar by François Lupot
ORLEANS, 1773.
*Photograph by courtesy of the Smithsonian
Institution, Washington DC.*

Overall length: 91cm
Scale length: 64cm
Body length: 44.2cm
Body width: upper bout 21.3cm
          waist 15.6cm
          lower bout 26.9cm
Body depth: increasing from 7.4cm at the
          upper bout to a constant 8cm
          over the waist and lower bout

There is conflicting information on François Lupot. Some sources give his date of birth in Plombières as 1725, others as 1736. He traveled to Stuttgart in either 1756 or 1758, and is recorded as being luthier to the court of Württemburg in 1766. He returned from there to France, setting up business in Orleans in 1770, and died in Paris in 1804.

The label of this guitar reads "Francisco Lupot fecit Orleano 1773." The spruce table extends over the neck in the normal fashion. The edge bindings are made of alternate bindings of ivory and ebony, and so is the soundhole inlay. Sides and back are made of a pale hardwood not commonly found in guitar construction, probably ash or elm. The bridge and pins are made of ebony with mother-of-pearl inlay, and the "moustaches" on the table on either end of the bridge are made of fretted metal.

This guitar appears to be the earliest surviving six-string guitar made in France. The five-course was still being made in considerable numbers at this time, and the six-string guitars were uncommon before the mid-1780s. Despite its early date, this guitar shows all the features we associate with the six-string instrument of the late eighteenth century. Although the body is still narrow, it has the typical rounded shoulders and wasp waist, in contrast to the less indented body which was still prevalent on five-course guitars.

The inverted figure-eight peg head is a feature associated with the majority of six-string guitars up until the second quarter of the nineteenth century, when tuning machines began to be widely used. It is interesting that the figure-eight form should have appeared immediately on the introduction of the single-strung guitar in the 1770s and 1780s.

The pegged bridge is typical of the six-string guitar before the standardization of the modern form of bridge which was first used in the 1850s. Naturally, the peg bridge was not suitable for double-strung guitars, which continued to use tied bridges, but the evidence of this guitar suggests that the peg bridge was used on some of the earliest of single-string instruments. It is possible, however, that the bridge seen here is not original: changes of bridge are common, and can be difficult to detect.

Six-string guitar by Antonio Vinaccia NAPLES, 1790.
Photograph by courtesy of the Smithsonian Institution, Washington DC.

Overall length: 90.2cm
Scale length: 64cm
Body length: 44.4cm
Body width: upper bout 22.3cm
           waist 16.3cm
           lower bout 29cm
Body depth: increasing from 6.3 to 7.4cm

The label reads "Antonio Vinaccia fecit Neapoli Anno 1790." The Vinaccia family was notable among Neapolitan luthiers during the late eighteenth century. Antonio I lived from 1734 to 1781, and his son Antonio II, the maker of this guitar, from 1763 to 1798. Of the other luthiers in the family, Vicenzo is also specifically mentioned as a maker of guitars.

The body of this instrument is wide in the upper and lower bouts for its date, and very sharply waisted. Sides and back are made of brown varnished fruitwood, and the table is pine or spruce. The decorative inlays on the table are made of mother-of-pearl set in bands of ebony and are typical of Italian workmanship of the period. The plaques on fingerboard and head are also made of mother-of-pearl, which has been ornately engraved.

The bridge is unusual. It appears to have been designed as a tied bridge, and the front and back are protected by strips of bone. The carving of the ends of the bridge is crude, and out of keeping with the level of craftsmanship shown in the rest of the guitar. This, and the presence of slight discoloration around the bridge area, suggests modification by another hand.

Six-string guitar by Gioacchino Trotto NAPLES, 1792.
Photograph by courtesy of the Instrument Museum of the Karl Marx University, Leipzig.

Overall length: 88cm
Body length: 43.5cm
Body width: upper bout 21.1cm
           waist 17.3cm
           lower bout 27.2cm
Body depth: 7cm

Trotto was another leading member of the Neapolitan school of luthiers in the late eighteenth century, and his label reads "Gioacchino Trotto fecit/Anno 1792 accosto le/grade di S. Demetrio."

The body of the guitar is lacquered a reddish brown, and the inlays to the sound-board are made of mother-of-pearl set in dark red mastic. The fingerboard is tortoiseshell, inlaid with mother-of-pearl.

This guitar has a smaller body than the one by Vinaccia, and is reminiscent in shape and decoration of late five-course guitars.

Six-string guitar by Grobert PARIS, *c.* 1820s.
Photographs by courtesy of the Paris Conservatory.

Overall length: 92cm
Scale length: 63.5cm
Body length: 44cm
Body width: upper bout 22.4cm
           waist 16.3cm
           lower bout 29.5cm
Body depth: increasing from 7 to 7.8cm over the upper bout, then constant at 7.8cm

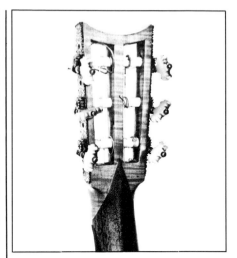

This guitar is famous for its association with Berlioz and Paganini. It was lent to Paganini on his second visit to Paris in the 1830s by J. B. Vuillaume, and then given by Paganini to Berlioz, at which time both great musicians signed it in token of their friendship and love of the guitar. Berlioz eventually gave it to the instrument museum of the Paris Conservatory, where it remains today.

The table has transverse as opposed to fan bracing, in the manner common to almost all non-Spanish guitars of the nineteenth century. Similarly, the body-to-neck junction is made by a V-shaped heel and plain end block in the manner of earlier European instruments. The sides are built of a light-colored rosewood, and the back is of pine with a thin external veneer of dark rosewood.

Six-string guitar by Louis Panormo
LONDON, 1822.
From the collection of John Roberts.

Overall length: 94cm
Scale length: 62.9cm
Body length: 44.8cm
Body width: upper bout 22.9cm
             waist 17.5cm
             lower bout 28.7cm
Body depth: increasing from 8.9 to 10.2cm

Louis Panormo was the fourth son of an Italian luthier, Vicenzo Panormo, and was born in Paris in 1784. He moved to London in 1819 and set up shop in Bloomsbury, where he built guitars, violins, cellos and double basses.

As his label states, Louis Panormo was "The only Maker of Guitars in the Spanish Style"—outside Spain, that is. The body shape and decoration of Panormo's guitars were closely copied from Pagés, and he used highly developed systems of fan strutting.

This guitar has a spruce table, fitted with seven light, symmetrical fan struts. The transverse bar immediately above the soundhole is stamped with the letter "P," a brand mark often used by Panormo in addition to his printed label. The sides are built of rosewood, while the back is made of rosewood veneer mounted on a sheet of maroon-painted spruce. Panormo followed the Spanish procedure of using a slipper foot, fitting the sides into grooves in the endblock formed by heel and foot, to make the junction between neck and body.

The neck, head and fingerboard show a distinct advance over Spanish procedure of the day. Panormo joined a maple head to a mahogany neck, and fitted superb tuning machines made by Baker. By using maple (which is very hard and durable), he could carve away large areas of the head to compensate for the weight of the machines. In this way he managed to obtain the accuracy of machine tuning without losing the lightness and balance of the small guitar.

The fingerboard is made of ebony, extends to the soundhole, and carries eighteen rectangular section frets. Panormo shaped the fingerboards of his guitars to a very slight curve, a most unusual feature on a nineteenth-century guitar. Most of Panormo's guitars are fitted with ebony pin bridges, with no separate saddle, and ebony mother-of-pearl inlaid lozenges on the soundboard at each end.

Louis Panormo's guitars are closer to the modern form of the instrument than those of any other maker of his day. They possess a beautifully rounded tone, with surprisingly warm basses for so small-bodied an instrument, and clear, singing trebles.

Six-string guitar by René Lacôte
PARIS, 1824.
From the Instrument Museum of the Paris Conservatory.

Overall length: 91cm
Scale length: 63cm
Body length: 43.5cm
Body width: upper bout 21.5cm
           waist 16.6cm
           lower bout 28.5cm
Body depth: increasing from 7.7 to 8.5cm at
           the waist, and constant at 8.5cm
           thereafter

René Lacôte was the most successful luthier in Paris during the first half of the nineteenth century. His output was considerable, but this did not affect the quality of the craftsmanship of his guitars, and he produced several innovations.

For the most part, this guitar follows the pattern common in French instruments of the 1820s and 30s. The sides are made of rosewood, and the back is built of pine with a

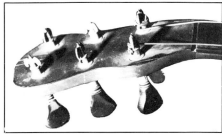

rosewood veneer. Decoration has been kept to a minimum. The fingerboard extends to the soundhole and carries eighteen narrow brass frets.

The most interesting feature of this guitar is the tuning mechanism incorporated in the figure-eight head. The strings are attached to metal capstans, which are turned directly by the pegs. Once the strings are brought to pitch, the pegs can be locked by screwing down the wing nuts tight on top of the capstans. This elegant mechanism is believed to be one of Lacôte's own inventions, although it appears on the guitars of several other makers who used it under license.

Six-string guitar by Johann Georg Staufer
VIENNA, *c.* 1825.
From the collection of Harvey Hope.

Overall length: 93.8cm
Scale length: 61cm
Body length: 43.4cm
Body width: upper bout 24cm
           waist 17cm
           lower bout 30cm
Body depth: increasing from 6.8 to 7.4cm

The label reads "Nach den Modell/Luigi Legnani/Von Johann Georg Staufer/Anno 18 in Wien No 480."

Staufer made several patterns of guitar, but the "Legnani" model, named after the famous Italian virtuoso and composer for the guitar, best shows the features for which he is famous.

The body is conventional enough in design, and is built of maple, with a spruce top. Staufer's design modifications were to the neck, head and fingerboard. The tuning machines are all mounted on one side of the head, the gears being set into the head itself and concealed by an engraved brass cover plate. The neck joins the body via a pivot, so that the

neck angle may be adjusted by the turning of a key at the base of the heel, and the ebony fingerboard carries over the table without touching it. There are twenty-two rectangular-section nickle-silver frets.

We would strongly suggest that references to Staufer as having "invented" the fingerboard extending to the soundhole are correct only insofar as they refer to the "flying fingerboard," separated from the table, and that the normal type of extended fingerboard was developed by others.

Six-string guitar by Nicolas Morlot
MIRECOURT, *c.* 1820s.
From the Victoria and Albert Museum, London.

Overall length: 93.7cm
Scale length: 64cm
Body length: 45.2cm
Body width: upper bout 21.9cm
         waist 16cm
         lower bout 28.8cm
Body depth: increasing from 7 to 8cm

"Enharmonic" guitar by Louis Panormo
LONDON, 1829.
Photograph by courtesy of the Instrument Museum of the Karl Marx University, Leipzig.

Overall length: 98cm
Scale length: not available
Body length: 48cm
Body width: upper bout 30cm
         waist: not available
         lower bout 36.5cm
Body depth: 8.5cm

The "Enharmonic" guitar was the invention of General T. Perronet Thompson, Fellow of Queen's College, Cambridge, from 1804 to 14, who in 1829 published a book called *Instructions to my Daughter for Playing on the Enharmonic Guitar.* General Thompson was dissatisfied with equal temperament on the guitar, and proposed an instrument that could be tuned and played in just intonation. Unfortunately, for just intonation the frets have to be placed in different positions for each key, and one fret cannot be made to serve all the strings. The guitar has, in effect, to be re-fretted every time there is a change of key.

To achieve this, the frets were made like croquet hoops, so they could be pegged into holes in the fingerboard, and were wide enough only for one string each. To provide the necessary positions, the octave had to be divided into fifty-nine divisions!

General Thompson's system was so ferociously complicated for the player and luthier alike that it is a miracle that any enharmonic guitars were made, and it has until now been thought that none survived. Although this instrument has been in the collection of the Leipzig Museum since the war (and in Cologne before that), it has not previously been recognized as an enharmonic guitar.

Louis Panormo was mentioned in the *Instructions,* published the same year as this guitar was built, as being able to supply the enharmonic guitar "Price in common wood 10 Guineas." As his normal guitars were avail-

The inside of the back carries the stamp "A La Ville de Cremone NICOLAS MORLOT," and the letters "NM." The sign "A La Ville de Cremone" was used by a number of luthiers working in Mirecourt in the Vosges area of France during the late eighteenth and early nineteenth centuries. During this period, Mirecourt was one of the leading European centers for the construction of both guitars and violins. Nicolas Morlot was active during the early part of the century, and had a reputation as a maker of violins after the style of Stradivari, as well as of guitars.

This guitar is typical of the better instruments made in Mirecourt. The sides and back are built of maple, and the back of the head and neck are stained black. Its construction details show no deviations from the general French style of the day.

able from two guineas to a maximum of fifteen for the most highly decorated, the price of the enharmonic guitar must have been an added disincentive to prospective purchasers.

The fingerboard of the enharmonic guitar is built strictly according to General Thompson's specifications; the original croquet hoop frets still survive, and there is a plaque on the head to indicate the key. Otherwise, the instrument deviates from Panormo's normal design only by being wider in the body (which is rosewood), by having a more ornately carved maple head, and by an unusual type of ebony and ivory pin bridge.

Six-string guitar by José Recio CADIZ, 1831.
From the collection of Harvey Hope.

Overall length: 94.6cm
Scale length: 64.9cm
Body length: 44.5cm
Body width: upper bout 22.5cm
         waist 17.5cm
         lower bout 29.2cm
Body depth: increasing from 10 to 10.4cm

The top of this guitar is made of spruce, with three fan struts, and the sides and back are made of a dark hardwood (possibly a form of rosewood). The neck is cedar.

It is interesting to compare the details of this six-string guitar, made by José Recio at

Six-string guitar by C. F. Martin
NEW YORK, *c*. 1836.
From the Martin Company Museum, Nazareth, Pennsylvania.

Measurements: not available.

The label reads "C.F.Martin & Schatz/ Manufacturers/of the Celebrated Spanish & Vienna warranted/GUITARS, VIOLINS, VIOLONCELLOS & DOUBLE BASSES/made in the best Italian Style No 1296."

C. F. Martin emigrated to the United States from Germany in 1833, and set up at

78 calle de S Leonora, with the six-course guitars built in Cadiz forty or fifty years earlier. The body shape and fan strutting show no significant development on the early instruments of Benedit, and are less advanced than some of the guitars by Juan and José Pagés. Although the bridge has quite a modern rectangular shape, the strings are simply tied to a raised center block, and there is no separate saddle. One innovation is in the

196 Hudson Street, New York, where he stayed until 1838. Henry Schatz was a friend of Martin's from Germany, and a business partner in the early years of the Martin Company.

Although the label mentions construction in the Italian style, C. F. Martin's guitars of the 1830s show the influence of Georg Staufer of Vienna, for whom he had worked.

Six-string guitar by Coffe-Goguette
MIRECOURT, *c*. late 1830s.
From the Mickleburgh Collection, Bristol.

Overall length: 92.4cm
Scale length: 62.5cm
Body length: 44.6cm
Body width: upper bout 23.8cm
          waist 17cm
          lower bout 30.6cm
Body depth: increasing from 7.5 to 8 cm

The guitar is signed "Coffe-Goguette à Mirecourt," and stamped "COFFE" in both capitals and script on the inside of the back.

head-to-neck junction. While this looks like that on six-course guitars, with a long tongue extending up the back of the head, it is functionally different. Whereas six-course guitars used a form of butt-and-V joint, this instrument uses a splice joint of the type found on classical guitars today. The tongue on the back of the head is simply a vestigial remain of the earlier type of joint, and is purely decorative.

The reference to the "Italian style" is, in fact, to Staufer's "Legnani" model.

The body of this guitar is of rosewood, with a spruce top, and the fingerboard and bridge are of ivory. The body bindings are also ivory, and the top edge is inlaid with the herringbone pattern strip which became a regular feature of many Martin guitars over the following century. The head and neck construction of very early Martin guitars follows Staufer. The tuning machine gears are concealed within the head, on the back of which there is an engraved silver cover plate, and the pegs all mounted on one side. The neck angle is adjustable by a mechanism controlled by a clock key, which turns a pivot mounted in the heel.

C. F. Martin's guitars of this period show a standard of constructional finesse and craftsmanship unsurpassed by any other nineteenth-century luthier. Martin was not the only important American-based guitar maker in the early nineteenth century and by no means the only one to come from Germany. Fernando Sor, writing in 1833, singles out Schroeder of Pittsburgh as being the equal of the leading European luthiers.

Coffe-Goguette won a bronze medal at the Exposition of 1839 for a well-made and tastefully ornamented guitar, which was also judged to have a superior tone to the others exhibited. In the revised 1951 edition of his *Dictionnaire Universel des Luthiers*, Vannes identifies Coffe-Goguette with Jean-Joseph Coffe (1799–1881), but not all authorities agree with this identification.

The guitar is a salon rather than a concert instrument. Despite its comparatively late date, the fingerboard only extends to the ninth fret, and in its mother-of-pearl decoration it seems designed to appeal as much to the eye as to the ear.

Six-string guitar by Louis Panormo LON-DON, 1843.
From the collection of John Roberts.

Overall length: 94cm
Scale length: 62.9cm
Body length: 44.8cm
Body width: upper bout 22.9cm
           waist 17.8cm
           lower bout 28.9cm
Body depth: increasing from 8.9 to 10.5cm

This guitar of Louis Panormo's is almost identical in size and construction to the other example we show (page 48), which was made over twenty years earlier. It differs only in having maple sides and back, a black

Six-string guitar by Beau MIRECOURT, *c.* 1840.
From the Instrument Museum of the Barcelona Conservatory.

Overall length: 84.5cm
Scale length: 63cm
Body length: 46cm
Body width: upper bout 25cm
           waist 18cm
           lower bout 32.5cm
Body depth: increasing from 7.7cm at the neck to 8.5cm at the waist, and then decreasing to 8.2cm on the lower bout. The arching of the back is great enough to be noticeable

We include this guitar for the sake of its scalloped fingerboard. The spaces between

the frets are scooped out, and the brass frets are set with their tops flush with the ridges so formed. Scalloped fingerboards had a vogue in the mid-nineteenth century. The most important luthier to build scalloped fingerboard guitars was René Lacôte, who is often credited with their invention.

The advocates of scalloped fingerboards claimed that they facilitated the playing of glissandos, but they could present problems of intonation. The tension of the string varies according to which part of the hollow it is pressed to.

Another sign of nineteenth-century experimentation is in the cutting away of the shoulders of the upper bout to make the high frets more accessible (as on modern electric guitars). Such modifications usually impair the tone of the acoustic guitar, and have never become common on the classical instrument.

lacquered head and neck, a pin bridge with saddle, and a soundhole decorated with concentric bands of purfling. These features bring it more into line with the French taste in guitar styling, although the design remains thoroughly Spanish in inspiration.

Louis Panormo continued to work in London until 1854, after which it is believed that he emigrated to join his son in New Zealand. Louis was not the only member of the family to make instruments in London. Two of his elder brothers, Joseph and George, and their respective sons, Edward and George Lewis, were also successful luthiers, and built guitars. None of them, however, was the equal of Louis.

Six-string guitar by Altimira
BARCELONA 1840s.
Photographs by courtesy of the Victoria and Albert Museum, London.

Overall length: 93.5cm
Scale length: 62.5cm
Body length: 45cm
Body width: upper bout 23.3cm
           waist 17.2cm
           lower bout 30.5cm
Body depth: increasing from 8.5 to 9.5cm

Altimira was active in Barcelona in the period 1840 to 1880, and was a maker of both

guitars and violins. In 1878 he won a silver medal at the Paris Exposition for a highly decorated guitar. The instrument shown here has a label reading "No 385 Fab^{ca} de Altimira. Calle Escudellers No 61. Barcelona ano 184.," and is said to have been made for the daughter of Don Manuel de Rosas, the one-time dictator of Argentina who fled to England in 1852.

Though built in the north of Spain, it is constructed on French lines. There is no sign of fan strutting, or any awareness of the constructional developments current in the south. The body shape is typically French, and Altimira has used concealed tuning

machines of the type introduced by Lacôte.

The major emphasis of this guitar is on decoration. There is a lavish use of mother-of-pearl, which appears both in the bindings and on the fingerboard. The spaces between the frets are occupied by engraved mother-of-pearl plaques showing miscellaneous scenes, including a huntsman, a man and a dog, a dog and sheep, boats on a river, a church, birds, and a fisherman.

The back of the guitar is made of bird's-eye maple veneer laid over pine. The love scene in the center is painted on wood with inlays of mother-of-pearl and painted ivory. One of the figures is playing a six-course guitar of late-eighteenth-century pattern.

The instrument is a good example of a boudoir instrument made for an influential client, a guitar in which almost vulgarly lavish ornament is the supreme consideration.

Six-string guitar, FRENCH, mid-nineteenth century.
From the Instrument Museum of the Barcelona Conservatory.

Overall length: 85cm
Scale length: 65.5cm
Body length: 44.5cm
Body width: upper bout 24.5cm
          waist 17.8cm
          lower bout 31.2cm
Body depth: increasing from 8.5 to 9.4cm

Although it has no visible maker's identification, the combined evidence of bridge design, body shape and machine head identify this instrument as French in origin, and dating from the middle of the nineteenth century.

The interesting feature of this guitar is its double back. The extreme back is made of rosewood, and has a small oval soundhole in the center of the lower bout. The intermediate back is made of pine, and is quite heavy. It has a circular soundhole immediately under the soundhole in the front.

Several guitarists and luthiers at different periods have felt that the guitar's vibrations are inhibited by the contact of the back with the player's body. Double-backed guitars have been made in an attempt to overcome this damping effect. However, the provision of a double back does not automatically overcome the problem. The air trapped between the two backs can itself act as a dampening spring, restricting vibration, and it is to overcome this effect that soundholes have been cut in the backs. The difficulty now arises that the back of the guitar no longer acts as a simple reflector, and there is a flow of air between the various cavities created. It is therefore not surprising that luthiers have on the whole been content to work on the formidable range of problems presented by the normal guitar, without further complicating the issue by adding a second back.

Six-string guitar by René Lacôte
PARIS, 1852.
From the Instrument Museum of the Paris Conservatory.

Overall length: 96.5cm
Scale length: 62.5cm
Body length: 44cm
Body width: upper bout 22.3cm
          waist 16.5cm
          lower bout 29.8cm
Body depth: increasing from 8 to 8.5cm

We were fortunate in being able to

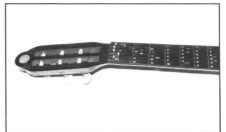

examine this instrument while it was undergoing restoration, and the photograph of the interior reveals the bracing and construction pattern typical of nineteenth-century non-Spanish guitars.

The head of the guitar is fitted with Lacôte's patent tuning machines, in which the gears are built into the head and fully concealed. This elegant system is common on his later instruments.

The most unusual feature of this guitar is its fingerboard. The frets are divided into six parts, one for each string. Each of these mini-frets is mounted on a small ebony block, and these ebony blocks slide in rectangular grooves cut in the ebony of the fingerboard. The exact location of every fret can be adjusted separately for each of the six strings by sliding the ebony block into position, and wedging it with a minute sliver of cork.

Problems of intonation and temperament have interested players and luthiers alike ever since the creation of the guitar. The adjustable frets of this guitar allow compensation to be made for changes in tension caused by depressing the string at each fret.

The sliding fret system was invented by Lacôte, and the construction of the fingerboard is a masterpiece of intricate craftsmanship.

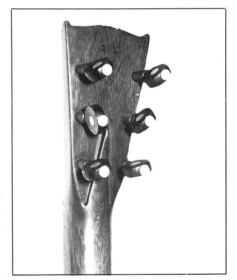

Six-string guitar by José Serrano SEVILLE, 1852.
From the collection of Harvey Hope.

Overall length: 94.3cm
Scale length: 65cm
Body length: 44.5cm
Body width: upper bout 20.9cm
           waist 16.5cm
           lower bout 29cm
Body depth: increasing from 9.4 to 10cm

The guitar's top is made of spruce, fitted with three fan struts, and the sides and back are rosewood. Rosewood has also been used for the fingerboard, and for the pegs (which are very neatly decorated with ivory inlay). The pin bridge, with a separate saddle, appears to be original.

Serrano's guitar is very well made, but retains the small body familiar from the late eighteenth century, simple strutting, traditional pegs and a tied bridge. It is of interest because it was made at the time when Antonio de Torres, also in Seville, was building the first "modern" classical and flamenco guitars (see pages 56–7). This guitar can therefore be taken (with caution) as a yardstick against which to assess the extent of Torres' innovations.

Six-string guitar, Style 2-27, by the C. F. Martin Company NAZARETH, PENNSYLVANIA, *c.* 1867.
From the collection of John Pearse.

The guitars made by the Martin Company from the 1850s onward are quite distinct from any made in Europe in the nineteenth century. They show the emergence of a truly American style of guitar.

Martin's guitars of the second half of the nineteenth century, which were built for gut strings, are transitional guitars in two senses. In size and tonal quality they fall between the early nineteenth-century guitar and the modern classical guitar developed by Torres in Spain from 1850. Where Torres was spurred on by the interest of leading concert virtuosi, the Martin company was building guitars for use in the home, largely for song accompaniment. The difference in patterns of use thus affected the paths taken in instrument design.

Martin's guitars are also transitional in that the design for the early gut-strung instruments proved to be the basis for the steel-string guitars which developed in the twentieth century. Martin developed around 1850 a revolutionary bracing pattern, based on diagonally placed bars with an X pattern under the waist and lower bout. Although less well adapted to the demands of gut strings than was Torres' fan strutting, this design later proved to be highly suited to steel-string instruments..

Although nineteenth-century Martins are small by modern standards, they are loud for their size, and are still sometimes used by leading folk musicians. John Pearse says that this guitar is one of the best balanced instruments he has ever played, and is ideal for recording.

Six-string guitar by Miguel Farfan PERU, 1874.
From the Instrument Museum of the Barcelona Conservatory.

Overall length: 96cm
Scale length: 62.5cm
Body length: 46.5cm
Body width: upper bout 22.3cm
　　　　　　waist 19.1cm
　　　　　　lower bout 30cm
Body depth: 12cm

The label of this instrument reads "Fabrica/por/MIGUEL FARFAN/1Aedo/Cuzco, año 1804."

By the South American standards of the day, this must have been a superior instrument, although it falls short of the sophistication shown by the very best of European luthiers. The combination of Spanish and French/Italian influences is peculiar. The body profile is generally Spanish, as is the shape of the heel, but there is an end block in place of the Spanish slipper foot, no fan strutting, and a French or Italian pattern figure-eight head.

The shape of the tied bridge has a character slightly similar to that of the pin bridge of the Gibson SJ200 made more than sixty years later. We are reminded of the influence of South American guitars on North American steel-string guitar design.

The modern classical guitar

The development of the modern form of the classical guitar is one of the few stages of the instrument's history that can be traced with reasonable certainty. When we examine closely those guitars built in the early years of the nineteenth century by luthiers such as Louis Panormo and the members of the Pagés family, it is clear that, although they possess some of the features of the modern instrument, they represent an earlier stage of development. But the instruments made by the Spaniard Antonio de Torres Jurado from the 1850s until his death in 1892 are immediately recognizable as classical guitars in today's sense.

Torres, who is often referred to as the "Stradivarius of the guitar," probably did more than any other luthier to develop the qualities of the instrument. The guitar, unlike the violin, does not keep its full acoustic properties over a period of centuries, so we cannot make a full assessment of the playing characteristics of old instruments. However, enough of Torres' guitars survive in playable condition to confirm the opinion of his contemporaries that his instruments possessed a tonal beauty and power of projection which were unusual by any standards, and in a different class from anything else known in his day.

Torres is a shadowy figure: few of the details of his life can be documented, while a considerable body of hearsay and legend has grown up around the small core of hard fact.

He was born on June 13, 1817 in La Cañada de San Urbino, just outside Almería. At the age of sixteen he moved to Vera, in an unsuccessful attempt to avoid military service. He was conscripted in 1835, but his discharge followed in a few months (probably on the grounds of ill health), and he returned to Vera to marry. He remained in Vera for some years, and worked as a carpenter.

Torres' whereabouts and career for the six or seven years after the death of his first wife in 1845 are a subject of dispute. The generally accepted story is advanced by Emilio Pujol in his book on Tárrega. Pujol states that Torres worked in Granada, where he learned guitar making from José Pernas. Granada was an important center of lutherie in the mid-nineteenth century, and Pernas one of the city's leading craftsmen. Pernas had a fondness for building pear-shaped guitars with no upper bout; at least one such instrument has been attributed to

Torres, and this has been taken as circumstantial evidence of a link between the two men.[1]

Unfortunately though, no evidence supporting Pujol's linking of Torres to Pernas (or even confirming Torres' presence in Granada) has yet been discovered. On the contrary a signed and witnessed document has recently come to light in which Torres swore that he had been resident in Seville since 1845—which would seem to preclude any connection with Pernas.[2]

Whatever the truth of Torres' whereabouts in the later 1840s, and the details of his training as a luthier, it is certain that he was established as a guitar maker in Seville by the early 1850s. During Torres' Seville period, he worked for the most part in the calle de la Cerragería[3] and achieved a considerable reputation. His instruments were adopted by the guitarist Julián Arcas, who then introduced Torres to Francisco Tárrega. Both Arcas and Tárrega played Torres guitars in their recitals in Spain and abroad.

This period seems to have lasted until 1869, at which point Torres was no longer able to support himself financially by guitar making. There are records that in 1876 he was back in Almería, married for a second time, and running a china shop to make a living. But in 1880 he started making guitars again, at 20 calle Real, La Cañada, Almería. This final phase of his career as a luthier was to last until his death in 1892.

Although his life is sketchy, Torres' achievements are clear. His revolution of the guitar was brought about less by the introduction of new features than by the development, perfection and combination of existing ideas whose full potential had not been realized. The most immediately noticeable difference between his guitars and those of his predecessors is to be found in the shape and size of the body. Torres' guitars had conspicuously larger upper and lower bouts, giving the guitar a fuller figure, and deeper sides. His most famous work, however, was in the development of fan strutting.

He demonstrated conclusively the acoustic importance of fan strutting, with the aid of his famous papier-mâché bodied guitar (see page 61), and through his many experiments, tested out a number of strutting patterns; one of these, the seven-fan system, eventually became his standard. Torres' pattern of strutting is still widely used, and remains the point of departure for any luthier wishing to develop alternative patterns of strutting design.

The combination of a judiciously strutted table with the larger body size gave Torres' instruments a stronger, richer sound, with a wider range of tonal response than any of their predecessors. Although they are not particularly loud by modern standards, Torres' guitars have a clear, balanced tone, firm and rounded, which carries well.

His other achievements include the standardization of the scale length at 65cm, a size that allows the guitar something approaching its maximum volume without either sacrificing clarity of sound or facing the player with excessive left-hand stretches. He also standardized the modern pattern of fingerboard—wider and thicker than that on earlier instruments—and a pattern of tied bridge almost identical to that found on all classical guitars today. Finally, he stripped the instrument of all extraneous decoration in favor of a simple rosette and the minimum of purflings and inlays.

The Torres guitar was so obviously superior to anything else in its day that its example changed the pattern of guitar building, first of all in Spain and eventually worldwide. Not only that, but the new sonorities and tone colors which became available on the modern guitar have inspired composers and virtuosi alike to explore new ways of making the most of them. The modern instrument, introduced by Torres, has proved to be an important catalyst in the development of music and technique.

Torres left no pupils or immediate successors. After his death, Madrid became the main center of guitar building. In the last part of the nineteenth century and the beginning of the twentieth, the Madrid school was led by three luthiers—Vincente Arias (*c.* 1840s–1912), José Ramírez I (1857–1923), and his brother Manuel Ramírez (1866–1942). Both the Ramírez brothers trained pupils who were to become outstanding guitar builders in their own right. Manuel Ramírez, who originally learned the craft from his brother, had three pupils two of whom, Santos Hernández (1873–1942) and Domingo Esteso (1882–1937), became almost legendary. It was José I, however, who really founded the family business which still flourishes. José I's pupils included his son José II (1885–1957) and Enrique García (1868–1922). García eventually left to set up in Barcelona, where he trained yet another famous luthier, Francisco Simplicio (1874–1932).

Back in Madrid, José Ramírez II took over the business on his father's death and trained his son José III (the present head of the firm) and Marcelo Barbero (1904–1955). Barbero worked for some years for the widow of Santos Hernández, and built some exceptional instruments. The first half of this century often seems a golden age for guitar construction, but it was not so easy for the luthiers themselves: their instruments sold for ludicrously small prices. It must also be remembered that the majority of their output at this period was made up of flamenco guitars, which were in much greater demand.

In Spain today there are good guitar makers in many of the chief cities. Madrid continues to be the principal center, with the workshops of Arcángel Fernández (who learned from Barbero), Marcelino López Nieto, the Hermanos Conde (who continue the business of their uncle Domingo Esteso), José Ramírez III, and the former Ramírez employees Paulino Bernabe, Manuel Contreras and Felix Manzanero.

In Barcelona, Ignacio Fleta is outstanding. Although Manuel Reyes of Cordoba is famous chiefly for his flamenco guitars, the few classical instruments he makes are also highly regarded. There is a flourishing school of luthiers in Granada among whom Antonio Marín Montero is the most widely known.

With this continuing activity, Spain remains the center of classical guitar construction—but it does not have a monopoly on luthiers making the instrument. One of the most influential of all makers in this century has been the German Hermann Hauser (1882–1952), whose business is now continued by his son. Robert Bouchet of France has made guitars for many leading recitalists; David Rubio has become the first Englishman to gain an international reputation for his guitars, and another English-based luthier, the Madrid-born José Romanillos, has recently come to the fore. In America, the two best-known makers have been Manuel Velásquez and Manuel Rodríguez (born *c.* 1930), the latter of whom settled in Los Angeles after training in Madrid with José Ramírez, but has now returned to Spain. The Japanese have, not surprisingly, extended their natural genius for both imitation and craftsmanship into the realms of instrument making, and produced a number of luthiers specializing in the guitar.

With so many fine individual craftsmen at work, guitars with very different sound qualities have naturally been produced. Two main trends can be identified. The first has resulted from the changed circumstances in which the modern guitar is played. Recitalists now have to make themselves heard in concert halls seating anything from a few hundred to two or three thousand people. Professional guitarists have become increasingly concerned with the problem of gaining volume—in addition to all the other difficulties of tone production and guitar technique. Volume and carrying power have become major concerns for the luthier. In the middle years of the century, the search for a more powerful guitar led to the adoption of a larger body size and greater string length. There was also a theory that guitars for use in big halls should have increased bass resonance to allow for the greater absorption of bass frequencies by the bodies of the audience and air spaces of the hall.[4] Unfortunately, a loud bass-responsive guitar is only achieved at the expense of some power and clarity in the treble range.

There is an opposite school of thought which holds that a perfectly balanced guitar sound, with less apparent volume but clear trebles and no undue bass emphasis, will carry better whatever the size of the hall.

In general, the Spanish-based makers have tended to go for the first option and build big, sonorous instruments. One suspects that there is also something in the Spanish temperament which is drawn to the sweeter, romantic, slightly syrupy sound such guitars often produce. The makers of the northern European countries have tended to follow a line of development from Torres through Hauser, aiming for clarity and balance in a smaller-bodied guitar. The performer can still gain a romantic sound by working with the right hand over the soundhole or even over the fingerboard, and the firmer tone can be of help in achieving the clarity of voices needed in some of the early music in the repertoire.

The argument about the effect of the audience in absorbing bass frequencies is a difficult one to assess. Musical acoustics is a complicated subject in which ideas frequently go in and out of fashion. But it should be pointed out that modern concert halls are carefully "tuned" acoustically, and are designed to allow for the effects of the audience on the acoustics. Also, leading authorities on the design of concert halls maintain that it is the *higher* frequencies, not the lower, which suffer in the larger hall, being absorbed by both the audience and the air itself.[5] The evidence of the architects and engineers favors the approach to guitar making of luthiers such as Hauser, Rubio and Romanillos who prefer a clarity of sound, with strong treble frequencies. It may be significant that in recent years José Ramírez has made a model with the shorter 65cm scale length and smaller body, in addition to his usual large concert model. The opinions of performers themselves vary considerably: guitarists are the most fickle of musicians where their instruments are concerned, and it can also be difficult for the guitarist on the platform to judge exactly how the sound will be heard by the audience.

Such a division of opinion points to the lack of conformity in modern guitar design. Modern classical guitars look similar, but they vary considerably in important details of internal construction. The guitar is unlike the violin in that the exact way in which it produces sound, and the best way of releasing tone and volume from the instrument, are still in dispute. In recent years, an American scientist Dr. Michael Kasha (Director of the Institute of Molecular Biophysics at Florida State University) has applied his skills to guitar acoustics and mechanics in an attempt to resolve the argument. Working in conjunction with luthier Richard Schneider, he has produced a series of guitars with revolutionary features in their strutting, bridge, neck and body design (see pages 83–84). Kasha and Schneider have reached a stage at which tests show that their guitars are significantly louder than conventional instruments. They are also confident that they can now "tailor" the strutting and thickness of a top to give any particular response and tonal characteristic requested by a performer. To date, their ideas have aroused great interest, but many players and luthiers are still doubtful of Dr. Kasha's theories. However, it is now inevitable that scientific methods of analyzing guitar behavior will be increasingly used, and the knowledge gained can only benefit instrument design.

One of the most important innovations of the postwar era has been the introduction of nylon in string making. Previously, classical guitar strings had been made of gut for the trebles, while the basses were metal wound on floss silk cores. Gut strings at their best provided a firm and brilliant tone, but suffered from considerable practical drawbacks. They are difficult to make true and regular, particularly in the lighter gauges; they often suffer from false vibrations, caused by inconsistencies in their diameter and structure, go out of tune easily, and fray quickly against the frets and under the impact of the guitarist's fingernails. Silk-floss-cored basses also had their problems. Silk floss has a comparatively low breaking strain, so that strings had to be heavily built to take the tension. The resulting mass diminished their powers of sustain.

The first commercially available nylon treble strings were produced after the war by the New York string maker Albert Augustine, who used the newly available monofilament nylon, originally produced for fishing lines. The basses were wound on nylon floss cores. Although flabbier than gut, monofilament nylon is cheap and can be made with a very regular diameter and absolute consistency of material. Nylon strings stay in tune better, do not fray, and last much longer—although they gradually lose their elasticity and tone. While some players still hanker after the extra brilliance of gut, the practical advantages of nylon strings have led to their universal adoption. Nylon-floss-

cored basses offer an absolute advance over the earlier silk-cored strings in that the greater tensile strength of the synthetic materials allows a lighter string with a better sustain.

In the last two decades there has been a boom in the mass production of inexpensive guitars to meet the enormous demand for instruments from beginners and students. Some of these guitars are very good within their own range, although they do not aim to compete with the best hand-built instruments. The better ones are entirely suitable for their purpose; a top-quality guitar needs a good player to reveal its potential, which is often not apparent to the novice.

The instrument gallery which follows shows some examples of concert guitars by luthiers from Torres to the present. It should be read with the understanding that no two instruments by the same maker are ever quite identical—and that even the greatest makers have had their failures. Specific comments about a particular guitar can refer to that guitar only, although they can often shed light on the luthier's approach and the general characteristics of his instruments.

José Ramírez's shop in the Concepción Jerónima in the old quarter of Madrid.

Guitar by Antonio de Torres SEVILLE, 1854. *From the José Ramírez collection.*

Overall length: 96cm
Scale length: 65cm
Body length: 46cm
Body width: upper bout 26.1cm
         waist 22.2cm
         lower bout 34cm
Body depth: increasing from 9.2 to 10.2cm

This is a guitar of exceptional historical interest, being one of the earliest of Torres' surviving instruments. In many ways it represents a formative stage in the development of his art, combining some features that are typical of his work with others that were either modified or eliminated later in his career.

Even at this early date, Torres was using the system of seven fan struts that is found on the majority of his guitars and the scale length conforms exactly to the standard he used throughout his life. The body is slightly shorter and narrower than on his later instruments, although the box is deeper. These proportions are not surprising, since the general trend of Torres' development was toward a wider but slightly shallower instrument.

The unexpected features of this guitar are the design of the head and bridge, the ornate rosette and inlay, and the address on the label (the unclassical *golpeador* may be discounted

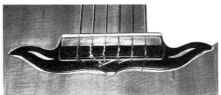

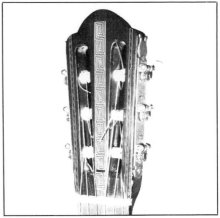

as a later addition). While the head, bridge and inlay do not accord with the standard ideas of Torres' classical simplicity, we do not feel that they cast doubts on the authenticity of this guitar: throughout his career, Torres built a small number of instruments with a greater than usual degree of ornamentation.

The address on the label is not recorded elsewhere, Torres' usual Seville address being in the calle de la Cerragería.

Although this guitar does not have quite the same degree of refinement found in Torres' instruments of a few years later, it is of a far higher quality than other guitars being made at the same period. While it is difficult to assess the playing qualities of an instrument as old as this one, it still has an attractively rounded singing tone.

Guitar by Antonio de Torres SEVILLE, 1859. *From the Instrument Museum of the Barcelona Conservatory.*

Overall length: 97.5cm
Scale length: 65cm
Body length: 47cm
Body width: upper bout 27cm
         waist 23cm
         lower bout 35.3cm
Body depth: increasing from 9 to 10cm

The perfection of proportions, quality of timbers, and the design of the head and bridge, mark this guitar as typical of Torres' production during his "first epoch."

The back is made of four strips of rosewood, divided by fine strips of plain inlay. The use of more than two pieces of timber for

the back is a common feature of Torres' classical guitars. It is usually suggested that this was forced on him by the difficulty of obtaining sufficiently wide boards of rosewood. However, Torres also used four-piece backs on many of his cypress-bodied flamenco guitars, and since wide planks of cypress are not difficult to find in Spain, we may assume that Torres preferred this form of construction.

It is not possible to see the strutting arrangement on this guitar because of a tone projector fitted inside the soundhole, which prevents access to the underside of the table. The tone projector consists of a tapered perforated metal cylinder, slightly separated from both back and front and supported on wooden pegs. It was thought to help the volume and projection of the guitar. Torres experimented with tone projectors on a number of his early guitars, but used them with decreasing frequency.

The street name and number are handwritten on the label, instead of printed. This suggests that Torres had only recently moved to his workshop in the calle de la Cerragería.

The guitar was formerly owned by the famous recitalist Miguel Llobet, who was so attached to it that, when the back split, he refused to let anyone repair it for fear that its character would be altered. He continued to give concerts on the guitar despite its damaged condition.

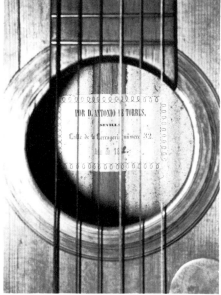

Guitar by Antonio de Torres SEVILLE, 1862. *From the Instrument Museum of the Barcelona Conservatory.*

Overall length: 99.6cm
Scale length: 64.5cm
Body length: 48cm
Body width: upper bout 26cm
         waist 21.5cm
         lower bout 34.7cm
Body depth: increasing from 8.9 to 9.5cm

This is the famous "papier-mâché" bodied guitar, which is so frequently cited as proof that the strutting of the table is of paramount importance in the determination of guitar tone. The table is made of high-quality spruce, and has the conventional Torres bracing pattern of seven fan struts in the lower bout. The sides and back are made of sheets of cardboard, stiffened with timber fillets. This construction makes the body unusually light; in order to maintain the balance of the instrument, Torres fitted it with a peg head, and used rosewood in place of the heavier ebony for the fingerboard.

The guitar's table is now so badly split that it can no longer be played. Domingo Prat was fortunate enough to hear the guitar before it was damaged, and described it as having an extraordinary sound, soft and deep though a little lacking in penetration. Taking Prat's description as accurate, Torres' experimental guitar demonstrated more than the importance of a well-strutted table in determining tone quality: it also proved the importance of the reflective surfaces of sides and back in providing projection and volume.

Torres refused to sell this guitar during his lifetime, and it came to the Barcelona Conservatory via first Tárrega and then Llobet.

Guitar by Antonio de Torres ALMERIA, 1883.
From the Instrument Museum of the Paris Conservatory.
Photographs of front and back by courtesy of the Conservatory.

Overall length: 99cm
Scale length: 65cm
Body length: 48cm
Body width: upper bout 27.2cm
           waist 23.4cm
           lower bout 36cm
Body depth: increasing from 8.9 to 9.3cm

This guitar was made during Torres' second epoch, after his return from Seville to his native Almería, and has maple back and sides in place of the conventional rosewood. It is strutted to the standard Torres pattern, the seven symmetrical fans being very light and delicately shaped.

The guitar belonged formerly to the recitalist Jean Lafon and has received heavy use, necessitating its repair first by Manuel Ramírez and then by Robert Bouchet. Even so, it retains a firm sweet tone, with an unusually long sustain.

It is often said that Torres guitars do not have enough power to be used under modern concert conditions. However, it should be remembered that they were played in public by several leading performers in the late eighteenth and early nineteenth centuries. Today, the Dutch guitarist Pieter van der Staak sometimes uses his Torres guitar for concert work, and finds the carrying power of its sound surprising—sufficient, indeed, for halls holding up to 700 people.

Guitar by Francisco González
MADRID, *c.* 1870s.
From the Instrument Museum of the Paris Conservatory.

Overall length: 97cm
Scale length: 64.5cm
Body length: 48.5cm
Body width: upper bout 28cm
           waist 23.5cm
           lower bout 36.5cm
Body depth: increasing from 9 to 10.4cm

Francisco González is not a well-remembered luthier, but he occupies a significant place in the history of modern guitar construction as the teacher of José Ramírez I, founder of the great family firm of Madrid luthiers. This guitar can be considered the direct ancestor of the instruments produced by the leading members of the Madrid school.

There are signs of the influence of Torres, but both design and construction are less refined. The table is of good-quality timber with five rather crudely made broad, shallow fan struts. The sides and back are built of rosewood, with inserts of maple. The timbers of the back are not book-matched, and the back of the guitar has at some time been repaired by the original maker. Unfortunately, after the repair a new label was inserted over the original, and the date of construction is obscured.

Although the proportions of the guitar are modern, neither the design of the head and rosette, nor the execution of the interior construction, approaches the standards expected in a modern classical guitar. The limitations of this instrument reveal the superiority of Torres over the other luthiers of his day.

Guitar by Vicente Arias CIUDAD REAL, 1874.
From the José Ramírez collection.

Overall length: 96cm
Scale length: 64.5cm
Body length: 45.5cm
Body width: upper bout 24cm
            waist 20.5cm
            lower bout 34.5cm
Body depth: increasing from 9.3 to 9.8cm

Vincente Arias was the only Spanish guitar maker of the late nineteenth century whose work came close to rivaling Torres, and a comparison between their instruments is revealing. Arias' guitars are individual in their overall style, as well as in certain construction details, and are slightly smaller and more lightly built than equivalent instruments by Torres.

This particular guitar is very narrow in the upper bout and waist, but has a generous lower bout. The timber of the table is of high quality, and the workmanship of both interior and exterior construction is immaculate. The strutting system is unusual: there are six major fan bars, symmetrically disposed in the lower bout, and two extra, very short fans which spring from the outermost bars on both treble and bass sides.

Although this is very definitely a classical guitar, with rosewood sides and back, Arias has fitted it with the flamenco pattern of tuning peg. One suspects that pegs were used for reasons of lightness: throughout the guitar, everything possible has been done to reduce its weight.

The fingerboard is of rosewood, and hooks out over the soundhole on the treble side, carrying nineteenth and twentieth frets for the top string. This is not a common feature, and may have been included at the request of a particular guitarist.

Guitar by Manuel Ramírez MADRID, 1911.
From the José Ramírez collection.

Overall length: 98cm
Scale length: 65.5cm
Body length: 48.6cm
Body width: upper bout 27.7cm
            waist 23.5cm
            lower bout 36.3cm
Body depth: increasing from 8.3 to 9.3cm

Manuel Ramírez learned his craft from his elder brother José Ramírez I, who in turn had learned from Francisco González. The comparison between this instrument and the González guitar of some thirty or forty years earlier reveals the advances made by the Ramírez family over the intervening decades.

Manuel Ramírez has here used a body shape that lies somewhere between the González guitar and a "second epoch" Torres guitar. The table is strutted with seven symmetrical fans, arranged according to the Torres pattern. The scale length is greater than that used by either Torres or González, and in this increase—as well as in the proportions of the body—we see evidence of an attempt to produce a more powerful instrument. The decoration around the soundhole is made of mother-of-pearl set in black mastic. Ramírez has followed Arias' example in combining a rosewood body with peg tuning.

This guitar gives the overall impression of being robust and forceful. Although it has neither the extreme delicacy of an Arias nor the classical perfection of a Torres, it is an instrument of real character.

Guitar by Santos Hernández MADRID, 1924.
From the collection of the Circulating Music Library, Madrid.

Overall length: 97cm
Scale length: 65cm
Body length: 48.2cm
Body width: upper bout 27.6cm
                    waist 23.5cm
                    lower bout 36.5cm
Body depth: increasing from 9 to 10cm

Santos Hernández, the greatest of Manuel Ramírez's pupils, is remembered today chiefly for his flamenco guitars. This instrument is evidence of his mastery of the classical form.

The spruce on the table is of exceptional quality, with a fine straight grain and pronounced figuration. The strutting system is peculiar to Santos. The transverse bar immediately below the soundhole does not go straight across, but is set slightly on the diagonal so that it descends on the treble side. Below this cross bar are seven symmetrically placed fans. The slant of the transverse bar is designed to give slightly greater stiffness to the treble side of the table in order to improve high frequency responses. The influence of Santos' work on this idea can be seen in the guitars of a number of other luthiers, including Ignacio Fleta and José Ramírez III.

The guitar belonged originally to Segovia, who gave it to the Circulating Music Library in support of their aim of building a collection of instruments which could be loaned to young musicians. The guitar is still in perfect condition, and is played at concerts organized by the Library.

Guitar by Francisco Simplicio BARCELONA, 1931.
From the José Ramírez collection.

Overall length: 97.5cm
Scale length: 65cm
Body length: 47.6cm
Body width: upper bout 28cm
                    waist 24.2cm
                    lower bout 35.8cm
Body depth: increasing from 9.4 to 9.8cm

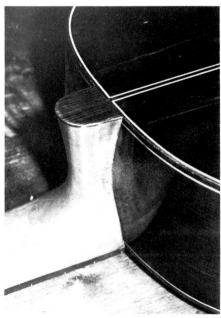

Simplicio was the only pupil of Enrique García. He made two models of guitar, which were similar save that the de luxe model had added ornamentation and an elaborately carved head.

Although Simplicio was linked to the traditions of the Madrid school by his teacher García, who had learned from José Ramírez I, his guitars have some distinctly individual features. The body of this guitar is wider in the upper bout and waist but narrower in the lower bout than those by Santos Hernández of similar date. The waist is accordingly less pronounced, with rounder curves. Simplicio's heel design is also distinctive, and offers an attractive alternative to the sharp-pointed ending of the traditional Spanish pattern.

This guitar has been damaged, necessitating considerable repair. However, it retains a very round mellow tone which has enough firmness in it not to sound flabby.

Guitar by Domingo Esteso MADRID, 1932.
From the collection of Bill Bogel.

Overall length: 99cm
Scale length: 65.5cm
Body length: 48.8cm
Body width: upper bout 27.6cm
            waist 23.5cm
            lower bout 35.7cm
Body depth: increasing from 9.3 to 9.7cm

The spruce table is, once again, of the highest quality with an exceedingly fine grain and a strong patterning of medullary rays. The quality of the timber on prewar guitars is often noticeably better than that on guitars being built today. Spruce was more plentiful then, and timber from very old trees (characterized by narrow grain) was easier to obtain.

Domingo Esteso was, like Santos Hernández, a pupil of Manuel Ramírez. Like Santos, he achieved great renown for his flamenco guitars, and also produced fine classical instruments. The chief difference between the two men's work is that Esteso's guitars are sweeter, mellower and less firm in their tone. The maple *golpeador* is a recent addition.

Guitar by Marcelo Barbero MADRID, 1934.
From the collection of Bill Bogel.

Overall length: 98cm
Scale length: 65cm
Body length: 48.5cm
Body width: upper bout 27.2cm
            waist 23.8cm
            lower bout 36cm

Body depth: increasing from 9.2 to 9.7cm

Although Marcelo Barbero trained with José Ramírez II, the chief influence on him was Santos Hernández, whose widow employed him for a time. This instrument predates that period, but the influence of Santos is already apparent in the shaping of the seven fan struts. These are very broad and flat, as are the struts on many of Santos' flamenco guitars of similar date. Barbero's guitars often possess an almost austere firmness of tone, very different from the romantic sweetness of sound that characterizes the guitars of so many of the present generation of Madrid luthiers.

Guitar by Hermann Hauser (Senior) MUNICH, 1935.
From the collection of Victoria Kingsley.

Overall length: 96cm
Scale length: 64cm
Body length: 47.4cm
Body width: upper bout 26.7cm
            waist 22.7cm
            lower bout 35.4cm
Body depth: increasing from 9 to 10cm

Hermann Hauser was the first non-Spanish luthier to make truly great modern classical guitars. His reputation as a maker of classical guitars is probably second only to that of Torres.

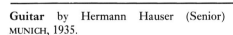

By the standards of today this is an unusually small instrument. The dimensions of the bodies of Hauser's guitars fall within the same range as those of Torres' instruments. Other similarities with some Torres guitars can be found in the shaping away of the fingerboard on the bass, and the projection of the bridge from the strings by a plate of mother-of-pearl.

Hauser's strutting pattern was developed from the basic Torres system of seven fan struts, but involved certain subtle modifications. This guitar has a shallow flat plate of timber, reinforcing the table under the bridge. The fan struts are unusually narrow and deep, those under the center of the table being deeper than those toward the outside.

Perhaps the most distinctive constructional feature of Hauser's guitars is the joint between head and neck. This is a V joint, reminiscent of the joint used on almost all pre-modern European guitars.

Hauser's guitars have been played in concert and on record by many of the great virtuosi of the century, including Andrés Segovia and Julian Bream. His instruments have demonstrated the perfection of tonal purity and focus of sound obtainable from a small-bodied guitar, and have shown that the carrying power of such an instrument can be out of all proportion to its size and apparent volume.

Guitar by Robert Bouchet PARIS, 1954. *From the collection of Victoria Kingsley.*

Overall length: 96.5cm
Scale length: 65cm
Body length: 48.5cm
Body width: upper bout 28cm
           waist 23.8cm
           lower bout 36.6cm
Body depth: increasing from 8.8 to 9.2cm

Lutherie is not Robert Bouchet's only art: he is primarily a painter, and spent many years as a teacher of painting. It was not until 1946, when he was already in his forties, that he made his first guitar. Bouchet had played the guitar since 1932, and was a friend of the Paris guitar maker Julián Gómez Ramírez (who had trained in the famous Madrid workshops with José Ramírez I). Bouchet's first guitar was made for his own use; although he had no formal training in instrument building, he had a natural aptitude for craftsmanship and made good use of his memories of visits to Ramírez's atelier.

Since then, Bouchet has become one of the most admired guitar makers in Europe. He only makes instruments when he wants to, and his production has always been very small. To date he has made no more than 144 guitars over a period of 30 years.

Robert Bouchet's guitars and procedures are unusual in a number of ways. The body shape, which has changed five or six times in the past, has always been determined by aesthetic considerations rather than by acoustic theory. The fingerboards are absolutely

flat, with no camber in any direction. The tuning machines are also distinctive: Bouchet buys the basic machines, silver-plates and engraves them by hand, then adds ivory buttons which he carves himself. He also engraves and prints his own labels.

Bouchet is famous for his work on guitar strutting. This instrument uses the system he employed up until 1956. There are seven symmetrically disposed bars under the lower bout. The cross bar immediately beneath the soundhole is arched slightly, and only attached to the table by its center third and at its extreme ends. For the remainder it is cut away so that two struts on the treble side and two on the bass may pass through into the area of the waist, where they connect to an oval pad around the soundhole. There are also two extra struts in the area of the waist which splay upward and outward from the main fan bars.

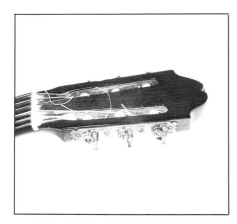

Bouchet modified this system in 1956 for one using five fan bars. These are also symmetrically placed, though not of equal shapes and sizes. The two outermost struts pass through the bar below the waist, to connect with the oval pad, as in the earlier system. What is really different about this system, however, is a transverse stiffening bar connecting the struts below the area of the bridge. This is heavier on the treble side than on the bass; by the way he shapes it, Bouchet can adjust exactly the response of the guitar to different frequencies.

Bouchet ascribes the greatest importance to the exact thickness of the timbers, and to the direction of the grain of the wood in the struts, in determining the guitar sound. He makes all adjustments to the response of the top by working on the bracing; the thickness of the spruce table is constant throughout.

Bouchet's guitars have considerable volume and sustain. The tone is generally firm rather than sweet, and they possess unusually good sound balance across the range. These qualities, combined with their aesthetic appeal, have made Bouchet's guitars sought after by players as diverse as Alexandre Lagoya, Julian Bream, Emilio Pujol, Turibio Santos and Manuel López Ramos.

Guitar by Ignacio Fleta BARCELONA, 1961.
From the collection of Malcolm Weller.

Overall length: 100.5cm
Scale length: 65cm
Body length: 49.5cm
Body width: upper bout 29cm
          waist 24.2cm
          lower bout 36.3cm
Body depth: increasing from 9.6 to 9.8cm

Fleta's guitars have several peculiar features. The neck-to-body junction is made by a massive bell-shaped end block in place of the typical slipper foot, and the strutting system incorporates a heavy diagonal treble bar, set at a very shallow angle to the transverse bar immediately below the soundhole. Below this are eight light fan struts, and a light flat plate under the bridge. Fleta is one of several luthiers to seal and lightly polish the inside of the back, with the aim of improving its reflective qualities. The body is very full in the upper bout, and rather stout in the waist. The fingerboard is only 5cm wide at the nut, and to compensate the frets are finished square with the fingerboard, instead of being beveled back.

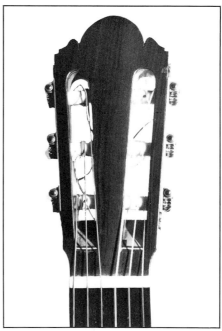

Fleta's guitars are probably more sought after than those of any other current maker. His waiting list is considerable, and his instruments sell for astronomical prices. They have the reputation of being difficult to play — they are guitars for the recitalist. Their most noticeable sound characteristic is their great power.

This particular guitar belonged formerly to John Williams, and may be heard on many of the records he made in the 1960s. Its tone is crisp and firm rather than mellifluous, and it demands a player with a strong technique to bring out its best.

67

Guitar by Manuel Hernández and Victoriano Aguado MADRID, 1966.
From the collection of Malcolm Weller.

Overall length: 100cm
Scale length: 65.8cm
Body length: 48.6cm
Body width: upper bout 28.2cm
 waist 24.8cm
 lower bout 37.2cm
Body depth: increasing from 9.6 to 10.2cm

The top is spruce, with seven symmetrical fan struts (this was not so on all Hernández y Aguado guitars), and the inside of the guitar is varnished. Even though it is quite a large instrument, it is very lightly built, and shows considerable attention to detail throughout.

Manuel Hernández and Victoriano Aguado formed a link with the prewar generation of luthiers: Modesto Borreguero,

Guitar by Arcángel Fernández MADRID, 1964.
From the collection of Malcolm Weller.

Overall length: 100cm
Scale length: 65.5cm
Body length: 49.2cm
Body width: upper bout 27.5cm
 waist 23.5cm
 lower bout 37cm
Body depth: increasing from 9.2 to 10.5cm

Although Arcángel Fernández learned his craft with Marcelo Barbero, this guitar shows little influence from the older luthier.

This is a bigger guitar than those made by Barbero, with a deeper box and larger bouts. The waist is, by contrast, rather small and sharply pulled in. The tone of the guitar is attractive, typically Spanish in its mellowness and sweetness.

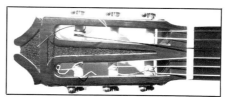

who trained alongside Domingo Esteso and Santos Hernández in Manuel Ramírez's business, once had a workbench with them. Their workshop in Madrid is still remembered as a haven of peace and contented craftsmanship.

The character of this guitar is difficult to summarize. It is neither very loud nor very soft, very harsh nor very mellow. It is the sort of guitar that would be boring if it were not very good of its kind. Its qualities represent a mean of many of the desirable features on a guitar, resulting in an attractive instrument which has a less clearly marked "personality" than many others.

The spruce table is strutted with five parallel bars in the lower bout. Fernández is one of several makers to have used a system of this sort in place of the usual splayed struts; although good results have been achieved, it is difficult to demonstrate any advantage over the more conventional fan arrangement.

Barbero thought highly of Arcángel Fernández, to whom he entrusted the training of his son.

Guitars by José Ramírez MADRID, 1969; and MADRID, *c*. 1960s.
(a) From the collection of Malcolm Weller.
(b) From the José Ramírez collection.

Overall length: 101cm
Scale length: 66.3cm
Body length: 49cm
Body width: upper bout 28.3cm
 waist 23.6cm

 lower bout 37.2cm
Body depth: increasing from 10 to 10.7cm
Label: "Constructor de Guitarras/José Ramírez/Concepción Jerónima no 2/1882 Madrid 1969/no.3.490 Class 1a." Also signature

Ramírez's current concert model has two immediately noticeable distinguishing features. The neck is reinforced with a central band of ebony to prevent warping, and the

rosewood sides are lined with cypress to stop them from going out of shape. Both of these features were introduced by José Ramírez III, the present head of the firm, who was also responsible in the 1960s for popularizing the use of cedar for guitar tops. His strutting system uses a diagonal bar below the sound-hole on the treble side, inclined at a much steeper angle to the transverse than Fleta's, and seven light fan struts. These, because of the diagonal bar, are much shorter on the

treble than on the bass side. The fingerboard is tapered away on the bass, to allow greater freedom for the string to move. Ramírez started shaping his fingerboards this way to satisfy recitalists who required the greatest possible volume, and buzz-free playing. Since he had already raised the bass side of the saddle as far as was compatible with a convenient playing action, the only remaining area for adjustment was in the fingerboard itself. All Ramírez's guitars are finished with a reddish spray lacquer.

The Ramírez family has played a dominating role in guitar making in Spain for three generations, and business is now thriving better than ever. Their top concert model is played by a host of recitalists including Segovia, for whom the three instruments in photograph (b) were made. They also do a brisk trade in the various student models which are made to their specifications by other workshops.

It is currently fashionable in some quarters to criticize the Ramírez approach to guitar building—but his instruments continue to be played by a large number of professionals all over the world.

(a)

(b)

Guitar by O. Raponi ROME, 1970.
Owned by Tim Walker

Overall length: 102.5cm
Scale length: 66.3cm
Body length: 49.8cm
Body width: upper bout 29cm
       waist 24.3cm
       lower bout 38cm
Body depth: increasing from 9.5cm to 10.3cm

The cedar top has six fan struts and a diagonal treble bar, which on the bass side extends beyond the transverse strut into the waist of the guitar. It is an exceptionally large instrument with an unusual shape, combining square shoulders with a very full, curvaceous lower bout.

Raponi is not a well-known luthier, but his guitars have been played by several leading artists including Alirio Diaz. Tim Walker, to whom this example belongs, chose it for its loudness, which is particularly important to him as much of his professional work is with ensembles such as the Fires of London. In addition to its great volume, the guitar has an attractive "middle-of-the-road" tone, which is bright and firm without being harsh or booming. The marks on the table are the result of the unconventional playing techniques demanded by some of the avant-garde compositions in Tim Walker's repertoire.

Guitar by Daniel Friedrich PARIS, 1972.
From the collection of Malcolm Weller.

Overall length: 100.5cm
Scale length: 65cm
Body length: 48.7cm
Body width: upper bout 27.8cm
         waist 24cm
         lower bout 36.8cm
Body depth: increasing from 9.7 to 10.7cm

Daniel Friedrich is one of the most experimental of modern guitar makers. He is keenly interested in technical aspects of guitar acoustics, and belongs to a small group of scientists and instrument builders in Paris who work together on problems of musical acoustics.

Daniel Friedrich has felt the influence of Robert Bouchet; this influence and his scientific turn of mind are reflected in his work on strutting. Friedrich has used a number of different systems; he records each exactly in a reference book, which contains details of all his guitars.

This guitar has seven fan struts to its spruce table. The center five are light, and extend backward from the transverse strut below the soundhole in the conventional manner. The outer two are much heavier, and pass upward through the main transverse bar to the soundhole, providing a triangular

stiffening for the table. All seven struts are connected by a scalloped transverse bar in the region of the bridge. The exact positioning of this bar depends on the timber of the top. Friedrich is one of those makers who are prepared to use either spruce or cedar, and adjust their procedures according to the different characteristics of the two types of wood.

This guitar is a powerful instrument with a rich tone and good balance across its whole range. The trebles are firm rather than singing, and hold their own well against the strong basses. Like all Daniel Friedrich's instruments, it is very finely made, attractive in the details of head and rosette, and immaculately finished.

Guitar by Richard Schneider, DETROIT 1973.
Photographs by courtesy of Richard Schneider.

Overall length: 104cm
Scale length: 67cm
Body length: 51cm
Body width: upper bout 27.8cm
         waist 23.7cm
         lower bout 36.7cm
Body depth: increasing from 9.3 to 9.8cm

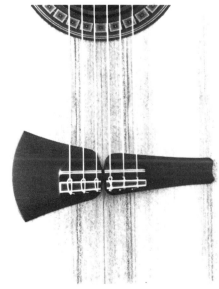

Richard Schneider learned guitar building with the Mexican luthier Juan Pimentel. Since 1969 he has worked with Dr. Michael Kasha on the development of a new guitar design based on scientific principles. At present, Schneider is consulting luthier to the Gibson company in Kalamazoo; he also maintains a workshop to produce classical and flamenco guitars on the Kasha system.

This guitar, named "Wanda," is one of the

"Long Models" designed for concert use. Although Schneider makes models with scale lengths from 64 to 67cm, he feels that the long scale gives considerably increased volume for the player who can handle the stretches it demands.

"Wanda" incorporates all the major ideas of the Kasha system (see pages 83–84). The lower bout of the redwood table is strutted with a transverse bar immediately below the saddle, and more than twenty small, asymmetrically shaped and asymmetrically placed struts radiating from around the edge of the bridge. The cross bar below the upper bout is cut away from the top to allow greater flexibility. This is because greater flexibility in the upper bout allows a fuller vibration in the *lower* bout, which provides greater volume.

The ebony bridge is shaped in accordance with Kasha's theories of impedance matching. The bass end is wide for the efficient transmission of high frequencies. The bridge is split at the center, with separate saddles for bass and treble strings, so as not to inhibit this mechanism.

Metal weights imbedded in the top of the neck and in the head act as inertia stops for the strings, ensuring that string vibrations are imparted to the table rather than wasted on the head and neck. To balance the guitar, there is a metal weight in the end block at the base.

The appearance of the guitar is visible expression of the unconventionality of the acoustic design. The curve of the base of the lower bout is a section of an ellipse having foci at the bridge and the soundhole. The head shape is also unusual, and tuning is by specially designed Schaller machines with sealed lubricated gears. Purflings, inlays and rosette are made of brilliantly colored dyed woods.

Richard Schneider's Kasha system guitars have been acoustically compared with conventional instruments, and proved to be significantly louder. He is also definite that they have dramatically better balance and sustain, and that the asymmetric Kasha strutting allows him to tailor the tonal responses of the instrument with much greater precision and consistency.

Guitar by José L. Romanillos SEMLEY, 1974. *Owned by Simon Munting.*

Overall length: 97.7cm
Scale length: 65cm
Body length: 48cm
Body width: upper bout 26.7cm
              waist 22.4cm
              lower bout 35.3cm
Body depth: increasing from 8.7 to 9.8cm

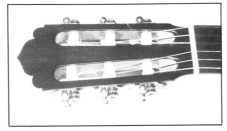

The spruce top has a conventional strutting system. As on all Romanillos guitars, the head-to-neck junction is by a V joint and Indian rosewood is used for the sides and back (as opposed to the Brazilian rosewood most makers use for their top concert models). The body shape is derived ultimately from a Torres pattern, and is smaller and much narrower than most modern instruments. Close attention has been paid to details such as the selection of purflings and inlays, resulting in a very pretty guitar.

Some players have reservations about the suitability of Romanillos' guitars for concert purposes, doubting that such a small-bodied instrument can have the volume to fill a large hall. However, those who own them disagree. Simon Munting, to whom this guitar belongs, says of it:

When you play it in a hall you think it's too quiet and that you're not doing enough, but you find it carries forever and everything can be heard. Also, on the treble, every note sustains equally. There are none which die on you. It has a lot of power at the beginning of the note, and a very clear, crisp tone. Romanillos is tough to play. You don't have big stretches, but you have to apply pressure.

Guitar by Masaru Kohno TOKYO, 1975.
Photographed at the Classical Guitar Centre, London.
Overall length: 101cm
Scale length: 66cm
Body length: 49.1cm
Body width: upper bout 28.2cm
　　　　　 waist 24cm
　　　　　 lower bout 36.8cm
Body depth: 9.7cm

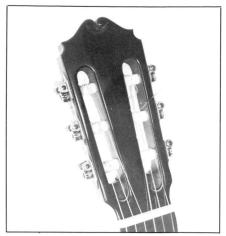

Masaru Kohno is the best known and longest established of the growing number of Japanese luthiers who make the classical guitar. This instrument is one of his top concert models, and guitars like this one command high prices in Europe and America.

It follows conventional European construction practice, having a spruce top with seven fan struts, and Brazilian rosewood sides and back. The one unusual feature is a pair of ebony reinforcing strips running through the neck. It has a powerful voice, with a tonal bias toward the bass frequencies. Craftsmanship and finish conform to the highest standards.

About one million people in Japan play the classical guitar—evidence of the extraordinary avidity with which the Japanese have embraced Western cultural forms at the expense of their own traditional arts. In the field of lutherie they have proved to be determined learners. Robert Bouchet remembers, with some alarm, the visit to his Paris workshop of a delegation of Japanese craftsman: they alternately bowed in respect and photographed everything in sight. A number of fine Spanish guitars have suffered dissection at the hands of Japanese instrument builders eager to learn their secrets. The Japanese demand for guitars of all classes has contributed in large measure to the shortage of good-quality timber, and some European luthiers are beginning to be worried by rivalry from the Orient. To date, however, the Japanese have not produced guitars as good as those of the very best European luthiers, despite their great skill as craftsmen. Whether they succeed in doing so will depend on the depth of their understanding of the instrument, its music and traditions.

Guitar by Marcelino López MADRID, 1975.
Owned by Simon Munting.

Overall length: 100cm
Scale length: 65.8cm
Body length: 49cm
Body width: upper bout 27cm
　　　　　 waist 23.5cm
　　　　　 lower bout 36.3cm
Body depth: increasing from 9.2 to 10cm

The spruce top has a system of six asymmetrically arranged fan bars. The center strut is much heavier than the rest, which are grouped two on the treble, three on the bass. There is a flat plate under the bridge, which is unusually shaped, with tapering "arms," and the body shape is smaller than on most Spanish-made instruments.

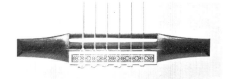

Marcelino López is an accomplished all-round luthier, building lutes and vihuelas as well as guitars, and also carries out instrument repairs for museums. Consequently his output of guitars is small, and they are hard to get. This instrument has an attractive tone of a noticeably Spanish character—sweet, rounded and romantic. While there is a slight bias to the bass frequencies, it has good balance and less bass boom than some of the larger instruments. Its owner finds it a very easy and pleasant guitar to play.

Guitar by Antonio Marín GRANADA, 1975.
Photographed at the Classical Guitar Centre, Bristol.
Overall length: 101cm
Scale length: 66cm
Body length: 49cm
Body width: upper bout 28.7cm
           waist 24.6cm
           lower bout 37.7cm
Body depth: increasing from 9.9 to 10.5cm

Antonio Marín is the best known of Granada's present-day guitar makers. While many of the luthiers of southern Spain are more adept at the flamenco guitar, and their experience with it colors their classical instru-ments, this is clearly a full-scale concert guitar.

The strutting pattern shows how widely Ramírez has been copied throughout Spain. There is a diagonal bar, starting in the area of the waist and extending down the treble side of the lower bout. There are seven fan struts, and those on the treble side extend both above and below the diagonal bar. This differs from the standard Ramírez pattern, in which the treble fans are confined to the area below the diagonal bar.

The guitar has a sweet, musical quality, and is very pleasant to play.

Guitar by Paulino Bernabe MADRID, 1975.
Photographed at the Spanish Guitar Centre, Bristol.
Overall length: 100cm
Scale length: 66cm
Body length: 48.5cm
Body depth: upper bout 28.5cm
           waist 23.8cm
           lower bout 36.8cm
Body depth: increasing from 9.7 to 10.2cm

The present generation of the Ramírez family continues to train notable guitar makers; Bernabe spent some years as principal craftsman in the Ramírez workshops before setting up on his own. He is a very fine craftsman, and the instruments he has made for his own personal collection are character-ized by exquisitely delicate inlay work. Bernabe is an experimenter with strutting systems, timbers and construction methods. In addition to making guitars with Brazilian and Indian rosewood bodies, and cypress for flamencos, he uses maple and pearwood. He is happy to use either spruce or cedar for the tables. In his opinion, a good spruce table will continue to improve over a period of thirty or more years, while a cedar table reaches its peak in two or three. The spruce table will probably be better ultimately, but many recitalists are more interested in the immediate performance of the guitar and prefer cedar.

This particular guitar has a cedar table and Brazilian rosewood body. The strutting sys-tem is one peculiar to Bernabe: there are three fan bars, of which the center bar is much the heaviest, and a small transverse pad under the bridge.

The sound of Bernabe's current guitars is different from those he made while working for Ramírez, being noticeably less sweet. This is a powerful guitar, with a strong treble, capable of making itself heard above other instruments.

Robert Bouchet playing one of his own guitars.

Construction

Among the bewildering changes in the world of the guitar over the last century, the luthier's patient hand construction of the true classical instrument is an enduring constant. Factories may turn out cheap guitars in their millions from the production lines, but the techniques by which high-quality instruments are made have remained virtually the same.

The best modern guitars come from small workshops. Sometimes a principal will oversee the work of several experienced craftsmen, occasionally there will be a collaboration and division of labor; often, though, the guitar will be made by one man working alone. This pattern of craftsmanship is the key to both the individuality and quality of the handmade instrument. Two men can sit at adjoining workbenches, working to the same design, with the same timbers and following the same procedures—but the instruments they produce will sound different. Every craftsman builds something of himself—his ideas and his personality—into what he makes, and every hand-built guitar has a distinctive character that derives ultimately from the individuality of the man who made it. In a factory-built instrument, assembled by different workers from mass-produced pre-prepared parts, such character is impossible.

The luthier's traditional way of working has other advantages. In developing his conception of the guitar he can draw on his previous experience and past results. He is free to experiment, making slight changes from instrument to instrument in the search for his ideal sound. He can, if he wishes, tailor a guitar to the requirements of a particular customer. He has the opportunity to discuss his work—the minute subtleties of tone color, balance, string tension and the like—with outstanding players who judge his success or failure. Above all he can select, cut and season timber to his exact requirements, and control quality at all stages of the work.

These advantages have to be paid for. The best materials are expensive; hand construction is slow and laborious; and a luthier's production is not large—commonly in the region of twenty to thirty instruments a year, sometimes less. Finally, the demand for good guitars has outstripped the supply and they have become subjects for investment. The price has risen accordingly.

Paulino Bernabe in his workshop in Madrid.

Any consideration of guitar construction must start with the raw materials, the timbers. The luthier's most important skill is his knowledge of wood and the way each piece can be worked to the best advantage. Individual preferences vary where timber is concerned, but all makers agree on the need for the highest quality of material. In the words of Manuel Reyes, one of today's leading *guitarreros*: "The most important basis for the making of the guitar is that you have a material which is exceptional and has been well cured or aged."[1]

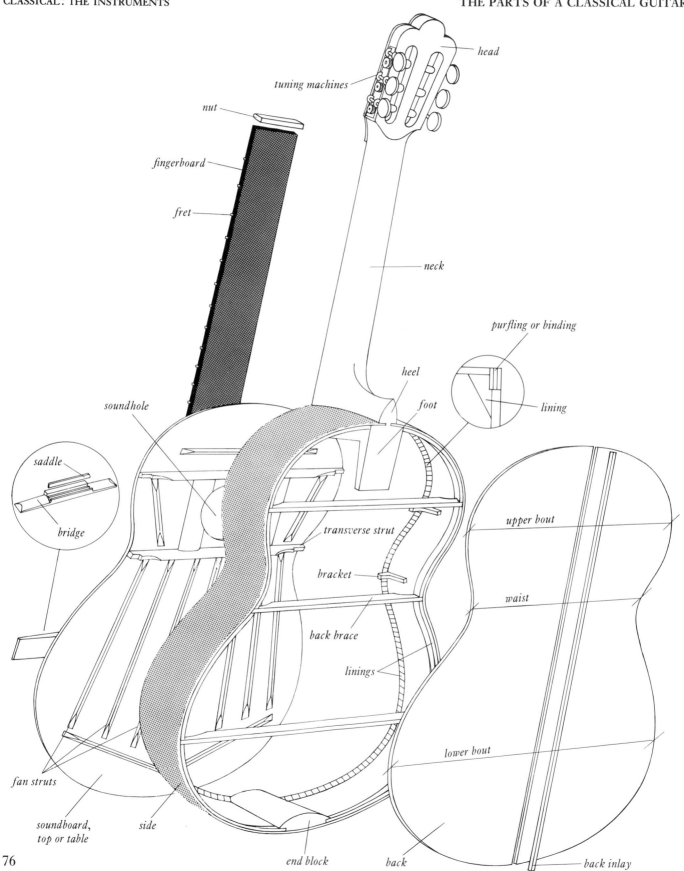

head

tuning machines

nut

fingerboard

fret

neck

purfling or binding

heel

foot

lining

soundhole

saddle

bridge

transverse strut

upper bout

bracket

waist

back brace

linings

fan struts

lower bout

soundboard,
top or table

side

end block

back

back inlay

The choice of timber for the soundboard is particularly critical. There are several "tone woods" available, of which spruce is by far the most sought after. Broadly speaking, two types of spruce are used in instrument building: Alpine spruce from the forests of Switzerland and Germany, and Sitka spruce from North America. Of these two, only the European spruce is used for top quality classical guitars.

Alpine spruce has been used for the soundboards of stringed instruments for many centuries. Only fully mature trees are used, and only the main trunk below the lowest branches. When cut and planed, spruce is a most attractive timber, blond in color, with a fine even grain. It is fairly soft and easy to work, yet resilient and dimensionally stable. One of spruce's features is the presence of strongly marked medullary rays, which grow from pith to bark, at right angles to the main grain. They consist of thin flat bundles of cells running between the main fibers, and their natural function is to store starch and circulate resin. In the finished guitar top these can be seen as fine silky waves, running across the grain. It is thought that, by providing a cross-linkage between the longitudinal fibers, the medullaries help to improve the tonal qualities of the soundboard. Their presence in timber used for musical instruments is therefore greatly prized.

There are several criteria by which the suitability of a piece of spruce may be judged. Most commonly used are the closeness and evenness of the grain. Each year's growth is marked by a wide, soft, pale ring of wood laid down rapidly in the spring, and a comparatively hard, dark, narrow ring marking the slow growth of late summer and autumn. It is these dark lines that we read as the grain of a finished plank. As a general principle, the closer the grain the more resilient the plank and the brighter the sound it can be made to produce—although, as with all general rules, there are many qualifying factors.

The luthier's choice of timber is ultimately subject to individual preference. In assessing the suitability of a thin board of spruce he will not only examine the grain, but will also flex the board to judge its resilience, and tap it to hear its "ring." The best spruce has an extraordinarily live quality which can be appreciated even by the non-expert.

Unfortunately, Alpine spruce is in short supply. Forests have been overcut, there are few sufficiently mature trees, and the top quality is both expensive and very difficult to find. Many guitar makers are now searching for alternatives. In recent years numerous luthiers (including José Ramírez and Ignacio Fleta, the two most famous Spanish constructors), have turned to Western red cedar as a substitute for spruce.

Despite its widespread use, the qualities of Western red cedar are still the subject of considerable controversy. In its immediate favor it has the advantages of being comparatively inexpensive and easy to obtain. Western red cedar is the largest of the North American cedars. Its trunk often grows twenty meters to the lowest branch and provides a staggering quality of straight-grain, knot-free wood. The American forests have been proportionally less heavily harvested than the European and many old trees (500–2000 years) survive, providing timber with an exceptionally fine grain. Cedar also possesses outstanding dimensional stability under changing conditions of temperature and humidity. On the debit side, it is much softer than spruce, and can be easily dented by a fingernail. It is less resilient and, although there is a light cross-grain patterning, has not the same lively medullaries. When cut, it gives off a fine aromatic sawdust which can be intensely irritant to sensitive lungs.

The real controversy about cedar centers on its behavior as a tone wood. Some luthiers are quite unable to make it work for them while others achieve good results. José Ramírez even goes so far as to say, "Stradivarius would have used the wood of America had he known of it."[2] It is difficult to make accurate comparisons, but careful listening to otherwise similar guitars by the same maker (one with a spruce, the other with a cedar top) suggests that the cedar is more responsive to low-frequency resonances. This makes it easy to achieve a sweet and mellow sound, but militates against firmness and clarity. It has also been suggested that a cedar top has less capacity for tonal improvement during the playing life of a guitar. Certainly some very good guitars have been built with cedar tops, but whether cedar has the qualities necessary for an outstandingly great instrument is still in doubt. Whatever the final verdict, cedar will continue to be widely used as long as the demand for guitars remains high and spruce remains scarce.

The sides and back of classical guitars are almost

always built of rosewood. Here again there is a choice, between the East Indian and Brazilian varieties. Although they share the same name, the two are actually different timbers. Both are dense, resinous, and very beautiful. Brazilian rosewood tends to be more highly figured and tawnier in color, while Indian is straighter-grained and often contains purplish streaks. Brazilian rosewood is more expensive and traditionally the first choice, though once again there is disagreement about their respective merits. While José Romanillos, for example, prefers the Indian, David Rubio holds it to be so inferior that "If I can't get Brazilian I won't make guitars."[3] Rubio believes that the Brazilian rosewood is less fibrous and works better for him as a sound reflector. Yet other makers will use either, putting a higher price on the instruments with Brazilian rosewood bodies as a reflection of the greater cost of the material, although the instruments are otherwise similar.

Maple enjoyed great favor for guitar bodies in the nineteenth century, but is now used only occasionally. The inherent strength of its cross-grain structure allows it to be planed down very thin, and a few luthiers still use this quality to produce a guitar with a sweet vivacious tone which is very attractive in the drawing room, although not so well suited to the larger spaces of the concert hall. Pear wood is another alternative, and Paulino Bernabe of Madrid has recently been experimenting with this for the bodies of both classical and flamenco guitars.

While the body timbers of the guitar are chosen primarily for their acoustic qualities, the considerations guiding the selection of timber for neck and fingerboard are chiefly structural. The neck of the guitar is under constant stress from the strings, which are always trying to bow it out of shape. The timber must be both strong and stable; even the slightest tendency to twist or warp will be accentuated by the pull of the strings. At the same time, it must be light, to maintain the balance of the instrument in the player's hands. The necessary combination of strength, stability and lightness is found in mahogany and in Honduras cedar.

The requirements for the fingerboard are that it be hard enough to resist the wear of the player's fingers over many years, and reasonably stable. Ebony has completely ousted rosewood as a material for fingerboards on the classical guitar, and is now the universal choice. Although

rosewood is more stable, the greater hardness of ebony has proved decisive.

Anyone who has worked with wood will know that it has a life of its own. It is constantly shifting and moving, responding to every change of temperature and humidity. In a musical instrument such as the guitar, which must be light and flexible to respond to musical vibrations, these tendencies cannot be restrained by massive construction. They must be controlled by the proper cutting and seasoning of the timber. All timbers for guitar construction should be taken from boards cut as nearly as possible along the radius of the log and must be thoroughly seasoned.

If a plank is cut radially to the log, so that the end grain runs straight up and down, the tendency to move will be purely along the three main axes of the plank. If on the other hand the plank is slab-cut, with the end grain running skew across the thickness of the wood, the forces exerted when it moves will twist and warp the plank.

To get as much of the timber as possible in the form of radially cut planks it is quarter-sawn. There are several ways of doing this, but in principle the higher the percentage of truly radial planks the greater the wastage, and the more complex the sawmill operation. José Romanillos' idea of splitting by wedges and axes is not a normal commercial procedure, and is only really practical where the luthier can work on the log himself (see page 89).

The proper seasoning of timber does more than reduce its tendency to warp: as it ages its strength increases and its tonal responses improve. Once the log has been cut the planks are carefully stacked and protected so that the moisture of the living tree can dry out. Air-drying is preferred to kiln-drying as it allows time for chemical changes which "cure" the wood. This is a very slow business: luthiers will season their timber for at least three to five years, and often for much longer—twenty or thirty years is favored for tops. Once it has been seasoned, the timber will be stored in the workshop until it has stabilized to the conditions of temperature and humidity under which it will be assembled.

The assembly of a classical guitar is determined by the instrument's dual nature: it is both a physical and a musical structure, and satisfying the requirements for both strength and responsiveness is not easy. The modern guitar has evolved to a point where it is sturdy enough to resist the pull of the strings on the neck and body without distortion, yet light and flexible enough to respond to the slightest musical vibrations.

In purely structural terms, the guitar's shape has inherent disadvantages. The body is essentially a flat box, and must be braced if it is to have any real strength. The full tension of the strings is transmitted directly to the flat top by the bridge. The top must resist this pull without distorting, but it must still be able to vibrate as a diaphragm. The difficulties created by this conflict have been further increased by the growth in size of the modern instrument.

The solution to the guitar's structural problems lies largely in the combination of two devices. The first is the special conformation of the heel and foot, into which the sides are slotted and which provides large gluing areas for the attachment of the front and back. This joint makes a rigid connection between the major components—sides, top, back and neck—at the point of greatest stress and potential movement, with a minimum of material, giving the instrument a center of stability.

The second critical feature is the highly developed system of fan strutting under the table, which braces it against the pull of the strings and controls its movement as a diaphragm. This allows the top to be thinned down for responsiveness and avoids lateral bracing under the lower bout of a kind that would inhibit its vibration. By his adjustments to the thickness of the top and subtle placement of the strutting bars the skilled luthier can "tune" the response of the top to the whole range of frequencies in order to get his desired sound.

The attention given to the table and its bracing might give the impression that it is the only important factor in sound production and tone response. But this is not so: a vibrating guitar string sets the top in motion and the vibrating top projects sound waves both outward and inward with equal intensity. The waves projected inward are reflected and focused by the body before being projected out through the soundhole. They must not conflict with the waves emerging directly from the top, and every part of the body space must be fully activated. The exact shape and size of the body, the size and location of the soundhole, the depth of the sides and the vibration characteristics of both front and back—all these factors

must be brought into balance. The interplay of variables is so complex that no exact rules can be formulated; the luthier must work for the most part by experience and intuition.

The relationship between size and volume is not altogether straightforward. Some of the most admired guitars are comparatively small-bodied. There is a limit to the amount of energy available from the strings, and to the amount of work it can do in activating the timbers and air spaces of the guitar. David Rubio has made the case that "It isn't the size that carries the noise. Perhaps if you had a machine which measured decibels of sound at a short distance from the guitar, the deeper box might come on stronger, but . . . the smaller guitar with beautifully balanced quality and good separation of notes will penetrate a much larger concert hall." Even so it must be admitted that a majority of the guitars heard in concert today are large instruments.

Luthiers are individualists and do not all follow exactly the same order of construction processes. Each has his own pet ways of carrying out different operations; however, the procedures of the traditional Spanish method remain the basis of classical guitar construction.

The first step is to prepare the sides. After they have been planed and scraped by hand to the right thickness—2mm or a little less—they must be bent to shape. The usual method is to work the timber round a heated bending iron. The traditional bending iron consists of an oval metal pipe heated by a charcoal brazier at the bottom; modern bending irons run on electricity. As the timber is heated it becomes malleable, and can be formed to the correct curve. It can be worked either wet or dry; it bends more easily the greater its moisture content, but working dry subjects the timber to fewer sudden changes of humidity, and saves time. Most luthiers work freehand, using a solid template or the marked-out shape of the top as a guide. Working freehand requires long experience, but gives the luthier freedom to modify the body shape of his guitars. Once the sides are shaped, they are put aside to settle for a day or two. If they spring out of shape, they can be worked again.

There is another method of shaping the sides, which involves steeping them in almost boiling water until they are fully malleable. Once they are soft they are clamped over a mold to give them the correct curvature. This technique has the advantage of simplicity, but restricts the luthier and prevents him from changing the body shape without remaking a basic piece of equipment.

José Ramírez employs an unusual side construction for his guitars, making them not of solid rosewood but of rosewood lined with Spanish cypress (the timber traditionally used for the body of the flamenco guitar). He believes that the lamination of dissimilar timbers inhibits warping or twisting of the sides, and the combination of rosewood and cypress must also be a factor in the distinctive sound of his instruments.

The neck is cut from a piece of Honduras mahogany or cedar, and the extra thickness of timber for the heel and foot can be laminated in layers. The foot is worked up and finished, but the neck itself is commonly left rough until it has been fitted to the body. Although the neck is usually built in one piece, Ramírez has introduced the practice of laminating it with a central spine of ebony as a further precaution against warping, and his example has been followed by several other luthiers.

The head of the guitar is often cut from the same piece of timber as the neck, and connected by a simple splice joint calculated to give the correct angle between head and neck. A V joint is still sometimes used instead of the simple splice and has the advantage of being essentially a compression as opposed to a shear joint. But it is difficult to make, and with the improved strength of modern glues has increasingly lost favor.

The guitar head may be veneered, worked to shape and prepared for the fitting of the tuning machines either now or at a later stage of construction, depending on preference. The head veneer can be a single sheet of rosewood or a sandwich of, for example, ebony, holly and rosewood. In either case the final layer of rosewood forms a visual complement to the bridge. The carving of the top and sometimes the front of the head is a distinctive feature by which the guitar's origin may be recognized. Each luthier has a design which, while he may occasionally change it, is as personal a signature as the name on the label.

Once the neck is prepared, the luthier can concentrate on the soundboard and back. They are usually worked more-or-less together, so that their resonant characteristics can be tuned together. Two thin, matched planks are glued together along a long edge which has been prepared perfectly smooth and flat, and the center inlay of the back is incorporated at this stage.

It is usual, though not universal practice, to glue the timbers for the top so that the narrowest—and therefore stiffest—grain is at the center. The reason is that the outer edges of the top are stiffened by their junction with the sides, and it is the center through which the critical vibrations are first transmitted. After gluing, the top will be planed to something approaching the correct thickness before the insertion of the rosette.

Rosette designs by José Ramírez. From the José Ramírez collection.

Rosette patterns vary from simple concentric rings of light and dark, to fantastically complicated patterns of multi-colored inlay.

The main part of the design is built from a mosaic of little slivers of wood, less than 1mm square, which can be either natural-color or dyed, and made by the luthier or bought from a supplier. The slivers are cut to the same length—usually about 15cm—sorted for color and glued into small square logs so that the different-colored elements make the desired pattern on the end grain of the log.

Once the logs have been glued, they are tapered so that they will fit snugly together to form a circular ring of the correct radius for the rosette.

The next step is to cut slices, about 3mm thick, from the ends of the logs, rather as you would cut slices from a piece of salami. The slices will now fit together to form a many sided polygon which closely approximates the final circle of the rosette. The other parts of the design are made from long thin strips of veneer, edge grain uppermost, which are cut

to length and bent to form continuous perfect circles of the right size. The strips are built up around a circular former and glued together until the mosaic part of the design is reached.

At this stage the slices are added. If a water-soluble glue has been used, they can be damped until it has softened. When pressed into place, the slivers will squidge around slightly and can be made to take on a circular alignment so that the pattern follows a true circle, whereas before it was made up of a number of small straight lengths. Finally, more ring strips are built up along the outside edge until the rosette is complete.

In many rosettes the ring strips are not just simple pieces of veneer, but incorporate a

pattern, often a herringbone. The pattern of such herringbone strips (which are also sometimes used in purflings) is, once again, formed by the end grain of slivers of different-colored woods, but in this case the slivers are glued to make a long thin strip instead of a compact log. Obviously strips like this are resistant to bending and inherently very fragile. They can, however, be given strength by sandwiching them between two long thin strips of veneer, and the resulting sandwich may be bent on a bending iron.

Since the construction of rosettes involves a large number of finicky, repetitive operations, the luthier may well make a year's supply at a time.

Once the rosette is in, the luthier can trim the top to its outline, plane and scrape it to thickness, and fit the strutting. This step is critical to the end result. The aim is to produce a guitar not only with quality of tone, but also with equal properties of sustain over the full range of its register. It must have a balanced response to both bass and treble and, ideally, every note should have equal loudness. Like any other resonating object, a guitar top has certain natural resonating characteristics of its own; the luthier must take care that these do not dominate and color the whole range.

The variables he has to work with are the thickness of the top, and the number, layout, size and thickness of the fan struts. The number of possible combinations is enormous—witness the variations of strutting found on good guitars today.

First, the luthier must assess the capabilities of the top, come to a judgment of its potential sound qualities and decide how to realize this full potential. If the board is stiff, it is more likely to have a naturally good treble response; if it is floppy, it will be bass-responsive. There is general agreement that it is not too difficult to achieve a good, rich bass. The real problem lies in getting a clear treble, one that has no "missing notes" and will stand up to the weight of the basses and ring through clearly. It is easy to produce a guitar which is good in parts, but not so easy to make one which is good all through. The problem becomes more acute as the guitar becomes larger, since bass resonance tends to increase with instrument size. Many of the strutting schemes tried out in recent years have been

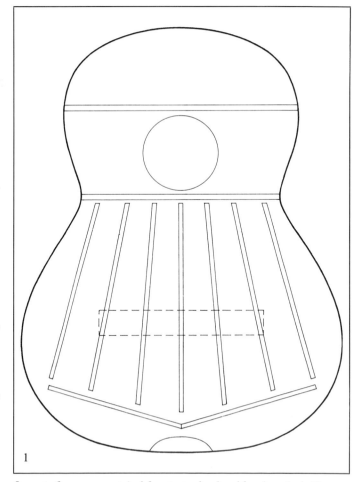

Layout of seven symmetrical fan struts, developed by Antonio de Torres.

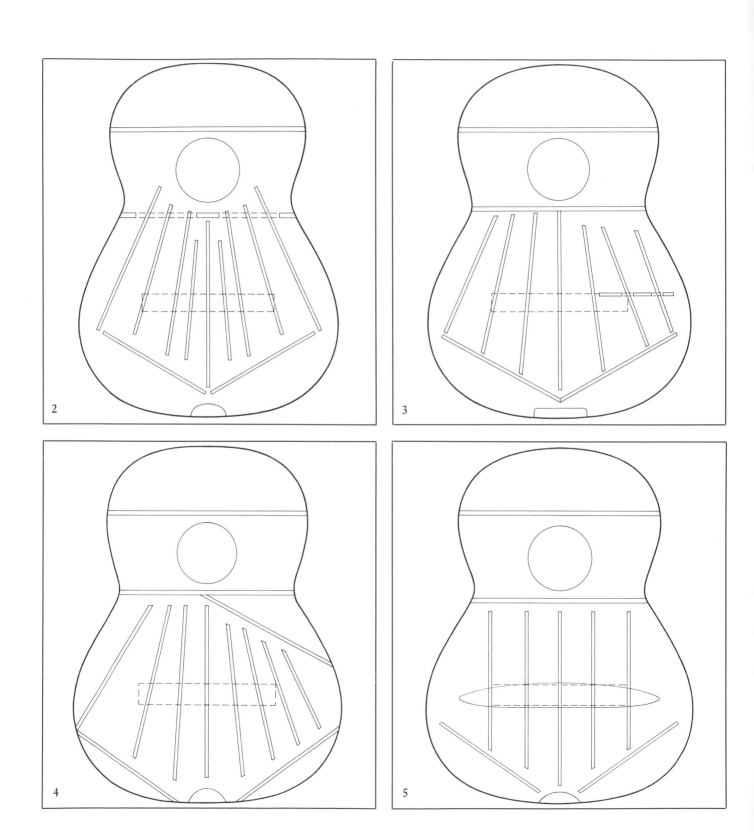

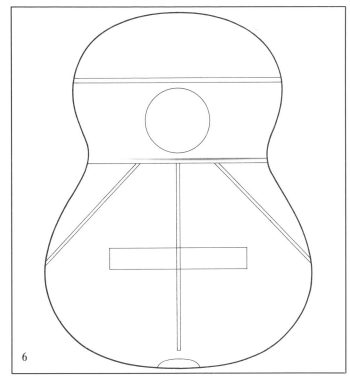

6

designed to stiffen up the treble side of the table and boost high-frequency responses.

The fan bars are not the only important struts on the underside of the table, although acoustically they are the most critical. There are also cross braces to give stability at the waist and upper bout, stiffeners round the edge of the soundhole, and sometimes a stiffening pad under the end of the fingerboard. All of these help to stop unwanted flutter in the upper part of the table.

Torres himself was a great experimenter, and tried out a number of different patterns — a fact which is sometimes overlooked. Some of his experiments (diagram 2) were

as strange as anything found on a modern guitar. This pattern, with nine fans, six of which pass through an arched transverse brace below the soundhole, comes from an instrument made in 1863. This guitar was also fitted with a sound projector (a copper cylinder with flared end) beneath the sound hole.

The system of strutting devised in 1956 by the French luthier Robert Bouchet uses a somewhat similar arched brace below the sound hole.

More recently David Rubio has modified the Torres strutting with a "nodal bar" across the two outer struts on the treble side, somewhere in the region of the bridge (diagram 3). He developed the idea from Bouchet's concept of a bar connecting the struts under the bridge, and finds that with careful placing he can use it to discipline the treble response.

The pattern of strutting from a guitar by Marcelino López (diagram 4) shows another way of stiffening the treble, with a diagonal bar just below the main cross brace. Variations on this theme are also used by Ramírez and Fleta. Here it is worth noticing the asymmetry of the fans themselves — four on the treble side, three on the bass, around a central longitudinal bar, the treble fans being noticeably lighter.

Felix Manzanero is one of a number who have used a system of parallel bars (diagram 5), but what can one say of Paulino Bernabe's three-strut design (diagram 6)? One wouldn't expect it to work at all; but Bernabe is a luthier of great skill, and his apparently outrageous ideas give surprisingly good results.

The variations in strutting patterns are almost innumerable, but this small selection should give some idea of the main avenues which have been explored.

At present, great efforts are being made in America to reduce the element of guesswork in soundboard design. Since the middle of the 1960s, Dr. Michael Kasha has been applying his formidable scientific skills to the problems of guitar acoustics. As Dr. Kasha is the first to admit, it is not easy to blend science and lutherie: theoretical physics describes idealized models, and both compromise and intuition are needed when applying its precepts. Accordingly, Dr. Kasha has col-

laborated with luthiers, guitarists and scientists to develop, test and execute his ideas.

Kasha's knowledge of physics suggested to him that traditional fan strutting inhibited the soundboard's vibration: the bridge of the guitar rocks back and forth, sending waves rippling through the top. Long, continuous bars passing under the bridge tend to reduce the amplitude of these waves and so restrict the sound output of the guitar. The first aim, therefore, was to produce a design that would

give the top stability but allow it to vibrate more freely. Later, Dr. Kasha started to work on ways of predicting and controlling tone quality, balance and response. The resulting designs depart radically from traditional strutting types.

All Kasha-design guitars have a transverse bar beneath the bridge saddle, which acts as a pivot about which the bridge rocks. This provides the essential stability without restricting the rocking motion. Comparatively

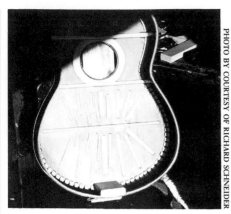

PHOTO BY COURTESY OF RICHARD SCHNEIDER

short struts then radiate over the lower bout from the bridge area, activating the soundboard. Theoretical plate mechanics provides the guidelines for deciding on the length and placing of these struts. In principle, a plate vibrates most forcefully at its natural resonant frequency; large plates have low frequencies, small plates have high ones. Accordingly, Kasha structures the soundboard into a series of different sized zones, each of which operates in the particular frequency band in which it is most efficient. These zones are both defined and activated by the radiating struts. The *The underside of the soundboard of a guitar made by Richard Schneider to Dr. Kasha's design.*

struts on the bass side of the soundboard are longer than those on the treble, so that low notes bring proportionally larger areas into play; some of the struts on the treble side are designed to reduce the area that can vibrate at high frequencies.

Dr. Kasha's theories have met with scepticism in many quarters, but are slowly gaining ground. Luthier Richard Schneider (who has worked with Kasha since 1969) is so convinced of their correctness, and the improvement they have brought to his instruments, that he says, "In five years' time it will be obvious there is no other way to build a guitar."[4]

The top of the guitar is clamped to the workboard while the struts are fixed and shaped. The struts themselves are made of the same timber as the top, whether spruce or cedar. Their gluing must be clean and thorough: loose struts can buzz, and will not do their job properly.

The cross braces are not completely flat, but have a slight curve on them which gives the table a very shallow arch. The back is also slightly arched since arching both increases the strength of the instrument and prevents the formation of standing waves, vibrations which can build up between two flat parallel surfaces, and become amplified until they dominate.

During the shaping of the struts the luthier gives the top its final tuning, constantly checking its resonant characteristics. Different makers have different procedures: some tune the top to a specific note (which can be sounded by tapping the top or drawing a violin bow across the edge), others listen to the patterns of harmonics, others are less specific about their systems but know when it sounds "right."

The back has three cross struts and a center fillet over the joint between the two halves, and is tuned in a similar way to the top. Ideas vary on the subject of the proper relationship between the characteristics of top and back. David Rubio, for example, tunes the back a semitone lower than the front, while others will not tune it to a specific note. The ultimate aim is a top and back which are acoustically compatible and capable of producing a clear sound from the final guitar.

Once the top and back are complete, the whole neck and body assembly may be glued together. One method is to glue the neck assembly first to the top (still attached to the workboard) and then bring in the sides. Alternatively, the sides may first be glued into the slots in the heel/foot and the top glued on after. The glue area between the sides and top is increased either by small triangular blocks, placed close together all round the junction, or a kerfed, or a solid, lining. (A kerfed lining is a strip of wood of triangular section, with slots cut at regular intervals so that it may be bent to the contours of the body.)

The glue area for the junction of sides and back is similarly increased by a lining, which is normally continuous and shaped on the bending iron before being glued to the sides. There is a theory that, as well as increasing strength, the linings aid the acoustic properties of the body by filling in what would otherwise be dead corners at the angles of the body junctions.

Once the neck, top and sides are together (still clamped to the workboard), the back can be glued in place and trimmed to size.

Attention must be paid during the body assembly to the correct alignment of the neck, and to its tilt relative to the body. The neck is sometimes set flat, in the same plane as the soundboard, but many makers give it a very slight upward tilt which produces a rise at the nut of anything up to 3mm. This helps to achieve a proper action and buzz-free playing, and reduces the amount of taper which has to be incorporated in the fingerboard.

The set of the neck, contour of the fingerboard, height of the bridge saddle, and even the behavior of the table, all affect the action of the guitar.

Once the body is together, the luthier can inlay the

purflings at the junctions between top and sides, and sides and back. The purflings, made of long strips of hardwood veneers, add greatly to the aesthetic grace of the guitar. They also seal the end grain of sides, top and back, and so inhibit the absorption of moisture from the atmosphere. A ledge or notch slightly smaller than the purfling section is cut at the top-to-side and side-to-back junctions with either a purfling cutter or a router. The purfling is fitted, glued, sanded and scraped flush with the body.

Now that the body is essentially complete, attention focuses on the neck and fingerboard. The head also will now be veneered, carved, and slotted for machines if this was not done at an early stage.

The fingerboard is more complicated than it looks. It has to be fitted, marked out, slotted and fretted. As usual, the precise order in which the operations are carried out varies from workshop to workshop. In shaping the fingerboard two conditions have to be met. The underside must fit snugly, without being forced, along the neck and over the table to the soundhole. Once this has been achieved it may be glued in place, and the top surface can be worked up. The pattern of the vibrating string must also be taken into account. When a string vibrates its greatest displacement occurs at the twelfth fret—the mid-point of its vibrating length—on the open string. It must have room to move or it will buzz against the frets, but if the action becomes too high the guitar may be difficult to play and its

tone may be changed. To take account of this the fingerboard thickness is tapered from the nut to the soundhole. The top of the fingerboard is not always made flat: the envelope of a vibrating string is curved, and this may be matched by a curve on the fingerboard. The curve on a well-adjusted fingerboard can give a rise of between 0.4 and 0.8mm between the twelfth and first frets. Finally, the bass strings vibrate with a larger displacement than the treble. To allow for this, the saddle may be raised on one side, or the fingerboard tapered away on the bass side, or both. The adjustments are very slight, but important.

The next step is to fret the guitar. The scale length is, obviously, one of the prime determinants of guitar design and construction. In recent years, some makers have increased the scale length from Torres' standard of 65cm to 66cm and more in the search for an instrument with greater power. This makes the guitar more difficult to play, however, as greater hand stretches are demanded, and there have been growing doubts about the apparent power of the larger guitar.

The luthier must be able to mark out and position the frets with great accuracy, so that the guitar will be in tune at all points. The musical scale which we now use is one of equal temperament, in which the octave is divided into twelve perfectly equal semitones. To show how this determines the fretting calculations of the guitar involves a little basic mathematics which are described in the box.

The pitch of a note is proportional to the frequency of vibration of a string, and inversely proportional to its vibrating length. Also, an octave increase in pitch is produced by a halving of string length, which doubles the frequency.

The relationship between frequency and scale length can be expressed as $F \propto 1/L$, or $F.L$ = constant, where F is frequency and L is string length.

Now if the octave is to be divided into twelve equal semitones giving frequencies F_0, F_1, F_2, ... F_{12}, then $F_0/F_1 = F_1/F_2 = F_2/F_3$ ... F_{11}/F_{12}. So $F_2 = F_1 \times F_1/F_0$, and the ratio of a whole tone $F_2/F_0 = (F_1/F_0)^2$. Three semi-

tones gives the ratio $F_3/F_0 = (F_1/F_0)^3$, and the octave, of twelve semitones, $F_{12}/F_0 = (F_1/F_0)^{12}$.

But the octave ratio represents a doubling of frequency, so that $F_{12}/F_0 = (F_1/F_0)^{12} = 2$, and F_1/F_0, the frequency ratio of the semitone interval, is $(2)^{\frac{1}{12}}$, or the twelfth root of two.

Similarly the lengths of the strings which produce these two notes a semitone apart are connected by the relationship $L_1/L_0 = 1/(2)^{\frac{1}{12}}$, since $F \propto 1/L$. The distance between the nut and first fret to give a distance of one semitone must be $L_0 - L_1 = L_0 (1 - 1/(2)^{\frac{1}{12}})$. If this distance is called x and calculated, the result is that $x_0 \simeq L_0/17.817$. Similarly, $x_1 = L_1/$

17.817, and so on.

This relationship is the basis of all fretting calculations. If L_0 is taken to be the scale length of the guitar, then x_0, the distance from the first fret to the nut is calculated as $L_0/17.817$, and the remaining frets can be calculated in the same way. In practice, when laying out a fingerboard in equal temperament, the scale length is divided by 17.817 to gain the position of the first fret. The remaining length is divided again by 17.817 to find the position of the second fret, and so on, until all the fret positions have been worked out.

When he has worked out the fret positions for the scale length he wants—or, more likely, obtained the results of

someone else's calculations—the luthier can make up a template marked with the positions. This can be clamped to the fingerboard and the fret positions transferred to the prepared ebony.

The frets themselves are made of T-shaped pieces of nickel silver wire cut from a roll. The tail or "tang" of the fret wire has a number of dimples. To fit the fret, grooves are cut in the fingerboard with a fine bladed saw. The cuts must be exactly the right depth and width, so that when the fret wire is hammered home the tang is fully housed and the dimples are securely gripped by the wood. It is purely a pressure fit, with no glue.

Most luthiers cut the slots one at a time, either by hand or on a power bench saw. There is a special bench saw available to the larger, more automated, workshop which can cut all nineteen grooves at once. This is like an ordinary circular saw, except that it has nineteen blades all spaced to give accurate fret positions. When using a bench saw, it is more convenient to slot the fingerboard before attaching it to the neck; working by hand the reverse is true.

Once the slots are cut, pieces of fret wire are snipped from the roll, slightly longer than needed, tapped home with a hammer, trimmed to length and filed smooth, so that the string makes firm contact with the precise center of the fret when depressed.

Once the fingerboard is fretted the neck can be given its final shaping, and the bridge and nut fitted. Neck and heel are carved with a chisel and spokeshave, and the speed with which a skilled luthier can transform a roughly shaped lump of wood into a perfectly smooth, correctly contoured neck is astonishing.

The bridge for the classical guitar is made from a rectangular block of rosewood. The center portion, where the strings are tied, is protected round its edges with ivory, and sometimes inlaid with a timber mosaic matching the rosette design. The Kasha bridge is wider on the bass than the treble side; this, it is claimed, helps to give a more balanced response.

The exact positioning of the bridge is as essential as the exact location of the frets if the guitar is to play in tune. In theory, the scale length is the distance between the string's bearing points on the saddle and nut. In practice the bridge has to be set a little further back, so that the string length is very slightly longer than the theoretical scale length. This difference between nominal scale length and actual string length is known as compensation, and works out at approximately 2mm, although it varies slightly from guitar to guitar according to scale length and action. Without accurate compensation the guitar will not play in tune. When a string is stopped, its tension is increased by the very action of pressing it down. The increase in tension raises the pitch of the note slightly from true, and this rise of pitch has to be corrected by the compensation. Once the bridge position is established, the bridge, which has already been sealed and polished, can be glued in place with the aid of two or three deep-throated clamps.

Both saddle and nut are made of bone or ivory. Ivory is much preferred, as it retains its beauty where bone will yellow with age. The shallow grooves in the nut, in which the strings are seated, are ranged slightly to the bass side of the fingerboard. This allows a little extra room so that the first string will not be pulled off the fingerboard in legato passages.

Finally, the guitar has to be polished. There are a few makers who temporarily fit the machines and string the guitar before polishing, to try it out and make any final adjustments, but this is tedious and most do not bother.

Opinions vary as to the effect of varnish on the tone of the guitar. On balance it seems that, provided the varnish is applied in normal quantities, the difference it makes is slight.

Applying the finish to the guitar involves several different processes. Rosewood is an oily timber, which must be thoroughly degreased with a volatile solvent before any finish can be applied. The entire guitar, with the exception of the fingerboard, is then sealed with a thin coat of shellac. After sealing, the rosewood of the body and the cedar or mahogany of the neck have to be worked over with filler to fill their open pore system. Only when the filler has thoroughly dried can the varnish or polish be applied. The whole guitar receives varnish, except for the fingerboard which remains in its natural state.

Several types of finish are available—French polish, oil and spirit varnishes, and lacquers. French polish, the traditional finish for the best guitars, is beautiful, durable and acoustically suitable—but slow and difficult to apply. It is a type of shellac, applied with a smooth, tightly wadded cloth pad. The polish is applied with long smooth strokes in progressively thinner layers. The last layers are very thin and worked up to a deep gloss. Finally the polish is "spirited off" with a little pure alcohol to remove excess oil and bring the gloss to perfection.

Varnishes are made of natural resins in solution in oil or spirit bases. They are applied by brush, rubbed down with fine silicone paper, and polished with a fine polishing compound. Oil varnishes are slower-drying and more flexible, and some makers suspect that they damp the vital treble responses.

Both nitrocellulose and acrylic spray lacquers (widely used on steel-string and electric guitars) are slowly finding their way into the classical workshop. José Ramírez was the first to popularize spray finishes on handmade guitars. Lacquers are durable, easy to apply, and work up to a very hard gloss. They can also look disturbingly synthetic, and care has to be taken in spraying to avoid ugly buildups in corners such as that between the junction of bridge and top.

When the varnish is hard, dry and polished, the machine heads can be fitted and the guitar strung. Many of the best machines are made in Germany, plated with gold or silver and chased by hand. There are others available in a blued finish, with the engraving picked out in gold. The gears should be free of play, and turn smoothly and easily—a point which can only really be assessed with the string tension released.

Finally the guitar is finished—or, rather, the construction of the guitar is finished, for the new instrument takes time to reveal its full qualities. It has to be played in, and every note should be equally exercised. Otherwise unnecessary "dead spots" may develop. Properly treated, the guitar will continue to improve for years; neglected or inadequately played, its powers will fade away.

Recitalist José Luis González trying out guitars in Paulino Bernabe's workshop.

Since 1970, the guitars made by José Romanillos have gained an international reputation. The following photographs of the various stages of classical guitar construction were taken, and the accompanying comments recorded, in 1975 and 1976 at his workshop in the English village of Semley, Dorset. Together they give an insight into the way in which one particular luthier approaches his work.

Romanillos made his first guitar on his kitchen table in London in 1959, because he wanted an instrument to play but couldn't afford to buy one. But, as he says, "Once I made a guitar and I proved to myself I could make some kind of sound out of a few pieces of timber, I got hooked." He has been making guitars ever since.

In 1970, Romanillos was introduced to Julian Bream and showed him examples of his work. As a result of this meeting Romanillos operated for a time in the instrument making studio which Julian Bream had set up at his farm in Dorset. Romanillos says of this period: "It did help me a lot; it produced a workshop, and he has this ability to inspire me."

The friendship with Bream, centered on the guitar, still continues, with a constant exchange of ideas about the instrument and how it can be improved. "It is a driving force, but it could also be a pitfall, because his standard is terribly high and one is trying to produce the ultimate instrument. I have to be very careful that I don't get, how shall I say, under the influence of Bream—that I don't get carried away."

Romanillos works alone, and carries out almost every operation by hand using traditional methods. As a result his output is small, between fourteen and seventeen instruments a year. He could produce more, but values his independence; he likes to be able to work in his own way, and to have time for his researches on the great nineteenth-century luthier Antonio de Torres Jurado and, in the summer, for cricket.

"The guitar is an instrument which lacks stability like the cello or fiddle. Some ideas work, some don't. There are two luthiers I revere: one is Hauser, who died in 1952, the other is Torres. These two are my guiding lights. I haven't heard any guitars which sound like Hauser anywhere. Torres sounds very good, but of course they are very old now and you can't make a true assessment of some of the sound qualities.

José Romanillos in his workshop

"I'm trying to create an instrument that is intimate and also to make it, aesthetically speaking, as beautiful as I can. I try to make an instrument which is light, which makes more resonance, but is controlled. I think with a smaller guitar the sound is more in focus. With a large guitar, you seem to be further away from it.

"Given an intimate instrument, you have to get the most out of it. For example, when they play the triangle in the orchestra, you can hear the sound through almost all the other instruments. It's a particular sound which cuts through, and this is what I try to achieve. They're very deceptive, my guitars. Some players say the output is not great, but it has *intensity* and the note carries through.

"You've got to get the sound out from the table. You have to make the body resonant by using the air cavities, and you only do that if you activate all the parts of the guitar. Otherwise you have a guitar on which one note lasts five minutes and another lasts five seconds. The instrument has to breathe. Some of these large instruments, they consume. They play, and they have great impact, but the sound tapers down. And this is my fight—I don't achieve it all the time. I'm too conceited; I always think the next one will be a greater instrument, so I'm always searching. The trouble is, some of the things I think will be right don't work out the way I want them to. Others . . . well, we always try to achieve the ultimate.

"Quality of sound is my driving force. Tone and balance are good things, but quality is most important. It depends on the timber above all, and on the way you approach it. I want excellence in every respect. How do you define excellence? I don't know. A guitar above all must have character, so it stands out. It's like human beings, in a way. All different, but you sometimes find a person who has a tremendous poise or warmth. The guitar, when you hear it, has to draw you to it, to its excellence. I have produced two or three guitars which have significance in that sense."

"It depends on the timber above all ..." Split wedges of Alpine spruce, which will go to make guitar tables when they are fully seasoned and matured.

"The timbers should be split rather than sawn. I used to buy the tables from good dealers in Switzerland and Germany, but two or three years ago I decided to go to Switzerland and buy the tree myself. I split it, and brought it here, and I chopped it and cut it. The best way, in my estimation, is to split the timber with wedges and a couple of axes. The idea is to get the radial line, with the medullary rays. They're very important in the qualities of sound and elasticity of the timber.

"Also by splitting you get the wood as straight as possible lengthwise. Microscopically, timber fibers are like a handful of drinking straws. If you deviate from the straight and chop the fibers you lose a bit of the strength. That's one of the reasons for splitting: you naturally split right along the fibers. When they're split, they come in wedges. Then, once you've got so far, you quarter-saw. The shed is full of wedges which are too small. I only use 30 to 40 percent of the wood from any log."

"There is a human element—it's the tree *I* cut. But also there is a continuity of material. I understand how certain materials work for my particular use. If I run out, I have to start again because every tree is different. If you buy two or three tops and work on them, the material is finished and you have to start fresh again.

"You get a piece of spruce cut, and you see all these lovely medullary rays, it has a grace and beauty. . . ."

"Practically speaking, it's more or less impossible for the back and side timbers to be split. But I do insist that they should be straight grain and quarter-sawn.

"Six years ago I bought four logs of rosewood and had them cut to my requirements. Since then I have found a place in India which will cut the timber as I want.

"I couldn't get Rio rosewood quarter-sawn, straight

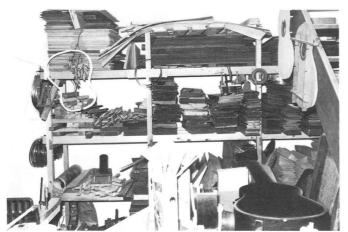

Timber stacked in the workshop storage racks

grain, of the same quality. Even if I could, the price would be prohibitive. Some people seem to think that Brazilian rosewood makes for a better sound, but I prefer the sound Indian gives. Of course, some people go for Rio rosewood because it's difficult to get, for its rarity value."

Timbers waiting to be used—the lighter timber is spruce for the tops, the darker is rosewood. A rough translation of the phrase penciled in on the rack below would be, "Guitar, something which caresses, and something which ruins."

"I keep it in my shed until a year before I use it. The timbers I'm using at the moment I've had for about six years. Not very much, but still . . . . One of my reservations about this country is that the weather is not very propitious for seasoning timber. I believe in the effect of the air and the wind. It's not only the moisture in the wood that counts, but also many different chemicals. I don't profess to understand what they do, but I believe in the effect of nature. When it's sunny I put the timbers in the sun, throw them about, all sorts of things. But humidity is a terrible thing. For timbers, humidity is a weakening factor: the more water in a timber, the weaker it is. In this country the humidity can be pretty disastrous."

Shaping the side of a guitar on the bending iron, an oval-shaped metal tube which is electrically heated.

"I work on four guitars at a time. I start with the sides. The planks are sawn to $\frac{3}{16}''$ or $\frac{1}{4}''$ at the mill and then I plane and scrape them to the thickness required. Even the sides I scrape and plane by hand.

"Once I've planed them I shape them on a hot bending iron. I work them dry, though occasionally I damp the wood slightly at the waist if it's going to buckle. I work free, although I have a template to give me guidance. Some people use either inside or outside molds, but I'm free from that.

"In developing my guitars I have worked with the depth of the box more than with the shape. How do you tell what differences one shape makes from another? One has to have intuition. . . . I have looked at the masters and I have adapted their shapes. But in order to prove the effect of different shapes one would have to be very scientific about it. I would like to know."

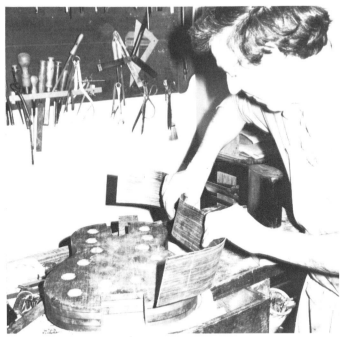

Checking the contour of the side against a template.

The neck in its rough state.

"I may have made it look easy, but that's only because I've had lots of practice!"

The heel and foot, showing the groove into which the side will be slotted and glued when the guitar is assembled.

"Then I glue all the components of the neck, the heel and everything. The neck is rough, just cut to shape on the bandsaw. The only thing for which I use the machines so far is to shape the neck.

"Before I put the neck to the side, I finish the inside part of the heel (the foot) and varnish it. But all the outside is rough.

"I use old Honduras cedar for the neck. This is light and very stable. Old Honduras mahogany is also good, and I wouldn't mind using if it I could find some light enough. But I bought a stock of cedar a long time ago and I love it. You've got to get the balance right and cedar works for me."

A circle cutter is used to take out the ring in the top where the rosette surrounding the soundhole is to be inlaid. The circle cutter, with its fine blade, is set to make a cut both of the right radius and also to the depth to which the timber must be removed to accommodate the thickness of the rosette.

Matched pieces of Alpine spruce hanging in the workshop, waiting to be worked up into guitar tops, and a finished top with the rosette inserted.

"Once I have the sides shaped and cut to length, and the neck and heel shaped with the grooves, I concentrate on the top.

"I don't give so much importance to the grain of the wood as to having it split the right way. Some people say that ten or twenty lines to the inch or whatever might be right, but I prefer to go by the feel, the look, the way the timbers reflect the light. Obviously, I don't want the grain too wide or the table will be weak.

"When I look at the timber I like to see plenty of character. If you have too uniform a top it is going to be characterless. I like a bit of human frailty in it. But we pick and choose according to our experience."

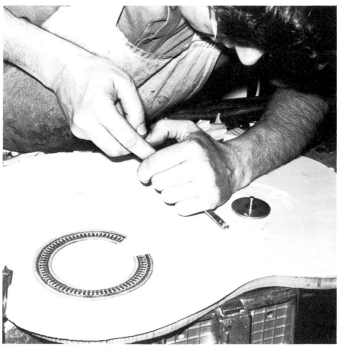

The excess material is cut away with a flat chisel. The marquetry rosette, which is about to be fitted, can be seen in the foreground.

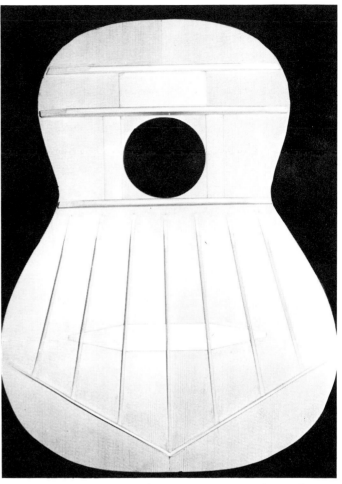

The soundhole itself is not cut until after the rosette has been fitted. The arch design was inspired by the arches of the mosque of Cordova.

"The two halves of the top are joined and glued, and then planed to near enough the right thickness, and the rosette is inserted.

"The rosette is already made. I make enough for twelve or fourteen guitars at a time. They're all natural woods, not dyed. The timbers in that rosette are rosewood, holly, yew, satinwood, Honduras cedar. I don't think there's any ebony. . . . The rosette, as you know, is usually made by joining slivers of different timber with the end grain up to form a pattern, in a little block. But the arches work on another principle, which involves so many facets I don't even know how to describe it. The trouble is, when I conquer one thing I have to tackle another so I'll probably change it.

"At a lecture I gave recently, I took a guitar along and I told them how difficult the rosette is and one of the boys came to me after and asked, 'If acoustically it doesn't enhance the guitar, why do it?' I thought it was a funny question."

The underside of the top, showing the pattern of cross-bracing and the seven fan struts.

"After I put in the rosette and the outer part of the top is clean, I work it to thickness and put the strutting inside. The thickness of the top is more-or-less uniform although I tend to thin a little bit toward the sides, particularly on the lower bout. It depends on the elasticity of the timber, but you have an area in the center where you want more wood.

"The struts are made of spruce, same as the top. Basically I use the Torres pattern of seven fan struts. Hauser copied Torres. I have examined both men's work and added my own ideas. I'm always working with thicknesses and slight variations, and different methods of putting things together. But the changes are very subtle.

"I have changed the strutting occasionally, and made two or three unusual guitars. They work in many ways."

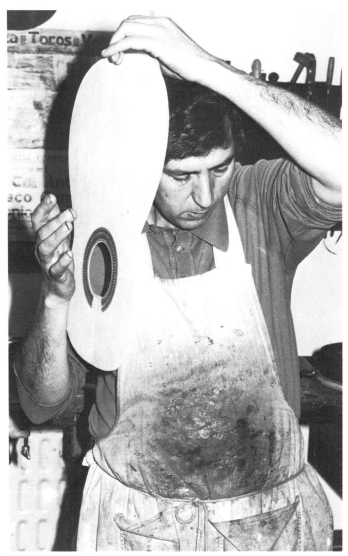
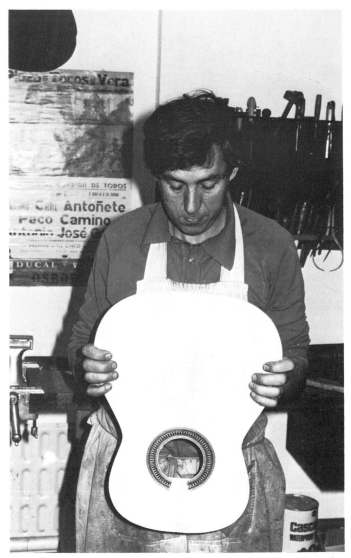

Tapping and flexing a partly finished top.

"I don't tune the top to a specific note, but try to kill the very high harmonics. If the guitar is coming out in G, G♯, or A, this note is very strong. If you don't control it, the instrument responds to that note and it colors everything. But by the way you place the fan braces on the top, you either increase or kill a harmonic.

"I don't profess to understand the method yet, but I work to a system. If there are too many high harmonics floating around, they color the whole range. That's one of the basics of the guitar.

"After a time you get a feeling, a pragmatic answer, and you make the instrument that way. I work by tapping, by tapping the soundboard. I also go by the feel. When I'm shaping the struts, I take the top and flex it. The feel of the timbers, and the tapping, will give you more or less what you're after, if you're lucky. Sometimes it doesn't work, because sound is not the sort of thing that's easy to understand. There's no physical law that tells you what you've got to do, you can only go by your own experience. You've got a sound in your ear and you try to get that sound out of the top.

"There's only one way to make it work: feeling it here, tapping it there."

Two partly finished backs.

"I work the back at the same time as the top because I have to match the sounds of both.

"I don't try to tune the back to a specific note, but I try to give it a sound which will work well with the front.

"The timbers are matched. They come from the same piece of wood, which has been opened like a book."

The assembly for gluing the sides to the neck and the sides to the top. The top is held to the workboard by a clamp through the soundhole. A notched jig over the struts allows firm clamping without bruising the delicate timber. The sides are glued in to the slots in the heel and the top surface of the foot is glued to the underside of the soundboard. The sides will be held down firmly to the underside of the top with additional clamps when the triangular blocks connecting sides and top are glued in place all around the junction.

"The neck is glued, and the end block. When I've got that, the sides come in and they're held to the top by little blocks. I use animal glue for that. You increase the gluing area of the sides to the back by putting in the lining. This is just over double the thickness of the side."

Gluing the back to the sides.

"You have to cut the struts away from the lining, so the back will fall in place. When that is done, it's more-or-less cut to shape and you glue all around it. The back is held to the side by the thickness of the lining. Once the glue is dry it comes out of the clamp—and the surplus of the back is trimmed off.

"This is the Spanish way of building."

The top of the rough-shaped neck, showing the male half of the V joint which will be fitted in to the matching cut-out V in the head.

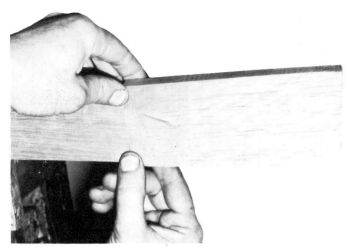

Fitting the head on to the neck. The rake of the head to neck makes this a difficult joint: compound angles have to be worked out and cut with a high degree of accuracy.

"After the back is glued, the tilt of the neck is checked—it's a few degrees in relation to the top. Then I work out the head.

"I like the V joint. First of all I enjoy making it. It's a nice challenge, a difficult joint to make. Second, it's the best joint I've found. Many makers use the splice joint, but this leaves a nasty glue line at the back which is unsatisfactory to me, and is not so strong."

A selection of purflings and inlays.

"Then I'll work the inlays and purflings. I cut out with the cutting edge and chisel. I pare away and take the bindings in. The back and front bindings are glued on to the instrument together.

"I use all sorts of things for the inlays, principally satinwood, which is a very beautiful wood."

"When the bindings are done, I clean the backs up, glue the fingerboard, which has to be shaped and cut to size, and face the head. I shape the head after it has been faced.

"Instead of increasing the saddle height to allow for the greater displacement of the bass strings, I taper the fingerboard to give clearance for the bass to move. If the saddle gets too high, it sounds banjoey and alters the tension of the instrument."

The wooden template, with fret positions marked on it, clamped to the fingerboard.

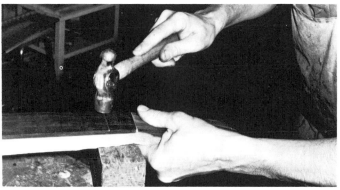

Tapping home a fret. The edge of the hammer head is radiused to protect both wire and fingerboard against indentations.

Transferring the fret positions from the template to the fingerboard.

"To fret the fingerboard I have a table marked out and I transfer the measurements. The scale length is 65cm unless someone specifies different. I've made 64.5cm. I know that over 65cm it doesn't work so well: for a start, the spread puts the player at a disadvantage. I've seen guitars at 67cm but . . . you've really got to have a big hand! If you go too short you change the character of the instrument. I think 65cm is probably the best compromise.

"I had someone make steel templates, slotted exactly for position and depth so I could just saw through, but they weren't accurate enough. So now I have just a piece of wood with the dimensions on."

Trimming down the fret to length.

"The saw cut is of the right width and depth and you just tap the frets gently. It's a little bit troublesome at the end over the table, where it's floating. There isn't very much support. Sometimes what I'll do is use a clamp inside.

"The fret wire is a standard 2mm nickel silver."

Cutting the slots for the frets. The back saw makes a cut of exactly the right width to grip the shank of the T-shaped fret wire firmly when it is hammered home, and the jig clamped to the blade ensures that the cut is of the right depth.

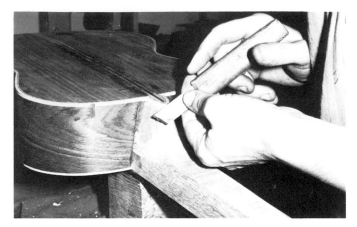

Carving the heel.

Shaping the neck with a spokeshave.

As the neck approaches its final contour, its depth is checked with a gauge.

"The neck gets its final shape when the instrument is put together. This is the last thing I do on the guitar apart from fixing the bridge."

Locating the bridge, with the same template used to mark out the fret positions.

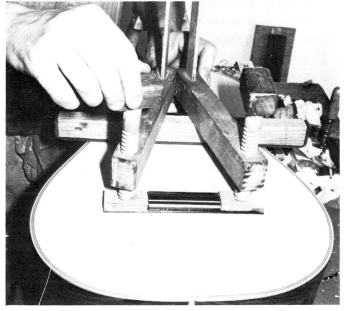

Gluing the bridge.

"The bridge has been shaped and is glued on to the table. I've got two deep-throated clamps, which I put under the soundhole to support it, and glue it together. The glue I use is Cascamite. In this life there are a lot of purists where glues are concerned, but I'm not one of them. Cascamite is very strong and acoustically I don't think it makes any difference."

"My contention is that the polish doesn't make any difference at all to the tone. Other people will shout me down on this, particularly the violin makers. Obviously if you put *too* much on, it makes a difference by changing the thickness of the plate. You have tuned two plates up to what you think is right, and too much polish will change it.

"It's the material which is critical — you must know the material and what to do with it. The timber is absolutely vital."

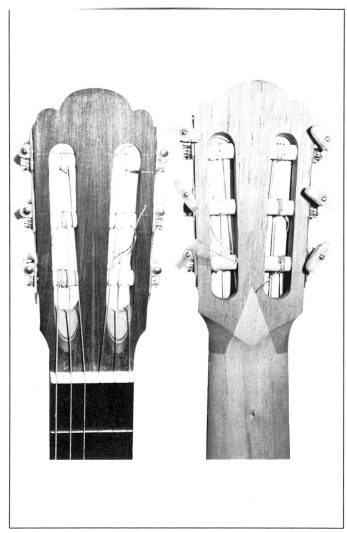

Two finished but as yet unpolished guitars, and one awaiting fretting, hanging in the workshop.

"I usually try my guitars before I polish them. I string them up and go through them note by note. Sometimes if I think they haven't worked out, the unpolished top allows me to alter them by scraping here and there and I can try to get the response that I want. I don't do that very often. Once I have tried them, I leave them hanging for a while, to get an idea of what they are like. Then, finally, I polish them.

"I use French polish, shellac dissolved in methylated spirits, put on with a rubber. It's a slow process.

The head of the guitar before polishing. The machine heads will have to be removed before the final polish is applied. The triple-arch head design is closely modeled on the pattern used by Torres.

The complete guitar. When he came to string up and try out this instrument (named "La Primera") before giving it its final polish, José Romanillos was particularly excited about its tone and tonal balance. The quality of the basses was most noticeable—lighter and less booming than on most modern guitars, but with great purity and a clear, bell-like ring.

"One mustn't forget that Stradivarius, the greatest of them all, lived to be ninety or ninety-two, and he started to make fiddles when he was eleven. He only made his best ones when he was fifty and had forty years of experience behind him. Many other people have had that sort of experience and haven't been a Stradivarius, but there's no other way. You can't beat that contact with the woods. And this is why I say life is very short. You must live to be a hundred!"

The label of "La Reina."

"I'm living in a foreign country, so I decided to name my guitars in Spanish—it brings me to reality somehow. It's probably silly, but it has a meaning for me.

"I have a directory for my guitars: I know where each one goes, and who has it."

MUSIC FOR THE CLASSICAL GUITAR

Music for the vihuela

Although only one vihuela is known to have survived, both the quality and the quantity of the music published for the instrument in mid-sixteenth-century Spain indicate its importance and popularity. No identifiable school of vihuelists existed; in fact, some of the earlier composers were totally unaware of the existence of previous vihuela books. Nonetheless they were able to draw on common sources such as the songs and dances of country and court, and the sacred music of both foreign and Spanish composers. From this basis they produced some of the finest of all polyphonic instrumental music, which had a style distinct from the lute music of the rest of Europe. As a solo and accompanying instrument, the vihuela filled the role in Spain which the lute occupied elsewhere in Europe. The music for vihuela matches the lute music of the period both in its beauty and in the significance of its compositional devices. Although a handful of vihuela pieces are now well known and frequently played on the concert platform, the whole surviving range of the music deserves greater exploration and wider performance. The vihuela books contain the earliest known written music for guitar-type instruments, and show us how these instruments were used for the expression of some of the most sophisticated musical thought of their age.

During a period of 41 years, from 1535 to 1576, seven main books were produced. With one exception, they were the work of professional musicians or courtiers attached to the most splendid households of Renaissance Spain. These magnificent books, containing between them about 700 compositions, printed expensively on the best paper and often charmingly decorated, were more than collections of music: they were also intended as instruction books,

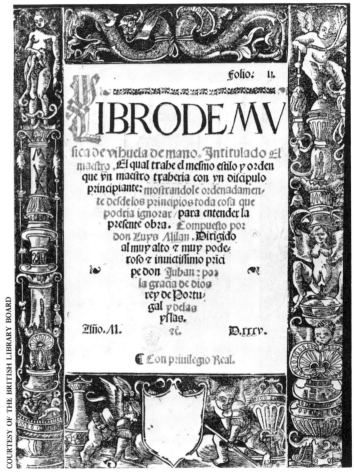

Frontispiece to Luis Milán's El Maestro, *1535.*

designed to lead the player from easy pieces to those requiring a much greater degree of technical and musical skill. The first vihuela composer, Luis Milán in *El Maestro* (1535), set out his purpose in the prologue: it is a "book . . . which has the same style and order that a teacher would have with a pupil who was commencing . . . showing it [the music] in orderly fashion." The seven music books, together with the *Declaración de Instrumentos Musicales,* a treatise of 1555 by the Franciscan friar Juan Bermudo, provide a fund of information on sixteenth-century technique and Spanish musical taste.

Because the books were intended for an aristocratic and educated audience, the vihuelists assumed a certain degree of knowledge on the part of their readers. For this reason, understanding of *compás* (beat) and *mesura* (the value of the notes) was not dealt with. Instead many of the books were concerned with the principles of string selection, tuning, reading tablature, and with advice on technique.

The six-course double-strung vihuela was tuned with the lute intervals of 4-4-3-4-4. In Spain, as in the rest of Europe at this period, pitch was a matter of practical convenience. It depended on a variety of factors: the tensile strength of the string used (which could vary enormously), the size of the instrument, the accuracy of the performer's ear, and even the state of the weather. One assumes that there was a range of octave tunings to suit the different sizes of instruments. Remembering the interval of a third between the third and fourth courses, the range could be from E-e', up to A-a' or even lower D-d' if one accepts the existence of a bass vihuela. Advice on tuning was practical: Luis Milán explained that the player had to tune the first string as high as it would go and use that as a guide to tune the others, which were then checked by comparing unison and octave sounds. If the tunings were incorrect, either the string could be slightly screwed up, or the tied gut fret adjusted. It was possible—and obviously an acknowledged skill—to play on a distuned instrument. One Luis de Guzmán was described as doing just that: "He tuned his vihuela in the usual tuning, and then lowered or raised one string of the third or fourth [course] and thus he played."[1]

Tempo directions were given at the beginning of many pieces: some should be played "somewhat joyfully" and others "with a beaten or fast measure." But the vihuelists were pragmatic and untyrannical teachers: "each one must conform to the disposition of his hands and the difficulties of the work. . . . And he who does not have enough freedom of the hands must play with a settled measure especially beginners, until he has knowledge of the work. . . . Neither does the measure go hastened nor very slowly."[2]

And naturally the kind of music acted as a guide. A song marked "of joyful merry nature" would be played at a different pace from some of the complicated *fantasias*, or the transcription of a hymn tune. The last of the vihuelists, Esteban Daza, gave no advice as to tempo and did not explain the two signs he used, which suggests that standardized conventions of notation and performance had become widely accepted by the 1570s. The detailed instructions given were important, for perfection of playing was the aim. The vihuela was a courtly instrument and the music had to reflect the cultured and polished circles that the players moved in. Miguel de Fuenllana in *Orphenica Lyra* of 1554 devoted a section of his introduction to *tañer con limpieza* (neat or clean play), dealing with problems such as avoiding touching a string not ciphered for. "Such playing is not only untidy but also it gives great offense to the ear,"[3] he warned. Other skills were necessary for pieces which involved internal changes of pace. Milán explained these in a passage of his introduction entitled *tañer de gala*, which dealt with alternating fast and slow passages. The player must "play all the *consonances* [chords] with a slow measure and all the *redobles* [scale movements] with a hurried measure." Playing *redobles* was explained most fully by Fuenllana. There were three ways of executing them: *dedillo*, played with the index finger alone, "easy and agreeable to the ear, but it is not to be denied imperfection"; *de dos dedos*, which contains "perfection in itself" but should only be used on the thicker strings; and *de los dos dedos primeros*, using the first and second fingers which if mastered properly contained "all the perfection of which the *redoble* is capable, as much in speed as in clarity. . . ."[4]

As to plucking the string, Fuenllana advocated using the fleshy part of the finger, so beginning the controversy over whether the fingertip or the nail should be used. "To strike with the nails is imperfection. . . . It is a great excellence to strike the string with a stroke which employs neither nail nor other invention. Only the finger, the living thing, can communicate the intention of the spirit."[5]

Vihuela music was written in tablature, an eminently practical system in use until the eighteenth century. The principle involved was very simple. Each line of the staff represented a string of the instrument. In Spanish and Italian tablatures the top line represented the bottom

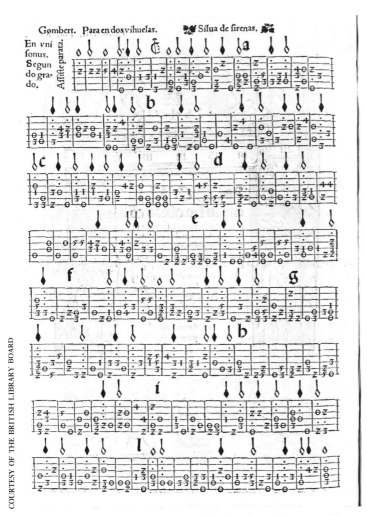

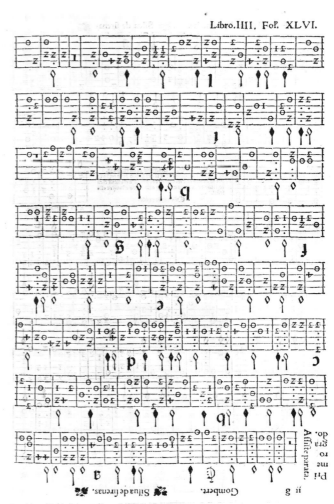

A duet from Enriquez de Valderrábano's Silva de Sirenas, *1547. One page is printed upside down so two players can share the same book.*

course, in French and English books, the top line represented the top course. (Perversely, Luis Milán used the latter system, although the other composers conformed to the Spanish convention.) Conveniently, tablature tells the player where to put his finger to play a note; the frets to be stopped are indicated by either numbers or letters. So 0 represents an open string, 1 the first fret, 2 the second, and so on. The value of the note was shown by the different note types written above the stave. This system contained the immense advantage of enabling the player to follow music without needing any knowledge of theory or sight reading. Many modern players are now learning to read tablature so that they can play music hitherto only available through transcriptions, which inevitably reflect the personal opinions of the transcriber.

Publishing in Spain was very expensive and it is therefore surprising that none of the vihuelists dealt with the art of intabulation, that is, how to render other music into tablature for the vihuela. Juan Bermudo—a musical theorist rather than a practical composer—was the only writer on the vihuela to advise on the subject. He recommended the novice to begin by setting songs to a simple chordal accompaniment. The more musically proficient were directed towards the masses of the religious composer Cristóbal de Morales. "He who gives himself up to this music will not only be wise but also an attached devotee."[6] Bermudo also recommends the music of famous foreign composers such as Josquin des Prez and Nicolas Gombert. Their music came to Spain with the Flemish musicians in the retinue of the Emperor Charles V, and the long periods these musicians spent in Spain influenced native music both in technique and in style.

The diligent pupil, after absorbing a mass of advice, was now ready to entertain his circle. In the vihuela books he had at his disposal some of the finest music of the Renaissance. To dip into the books is to discover the wide-ranging interests of the composers. Popular songs, epic ballads, sacred masses and Italian madrigals were just some of the sources drawn on by the inventive minds of the vihuelists.

There were several main forms used by all the vihuela composers. One of the most important was the *fantasia*, a form originally based on polyphonic vocal patterns. A *fantasia* indicated an original piece of composition, whose subject could either be the composer's own or a parody of another's. Alonso Mudarra begins his *Tres Libros de música en cifra para vihuela* (Seville 1546) with ten *fantasias*. These were grouped according to technical difficulty, some being specifically designed "with extended *passos*" which were to "develop the hands." The last *fantasia* in this group is the charming "Fantasia que contrahaze la harpa en la manera de Luduuico." Luduvico was a well-known harp player who could, according to Bermudo, perform wonders on the instrument: "It is said that when the famous Luduvico came to a cadence, he placed his fingers below the string, altering it by a semi-tone, and made the cadence using a sharp note."[7] Halfway through this *fantasia* comes a comment referring to the false relations which help make the piece so interesting: ". . . from here to the end there are some dissonances; if you play them well, they will not sound bad." The clashing of D sharp and E natural which occurs must have sounded strange in the sixteenth century.[8]

The *tientos* were less ambitious, and were included as practice pieces in a given mode. Apart from Milán, whose compositions were all his own, the vihuelists made extensive use of intabulations, transcriptions which either faithfully represented the original, or used only a part of it. In this way some of the most beautiful sacred music written by the great north European composers found its way into the vihuela repertoire. Masses and hymns from Morales,

Villancico *by Guerrero, from Esteban Daza's* El Parnaso, *1576.*

Josquin, Gombert, Philippe Verdelot, Adriaan Willaert and Thomas Créquillon among others were used. Generally the vihuelists were faithful to the original, and were less inclined than the lute composers to embellish the music. In a lighter mood, secular French chansons, Italian madrigals and Spanish songs appeared in the books.

Unlike the lutenists, the Spanish composers almost completely ignored the numerous dance forms. Milán's six *pavanas* are an exception and are probably the best known of all vihuela pieces. The *pavana* was essentially a solemn processional dance in exact time, but Milán directs that his should be played as free rather than strict works. His are set to a harmonic vocal line and are lighter and gayer than is usual for this normally stately form. Fuenllana and Esteban Daza (*El Parnaso*, 1576), composed no dance music. Those by other composers—Enriquez de Valderrábano (*Silva de Sirenas*, 1547) and Diego Pisador (*Libro de Música de Vihuela*, 1552)—are really sets of variations on the *folia*. Originally mentioned as a "fool's dance," or a Portuguese carnival dance of the late fifteenth century, the *folia* later became famous as the *Folies d'Espagne*. In his dictionary of 1611, Covarrubias referred to it as fast and noisy, bearing the name "mad" or "empty-headed." The *folia* was to be found all over Europe; in England it was used as an accompaniment to a popular song: "Vaine is worldlye pleasure."

One form native to Spain was the *villancico*, a popular song invariably treating of love which, by the sixteenth century, was sung by prince and peasant alike. Milán's *villancicos* are brief and follow the traditional pattern of the form, which is a refrain of two or three phrases modified in the second section (called *la vuelta*) and then repeated again for the last section. He gives two versions of each *villancico*. The first is slow with a chordal accompaniment which allows the singer to *hacer garganta* (to use the throat, literally) or embellish the vocal part. The second version is faster with more scale passages for the vihuela. The catchy tunes of all the *villancicos* became as popular in Spain as ballads in Tudor England. They feature strongly in the vihuelists' books. Some of the verses were borrowed from the great poets of the age such as Juan Vásquez who published collections in 1551, 1559 and 1560; others were anonymous, becoming quickly absorbed into popular tradition.

The other typical Spanish poetic and musical form much loved by the vihuelists was the *romance*. Again of popular origin, the form was taken over by the aristocracy. Adapting it by writing *romances* which were *eruditos y artisticos* (that is, an artistic imitation of a popular theme), they added to the vast repertoire already in existence, and helped to keep the form vital. The *romances* had originally been medieval epic poems, distinguished by a particular meter, and telling of historical or biblical events in a dramatic form. Tales of treason, war, murder and revenge were adapted and set to music.

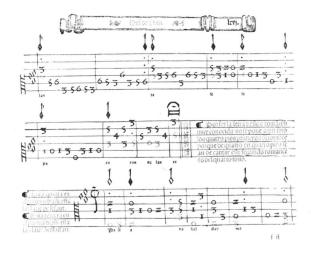

Passeavase el Rey Moro, *a romance from Luis de Narváez's* Delphin de Música, *1538. The tale tells of the fall in 1492 of Alhama, the gateway to Granada, and the Moorish king's lament for it. Narváez included only the opening lines from the* romance, *which, in its complete form, had at least twenty-three verses.*

A double page of romances *from Diego Pisador's book of 1552. As with all the* romances *the text was shortened as the events passed into common folklore. The story tells of the murder of Don Sancho, the King of Castile, during the siege of Samora. The "traitor bold" of the text is Vallido Dolfos, hired by Sancho's sister Urracca. The story begins:*

> *Rey don Sancho, Rey don Sancho*
> *Never say you've not been told,*
> *From this city of Samora*
> *Has gone forth a traitor bold.*

One type of *romance* was the *romance fronterizo*, or border ballad, whose subject matter was the final expulsion of the Moors from Spain in the campaigns of 1481 to 1492. The ballad is unusual in that it was one of the few composed for the defeated moorish armies. Another type was the *romance viejo*. Diego Pisador included *Guarte guarte rey don Sancho*, one of a group about El Cid. The *romance* included a purely instrumental introduction and ending, a feature also used by Fuenllana to good effect.

One of the problems raised by the songs in the books is whether the vihuelist was expected to accompany the singer with the melody which is marked either by a dash or red numbers in the vihuela part: none of the composers states plainly whether there should be an accompaniment or not.

The *romance* gave rise to the variation or *diferencia*. Narváez was the first composer to exploit the variation as a separate form of music and was followed by the other vihuelists. The need for variations arose from the monotonous nature of the accompaniment of many long *romances*. By the sixteenth century the form was a purely instrumental one. Two of the most popular themes were the medieval *romance* called *Conde Claros*, which originally had 206 lines, and the *romanesca* theme which became known in Spain as *Guárdame las Vacas* from the opening words of the song. A folk tune known all over Europe, it appeared in England as *The Shepherd Carillo his Song*.

Consort music was very popular in the sixteenth century, and there are scattered references to vihuela consorts in Bermudo's treatise. Valderrábano, with an eye for practicality and the high cost of music books, printed the second part upside down so that two players could share a book.

The period when the main surviving vihuela books were published was surprisingly short, although the sudden emergence of so much technically advanced music indicates a long period of cultivation.[9] The briefness of the vihuela's flowering was in no way a reflection of the quality of the music, but has more to do with the caprices of fashion.

Vignette from Diego Pisador's book of 1552.

Four-course guitar music

During the sixteenth century, the four- and five-course guitars co-existed in Spain with the courtly vihuela, and were immensely popular. The guitar was the most widely used instrument in the theater, and was played by the numerous strolling players of the period. However its simple music was learned by ear, and it was not until the following century that popular pieces were written down. It appears that, as in Italy (where only four *fantasias* for the four-course guitar were known at this period), the guitar was not considered important enough to have a work devoted solely to it.[1]

This does not mean, however, that the guitar was ignored by professional musicians in Spain. Indeed, the first surviving published music for guitar is to be found in the vihuela books. Alonso Mudarra included pieces for four-course guitar in the first book of his *Tres Libros de Música* of 1546—four *fantasias*, a *pavana*, and sophisticated variations on an old favorite, the *romanesca* theme, *Guárdame las Vacas*. Mudarra indicates two tunings (*temples*) for the guitar. The first *fantasia* is to be played *al temple viejo*, the other *al temple nuevo*. These tunings were later explained by Juan Bermudo. The old tuning was held more suitable for "old romances and strummed music than

Two pages of four-course guitar music from the vihuela book by Alonso Mudarra of 1546.

A page of four-course guitar music from the vihuela book by Miguel de Fuenllana, 1554.

for music of the present time," and had intervals of a fifth, major third, and fourth. The new tuning required intervals of a fourth, major third, and fourth, and was suitable for those who "cipher good music for the guitar."[2]

The other vihuelist to include works for four-course guitar was Miguel de Fuenllana. Book Six of the *Orphenica Lyra* contains a setting of the hymn *Crucifixus est*, the *villancico Covarde Cavallera* of Juan Vásquez, the famous *romance Passeavase el rey moro*, and six *fantasias* by Fuenllana himself. Neither of the vihuela books gives any instructions on playing the guitar. Perhaps the pieces were added merely as an acknowledgment of the presence of the smaller and humbler instrument, perhaps some of the courtiers who normally played the vihuela were curious about the instrument, or possibly the vihuelists wanted to try their hands at something new.

If the four-course guitar did not receive a great deal of attention in Spain and Italy, elsewhere in Europe the situation was different. In France in the 1550s the instrument was coming into its own, and between 1551 and 1555 nine books of music for the four-course guitar were published.

A quick glance at the music reveals the differences between French and Spanish tastes. Most of the pieces are either intabulations of *chansons* or popular dance tunes. Enthusiasm for the pleasures of dancing was affecting most of Europe, and for the next two centuries dance tunes were to form the basis of the repertoire for both guitar and lute, as well as for keyboard instruments. In the sixteenth century many of the dances which were later incorporated into the suite form were already in favor.

The allemande was an old German dance, of simple binary origins, given a serious quality by its moderate 4/4 measure. In the next century the allemande became a stylized type, often used as the first movement of the suite and usually followed by a lively courante.

From France came the popular branle, an old round dance in simple 2/4 measure, although 4/4 measure was later adopted in the courts of France and England. There were as many as twenty local varieties, many of which appear in the French guitar books.

The popular and gay galliard came from Italy; the five basic dance steps fitted into six beats of the simple triple time, ending with a high leap in the air. The galliard was conventionally paired with the pavan in 4/4 time, ". . . a kind of staid music, ordained for grave dancing, and most commonly made of three strains, whereof every strain is played or sung twice."[3]

Closely related to the pavan was the *passamezzo*, an Italian dance described by Thoinot Arbeau as a "pavan played less heavily to a lighter beat."[4]

In addition, the French four-course guitar books also included intabulated Italian songs, and the usual transcriptions (often note-for-note) of lute pieces. Most of the *chansons* have been traced to publications by Pierre Attaignant (*c.* 1494–1552), who ran one of the most successful music businesses in Paris. Despite copyright restrictions, there was much wholesale pirating of other publications—which went, naturally, unacknowledged.

In 1551 Simon Gorlier published *Le Troysieme Livre . . . mis en tablature de Guiterne*, a collection of intabulated *chansons* from the highly successful publishing house of Robert Granjon and Michel Fezandat in Paris. This, and three other books by one Guillaume Morlaye were discovered fairly recently, and have added some 110 pieces of music to the known repertoire of the four-course guitar.[5] The demand for guitar music was obviously high, for in August of 1551 royal permission was granted to the rival firm of Adrian LeRoy and Robert Ballard (also in Paris) to publish music for the instrument. Between 1551 and 1555 their publishing house produced five books of tablature, four by LeRoy and one by Grégoire Brayssing, a German who lived in Paris after 1547.

Their first publication, LeRoy's *Premier Livre de Tabulature de Guiterne* of 1551, presented a more varied selection of pieces than that of Simon Gorlier. Two opening pieces were followed by a typical selection of "*plusieurs chansons, fantasies, pavanes, galliards, almandes, branles.*" In the same year LeRoy produced an important guitar tutor.[6]

The nine books that appeared in the short space of five years were less ambitious than the vihuela books. The books were produced for a popular, amateur audience rather than a small and cultured circle, and this commercial consideration largely determined the style and content of the music.

The level of demand meant that music had to be produced quickly and many of the composers were forced

Four-course guitar music from the Second Livre de Guitarre *of Adrian LeRoy, 1555.*

to look abroad for foreign sources. Morlaye in his *Second Livre* of 1553 took a *fantasia* from Melchior de Barberiis' lute book, renaming it a branle, while his *Quatrième Livre* of 1552 contains two versions of the Spanish favorite *Conde Claros*, one for guitar and one for cittern. Another foreign piece appeared in his *Second Livre*, the *Hornepipe d'Angleterre*. Grégoire Brayssing's *Quart Livre de Tabulature de Guiterre*, published by LeRoy and Ballard in 1553, is the only book containing no dances, having instead six *fantasies*, intabulations of *chansons* and several psalms. LeRoy's *Second Livre*, published in 1555, was a collection of songs with a short text, invariably treating of love and sung to a simple popular melody—in LeRoy's case to well-known branles.

The most attractive pieces in the books are the longer *fantasies* and particularly those by LeRoy, but the majority of the shorter works are musically and technically limited. The four-course guitar was a small and delicate instrument, with less scope than the lute or the six-course vihuela for complex harmonic effects, so the instrument was easier to play and therefore popular among amateurs. Historically, the books are important for they mark the shedding of the guitar's earlier folk origins, and its emergence into genteel society.

After this burst of publishing fever in mid-century France, relatively little was composed for the four-course instrument. Although the last known work (John Playford's *A Booke of New Lessons for the Cithern and Gittern*) appeared as late as 1652, the four-course guitar's popularity was only short-lived.[7]

Five-course guitar music

During the sixteenth century a fifth string was added to the four-course guitar. The four- and five-course instruments coexisted for a time, but the newer guitar rapidly surpassed the earlier instrument in popularity. The first five-course guitar music appeared in a vihuela book, Fuenllana's *Orphenica Lyra* of 1554. There is a gap of some forty years before the next publication, and during this time the great polyphonic heritage of instrumental music was discarded in favor of an exclusively strummed style.

This new style was announced in 1596 by Dr. Juan Carlos y Amat, a doctor of medicine and author of medical texts. Amat could hardly have foreseen the extraordinary and far-reaching effect his little book *Guitarra Española y Vándola* was to enjoy when it first appeared.[1] The sixty-page treatise is a modest book, and will teach the pupil "to tune and play *rasgueado . . .* with marvelous style."

With the guitar tuned Aa dd' gg bb e', the pupil was ready to learn a system of notation set down by Amat which would enable him to strum his way through the short popular dances that dominated guitar music at this time. The method, a kind of musical shorthand, was simple: the pupil memorized a series of twenty-four numbered chords. These chords—twelve major and twelve minor—were explained in detail so that the reader would know how to finger them on the guitar. They were arranged in a circle of fifths, with the major chords in the upper part and the minor chords in the lower. The five boxes within each chord represent the strings, the innermost circle of boxes indicating the first, and so on. Within the boxes frets were shown by the numbers, while the letters beside show which fingers are used to stop down the strings: a, e, i, o, represent the first, second, third and fourth fingers. So, explains Amat, the musician can assemble his music, as "The good and practiced painter has ready all the colors necessary so that he may paint a man, or a lion or a bull."[2] This rigid system of "music by numbers" had a huge following. Within a few years the strummed style was firmly established.

Chord table and finger positions for the coded chords in Dr. Juan Carlos y Amat's Guitarra Española. *The positions labeled "n" refer to the major chords in the upper half of the circle, those labeled "b" to the minor chords in the lower half. This edition was published in Gerona in 1639.*

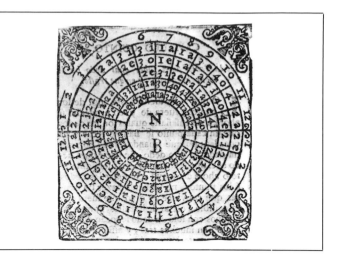

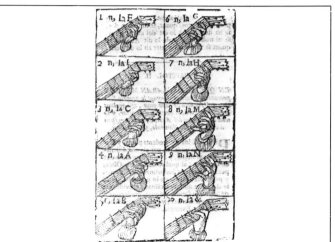

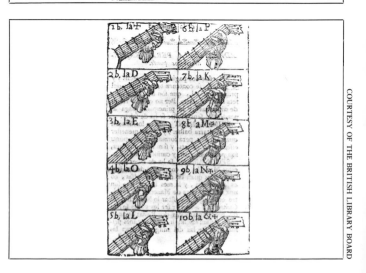

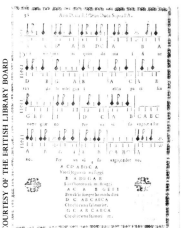

A song from Benedetto Sanseverino's book Intavolatura Facile, *1620. Letters indicating which chords to play refer to the chord alphabet given at the beginning of the book.*

In the early years of the seventeenth century the center of guitar activity shifted to Italy. In 1606 Girolamo Montesardo published *Nuova Inventione d'Intavolatura per sonare li balleti sopra la Chitarra Spagnuola, senza numeri e note*, a work which adopted Dr. Amat's system for producing strummed music, but changed the numbers for letters. From that date to 1629 guitar music was exclusively concerned with the *rasgueado* or strummed style. This was an interesting development. In the sixteenth century the guitar had made itself respectable and become incorporated into upper-class life, but now it harked back to its humble origins as a simple strumming instrument used only for accompaniment. Concentration on chordal texture and basic rhythm replaced the contrapuntal style of the older vihuela and four-course guitar.

Simplicity of style meant facility of printing, and notation became simplified to a series of letters indicating the chord to be played, lines to show which way the stroke should be played — for upward, and — for downward—and occasional hints on meter and beat.

The Italian publishing houses of Florence, Rome, Milan and Naples produced strummed guitar books in quantity. The music consisted of popular songs and dances but with a wider range than in the previous century. Many of the dances came from Versailles, one of the most brilliant centers of entertainment in Europe.

One new dance popularized through the French court was the gavotte. Originally a peasant dance—named, it was

believed, after the "gavots" or inhabitants of the Pays de Gap—it rapidly spread to all parts of Europe. It found its way into the suite, usually following a saraband. This dance, also known as the *zarabanda*, was an interesting example of the musical influences which came from the New World. In its earlier state it was highly erotic and exciting: "A dance so lascivious in its words, so ugly in its movement, that it is enough to inflame even very honest people."[3] In Spain in 1593, anyone performing it in public could be punished with 200 lashes. The saraband first appeared in Montesardo's book of 1606 and by 1618 was danced in sober form in most of the courts of Europe.

Another of the dance forms to come from the New World was the chaconne. Originally a wild sensual dance, it too lost its unbridled character in Europe. It was first recorded in 1599 when it was danced at the wedding of Philip III of Spain, and from 1606 appeared in guitar and lute music. With its close relatives, the *passacalle*, the *zarabanda* and *folia*, it passed from being a form exclusive to the guitar into the art music of the baroque era.

The *passacalle* came from Spain, getting its name from the Spanish words *pasar* and *calle* meaning "street song." Examples of this dance first appeared in Spain in Amat's instruction book, and in Italy in Montesardo's book of 1606. Based on the simple chord progression I–IV–V–I, it was played between rounds of a dance or used as an introduction to a song. The *passacalle* still survives as a ritornello in the folk music of Latin America.

The bourrée was first mentioned by Praetorius in 1619, and became popular in the 1660s. In quick double time, the bourrée was lively, somewhat similar to the gavotte. The courante first appeared in a lute book of 1577 but was extensively used in guitar music from 1606 onward. Later in the seventeenth century it formed a standard movement of the suite. There were two versions: the Italian courante in quick triple time and a rather more refined French version in moderate 3/2 or 6/4 time. The gigue came into fashion in the seventeenth century, although it had been known and liked in England a century earlier. In France it reached its height in the court of Louis XIV. Incorporated into the suite, it often formed with the bourrée a lively ending piece.

The minuet, originally a French country dance in triple time, was used by Lully in 1653 and adopted as the official dance of Louis XIV's court. It then became immensely popular throughout Europe. Some beautiful examples are found in the guitar works of the Frenchman Robert de Visée (see page 113).

Dances which were popular but did not appear in the suite form included the *marizápolos*, a popular Spanish song; *canarios*, a dance in quick 3/8 or 6/8 time, usually having a dotted note on each strong beat to give it a lively effect; and the *jácara*, a popular ballad or dance.

These dances were all particularly suited to the guitar's strummed style, resulting in a flood of dance books, particularly in Italy where over fifty works are known to have appeared between 1606 and 1629.

Outside Italy during the first quarter of the seventeenth century, little guitar music was published. One publication on the guitar did appear in Paris in 1626: Luis de Briceño's *Método mui facilissimo para aprender a tañer la guitara a lo Español*. This was an elementary work, giving sixteen chords and no indication of rhythm, and providing only simple Spanish songs and dances.

In 1629 the Italian Giovanni Paolo Foscarini heralded a return to the use of *punteado* technique (the plucking of notes on single courses). Foscarini signed his work rather bombastically, "L'Academico Calignoso detto il Furioso" ("The Obscure Academician known as the Furious One"), but was apologetic when introducing pieces written in a style using contrapuntal lute techniques:

> Of the sonate, called pizzicato, I say no more than that, having put them in more for the embellishment of the work than for other reasons, since I know well that they are more suited to the lute than to the guitar.[4]

His book is the first known work to contain a mixture of the *alphabeto* system (played *rasgueado*) and tablature, indicating *punteado* playing.

Foscarini's compositions fall into two basic styles. He produced works which use the *alphabeto* system exclusively and works which in their ornamentation reflect the influence of French lute music. Apart from its purely historical significance, his music is both original and exciting and would be well worth more serious attention.

Foscarini was followed in Italy by further mixed tablature writing, of which the works of Giovanni Battista Granata (published between 1646 and 1680), Domenico

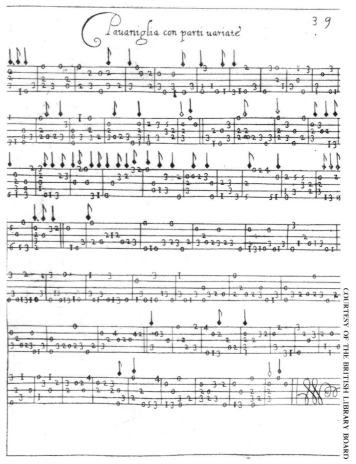

A pavan from Giovanni Paolo Foscarini's book Il primo, secondo e terzo libro della Chitarra Spagnola *of c. 1629. This book is the first known to use both* alphabeto *and* tablature. *Some of the music, such as this pavan, discards the* alphabeto *system altogether.*

Pellegrini (1650) and Ludovico Roncalli (1692) are the best known.[5] But it was another Italian composer, Francesco Corbetta, who really encouraged interest in the guitar. He traveled widely and published his music books in various European cities, including Bologna, Milan and Brussels. The first book was simple and old-fashioned in its complete reliance on the *rasgueado* style. But with the next two works he began to reflect the changing and increasing sophistication of musical taste. The old *alphabeto* system was used only occasionally, the typical dance forms were arranged in loose suites and both the books made use of *scordatura* (altered tunings).

A page of instructions from Francesco Corbetta's La Guitarre Royalle *of 1671.*

Two dances by Corbetta from La Guitarre Royalle.

Corbetta's two best known works, which fired the enthusiasm of two kings and inspired a whole host of later composers, were the collections named *La Guitarre Royalle* dated 1671 (dedicated to Charles II of England) and 1674 (dedicated to Louis XIV of France). The two differ in some ways, but certain elements in both collections point the way forward to the later masterpieces of Robert de Visée. The natural and essentially percussive character of the instrument is retained in the use of rapid successions of strummed chords. But Corbetta, like Foscarini, indicated the individual notes of a chord, and thus allowed himself greater freedom to produce new and unexpected effects. There is considerable lute influence in his use of ornamentation, with trills and rebattements.

The year after Corbetta's death in 1681 saw the first publication by one of his pupils, Robert de Visée. De Visée was a proficient composer and player, equally at home on the guitar, lute and theorbo. Among his many published works are two books devoted exclusively to the guitar. These books contain some exciting and often extremely difficult pieces. De Visée was the first guitar composer to use the suite form extensively and systematically, and had an important influence on its structural development. His suites frequently start with a prelude, usually to be played quite fast, which is followed by such contrasting dances as the slow allemande and the lively courante. He also used contrasting relative keys within the suite.[6]

In Spain, although the first half of the century was dominated by guitar music from Italy, there are some native works. Don Antonio de Santa Cruz produced a

The chord alphabet in Don Antonio de Santa Cruz's Música de Vihuela.

A page of music from Gaspar Sanz's Instrucción de Música sobre la Guitarra Española *of 1674.*

beautifully decorated handwritten book. There is a copy of the *alphabeto* at the beginning of the book, but the tablature calls for the *punteado* style. Typical Spanish dance forms of the early seventeenth century appear: *jácaras, canarios, marizápolos,* as well as *pavanas, gallardes* and *passacalles.* A further set of pieces, also in manuscript form, came from the pen of Don José Marín (1619–1699). Little is known of him, but in 1644 he was employed as a singer in the royal chapel of the Convent of the Incarnation, Madrid. His work consists of fifty *tonos* and *passacalles,* the words written by a fellow monk and the music of the guitar by Don Marín; all were originally intended for the theater.[7]

One of the most important publications of the seventeenth century was Gaspar Sanz's *Instrucción de Música sobre la Guitarra Española* (1674). Sanz's book must have reached a wide audience, for eight editions are known to have appeared between 1674 and 1697. The remarks he makes in the Prologue and the explicit instructions, particularly for *punteado* playing, suggest that guitar music in Spain had not yet broken free from the emphasis on the strummed style. Sanz lists as his influences Foscarini, Kapsberger (published 1604), Granata, Lorenzo Fardino and Corbetta *el mejor de todos.*[8] He was well traveled and could have heard the music of these composers during his stay in Italy. (It is also possible that these were names known to Spaniards, for the lack of native sources would drive guitarists to look naturally to Italy for music.)

Sanz begins the music of his first book with simple dances entirely in *alphabeto* setting, but then moves firmly into the style of the late seventeenth century. Part of Sanz's impact came from his use of native sources: both popular music and music that imitated "all the sounds of the palace." Within the first category came the dances of *las Hachas* (torch dance), *españoletas, zarabandas* and *canarios,* all well known through the theater and the street singers. In a slower more aristocratic vein were such pieces as "The Trumpets of the Queen of Sweden" and "The Comedy of Naples." Sanz helped to create a body of music essentially Spanish in character—his use of triplets, for example, resembles the *falseta* found in flamenco—and his works are still extensively played today.

In the late seventeenth century two further works appeared in Spain. Don Lucas Ruiz de Ribayez published *Luz y norte musical* (1677), a work devoted to the guitar and harp, containing a repertoire of dances based on folk melodies, and relying heavily on the work of Sanz. In 1694 appeared Don Francisco Guerau's *Poema harmonica.* Guerau includes a description of posture which suggests that guitar technique was well advanced.[9]

Interest in the guitar had spread in Europe in the second half of the seventeenth century, enormously helped by Corbetta's influence. Nicola Matteis followed Corbetta to London and in 1682 produced *The false consonances of musick or Instructions for the playing a true Base upon the Guitarre.*[10] A publication of 1705 by the Frenchman François Campion, *Nouvelles Découvertes sur la Guitarre,* encouraged the taste for guitar playing in France and continued the trend set by Corbetta in developing guitar music away from its chordal emphasis.

In Bavaria Princess Adelaide brought her instrument, and a manuscript collection of music, to Munich on her marriage to the Elector. Later in Germany, in 1689, Jacob Kremberg's *Musikalischen Gemüths-Ergötzgung* combined the guitar with the lute, angel lute and viol to accompany the voice. But all these were isolated examples in northern Europe and the guitar in no way rivaled the lute for popularity.

With the publications of the seventeenth century in France, Spain and Italy, and particularly those of Foscarini, Sanz, Corbetta and de Visée, an important stage in music for the guitar was reached. These compositions represent a transitional and creative point: they both look back to the guitar's humbler use as a provider of strummed accompaniments and, at the same time, in their sophisticated exploration of the *punteado* style, look forward to the instrument's solo role. But during the eighteenth century the guitar and its music were eclipsed by the pianoforte and harpsichord, which became the favored instruments of the aristocracy. This is not to say that guitar books ceased to appear. Brussels saw the publication of *Recueil de pièces de guitare* by François LeCocq in 1729. In Spain Santiago de Murcia, guitar tutor to the first wife of Philip V, composed a *Resumen de acompañar la parte con la Guitara*. This was handwritten, dated 1726, and included the *alphabeto*. In 1752 Pablo Minguet y Yrol produced an instruction book for various instruments, including the guitar. Instructions on *rasgueado* playing are still included, and the music consists of such popular Spanish dances as a *jota aragonesa*, *fandangos*, and *folias*. Dances like these were the staple diet of popular music in eighteenth-century Spain, heard in the theaters, in cafés, inns and at private parties.

However, at least one notable development took place in the latter part of the century—the beginning of the change from tablature to modern notation. The first example of this appeared in Michel Corrette's *Les Dons d'Apollon* (published in Paris in 1763), a method which included learning the guitar from both tablature and music. At first violin notation was used, and following this convention the G or violin clef was adopted, with the

Les Dons d'Apollon by Michel Corrette, 1763, shows the first known music for guitar written in modern notation.

sound, as on the modern guitar, an octave below the written pitch. The notation was imprecise: no consistent attempt was made to denote the separate voices. This primitive notation appears in early nineteenth-century guitar music, and it is not until well into that century that notation became accurate and advanced. Even so, notation became rapidly widespread in some parts of Europe. In 1768 Jean-Jacques Rousseau wrote in his *Dictionnaire de Musique*:

> . . . As the instruments for which one employed tablature are for the most part no longer in use, and as the ordinary note has been found more convenient for those which are still in use, tablature is now almost completely forsaken, and only serves for students' beginning lessons.[11]

Little music of note appeared in the last thirty years of the century, although in both France and England there was a spate of trivial works for the female amateur. The guitar had sunk to the level of a pretty ornament, and the music reflected its new status. The introduction to F. Chabran's *New Instructions for the Spanish Guitar,* published about 1795, begins:

> The tone of the Spanish guitar is much like the Harp, very harmonious, is esteemed the most complete accompaniment to the female voice, and is capable of producing all the desired beauties of harmony.

The music varied from such stirring tunes as "Rule Britannia" (this was the time of the Napoleonic Wars) and "God Save the King" to sentimental songs such as "A Shepherd lov'd a Nymph so fair." No doubt very pretty to sing, but the typical late eighteenth-century repertoire hardly advanced the guitar as a serious musical instrument.

Title page from a popular nineteenth-century guitar tutor.

Music for the transitional guitar: six courses and the pre-modern six single string guitar

The appearance of the six-course guitar in Spain in the late eighteenth century was accompanied by the publication of Antonio Ballesteros' *Obra para guitarra de seis órdenes* in 1780. In 1799 two further methods were published: Federico Moretti's *Principios para tocar la guitarra de seis órdenes* and Fernando Ferrandière's *Arte de tocar la Guitarra española por Música*. Ferrandière's manual explained how to read the new notation, setting out some of its advantages:

> The guitar can play together with any of the instruments of the orchestra . . . it can easily imitate other instruments, such as flutes, trumpets or oboes, and has the ability to accompany singing as though it were a pianoforte.

Rivalry between the guitar and the pianoforte continued throughout the nineteenth century.

The first signs of a serious revival of interest in the guitar had appeared a few years earlier, when Miguel García, a Cistercian monk known as Father Basilio, achieved great fame for his *punteado* playing and his approach to contrapuntal music. Moretti was one of his pupils and extended his master's work, and Moretti in turn had an enormous influence on two famous figures, Fernando Sor (1778–1839) and Dionisio Aguado (1784–1849).

Fernando Sor was one of a number of minor classical composers, followers of Mozart and Haydn who never approached the greatness of their exemplars. One of Sor's pupils, Napoleon Coste, wrote that Sor caused "a lively sensation in the musical world. He had astonished and delighted by the charm and novelty of his creations, which will remain as models of science and good taste."[1] Coste was unintentionally pointing out the problems of Sor's music, for little of his vast output for the guitar rises above "good taste." Even his admirers acknowledge the limitations of his work. As Emilio Pujol has remarked: "His concert pieces, as well as his Method, reveal a musical mind tending to brilliancy in technique rather than depth of feeling and elevated conception."[2] Sor, like so many of his fellow guitarists, was forced to earn a living through teaching and writing for amateur players. In the introduction to his guitar tutor, he was aware that economic necessity could have a detrimental effect on his art:

> A very celebrated guitarist told me that he had been obliged to give up writing in my manner, because the editors had openly declared to him, "it is one thing to appreciate compositions as a connoisseur, and another as a music-seller; it is necessary to write silly trifles for the public. I like your work, but it would not return me the expenses of printing." What was to be done? *An author must live!*[3]

Nevertheless some of Sor's work is very enjoyable, in particular the famous *Variations on a Theme by Mozart* (the theme from the first act of *The Magic Flute*) and his guitar sonatas. Among his instructional exercises, many succeed brilliantly by emphasizing particular technical difficulties without letting the musical content fall to banality or boring repetition.

Like Sor, Mauro Giuliani (1781–1829) was a pioneer in writing for the guitar, attempting to create a worthwhile repertoire for a "new" instrument whose potential had been little explored. Both men wrote for the guitar in a way that brought out fresh musical textures, avoiding the cliché-ridden effects of so many contemporaries. Giuliani wrote a wide variety of works, and was an extremely popular composer, producing many of his pieces at the explicit request of his avaricious publishers. His music reflects the tastes of early nineteenth-century Europe, and particularly of Vienna, the city where most of his works were published.

His solo guitar works range from studies—short private pieces aimed at improving the skill of his pupils—to ambitious works for public entertainment. He wrote works in the form of "theme and variations"; one sonata, Opus 15, in the classical idiom of Haydn and Mozart; and, in keeping with the ruling Viennese passion, a number of dances.

Giuliani's guitar duets fall into two main types: those in which a principal guitar is accompanied by a subordinate secondary guitar, and those in which each guitar plays an equal part. In three works he took on the difficult task of combining the guitar with a chamber orchestra. This combination presented even more prob-lems to the composer in Giuliani's day than it does now. For while the other instruments in the chamber orchestra were highly developed, the early nineteenth-century guitar was an instrument with a very quiet voice. Giuliani intelligently sidestepped the problem of balance by passing the main thread of musical argument back and forth between soloist and ensemble, keeping up a continual shift of interest.

Both Sor and Giuliani were virtuoso performers who wrote their own display pieces. Nonetheless a number of composers concerned primarily with other instruments did write guitar music, with varying degrees of success. Niccolò Paganini, who called the guitar "my constant companion in all my travels,"[4] wrote numerous works for it. None of these come near his violin compositions, however, and have not stood up well to the test of time. Hector Berlioz also had a real love for the instrument, playing well enough to give lessons in Paris while a penniless student. He includes the guitar in his *Treatise on Modern Instrumentation and Orchestration*:

> It is almost impossible to write well for the guitar without being a player on the instrument. The majority of composers who employ it are, however, far from knowing its powers; and therefore they frequently give it things to play of excessive difficulty, little sonority, and small effect.[5]

He recommended the works of Zani de Ferranti, Huerta and Sor, all virtuoso performers.

The hardworking professional guitarist was not affected by the wave of Romanticism which was sweeping across Europe in the early nineteenth century. But to the casual amateur there was no better instrument. His insatiable appetite for music making was met by huge amounts of music, both for solo and ensemble playing. The large publishing houses were printing works by a host of half-forgotten figures like Simon Molitor, Felix Horetzky, Leonhard von Call, and Wenzel Thomas Matiegka. Their pieces were destined to be performed in the drawing room to entertain a small gathering, and regarded as nothing more than a pleasing break from card playing or polite conversation.

Many of the pieces were taken from favorite operas, ballets, ballads and popular songs. It was this "drawing

Sor's recommended playing position, with the little finger braced against the guitar, and the guitar resting on a table.

PL. III.

The French and Italian playing position, according to Sor's Méthode.

room" music which was so popular with the genteel strummers of the day. In England the level of guitar playing in mid-century was summed up when Madame Pratten (see page 158) found that the amateur pupil was not inclined to devote sufficient study to the instrument to gain the technique necessary to grapple with the difficulties of the music of the classic authors of the guitar. The works of Giuliani and Sor, Legnani, Nüske and Schulz were beyond the powers of the average student.[6]

It is surprising that in a century of such intensive theorizing and scientific experimentation only one work — Carulli's *L'Harmonie appliquée à la Guitare* — dealt theoretically with the guitar. But even this work was intended for amateurs and was "not at all a complete treatise of Harmony or Composition." So the composer without a thorough knowledge of the instrument received little help and encouragement in writing good music, and the idea that only guitarists could write for their instrument became firmly established. On the concert platform the professional guitarists performed either their own works or those by their fellow virtuosi, and unfortunately their skill as composers rarely matched their ability as performers.

A prerequisite for the amateur was the guitar tutor, numbers of which were produced throughout the century. Every aspect of guitar playing, both theoretical and practical, was set out with admirable clarity.

The most striking aspect of the tutors is their lack of agreement on various aspects of technique. For example, no single way of holding the instrument had emerged; it could be supported on the left leg which rested on a footstool, or on the right leg, or even supported on a table. A ribbon was sometimes recommended to hold the guitar

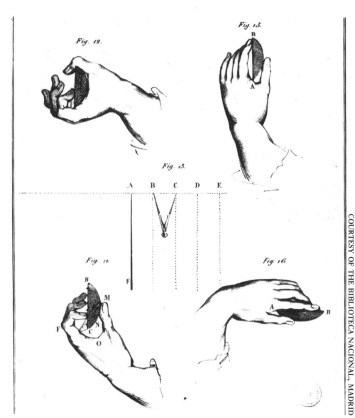

Hand positions from Sor's Méthode pour Guitare, *published in Paris, 1830.*

Dionisio Aguado playing the guitar. Like Sor he braced his little finger against the guitar, but used his patent tripodion for support. From the Nuevo Metodo para Guitarra, *published in Paris and Madrid, 1843.*

steady: "This is necessary, because in playing, both hands are engaged, and must go backwards and forwards on the instrument."[7]

The most sophisticated invention to hold the guitar was the "Aguado Machine," or tripodion—a stand to support the guitar firmly while leaving the hands free. The theory was that it would also eliminate the dampening effects of the player's body so that "the whole instrument can vibrate without interference," allowing a greater volume to be produced. It had the added advantage, according to the inventor, of leaving the player free to concentrate all his energies on playing, and enabling him to adopt an elegant posture, making even the most difficult piece look easy to the onlooker.[8] Despite the claims of its inventor, the tripodion was never universally adopted.

Controversy arose from the common practice of resting the little finger of the right hand on the table of the guitar. One tutor said that "The little finger is never used in playing, but is left free without leaning on the guitar,"[9] while another tutor advised ladies of delicate hands that "The little finger of the right hand is placed on the sounding board, to give that hand a firm position."[10]

Advice on the action of the fingers, the use of various fingers in the right hand and the use of *apoyando* for the thumb were touched on in the tutors. The level of sophistication varied widely, one writer feeling it necessary to give the following advice: "To play well, it is absolutely necessary to play in time. To attain this it is advisable to count, and if possible aloud."[11]

Another controversy, which had been continuing for centuries, was whether to pluck the strings with the nails or the fingertips. Sor and Aguado, in agreement on most other

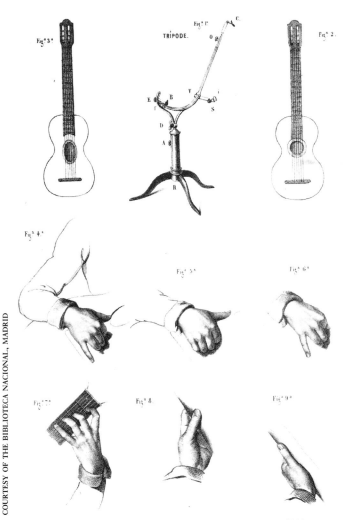

Illustration from Aguado's Nuevo Metodo para Guitarra, *1843.*

matters, found this a real point of difference between them. Sor maintained that the nails should not be used and boasted that he had convinced Aguado on this point: "Aguado ... himself would willingly have given up the use of nails had he not acquired with them such great dexterity, and had he not reached a period in life when it was too difficult to alter the habitual action of his fingers." But Aguado in the last edition of his method, printed in Madrid in 1843, gives a different story; he had in fact only made one concession, by stopping using the thumb nail. But he stated: "I consider it preferable to play with the nails in order to obtain from the guitar strings a tone unlike that of any other instrument."[12]

Most of the guitar tutors have now disappeared from use, and are of interest only to historians. Some, however, have continued to be used, notably that by Matteo Carcassi (1792–1853), an Italian who was both a brilliant performer and teacher. His exercises are tuneful and have an interest beyond that of simple studies, and he further encourages the pupil by arranging some of the pieces as duets to be taken by pupil and teacher together. His exercises, along with those by Sor, Giuliani and Ferdinando Carulli (1770–1841), were used in many other contemporary tutors.

Ease of playing and listening were important criteria. Madame Sidney Pratten's remarks concerning her method of composing give some idea of the sentiments which inspired her:

> I do think that "Eventide" is one of my most lively inspirations. I cannot say that I composed it. ... I simply take up my guitar and out of the tips of my fingers tumble out the sounds on the strings ... and then I play it over and over again until my brain retains it; then sketch it down. Then I leave it, and return to it and put it "ship-shape." Then with my "little bricks" collected, I build up a romance, or a story.[13]

Modern guitar music

Just as Torres is credited with the introduction of the modern classical guitar, so Francisco de Asis Tárrega Eixea (1852–1909) is associated with its musical and technical foundation. Tárrega was a great player who standardized technique in vital ways. Playing on a larger guitar, he supported the instrument on the left leg. He also established the *apoyando* stroke, abandoning the old practice of resting the little finger of the right hand on the table. He was here formalizing a practice already known; when Emilio Pujol asked Tárrega if he was the inventor of the *apoyando* stroke, he replied: "No, Julián Arcas used it in rapid scale passages, but without establishing any fixed order of fingering."[1] Realizing the need for new music for the new instrument, Tárrega transcribed the music of Beethoven, Chopin, Bach and Schumann and composed numerous pieces himself. Most of these—of which the most famous is the tremolo study *Recuerdos de la Alhambra*—are musically light, but characteristically combine frippery with a formidable technique.

Tárrega was living at a period that saw a great flowering of Spanish composition, heard in the music of Isaac Albéniz (1860–1909), Enrique Granados (1867–1916), and Manuel de Falla (1876–1946). Many of their works have been successfully transcribed for the guitar. Tárrega died at the age of fifty-seven, but his pupils Emilio Pujol, Miguel Llobet, Rita Brondi, Daniel Fortea, and Alberto Obregón continued his work. Emilio Pujol in his tremendous *Escuela Razonada de la Guitarra* has passed on the elements of Tárrega's teaching. With the new advanced technique, particularly that of the right hand, the guitar's music was once again ready to develop.

The twentieth-century repertoire of the guitar begins with a work by Manuel de Falla, his *Hommage pour le Tombeau de Debussy*. Miguel Llobet had wanted Falla to write a piece for guitar for some time. Debussy had recently died, and one day after a concert in Paris, Falla met the editor of the *Revue Musicale*, Henri Prunières, who was planning to devote a complete issue of the magazine to Debussy's memory. He asked Falla for an article, but Falla preferred to write a piece of music. But of what kind?

. . . he had only one fixed idea, that it should end with Debussy's *Soirée dans Grenade*. Then it occurred to him that he could make it a work for the guitar, thus satisfying Llobet at the same time. So, on his way through Barcelona, when returning from Paris to Granada, he told Llobet of his decision.[2]

Falla set himself to study the guitar in order to appreciate its technique fully. A fortnight later, to his great surprise, Llobet received the *Hommage pour le Tombeau de Debussy*.

Despite wanting to write another piece, the *Hommage* remains Falla's sole contribution to the music of the guitar, although other works of his have been successfully transcribed for guitar, most notably pieces from his ballet *El Sombrero de Tres Picos*.

It was during the 1920s that the foundations of the modern classical guitar repertoire were laid. Andrés Segovia has been the greatest single influence in the establishing of the instrument and one of his most important and long-lasting contributions has been to the music, first by transcriptions and second by his direct encouragement to composers for new works. Segovia's most famous transcriptions include the *Chaconne* from the *Second Partita in D Minor* by J. S. Bach, originally written for violin, and Bach's lute suites, but he also took the music of Handel, Mendelssohn and other composers and set it to the guitar.

From Segovia's first public appearance in Paris in 1924, he has commissioned and inspired works from both European and Latin American composers. During the twenties and thirties he collaborated with the Spanish composers Federico Moreno Torroba (born 1891) and Joaquín Turina (1882–1949) to produce works that, through their strongly rhythmic character and lively melodies, have become standard works. Torroba's *Suite Castellano* (1926) and his *Pièces Characteristiques* (1931), Turina's *Fandanguillo* (1926) and *Sonatina* (1935) have an essentially Spanish flavor, and some of the pieces such as Turina's *Hommage à Tárrega* of 1935 contain flamenco effects.

In 1932 Segovia met the Italian Mario Castelnuovo-Tedesco (1895–1968). Segovia sent him a note with two pieces for him to look at: Sor's *Variations on a Theme by Mozart*, and a piece by the South American Manuel Ponce: *Variations sur Folia de Espana et Fugue*.

Andrés Segovia

Castelnuovo-Tedesco was inspired by these pieces to write his first guitar music, *Variations* (opus 71). Six years later, after composing several guitar pieces, the first twentieth-century guitar concerto appeared: the *Concerto in D* (opus 99), dedicated to Segovia. In 1951 he published the *Quintet for Guitar Strings* and ten years later a meeting arranged by Segovia with the guitar duetists Alexandre Lagoya and Ida Presti led to the composition of a series of works for two guitars. Castelnuovo-Tedesco was a prolific composer and his guitar works include pieces for solo guitar, duets and string quartets, as well as works for guitar and voice and guitar and other instruments.

Alexander Tansman (born 1897), a composer of Polish extraction, wrote a small number of guitar works in a highly individual style. In 1951 his *Cavatina Suite* won the first prize in the Concours International of the Academia Musicale Chigiana in Siena. The work originally consisted of four movements, but a fifth was added at the request of Segovia to give the work a more lively and positive ending.

Perhaps one of the best known and most popular twentieth-century European composers for guitar is Joaquín Rodrigo (born 1902). His most famous works are two long pieces: *Concierto de Aranjuez*, dedicated to and first performed by Regino Sainz de la Maza in Madrid in 1940; and the *Fantasia para un gentilhombre*, written in 1954 for Segovia. The *Concierto* was greeted with instant enthusiasm. The name *Aranjuez* refers to the ancient palace of the Spanish kings near Madrid. The site is considered the most beautiful of the royal palaces, and Rodrigo has said that his concerto "is meant to sound like the hidden breeze that stirs the treetops in the parks; it should be only as strong as a butterfly, and as dainty as a veronica."[3] His *Fantasia para un gentilhombre*, dedicated to Segovia, is based on music by the seventeenth-century Spanish composer Gaspar Sanz. "My ideal," Rodrigo has said, "was that if Sanz could hear this work, he would say, 'While it isn't exactly me, I can recognize myself.' "[4] The *Fantasia*, in five movements, recreates a variety of Sanz's dances. The universal popularity of both these romantic pieces has unquestionably widened the audience for guitar music. However, when judged by the standards of the classical repertoire as a whole they appear as entertaining, but essentially lightweight works.

In this century there has been a considerable interchange of ideas between European and Latin American composers. Within the last few decades especially, the works of Manuel Ponce (1882–1948), Heitor Villa-Lobos (1887–1959), Augustine Barrios (1885–1944), Vicente Emilio Sojo (1887–1974), and Antonio Lauro (born 1913) have introduced Latin American forms and rhythms into the classical guitar repertoire.

Manuel Ponce was the first Mexican composer to achieve international fame. Encouraged by Segovia's visits to South America in the twenties, he produced a number of attractive works. Some of these use interesting new textures in a modern idiom, while others rely on traditional devices. His *Sonata Romantica*, (sub-titled "Hommage à Franz Schubert qui aimait la guitare") contains many echoes of Schubert's style, and his two-movement *Suite Antique* so effectively imitates baroque music that for some time it was accepted as the work of the seventeenth-century composer Leopold Weiss. (Since the discovery of its real author it has become known as "Ponce's Secret Weiss.") Other of Ponce's works are widely played: *Thème Varié et Finale, Twelve Preludes* and the three-movement *Sonatina Meridional*. Ponce is well liked and rarely does a performance go by without one of his pieces being played. Segovia has called him "probably the best composer for the guitar."[5]

Heitor Villa-Lobos, a Brazilian, is also a household name among guitar enthusiasts. He wrote works for all combinations of instruments and voices, sometimes building on traditional Brazilian forms, sometimes using European conventions. His *Douze Etudes* of 1929 were written for Segovia, who has compared them to those of Scarlatti and Chopin for their technical skill and abstract musical beauty. They remain among the most advanced studies written for the guitar. Each develops a figuration designed specifically to exploit and stretch the natural possibilities of the instrument. In 1940 Villa-Lobos wrote the *Cinq Préludes,* another popular standard work. These preludes are remarkably attractive mood pieces, moving from a distinct and melancholy theme in Number One through a searching and meandering Number Three and finishing with a syncopated piece strongly suggestive of dance rhythms. In contrast, his Brazilian qualities come out most strongly in *Choros Number One* for guitar.

Segovia has said on one occasion that he is "interested in only one direction. It is the classical direction."[6] He is most at home with pieces that do not depart from traditional forms, and the works composed under his inspiration reflect this predilection. The music of the first generation of composers for the modern classical guitar is essentially romantic and melodic, and displays none of the toughness of later more experimental composers.

There is a noticeable lack of important guitar works from the first great generation of modern composers—Stravinsky, Schoenberg, Bartok, Berg and Webern. It was not until the 1920s that the guitar began to be established as a concert instrument and at this period there was no virtuoso with sufficient interest in avant-garde music. The small guitar pieces written by Schoenberg, Stravinsky and Webern suggest a latent interest in the instrument. But one cannot help but wonder how the repertoire for the guitar might have developed had such great composers been encouraged to pursue it seriously.

The first work to make consistent use of modern compositional techniques on the guitar is Frank Martin's *Quatre Pièces Brèves*, written in 1933 but not extensively performed until recently. For it is the younger generation of guitarists such as Julian Bream, John Williams and Tim Walker which has encouraged major contemporary composers to write for the guitar. These three in particular have been associated with certain specific composers, and the collaboration and interchange of ideas between composer and performer have led to some outstandingly inventive new works. At last the guitar is being accepted as a respectable member of the musical family and has attained the status of a serious musical instrument among major composers.

For composers who are not guitarists the advice of leading performers is important. The Englishman Stephen Dodgson (born in 1924) has written several important works for guitar.

> Like Rodrigo, I don't play the instrument. In fact, a direct confrontation with its formidable technique would be far more likely to inhibit than assist my developing sense of its resources. My tutelage began with Julian Bream and has continued under John Williams—as fortunate a combination of teachers as any composer would wish for.[7]

In 1956 Stephen Dodgson wrote a *Concerto for guitar and chamber orchestra,* first performed by John Williams in 1959. The scoring of the work takes into account the relative weakness of the guitar sound in comparison with that of other orchestral instruments. So the orchestra has no oboes but three clarinets, chosen for their tonal contrast with the guitar.

Other works followed: the *Duo Concertante* for guitar and harpsichord was commissioned for a series of recitals given by John Williams and Rafael Puyana in 1968. The brooding opening is followed by a more lively contrapuntal passage where the two instruments are directly contrasted, and the piece ends with a long cumulative coda. In this piece the two instruments are used in a way that emphasizes the individuality of their respective sounds as opposed to one that creates a pseudo-ensemble effect.

In 1959 Stephen Dodgson wrote his *Fantasy-Divisions,* a technically demanding piece. The *Fantasy* provides the

John Williams.

Julian Bream.

basis for a set of five variations, conceived in the tradition of sixteenth-century divisions. Though the overall mood is contemplative, there are passages of very rapid flourishes and an attacking *rasgueado* style.

Stephen Dodgson has always been a varied and inventive composer, using different effects to suit the piece. In *Four Poems of John Clare* of 1962, he succeeds in adapting the guitar sound to the mood of the four poems: "Trotty Wagtail," "The Peasant Poet," "Turkey" and "The Fox." In recent years he has written a series of instructional pieces for the guitar in collaboration with Hector Quine, and works for guitar and cello.

Julian Bream became associated with Benjamin Britten through the *Songs from the Chinese*, which were written for him and the English tenor Peter Pears in 1958. These poems have an elusive quality which is echoed in the writing of the guitar part. Specific effects appear in the imitation of the flute and drum when mentioned in the lyrics. An interest in sleep and dreams runs through several of Britten's works and in 1963 he composed his famous *Nocturnal*. This piece, written for Julian Bream, is based on a song from John Dowland's *First Book of Songs or Ayres of Four Partes* of 1597, which begins: "Come, heavy sleep, the image of true Death."

The eight parts of this work marked *Musingly, Very Agitated, Restless, Uneasy, Marchlike, Dreaming* and *Gently Rocking* are intensively evocative. The work begins with a single melodic line, to be played very freely, then suddenly moves into a complete contrast of brilliant running arpeggios and scales played over the whole fingerboard. The *Nocturnal* is in a sense an inverted set of variations in which disparate moods and elements finally resolve into a statement of Dowland's original theme. Toward the end, the melody is subdued to a single line, and then trails into silence. Julian Bream has called this the greatest single work for guitar yet written.

Many works are now being written for guitar by avant-garde composers, who often demand a considerable intellectual effort on the part of both performer and listener. Some works are primarily intellectual in inspiration; others explore new textures, rhythms and unusual effects. Even in the most emotionally forceful of new works, the feeling is not immediately apparent to the listener, who must become familiar with the idiom before he can appreciate the music.

The guitar in ensemble has received a great deal of

serious attention recently. Hans Werner Henze's works—*Kammermusik*, *Voices*, *El Cimarrón*, and his recent opera *We Come to the River*—all include sizeable guitar parts. Pierre Boulez's *Le Marteau sans Maître* (1959), which gave Boulez an international reputation as a composer, is scored for flute, xylophone, vibraphone, percussion, guitar and viola—instruments which play alternately as an ensemble and as an accompaniment to a mezzo-soprano. *Le Marteau sans Maître* has become accepted as one of the masterpieces of postwar music, but when it first appeared it horrified both musicians and critics by its difficulty and apparent incoherence. Tim Walker, a contemporary British guitarist involved with ensemble work, particularly with the Fires of London and the London Sinfonietta, has described it as

> A fantastic work, and possibly the most difficult piece I've come across.... The *Marteau sans Maître* is sympathetically written as far as the physical side is concerned, but rhythmically and dynamically it's extremely complex. Even when you're not playing your own part, you have to concentrate very carefully or the ensemble goes to pieces. This can happen very easily....[8]

Tim Walker has become associated with two British composers: David Bedford and Peter Maxwell Davies. As he explains, they exemplify two approaches. In one the composer takes as his starting point the specific qualities and effects inherent in the guitar as a musical instrument—both those that are established and any new ones he can discover. In contrast, some composers write music which, though set for the guitar (falling within its compass and fingering patterns), is not specifically guitaristic. These pieces are examples of pure music which is written to be played on the guitar.

You asked for it, commissioned in 1969 by Tim Walker from David Bedford, is an example of the first approach. Though serious in intention Tim Walker will allow that "The listener and/or performer is allowed to smile during this piece."[9] As David Bedford explained in an interview, all the basic material in *You asked for it* is contained in the series of chords which open the piece. These are ordinary guitar chords which have been modified by the displacement of one or two fingers to produce discords. These four

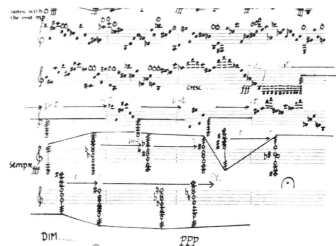

From the manuscript of David Bedford's You Asked For It. *Owned by Tim Walker.*

chords are treated in a number of ways. In one section the notes are played rapidly as single notes with an accented rhythm created by snapping the string against the fingerboard. Other techniques include *glissando* chords, passages of very high harmonics, and the use of a bouncing teaspoon to sound the strings. In the middle of the piece there is a percussion section in which the guitarist has to improvise with his fingers on the guitar body. In David Bedford's words:

I thought that if someone commissions a piece it's nice to give him an area of freedom where he can improvise. Here he has to improvise with wet fingers on the back of the guitar to make it squeal and make strange noises. This gives him something interesting to do in the middle of all this discipline.[10]

All of the effects used stem from the intrinsic nature of the guitar. Although the more unusual techniques may horrify some guitarists, they are in line with the approach to instrumental sound adopted by many composers today.

In contrast, Peter Maxwell Davies' *Lullaby for Ilian Rainbow*, written for Tim Walker in 1973, is concerned less with exploiting specific guitar techniques and more with presenting musical ideas that can be produced on the guitar. As Tim Walker explained, "Max writes the piece and then says, 'Is this possible?' " All *is* technically possible, but less consideration is paid in the writing to comfort and ease of playing.

Like much of the best modern music, the *Lullaby for Ilian Rainbow* is difficult to listen to and difficult to play. Instead of relying on immediately recognizable melodic lines or sensuous tone colors, it succeeds through complex use of rhythmic and dynamic effects. However, it can be appreciated emotionally once it has been assimilated intellectually by repeated listening.

The *Lullaby* is strictly notated; the dynamic of almost every note is specified. Each bar has a separate time signature, which is not marked but which must be worked out and exactly followed by the player. The music is made up of a web of foreground and background sound which the player must balance to give the piece its particular character.

Although it is not exceptionally hard to finger, Tim Walker finds the *Lullaby* the most difficult piece in his repertoire. But the problems it poses for performer and audience are of a type common in modern music generally, problems which guitar enthusiasts will have to face increasingly.

Alan Rawsthorne's *Elegy* (1971), Lennox Berkeley's *Sonatina* (1958), Richard Rodney Bennett's *Concerto for Guitar and Chamber Ensemble* (1970), William Walton's *Five Bagatelles* (1952) and Reginald Smith-Brindle's *El Polifemo de Oro* (1958), further works by Peter Maxwell

A page of the original manuscript of Peter Maxwell Davies' Lullaby for Ilian Rainbow. *Owned by Tim Walker.*

Davies and many others have all helped to build up what is now a formidable repertoire of modern guitar music. The inspirations behind these new works are, as might be expected, extremely varied. Part of Malcolm Arnold's *Guitar Concerto* was written as an elegy in memory of the French jazz guitarist Django Reinhardt.

It is no coincidence that all the composers discussed in this last section are European. Europe, and especially London, is still the center of much guitar activity. More people than ever before are playing the classical guitar and many of these are writing music for it. But the greatest hope for the instrument's future lies in the fact that composers who are not themselves guitarists have started to produce major guitar works. Herein lies a sign that the

127

guitar may at last be fulfilling its potential as an important musical instrument. The guitar's status has in the past been restricted by the lack of serious and significant works, so the concert artist has had to rely too much on transcriptions and salon pieces. This is not to decry much of the guitar's repertoire, but while these pieces are often pretty and appealing, they grow tedious if played too often. It is surely for this reason that the guitar has been treated so lightly in the past by serious critics.

Now the responsibility lies with performers and the listening public. Many of the best new pieces require repeated listening before they become fully comprehensible and therefore enjoyable. New works must be played often enough to become established in popular taste. If they are not, there is a danger that composers may become discouraged, and the guitar may be thrown back on the existing repertoire. If this happens, the instrument in its classical form could all too easily be condemned to yet another of its periods of eclipse.

SOCIAL HISTORY OF THE
CLASSICAL GUITAR

From Luis Milán's music book El Maestro *of 1535, depicting Orpheus serenading animals and birds on a vihuela.*

Prince and peasant

The Renaissance in Europe has come to be thought of as a golden age for the rediscovery of classical learning, and for the development of philosophy, literature and the visual arts. Historians have tended to accord music a comparatively minor place among the creative glories of the period. But for the Renaissance man, music was one of the principal splendors of life. The magnificent palaces of the high-born, symbols of the owner's wealth and standing, were embellished by the presence of musicians as much as by masterpieces of painting and sculpture. The most wealthy and powerful of aristocrats, the princes temporal and spiritual, employed full companies of musicians to play sacred music in the chapels and secular music for the entertainment of their leisure hours. Music was regarded both as a science and an art, and its study and practice a necessity for any educated man.

The sixteenth century was a time of great sacred vocal music: composers like Cristóbal de Morales, Josquin des Prez, Claudio Monteverdi and Thomas Tallis represent an upsurge of creative musical writing. The development of polyphony, together with a belief in the value of worship through music, stimulated composers to greatness. But the period 1400 to 1600 also witnessed the beginning of a trend that was to cause a great change in musical emphasis. Composers began to adapt forms that had once been purely vocal for solo instruments. Music for instrumental consorts also became popular and both the development of new instruments and the refinement of older ones were naturally encouraged.

Instruments of all kinds were blown, struck, bowed and plucked, with those suited to the new art form of solo playing becoming increasingly popular. Of the plucked instruments, the lute was the main favorite. Developed

129

over a long period, it achieved in the sixteenth century a structural and musical perfection. Europe gloried in the music of lutenists such as John Dowland, Pierre Attaignant, Adrian LeRoy, Francesco da Milano and Hans Newseidler.

One country that did not share this enthusiasm for the lute was Spain. The instrument was known there—it is referred to as the *vihuela de Flandes* by Juan Bermudo in his musical treatise of 1555—but no music appears to have been published for it and there is little documentary evidence for its use. The Spanish aristocracy preferred the vihuela, which, while sharing the lute's stringing and tuning, was shaped like a guitar. One theory for this apparent eccentricity is that the lute was unpopular for its Moorish associations, and was seen as a reminder of conquest and occupation.

The vihuela was played both by the aristocracy and by the professional musicians in their employ. Players and composers were to be found all over Spain: "Now there lives Torres Barroso, resident of Salamanca, admirable in the composition of this music...."[1] Luis de Guzmán played so well that he "made the strings speak."[2] Some of the music they might have played is contained in the seven major vihuela books published between 1535 and 1576 and comprising about 700 works (see pages 101–6). The composers were themselves skilled players on an instrument that inspired music comparable, both in technical difficulty and musical beauty, to that written for the lute.

The amount of music produced for the vihuela is low considering the instrument's obvious popularity. Music publishing in Spain had not reached the level it had in Paris, where the development and exploitation of movable type had rapidly led to a flourishing publishing industry. Moreover, Spain was suffering from severe inflation brought about by an influx of gold from her colonies in the New World. Some projects had to be abandoned altogether, such as Bermudo's proposed addition to his treatise. The vihuela composer Diego Pisador, who was not attached to any of the great courts or households and hence lacked a patron, had to meet the whole cost of printing himself, much to his father's displeasure:

> ... cure yourself of this folly of the book, and sell it to the printer and clear yourself of fantasia and consider that you are now forty and no longer a boy.[3]

Bronze figure playing a vihuela, from the lectern by Juan Nicolas de Vergara in Toledo Cathedral, c. 1565.

The other vihuela composers were in more favored positions: Don Luis Milán was a member of the court of Germaine de Foix at Valencia; Luis de Narváez became *maestro de vihuela* to King Philip II and accompanied the king when he traveled abroad in 1548; the blind Miguel de Fuenllana was in the service of the Marquesa de Jarifa; Enriquez de Valderrábano was attached to the Count of Miranda; and Alonso Mudarra, a canon of the cathedral of Seville from 1547 to his death in 1580, composed his music while in the household of the powerful Duques del Infantado.

Detailed information on the lives of the leading vihuelists is scarce. The best-documented life is that of Don Luis Milán. From the mid-1520s onward the palace at Valencia was a center of culture, boasting an extensive library, a large collection of musical instruments and one of the finest chapels of musicians in Spain. Luis Milán was the perfect example of the Renaissance ideal: courtier, poet and first-rate musician, he combined a lively interest in all the arts with an appreciation of life's pleasures. Entertainment at court was an important part of daily life, and here the vihuela played a major role, for it was an aid to courtship and religious devotion, and was also used extensively in dramatic representations and pageants, a form of entertainment at which Milán himself excelled.

The golden age of the vihuela was remarkably short, although the instrument continued in use for some time. Pedro Cerone, a nobleman who spent time at the court in Madrid, described in his book *El Melopeo y Maestro*, published in 1613, how he heard a number of musicians, among them vihuela players, play at a fête given for the courtiers of Philip IV. In 1633 there is a mention of two vihuela players in the Chapel Royal, but after this the instrument seems to have disappeared.[4] The main cause for its disappearance was the rapid rise of its country cousin, the smaller and less ambitious guitar.

An early mention of the guitar in Spain occurs in Johannes Tinctoris' musical treatise of 1487:

Furthermore there is the instrument invented by the Catalans which some call the *guiterra* and others the *ghiterne*. . . . The *guiterra* is used most rarely because of the thinness of its sound. When I heard it in Catalonia, it was being used much more often by women, to accompany love songs, than by men.[5]

Despite this unpromising debut the guitar rapidly came to play an important part in the musical life of all classes of Spanish society. The spread of its popularity was helped enormously by its use in the theater. Just as the people of Tudor England flocked to the plays of Marlowe and Shakespeare, so in Spain the strolling players who set up their rudimentary equipment in the courtyards of large houses were sure of an audience. Audiences were often vociferous and rowdy; and what better way to keep them entertained than to introduce a player singing a popular *villancico* to the sound of a guitar? The guitar, like the small harp and violin, was cheap to obtain and easy to handle. Lope de Rueda (1500–1565), writer and actor-manager, played the guitar on stage himself, although referring to it as a "squeaky" instrument.[6] But the guitar was improving rapidly, and the addition of the fifth string gave it a broader range and greater sound, making it the ideal instrument to accompany the popular ballads and dances of the day (see page 110). For a long time the poet Vicente Espinel (1551–1624) was credited with the improvement, the legend beginning in 1632 when a character in Lope de Vega's play *Dorotea* declares:

May Heaven forgive that Espinel! He has brought us those new verses, *décimas* or *espinelas*, and the five strings of the guitar, so that now everyone forgets the old noble instruments as well as the old dances, what with these wild gesticulations and lascivious movements of the *chaconne*, which are so offensive to the virtue, the chastity and the seemly silence of the ladies.[7]

In fact Espinel was not the inventor, although he played a large part in popularizing the five-course guitar.

While polyphonic music for the four- and five-course guitars was included in two of the vihuela books (see page 107), the music played by the majority of guitarists was undoubtedly the easily learned strummed style mentioned as early as 1555 by Bermudo. To the music theorist this was elementary: ". . . it is not desirable music and the ear is not made for them. The strummed *villancicos* do not have a very good basis in music. . . ."[8] Although Dr. Juan Carlos y Amat's instruction book on the strummed style proved immensely popular when it first appeared in 1596 (see page 110), guitarists learned mainly by ear and imitation. The

barber in Espinel's novel *La Vida del escudero Marcos de Obregón* would certainly have been both poor and illiterate:

> There came almost every Night a young Barber of my Acquaintance to visit me. He had a good Voice, and bringing with him a Guitar, he seated himself in the Porch of our House, and sang some little Airs, to which I added a bad Second, but well in tune; and our Neighbors were so well pleased with this little concert, that they used to assemble about the Door and listen to our Harmony.[9]

Evidence for the continuing use of the guitar is also found in the works of Miguel de Cervantes. He loved the music and dances of his native Spain, and shared the opinion of Sancho in *Don Quixote*, who declared: "Madame, where music is, no evil thing can be."[10] Cervantes' characters are not players of the aristocratic vihuela; they strum the humble guitar.

Musicians by Guercino (1591–1666). Private collection.

By the early seventeenth century, the Spanish guitar was not a wholly plebeian instrument. Although we have very little evidence of its form, its music or its players at this date, Pedro Cerone's list of royal musicians in 1613 includes guitarists. These probably played for the theatrical productions which were as popular at court as among the populace.

In sixteenth-century France the four-course guitar enjoyed a brief but spectacular vogue. Henri II (1519–1559) is reported to have set the fashion by serenading his mistress, the beautiful Diane de Poitiers, on the instrument. The music Henri and his courtiers played was probably that of Adrian LeRoy, Grégoire Brayssing, Guillaume Morlaye and Simon Gorlier (see page 108). "In my earliest years," mourned an anonymous writer in Poitiers in 1556, "we used to play the lute more than the guitar, but for twelve or fifteen years now everyone has been guitaring, and the lute is nearly forgotten in favor of Heaven knows what kind of music on the guitar, which is much easier than the lute."[11] Strong words and not entirely true: the lute had a formidable following and Adrian LeRoy, for example, is better known for his lute music than for his guitar pieces. Nonetheless, all over France people were "guitaring."

The guitar was already acquiring, in contemporary literature at least, an association with loose living. The poet Ronsard wrote:

> It is the ideal instrument
> For ladies of great learning.
> Lascivious ladies also play,
> To show off their yearning.[12]

In France as in Spain the guitar was proving its suitability for accompaniment. Throughout the sixteenth century, dance books were produced in quantity. They usually contained a history of the dances then in fashion, explanatory pictures and notes, and sometimes music. It made little difference where in Europe these were produced for the dance repertoire was truly international. In 1597 Thomas Morley's *A Plaine and Easie Introduction to Practicall Music* described various dances. "The Alman is a more heavy dance," he stated rather rudely, "(fitly representing the people whose name it carrieth)."[13] The most popular dances often gave rise to a number of variants: the branle had over twenty local varieties. It was known in England as the "French brawl" and danced at both village fairs and at court. Shakespeare, a valuable guide to the fashionable dances of the age, mentions it in *Love's Labours Lost*:

MOTH: Master, will you win your love with a French brawl?

ARMADO: How meanest thou? brawling in French?

MOTH: No, my complete master, but to jig off a tune at the tongue's end, canary to it with your feet, humour it with turning up your eyelids. . . .[14]

"Canary" may be a reference to the *canarios*, an extremely popular dance through the sixteenth and seventeenth centuries.

Another lively dance was the Italian galliard: "The

Cap. Bellauita.   Cap. Mala Gamba.

Franca Trippa.   Fritellino.

The clowns Franca Trippa and Fritellino from the Balli di Sfessania *series of commedia dell'arte engravings by Jacques Callot (1592–1635).* Sfessania *are obscene Neapolitan carnival dances. From the collection of the Victoria and Albert Museum.*

galliard is so called because one must be blithe and lively to dance it,"[15] wrote Thoinot Arbeau. But fashions in dancing came and went rapidly:

> When we gave our *Aubades* at Orleans we always played on our lutes and guitars the *Gaillarde* called *La Romanesca*. But to me it has come to seem stale and trivial.[16]

It was not just the aristocracy who were playing the guitar throughout France: the bourgeoisie were aping the customs of the court, and merchants, wine dealers, carpenters and joiners were buying and playing the instrument. The many inventories in existence suggest that guitar making had become a profitable business. In Paris in 1551 one Philippe de la Canessière possessed "three guitars, of which one has eleven strings [a six-course guitar], and two small ones." Throughout the century such references point to a great deal of interest in the guitar. The successful father-and-son team of Robert and Claude Denis ran a flourishing business. In their Paris shop in 1587 they had: "250 planks of spruce to make guitars... 2 guitars from Aubry ... one old Spanish guitar ... 24 common guitars ... seven guitar necks," and there is also a reference to "4 guitars from Lyon, of which one has a lute back."[17] Lyon was the great guitar making center next to Paris, particularly known through the work of the famous Bavarian luthier Gaspard Duyffoprucgar and the German Philippe Flac.

Guitar making in France was organized into guilds, tightly controlled to protect makers, and much of the evidence for the guitar's popularity comes from the numerous court cases involving the faking of famous makers' instruments. Buying a guitar followed the same pattern as in Spain today. The customer went to a maker's shop where he could either buy an instrument off the hook, or order one to be made specially for him. An alternative was to go to the annual fairs held in such places as St. Germain des Prés in Paris where manufacturers set up booths to display their instruments.

The wealth of small details show that guitar playing was popular in France. But the apologetic tone of Simon Gorlier's introduction to his 1551 book of guitar music suggests that the guitar remained a minor instrument compared to the lute:

> The Ancients were satisfied with such instruments as the Guitar.... Not that I claim to prefer it to other instruments, but at least, if merely in honor and memory of antiquity, I wanted to show that it had its own limits proper for reproducing music in two or three voices or parts as well as does a larger instrument.

In England there is less evidence of activity, but the guitar was obviously played there. In 1548 Thomas Whytehorne, later to become master of music for the Archbishop of Canterbury, wrote of his youth: "I went to the dancing school ... and also learned to play on the gittern and cittern, which instruments were then strange in England, and therefore the more desired and esteemed."[18]

Later he described how a young lady had fallen in love with him:

> ... she devised certain verses in English, writing them with her own hand, and did put them between the strings of a gittern, the which instrument as a sitting mate, lying mate, and walking mate, I then used to play on very often, yea, and almost every hour of the day for that it was an instrument much esteemed and used of gentlemen, and of the best sort in those days.[19]

There is no definite evidence that the vihuela was known in England, although an inventory of Henry VIII's musical instruments mentions four "guitterons with 4 cases to theim they are called Spanish Vialles."[20]

In England as in France the aristocracy led the fashion of playing the guitar. "Sumtyme I foote it with dauncing—now with my Gittern, and els with my Cittern"[21] wrote Robert Laneham, a favorite of Robert Dudley, Earl of Leicester, who was himself a player. A portrait of the Earl on the front of the so-called Bishop's Bible of 1568 shows him surrounded by the objects of his interests, which included a four-course guitar. He is known to have patronized James Rowbotham, who printed a translation of Adrian LeRoy's instruction book to play "unto the Gitterne."

Most of the music played in England at this period must, like the instruction book, have come from France, for the only evidence of English composition for the four-course guitar is a pavan and galliard in the Mulliner book —

a manuscript collection of mainly keyboard pieces — and some pieces for guitar in the Lord Braye manuscript, both dated around 1560.

Once the guitar appeared in England, it spread to other classes. A farmer named Leonard Temperlaye left, on his death in 1577, an old "syttrone" and one broken "gyttrone." John Feld, a servant in Norwich, did in 1561 "absent himself from his master his service and went running about the country with a gittern." Complaints of the Merchants Adventurers Company in Newcastle in 1554 over the "lewd liberty" of their apprentices show that not all of English society approved of the instrument. The list of the apprentices' misdemeanors included "dicing, carding and mumming, what tippling, dancing, and brazing of harlots . . . what use of gitterns at night — what wearing of beards."[22]

By the end of the sixteenth century the guitar had become known throughout western Europe, but the extent of interest is difficult to determine exactly. Compared to the popular lute it was obviously a minority instrument. But it had come to stay and in the next century the five-course guitar became established as a serious musical instrument.

Baroque glory

The early seventeenth-century guitar began its career humbly. It was used purely as a strummed instrument, for its five courses, tuned in octaves, made it the ideal accompaniment to the popular songs and dances of the age. In this capacity it achieved enormous popularity all over Europe.

In Spain the strummed style caused the Spanish Inquisitor Don Sebastián de Covarrubias Orozco to declare sadly in 1611 of the vihuela:

> This instrument has been highly regarded until the present time, and has had most excellent musicians, but since guitars were invented, those devoting themselves to a study of the vihuela are small in number. It has been a great loss, as all kinds of plucked music could be played on it: but now the guitar is no more than a cowbell, so easy to play, especially *rasgueado*, that there is not a stable lad who is not a musician on the guitar.[1]

In France, Pierre Trichet attacked the guitar for the "grotesque and ridiculous" dances that it accompanied, especially in Spain. But:

> . . . even in France one finds courtesans and ladies who turn themselves into Spanish monkeys trying to imitate them, demonstrating that they prefer foreign importations to their native products. In this they resemble those who, though they could dine well at their own table, would rather go out to eat bacon, onions and black bread. For who is not aware that the lute is what is proper and suitable for the French, and the most delightful of all musical instruments? Still there are some of our nation who leave everything behind in order to take up and study the guitar. Isn't this because it is much easier to perfect oneself in this than in lute playing, which requires long and arduous study before one can acquire the necessary skill and disposition? Or is it because it has a certain something which is feminine and pleasing to women, flattering their hearts and making them inclined to voluptuousness?[2]

There is a further element in this violent dislike of the guitar. The lute was exclusively an upper-class instrument but the guitar had no such pretensions, and its associations

The Night *by François Mazot (mid-seventeenth century).*

COURTESY OF THE BIBLIOTHEQUE NATIONALE

with wandering players in particular helped foster its somewhat unsavory reputation. Actors were linked in people's minds with vagabonds and thieves, and indeed their professions were often interchangeable.

Nonetheless the guitar did have certain advantages. The lute was becoming increasingly complicated and more difficult to play; furthermore the lutenist found himself spending more time tuning his instrument than playing it. As Luis de Briceño pointed out in 1626, the guitar:

> . . . has none of the inconveniences to which the lute is subject; neither smoke nor heat nor cold nor dampness can incommode it. It is always fresh as a rose. If it gets out of tune easily, it is just as easy to tune it again.[3]

And so he claims that everywhere people were abandoning the lute for the guitar. This was certainly the case in Italy, where a flood of exclusively strummed music books appeared between 1606 and 1629 in Florence, Milan, Rome and Naples. Collections of sonnets and madrigals were set to simple chords and proved instantly popular. As a gentleman amateur wrote in 1628:

> Furthermore the Spanish guitar came into favor at the same time throughout Italy, especially in Naples, and it seems almost as though the guitar and the theorbo have conspired to banish the lute altogether.[4]

The patrons of the music of Benedetto Sanseverino (published 1622), Ambrosio Colonna (published 1627), and many others, were well-born and wealthy enough to afford the expensive and ornate guitars being built for them by the leading Italian makers of the early seventeenth century (see pages 24–33). But the guitar continued to have humbler players too. Performing in public theaters, at private parties or in booths set up beside the road, the strolling commedia dell' arte actors were seldom seen without a guitar. The diversity of players in Italy caused the composer Michael Praetorius to write of the guitar in 1619.

> Some have five courses, and are used in Italy by Ziarlatini and Salt'in banco [charlatans and mountebanks] only for strumming accompaniments to *Villanelles* and other foolish low songs. Nevertheless it can be used to good effect in other graceful *Cantiunculae* and delightful songs by a good singer.[5]

The strolling players went far afield and were to be found all over Europe from Venice to Munich to the busy Pont Neuf in Paris. Here all kinds of tradesmen, wrestlers, quack doctors and actors gathered along the bridge to earn a living by entertaining the aristocracy who passed by on foot or in their carriages and sedan chairs.[6]

Though the guitar in early seventeenth-century France was not as popular as in Italy, it did not disappear entirely. As a youth, Louis XIV was so enthusiastic a player that in 1656 Cardinal Mazarin sent to Italy for a guitar teacher, the well-known composer and player Francesco Corbetta. Born in Pavia around 1615, Corbetta began his career by teaching in Bologna. As a peripatetic musician he did the rounds of the courts of Europe. By 1643 he had moved to the court of the Duke of Mantua and five years later was publishing in Brussels. His arrival at the French court must have done much to enhance the prestige of the instrument, and he was immediately asked to compose the interlude guitar music for a ballet by Jean Baptiste Lully (1632–87), the King's Master of Music and himself a talented guitarist.

To satisfy such noble patrons, a fine tradition of instrument making was established in Paris, where the most prolific and best-known makers were the Voboam family. Many guitars of the later seventeenth century were richly ornamented, as is shown by two guitars in the Conservatory in Paris made for Louis XIV's daughters.

ABOVE: *Giovanni Everisto Gherardi as Brighella (The Intriguer). He played this under the name of Flautin (The Flute Player) in a troupe of the commedia dell' arte. Engraved by Nicholas Bonnart I (1637–1718). From the collection of the Victoria and Albert Museum.*

BELOW: *Seventeenth-century engraving of the Pont Neuf. From the collection of the Musée Carnavalet.*

ABOVE LEFT: Dame de qualité en habit de chambre, *by H. Bonnart (c. 1642–1711). From the collection of the Bibliothèque Nationale.*

ABOVE: Dame jouant de la guitarre, *by Robert Bonnart (1652–c. 1729). By the mid-seventeenth century, there were innumerable engravings of fashionable ladies strumming the guitar. From the collection of the Bibliothèque Nationale.*

LEFT: The Guitar Player *by Jacob van Schuppen (1670–1751). The man is playing a five-course guitar which strongly resembles those made by the French Voboam family in the latter half of the seventeenth century.*

One, made in 1687 by Jean Voboam for Mademoiselle de Nantes, Duchesse de Bourbon, has an elaborately decorated tortoiseshell back (see page 30). The other, which was made for her sister, Mademoiselle de Chartres, Elizabeth-Charlotte d'Orleans, in 1676, shows an equal concern for fine craftsmanship and intricate detail.

Guitars made in Germany in this period were equally ornate. Although there was little music published in Germany and few mentions of guitar activity, there were some famous makers. In Munich in the first half of the century Jacob Stadler was producing many outstanding instruments. In Hamburg the tradition of guitar making was set by Hans Christoph Fleischer and carried on by his son-in-law Joachim Tielke. Traditions of guitar making frequently run in families and it is believed that Tielke's elder brother was also a maker. Guitar makers of this period were often men of high social standing. Joachim Tielke was a well-known member of the community in Hamburg, and his friends included the musicians Buxtehude and Andreas Kneller.

In England too the guitar was popular among aristocratic amateurs. Interest was stimulated by the contact with the French court of many English aristocrats who fled during and after the Civil War (1640–45). Two of these exiles were Sir Ralph Verney and his wife Lady Mary, who left Claydon, their home, in 1642 and spent most of the next few years in France. The letters that passed between them and their friends—and, later, when Lady Mary had returned to England in an attempt to get a pardon, between Sir Ralph and his wife—give an insight into one English family's preoccupation with the guitar.

Lady Mary took her precious guitar of "ebony inlayed with mother pearle" with her into exile. To Lady Mary the guitar was a solace, and she passed some of her time in composing songs for the instrument which were later sent back to Claydon. On her return to England she took her favorite guitar with her. Later Sir Ralph wrote to her jokingly from Blois: "For your Gittar, if you forgot any one lesson, nay if you have not gotten many more than you had, truly I shall breake your Fiddle about your Pate. . . ."[7] The separated couple exchanged many letters about the education of their children. Learning an instrument had now become a standard part of any upper-class child's education, and the guitar was an obvious choice for a young boy. Mun, their eldest son, took up the guitar rather than the lute "for the lute is soe tedious a thing that I doubt . . . hee would never play well,"[8] and Sir Ralph ordered a "fine Gittare" from Paris for his son.

In 1648 Sir Ralph was pardoned and the family reunited at Claydon. Later, in 1656, their second son Jack remembered his mother's guitar that she had taken to France with her and wrote to his father from school asking him

> to bestow the gittarre which was my Mother's on mee; you did give it mee when you went out of France, and then when I came over, you sayed I should not have it because it would bee broked att schoole.

He explains triumphantly that he now sleeps in a room with only a small number of fellow pupils and has his own closet, so he can look after the instrument. Moreover he does not like the guitar he has at present: "That Gittarre which is in the wooden casse is of noe sound att all almost, and then it is very ugly—it is very coarse and rude."[9]

The instrument occupied much of the lives of families such as the Verneys, who owned at least four or five guitars. Lady Mary's guitar was obviously a fine one, which suggests that the beautifully decorated instruments of this period were in fact meant to be played and not merely regarded as pieces of furniture.

In 1660 Charles II, who had left England in 1645, was summoned back from fifteen years of exile on the Continent. The new King's taste set the pattern of his court, and his liking for the guitar was immediately followed. He traveled to Dover on his triumphant return accompanied by his guitar—much to the disgust of Samuel Pepys, who was given charge of it. "I troubled much with the King's gittar and Fairbrother the rogue, that I intrusted with the carrying of it on foot, whom I thought I had lost." Pepys was a member of the lute-playing faction and regarded the guitar with a good deal of disdain: "methinks it is but a bauble."[11] With the summoning of Francesco Corbetta to Charles' court in 1662, Pepys' discomfort increased. In 1667 he wrote:

> After dining with the Duke of York, and coming out through his dressing room I there spied Signor

He persuaded the lady's brother, the Earl of Arran, to take him to her apartments at court, ostensibly to hear the Earl play a sarabande. Unfortunately they also found the lady's husband there, and:

> Jealousy, like a malignant vapour, seized upon his brain: a thousand suspicions, blacker than ink, took possession of his imagination, and were continually increasing; for, whilst the brother played upon the guitar to the duke, the sister ogled and accompanied him with her eyes, as if the coast had been clear, and no enemy to observe them. This sarabande was repeated twenty times; the duke declared it was played to perfection; Lady Chesterfield found no fault with the composition; but her husband, who clearly perceived that he was the person played upon, thought it most detestable.[12]

COURTESY OF THE WALLACE COLLECTION, LONDON

Lady playing a guitar, *1669, by Caspar Netscher (1639–1684)*.

Francisco tuning his gittar and Monsieur de Puy with him. . . . I was mightily troubled that all that pains should have been taken up on so bad an instrument.[11]

In 1665 Charles sent some of Corbetta's music to his sister Henrietta, Duchess of Orleans. In return for such royal patronage, Corbetta dedicated his *Guitarre Royalle* of 1672 to the king.

How much the courtiers who affected to like the instrument were really enthusiasts and how much they were trying to curry favor with the royal family is impossible to tell. In any event, the guitar became part of every courtier's life. As such, it was bound to be caught up in the various sexual intrigues that enlivened court life. Anthony Hamilton's *Memoirs of the Count of Gramont* chronicled one affair. The Duke of York was interested in Lady Chesterfield, who possessed a "wonderful guitar."

COURTESY OF THE COURTAULD INSTITUTE OF ART

The actress Mary Davis by Sir Peter Lely (1618–80) who came to England during the 1640s. From the collection of Lord Bradford, Weston Park.

Louis XIV's Musicians *by François Puget, 1687. Musée du Louvre.*

In 1681 Corbetta returned to France, dying there the same year. His influence had been enormous. Throughout Europe he had established the guitar as a serious and respectable instrument, and encouraged other composers to write for it. Because of him a regular position of guitar tutor to the King of France was established, and he was followed in this post by the eminent musicians L. Jourdan de la Salle and, in 1719, Robert de Visée.

In England, the audience for the guitar that Corbetta had helped to establish encouraged other foreign musicians to seek patronage. The Italian violin virtuoso Nicola Matteis, whose playing on the guitar was powerful enough "to stand in consort against an Harpsichord,"[13] made his home in the courtly circles of Restoration England. In 1682 he published *The false consonances of musick or Instructions for the playing a true Base upon the Guitarre*, stressing the universal popularity of the instrument in his introduction: "The Guitarre was never so much in use and credit as it is at this day, and finding it improved to so great a Perfection it is my present design to make it company for the other Instruments."

Fashions set by the aristocracy were copied by the common people. John Playford, in a last-ditch stand to defend the old cittern, produced *Musick's Delight on the Cittern* (1666):

It is observed that of late years all Solemn and Grave Musick is much laid aside, being esteemed too heavy and dull for the light Heels and Brains of this Nimble and Wanton Age; Nor is any Musick rendered acceptable, or esteemed by many, but what is

presented by Forreigners: Not a City dame, though a Tapwife, but is anxious to have her daughter taught by Monnsieur la Novo Kirkshaivibus on the Gitar.

Spain remained the one country where the guitar, once established, never lost its popular appeal. While aristocratic tastes in music fluctuated, the guitar was still used to accompany the songs and dances of ordinary people. For most of the seventeenth century, little serious guitar music appeared in Spain. However, in 1674 Gaspar Sanz published his *Instrucción de Música sobre la Guitarra Española,* a book that remains popular today.

Little is known of Sanz's life and what little there is has been continually disputed. Born in Calanda in Aragon around 1640, he studied the humanities in the typical mixture of music, philosophy and theology at the University of Salamanca. He received the degree of Bachelor of Theology, and later traveled to Italy to fill the prestigious post of organist in the Royal Chapel in Naples.[14] Sanz returned from Naples to become guitar tutor to Don Juan, the illegitimate son of Philip IV and the actress Maria Calderón, and it was for Don Juan that Sanz composed his music and wrote his tutor.

Sanz had been heavily influenced by Italian guitar music, which by this time had broken free of the earlier strummed style, and his book was a successful attempt to introduce the Italian style into Spain. His detailed instructions and delightful music, a mixture of a courtly aristocratic style and a popular one with its origins in folk music, inspired others to follow him.

The composers whom Sanz inspired and his elevated position as tutor to the aristocracy indicate his success in creating a following for the guitar. But guitars made in Spain are extremely rare for this period (see page 37). It is therefore likely that Italian guitars were imported for the rich while the makers of folk guitars remained, as always, anonymous.

As the seventeenth century drew to a close, it appeared that the guitar had achieved a permanent place among plucked stringed instruments. Guitar making had become a highly skilled profession, with luthiers of the worth of Joachim Tielke, the Voboam family and the Sellas family working throughout Europe. The music had evolved from the purely strummed chordal style of the early century to the highly complex contrapuntal styles of Foscarini, Corbetta, Gaspar Sanz and Robert de Visée. Moreover, the patronage of the nobility of Europe would seem to have set the final seal of approval on the guitar. But the guitar's history has always been unpredictable: in the next century, the instrument was to fall from favor yet again.

The Guitar Player by Jan Vermeer (1632–1675), one of the most famous guitar paintings.

COURTESY OF BULLOZ

La Leçon de Musique *by François Boucher (1703–70). Musée Cognacq-Jay, Paris.*

Fashion and sentiment

Fashions in music are as ephemeral as all other fashions set by the aristocracy, and the eighteenth century saw shifts in musical tastes which were not helpful to the guitar. In the first place, the guitar's position as a solo instrument for the amateur was successfully challenged by the harpsichord and pianoforte. Second, there was an increase in interest in chamber music where the guitar, with its smaller sound, could not compete. And third, the passion for opera which gripped both the Italians and Spanish later in the century utterly precluded the guitar's use.

These disasters did not overtake the guitar at once, nor did they lead to its complete disappearance. For a time the guitar kept its status as an instrument of the aristocracy. In France the paintings of Antoine Watteau (1684–1721) and Nicolas Lancret (1690–1743) show it as a romantic plaything, a gentle accompaniment to seduction or a means of showing off an elegant posture. The upper classes above all wanted to be amused, and for such entertainment the guitar was perfect. In mid-century Diderot and d'Alembert's *Encyclopédie* recorded this interest:

> The sound of this instrument is so gentle, that the greatest silence is necessary to experience all the subtleties of a good player. It is made to be played alone, or to accompany a voice with similar instruments. Some amateurs have revived it and at the same time reawakened a taste for our *vaudevilles, pastorales* and *brunettes* which have given it a new charm.[1]

Elsewhere the general lack of professional interest in the instrument helped foster attitudes of contempt. In England, the Reverend Dr. John Brown viewed the guitar as

> . . . a trifling instrument in itself, and generally now taught in the most ignorant and trifling manner . . . while the theorbo and the lute, the noblest because the most expressive and pathetic of all accompaniments, are altogether laid aside. What is the reason for this? Because the guitar is a plaything for a child.[2]

In 1771 Dr. Charles Burney said that "there is hardly a private family in a civilized nation without its flute, its fiddle, its harpsichord, or guitar."[3] But as a serious solo

La Gamme D'Amour *by Antoine Watteau (1684–1721). Watteau's many paintings of guitarists perfectly convey the sense of idyllic happiness. In the hands of a lover, or lying abandoned on the grass, the guitar becomes an integral part of his outdoor scenes.*

ABOVE: Conversation Galante *by Nicolas Lancret (1690–1743).*
Lancret was one of the principal followers of Watteau.

ABOVE RIGHT: *Plucked stringed instruments. From Diderot and*
d'Alembert's Encyclopédie.

BELOW RIGHT: *The interior of an instrument maker's shop. Diderot and*
d'Alembert's Encyclopédie, *published in Paris from 1751. From the*
collection of the Victoria and Albert Museum.

Gilles and his Family *by Antoine Watteau (1684–1721). Watteau*
worked in Paris between 1704 and 1707 for Gillot, a painter of theatrical
scenes.

instrument, it was largely replaced by the harpsichord and pianoforte.

In Italy, guitars continued to be played by itinerant musicians. On a visit to Venice, Dr. Burney reported hearing "a great number of vagrant musicians, some in bands, accompanying one or two voices, sometimes a single voice and guitar, and sometimes two or three guitars together."[4] But the upper classes had developed a passion for opera and in the plush opera houses the guitar was completely out of place (as well as being inaudible).

Italian fashions had an effect on musical taste in Spain, the country above all others where the guitar had become the national instrument. In 1700 the French house of Bourbon took the throne, in the person of Philip V, the non-Spanish-speaking grandson of Louis XIV. His first wife, the Italian Maria Luisa Gabriela of Savoy, employed Don Santiago de Murcia to teach her the guitar, but for some decades after her death in 1714 no more is heard of aristocratic guitar players. As in Italy, the dominant musical love of the court was for opera.

The most significant composer in Spain in the early century was Domenico Scarlatti (1685–1757) who lived and worked in the country for nearly forty years. Scarlatti wrote no music for the guitar, but its rhythms and textures are vividly reproduced in his music, and "surely no composer ever fell more deeply under its spell."[5] Much of his music has been transcribed and is today played most successfully on the modern guitar.

Outside the court, the guitar remained an essential part of Spanish life. "The flat guitar with its strum, strum, we shall happily leave to the garlic-eating Spaniards,"[6] wrote a German rudely in 1713 from the safety of Hamburg. At street corners, fairs and in drawing rooms the guitar was always to be heard. In 1776 Sir John Hawkins recorded that overworked cliché of the romantic young Spaniard serenading his lover:

At Madrid, and in other cities of Spain, it is common to meet in the street, young men equipped with a guitar and a dark lanthorn, who taking their station under the window, sing and accompany themselves on their instrument; and there is scarce an artificer or labourer in any of the cities or principal towns, who when his work is over does not go to some of the public places

Dance on the banks of the Manzaneros, *by Ramón Bayeu (1746–93), Goya's brother-in-law. Museo Municipal, Madrid.*

COURTESY OF ARCHIVO MAS

and entertain himself with the guitar. . . .

But despite all this, he noted, "few Spaniards are composers of music."[7] Little new guitar music was written and Dr. Juan Carlos y Amat's book, which had first appeared in 1596, was still being republished well into the century. It was so popular that in 1764 a certain Andrés de Sotos published it in Madrid under his own name in an "augmented" version. One other book of music appeared in 1752, that of a dancing master Pablo Minguet y Yrol. A section on the guitar was included along with "all the best instruments," such as the clavichord, organ, harp, psaltery and many others. His guitar music included such forms as the *jota aragonesa*, *fandango*, *folia*, and *seguidillas*, dances which were recorded time and again by travelers who took in Spain as part of the "Grand Tour" of Europe. By the mid-eighteenth century the theater had caused such dances to invade fashionable society ballrooms, a process which broke down the old distinction between aristocratic and popular dances. Sometimes, however, the dances seen in a Madrid ballroom were completely different from those danced in inns and cafés. An English traveler recorded in 1772:

> . . . I was agreeably entertained with seeing my landlord and landlady dance the *fandango* to the music of the guitar. The person who played on it struck merely a few chords in triple time, and beat time with the same hand on the belly of the instrument. The dance itself is for two persons. . . . Every part of the body is in motion, and is thrown into all postures, frequently into very indecent ones. Stamping the time with the feet and playing all the while with the *castanetas*.[8]

The *bolero* was another dance enjoyed throughout society, performed in the smallest cafés and at grand balls such as the one attended by William Beckford in December 1787. The company was distinguished: the Cardinal Archbishop of Toledo, the Turkish ambassador Admet Vassif and a multitude of other VIPs.

> A circle was soon formed, a host of guitars put in immediate requisition. . . . The quicker we moved, the more intrepidly we stamped with our feet, the more sonorously we snapped our fingers. . . . The rest of the company, the Spanish part at least. . . were so much animated, that not less than twenty voices accompanied the *bolero* with its appropriate words in full chorus, and with a glow of enthusiasm that inspired my lovely partners and myself with such energy, that we outdid all our former out-dancings.

One member of the party was not made happy by such native music, the Italian Luigi Boccherini (1743–1805). He had arrived in Madrid in 1768 to become part of the household of the powerful Benavente-Osuna family, who ran a salon to which leading figures in all fields were invited on selected evenings. Boccherini on occasions expressed a positive dislike of the guitar. At this same party he turned to Beckford and whispered:

> If *you* dance and *they* play in this ridiculous manner, I shall never be able to introduce a decent style into our musical world here, which I flattered myself I was on the very point of doing. What possesses you? Is it the devil?[9]

But to please his patron, an enthusiastic player of the guitar, Boccherini produced twelve quintets scored for two violins, guitar, viola and cello, and one symphony containing a guitar part. One of his quintets contains "the fandango which was played on the guitar of Padre Basilio," a Cistercian monk whose inspired music helped start a serious revival of interest in the guitar.

This revival was conducted against a background of genuinely popular guitar music. "The real opera in Spain is in the shop of the *Barbero* or in the courtyard of the *Venta*,"[10] wrote Richard Ford in his travel diary of 1796.

Throughout Europe during the late seventeenth and early eighteenth centuries forms of musical entertainment were changing. Private parties and public performances rapidly became fashionable throughout the continent, and music became a recognized profession. But with this the status of the musician and his music also generally changed. In 1778 the young Mozart wrote of a party he played at:

> After an hour's wait in the cold I began to play upon a wretched and miserable pianoforte. The most annoying thing about it was that Madame and all the gentlemen never for one moment interrupted their occupations but continued them the whole time, so that it was to the chairs and tables that I was playing. I had begun some of Fisher's *Variations*. I played half and rose. Then a burst of applause. Give me the best piano in Europe and for an audience people who neither understand nor wish to understand music, who feel nothing with me that I am playing, and I lose all my joy in performing.[11]

The indifference prevailed all over Europe: at the British Embassy in Berlin the conductor of the orchestra, so incensed at such behaviour and seeing no reason to put

An English Tea Party at a Salon, *by M. Barth Ollivier. Detail of a painting showing the young Mozart with a guitarist and cellist playing in 1776 to the Prince de Conti.*

BELOW: *Watercolors by Carmontelle (1717–1806). From the collection of the Musée Carnavalet.*

Un oiseleur accordant sa guitare. (*A bird catcher tuning his guitar*).
Engraving by P. E. Moitte from a painting by Jean Baptiste Greuze (1725–1805). The original painting was exhibited in the Paris Salon of 1757. From the collection of the Victoria and Albert Museum.

himself to any great trouble, performed the same piece of music under different titles throughout the evening. No harm was done—indeed, he was complimented at the end for the variety of his program. Music in the late eighteenth century provided an excuse for social gatherings and a pleasant background for polite conversation. In these circumstances the guitar could not compete, and indeed was not asked to, for it was purely an amateur instrument.

In France such musical evenings as the one described by Mozart (which took place in the Duchesse de Chabron's house in Paris) were brought to an abrupt end by the Revolution of 1789. Evidence that the aristocracy had played the guitar came in the Inventories made by the Committee of Public Safety which listed the possessions of those aristocrats who had fled abroad or lost their heads on the guillotine.[12] But the guitars were overshadowed by the hundreds of violins, flutes, harpsichords and pianofortes which had provided the nobility with musical entertainment.

The eighteenth century was a quiet period for the guitar, a time when little serious music appeared for the instrument and it came to be regarded only as a pleasant way of passing a few hours. But from the 1780s onward the groundwork was being laid for its revival in the following century.

Un concert sous le Consulat, *1812, by Nicolas Antoine Taunay (1775–1830). Private collection.*

Virtuosi and enthusiasts

The guitar's spectacular rise in popularity was one of the great success stories of the early nineteenth century, and happened for a number of interacting reasons. The development of the new and improved six-string and six-course instrument (see pages 40–2) coincided with a new interest in its musical possibilities, brought about largely in Spain by the exciting *punteado* style of Father Basilio. Originally organist at the Escorial palace, he soon became guitar teacher to Queen Marie-Louise and many of Spain's aristocrats. More important for the future of the guitar, however, he inspired two of his pupils, the Italian Don Federico Moretti and the Spaniard Fernando Ferrandière, to write methods for the new guitar.

But it was Fernando Sor and Dionisio Aguado, two Spaniards, who were directly responsible for the widespread cultivation of the instrument. Fernando Sor, or Sors as he was known in Spain, was born in Barcelona in 1778, the son of a merchant who was himself an enthusiastic amateur guitar player. Sor was educated at nearby Montserrat monastery, receiving an excellent musical training in composition and performance. Leaving at the age of seventeen, he returned to Barcelona and almost immediately began composing. His first work—an opera called *Telemaco on the Island of Calipso*—was performed in Barcelona on August 25, 1797. It was highly acclaimed, the young Sor acquired a certain celebrity, and on the strength of this was invited to Madrid. There the Duchess of Alba, who conducted a bitter cultural and social war with Boccherini's patrons, the Benavente-Osuna family, appointed him organist of her chapel and teacher of the guitar to her daughter. The Duchess died in 1802, but Sor was taken up by the Duke of Medina-Celi. Patronage at this period of Sor's life was of the best kind: his duties were so few that he was able to spend most of his time composing. But in 1812 the re-establishment of the Spanish monarchy—which Sor had opposed—forced him to flee to Paris. His first publications for the guitar date from his two-year stay in the French capital. Like most guitarists, he had to teach to earn a steady living, and, finding no suitable guitar music for his pupils, began to publish his own compositions.

Sor was an outstanding player, and on his London debut in 1815 made an instant and amazing success. One critic wrote afterward:

> It is a fact that, until the arrival of Sor in this country, which took place about fifteen or sixteen years ago, the guitar was scarcely known here, and the impression he made on his first performance at the Argyll Rooms, which I attended, was of a nature which will never be erased from my memory; it was at once magical and surprising; nobody could credit that such effects could be produced on the guitar! Indeed, there was a sort of suppressed laughter when he first came forth before the audience, which, however, soon changed into the most unbounded admiration when he began to display his talents.[1]

Sor had sparked off the English love affair with the guitar, which lasted throughout the nineteenth century. *La guitaromanie* was experienced throughout Europe, for the intimate nature of the instrument, together with its portability, made it the ideal instrument for the writers and

musicians of the Romantic age. While Hector Berlioz was studying in the Conservatory at Rome, he met the young Felix Mendelssohn. In the evenings they and some of their friends gathered in the garden, "where my wretched voice and paltry guitar were often requisitioned."[2] Whenever he felt depressed, Berlioz took a trip to the village of Subiaco as a remedy.

> An old gray suit, a straw hat, a guitar, a gun and six piasters were all my stock-in-trade. Thus I wandered, shooting or singing, careless where I might pass the night. Sometimes a glorious landscape spread before me. I chanted, to the guitar accompaniment, long remembered verses of the *Aeneid*, the death of Pallas, the despair of Evander, the sad end of Amata and the death of Lavinia's noble lover, and worked myself up into an incredible pitch of excitement that ended in floods of tears.[3]

Other composers also found the guitar an instrument which afforded them a great deal of amusement. Two oddly dressed blind street beggars who walked through the streets of Rome during the Carnival in February 1822 were Rossini and Paganini, singing songs composed by Paganini and accompanying themselves on guitars. Paganini was by all accounts almost as formidable a player of the guitar as of the violin.

Interest in the guitar in the early nineteenth century was so widespread and sudden that even countries with no tradition of guitar playing found themselves caught up in the enthusiasm. Although some guitars and their makers are known in Germany, for instance, the instrument had never been widely popular. However, early in the nineteenth century, Herr Jacob Augustus, a violin and guitar maker was writing:

> The late Duchess Amalia of Weimar having introduced the guitar in Weimar in 1788, I was obliged to make copies of this instrument for several of the nobility; and these soon became known in Leipzig, Dresden, and Berlin. So great a demand rose for them that, for the space of sixteen years, I had more orders than I could execute.[4]

At about the same time, a Frankfurt publication of 1802 claimed that "Here in Germany [the guitar] has risen to being the 'darling' instrument of the ladies."[5]

Within this climate of rapidly increasing respect for the guitar, Sor became the instrument's greatest exponent. In the early 1820s he traveled to Russia, where he gave successful performances, produced several of his ballets, appeared at the Imperial Court in St. Petersburg and composed the funeral march on the death of the Czar.

Sor divided the rest of his time between Paris and London, teaching, performing and composing hundreds of guitar pieces. Later in the 1820s he met his fellow countryman Dionisio Aguado, who had traveled to Paris specifically to meet him. The two instantly became friends, and Sor commemorated their friendship with a guitar duet, *Los Dos Amigos*.

Aguado, besides being a brilliant player, was also an outstanding teacher, and his method and studies remain his lasting achievement. Aguado spent most of his life in Spain where the guitar, although facing competition from the pianoforte, remained very popular. In 1829 a correspondent of the music magazine *The Harmonicon* wrote that, in Spain,

> The guitar is the instrument most generally employed, it is quite as national as their beads and their chocolate, and is to be found in every house, from that of peer to the barber. . . . All play the guitar; all have a facility in playing it, from the amateur who performs *pro musica*, as they express it, to the artist who employs it professionally (*aficionado*).[6]

Sor and Aguado, and the Italians Ferdinando Carulli (1770–1841), Matteo Carcassi (1792–1853) and Mauro Giuliani (1781–1829) were only a few of the early nineteenth-century players who helped create the enormous following for the guitar. But social conditions were in their favor. For the first time there existed a large, predominantly middle-class public whose tastes, inclinations and purses provided the kind of conditions where the guitar could flourish.

Their new wealth gave them leisure to cultivate music as a social amenity, and a guitar course became a compulsory part of a proper education. The taste for performances was satisfied in small salons in Vienna, private musical evenings in London and Paris, and larger concerts in public rooms where the virtuosi astonished

TOP: *"Valencian characters," from a drawing by Señor Ortego. From the newspaper* El Museo Universal, *August 29, 1868. From the collection of the Victoria and Albert Museum.*

BOTTOM: A Guitar Player, *1873, by Giovanni Boldini (1845–1931).*

Sheet music cover, La Plainte Moresque, *drawn by Edouard Manet (1832–83).*

The Street Singer *by Norbert Goemuette, 1885.*

their audiences with startling technical displays. Gone were the days when music making was largely confined to the upper classes; now for the price of a ticket, anyone could hear the playing of Zani de Ferranti (1802–1878), Luigi Rinoldo Legnani (1790–1877), Sor, or "the sublime Barber," an eccentric man called Don Trinidad Huerta y Caturla (1804–1875) who went to America and Russia on concert tours.

Vienna and Paris were the two main centers in Europe to which guitar players were attracted. Many of the players settling in these cities originally came from Italy, a country which at the beginning of the century appeared to hold considerable attraction for guitarists. Italy was in the forefront of the development both of the new six-string instrument (see pages 41–2) and in the adoption of modern notation. Federico Moretti, in his work for the six single-string guitar of 1799, mentions earlier editions of 1788 and 1792 published in Naples. In 1805 the Italian correspondent of the newspaper the *Leipzig musicalischer Zeitung* wrote:

. . . no instrument is so cultivated as the guitar. Furthermore, it is a fact that there are good composers here for this little creature, and excellent virtuosi, in a

155

more elevated sense than one should expect for the guitar. In order to meet the demands of the amateurs there are countless teachers, and workshops which construct guitars of all types. It is already well known that there are several concerns here which manufacture the best strings in the world, and export them to every nation.[7]

But the very popularity of the instrument, particularly in Naples, intensified competition for audiences. Moreover there was the physical difficulty of giving public performances on the relatively small-sounding guitar in the great opera houses of Rome, Milan and Venice. And as early as the 1770s Dr. Burney had noticed the strange state of music publishing. "The art of engraving music there seems to be utterly lost, as I was not able to find a single work printed in the manner we print music in England."[8] The establishment of the House of Ricordi in Milan in 1808 helped the situation, but it was still possible for a correspondent to write in *The Harmonicon* of 1823:

It is a sad tantalising thing to hear music in Italy which you may wish to carry away with you, for they have no printed music! This alone is sufficient to indicate the low state of the art. From Naples to Milan, I believe there is no such artist as an Engraver of Music, and you never see a Music shop. You must therefore go without it or employ a copier.[9]

This was expensive and, as the copier charged by the amount of paper used, all Italian music was written as large as possible. The final blow to Italy's chances of becoming a guitar center was delivered by Napoleon, whose campaigns so disrupted cultural and social life that many of the main conservatories were forced to close. The most famous Italian guitar players left early in the century: Giuliani to Vienna in 1806, Carulli to Paris in the same year, Carcassi in 1820 and Zani de Ferranti to Brussels in 1827.

Vienna held out promise for a good musical career. Austria had been one of the few countries with a genuine and informed love of music, particularly encouraged by the Empress Maria Theresa. Conditions for guitarists were favorable: there were good guitar makers, led by Johann Georg Staufer, a large number of publishing houses and, most important of all, a wealthy public who delighted in

the kind of intimate, light entertainment which the guitarists supplied.

Giuliani took advantage of these circumstances and his rise to fame was rapid. Soon after his arrival, a newspaper was commenting that his playing was changing the instrument's status from a "frivolous galant music-box" to something worthy of serious consideration. For Giuliani was a virtuoso, renowned at a time when virtuosi were fairly common—Paganini and Liszt were thrilling audiences all over Europe. Of Giuliani an English critic wrote:

Giuliani's performance on the guitar in Vienna, in the very seat and center of musical learning, was the wonder and delight of the most distinguished dilettantes. The announcement of his performance at a concert was the sure source of a numerous audience. In short, Giuliani was the Paganini on his instrument.[10]

Comparisons like this should not, however, be taken too seriously—they seem to have formed the mainstay of nineteenth-century music criticism. Composers and players must have rapidly become confused as to their own particular qualities: Sor was "the Beethoven of the guitar" and not surprisingly Beethoven was nicknamed "the Sor of the piano." Sor was even hailed as the "Racine of the guitar."

The musical circle to which Giuliani belonged in Vienna was a closely knit one. Beethoven is known to have attended Giuliani's concerts, and in 1813 and 1814 Giuliani performed Beethoven's music with other well-known musicians. Some performances were private, arranged by members of Austrian high society for their friends and often attended by the royal family; others were subscription or charity concerts run on the same principles as today—that is, expensive occasions when the foremost musicians were invited to play, a few famous figures to listen to them, and the rest of the tickets sold to a public anxious to be seen in the best company.

In Vienna, as elsewhere in Europe, amateurs enthusiastically took to the instrument, stimulating a host of minor figures to produce music both for solo guitar and for the instrument in chamber works. Giuliani was himself doing his best to satisfy such a public—between 1806 and 1819 he wrote over a hundred works. But the very diversity and quantity of the demands made on him—music for professional players, both solo and ensemble works, studies for his pupils, and technically brilliant pieces for his own performances—was exhausting and not very lucrative. In 1819 he was forced to leave Vienna because of financial difficulties. Some of his difficulties were caused by the rising popularity of the pianoforte, but some were undoubtedly caused by his fellow guitarist, composer and publisher Anton Diabelli, who had the reputation of being the worst paymaster among publishers—Schubert also suffered from his avarice. In 1824 Giuliani angrily described Diabelli and his partner as "these two super-braggarts who pride themselves on having the best music store in Vienna," and later they appear in his correspondence as "two false businessmen."[11]

On his departure from Vienna, Giuliani was determined to travel around his native Italy giving concerts, but his letters of 1819 to his friend the publisher Domenico Artaria indicate both Giuliani's personal despondency and the state of music in Italy at this time. From Venice he wrote:

I doubt I shall go to Naples and Rome inasmuch as, dear friend, the misery is great, and above all the taste in instrumental music is so abased that it makes one ashamed. . . . At Verona all my best friends advised me not to give a concert, being certain of not making anything, as even poor Paganini did not even make expenses and thus had to make up the difference out of his own pocket. . . .

Things were little better elsewhere. At Vicenza "everyone was away in the country," Padua was "the same story, since the mania of poverty is rampant in the streets." In Venice itself where he had hoped to do better, "Paganini . . . only sold 300 tickets at three francs. . . ."[12] If the great Paganini, whose powers were so impressive that he was forced to carry a birth certificate to prove his mortality, could not fill a concert hall, then music in Italy was in a very sorry state indeed.

In Rome between 1820 and 1823 Giuliani's fortunes began to improve, but his later career never reached the heights of his youth, and although the notices he received were as fulsome as ever, they appeared less and less frequently. He died in Naples on May 8, 1829, his obituary

containing a hidden insult to the guitar: "the guitar was transformed in his hands into an instrument similar to the harp, sweetly soothing men's hearts."[13] After all his efforts, the guitar still could not stand on its own merits. But he had done much to foster interest in the instrument, and in England a magazine, *The Giulianiad*, was started as a direct result of his playing. In *The Giulianiad* there are the beginnings of the tendency to sentimentalize the instrument which culminated later in some extraordinarily banal music.

Of all kinds of music the Guitar is the instrument of romance and sentiment; its name is handed down to us associated with deeds of chivalry and love, and awakening in the memory a thousand traditions of its enchanting power.

So ran the introduction to the first issue. The magazine attempted seriously to promote the guitar, but its tone was defensive. One article was written "On the comparative merits of the pianoforte and guitar, as an accompaniment to the voice." It was here that the two instruments really clashed, for the most popular form of amateur music-making was accompanied song. *The Giulianiad* stated the case for the guitar as the ideal accompanying instrument: though less powerful an instrument, it was sweeter and had more variety, was easily tuned, and well adapted to the voice. It was easy to extemporize on tunes originally written for the piano—a dangerous claim, since extemporizing often meant the eternal strummed chords. It taught the performer to play with feeling, due to the great variety of tones that could be produced. Finally, it was portable compared to the piano, "whose unwieldiness may prove rather a cumbersome escort in a short journey to the country."[14]

This kind of justification for the guitar is met with time and again. Flamini Duvernay, the "Guitarist to the King's Theatre," asserted:

The guitar possesses many important advantages in addition to portability, among which may be enumerated, facility of tuning, Graceful and Elegant position of the Player, and sweet Tone, which sounds with great effect in Garden and Boating Parties, as well as at Home; forming a delightful accompaniment to the Voice at all times.[15]

One of Madame Sidney Pratten's many guitars. From the collection of Keith Johns.

In a later article in *The Giulianiad*, the disadvantage of the small sound of the instrument was discussed. Although concert halls were smaller and performances more intimate than today, the instrument at this time could not produce a large sound. The writer of the article offered advice to players trying to make the instrument louder:

> Playing generally in a large room, they naturally wish that every part of the audience should hear, and in doing this they wholly mistake the manner in which it be successfully effected. They pull the strings with so much force, for the purpose of producing a *loud* tone, that, although they produce more noise, they in fact lessen the real tone of the instrument. A mere whisper, if the tone is sweet and compact, will find its way to every corner of a large theatre, while an overstrained string will produce a tone which will fall, so to speak, dead and lifeless.[16]

In the mid-nineteenth century, London was a center of guitar playing. In 1862 the celebrated Spanish guitarist Julián Arcas visited London and under the patronage of the Duke of Wellington, performed at Apsley House. He was enthusiastically received and the Duchess of Cambridge, Queen Victoria's daughter and her daughter Mary Adelaide arranged two more concerts in the Brighton Pavilion.[17] Arcas was an exceptional guitarist, and probably influenced the great Spanish player Francisco Tárrega (see page 122). Jules Regondi (1822–1872), an infant prodigy, also settled there after 1831. Another child wonder living in London was Catherine Pelzer, later Madame Sidney Pratten. She had an early success as a concert guitarist both in England and on the Continent, but her fame lay in her teaching of the nobility. She was a lady of great delicacy of feelings. Her biographer Frank Mott Harrison wrote: "I have known her to be unable to play when facing an ill-shaped piece of furniture, so sensitive was her mind."[18] It is unfortunate that he should have been such a shining example of high Victorian sentiment, for Madame Pratten was certainly a great teacher. But the biography gives an excellent picture of the guitar's place in genteel society. Madame Pratten's patron was Lady John Somerset, who set her up in an apartment, and launched her into society as a guitar teacher. Her pupils included two daughters of Queen Victoria, Princess Louise and Princess

Beatrice, and a "large percentage of our titled ladies."

The guitar had come a long way from its humble origins—and was encouraged further by Madame Pratten:

> . . . it was always Madame Pratten's desire to maintain the prestige of the guitar . . . she dreaded the idea of her instrument becoming in any way vulgarized, and insisted upon it keeping its place exclusively in the gentlewoman's drawing room.[19]

And in the drawing room the guitar might have remained, but it was saved by the appearance of dedicated and brilliant figures in Spain.

COURTESY OF THE WALLACE COLLECTION

The Dead Mouse *by L. L. Boilly (1761–1845)*

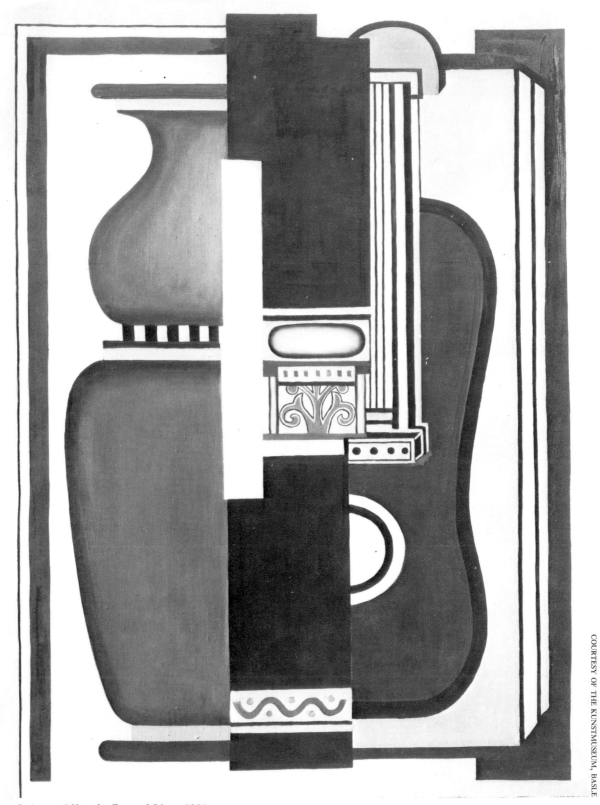

Blue Guitar and Vase *by Fernand Léger, 1926.*

The widening audience

The beginnings of serious interest in the modern classical guitar were laid by Francisco de Asis Tárrega Eixea (1852–1909) and the pupils who carried on his work. Tárrega was a brilliant player, so obsessed with the guitar that he played and practiced all day. An hour for scales, an hour for arpeggios, an hour for trills, an hour or longer if needed for difficult passages and position:

> Thus passes the morning. After lunch, once more the guitar, but the work is different. The complete works of Schumann for the piano are on the table. . . . Tárrega skims through them, stops at a page, and tries it on the guitar to see if it will lend itself to transcription. . . . Every day, toward evening, some intimate friends and *aficionados* come to hear him play. . . . Then at night, after dinner, when everybody is asleep in the house, Tárrega plays for himself.[1]

Drawing of Tárrega by Morco. From the collection of the Instrument Museum of the Barcelona Conservatory.

He made some concert tours, and went to London in the 1880s to perform with Madame Pratten, but was happiest while playing for a small circle. His friends and acquaintances "venerated him as artist and adored him as friend"[2] and it was through his personal inspiration and teaching that he had the greatest effect.

One of those whom Tárrega directly inspired was Emilio Pujol, who met him in 1902. Pujol never forgot this first meeting:

> . . . for me, who had a presentiment of [the guitar's] beauty but had never imagined its enchantment in the hands of a great artist, this was an unsuspected revelation which enslaved my will and fixed the course of my destiny for the rest of my days.[3]

Pujol in his turn has become a great, though modest, figure in the guitar's history. He has given concert tours and conducted courses in both the guitar and the vihuela. It was Pujol who first found the vihuela in the Jacquemart-André Museum in Paris (see page 21). Playing on a replica at a concert in Barcelona, he opened up a vast new field of interest to guitarists and lutenists. He also helped foster interest in early music, when in 1926 he began to publish a series of transcriptions from the seven Spanish vihuela books and from five-course guitar books. In 1934 appeared the first of four volumes of *Escuela Razonada de la*

Miguel Llobet, drawing by Charles Léandre from Mercure Musicale, *1906.*

Guitarra, the distillation of Tárrega's teaching. As player, teacher and musicologist Emilio Pujol's contribution has often been overlooked, perhaps because of his more flamboyant contemporaries Miguel Llobet and Andrés Segovia.

Miguel Llobet, another of Tárrega's pupils, was born in Barcelona in 1878. Segovia later commented on his playing:

> Among all the pupils of Tárrega the best was Llobet. A better musician than the others, a better technique—the sound was not so good, but a great expressive sympathy.[4]

Llobet's approach differed from that of Tárrega:

> . . . in spite of his profound admiration for Tárrega, his master, the aesthetic feeling of Llobet was not the same; it differed for reasons of their nature of looking at things, age, and surrounding circumstances. And while Tárrega, enamored of the purity of the classic quartet in its homogeneous variety, would have unified the six strings of the instrument, Llobet, attracted by the diversity of timbre of the orchestra, would have made a separate guitar out of each string.[5]

Llobet differed from Tárrega in one other important aspect: he played with the fingernails.

Llobet was successful at the beginning of the century in Spain, but the lack of opportunities for guitarists persuaded him to move to Paris in 1904. Six years later Domingo Prat invited him to Argentina and from then on he traveled, giving concerts in North and South America and throughout Europe (he was particularly successful in Germany). In the 1930s he returned to Spain, but appeared to have been completely crushed by the Civil War and died in Barcelona in 1938.

Among serious Spanish composers there was considerable interest in the guitar. Manuel de Falla had a great admiration for the instrument and its music, and spent many hours in the company of the composer and player Don Angel Barrios in Granada.

But the greatest single figure in the classical guitar world for over half a century is Andrés Segovia. He was born in Linares, near Jaen, in the province of Andalucia on February 21, 1893. He began his musical career on the piano, but rapidly rejected this and other instruments for the guitar. Self-taught because of the lack of adequate instructors (he moved north too late to become a pupil of Tárrega), he gave his first public concert at the age of sixteen in Granada and then in Cordova and Seville. He continued to Madrid, where Manuel Ramírez, impressed by his playing, offered him one of his guitars for his debut at the Ateneo Theater. In 1918 he traveled to South and Central America, and in 1924 played at the Paris Conservatory before an audience that included Falla, Paul Dukas and Albert Roussel whose piece *Segovia* was given its first performance. During those early years Segovia was acutely aware of the need for a new repertoire. The basis had been laid down through the work of Tárrega, Llobet and Pujol, but during the next few years Segovia tirelessly transcribed early music himself and encouraged composers to write new works. At times he met considerable opposition as Bernard Gavoty, music critic of *Figaro*, described:

> The program on that occasion announced one work that made the violins start and tremble: Bach's *Chaconne*. Horror of horrors! The *Chaconne* for solo violin, the sacred *Chaconne*—were we going to hear—nay, endure—its profanation by a guitarist? They covered their faces, as Spanish ladies do when watching a bullfight—that is, with their fingers slightly parted so as to see through the spaces. . . . Be that as it may, the violinphiles arrived in profound gloom to witness the "murder." As for myself, my enjoyment of the performance was unclouded. . . . No painter's palette was ever richer in colors than Segovia's guitar in tones and nuances on that particular evening.[6]

In 1925 Segovia traveled to the Soviet Union and three years later he gave the first guitar recital ever held in New York. Since then he has played throughout the world and is only now abandoning long and tiring tours which involve a lot of traveling. He has also spent much time teaching at master classes at Santiago de Compostela, the Academia Musicale Chigiana in Siena and the University of California at Berkeley.

Segovia's numerous records range over the guitar repertoire from the music of the early vihuelists to the modern composers whom he directly encouraged.

Andrés Segovia receiving an honorary Doctor of Music degree from Florida State University on February 27, 1969.

ABOVE: *Mario Maccaferri in 1932. He is playing one of the classical guitars made to his design and under his supervision, by Selmer of Paris. Maccaferri (born in 1899) enjoyed a successful career as a concert guitarist in the 1920s and 30s, which was ended by an injury to his right hand in 1933.*

LEFT: *Mario Maccaferri's right-hand position. Maccaferri's use of a thumb-pick, learned from his teacher Luigi Mozzani, allowed him to develop tremolo and arpeggio techniques to a degree not normally possible. Maccaferri designed the nine-string guitar he is playing here, with three extra bass strings clear of the fingerboard, to facilitate the playing of lute music on the guitar.*

The Mexican composer Manuel Ponce was one of Segovia's great favorites and Segovia later recalled their collaboration:

> I had to tell him how to approach the technique of the instrument and although he didn't play the guitar he immediately took to the spirit of its technique and musical possibilities. But of course one can never really know what is possible on the guitar and the last piece he wrote for me, the *Sonatina Meridional*, was fine until he presented me with the last movement in Paris. It was impossible, and after so many pieces he had composed. I told him I was sorry, but I couldn't adapt it for the guitar. He said, don't be sorry, tomorrow you will have another one. And he did, and it was wonderful.[7]

To hear Segovia play is an unforgettable experience, and even past the age of eighty the tones and nuances he can produce are astonishing. Whether playing to five people or to five thousand he can draw the audience into the music so that they become totally absorbed by it:

> . . . my idea always is to reduce this enormous quantity of people to the intimacy of eight or ten persons. To obtain from the audience the quality of silence and attention that the guitar needs and then transform the whole audience into an intimate gathering.[8]

Segovia has been a great inspiration not only because of his superb playing but also because of his personality. Always supremely confident of the potential of the guitar, and of his own ability to exploit that potential, he had the courage and conviction to persuade people that the guitar was a serious instrument at a time when it was not highly regarded.

Segovia has directly influenced and taught generations of guitarists. The Venezuelan Alirio Diaz (born 1923) was Segovia's outstanding pupil at the Academia Musicale Chigiana in Siena and has since become one of the world's leading players, being particularly successful at interpreting Latin American music. The two have taught together at Siena, but although Segovia is always the *maestro* their approaches have been sufficiently different to be interesting. The Italian player Oscar Ghiglia attended some of these master classes, and explained the contrast between the two:

> Diaz wanted things to be just right. He wouldn't admit a change in fingering or a faulty position. Whereas Segovia would admit these things, he emphasized musicality. Diaz emphasized both—musicianship and technique. He demonstrated, which was inspiring; Segovia demonstrated but said little and encouraged when necessary.[9]

Segovia's fellow Spaniard Narciso Yepes (born 1927) is another player whose technique is impeccable. He was taught by Vicente Asencio, a music teacher whose belittling of the guitar spurred the young Yepes on to prove him wrong:

> He showed me on the piano what I was to play on my instrument. One day, for example, he told me to play my scales *prestissimo*, just as he did on the keyboard. "But that's impossible. . . ." "Impossible?" He banged the piano lid angrily. "Impossible? Then change your instrument if nothing can be done with that one!"
>
> At home I pondered over the problem. The main reason why I could not play scales as quickly as a pianist was that, like all other guitarists, I plucked the strings with only two fingers of the right hand, whereas a pianist uses five fingers. I shut myself away for a month, and tried in complete privacy to increase the agility of the three hitherto idle fingers of my right hand. Then I went back to Asencio and played him the scales at the speed he wanted. "Good, good," he exclaimed. But he at once demanded new subtleties, such as making a particular note stand out from a chord, and he thus constantly forced me to evolve new techniques.[10]

Yepes gave his first public concert at the age of twenty and since then he has become a player with an international reputation.

Players of international stature have come from other countries too; many of them combine playing with teaching. Karl Scheit was formerly professor of music at Vienna, a position now taken over by Konrad Ragossnig, who is also a superb lutenist. From North America Alice Artzt and Christopher Parkening are two players with established reputations, while the numbers of good South American players grow each year.

Narciso Yepes with his ten-string guitar.

John Williams and Julian Bream.

The interests of the two English players, John Williams (born 1941) and Julian Bream (born 1933) are wider-ranging than those of Segovia and his other pupils. Julian Bream's first instrument was the piano but his father, a keen musician, played the plectrum guitar in a small dance band, and it was through jazz that Bream was first introduced to the guitar. He learned by listening to the radio and by watching other players. Brought up on the sounds of Django Reinhardt and the Hot Club of France, Charlie Christian and Benny Goodman, he still retains a keen interest in jazz. His formal training at the Royal College of Music was in piano, cello and composition. There was no guitar course offered at that time and prejudice against the instrument was so great that the Principal forbade Bream to play it within the hallowed precincts of the College.

Bream's first London concert took place at the Wigmore Hall in 1951 (when he played on an old Martin guitar), an occasion which he vividly remembers. Since then he has led the life of a busy and successful musician, dividing his time between his country home in one of the most beautiful parts of England, the recording studio, and the concert hall.

Julian Bream's musical tastes are varied and his fame as a lute player is as great as his reputation as a guitarist. From his meeting with the English tenor Peter Pears came a series of concerts, specializing in Elizabethan lute songs, and later in works specially written for them by Benjamin Britten, William Walton and Hans Werner Henze. His repertoire on the guitar ranges from the Bach *Chaconne* to works by contemporary composers—in 1976 he gave the first performance of a thirty-minute piece written for him by Henze. He has done a great deal toward promoting contemporary music on the guitar, but it has to be music

165

which he can assimilate and appreciate:

> I couldn't possibly play pieces for the guitar that I wouldn't begin to understand. As a performer your job is to try and elucidate and present music to people who love music, not because they are professional musicians but because they *love* music. Your job is to make it *clear* to them, or as clear as possible. But you won't stand a dog's chance if you're not clear from the outset what the composer is trying to do.[11]

He recognizes the problems involved for both player and audience in performing contemporary music:

> ... you really have got to create as much conviction in your performance as possible ... modern music tends to use more effects. There can be abrupt changes of color, colors that may sound ugly in classical music, but have a great pertinence in contemporary music.[12]

Julian Bream's playing has a quality which sets him apart from other guitarists. Technically he is brilliant, but the listener forgets the intricacies of technique in the emotional force of his playing. His ability to communicate the essential qualities of a piece of music stems in part from his feelings for the guitar as a musical instrument:

> ... the guitar is an immensely beautiful and valuable instrument in our musical heritage in its *sounds* and its ability to evoke atmosphere .... The guitar has a uniquely evocative character in its ability to cast a spell.[13]

John Williams, born in Melbourne, Australia in 1941, began learning the guitar from his father, founder of the Spanish Guitar Centre in London. In 1952 when the family came to England, Williams was introduced to Segovia, who, immensely impressed, took him on as a pupil. On Segovia's advice he entered the Academia Musicale Chigiana at Siena and held a scholarship there for the following five years. Back in England he suffered, like Bream, from lack of a guitar course at the Royal College of Music and studied piano and musical theory from 1956 to 1959. His London debut at the Wigmore Hall took place in 1958. After the occasion Segovia wrote: "A Prince of the guitar has arrived in the musical world ... it will not be

long before his name becomes a byword in England and abroad."[14] His prediction was right; today John Williams is one of the most skilled classical guitar players with an outstandingly fluent technique. His repertoire varies from transcriptions of early lute music, through works by de Visée and Sanz, to South American composers and contemporaries such as Stephen Dodgson. His music has recently taken a non-classical turn, which is perhaps surprising for Segovia's outstanding pupil, but John Williams is particularly concerned that the classical guitar should come out of its somewhat "conservative" image.

> ... the guitar has always been basically a popular instrument. And I think that in our enthusiasm one doesn't want to forget the fact that just as much good music is done in all the forms of popular music as is done in classical music. It's different but it's just as good.[15]

In July 1969 Williams appeared with the jazz guitarist Barney Kessel at Ronnie Scott's Jazz Club in London playing works by Bach, Scarlatti, Villa-Lobos and Albéniz. He has taken part in a concert at the Albert Hall held in aid of the families of Greek political prisoners, and recorded the music of Mikis Theodorakis with the singer Maria Farandouri. He has played the guitar on several popular British television shows.

John Williams has also ventured into the electric guitar and pop fields, which presents problems for a classically trained, basically solo musician. He has found that there are considerable limitations in the transfer of a classically based finger-style playing to the electric guitar. The narrow fingerboard demands a total readjustment of approach. Few classically trained musicians understand the range of sounds and techniques supplied by the electric guitar. The temperamental adjustment is just as difficult as the technical, as he has explained:

> The technique and feeling of playing pop is instinctive in the same way that it is in the blues. ... I would never ... want to play any sort of guitar that a hundred people—not just the five or six best rock players—can do much better than I can.[16]

The search for new effects and new roles for the classical guitar continues with the work of such guitarists as

Tim Walker, Leo Brouwer and the Omega Quartet of Gilbert Biberian, all of whom play as soloists and in ensemble. Duo playing was made popular by the team of Alexandre Lagoya and Ida Presti (died 1967); since then, the number of duos has grown, and with it the amount of music written for them.

The general public has mainly heard of the few big names; yet it is the lesser known but highly talented body of musicians who sustain the general enthusiasm for the guitar.

Opportunities to learn the guitar are greater now than they ever have been. In response to demand there are good teachers in schools, colleges and guitar centers. Many of the music conservatories now offer courses, and for the talented and lucky few there are master classes held by the top guitarists. Guitar competitions are held all over the world, often giving younger players a start in their careers. But despite all the openings that exist it is still difficult to become established as a performer. One young English player, Simon Munting, combines giving concerts both in and outside London with teaching, recording, writing articles and editing music. At this early stage in his career, he regards concerts as a means of becoming known to potential pupils, music publishers, and record, television, and radio producers.

A most important figure in the guitar world, but one who usually remains anonymous to the general public, is the session musician. Being a session guitarist requires a different approach; the guitarist must be able to play with other musicians and follow a conductor's beat. He must also be able to play in any idiom — in one session he may be asked to play a piece of jazz or a classical guitar solo. He has to be able to work quickly: to go through a piece, possibly make alterations and then record it. Top session players must be completely professional and it requires a calm, versatile and experienced musician to be successful.

Roland Harker, a Londoner, plays both electric and classical guitar in session and in live performances.

Three Musicians, *by Pablo Picasso, 1921.*

Consequently he has a vast repertoire: he has played the guitar part in Mahler's *Seventh Symphony* with the New Philharmonia, was guest artist with the Fires of London in 1975 when he performed a piece called *Pantomimes* by Bruce Cole, played Webern's *Five Pieces for Chamber Group* under Daniel Barenboim and can be heard as the background music to numerous films, particularly Westerns shot in Mexico.

It has become an established pattern that the classical guitar should enjoy a period of popularity and then disappear again. But while it is difficult and dangerous to make predictions, the instrument's future looks promising. During the last forty years the guitar has become firmly established as a respectable classical instrument. Interest in it is constantly growing, many of the best contemporary composers have helped widen its repertoire and there are both more and better players, amateur and professional, than at any other time in its chequered history.

THE FLAMENCO GUITAR

Cantaor y guitarrista

THE ORIGINS AND DEVELOPMENT OF FLAMENCO

The great body of music known as *flamenco* is the product of a living tradition of great antiquity, centered in the Andalucia region of southern Spain. Over the centuries it has evolved into a highly organized, tightly structured art form which makes use of the elements of song (*cante*), dance (*baile*) and guitar playing (*toque*). There are hundreds of different types of pieces within flamenco, which have generic names such as *seguiriyas, soleares, alegrías, malagueñas, fandangos, zapateado, rondeña* etc. They are defined by characteristic melodic, rhythmic, and harmonic structures; each has a characteristic mood (and sometimes subject matter) and many are regional variants of essentially similar forms.

The study of flamenco and its history is bedeviled by difficulties and confusions. On the one hand it is a genuine folk art, an art of the people: shaped and molded by experiences of joy, hardship and suffering, it deals with the deepest emotions that lie at the roots of human experience. In this way it has a universality of appeal which operates far beyond the confines of its native Andalucia. But on the other hand, the feelings in which flamenco deals are expressed in musical forms of extraordinary complexity and sophistication which, while allowing great scope for improvisation, are governed by rules as strict as any in classical composition.

Flamenco is therefore at one and the same time a way of life, a true folk music, and a form of high art. The purely musical interest and complexity of flamenco suggest that a precise critical description of its qualities should be both possible and rewarding. However, the profound emotions generated by the best flamenco frustrate attempts at such an analysis. When a great singer, dancer or guitarist is truly inspired, emotion and conscious art are fused in a musical ecstasy. The attainment of this state is referred to by the term *duende* (literally *elf* or *spirit*), which is used almost mystically to describe the performer's immersion in his deepest feelings, and the communication of this state to the audience. The term has been over-used in the past (more frequently by intellectuals in love with the music than by *flamencos* themselves) in a way that tends to surround with mystery what is, after all, a fundamental experience common to many forms of musical expression. The late Manolo de Huelva (who was widely reverenced by those who heard him as the outstanding flamenco player of his time, and was once described by Segovia as the greatest living guitarist) so hated the term, whose use he blamed on his friend García Lorca, that he denied its validity altogether. However, in his denial he gave what is probably the best succinct definition of the awkward word: "There is no such thing as *duende*. There is, however, the transmission of feeling from guitarist to listener."[1]

Throughout its history, an appreciation of the true qualities of flamenco has been further impeded by a strong element of conservatism. Many *aficionados* look back to the flamenco of a generation or two ago for an ideal of purity and force of expression. This tendency is not just a modern one, but can be found in the works of many writers on the subject over the past century. It represents a serious misconception of the history of flamenco, which is fundamentally one of change and growth. As a living tradition, flamenco is constantly affected and modified by the circumstances of the society in which it is rooted—as indeed it must be if it is to remain a vital musical force. Paco de Lucia, the most exciting and widely popular flamenco guitarist to emerge for decades, is surely right when he says: "Flamenco has too much personality, and too much character and emotive force, to stay in the same form all its life."[2] In trying to trace its history, the better to understand what flamenco is and what it may become, we are faced with yet another serious problem. As a folk art, flamenco has very little written history, and the legends about it are often cloudy and confused. The forms, songs, musical structures, and reputations of former masters have been passed down from generation to generation, often from father to son, only by word of mouth and direct imitation. Very little of the music has ever been notated, and many players read neither notation nor *cifra* (a form of tablature). Until the advent of the record player—a device that many of the older players have distrusted—there has been no way of making a permanent record or description of the state of the art at any given moment. All too much of the history of the development of flamenco, and the art of its past masters, relies on circumstantial evidence and memories. The absence of reliable factual and musical record means that in many cases we can only be sure of what lies in actual living memory, and the further back in time we go the greater the area of conjecture.

Even the origins of the word *flamenco,* and its first use to describe the music, are unknown. There are several theories of the derivation of the word. One holds that it is a corruption of the Arab *felag mengu,* meaning "fugitive peasant," which came to be applied to the gypsies and their music following their proscription after the Moors' expulsion from Spain. Another, less probable theory holds that the word comes from a mispronunciation of *flameante* ("flaming") and was used as a description of the wild, fiery character of the music and musicians. Other theories are based on *flamenco*'s literal meaning of "flemish" and postulate a connection with the servants who came from Flanders in the coronation retinue of Charles V in the sixteenth century. These men were apparently the cause of considerable resentment and jealousy, and it has been suggested that *flamenco* became a general term of abuse which was then applied to the gypsies. But, in truth, no one is really certain.

The conjectural nature of so much of the background to the present art of flamenco is compounded by its origins as a music of the gypsy, the outcast, the poor and the oppressed. For centuries, secrecy and deliberate mystification were essential for the gypsies' survival, and secrecy is an element in the character of many *flamencos* to this day.

A variety of cultural influences present in Spain over

A gypsy guitarist and dancer. Engraved from a drawing by Gustave Doré, who visited Spain in 1862 to make a series of drawings for the travel magazine Le Tour du Monde. *His eye was particularly caught by gypsies and musicians, whom he represented with acute observation and a complete lack of sentimentality.*

FROM THE COLLECTION OF THE VICTORIA AND ALBERT MUSEUM, LONDON

the centuries have left their mark on flamenco. There are several features of the music that give hints as to its ultimate origins. One of the most important of these is the constant use of early scale systems and, in particular, of the Phrygian mode. This is one of the modal scales of the early Christian church, codified in the eighth century and built on the same fifteen sounds as the ancient Greek diatonic scale. Each was formed of the seven natural notes of the scale (and their octaves), subject to the rule that the fifths and fourths of which the scale is composed must be perfect. It is almost certain that ancient Hebraic music, going back some three thousand years, used very similar modal scales. Accordingly, the persistence of modal scales in flamenco has tempted some writers to see its origins variously in Hebraic, Greek and early Christian music. However, modal structures are fundamental to so many forms of ancient music that we can only say that flamenco numbers some of the oldest known musical forms among its ancestry. But it is worth asking why modal scales have persisted in flamenco so long after their disappearance from most other Western music.

The answer probably lies in the vital influence of Islamic culture on Spain, and in the events that followed the expulsion of the Moors. The Moorish conquest of Al-Andalus ("The Land of the Vandals," now Andalucia) took place in 711, and the Moors dominated the Iberian peninsula until their final expulsion from Granada in 1492 by King Ferdinand and Queen Isabella. By the middle of the eighth century Spain had become part of an Islamic empire which stretched as far east as the Indus, an empire which encouraged the arts and learning. In the fields of science, philosophy, literature, the visual arts and music, Spain developed into one of the great centers of Islamic civilization. The Mosque at Cordova and the Alhambra palace in Granada still stand witness to the greatness of this age. The invaders assimilated rather than destroyed; conquered nations were allowed to maintain their own religions alongside Islam, and the Arabs cultivated not only their own learning but also that of the peoples with whom they came into contact. The musical benefit for Spain was great, and the Arab influences can still be heard in flamenco.

During the reign of Abd al-Rahman II, from 822 to 852, the court of Cordova was graced by one of the greatest of all Islamic poets and musicians, Ziryab of Baghdad. Ziryab brought with him musical systems originating in India which emphasized enharmonic techniques (using intervals smaller than a semitone) and a reiterative ornamental style. Traces of these can still be heard in flamenco, alongside other Moorish characteristics such as the extensive use of melismas by the singer, who constantly ornaments a note with higher and lower *appogiaturas*. The hand movements in the flamenco *baile* are also strikingly similar to those in some forms of Indian dance.

In addition to bringing new cultural forms with them, the invaders tolerated both the Christian and Jewish religions and their associated music. Finally—and of great importance to flamenco—during the period of Islamic rule the gypsies, originating in India, reached and were allowed to settle in Spain.

The cultural tolerance practiced by the Moors did not survive their leaving. Gypsies have rarely been accepted by their host societies, and Spain proved no exception. Inspired by their success against the Moors, the Spanish authorities set out with a crusading fervor to purge the country of those it considered its dissidents and undesirables—the gypsies and the Jews. The first laws against the gypsies were passed in 1499, heralding centuries of persecution. The traveling way of life was outlawed; those without a settled habitation became liable to punishment by transportation, the galleys, or death. The gypsies were banned, at one time or another, from their traditional occupations of smithing, horse dealing, sheep shearing and fortune telling. In the seventeenth and eighteenth centuries, even their language (*caló*) was made illegal. Persecution bred fear and suspicion; the gypsies withdrew from the cities to live in the surrounding hills and caves. Their isolation from society enforced on them a separate artistic development. Their *cante gitano* (gypsy song), which is one of the two principal elements of flamenco, retained many strong Eastern and Moorish characteristics unaffected by the mainstream of European musical influences.

Flamenco was eventually created by the fusion of the *cante gitano* with Andalucian folk music. Our first descriptions of the latter come from travelers to Spain in the late eighteenth century. In these travelers' books we read of dances such as the *fandangos*, performed to an accompaniment of various instruments, most importantly the guitar.

It was also in the late eighteenth century that the official attitude toward the gypsies began to ease. In 1780 comes the first mention by name of a gypsy singer, El Tío Luis el de la Juliana, from Jerez de la Frontera. But the gypsies were still highly secretive about their music, which was usually performed in private and almost never heard by outsiders. One of the first explicit descriptions of gypsy

A Spanish folk dance, accompanied on the guitar. This oil sketch, probably dating from the 1770s, has been attributed to Francisco Goya.

some resemblance to Malbrun (Malbrouk) and as he strummed, repeating at intervals the gypsy modification of the song.[3]

Here we can detect the basic elements of modern flamenco— the *cante* and *baile*, the percussive finger snapping (*pitos*), and the accompanying guitar.

The Russian composer Mikhail Ivanovich Glinka (1804–57) was another traveler fascinated by the music of Spain; he tells how, in Seville:

> The winter of 1846–7 was a pleasant one for us; we visited the dance shows of Felix's and Miguel's, where during the dances the best national singers would burst out in the Eastern manner, while the dancers would continue their intricate steps, so that it seemed we were hearing three different rhythms, that is, the singing went on by itself, the guitar separately, while the dancer would clap her hands and stamp her foot as though entirely apart from the music. The eminent although aging national singer Planeta visited us and sang for us.[4]

El Planeta (*c.* 1785–1860), who came from Triana, was renowned as the "King of the *Polo*," a gypsy *cante* which survives in flamenco today.

Glinka was particularly struck by the Eastern sound of the music, a legacy of the Moorish occupation. Another traveler of the 1840s noticed the same characteristics in the *caña* (a type of gypsy flamenco song which is still performed):

> During the lucid intervals between the ballet and the brandy, La Caña, the true Arabic *gaunia*, the song, is administered as a soother by some hirsute artiste, without frills, studs, diamonds or kid gloves, whose staves, sad and melancholy, always begin and end with an *ay!* a high pitched sigh, or cry. These Moorish melodies, relics of auld lang syne, are best preserved in the hill-built villages near Ronda, where there are no roads for the members of Queen Christina's *Conservatorio Napolitano.* . . .[5]

During the period 1800 to 1860 there are mentions in travel books of a number of recognizable flamenco forms, including the *fandangos, malagueñas, peteneras* and *rondeña* of the *cante andaluz,* and the *polo* and *caña* of the *cante*

music is to be found in the works of the English writer George Borrow. Borrow had extensive experience of the gypsy life before he went to Spain; he had traveled the roads of the British Isles with the gypsies and spoke their languages. In Spain too he was accepted, and in *The Zincali* (published in 1841) he tells of a wild wedding celebration:

> The men sprang high into the air, neighed, brayed and crowed; whilst the *gitanas* snapped their fingers in their own fashion, louder than castanets, distorting their forms into all kinds of obscene attitudes and uttering words to repeat which were an abomination. In a corner of the apartment the while Sebastianillo, a convict gypsy from Melilla strumming the guitar most forcibly and producing demoniacal sounds which had

Gypsies dancing the zorongo *in a patio in Seville, 1862. Engraved from a drawing by Gustave Doré. Doré's sympathies are obviously more with the gypsies than with the smart and supercilious party they have been hired to entertain. The* zorongo *is still a part of modern flamenco.*

An improvised seguidilla. *Engraved from a drawing by Gustave Doré, 1862.*

gitano. Although there is little firm evidence, most modern writers agree that the profoundly emotional *jondo** forms of the *cante gitano* were established by this time, but were kept secret. It is widely held that the *cante gitano* was almost invariably sung without accompaniment, but Borrow's evidence proves that the guitar was used at least sometimes by the gypsies. The Andalucian *cante* was more openly and widely performed; its folk origins were, though humble, quite respectable. Andalucian folk songs had in the past been accompanied by a considerable variety of instruments, including the bandurria, violin and tambourine, but now the guitar predominated. Exactly how the gypsy and Andalucian *cantes* were related, and how much interchange there was between the two at this date, remains a matter for conjecture.

Flamenco first became a public, performing art in the second half of the nineteenth century, with the emergence of the *café cantante.* The first *café cantante* opened in Seville in 1842, and attracted very little attention. But by the 1860s similar cafés were established not only in the major cities of Andalucia—Seville, Granada, Cadiz and Jerez—but as far afield as Madrid, and beyond. The typical *café cantante* consisted of a large room lit by oil or paraffin lamps. At one end would be a small stage for the performers, perhaps with a backdrop of paintings of typical Andalucian scenes and landscapes. The rest of the room would be crammed with small tables, which filled up early as the customers crowded in to get the best seats. Seated in

the flickering, smoky half-light, an audience of *aficionados* from all classes and occupations watched the performance. They could expect to be entertained by a group comprising perhaps one or two singers, three or four female and two male dancers, accompanied by two guitarists. The second half of the nineteenth century was one of the great ages of flamenco performance, and the finest performance was often to be heard in the *café cantante.*

In addition to bringing flamenco to a wider public, the *cafés* also served to draw together the Andalucian and *gitano* traditions. Gypsy singers, who were able at last to make a living by the public practice of their art, tended to specialize in the deeply emotional forms of the *seguiriyas, soleares* and *martinetes,* but also dominated the performance of the bright and lively *bulerías* and *tangos.* Their raw, earthy, unadorned style and harsh voices contrasted with the cooler, smoother, virtuoso style of the non-gypsies who specialized in the Andalucian *cantes* such as the *malagueñas, verdiales, granadinas* and *tarantas.* Before the era of the *cafés,* many artists were expert in only one or two forms, the *cantes* of their native regions. But the intense competition in the *cafés,* and the wide contact between performers, led to the appearance of singers who were masters of many different forms from both the *cante gitano* and the *cante andaluz.* Silverio Franconetti (*c.* 1825–93), who had his own *café* in the calle Rosario in Seville, made a huge reputation and large sums of money from his ability to sing a wide variety of forms. Although

* *Jondo* is an Andalucian dialect variant of *hondo* (*deep*), and is used to indicate the emotional and spiritual depth of flamenco music.

Scene in a café cantante *in Madrid. A painting by Alfredo Palmero.*

not himself a gypsy, he learned the *cante gitano* thoroughly, and his great success prompted other singers to try to follow his example by extending their repertoires.

So the demands of the *café cantante* developed the skills and range of the singers, and brought together the *cante gitano* and *cante andaluz*. They also expanded the role of the guitar, which became tremendously popular in the *cafés*. Each would employ a regular first and second guitarist, who had to know how to accompany many different forms of song and dance, and be able to follow the styles of different singers with sympathy and flexibility. While the singer remained the leading figure, the guitarist came to take a less subservient part as time went on. Good guitarists were in great demand, the crowds loved them and competition was fierce. In their efforts to outdo each other the players introduced new techniques, and sometimes even resorted to tricks and outrageous acts of showmanship such as playing with a glove on one hand or with the guitar held above their heads. Such absurdities aside, the general level of technical skill increased, and the *cafés* fostered a series of fine guitarists culminating in Ramón Montoya (1880–1949), who was later to be the founder of the modern style of flamenco solo guitar (see page 192).

The *cafés cantantes'* greatest days were over by the turn of the century, and by the 1910s they were in serious decline. The years up to the start of the Spanish Civil War in 1936 were to be the years of the theatrical presentation of flamenco, of the "Opera Flamenca" and "Flamenco Ballet." Theater performances varied from straightforward song recitals to exhibitions which were little more than variety acts with a vaguely flamenco flavor. Public taste turned toward a smoother type of voice, as typified by Antonio Chacón (1865–1929), toward the lighter Andalucian *cantes* (the *fandanguillos* in particular), and away from the harshly emotional gypsy *cante* exemplified by Manuel Torre (1879–1933), the great master of the *seguiriyas*.

Antonio Chacón has been blamed for popularizing a lighter style of performance and so contributing, albeit indirectly, to the trivialization of the art at this time. Chacón, however, was a great singer with a knowledge of all branches of the *cante*. Though not himself a gypsy, and the most famous master of the Andalucian forms, he had learned the *cante gitano* to become an all-round performer

in the tradition of Silverio Franconetti. Chacón suffered from the change of public taste, and late in his career expressed his resentment at the singers who pandered to it: "Variety-show flamencos, the youngsters that have come up, have killed serious *cante*. They don't know how to listen."[6] But the public was avid in its demands, and flamenco companies with their "folkloric" songs and "balletic" dances trundled their way around the theaters of Spain, Europe and the Americas.

The plight of the *cante* caused great concern to the small group of intellectuals who loved the art. In 1922 the composer Manuel de Falla was so desperately worried by the state of the *cante jondo*, which he believed to be on the point of extinction, that he became the moving spirit in organizing a competition which he hoped would re-establish the art in its primitive purity. With the help of a group of like-minded *aficionados*, which included the poet Lorca and the painter Ignacio Zuloaga, he organized a two-day "Primer Concurso de Cante Jondo," held in Granada in June of 1922. The contest was divided into three sections. The first was for the *seguiriyas*, which Falla held to be the fountainhead of all true flamenco; the second was for the *serranas*, *polos*, *cañas* and *soleares*; and the final category was for the forms sung *a palo seco*, without guitar, the *martinetes*, *carceleras*, *tonas*, *livianas* and *saetas*. In accordance with Falla's theories of the *cante* as an art of the people which had been perverted by professional performance, only amateur competitors were allowed. It was hoped that the contest would be the first of many, and would lead to schools of flamenco throughout Andalucia in which the old men would hand on the traditions to succeeding generations.

The idea of a competition in an "art of the people," designed to produce a kind of academy for its preservation, would seem to be inherently self-contradictory. In the event, it was a disaster. Most of the amateurs proved lamentably ignorant, and the prize for the *seguiriyas* was not awarded. Falla was so disillusioned that he abandoned the *cante* to its fate, and left Andalucia for good.

As it turned out, flamenco's artistic and intellectual well-wishers had less to worry about than they thought. The leading professional singers of the time, Chacón, Torre and the young Pastora Pavón ("La Niña de los Peines"), were some of the greatest in flamenco history.

A flamenco performance in about 1930, with the dancer "La Macarrona," the most renowned interpreter of the baile. *The young guitarist on the left of the photograph is Niño Ricardo, who was destined to become one of the greatest performers in the history of flamenco; standing behind him is Curro de la Jeroma, who was unique in being equally brilliant as a singer, dancer and guitarist.*

There was no real shortage of true artists in the dance either, and such fine guitarists as Javier Molina, Ramón Montoya, Manolo de Huelva, and Perico el del Lunar were all active. The true *cante jondo* was not in fashion with the wider public, but it survived in a few cafés and inns, and in the homes of the performers and their friends.

Even the despised theatrical flamenco shows did some good. They provided a means of support for artists who would otherwise have been hard put to keep going, and the

efforts of the touring companies spread the interest in flamenco far beyond Spain. Some of the traveling shows, particularly those to South America, encountered rhythmic and formal influences which actually remained to enrich flamenco after the theatrical dross had fallen away.

Some of the most successful foreign tours were those arranged by the dancer "La Argentinita" (1900–45), born in Buenos Aires but resident in Spain from an early age, whose company caused a sensation on its first visit to the United States. In 1933 she took to New York a show called *Las Calles de Cádiz*, which was considered to be the high spot of theatrical flamenco. In her effort to present some authentic flamenco, and portray the life of the *barrio* Santa María in Cádiz, she gathered together many notable performers. She even persuaded the guitarist Manolo de Huelva, a purist among purists, to make his only appearance in a theater (although he hated it and walked out before the end of the engagement). La Argentinita's efforts in New York were so well received that she was honored by a statue outside the Metropolitan Opera House alongside Pavlova and Caruso.

The years that Carmen Amaya (1913–63) spent in Buenos Aires, from 1929 to 1940, were important for more than her company's success and the foundation of her personal fortune: the influence of Latin America was expressed particularly through her performance of the *colombianas,* a form that she and the guitarist Sabicas made widely popular.

With the movement of flamenco into the theater, and the growing popularity of classical guitar concerts, it must have seemed inevitable that sooner or later the flamenco guitar should make its solo debut on the concert platform. This event was long delayed by the feeling of most players that the guitar's role in flamenco was one of accompaniment, but in Paris in July 1936 a series of concerts, recitals and records by Ramón Montoya established the guitar solo as a legitimate form.

War in Europe and the aftermath of civil war in Spain made the 1940s an unpropitious decade for flamenco, with little opportunity for paid performance outside the Americas. Thus in 1942 Carmen Amaya was appearing in the scarcely flamenco atmosphere of Broadway revue, and, in 1944, filming in Hollywood. The art of *cante jondo* began to seem beyond resurrection.

However, a concern for true flamenco began to reappear in the 1950s, bringing with it new (if limited) opportunities for serious performance. Festivals in Cordova, Jerez and Malaga in the late fifties and early sixties stimulated public interest and encouraged a new generation of artists. The long-playing record also made an important contribution to the preservation and revival of flamenco. In the early 1950s, the guitarist Perico el del Lunar was approached by recording interests and asked to make an anthology of the old *cantes.* At first he was dubious: "I thought we would put the people to sleep, and told the record people so."[7] But he agreed to go ahead.

Perico was the ideal man for the job. He had learned the guitar with Javier Molina, and from his accompaniment of all the great singers of his lifetime, including Antonio Chacón and Manuel Torre, had gained an encyclopedic knowledge. For the records he selected a number of the finest living singers, including Rafael Romero and El Niño de Almaden, and those *cantes* which they had forgotten, or never known, he taught them himself. The resulting three-volume *Anthology of Cante Flamenco* saved some forms from oblivion, and awakened fresh interest in others. The success of the venture encouraged the issue of records by other great masters such as Antonio Mairena and La Niña de los Peines, and slowly the *cante jondo* began to win back lost ground. In the same period the guitar records of Sabicas and, above all, Manuel Serrapí ("El Niño Ricardo") inspired a fresh generation of players.

Foreign interest in flamenco continued to grow, to the point where the gypsy guitarist Roman el Granaino could say: "The foreign public appreciated the true flamenco more than the Spanish public. It is far more rewarding both artistically and monetarily to perform outside Spain. Except for the non-flamenco atmosphere of course. . . ."[8] But the scope for foreign tours was obviously limited and it remained difficult for flamenco performers to find suitable work in Spain. The ideal venue for flamenco remained the private *fiesta,* organized and paid for by some rich *aficionado,* with a congenial group of fellow performers, a small and knowledgeable audience, unlimited drink, and a fee at the end. As paying alternatives there was little beside the *tablao flamenco* (flamenco nightclub) or occasional tour.

Recent changes in flamenco are still too close to us for an easy assessment of their outcome. The Spanish tourist boom in the last fifteen years has brought new influences and new wealth to the country. Attitudes are rapidly changing as the main tide of European popular and consumer culture flows into the country. These changes are bound to have an effect on the circumstances, performance and musical style of flamenco.

Tourists to Spain have seized on the notion of flamenco as typical of Spanish "local color." In response to this demand a crop of *tablaos flamencos* has sprung up in the chief cities and along the tourist coasts. What of their effect? In the opinion of the guitarist Juan Martín:

> Personally, I think the *tablaos flamencos* are a dreadful bore. You can't produce flamenco by pressing a button. And this is what they expect of these artists, who are good artists. But it is against the whole nature of

The fair at Seville, as pictured in El Museo Universal *in 1869. The great Easter fair, at which parties rent booths or* casetas *for the duration, remains a great occasion both for the* sevillanas *(the folk dance which takes its name from the city) and for the performance of true flamenco.*

flamenco, performing at a set hour every night. So the artists are very disciplined, and they do incredible *palmas* [rhythmic hand-clapping], and it impresses the tourist public. There are *tablaos flamencos* with good artists, but it's very much a money-making thing. You *can* get an inspired night in a *tablao flamenco*, but you can imagine, to sit there seven nights a week, playing a set routine. . . .[9]

What are the alternatives? Flamenco still survives in its traditional habitats in Andalucia: the fairs and festivals, the private *fiestas* and celebrations. Such events necessarily reach only a fraction of those interested in flamenco, so once again flamenco has taken to the halls. But the flamenco now appearing on the concert platform and in the theaters is very different from the old Spanish ballet and "Opera Flamenca." Audiences everywhere increasingly demand purity of style and material from the group—even if they don't always know what they mean by "purity." Foreign audiences are becoming particularly concerned to get "the real thing." The variety turns and story-telling shows of the past have almost completely been replaced by an unadorned presentation of the chief *cantes, bailes* and *toques.* There has been an astounding increase in popularity of solo guitar concerts, which are even more popular abroad than in Spain.

Many guitarists have toured all over the world, going as far afield as South Africa and Japan, and several have settled in the United States and England, attracted both by the wider possibilities of concert performance and, in some cases, by the possibility of contact with other types of music. The influence of phonograph records has also increased enormously, though one could wish that the British and American companies were more willing to issue records other than guitar solos by a handful of the better-known players.

In response to such changes of circumstance, two main tendencies within flamenco are detectable. On the one hand there are the traditionalists who cling to well-established styles, and who aim for a certain elemental simplicity in the search for *duende* and a *jondo* expression. Alternatively there is the "modern" school of performers, grouped around the younger stars. In response to the increased internationalization of Spanish life, and of the appeal of flamenco, they are starting to introduce fresh elements to modernize the art without losing its essence. Today we are hearing the introduction of harmonies and chord sequences, some of them influenced by jazz and Latin American music, which would have been unthinkable ten years ago.

Each of these tendencies has its advantages and its dangers. If flamenco does not renew and modernize itself, it runs the risk of dying by internal ossification and by

The guitarist Paco Peña on stage with his group "Flamenco Puro."

Paco de Lucía in the recording studio.

divorce from the life and interests of its audience. But how many innovations of that type can be made without losing the fundamentally Moorish sound of the music, and its ability to express deep and complex feeling? On the evidence of the past, flamenco is a hardy survivor, capable of surviving as long as there exist performers who understand its qualities and feel the need to express themselves through its forms—and as long as there is an audience, however small, which is prepared to listen. It can be argued that there has been some bastardization and trivialization of the art for the tastes of a keen but largely ignorant public. It is also true, however, that a new generation of performers is maturing, performers who combine a deep knowledge of the tradition with a concern for new possibilities, and they are reaching an audience which is world-wide. There are signs that flamenco may be growing into an international art, without losing its Spanish roots. Whatever the outcome, the possibilities are exciting.

THE MODERN FLAMENCO GUITAR

The modern flamenco guitar is first cousin to the modern classical guitar. The two have a common ancestry, and are handbuilt by essentially the same methods. The flamenco guitar, however, has a particularly distinctive sound and playing action of its own, achieved by the use of different timbers for the body and subtly different dimensions and proportions.

Like the true classical guitar, the flamenco guitar is an instrument of comparatively recent invention. In the guitars of late eighteenth-century Spain, the common forebears of both types, we find no division between "classical" and "flamenco" models. These instruments had six courses tuned by pegs, pine tables (with rudimentary fan strutting in some cases), and narrow bodies constructed from either the indigenous Spanish cypress or imported Brazilian rosewood. From the instruments that survive, no essential design differences can be discerned between the cypress- and rosewood-bodied models. The pictorial, written and musical evidence of the period shows the same basic pattern of six-course instrument being used by all classes for all purposes, from the peasant's accompaniment to folk song and dance to the elegant young ladies' drawing room entertainment. In essence, these are *Spanish* guitars, without further division or classification — save that of price, to match the pocket of the buyer.

Much has been written about the development by Antonio de Torres Jurado of the modern pattern of classical guitar, with its full body made of rosewood, fan-strutted top and mechanical tuning machines. What has not been so widely discussed is the emergence of the flamenco guitar as we know it today. Available evidence suggests that Torres should be credited with the development and stabilization of the flamenco guitar in the 1850s, at the same period and in the same way as he defined the classical type.

Flamenco guitar by Antonio de Torres, 1867.

There are several reasons why we might expect to see the flamenco guitar's emergence as a separate instrument at this time. The date corresponds with the emergence of flamenco as a popular musical form, with the establishment of the *cafés cantantes* (see page 174). With the demand for the guitar as the essential accompanying instrument for flamenco, and the income from performance to pay for it, it is not surprising to find the appearance of a type of instrument specially adapted to flamenco's needs. Equally, there was no one better equipped than Torres to make such an instrument.

An examination of an early flamenco guitar, made by Torres in 1867, reveals the basic characteristics of the type. The six strings are tuned by wooden pegs, which are preferred to machines, and the body is a little smaller than the equivalent classical model. The two most important characteristics of the typical flamenco guitar, however, are the use of Spanish cypress for the back and sides, and the extreme lightness of the construction. The physical properties of cypress, an attractive blond wood, allow it to be worked considerably thinner than rosewood without danger of distorting or cracking. The use of very thin, light cypress sides and backs helps to give the flamenco guitar its distinctive sound, and is a conditioning factor in several of the other special constructional features. In keeping with the overall aim of lightness and vibrancy, the whole internal construction is simpler than on the classical model. Torres, for example, used a system of only five fan struts on his flamenco guitars in place of the seven usually found in his rosewood guitars. The peg head has also persisted for the sake of overall weight and balance, to match the lightweight body. For the same reason Torres even went to the length of using rosewood for the fingerboards of his flamenco guitars, in place of the more durable but heavier ebony.[1] The action of the flamenco guitar is set lower than that of the classical, with the strings closer to the frets for rapid fingering, and the fingerboard itself is usually slightly narrower. Finally, the table carries the distinctive *golpeador* or tap plate to protect it against the drumming and slapping of the guitarist's fingers, which forms an essential part of flamenco technique.

It has been suggested that many of the characteristics of the flamenco guitar initially arose from the need for an inexpensive instrument. There is an element of truth in this argument: flamenco guitarists have not, traditionally, been rich men. Cypress is much cheaper in Spain than imported rosewood, pegs cost less than tuning machines, and in consequence a luthier's flamenco guitars cost less than his equivalent classical models. But economics are only part of the story. Flamenco is a complex music which places unique demands on the guitar's performance. It is quite possible to explain and justify every one of the flamenco guitar's special features as a response to the demands of flamenco music.

The flamenco guitar evolved as an accompanying instrument to the *cante* and *baile*. It had, therefore, to be able to provide a driving rhythmic beat, a harmonizing background to the voice, and linking melodic passages in the form of *falsetas*. To do this it must combine, in Manuel Reyes' phrase, "potency and sweetness," but above all it must be capable of pushing out a strong percussive beat which will not be swamped by either the harsh voice of the singer, or by clapping hands and drumming feet. The light, vibrant body of the flamenco guitar is ideally suited to this purpose, imparting a harsher, more brilliant sound than the classical, with emphasized treble frequencies and a shorter sustain. Where the sound of the classical guitar is round and mellow, the flamenco is crisp and percussive. The harsher sound matches ideally the rough-edged voice which is so typical of the flamenco *cantaor*, and the shorter sustain helps to maintain a clarity and brilliance of sound in passages built on the rapid succession of either chords or single notes. Even the low action of the strings assists the percussive element.

Over the last century and a quarter, the basic flamenco guitar has undergone few modifications, although it has, like the classical, increased a little in size. Several variations on the basic pattern have been tried, however. During the latter part of the nineteenth century, it was quite common to find flamenco guitars made with maple rather than cypress bodies. Vicente Arias (*c.* 1840s–1912) was particularly fond of this type of guitar, and made some very beautiful instruments. Maple can, like cypress, be worked very thin, and produces a sound which is a little fuller without being as mellow as that of the rosewood-bodied classical guitar. Maple continued to be used for flamenco guitars up until the Spanish Civil War, but has now gone out of favor.

During the last fifty years, an increasing proportion of flamenco guitars have been made with tuning machines instead of the traditional pegs. Although the balance is not quite as good, and the peg head is a perfect aesthetic complement to the flamenco guitar, machines tend to be easier to tune and hold their tuning better. There is some controversy as to whether the use of machines affects the sound of the guitar. Guitarists who swear by pegs believe that machines interfere slightly with the overall vibrancy of the instrument, but most players are happy to use either type of tuning mechanism.

The most significant recent introduction has been the hybrid "concert flamenco" guitar, which combines the flamenco fingerboard and *golpeador* with the classical rosewood body and machine tuning. Naturally, the alliance of a flamenco action to a classical body requires delicate adjustments to the strutting and thicknessing of the table. The "concert flamenco" guitar's tone is consequently almost exactly halfway between that of the true flamenco and the true classical guitar, not as harsh as the one nor as sweet as the other. The demand for such a guitar has arisen from some of the specialists in concert performance of solo flamenco guitar, who feel the need for an instrument with the traditional fast action but want a slightly warmer, bigger sound. This is the type of instrument favored at present by Spain's leading young players, Paco de Lucia and Manolo Sanlúcar.

The technicalities of the construction of a flamenco guitar may be very slightly simpler than those of the classical—in Spain, the apprentice's first guitar is traditionally a flamenco model—but achieving the true flamenco sound is not easy. It is noticeable that, while some of the best classical guitars are now made by luthiers in other countries, the Spanish retain absolute preeminence in the construction of the flamenco model. Even within Spain, while most of the leading makers build both types, the construction of the flamenco guitar is dominated by a small number of *guitarreros*. This has been the case since the days of Torres. It seems that a luthier needs a certain feeling for the sound and spirit of flamenco to be able to build its guitars.

Most of the great flamenco guitar builders of the past have been equally famous for their classical guitars. Of the early luthiers, Torres himself, Arias, and Manuel Ramírez (c. 1866–1916) excelled at both forms. During the first half of this century, before the extraordinary post-war growth in the popularity of the classical guitar, the flamenco guitar provided the Spanish luthier's main livelihood, and three builders stand out above all others.

Santos Hernández (1873–1942) has undoubtedly been the most famous maker of flamenco guitars this century. He was a pupil of Manuel Ramírez, and continued to work for Ramírez's widow for some years after her husband's death. In the 1920s Santos Hernández set up on his own in Madrid; his shop at Aduana 27 became a gathering place for the leading performers of the day, including Ramón Montoya and Antonio Chacón, and was known as the "Parnassus of the Guitar." Santos' instruments were eagerly sought by the best flamenco guitarists during his lifetime. Even now, more than thirty years after his death, they are in great demand and fetch enormous prices, not as museum pieces but as playing instruments.

Santos' one contemporary rival as a maker of flamenco guitars was Domingo Esteso (1882–1937), another protégé of Manuel Ramírez. Esteso's guitars have a different character, mellow and sweet without being flabby, and were well suited to the apparently simple but deeply emotional style of players such as Perico el del Lunar.

The third almost legendary constructor of flamenco guitars in this century was Marcelo Barbero (1904–55), who learned his craft with José Ramírez II. Barbero was employed for a time by Santos Hernández's widow. To the benefit of his own work, this gave him the opportunity to examine and repair a number of the old master's instruments. By the time of his death in 1955, Barbero had built guitars for most of the leading guitarists, and passed on invaluable advice to Manuel Reyes of Cordova, perhaps the best known of today's makers of flamenco guitars.

Since the war, the demand for classical guitars has completely outstripped that for flamenco. There remain nevertheless a few makers who specialize in the flamenco guitar, and who have particularly high reputations among professional guitarists. Manuel Reyes is not alone in preferring the flamenco form. He is rivaled by the Conde brothers in Madrid (who maintain the workshop of their uncle Domingo Esteso), and the young Gerundino Fernández in Almería. These craftsmen are well able to provide instruments which do full justice to the exceptionally high standard of virtuosity prevalent among today's leading players.

Flamenco guitar by Antonio de Torres
SEVILLE, 1860.
From the collection of Malcolm Weller.

Overall length: 97cm
Scale length: 65cm
Body length: 46.5cm
Body width: upper bout 24.7cm
            waist 20.6cm
            lower bout 33cm
Body depth: increasing from 8.5 to 9.2cm

This instrument shows the perfection which the flamenco guitar reached very early in its existence. It is an outstanding guitar even among Torres' remarkable *oeuvre*.

Aesthetically, it is one of the most perfect guitars ever made. The purity and balance of the proportions of the body, neck and head are exceptionally beautiful. Here we can see that the beauty of the guitar lies more in the perfection of its basic form than in its decoration. The complete lack of adornment (Torres has used the simplest possible sound-hole decoration, of alternating dark and light wood bands), enhances its visual appeal.

The construction shows several features typical of Torres' flamenco guitars. The body, which has cypress sides and a four-piece cypress back, is narrower than his classical guitars of the same epoch. The lightness of the construction is exceptional, and the table is strutted with only five fans as opposed to the seven we would expect on a classical model. In these characteristics we can see that Torres had very clear ideas about the essential differences between the classical and flamenco instruments, and about the constructional methods appropriate to each.

The table of this guitar has warped slightly, with the result that a high saddle has had to be inserted to correct the playing

action. This must have had an effect on the guitar's tone, but it is otherwise in exceptional condition for an instrument of its age, and still performs well. Although its sound is not as robust and attacking as that of a modern instrument, it is firm, dignified and very well balanced. The tone is rich and varied, tender without being lush, and incisive without being harsh. In fact, the sound of the guitar fulfills the promise of its looks.

Flamenco guitar by Vicente Arias
CIUDAD REAL, 1878.
From the collection of Bill Bogel.

Overall length: 95cm
Scale length: 65cm
Body length: 45.8cm
Body width: upper bout 24cm
            waist 20cm
            lower bout 33cm
Body depth: increasing from 9 to 9.6cm

In the flamenco as in the classical guitar, Vicente Arias was the only luthier of the nineteenth century to rival Torres in the elegance and constructional quality of his instruments.

By contrast to Torres' guitars, Arias' instruments have an extreme lightness and delicacy which gives them a slight feeling of softness. This quality is difficult to describe, but it is strongly apparent on actually handling one of the instruments. We feel that it is the

Flamenco guitar by Vicente Arias
CIUDAD REAL, 1889.
From the José Ramírez collection.

Overall length: 95cm
Scale length: 63.6cm
Body length: 45.8cm

Body width: upper bout 25cm
            waist 20.2cm
            lower bout 33.2cm
Body depth: increasing from 8.2 to 8.8cm

slightly greater robustness and firmness of Torres' work which gives his guitars that last degree of perfection which is not found in those by Arias.

This particular instrument has a fine spruce table, with six very light fan struts, and back and sides of maple. As one would expect from a guitar of this period and construction, it is not very forceful, and has a less incisive sound than the Torres guitar of 1860. Aggressive playing, in fact, kills its qualities. If, however, it is played simply and cleanly (after the fashion of much early flamenco guitar technique) it responds well.

Several comparisons can be drawn between this cypress-bodied guitar and both the maple-bodied guitar of 1878 by the same maker and the Torres guitar of 1860. Here Arias has gone to the absolute extreme in his search for lightness and vibrancy. He has followed Torres in reducing the number of fan struts—down to only four, in this case. Naturally this weakens the construction. To compensate, Arias has shortened the scale length to reduce string tension and stress on the table. This has enabled him to keep a fairly full body shape with a full lower bout.

It is worth remarking here that it is almost impossible to find two guitars by either Torres or Arias which have exactly the same body shape. These early makers were constantly experimenting and they varied their guitars much more than do modern luthiers. This does not necessarily imply that they knew less, but is in part a reflection of their dedication to their craft and an indication that they were under less commercial pressure to produce a steady stream of instruments.

This guitar is as beautifully put together as all Arias' instruments. The head has a triple arch somewhat similar to Torres' guitars, and the heel is much smaller and more reminiscent of those on the earlier Spanish six-course guitars.

Flamenco guitar by José Ramírez
MADRID, 1927.
From the José Ramírez collection.

Overall length: 98cm
Scale length: 65cm
Body length: 48cm
Body width: upper bout 27.8cm
            waist 24cm
            lower bout 37cm
Body depth: increasing from 8.2 to 9cm

On the death of José Ramírez I in 1923, the direction of the family firm was taken over by his son José II. José II was successful in building up the business, and his flamenco guitars of the 1920s and 1930s were held in high regard by many players.

The flamenco guitar had become much larger by the 1920s. This guitar has a wide body even by today's standards and is about half a centimeter wider than most other instruments of the 1920s. At this date, though, the body of the flamenco guitar was still noticeably shallower than that of the classical: the recent trend has been toward an increase in depth of the box.

The table carries eight fairly heavy fan

struts. It has been heavily repaired, and the marks on the interior suggest that there were originally nine fans.

The fingerboard is made of rosewood. Since this is a heavy-bodied guitar, there can be no suggestion that rosewood was preferred to ebony for the sake of balance. In this case the consideration would have been solely one of cost.

In comparison with the guitars of similar date by Santos Hernández and Domingo Esteso, this is rather a coarse instrument, one of power rather than refinement. One would expect it to have given good service in a *cuadro*.

Flamenco guitars by Santos Hernández
MADRID, 1930.
The guitar whose measurements are given is the one on the left.
From the José Ramírez collection.

Overall length: 99cm
Scale length: 65cm
Body length: 48.3cm
Body width: upper bout 27.5cm
            waist 23.5cm
            lower bout 36.5cm
Body depth: increasing from 8.8 to 9.2cm

Santos Hernández's flamenco guitars are so prized that the sight of three together is enough to make any *aficionado*'s mouth water! The three instruments were all made in different years: that on the left (whose label we reproduce) is dated 1930, that on the right 1927. The guitar in the center was made some years earlier while Santos was employed by Manuel Ramírez's widow. The label of this guitar reads: "Fabrica de Violones y Guitarras/de la/Viuda de Manuel Ramírez/ Arlaban 8," and is stamped with the initials

"S.H." Forgeries of Santos Hernández's guitars have been made in the past, a practice encouraged by the widespread belief that he did not sign his instruments. It should be noted, however, that all three of these guitars carry his signatures. Those on the left and in the center are signed on the underside of the table, that on the right carries a signature on the label.

The guitars on left and right are strutted with seven very broad flat fan bars in the lower bout, a feature common to Santos' mature instruments. The one in the center also has seven struts, but these are lighter and narrower. In all of the guitars, the transverse bar immediately below the soundhole runs straight across instead of being set on the diagonal, as was often the case on Santos' classical model.

Santos Hernández's guitars were the automatic first choice of many of the leading players of his day, including both Ramón Montoya and Niño Ricardo. The guitar whose measurements we give is an instrument of firmness, with great reserves of power. It has a slighter harder action than many flamenco guitars and is capable of a really biting attack. At the same time, the top string has a surprisingly lyrical capability.

Flamenco guitar by Domingo Esteso
MADRID, 1934.
Owned by Juan Martín.

Overall length: 98cm
Scale length: 65.5cm
Body length: 49cm
Body width: upper bout 27.2cm
      waist 24cm
      lower bout 37cm
Body depth: increasing from 9.4 to 9.6cm

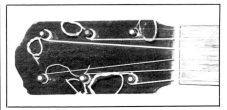

Although this is a large guitar with an unusually deep box, it is exceptionally lightly built for a modern flamenco guitar. Such weight reduction was made possible largely by the quality of timber: both the spruce of the table and the cypress of the body are excellent, and this has allowed the luthier to work them thinner than is often possible. The table is braced with seven light fan struts.

Domingo Esteso's flamenco guitars have a character quite different from those of his contemporary rival Santos Hernández, being generally more mellow. The owner of this example says of it: "It has a very big full sound, and amazing vibrato as well. If you play high up, it has a vibrato that modern flamenco guitars don't have. It is a sound which was very well suited to some of the older players such as Perico el del Lunar."

Flamenco guitar by Marcelo Barbero Sr.
MADRID, 1954.
From the collection of Malcolm Weller.

Overall length: 99cm
Scale length: 65.5cm
Body length: 48.2cm
Body width: upper bout 28cm
      waist 24.2cm
      lower bout 36.8cm
Body depth: increasing from 8.7 to 9.5cm

Although Marcelo Barbero trained under José Ramírez II, and was later influenced by Santos Hernández, his guitars are highly individual in their qualities. Their appearance is characterized by neatness and restraint, which is apparent in the shape of the body, and the design of both head and rosette. In some of his guitars he used an unusual system of neck reinforcement in which he inserted six small transverse pieces of ebony into the neck immediately below the fingerboard. The table of this guitar is braced with five rather rounded fans.

This is one of only four guitars which Barbero made during the last year of his life. It is known as *La Sevillana* and was built originally for Pepe Martínez. Its tone is very clear, particularly on the top string. Every note is distinct, and there is a matching of sound quality across the instrument's range which is unusual in a flamenco guitar. Perhaps in deference to Pepe Martínez's lyrical style of playing, it is very slightly mellower than some others of Barbero's guitars which we have heard, which have a sound that can be best described as austere.

Flamenco guitar by Manuel Reyes
CORDOVA, 1972.
From the collection of Terry Lewis.

Overall length: 100.5cm
Scale length: 65.6cm
Body length: 49cm
Body width: upper bout 28.1cm
      waist 24.2cm
      lower bout 37.2cm
Body depth: increasing from 9.2 to 9.9cm

The label reads "Manuel Reyes/Constructor de Guitarras/Plaza del Potro 2. Cordoba (España)/Año 1972." Manuel Reyes was greatly influenced by Barbero; although the two men never worked together, they were introduced at the end of Barbero's life, and Barbero passed on much valuable advice. Reyes said that Barbero made the best of all flamenco guitars. Today, Reyes himself is possibly the best known living flamenco constructor.

The guitar's table is braced with seven light fan bars which extend right back to the bottom of the guitar. The body shape shows the influence of Barbero, being similar in its

curvature, though fuller in the lower bout.

The sound of this guitar is quite different, however, from that of a Barbero. It is very loud and intensely aggressive throughout its range, with a particularly incisive treble.

Flamenco guitar by the Hermanos Conde (Sobrinos de Domingo Esteso) MADRID, 1972.
Owned by Juan Martín.

Overall length: 99cm
Scale length: 66.5cm
Body length: 49.2cm
Body width: upper bout 27.5cm
      waist 24cm
      lower bout 37cm
Body depth: increasing from 8.8 to 9.2cm

The label reads "Sobrinos de Domingo Esteso/Construcción de Guitarras, Gravina 7—Madrid/Año 1972."

The three Conde brothers maintain the workshop which belonged to their uncle Domingo Esteso. The guitars they make are played by many of today's professional flamenco guitarists.

The spruce table of this guitar has seven fan struts, of which the five central ones are set parallel. The width of the body is very similar to that of guitars made by Domingo Esteso, but the body is considerably shallower. The Conde brothers finish their instruments in an orange-colored varnish, which seems to be

popular at present but, because it masks some of the natural beauty of the wood, is aesthetically regrettable.

The sound of the Conde brothers' guitars is very different from the sound of those made by their uncle. This instrument has an extremely bright, attacking, almost brittle sound, although it is capable of a surprisingly lyrical tone on the top string.

Flamenco guitar by Paulino Bernabe
MADRID, 1974.
From the collection of Malcolm Weller.

Overall length: 100.5cm
Scale length: 66cm
Body length: 44.8cm
Body width: upper bout 28.4cm
          waist 24.5cm
          lower bout 36.3cm
Body depth: increasing from 9.8 to 10.5cm

Paulino Bernabe's guitars have several peculiar features, which are well illustrated by this example. The sides and back are made of pear wood, which Bernabe sometimes uses on flamenco guitars as an alternative to cypress or maple. The cedar table uses a most unusual type of strutting, which can hardly be called fan strutting at all. The chief elements in the lower bout, below the cross bar, consist of a long center bar, a thin transverse plate under

Flamenco guitar by José Ramírez
MADRID, 1973.
From the collection of Malcolm Weller.

Overall length: 100.5cm
Scale length: 65cm
Body length: 48.8cm
Body width: upper bout 27.4cm
          waist 23.4cm
          lower bout 36.4cm
Body depth: increasing from 9.2 to 10cm

The Ramírez firm is now much better known for its classical than for its flamenco guitars, but it still produces quite a considerable number of the latter.

The comparison between their top classical and flamenco models shows some fairly large differences in construction. This Ramírez flamenco guitar is very much smaller than their classical instruments, having much narrower bouts and a shallower body. Unlike the classical, the neck of the flamenco model has no ebony reinforcing strip down the center. The sides are traditionally built of Spanish cypress, and the cedar table has only five simple fan bars (in place of the complex strutting of the Ramírez classical). Where the classical model is heavily built, and involves some innovatory features, the flamenco model is light and traditional.

In its tone this guitar shows something of the Ramírez tradition. It possesses a rather romantically sweet treble, while the basses are more crisp and incisive.

the bridge, and two very widely splayed "fan" bars high up under the waist.

The photograph of the back shows clearly the reinforcement strip up the back of the neck, and the central band of cypress running up the back of the body. The detailing of the center strip and the top ending of the edge bindings are typical of Bernabe's craftsmanship.

This guitar, though unconventional, is a fine instrument. It is not particularly vibrant, but it produces rich overtones. The sound is mellow and dignified, rather than harsh or rough-throated, but the instrument is also capable of the vitality and attack essential for a flamenco guitar.

Flamenco guitar by Gerundino Fernández
ALMERIA, 1974.
From the collection of Nick Cousins.

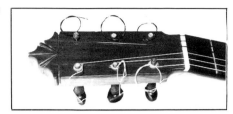

Overall length: 100cm
Scale length: 65cm
Body length: 49cm
Body width: upper bout 28.5cm
        waist 24.5cm
        lower bout 36.5cm
Body depth: increasing from 8.7 to 9cm over
        the upper bout, and constant at
        9cm thereafter.

The body shape of this guitar is unlike most flamenco instruments, having very well rounded bouts. The table is made of cedar, and there are seven fan struts. The center strut is quite substantial, but the remainder are all very light. The fans are arranged so that the central five are parallel and only the outermost two are splayed.

In this guitar the fingerboard is, at 5.3cm at the nut, wider than is usual on a flamenco model, which facilitates *ligado* playing. The body is finished in a spirit varnish, which is soft and marks easily.

Gerundino is a young maker of flamenco guitars, little known outside Spain, who has recently made a considerable reputation. His instruments vary considerably in their tonal qualities, which is probably why they can be found in the hands of guitarists as stylistically different as Paco Peña and Juan Martín.

This guitar is very light and vibrant, with considerable attack on both treble and bass. However, it can produce a surprisingly wide variety of tonal responses throughout its range, and a greater mellowness than one would at first expect.

Concert flamenco guitar by the Hermanos Conde (Sobrinos de Domingo Esteso) MADRID, 1974.
From the collection of Terry Lewis.

Overall length: 100cm
Scale length: 66.5cm
Body length: 49cm
Body width: upper bout 28cm
        waist 23.4cm
        lower bout 36.8cm
Body depth: increasing from 8.8 to 9.9cm

The concert flamenco guitar, with its flamenco action and rosewood body, presents special problems for the constructor. The luthier has to resolve essentially opposite characteristics of both classical and flamenco guitars into a musical form. The Conde brothers have done this with some success, and their concert flamenco guitars are played by several of Spain's younger flamenco guitarists—most notably, by Paco de Lucia.

This guitar has a shape somewhat different from the traditional flamenco model by the same firm which we include earlier. It is larger in the bouts and smaller in the waist. The seven fans are evenly splayed under the cedar table, which is protected by a clear celluloid *golpeador*.

Opinions on the sound of the concert flamenco guitar are varied. It has come about with the rise in popularity of solo performance, at the request of players who still need a very light fast action but who fear that the short sustain of a flamenco guitar is not well suited to the concert hall. There is perhaps also a suspicion that the rosewood-bodied guitar is somewhat classier than the traditional flamenco guitar, and therefore more appropriate.

The sound of the concert flamenco guitar is mellower than that of a cypress-bodied instrument, with less "rasp," but brighter than that of the full classical model. There is a danger that, in some hands, such a guitar may not have quite the necessary cutting edge to bring out the full "tang" of flamenco.

THE GUITAR IN FLAMENCO

The history of the guitar in flamenco is to a great extent the history of the leading guitarists. Some have contributed small things, such as a particular phrase, but others—the greatest—have by their influence revolutionized the whole style of playing.

While there are many stories of the great singers of the early years of flamenco, the guitarists who played with them are but shadowy figures. Consequently, for most of the history of flamenco, all attention has been focused on the *cantaor* (singer), and the importance of the guitar has been played down. But subordinate though the accompanist may be, his role is critical. Paco Peña, one of today's leading flamenco guitarists, asserts that:

> The guitar has not been given enough credit for what it does in a group. Historically, it is so significant in the development of flamenco music. It decides rhythms, it decides the direction of the melody, of the singer, by creating patterns which did not exist with just the voice. In practical terms, the guitar provides all the music—but in Spain nobody ever watched the guitarist in a show.[1]

One of the first *tocaores* (guitarists) we know by name was Francisco Rodríguez, "El Murciano," who died in 1848, when he was in his fifties. It is said that he accompanied Andalucian singers on a small guitar, and played with great fluency. Mikhail Ivanovich Glinka met him in 1847, and spent many hours unsuccessfully trying to notate his *toques*. This fragment of information, and George Borrow's description of the gypsy guitarist Sebastianillo's "demoniacal strumming" and "repeating at intervals the gypsy modifications of the song," indicate something of the guitar's early place in flamenco. Glinka's failure to transcribe the intricacies of El Murciano's

playing, and Borrow's description of the guitar's strumming and musical ornamentation, suggest that the two main elements of flamenco playing, the *rasgueado* and *falseta*, were both already quite well developed. The flamenco *rasgueado* (or *rasgueo* in Andalucian dialect) is much more than a simple strum. More than twenty types of *rasgueado* exist, which can be used for the expression of harmony, melody, rhythm and counter rhythm. The *rasgueados* of a good player provide much of the attack, drive and percussive force of the flamenco guitar, but never obscure or interrupt the flow of thc music. The *falseta*, by contrast, is a mainly melodic passage which is often embellished with complex variations. The *falseta* developed as the guitarist's commentary on the *cante* and, however involved it becomes, should never lose sight of the song's underlying character, or its rules of rhythmic and melodic progression.

In the early days of the flamenco guitar, technique was limited: left-hand fingering was relatively simple and right-hand technique was heavily dominated by the use of the thumb. Complex *picado*, arpeggio and tremolo passages were unknown. But with the era of the *café cantante*, the guitarist's task assumed greater importance, and technique developed rapidly.

"El Maestro Patino" (*c.* 1830-1900) is remembered as the first of the succession of outstanding players who were fostered by the *cafés*. But although his place in flamenco's pantheon is secure, little is recorded of his achievements save that he was a fine accompanist and famous for his use of left-hand *ligado*.

The guitarists in the *cafés cantantes* were spurred to develop their playing by the desire to compete with the singers for public attention. Francisco Sánchez of Cadiz, who lived from 1840 to 1910 and was known as "Paco el

Barbero," experimented with the idea of running several *falsetas* together to produce extended solo passages. He is said thus to have become the first flamenco guitarist to play solos in public, in the *cafés*, and eventually made enough money to buy his own tavern in Seville.

Another way to attract notice was to develop a more complicated and impressive technique, and the *cafés cantantes* witnessed the emergence of the first real virtuosi of the flamenco guitar. One of these was "Paco de Lucena" (Francisco Díaz, *c.* 1855–1930), who was born in Cordova, learned most of his flamenco in Malaga, and achieved fame as a star performer at the Café Silverio in Madrid. Although his playing was essentially based on the use of the thumb and *rasgueado*, he introduced right-hand techniques that originated in classical playing. He is believed to have popularized the flamenco use of *picado*, three-fingered arpeggio, and the classical type of tremolo, fingered p,a,m,i (thumb, ring finger, middle finger, index finger).

The Café Silverio, which was owned by the singer Silverio Franconetti, was a showcase for the finest talents in flamenco. One of Paco de Lucena's successors as a principal guitarist of the *café*, in the late 1880s, was Javier Molina (*c.* 1868–1956) from Jerez. Molina was a child prodigy, like so many other great flamenco guitarists, and was supporting his family on the proceeds of his playing by the age of twelve. He left home at seventeen for Seville, the center of the flamenco world at that time, in the company of his brother and the singer Antonio Chacón, who came to be regarded as the supreme master of the *cante*.

Javier Molina's playing earned him the nickname of "El Brujo de la Guitarra" (the Magician of the Guitar). He is a figure of great historical importance, forming a link between the styles of the nineteenth century and those of modern players. Molina's connection with the relatively simple, deeply felt playing of the early flamenco guitarists came through Paco el Barbero, from whom he took lessons after arriving in Seville. Molina evolved from Barbero's teaching a style that combined great skill with a directness and earthiness of expression, which influenced first Ramón Montoya and, later, Niño Ricardo—the two most famous of all flamenco guitarists.

Ramón Montoya was born on November 2, 1880, not in one of the cities or villages of Andalucia, but in Madrid. His parents were gypsies who dealt in livestock, and the

Ramón Montoya.

young Montoya appeared in the circus as a bareback rider at the age of five. The course of his life was changed by hearing a blind man playing the guitar in the streets, after which he determined to become a guitarist himself. By the time he was fourteen he had taken lessons from the "Maestro Malagueño" and Miguel Borrull, Sr, and was sufficiently advanced to be hired as second guitarist in a *café cantante* called La Mariana.

During his apprenticeship in the *cafés*, Montoya came to know the famous singers of the day. He came to be particularly associated, as accompanist, with Antonio Chacón. After the decline of the *cafés*, Ramón Montoya's

192

professional success continued. He was in great demand for private *fiestas*, often being entrusted with the formation of the troupe, and was the central figure around whom guitarists and enthusiasts gathered at Santos Hernández's workshop, and in the Villa Rosa in the Plaza Santa Ana, Madrid.

In the course of a long career, which ended with his death in 1949, Ramón Montoya enriched the flamenco guitar with new musical concepts, new *falsetas,* and new techniques.

His technical innovations included a more complex use of the left hand (in which he was influenced by the classical playing of Tárrega and Llobet), more complex arpeggios, a greater use of *picado,* and a "four-finger" tremolo played p,i,a,m,i. Although it is difficult to play smoothly, Montoya's tremolo has become standard in flamenco, as it allows the guitarist to produce a full sound while keeping a slow tempo with the thumb.

While Montoya's technical innovations turned the flamenco guitar in the direction of more complex playing styles and brought it to a new level of virtuosity, he was much more than a technician. He was, indeed, one of the few great creators in flamenco. Where so many guitarists rely on other men's *falsetas* (often without knowing it), Montoya was prolific in the creation of new material. He introduced many phrases which have since passed into every guitarist's repertoire of "traditional flamenco." He was also the inventor of the solo *rondeña,* which was the first *toque* to be created specifically for the guitar: all other guitar solos had been derived from the *cante.*

Ramón Montoya's recording of the *rondeña* (made in Paris in 1936 and now reissued on the Hispavox LP *Arte Clásico Flamenco, Ramón Montoya*) demonstrates his virtues as a soloist. The *rondeña* has a somber but lyrical grace; it is played with the sixth string tuned a tone lower, and the third a semitone lower than usual. Montoya used his controlled virtuosity not just to decorate the piece but actually to shape it, and it is characterized by unexpected phrasing and a use of harmonics rare in flamenco.

Ramón Montoya's series of ten recitals at the Salle Pleyel in Paris in 1936 brought the solo flamenco guitar onto the concert platform, and won him great critical and public acclaim. Despite this success, and his warm memories of the occasion as a highlight of his career, he is said to have continued to regard solo playing as a sideline, of little importance when compared with the guitarist's main task of accompanying the *cante.* However, the Paris concerts and recordings laid the essential foundation for the establishment of the solo guitar as an accepted branch of flamenco.

Montoya's influence can be heard directly in the subtly moving, lyrical guitar of Pepe Martínez (born in 1922), who sat at his feet as a youth and toured with him at the age of twenty-one, and in a recorded tribute by Manuel Caño called *Evocación de la Guitarra de Ramón Montoya.* Indirectly, almost every guitarist today has been influenced by Montoya, although many are not conscious of the extent of the debt.

Although Montoya confirmed the trend toward a greater expression of technical virtuosity, which has continued since the war, some of his outstanding younger contemporaries developed styles that owed more to earlier manners. This was not the result of a lack of ability, but of a belief that an apparently simpler style of playing allowed for a more powerful expression of deep feeling. Thus "Perico el del Lunar" (Pedro del Valle, 1894–1964), who started his career as a pupil of Javier Molina and a devotee of Ramón Montoya, later developed a slow but moving style, based on a deliberately restricted right-hand technique. Similarly, the famous gypsy guitarist Diego del Gastor (Diego Amaya Flores, *c.* 1906–73), from Morón de la Frontera, was convinced that "It is bad to be too dexterous and play fast, empty nothings." Although he had a highly developed technique, and quite a considerable classical guitar repertoire, his *aire*—the word flamencos use for the spirit of the music—was "primitive" and urgent.

One of flamenco's legendary guitarists, Manolo de Huelva (*c.* 1892–1968)—whose admirers have ascribed to him every possible virtue of creativity, spontaneity, drive, technique and expressive power—is said to have subordinated his entire right-hand technique to the use of the thumb and *rasgueado.* He apparently made only occasional use of *picado* and arpeggio, and utterly despised tremolo. Unfortunately, Manolo de Huelva was legendary as much for his eccentricity as for the brilliance of his playing: he grew increasingly secretive as he grew older, refusing to play for an audience save at private *juergas* (and then only if the singers, the company, and his mood were right), rarely

Guitarist Melchor de Marchena with singer Gordito de Triana.

Niño Ricardo.

exposing his best material when other professionals were present, and recording no more than two insignificant accompaniments. Thus, sadly, his music has died with him, and has not been handed on to enrich the flamenco of succeeding generations. Echoes of his style linger on in the impassioned playing of Melchor de Marchena, one of the most successful of accompanists.

Melchor de Marchena has stated that "The flamenco guitar, in its great advance in virtuosity, is losing its vitality and soul." Despite this fear, and the resistance of a small number of fine players to the trend, the virtuosi have come increasingly to dominate the flamenco guitar during the past thirty years. During this time the art of flamenco has seen a considerable revival, and its vitality seems to have survived intact.

The outstanding guitarist of the post-war era has been Niño Ricardo (Manuel Serrapí, 1909–72), who was born in Seville and worked in his youth as second guitarist to Javier Molina. In the course of his career, Ricardo worked with all the finest singers, and built up an extraordinarily wide knowledge of flamenco. His knowledge and feeling for the art, both as soloist and accompanist, were combined with an innate sense of the guitar's possibilities, and an abundant musical creativity amounting to genius. From this combination of gifts and experience, Ricardo developed a style of playing and a range of *falsetas* which have influenced virtually every one of the current generation of professional flamenco players. The reasons for Ricardo's overwhelming influence are summed up by one of these, Juan Martín, who says:

Ricardo was a great creative player. His conception was the brilliant thing. He added a new intensity of expression. . . . The beginning of his *soleares* was completely new, and his intensity in *tientos* also, to which he gave a totally different *aire*. The use of the *rasgueo* with the thumb following on the fingers was typical of Ricardo, and in the *seguiriyas* he used it to give a sound which was much more earthy and which to me expresses the thing more nearly. There are moments which are sweet, of course, but for an oppressed people the expression is harsh as well. . . . Ricardo gave to flamenco; he gave new chords, new ideas of rhythm and harmony, which we could learn from.[2]

194

Although Ricardo's ideas are often very difficult to execute, and demand a sophisticated technique, he was scornful of the people whom he called "string-breakers"—flashy technicians with no real musical feeling. He himself was not a virtuoso player by today's standards; a new phrase would often occur to him before he could polish the one he was playing, and his fingers could sometimes hardly keep pace with the flow of his ideas. Ricardo's playing can, at first, seem harsh and jumbled to ears accustomed to the polish of classical guitarists, but attentive listening can hardly fail to reveal the power and originality of his music.

While Ricardo dominated the flamenco guitar in Spain for the last twenty years of his life, he was not the only great player of the period, nor was he the only one to influence the development of the instrument.

Agustin Castellón, "Sabicas," was born a gypsy in Pamplona in the extreme north of Spain. Though far removed from flamenco's homeland in Andalucia, he proved to be a child prodigy on the guitar. Fernando el de Triana relates in his book *Arte y Artistos Flamencos* that Sabicas started to learn the repertoire before he had a guitar by listening to the playing of a neighbor. When his parents bought him an instrument, he made such rapid progress that he made his debut in Pamplona at the age of eight, and was winning contests in Madrid before he was in his teens. Sabicas says of his early years: "There were other guitarists who influenced me, for example Ramón Montoya and the Niño [Manolo] de Huelva, but I studied alone and it was I who taught myself to play."[3]

Sabicas' career was interrupted by the outbreak of the Spanish Civil War and in 1937, while still in his twenties, he left Spain for the Americas. He has lived in New York since 1940, and had not returned to Spain until 1967, when he visited his homeland to receive the Gold Medal of the Flamenco Guitar.

Sabicas was largely forgotten by the Spanish public for many years, until the release of a sensational record called *Flamenco Puro* in the late 1950s. Since then he has influenced many other players, but his continued absence from Spain and his prolific recording career in America have produced a number of ironies. While he is less renowned in Spain than he deserves, he is famous abroad to audiences who have never heard of Niño Ricardo. Most

COURTESY OF SABICAS

Agustin Castellón, "Sabicas."

strangely, Sabicas is less widely popular in America than Carlos Montoya (nephew of the great Ramón), a player who does not approach his class.

Sabicas occupies a place of great importance in the history of flamenco. He was the first guitarist to devote himself to making a career as a soloist, and the first to win widespread acceptance for the flamenco guitar in the concert hall. He claims, with pardonable exaggeration:

In the last thirty years I have transformed the flamenco guitar, taking it from the tavern to the concert hall. . . . When I first presented myself to impresarios they used to ask, "And what do you do?" And I said that I was going to play the guitar. "Accompanying someone?" "No, señor, I am going to play solo." I was only a street urchin when I started, but they allowed me to, and little by little I became known. The other guitarists laughed at the idea of playing flamenco solo, but 90 percent of the mechanisms used in flamenco playing today are mine.

Sabicas is a very different type of player from Ricardo. His technique is uniquely polished, and he has developed every facet of technique to an equally high level. In particular, he has demonstrated the possibilities of arpeggio on all the strings, *picado* on the three bass strings, and *alzapua* (using the thumb as a plectrum with alternating up and down strokes) across all six strings. Paco Peña gives a fellow-artist's appreciation:

> Sabicas has investigated the guitar. He has introduced many harmonies and diminished chords which were unheard of when he started to play, but which *are* flamenco now. Sabicas is moving all the time, and to me he is as much of a genius as Ricardo was. He has a wonderful technique and uses it. I admire his ease and delivery, the facility and fluency of his playing and ideas. The richness and flow of his ideas is not immediately obvious, because he does everything so smoothly.

The leading younger players in Spain today, such as Paco de Lucia, Victor Monge ("Serranito"), and Manolo Sanlúcar, have benefited greatly from the examples of Ricardo and Sabicas. Technical virtuosity has developed to a previously unimaginable degree, not as a goal in itself but as the vehicle for the expression of fresh ideas. Paco de Lucia in particular has evolved a style which is already shaping the playing of his juniors with the degree of influence formerly exerted by Niño Ricardo.

Paco de Lucia, whose real name is Francisco Sánchez Gómez, was born in Algeciras in December, 1947. His entire family was involved with flamenco; Paco's father was formerly a professional guitarist, and his brothers and sister have all become performers. Paco started to learn the guitar at the age of seven, by which time he was already well grounded in the essential rhythms of flamenco. Under the direction of his father, he practiced the guitar intensively until he was twelve, developing both an outstanding technique and a thorough knowledge of the *toques* of Niño Ricardo.

At the age of thirteen Paco de Lucia was taken to America with José Greco's company, and met Sabicas and

Paco de Lucia in performance, accompanied by his brother Ramón de Algeciras.

Mario Escudero, who encouraged him to break away from Ricardo's material in order to develop his own *falsetas*. In 1962, when he was fourteen, Paco de Lucia tried to enter the famous competition of *La Cátedra de Flamencología* in Jerez, but was held to be too young to compete for the main prize. He made such an impression, however, that he was given a special prize, *El Premio Internacional de Acompañamiento*, and the episode added as much to his prestige as if he had won the main contest. A year later he was recording, and was well and truly launched on a career that has made him a legendary reputation while still in his twenties.

Paco de Lucia's playing is distinguished by a ferocious intensity and attack, an enormous facility in the left hand,

and a blindingly fast *picado*. His early years of training and his natural talents have taken him to the point where, as he himself says, technique is no longer a problem. He is more concerned to find new chords and harmonies, and to open new paths for flamenco without losing its essential qualities.

In this area he has had considerable success. In the words, once more, of Paco Peña,

> Paco de Lucia is a genius, like Sabicas is a genius and Ricardo was a genius. He is using a lot of Latin American and jazz harmonies and chords, but he is doing it very intelligently. He is looking for more excitement, but in the idiom of flamenco.

Paco de Lucia has come to be idolized throughout Spain, and has done much to bring to flamenco a new young audience who might otherwise be interested only in pop music. But despite his acknowledged genius, not all guitarists and *aficionados* are entirely happy about the effect of his influence. Paco de Lucia's knowledge of the traditions of flamenco allows him to make valid use of chord progessions borrowed from other types of music; some critics fear that, in the hands of lesser players, such importations may vitiate the force and spirit of flamenco. Similar worries have attended the innovations of all great creators of the flamenco guitar, and whatever may be the ultimate effect of his influence, Paco de Lucia is surely justified in feeling that, for himself,

> I was brought up in a flamenco atmosphere, and I only really feel flamenco, and after that I play what I want to play without worry.... People tend to confuse the pure and the old. The old to me is the art of the museum and the archive, and the pure is what the artist feels at the time of playing.[4]

Victor Monge, "Serranito," is another guitarist who, like Paco de Lucia, is using a wonderful technique to make flamenco with a new and personal *aire*. While he too likes to introduce unconventional chords, his playing has a different character, with a greater degree of introspection, an interplay of longer melodic lines, and a wider variation of dynamic intensity. Serranito uses technical skill to combine an almost classical neatness and subtlety of phrasing, and unexpected accents on particular notes, with

COURTESY OF HISPAVOX RECORDS

Victor Monge, "Serranito."

the ability to express the essential emotion of a *toque*—be it light and frivolous, or somber and tragic.

The worldwide growth of enthusiasm for the guitar in all its forms over the last twenty years has helped to spread the taste for flamenco, although new audiences have sometimes shown a distinct liking for work that falls outside the strict canons of the music. During the 1960s, the performances of Manitas de Plata, a gypsy from Sète in the south of France, roused audiences throughout Europe and America to a fever pitch of excitement—while flamencos decried his playing as a succession of flashy tricks which do not obey the rules of the art.

The existence of large audiences outside Spain has encouraged some artists to settle abroad in countries which give a warm reception to their particular style of playing. Juan Serrano's brilliant technique, which he has developed

Juan Serrano.

Paco Peña on stage with his group "Flamenco Puro."

in the belief that increasing the number of notes per second increases the excitement of the music, brought him immediate success on his Carnegie Hall debut in 1962, and he has lived in America since 1963. The different cultural attitudes which guitarists find outside Spain can sometimes provide fresh musical ideas which can legitimately be fed back into flamenco, enriching the old forms. Two leading players who have made their homes in England, Paco Peña and Juan Martín, have both been helped in the creation of their own personal styles by contact with music not easily available in Spain.

Paco Peña was born in Cordova in 1942, and started playing the guitar as a small child. By the age of twelve he was playing professionally, in a folk music group, from which he soon went on to make a career as a flamenco

accompanist. He first went to London in 1963, and it was there that he played his first engagements as a soloist. London audiences "adopted" him, and he has lived there (in between numerous international tours, and return visits to Spain) since 1968.

Paco Peña shares with Sabicas the aim of cultivating every branch of flamenco guitar technique, and is at pains to project a good tone in his playing. His music is full of grace, and projected without any feeling of rush or strain. Although he has remained closer to the traditions of Sabicas and Ricardo than have players such as Paco de Lucia and Serranito, he is very definitely a creative musician, who says that "if ever I feel I have nothing more to give to flamenco, I shall stop playing."

Paco Peña has come into contact in London with many

classical musicians, and has frequently appeared with John Williams. While his playing has remained undilutedly flamenco, contact with classical players has strengthened his natural tendency to give each piece, and each concert, a definite shape:

> Many solo guitarists just play what they have played for dancers without shaping it properly. But the music must have a structure—a beginning, a middle and an end. I don't like to play disjointed *falsetas*. I think *falsetas* must follow inevitably one from another, and I also like each piece to follow from the other, so the concert makes an impact as a whole.

In addition to stressing the need for order and shape to the performance, Paco Peña is adamant about the importance of improvisation. The compulsion toward both polish and spontaneity sets high standards, which are not always easy to meet:

> You have to improvise if you want to be any good, and you have to be able to do it on the spur of the moment. I like to be free to improvise on stage, but still to be polished, to play with both feeling and accuracy. For this to work, my technique must be in good shape and I must be feeling good in myself. On a few occasions I don't feel like this, and I have to fall back on what I know—and for me this is failure, although the audience may feel I have played very well!

Although London might seem an unlikely milieu for a flamenco guitarist, Juan Martín, who was born in Malaga and has also worked extensively in Madrid, came to settle there because

> London is an art center, a cultural center, and, above all a musical center. Being in London you are exposed to a lot of different music, you learn about concerto form, symphonic form, and even these things give you ideas. Our ancestors in Andalucia maybe only heard very regional music. But now—I go to hear jazz, I go to classical concerts. The modern guitarist, if he has any imagination and is alive, hears sounds which must influence him. You can't say, no, I'm a pure flamenco and I'm not going to listen.

While Juan Martín has been brought up in the modern school of virtuoso playing, he is certain that the future of the flamenco guitar lies in the development of greater musicality, rather than in extending technique still further.

> For me, and this is a very personal thing, flamenco's future is not so much in playing more notes per second—it has reached a ridiculous state, and is almost vulgar—but in starting to play *music* while keeping it flamenco. In my conception of flamenco, I feel that contrasts in intensity, in dynamic, in tone, must be good. The most impressive techniques in flamenco are much more impressive if you contrast.

Juan Martín shares with many older players the feeling that the right-hand techniques involving the thumb and *rasgueado* have a special character, a force that is essential to the expression of excitement and deep emotion in flamenco. He also believes that to move too far from the Moorish sound, too far in the direction of jazz and Latin American chording, is to lose some of flamenco's power and character. These convictions do not stem from a desire to put the clock back or to deny the creative discoveries of modern flamenco, but from the wish to develop flamenco by allying a wide range of musical experiences with the traditions of those parts of Andalucia where

> You get a very pure type of *cante* and guitar playing, and if you play tremolo too much it's called *floreo* (idle talk) and people just look the other way. You start very much with the idea that good flamenco playing is thumb and *rasgueo*. Fast runs and *picados* are fine, but not what the very pure *aficionado* will admire, which is much more the thumb and *alzapua* technique. I too find this more exciting. You play *tientos, bulerías*, all these pieces which are in the *por medio* keys, and it's the *aire* you play with which counts. It is the drive you give to a *bulerías* or *soleares*, the evenness and control of rhythm which will give excitement.

Every creative guitarist has his own style and exploits different possibilities of the flamenco guitar, but the conditions in which flamenco is performed affect all players. One of the most important forces in flamenco at present is the extraordinary popularity of the solo guitar. To some audiences, indeed, the solo guitar *is* flamenco. The more conservative *aficionados* and critics have overreacted to this heresy by declaring that the guitar's only legitimate role is to support the *cante*, but, as is usually the case, the truth lies somewhere between these two extreme viewpoints. Paco de Lucia puts the guitarists' case that "guitar solo is a new form of expression in flamenco. The voice is the oldest, and therefore the most traditional and poetic. The guitar is new, and we are working and fighting so that it sounds as [sic] important music." While flamenco solo is a new form, a branch off the parent trunk, it is still closely connected with the main flamenco traditions. There are few who would disagree with Paco Peña when he says that "To play solo you have to play authentic flamenco, and the closer you are to the real atmosphere—that means singing, dancing and accompanying—the better off you are."

Naturally, playing solo and accompanying place different demands on the performer. The soloist has no other performers with him to share the responsibility, to give and receive inspiration. Where the performance of the traditional troupe combines with the guitar the percussive element of the *baile* and the melodic element of the *cante*, the solo guitarist has to create flamenco's musical drama by himself. Although he has, perhaps, a little more expressive freedom than if he were with a group, the soloist who takes too many liberties with the traditional structures of flamenco will find that his reputation suffers.

Those who deny the legitimacy of the solo flamenco guitar have frequently argued that the demands on the soloist (who must be his own composer or, at least, arranger) are too great, and that solo players are deficient in musical feeling in comparison with their fellows who remain faithful to the accompanist's role. The post-war history of flamenco hardly bears this theory out: the great players, such as Niño Ricardo and Sabicas, have proved themselves equally in solos and with the *cante*.

The problems of the guitarist, and the soloist in particular, have been increased by the tendency toward performing flamenco in concert. He has to create the excitement and spontaneity essential to the music in the cold, formal atmosphere of the concert hall. It is easy to understand why *aficionados* fortunate enough to be able to hear flamenco in intimate surroundings sometimes doubt that a stirring performance can be given on a stage. But concert halls are now an inevitable setting for flamenco, and the only one in which many of the audience will ever witness flamenco "live." Somehow the artist must find a way to surmount the barriers and generate an atmosphere in which the spirit of flamenco can be communicated.

Paco Peña sees the problems from the guitarist's point of view:

A stage is an artificial place for any music, and flamenco in particular. You're isolated, dressed up, and everybody's looking at you. But what can you do? We are conditioned to stages, and on stage I can bring flamenco to a public which otherwise wouldn't be able to see it.

When I am on stage, I try to create for myself an atmosphere which inspires me to play music, whether I am playing on my own or with the group. I feel the presence of the audience, but I don't want to see them. If I create an atmosphere which inspires me, which I enjoy, this will project on to the audience.

Most members of flamenco's new international audience will never have the chance to attend a private *fiesta* in Andalucia, to witness flamenco in its most traditional setting. But in compensation they will be able to hear, abundantly, in concert halls and on record, flamenco guitar playing of a higher standard than ever before.

Juan Martin accompanying Rafael Romero.

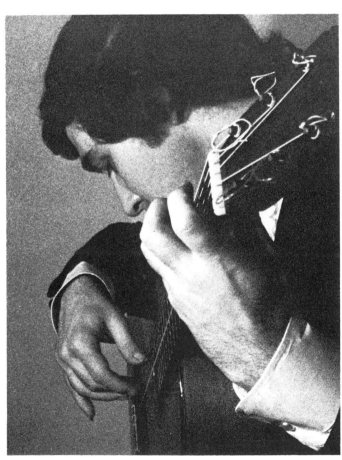

Juan Martín.

Introduction to the *toques*

There are scores of different flamenco *toques*, almost all of them derived from equivalent *cantes*, and each has its own *aire* and characteristic musical structure. Traditionally the *toques* have been divided, like the *cantes* and *bailes*, into three groups: *jondo* (profound), *intermedio* (intermediate) and *chico* (little). Many performers, however, have reservations about classifying the music in this way. A *cante* or *toque chico* is not necessarily easier to perform than one which is *jondo*. It just has a gay, lively emotional character instead of a tragic one. Also, a poor performance of a *jondo* piece can be completely without feeling, while an inspired rendering of a *cante, toque* or *baile chico* can be an incredible experience. Some pieces which succeed well as a *cante* are less impressive as a *toque*, and vice versa.

Guitarists tend not to classify pieces as *jondo, intermedio* or *chico*, but instead to distinguish between the *toques libres* and *toques a compás*. Every *toque a compás* has a fixed pattern of rhythmic beats, often with most complicated emphases. Although the guitarist can manipulate *compás* to a certain extent, he must never step completely outside it. To the uninitiated, the subtleties of *compás* are rarely apparent, but they are critical to the performer. As Juan Martín says, "In *compás* you must know every second where you are, and it's the same for the singer. People listen to the *cante* and hear *AHaiiieee...*; but every one of these, every *aiiee* is measured!" The guitarist has more freedom in the *toques libres*, which do not have rigid rhythmic patterns.

The professional guitarist needs a complete knowledge of the characteristics of all the major *toques*, whether he is working as a soloist or accompanist. To be a creative player, he must know how to work within the framework of a *toque* in such a way as to play material which is new without disrupting the essential structure.

To show the nature of these structures, and the considerations which affect the performer at the highest levels of flamenco, the guitarist Juan Martín has written the following notes on the characteristics of six of the most important of the many *toques*.

Señor Martín prefaces his remarks with a memoir of the flamenco world of Madrid in the 1960s.

When I was eighteen, I left Malaga by train for Madrid, and said goodbye to Andalucia—"La Bella"—to learn what I could from the *fenomenos* who all gathered in the Capital. I already played a guitar made by the Conde brothers, or "Sobrinos de Domingo Esteso" as they are also called, so when I went to Madrid I made my way to their shop at Gravina 7, to get them to check the *hueso* (saddle) of the bridge, and to meet Faustino and Mariano. (The third brother, Julio, worked in their other shop in the calle Atocha.)

While I was waiting, they gave me various instruments of theirs to try and were very friendly, knowing I had just arrived in Madrid. I started to play some material as well and as confidently as I knew. There were only two people in the shop, a case maker and a middle-aged man standing by Faustino's work bench. When I was halfway through playing a *serranas*, the middle-aged man approached me and said, "What's your name, son?" "Juan Martín," I answered. "And where did you learn that material?"

"From a Niño Ricardo record," I answered. And in an inimitable, tobacco-roughened voice came the statement: "*I am Niño Ricardo!*" I felt so small that I wanted to disappear through the floor. He then took the guitar from me and corrected the variations I had learned by ear, and I was amazed to find that he was sometimes playing the same notes I had learned in totally different positions. In spite of everything, we went into the bar opposite to drink some good Madrid *tintorro,* and I explained how I had learned his material by slowing the speed of the record player from 33 to 16rpm, making the notes almost an octave lower and slow enough to hear his cascading runs.

From then on, to go to the guitar maker's shop of the Conde brothers was to learn something new each time. Many famous *tocaores* gathered there in the mornings, but mainly at five in the afternoon. One would meet and talk with fellow professionals and Ricardo, who lived round the corner, would often be in for a quick chat and a smoke. He filled an ashtray in minutes, and in between would play his latest variations. I would follow closely, and then rush home to my *pensión* in the Antón Marín to work out while the notes were ringing in my head. What days those were!

Notes on some *toques*.

Toques a compás: soleares, bulerías, seguiriyas.
Toques libres: tarantas, malagueñas, granadinas.

The *soleares* is a good *toque* to start my thoughts on music I have played all my life, but about which I have never been persuaded to write before now. In my experience, the *soleares* creates an immediately serious *ambiente* whether used as the first *baile* in a *cuadro*, the first *cante* in a *juerga* or the first *toque* in a solo recital. It is also a good *toque* to start learning the guitar, since its *compás* of twelve beats, with accents on the third, sixth, eighth, tenth and twelfth, is the rhythmic origin of so many other styles. The *bulerías, alegrías,* and even *guajiras* and *peteneras,* which sound very different from the *soleares* due to their different chord sequences and *aires,* are nevertheless of the same basic rhythmic pattern.

The *soleares* is played in the Phrygian mode which, in the key of 'Mi' or E, gives the scale E F G A B C D E, and in the key of 'La' or A gives A B♭ C D E F G A. These are neither major nor minor scales, and as the Mi chord is very much the dominant chord in the sequence La menor (Am), Sol (G), Fa (F), Mi (E), I refer to it as being in the key of Mi (E), and not in La menor (Am) as some non-flamencos would do.

The *aire* of the *soleares* or *soleá*—a corruption of *soledad,* meaning solitude or loneliness—is solemn, grand, and played with a marked and repetitious rhythm. The most profound playing style of *soleares* should not have too much *floreo,* and should be played in a slow but pulsating way. Too much classical harmony in thirds or sixths tends to make the *aire* less *jondo,* and the more the roots are kept to the Phrygian mode and Moorish sound—though not too many arabesques—the more earthy the *aire.*

Triana was the main center for the development of the *soleares,* and there are now more than twenty types.

The *bulerías* for me is the most exciting rhythm in flamenco, and perhaps the most difficult to control perfectly. I prefer to play it in the *por medio* key, or Phrygian mode A, for excitement, *aire* and interest, though it can be played in any key. The *bulerías* can be played with many different *aires: al golpe* (with tapping), *estile campero* (country style) that Diego del Gastor often played, or in the modern style using many diminished and augmented chords within the traditional Phrygian mode sequence. Much of the modern sound is gained through bridging chords such as G7 and F7, which join the traditional Dm C B♭ A to give a sequence Dm G7 C F7 B♭ A. Paco de Lucia is particularly fond of this type of harmony. Juan Maya, on the other hand, has a rhythmic drive and force *por bulerías* of the sort typical among the Madrid professionals in the early 1960s. To hear La Paquera sing *bulerías* with Juan Maya and Manolo Sanlúcar accompanying *te quita el sentido* ("destroys your senses"), as we say in the language of flamenco.

The *bulerías* developed from the *soleá* being played at a faster tempo, mainly by the *gitanos* of Jerez de la Frontera who particularly favored the *por medio* key.

The *seguiriyas* is the most profound form in flamenco, whether sung, played or danced, and to hear the *seguiriyas* sung with true intensity and depth of sadness is one of the most heart-rending experiences possible in music. This happens very rarely even at private *juergas* where all those present are *aficionados de pura cepa* who have the music in their blood, and almost never in the commercial *ambiente* of the *tablao.*

The modern chords of today seem to give the *seguiriyas* a less serious tone; too much fast *floreo* will kill it dead. Its *compás* is counted 1 and 2 and 3 and a 4 and a 5 and, or *1 2 3 4 5* 6 *7 8 9* 10 *11* 12. Again, it is nearly always performed in the *por medio* key.

Among the greatest *tocaores* Niño Ricardo has given many wonderful *falsetas* to the *seguiriyas.* The older generation of *tocaores* such as Ricardo, Melchor de Marchena, Andrés Heredia, Diego del Gastor and Manolo de Huelva seemed to have a slight roughness of attack that suited this *cante* or *toque primitivo.* Though the polished techniques of today may be better guitaristically, and even more accurate in *compás,* they do not seem to produce the same *duende por seguiriyas.* Ricardo understood how to cut a chord just short of the measured time without losing the *aire* of the *seguiriyas compás.* This is true flamenco rubato.

The great gypsy *cantaor* Rafael Romero, whom I have presented in recitals of the *cante,* tells me that Curro de la Jeroma was the most wild and earthy *tocaor por seguiriyas,* with such a rhythmic feeling and flamenco thumb that, according to Rafael, *Sabicas se puso de rodillas* ("Sabicas went down on his knees") when he heard him before he left for America—and will do so even now when Curro's name is mentioned.

Seguiriyas are sung best in the province of Seville, and particularly in Mairena del Alcor, Utrera, Morón, Lebrija, Marchena, and of course—before they built the modern apartment blocks—Triana.

Before moving on to the *toques libres*, here are examples of several bars from each of a *soleares*, *bulerías* and *seguiriyas* which show the musical character of each of these *toques*.

SOLEARES

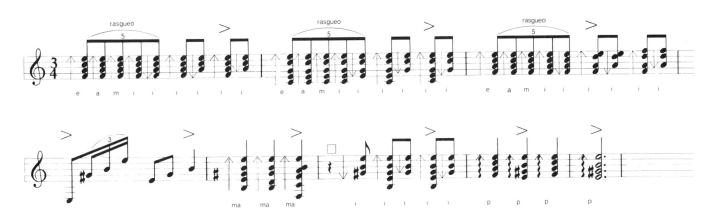

☐ = *golpe* (a tap on the *golpeador* with the third finger of the right hand)

BULERIAS

SEGUIRIYAS

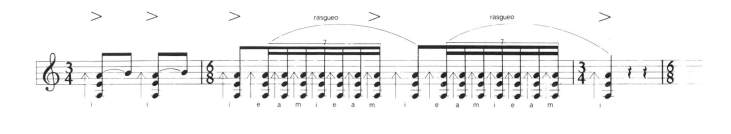

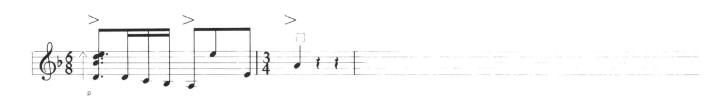

A *toque libre* does not have to mark time with a fixed rhythmic pattern the whole way through. It may, though, adhere to certain patterns for a period of time and then change into a freer mood, or echo the *fandangos* rhythm in some way, or have some underlying feeling of *fandangos*. I mention *fandangos* particularly, since most *toques libres* are derivatives of the *fandangos grandes* of particular regions — the *granadinas* from Granada province, the *malagueñas* from Malaga, and so on.

The Levante region has produced the *tarantas*, which is a *cante* heard best in Almería, Cartagena and Linares. As a *toque*, the *tarantas* has one of the richest natural harmonies and marvelous "dark sounds." The *tarantas* (which is a *cante intermedio*) can be even more profound as a guitar solo than some pieces of the *cante jondo*.

The variations in a *toque libre* which follow the *cante* are often the most popular within flamenco circles because they are recognized, but they lack the primeval force which a good *cantaor* gives. The most effective variations are often those that hark back to the *cante*, using the naturally good textures and sounds of the guitar, but do not imitate the human voice.

Because a *toque libre* is less rhythmically marked, it can be given a more melodic flow and these *toques*, with a lot of arpeggio and tremolo, always seem to go down well at concerts. The more vital and urgent *toques a compás* require more flamenco understanding, though it is possible that someone who is involved in jazz, rock or blues would feel the beauty of a *bulerías* that really swings. Like Ella Fitzgerald says, "It don't mean a thing if it ain't got swing" — and the same is true of flamenco *toques a compás*. But back to *toques libres*.

The good guitarist can bring a strong melodic line to a *granadinas, tarantas, malagueñas* or the *rondeña* and, if mixed with good harmony, this makes for a more balanced musical experience than if he plays nothing but *toques a compás* all evening or for the whole of an LP. Certainly, the playing style for *toques libres* is much closer to classical guitar playing than is the mainly thumb-and-*rasgueo* attack of a good *bulerías* or *seguiriyas*. I have played for singers who know nothing of the guitar, but can play two chords in the *por medio* key and keep a very flamenco *pulsación* in the right hand. This is another world to a *clásico*! *Hay que llevarlo adentro* (one must carry it inside one), as we say in Andalucia.

Finally, here are some phrases particularly associated with the *tarantas, malagueñas* and *granadinas*.

TARANTAS

MALAGUENAS

GRANADINAS

THE GUITAR
IN LATIN AMERICA

A brief survey

The subject of the guitar in Latin America is an enormous one, embracing many variants of the instrument and a vast field of musical and folkloric history. It is unfortunately beyond the scope of this book to do more than indicate very briefly the diversity of the subject and to place certain important figures within their historical context.

Guitar-type instruments were first introduced to Latin America by the Spaniards in the sixteenth century, and much of their history parallels that of the instrument in Europe. But whereas the strong aristocratic tradition of Europe tended to elevate the classical instrument and its music at the expense of others, the native influences in Latin America have encouraged a wider variety of guitars and a rich folk music.

The history of the guitar in Latin America begins with the first Spanish conquistadores. When Cortés landed in Mexico in 1519, he brought with him one Ortiz, a "*toceador de vihuela*," a vihuela player.[1] The instrument was an obvious choice to bring: it was light, portable and provided entertainment of the kind heard in the courts and households of Spain. But those who followed Cortés and his fellows saw music in a different light. For music — an effective persuader for an uneducated audience — was an important tool in the process of colonizing and Christianizing the indigenous population. By 1524 a church school had been set up to teach Spanish music, and the school also taught the art of building instruments, including the vihuela and possibly the guitar.

Mexico City developed rapidly. By 1574, aside from the Indian population, there were 15,000 Spanish residents. To cater for their needs, churches, schools, monasteries and hospitals were built. A printing press was set up in 1539, but printing was slow and costly; to bring a taste of the Old World to their new homes, the colonists imported a shipment of books yearly from Spain, and the vihuela books of Esteban Daza, Luis de Narváez and Miguel de Fuenllana were among the imports.[2]

The brutal Spanish colonization virtually obliterated indigenous Indian music, which was frowned upon by the Spaniards as belonging to a heathen culture. As the conquerors spread out from the main population centers, the missions followed, establishing small settlements. Here, as in the cities, instrument building and music making were among the first things to be taught. The evidence for the use of the guitar for the sixteenth and early seventeenth century, though scarce, indicates that the instrument was widely played. Before 1600 the nuns of a house at Encarnación, a settlement near Lima in Peru, were famed for the music they played on viols, harps, vihuelas, bajones and guitars.[3] In Argentina the Jesuit missionaries who founded settlements in the Parana River region brought musicians there as early as 1595, and the instrument was played by both Spanish and native musicians. In 1650 a Spanish army officer ". . . went to a wedding and sang to the accompaniment of a guitar."[4] An Englishman named Thomas Gage, during his travels in the 1620s and 1630s, visited a monastery just outside Mexico City. The monks, anxious to be hospitable, "made shew onto us of the dexterity of their Indians in music . . . whom they had brought up to dancing after the Spanish fashion at the sound of the guitarra."[5]

The music taught to the Indians was that of aristocratic Spain, although by the seventeenth century this music was changing through a reassertion of native culture. As settlements became established, Spanish and Indian cultures mingled through intermarriage, while in some areas of the continent, further influence came from the African slaves brought by the Spanish. New musical ideas gave the imported European dances a different character and also inspired original forms, some of which—such as the chaconne—found their way back to the courts of Spain.

Evidence for this intermingling of peoples can be found in the music. The Biblioteca Nacional in Mexico City possesses an interesting *Tablatura de Vihuela* of 1740.[6] The book contains over fifty dances, mainly the popular Spanish ones such as the *jota*, *fandango*, *folia*, and

An Indian playing a charango.

zarabanda. But there is also mention of dances called *cumbeas a cantos negros*, and tablature for "zarambeques," the name the black slaves called all the four-course variants of the guitar.[7]

The standard European guitar was the instrument played by the wealthy Spanish colonists in the cities. It was used to accompany songs, dances, and as in Spain for *tonadillos* in the entr'actes in the theater. In El Teatro de la Ranchería, founded in 1778 in Buenos Aires, the music was provided by a complete orchestra of guitars. Outside the cities, however, the picture was different. From their first introduction, guitar-type instruments had been en-thusiastically adopted by the native population, and in the poorer rural areas, a large number of variants arose. Many of these are still popular today. In size and scope, they range from the Cuban *tres*, a small, primitive guitar with only three strings, through the Brazilian *violao*, to the enormous Mexican *guitarrón*, the bass guitar of the *mariachi* bands. Most of these instruments are simply built from whatever materials are available locally. We include here a small selection of instruments drawn from across the continent to show something of the variety of guitar types in popular use to this day in the guitar-oriented folk music of Latin America.

Vihuelita, MEXICO. 1960s
From the collection of Peter Sensier.

Overall length: 76cm
Scale length: 49cm
Body length: 40cm
Body width: upper bout 21.5cm
　　　　　　　waist 17.5cm
　　　　　　　lower bout 29.5cm
Body depth: approx. 18cm
Five frets.

The *vihuelita* comes from Mexico. It is small, has a deeply arched back, and was probably made originally from a turtle, tortoise or armadillo shell.

The *vihuelita* is a *guitarra de golpe*, or strummed instrument, and is used in *mariachi* bands with the big bass guitar (*guitarrón*), whose five courses are tuned an octave below the top five strings of the standard European guitar. The *vihuelita*'s five single strings are tuned a d' g b e'.

Jarana jarocha, VERA CRUZ. 1960s.
From the collection of Peter Sensier.

Overall length: 84.5cm
Scale length: 54.5cm
Body length: 40cm
Body width: upper bout 19cm
            waist 15.5cm
            lower bout 24.5cm
Body depth: increasing from 7 to 8cm.

The *jarana jarocha* is used extensively in the music of Vera Cruz. It is a small guitar whose back, neck and sides are traditionally carved from a solid piece of wood. The placing of the *golpeador* (above, rather than below the soundhole) shows that the *jarana jarocha* is strummed with a very high right-hand position. The flashy style of the *golpeador* is typical of many Latin American folk instruments.

The *jarana jarocha* is often played in a group with the *requinto Vera Cruzana,* and harp. Its tuning is: a d'd' gg bb e'.

Cuatro, VENEZUELA. 1960s.
From the collection of Nick Cousins.

Overall length: 75.4cm
Scale length: 51cm
Body length: 31.8cm
Body width: upper bout 16.2cm
            waist 14.1cm
            lower bout 22.5cm
Body depth: increasing from 9.5 to 9.7cm.

The *cuatro* is a four-stringed folk guitar. It is often used with maracas to give the basic rhythm of many Venezuelan folk dances.

This *cuatro* has a pine top, which looks as if it might have come from an orange crate, and a body of some type of native cedar. Although unsophisticated materials are used and the construction is simple, the head is joined to the neck by a V joint, which demands highly skilled workmanship.

The marquetry *golpeador* on the upper bout indicates that the *cuatro,* like the *jarana jarocha,* is powerfully strummed with a high hand position; played in this way it has a surprisingly loud voice for so small an instrument.

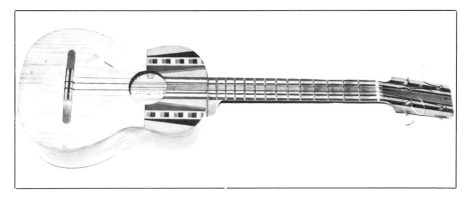

Tiple by Peter Sensier, *c.* 1963.
From the collection of Peter Sensier.

Overall length: 83cm
Scale length: 54cm
Body length: 41.2cm
Body width: upper bout 26cm
            waist 23.8cm
            lower bout 33.5cm
Body depth: 10.5cm

The *tiple* is a descendant of the four-course guitar played in Colombia, some parts of Venezuela, and Argentina. It is difficult to say when the *tiple* evolved, but José Espinosa, a traveler in Argentina in 1794, described hearing the *seguidillas* sung to the accompaniment of a *tiple*.[8] In Venezuela and Colombia, the *tiple* is used alongside the *bándola* to accompany a dance-song known as the *bambuco*, a "pursuit" dance of African origin which (like the *seguidilla*) alternates 3/4 and 6/8 rhythms.

The four courses each have three metal strings tuned: cCc e'ee' a'aa' d'd'd'.

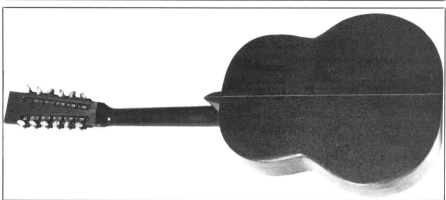

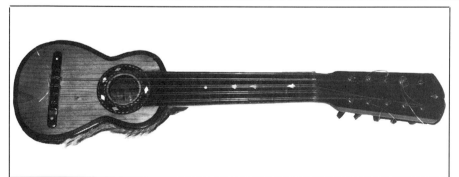

Charango
From the collection of Victoria Kingsley.

Overall length: 58cm
Scale length: 33cm
Body length: 20.5cm
Body width: upper bout 11.3cm
            waist 9.6cm
            lower bout 14.5cm
Overall length: 7.6cm

The *charango* is found in Ecuador, Bolivia, and the northwest Andean region of Argentina. It is characterized by the use of an armadillo shell for the body; *charangos* differ from one another according to the size and shape of the armadillo.

The *charango* is particularly favoured by the Indians, who can play it with great virtuosity alongside the flute, pan-pipe and guitar. The five double courses are tuned: e'e' aa ee' cc gg.

The popularity which the classical guitar enjoyed in Europe from the beginning of the nineteenth century was also felt in Latin America. The repertoire was essentially the same: in August 1822 a series of concerts held in the newly founded Academy of Music in Buenos Aires, consisted of two pieces by Carulli—a duet for guitar and piano and a quartet for guitars—and a quartet for guitars and piano adapted from a piece by Haydn. In October of the same year a Professor of Guitar was appointed to the Academy, and he and his pupils helped to popularize the music of the European composers Fernando Sor and Dionisio Aguado.

From this period onward, there was a greater cultural and musical exchange between Europe and Latin America than ever before. Domingo Prat, a central figure in the history of the guitar, was born in Barcelona in March 1886 but settled in Buenos Aires, and did much to encourage guitarists there. When the Spanish virtuoso Miguel Llobet visited Argentina in 1910 (at Prat's invitation), he found a public as knowledgeable and discriminating in European classical guitar music as in any major European city.

By 1928, when Andrés Segovia visited Mexico for the first time, there already existed a body of classical music based on native folk forms. And this was steadily growing: in February 1933 Rafael Adame, Professor of Guitar at the National Conservatory, gave the first performance of his *Concerto for Guitar and Orchestra*. But it was Segovia who was responsible for bringing much Latin American guitar music to a wider public outside the continent, through his encouragement of Manuel Ponce of Mexico, and Heitor Villa-Lobos of Brazil (see page 123). More recently John Williams has been a great influence in popularizing the music of other Latin American composers for the guitar: Gómez Crespo of Argentina, Vicente Emilio Sojo of Venezuela and his pupil Antonio Lauro, and the Paraguayan Indian Agustine Pio Barrios.

Barrios is a particularly interesting figure in the history of the guitar because of the way he combined European and Latin American cultural influences. He was born in 1885 and learned the guitar at an early age from Gustavo Sosa Escalada, the man who had done much to introduce the classical guitar to Paraguay. Barrios then studied at the National College in the capital and in 1908 gave his first public performance. Two years later he left Paraguay to visit and play in Uruguay, Brazil and Chile before returning home in 1924. In his concerts he had some trouble being accepted as a classical guitarist, particularly in Chile where the critics attacked him for his technique, his repertoire and his use of metal strings (the best choice when playing in hot humid atmospheres). During a later concert tour of Mexico, he met the Paraguayan diplomat Don Tomás Salomini and his wife; in September 1934, sponsored by them, Barrios went to Europe. In his first concert at the Royal Conservatory in Brussels, he began his program with standard guitar works or classical transcriptions. These were greeted politely, but when Barrios presented his own works the enthusiasm was genuine. This was the first time many of the audience had heard music based on Latin American folk forms, and they were caught up in its fresh exciting rhythms and new textures.

In the next two years, Barrios traveled and worked in Berlin and Spain. In 1939, having returned to Latin America, he was made Professor of Guitar at the National Conservatory of San Salvador, a post which he held until his death in 1944.

Barrios wrote over one hundred pieces for guitar, few of which have yet been published. He wrote virtuoso guitar music in the earlier nineteenth-century tradition of Sor, Giuliani and Paganini, and much of his music has the same virtues and vices as theirs. It appears exciting and attractive (and is often extremely difficult to play well), but is ultimately "salon" music. Nonetheless Barrios' music displays an interesting mixture of stylistic tendencies. He was heavily influenced by Chopin and Mendelssohn, and echoes of their music appear in his pieces; he also relied, however, on rhythms and harmonies drawn from many parts of Latin America.

Many of the typical dances and songs of Latin America have evolved from the guitar. In Argentina all the arts, including music, revolved around the colorful figure of the *gaucho*. The best singers and players among them formed a clan of *payadores* who entertained at inns and parties. A writer in 1942 described seeing them on one occasion:

Possibly the most interesting form of the *payada* was the one called the *contrapunto*, which was performed in the following manner: Two *gauchos* would sit on the skulls of oxen, tuning their guitars, while bystanders stood

The brilliant young Brazilian guitarist Baden Powell.

around them in a circle and urged them with yells and applause into a singing match.[9]

A wide range of devices is used by guitarists to express the rhythms of a song or dance. They can include full *rasgueado* using thumb and various fingers, played either up or down; taps on the body or bridge; stressing the bass note of a chord, or playing a fast arpeggio, which can be further accented by the use of right-hand damping.

For a long time, the Latin American musical forms best known outside the continent have been the samba and bossa nova. These Brazilian rhythms have provided the basis of much of the music of Antonio Carlos Jobim, Luis Bonfa, Baden Powell, Joao Gilberto, Laurindo Almeida and a host of other composers and players. When Jobim's "One Note Samba" and "The Girl from Ipanema" were first heard in the late 1950s and early 1960s, his distinctive chordal style and bossa nova rhythms brought about a new stylistic development on the guitar. The subtle harmonic shading combined with gentle rhythmic chords and chromatic melody of Jobim and his fellow composers produced a music that was instantly popular.

Four centuries of contact and exchange between different cultural traditions has resulted in an enormous wealth of music. Much of this, however, is regionally based: there may exist over twenty local variations of a dance within one country. But for a long time now, a considerable amount of interest has been shown in Latin American folk music and much of it has been discovered and documented. In the development of this music, the guitar has played a key role, for it has been the most widely used, and often the only locally available instrument for accompaniment. The music both of the early twentieth-century composers and of present-day guitarists points towards a fusion of folk and art music. To ignore this treasury of instruments and music is to reject traditions which are as vital and important as any produced in Europe or North America.

THE STEEL-STRING ACOUSTIC GUITAR

THE INSTRUMENTS

Introduction

Metal-strung guitars have a long history, both as "folk" and "art" instruments. They have been made in many countries over a span of centuries, and played by many different classes of people. But all the main types of steel-string guitar now in use are essentially of American origin, and were developed in the late nineteenth and early twentieth centuries.

The two principal forms of the modern steel-string guitar are the arch-top and the flat-top. There is a fundamental difference in the mechanical and acoustical operation of the two types. On the flat-top guitar, whose strings terminate at the bridge which is glued to the soundboard, the string vibrations are transmitted to the table by a rocking motion of the bridge. On the arch-top guitar, whose strings pass over the bridge and are attached to a tailpiece, the soundboard is activated more by vertical oscillations. The internal construction of the two types of guitar differs in accordance with the different mechanical forces on them. The soundboard of the flat-top guitar needs considerable strutting to resist the pull of the strings and distribute the vibrations from the bridge. The soundboard of the arch-top guitar, in contrast, needs only to resist vertical pressure from the strings; their longitudinal pull is taken by the tailpiece, which is attached to the endblock. The arch of the soundboard also has considerable inherent strength. These two facts, allied to the simpler mode of vibration of the arch-top, allow for a much simpler bracing (which often consists of nothing more than two longitudinal bars). The carving or shaping of the top itself is, however, of considerable importance in determining the quality of the instrument.

In both the arch-top and flat-top, the use of steel strings produces a loud volume and twanging, jangling tone. It is well understood that steel strings have a higher tension than gut or nylon, and so transfer more energy to the top and thus produce a louder volume. While it seems self-evident that steel strings should produce a twanging tone, the reason they do so is complicated.

Steel strings differ from nylon in being very true and efficient vibrators: whereas a nylon string produces a note with perhaps six to ten overtones, a note struck on a steel string can have forty, fifty, or even more. Now the air around a vibrating string, which transmits the sound to our ears, has a cushioning effect that modifies the vibrations. As a result, the frequency of each overtone (and therefore its pitch) comes over at slightly less than its theoretical true value. The regression of the overtones from their theoretical values introduces impurity and dissonance into the note. The greater the number of overtones present, the greater the clashes between them as they become less and less "in tune" with each other. It is this effect of internal discord among the overtones of the note which gives the steel-string guitar its characteristic sound.

The arch-top guitar is also sometimes known as the f-hole, orchestra, plectrum or cello guitar; those made with a top carved from a solid piece of wood (instead of being press-formed) are often called carved-top guitars. Although the arch-top acoustic guitar has gone out of favor since the war, it enjoyed great popularity for many years. Unlike the flat-top, which developed from earlier gut-strung models, the arch-top guitar has always been associated with steel strings.

Orville Gibson (1856–1918), the founder of the Gibson company, was the man most responsible for the early development of the arch-top guitar. Gibson first made instruments in his spare time while working as a clerk in a shoe store in Kalamazoo, Michigan, during the 1870s. He was struck by the inadequacies of the guitars and mandolins of his day, and by the comparative perfection of the violin. He decided to try to improve the guitar and mandolin by adapting to them some of the concepts of violin design, most importantly the carved top and back.

This importation of violin features was the starting point of the development of the modern arch-top. Orville Gibson's early guitars did not as a rule incorporate the violin bridge principle but used a conventional guitar pin bridge, which was sometimes strengthened by a metal stay passing to the base of the instrument. Throughout the nineteenth century, the American guitar was essentially a boudoir instrument played mainly by ladies. As such, it was naturally strung with gut or silk strings. It is likely that Gibson got the idea of trying metal strings from his work with mandolins; certainly, he was one of the first professional guitar makers in America to build a steel-string guitar.

By 1894, Orville Gibson had progressed to a point where he was able to set himself up as a one-man business. His unconventional instruments, which were large, sturdy and loud, soon created a demand he was unable to fulfill. In 1902 the Gibson company, with a staff of thirteen craftsmen, was formed in Kalamazoo thanks to the backing of a group of local businessmen. Since then the Gibson company has become America's largest manufacturer of guitars and mandolins.[1]

Information about the guitars produced in the first decade of the Gibson company is sparse. The first catalogue, for 1902–3, shows two ranges of models closely based on Orville Gibson's hand-built originals, offered with either gut or steel strings. The two styles, designated "L" and "O," were very similar at this date, with carved tops and backs, oval soundholes and pin bridges.

The first important modifications of Gibson's designs occurred in the period 1909–1911 with the introduction of tilted necks, raised "floating" pickguards, high bridges, and trapeze tailpieces to hold the strings (in place of the earlier pin bridges). These features bring the arch-top guitar closer still to violin principles. The strings now pass over the bridge and continue to the tailpiece, and the table is vibrated by vertical oscillations. The tilted neck allows a higher bridge, which increases the angle of the strings as they pass across it and thus the vertical pressure on the table. The increased vertical pressure helps to transmit

Lloyd Loar (third from the left) in the early 1920s.

more string vibration to the top, and gives the guitar greater volume.

The final major development in arch-top guitar design took place in 1924 with the introduction of the L-5, which had violin-type f-holes in place of the round soundhole. The L-5 was designed by Lloyd Loar, who worked for Gibson between 1920 and 1924. Loar's other guitar innovations included the two-footed adjustable arch-top bridge, and the first known pickup.

The 1920s and 30s were the heyday of the arch-top guitar. Its powerful volume and short sustain made it an ideal instrument for the dance bands and jazz orchestras of the period. Played with a pick, it could provide a firm, incisive rhythmic beat, and play rapid chordal passages or fast solo runs.

Having pioneered the carved-top guitar, Gibson never lost its dominance of the market. The L-5 became the definitive f-hole guitar and was Gibson's only f-hole model until 1932, when a range of less expensive models was introduced. The 1930s saw a proliferation of arch-top guitars not only from Gibson but from other leading manufacturers, including Martin and Epiphone. This was due to more than the demand for the guitar in the music of the day: in the grim economic circumstances of the Depression, many companies tried to tempt the customers with new models.

Some of the finest f-hole guitars of the 1930s were built in very small numbers, by independent makers such as

Charles Stromberg and John D'Angelico, who produced hand-carved guitars which are now collector's items. Surprisingly for such an essentially American instrument, some of the most famous of all arch-top guitars were built in Europe to the designs of a classical player, Mario Maccaferri. Maccaferri was associated with the Selmer company of Paris in the period 1930 to 1933, during which time he designed and supervised the construction of a range of revolutionary guitars. The quality of his arch-top model, which was played by Django Reinhardt, has become legendary.

The mass popularity of the acoustic arch-top guitar did not survive the war. Guitar production in America slowed to a trickle between 1941 and 1945 as the factories turned their resources to the war effort. When they returned to building guitars, the day of the dance band was almost over, and jazz and popular guitarists were turning to amplified instruments.

The steel-string flat-top, which has dominated the acoustic guitar market since the war, developed independently of the arch-top. Its origins lie in the gut-strung guitars of the nineteenth century.

The Martin company is the oldest American guitar manufacturer and the most highly regarded maker of steel-string flat-tops today. The company's history spans the whole period of development of the American acoustic guitar, and illustrates the changes it has undergone in the last 140 years. C. F. Martin I (1796–1873) was born in Mark Neukirchen, Germany, where he learned guitar making from his father before working for the celebrated Viennese luthier Johann Georg Staufer. Martin emigrated to America in 1833, following a long industrial dispute between the guitar makers of Mark Neukirchen and the local branch of the violin makers' guild.[2] On arriving in New York, Martin set up shop at 196 Hudson Street. In 1839 he moved his business to Nazareth, Pennsylvania; the company has remained there ever since.

Martin's earliest surviving guitars, made at Hudson Street in the 1830s, are noticeably European in design and show the influence of Staufer. During the 1840s and 50s, Martin's designs underwent radical change, and the flat-top guitars that resulted are recognizably the ancestors of these produced by the company today. Martin guitars of the mid-nineteenth century are small-bodied and finely crafted, with delicate inlays of wood or mother-of-pearl, and tuned either by German-made machines or ivory pegs. At some date in the 1850s C. F. Martin I invented the X-bracing pattern which has become the standard for steel-string flat-tops, in the same way as Antonio de Torres' fan bracing (developed at about the same time) has become the basis for classic guitar soundboard design. The Martin company did not start to build steel-string guitars before 1900, however: all its early instruments were designed for gut treble strings and silk-cored basses. Martin's first steel-string models were made on custom order, and it was not until 1922 that steel strings were offered on a standard production model.

The change to steel strings produced no externally visible alteration in the design of the guitars. Internally, the soundboard's bracing was made heavier and the number of bars increased. Thus the steel-string flat-top, a quite individual form of guitar, grew out of the gut-strung guitar almost as if by accident. Other companies adopted steel strings for flat-top guitars in a similar way, at various dates from the early 1900s to the mid-1920s.

While the Martin and Gibson companies are quite different in character, their early histories have one striking similarity. Both companies were founded on the skills of a single man whose growing reputation as a luthier produced a stream of orders which soon exceeded his output. With true entrepreneurial spirit, companies were formed which expanded from workshops into larger and larger factories. Once it was accepted that guitars could be built in factories, it became increasingly difficult for individual makers to compete economically—the pressure was on any successful craftsman to expand. The demand for more guitars—first for home entertainment, vaudeville and popular music orchestras, later for blues, country, jazz and folk music—changed the essential nature of American guitar production. The same demand for a guitar suited to essentially popular music also encouraged the adoption of steel strings, through the pursuit of a louder instrument for accompaniment and ensemble use.

During the latter part of the nineteenth century and early decades of the twentieth, there were many companies in America making flat-top guitars similar in shape and size to those built by Martin. Martin's most serious rival as a maker of high-quality guitars was the Washburn company, founded in the 1890s by George Washburn Lyon of the Lyon and Healy company. From its founding through the 1920s and 1930s, Washburn made a comparatively small number of very finely constructed instruments which are now rare and highly prized.

Many guitars were cheaply built, and two of the most important makers of less expensive instruments were Harmony and Stella. Stella guitars were particularly popular among blues players during the 1920s and 1930s. Although Stella guitars were made in large numbers, for sale by mail order, few have survived. Those that do survive testify to the high quality which American manufacturers could achieve on inexpensive instruments.

Gibson, sustained by its success with the arch-top guitar, was a comparative latecomer to the flat-top market: the 1921 catalogue shows no flat-top models. However, in the late 1920s and 1930s the company introduced a range of flat-top guitars designed largely for accompaniment and country music.

While the flat-top guitar became established in blues, country and folk music during the 1920s and 1930s, its real growth in popularity did not come until after the Second World War. The folk boom of the late 1950s through 1960s, which was reinforced by the use of acoustic guitar by some pop and rock stars, had a dramatic effect on the guitar industry. In the late 1950s, Martin's annual guitar production was in the region of 5,500; by the early 1970s, it had increased to something around 20,000. For Gibson, the post-war decline of the arch-top and rise of the flat-top has meant a considerable change in production patterns. From being a sideline before the war, flat-tops now make up almost the whole of Gibson's very considerable acoustic guitar production.

The guitar boom of the 1960s had the effect of rejuvenating several established companies and promoting the success of new ones. Guild and Ovation are two important American guitar manufacturers who first made their mark in the 1960s.

The Guild company was founded in 1952 by Alfred Dronge, the owner of a New York music store, who brought together five craftsmen to build a small number of guitars. Dronge was a classical player himself and Guild's early production reflected this interest. Since then, impelled by a switch to flat-tops in the folk boom of the early 1960s, Guild has followed the typical growth pattern from craft-based cottage industry to public-owned manufacturing company to corporation subsidiary.

Ovation, by contrast, started as a subsidiary of the Kaman corporation, whose primary interests are in aeronautics and related fields. Charles Kaman, company president, is a guitar enthusiast. The Ovation company grew out of his instruction to the corporation's aerospace division to investigate guitar design with a view to making improvements. The results emerged in 1966 with the first of Ovation's fiberglass-bodied, bowl-backed acoustic guitars.

During the 1960s the popularity of the acoustic flat-top became truly international. In consequence, the American manufacturers have had to face a number of challenges over the last decade. Their most formidable rivals have been the Japanese, who have applied their manufacturing skills to instrument building with increasing success. Through efficient factory work, low labor costs and determined marketing, Japanese firms have succeeded in capturing much of the market for cheap guitars. Their more expensive instruments are generally closely based on the designs of Martin and Gibson. However, the American companies continue to be successful despite the competition from often very much cheaper copies. Old established companies such as Martin and Gibson can sell large numbers of guitars on their name alone. More importantly, they have built up considerable expertise over the years; their instruments have an undeniable edge of quality, which for most serious musicians is sufficient to justify the high price. In recent years, Japanese labor costs have started to rise, and Japanese guitars are slowly losing their price advantage over American-made instruments. The competition is shifting more to the grounds of quality alone. In these circumstances, the pressure is on the Japanese makers to originate new designs and produce guitars with distinctive looks and sound qualities.

As the two largest American manufacturers of flat-tops, Gibson and Martin have been unwilling to abandon the mid- and low-range markets. Unable to produce good guitars inexpensively in America, and unwilling to compromise their reputations by putting their own names on lower-quality guitars, both companies make use of foreign subsidiaries. Martin has taken over the Levin company in Sweden to produce a mid-price range of guitars, and also uses the Japanese Sigma company to produce a line of inexpensive instruments. Gibson has since 1969 applied the Epiphone name (which it acquired in 1957 on the death of Epi Stathopoulo) to a range of Japanese-made guitars.

American manufacturers have been comforted in the 1970s by an increase in the demand for their more expensive models. Martin, for example, has found that its highest-priced models (which also carry the highest profit margins) are now forming a larger percentage of total production than ever before. The increased demand for high-price and often highly decorated guitars has also encouraged a reappearance of the individual luthier building individual steel-string instruments, and carrying out custom inlay work which the large companies now find uneconomical.

It is often said that the quality of modern steel-string guitars has fallen to far below that of guitars of the inter-war years. Certainly, changes in musical fashion have led to changes in guitar sound and design: large sturdy instruments are now preferred to the smaller delicate guitars of fifty years ago. However, it is often difficult to make direct comparisons between instruments of different ages: as a guitar grows older, it mellows and matures. The changes which take place in the sound of a guitar over the first two or three years of its life can be dramatic, and slow improvement can continue for as long as twenty or thirty years.

While the arch-top and six-string flat-top are the main types of modern steel-string guitar, two other variants deserve mention here. Of these, the most important is the Dobro or resonator guitar. The Dobro takes its name from its inventors, the Dopera brothers, who developed their first successful resonator guitar in 1926. The aim of the resonator guitar was to produce an increased volume; it also has a significantly different tone from other steel-string guitars. In the resonator guitar, the strings pass over a bridge which is supported on an aluminum "spider" and transmits the vibrations to a thin spun-aluminum resonator inside the guitar body.

The earliest and most expensive model of the Dobro was the "Tri-Plate," which incorporated three separate resonators activated by a triple-armed bridge. In 1928–29 single-resonator models were introduced, and single-resonator Dobros have since then been the most widely manufactured.

The Dobro patents have changed hands several times, giving the resonator guitar a particularly confused manufacturing history. Both wood- and metal-body models have been made, some with multiple slotted soundholes in the upper bout, some with f-holes, and some with two small circular soundholes.

The other significant variant of the steel-string guitar is the twelve-string. The modern twelve-string guitar was introduced into North America from Mexico; Latin America has a tradition of double-strung guitar-family instruments which dates back to the Spanish Conquest. Almost all twelve-string guitars have flat tops, although Martin has made two arch-top twelve-strings.

Twelve strings give the guitar a very full sound with interesting harmonic possibilities, but they make it more difficult to play. The pull of the strings also makes life more difficult for the guitar builder, who has to produce a stronger neck and more heavily braced top. The twelve-string guitar was first popularized by blues singers, notably Leadbelly and Blind Willie McTell. But despite occasional bursts of publicity, when it has been used by various pop stars, the instrument has never gained widespread popularity.

The Guitar Gallery which follows is divided into separate categories—arch-top, flat-top, resonator, and twelve-string guitars. Within each category, the entries are grouped chronologically.

The Martin company has used a system of standard sizes since the mid-nineteenth century, designating the size of the instrument by a prefix (2,1,0,00,000,D, etc). The dimensions of any Martin guitar vary only slightly from the standard for that model. Accordingly we have designated Martin guitars by their reference codes in the gallery, and grouped all the standard dimensions in the table in Appendix 1.

Carved-top guitar by Orville Gibson
KALAMAZOO, 1898.
From the collection of the Gibson company.

Overall length: 101cm
Scale length: 65cm
Body length: 48cm
Body width: upper bout 29.5cm
          waist 24.5cm
          lower bout 40cm
Body depth: increasing from 7 to 7.5cm

This guitar was built by Orville Gibson before the formation of the Gibson company. It has a handwritten label which reads: "The Gibson/Mandolins & Guitars/Patented Feb 1st 1898/Made by O. H. Gibson/Kalamazoo."

The top is hand-carved from one piece of Norwegian spruce. It is quite thick and has a pronounced arch with no bracing except for a single transverse bar below the soundhole. The back is also hand-carved from a thick plank. The sides are not bent but sawn to

shape from a solid plank, and extend up into the base of the neck, eliminating the need for a separate endblock or heel. The neck itself, as on many of Orville Gibson's hand-made instruments, is partly hollow and contains a resonant air cavity. Other unconventional features include the bridge, which is a combination of the usual nineteenth-century pin bridge with a metal reinforcing stay, and the solid flat headstock fitted with banjo-type ungeared tuning pegs.

Carved-top guitar by Orville Gibson
KALAMAZOO, *c.* 1898.
From the collection of the Gibson company.

Overall length: 106cm
Scale length: 65cm
Body length: 54cm
Body width: upper bout 31cm
          waist 25.5cm
          lower bout 44cm
Body depth: 10cm

The printed label of Orville Gibson's "De Luxe 'O' Style" guitar reads "The Gibson Mandolins and Guitars Are Acknowledged by leading Artists as World Beaters. Every Instrument Warranted. Correct Scale. Easy to Play. Beautiful Model. Powerful Tone. Originated & Patented February 1898 by O. H. Gibson. Kalamazoo. Mich."

This is an extraordinarily large guitar by the standard of the period, and is actually bigger than many of the large arch-top plectrum guitars built in the 1930s. The construction is similar to that of the preceding example. Top and back are similarly carved, the walnut sides sawn from a solid plank, and the neck is hollowed out. The body finish is a black lacquer.

The upper edge of the body is bound with alternating parallelograms of ebony and abalone, and the butterfly inlay on the soundboard is made of pieces of tortoiseshell, mother-of-pearl and abalone. The headstock inlay design of star and moon is found on many of Orville Gibson's instruments.

This guitar has a large, powerful tone with a character of sound and sustain somewhere between that of the standard f-hole guitar and the steel-string flat-top.

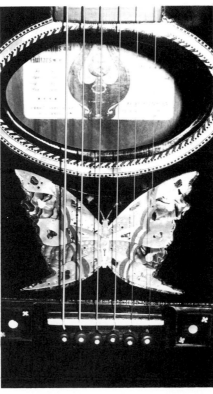

Gibson carved-top guitar, Style O "Special Grand Concert Guitar, Artist Model," *c.* 1918. *Photographed at Gruhn Guitars, Nashville.*

Overall length: 107cm
Scale length: 63cm
Body length: 51cm
Body width: upper bout 31cm
        waist 26cm
        lower bout 44cm
Body depth: 9.5cm

The top of the guitar is carved from spruce, and the sides and carved back are maple. The whole body is finished in a mahogany-colored stain. The neck has the heavy, chunky V section common to all Gibson guitars made before the introduction of the adjustable truss rod in 1925, after which a slimmer section was adopted.

The neck-to-body junction occurs at the fifteenth fret for easy access to high positions, and the unusual body design allows a long neck to be combined with a normally placed bridge. In effect, the Style O Artist Model was the first steel-string guitar with a cutaway shoulder, a feature of guitar design that was

not generally adopted until after World War II. The pattern of the shoulder curlicue is derived from Gibson's mandolin design, as is the extension of the fingerboard to give an extra two frets under the two top strings.

The two-footed bridge is not adjustable for height, which helps to date this guitar: the adjustable two-footed bridge was introduced by Lloyd Loar, who joined Gibson in 1920, and is specified on guitars in the 1921 catalogue. At the time of its introduction, the Style O Artist Model was Gibson's most

expensive guitar, and in 1921 it retailed for the princely sum of $265.95—when Martin's abalone-inlaid 000-45 cost a mere $150.

Despite its price, the style O found use in several fields of music. It was played by vaudeville stars and members of amateur guitar and mandolin orchestras, and was used for Hawaiian music (a special conversion kit was available free of charge). There is even a photograph of the young Bill Broonzy with a Style O—but this may just have been a prop in the photographer's studio.

Gibson L-4 carved-top guitar, *c.* 1920. *From the collection of the Gibson company, Kalamazoo.*

Overall length: 100.5cm
Scale length: 62.5cm
Body length: 51.5cm
Body width: upper bout 29.3cm
        waist 23.5cm
        lower bout 40.7cm
Body depth: 9.5cm

The L-4 model first appeared in Gibson's catalogue G, which the company believes to have been issued in 1910, and was the top model of the L series until the introduction of

the L-5 in 1924. Probably the most famous guitarist to use the L-4 was Eddie Lang.

The L-4 was built with a carved spruce top, carved maple back, and maple sides. Prior to 1925, when the adjustable truss rod was introduced, the necks were reinforced with a center strip of ebony. There is some confusion about the date of the introduction of the raised pickguard, as on this guitar. Lloyd Loar is usually credited with the design, but early Gibson catalogues state that it was patented in 1911, nine years before Loar joined the company.

This L-4 has been restored and refinished by Gibson: the bridge and tailpiece are not original.

Arch-top guitar designed by Mario Mac-
caferri for Selmer PARIS, 1932.
*Photograph by Tony Gilbert, courtesy of
Maurice Summerfield. Detail photograph of
another example, from the collection of Mario
Maccaferri.*

Overall length: 97.3cm
Scale length: 63.8cm
Body length: 47.3cm
Body width: upper bout 28.9cm
                     waist 25.4cm
                     lower bout 39.8cm
Body depth: 8.9cm at the neck, 11.1cm at the
                     waist, 9.5cm at the base

Mario Maccaferri has had notable careers
as a concert guitarist, luthier, engineer and
businessman, but is best known today as the
inventor of one of the most successful of all
steel-string guitars.

Maccaferri was born in 1899, near Bologna, Italy. He was apprenticed in 1911 to
Luigi Mozzani, guitarist and luthier. Mozzani
encouraged Maccaferri to take up the guitar
seriously, and he studied at the academy of
Siena before going to Paris in 1919 where he
met the great classical guitarists Miguel
Llobet and Emilio Pujol. In the 1920s
Maccaferri started to give recitals, and built a
successful career as a concert player, which
was abruptly terminated in 1933 when he
broke his right hand in an accident.

Maccaferri developed the first prototypes
for his famous guitar design in the late 1920s,
at a time when he was living and working in
London. After an introduction to Henri
Selmer, head of the firm of French instrument manufacturers, Maccaferri was offered a
contract to design a series of guitars for the
company and set up a factory to build them.

Production started in the latter part of
1932. Three models were offered in the
catalogue: Classical, Hawaiian and Orchestra.
The labels of the guitars bore the legend
*Fabriqué en France sous la direction technique de
M. Maccaferri, Selmer & Cie, Paris.* However, just as everything was getting underway,
Maccaferri discovered that his contract was
for only six months and after a bitter dispute,
parted company from Selmer early in 1933. As
a result, fewer than 300 Maccaferri guitars
were built, most of which were steel-string
arch-tops.

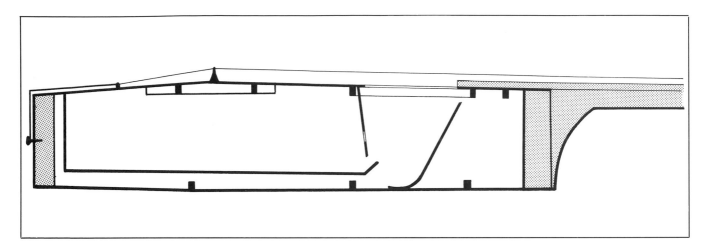

Maccaferri's guitars had a number of innovatory features, the most immediately noticeable being the cutaway shoulder and large D-shaped soundhole. The most radical innovation, however, is concealed inside the guitar. The body contains an internal soundbox, which is very lightly built and attached to the guitar sides at four points. In front of the soundhole is a shield, designed to project the sound vibrations from the body cavity. The purpose of the soundbox, which vibrates as a diaphragm, is to break the column of air within the guitar body and prevent wolf notes. In this it was highly successful, and Maccaferri's guitars are renowned for evenness in volume from note to note.

Although the guitars were mass-produced, great attention was paid to the construction of the soundboard. Maccaferri insisted that the wood be split rather than sawn, so that its fibers would not be cut. He also believed that the climatic conditions during construction are important: "Changes in temperature and humidity can result in stresses being built into the top which can affect the tone. How they do so is mysterious, and the effect is impossible to calculate, but these effects and the quality and type of timber are just as important as the strutting to the sound of the guitar."[3] While the tops of all models were made of spruce, the sides and back of the jazz guitar were built of a laminate of rosewood veneers with a core of spruce.

There were unusual features in the head, neck, fingerboard and bridge. The tuning machines were revolutionary in their day,

consisting of sealed lubricated units in which the circumference of the gear used the casing as a bearing surface. A similar principle is used today by the Schaller, MkVI, and Grover Rotomatic machines.

Maccaferri used a neck reinforcement of duralumin plates running longitudinally, and fitted the fingerboard with a zero fret, which helped give perfect intonation. The nut is retained as a string spacer. The fingerboard extends over the soundhole on the treble, giving twenty-four frets on the top string.

The bridge was designed to a helicoidal curve, for perfect compensation, and a choice of seven different bridge heights was offered to help the player obtain the action that suited him best. The tailpiece design accepts either loop or ball-end strings, and makes rapid string changes simple.

Maccaferri arch-top guitars had a most unusual tone, and great projection. They were mellower and less steely-sounding than a steel-string flat-top, but sang out more and sustained longer than any f-hole arch-top. The few that survive are highly sought by collectors and players, and replicas are now being made in Japan, with Maccaferri's approval, for Maurice Summerfield's CSL Company.

Maccaferri guitars were particularly associated with the great French guitarist Django Reinhardt (see page 330). Ironically, the two men never met. At that time, Maccaferri did not know Django's playing: the worlds of classical and jazz guitar did not touch, and the very idea that a gypsy with only two usable fingers on his left hand should be a great guitarist seemed too bizarre to be true!

Martin 00-18S arch-top guitar, 1932.
Photographed at Gruhn Guitars, Nashville.

Martin introduced the 00-18S arch-top guitars in 1932. Only nine had been made when, in 1933, the designation was changed to R-18, and the series was finally discontinued in 1941.

The top of this guitar is press-shaped in a mold from a bookmatched pair of thin sheets of spruce. The X bracing to the top, which is simpler than that on a flat-top guitar, is shaped to help maintain the arch. Press-molding was a cheaper way of forming the top than carving, but Martin found the technique unsatisfactory and abandoned it in 1935. The sides and back of the guitar are maple, and it has a dark sunburst finish. The bridge is adjustable for height at one end only, and is fitted with a slanting saddle.

Martin entered the arch-top plectrum guitar market in 1931, and produced three ranges of models (designated C, R and F) through the 1930s. The company wanted to broaden its range of products, the better to be able to compete in the hard times of the

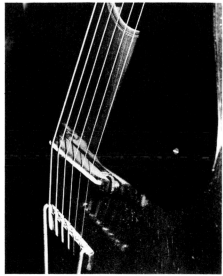

Depression. Although Martin's plectrum guitars were well made, they never seriously challenged Gibson's dominance of the market. The introduction of the C and R series with round soundholes was an error of judgment, and in 1934 the design was changed to f-holes.

Gibson L-50 carved-top guitar, *c.* 1932.
From the collection of the Gibson company.

Overall length: 104cm
Scale length: 62.2cm
Body length: 51.7cm
Body width: upper bout 29.3cm
waist 23.5cm
lower bout 41cm
Body depth: 10cm

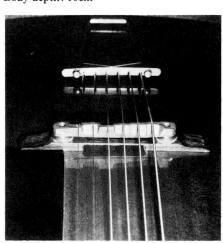

Despite the success of the L-5 from its introduction in 1924, it was not until 1932 that Gibson extended its range of f-hole carved-top guitars with the introduction of the L-12, L-10, L-7 and L-50. The range was redesigned with larger body sizes in 1934.

Although it was the least expensive of the line, the L-50 still had a carefully carved fine-grain spruce top, maple body, and two-footed height-adjustable bridge with individual compensation for each string. The neck incorporates the adjustable truss rod invented by Ted McHugh, which is still used on all of Gibson's current models.

Although Gibson's L-series f-hole guitars are remembered today for their use in jazz bands and dance orchestras, they were also widely used by country and blues musicians.

Epiphone Deluxe carved-top guitar, *c.* 1934.
Owned by Ray Gallo.

Overall length: 105.5cm
Scale length: 64.5cm
Body length: 52.5cm
Body width: upper bout 29.5cm
             waist 24.5cm
             lower bout 42.5cm
Body depth: sides 9cm, overall 11.5cm

Epiphone Olympic carved-top guitar, *c.* 1933.
From the collection of Paul Godden.

Overall length: 103cm
Scale length: 64.5cm
Body length: 49.4cm
Body width: upper bout 27.5cm
             waist 22.8cm
             lower bout 37.6cm
Body depth: approximately 11cm overall

The Epiphone Company of Long Island, New York was Gibson's main rival as a manufacturer of f-hole plectrum guitars. The top Epiphone models, such as the Deluxe, were designed to compete directly with Gibson's range, but the company also produced a number of simpler and less expensive guitars, including the Olympic and Zenith models.

This guitar is neatly but simply built, with a carved spruce top, mahogany back and sides, and mahogany neck. The legend "Epiphone Masterbilt" is applied to the headstock as a decal, where the more expensive models had the name scrolled in mother-of-pearl.

The Epiphone Deluxe was built from about 1930 to 1938, during which period it gradually became more highly decorated. This example has a spruce top with unbound f-holes, and sides and back of fine-quality maple. The flame on the back has been perfectly matched on the two halves of the body. The head detailing, with its asymmetrical shaping, is very pretty, and typical of Epiphone design at this period.

This guitar is still in service, and possesses an unusually loud, steely tone, which makes it an ideal orchestra guitar.

"Style A" carved-top guitar by John D'Angelico NEW YORK, c. 1935.
Photographed at Gruhn Guitars, Nashville.

Overall length: 107cm
Scale length: 63cm
Body length: 51cm
Body width: upper bout 31cm
waist 26cm
lower bout 44cm
Body depth: approximately 10cm

John D'Angelico (1905–64) started to build carved-top guitars in 1932, and by 1934 was making a range of four models, Style A, Style B, Excel and New Yorker. He discontinued the Styles A and B in the late 1940s, but continued to build the other two until shortly before his death. In his career, D'Angelico hand-built 1164 carved-top guitars. Most were built to order, and many had individual features to the customer's special requirements.

This is one of D'Angelico's earlier guitars. The top is carved from spruce, the sides and back are maple. D'Angelico guitars are still highly sought both as collector's pieces and as

Vega arch-top guitar, *c.* 1935.
From the collection of Louis Gallo.
Photographed at Top Gear, London.

Overall length: 105.2cm
Scale length: 63cm
Body length: 51.5cm
Body width: upper bout 30.8cm
waist 25.5cm
lower bout 43.1cm
Body depth: sides 9cm, overall 11cm

playing instruments. Although they are not the loudest of arch-top guitars, they have a particularly round and mellow tone, and are regarded as among the finest jazz guitars ever built. D'Angelico passed on his skills to Jim D'Aquisto, who worked for him from 1951 and has continued the tradition of high-quality hand-carved plectrum guitars.

The Vega company was famous for exquisitely made and decorated banjos. It is less well known that Vega also produced a range of inexpensive flat-top and arch-top guitars.

The top is built of spruce and the body of maple; even the cheaper guitars in the Depression era were often made with high-quality materials. Money was saved in their building by the use of simpler bindings, inexpensive tuning machines, and rosewood in place of ebony for the fingerboard.

"Eddie Freeman Special" four-string arch-top guitar by Selmer, *c.* 1937.
From the collection of Louis Gallo.

Overall length: 95cm
Scale length: 64cm
Body length 47.5cm
Body width: upper bout 29cm
          waist 25.8cm
          lower bout 40cm
Body depth: sides increase from 9.2 to 10.2cm

The "Eddie Freeman Special" was made not as a tenor guitar but as a four-string instrument specially suited for chord playing in an orchestra, and was designed for a reentrant tuning. Eddie Freeman's idea was that since an orchestra player spent much of his time playing four-string chords, a specially designed guitar could be made which was easy to play and would cut through the sound of the other instruments. This instrument is extremely loud and has an incisive tone.

The guitar's design is very close to that of the famous Maccaferri guitar, although there is no internal soundbox and the lower bout is braced only with two transverse bars.

The "Eddie Freeman Special" met with considerable opposition from orchestra guitarists in England, the country where it was introduced. The leading members of the profession decided that it was a bastard instrument, and a threat to their livelihood. They mounted a coordinated publicity campaign, writing a string of articles condemning the guitar, which killed its chances of success. Very few examples survive in their original state, most having been profitably converted into six-string guitars by widening the neck and putting on a new fingerboard.

Arch-top guitar by Selmer PARIS, *c.* 1937.
Photographs by courtesy of the Paris Conservatory.

Overall length: 102cm
Scale length: 67cm
Body length: 47.3cm
Body width: upper bout 29cm
          waist 25.5cm
          lower bout 40cm
Body depth: varying between 9.2 and 10.2cm

After Mario Maccaferri left Selmer, Selmer continued to build jazz guitars that look somewhat like the Maccaferri models, and are sometimes mistaken for them. There are a number of important differences, however. The later Selmer guitars had a twenty-one-fret fingerboard, joining the body at the fourteenth fret, and a small oval soundhole in place of the large D-hole. Maccaferri believes that Selmer introduced the smaller soundhole so that a small pickup unit the company was marketing could be easily fitted over it, and screw holes for such a pickup can be seen in the top of this guitar. The bridge, which at first glance appears identical to the Maccaferri bridge, is also different: the center section stands on two small feet, whereas the Maccaferri bridge made contact with the table over its whole length.

The most serious differences between the two types of guitar lie in their internal construction. The Selmer guitar uses a very simple bracing of transverse bars, and is not fitted with the internal soundbox, which was difficult and expensive to build.

The head of this particular guitar is stamped with Django Reinhardt's name. It belonged to him, and was given to the Conservatory by his widow. It now rests in a glass case, alongside classical guitars by the great makers of the seventeenth, eighteenth and nineteenth centuries.

Martin F-7 carved-top guitar, 1937.
From the collection of John Pearse.

Martin's F series were the largest carved-top guitars the company made, and seem to have been designed to compete with Gibson's L series.

The F-7, introduced in 1935, was built with a carved spruce top, and rosewood sides and back. The fingerboard is decorated with "pearloid" position markers, and has a decorative white inlay 6mm in from the binding on each edge. The headstock is inlaid with the C. F. Martin legend in the same way as the modern style 45 flat-top. All the fittings on this example are original.

Martin guitars have never been fitted with an adjustable truss rod: the company's aim is to make necks that will not distort, rather than ones whose curvature can be adjusted. Early steel-string Martin guitars were reinforced with an ebony strip. From 1934 to 1967, a T-section metal bar was used as reinforcement; since 1967, the neck rod has consisted of a hollow, square-section metal tube.

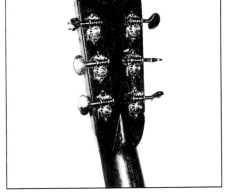

Carved-top guitar by Charles A. Stromberg & Sons BOSTON, *c.* 1938.
From the collection of Derek Weskin.

Overall length: 110cm
Scale length: 63cm
Body length: 55.5cm
Body width: upper bout 33.5cm
          waist 27.6cm
          lower bout 48.5cm
Body depth: sides 9cm, overall front to back
          11.8cm

The Stromberg firm hand-built carved-top guitars, in very small numbers, during the 1930s. Almost all its instruments were custom-made for specific players, the majority of whom were guitarists with the leading bands of the day. Irving Ashby, who was later to work for Nat King Cole and Oscar Peterson, spent some time in the Stromberg factory in Boston "breaking in" new guitars: those he handled included three for Freddie Green of Count Basie's band, and one for the guitarist with Paul Whiteman.

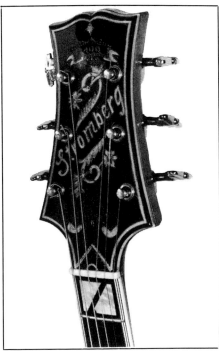

233

This instrument is one of Stromberg's 400 model guitars, the largest model the company built, which was designed to compete with the Gibson Super 400 which had been introduced in 1934. It has a hand-carved spruce top, and maple sides and back. The maple is of the highest quality, with a pronounced flame, and the grain of the two halves of the back is perfectly matched. The neck is also made of maple with an ebony center strip and joins the body between the fourteenth and fifteenth frets. Although it is thinner from front to back than most guitars of the period, there is no sign of any bow or warping.

Stromberg guitars had the reputation of being the loudest of all carved-top instruments. This superb example possesses, in addition to considerable volume, a wonderfully rich bass and mellow treble.

Gibson L-5 carved-top guitar, 1947.
From the collection of Harvey Hope.

Overall length: 107.5cm
Scale length: 64.5cm
Body length: 53.2cm
Body width: upper bout 32cm
        waist 26.5cm
        lower bout 43.2cm
Body depth: depth of sides 8.6cm, 11.5cm
        overall

Since its introduction in 1924, the L-5 has enjoyed greater success than any other f-hole guitar, and remains in production (on custom order) to the present.

The L-5 was modified from its original design in 1934, when the body size was enlarged, extra inlay was added to the fingerboard and the tailpiece was modified. Since then the design has been little changed, apart from the introduction of a cutaway shoulder as standard at the end of the 1940s.

This L-5 is in its original condition, save that a Rowe De Armond pickup has been fitted and the bridge position slightly altered. It has a sunburst-finish carved-spruce top, with exceptionally fine grain, maple sides and bird's-eye maple back. The L-5 was fitted with gold-plated Kluson De Luxe machines, and the tailpiece is also gold-plated.

Model G-40 arch-top guitar by Mario Maccaferri NEW YORK *c.* 1954.
From the authors' collection.

Overall length: 93.4cm
Scale length: 62.3cm
Body length: 43.8cm
Body width: upper bout 25.4cm
        waist 22.3cm
        lower bout 33.7cm
Body depth: approximately 10.2cm

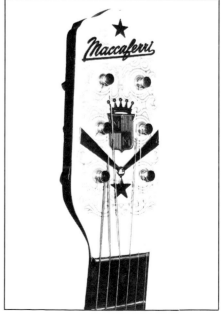

Maccaferri emigrated to America just before the war, and set up a successful business making clarinet and saxophone reeds. After the war, he founded a plastics manufacturing company, Mastro Industries.

In the early 1950s, Maccaferri decided to combine his experience of guitars and plastics to build a plastic guitar, and between 1953 and 1954 invested $300,000 in the tooling necessary to produce an arch-top and a flat-top model. His aim was not to produce a toy, but

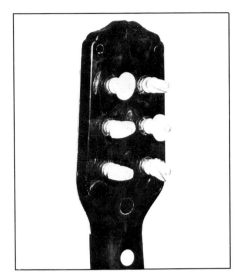

to make good playing instruments at a low price.

The body of the guitar is molded from polystyrene, with a cream-colored top and imitation rosewood back. A system of wooden struts is incorporated in the soundboard molding. The neck has a wooden core, sheathed in steel to resist the string pull, and is finished in plastic, as is the fingerboard. The wooden core carries through the body to the end block, so that the neck angle can be adjusted by turning a screw beneath the tailpiece, rotating the neck about a pivot at the heel. Tailpiece and bridge are essentially similar to those of the famous Maccaferri guitars of the 1930s—although the bridge is now plastic. The head of the guitar conceals a system of planetary-gear tuning machines, which have a 14:1 ratio. The "nut" is cast into

the front of the head, but acts only as a string divider: the fingerboard has a zero fret.

Maccaferri's plastic guitars represented a remarkable feat of engineering. More than that, they possess a remarkably good tone and loud volume, and, at $29.50 for the flat-top and $39.50 for the arch-top, offered very good value. Despite everything, the guitars were a commercial failure, and few were built. Maccaferri attributes their lack of success largely to his misjudgment of the market: in an attempt to reconcile people to the idea of a plastic instrument, he tried to give it a familiar form by making the guitars with f-holes. But by 1953 the days of the f-hole guitar were over. Maccaferri was more than compensated for his losses on the plastic guitars, however, by his success with plastic ukuleles, more than nine million of which were sold.

FLAT-TOP GUITARS

Guitar by Martin and Coupa, *c.* 1845
Photographs by Mick Dean.
Measurements not available.

Through the 1840s, C. F. Martin was in partnership with John Coupa, a guitar teacher with a studio at 385 Broadway, New York. The arrangement seems to have been that Martin built the guitars in Nazareth for Coupa to sell in New York under the joint name of Martin and Coupa.

Martin and Coupa guitars, now very rare, are of great significance in the development of Martin's designs. It was in the period 1840 to 1850 that Martin ceased to build guitars in the Viennese style of his mentor Georg Staufer, and started to move toward guitar styles which have essentially been maintained by the company to the present. Several of Martin's guitars of this period (some branded C. F. Martin & Co., New York, others bearing the Martin and Coupa label) show experimental features, and through them we can chart the course of the evolution of Martin designs.

This instrument has a combination of features that is, to our knowledge, unique on a Martin guitar. The head design is similar to that used by Martin in the 1830s, with the tuning machines concealed under a metal plate and buttons on one side, after the manner of Staufer. The body, however, does not have the Staufer-inspired, wasp-waisted

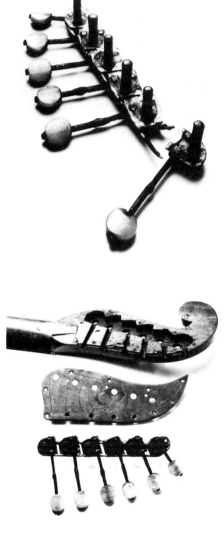

shape of the 30s, but is closer to the mature Martin style of twenty years later. The shape suggests strongly that Martin had had the opportunity to examine a Spanish-made guitar of about 1840, and was experimenting with Spanish-style construction.

This supposition is reinforced by the presence of Spanish features such as we have seen on no other Martin guitar, including simple fan bracing with three radiating struts, and a Spanish heel and slipper foot into which the sides are slotted. The division of the rosewood sides by a narrow decorative hardwood strip is another feature borrowed from nineteenth-century Spanish guitars. The presence of this strip weakens the sides; to give them strength, Martin fitted several vertical braces, and vertical brackets into which the cross struts of top and back are notched, framing up the body.

The design of the bridge is very modern for its date. In shape it conforms to the "pyramid" bridge pattern used by Martin throughout the latter half of the nineteenth century and the first quarter of the twentieth. But this is one of the very few nineteenth-century Martin guitars to be made with a tied rather than a pin bridge. The strings pass over a broad, backward-sloping ivory saddle-piece before being secured at the rear of the bridge.

This guitar proves that C. F. Martin was one of the few makers outside Spain in the early nineteenth century to be aware of the possibility of fan strutting on the guitar, and that he experimented with it before developing his own famous X-bracing system. It shows the American gut-strung guitar, the ancestor of the steel-string guitar, at a critical point of its evolution, about to break away from the diverse European influences to which it owed its beginnings.

Martin model 2-27, *c.* 1860.
Photographed at Gruhn Guitars, Nashville.

The earliest record of the use of numbers by Martin to denote standard sizes dates from 1852, by which time sizes 3, 2, 2½ and 1 had been defined. Sizes 5 and 0 were recorded in 1854, and size 4 in 1857.

Size 2, as shown here, was the smallest standard guitar built by Martin: sizes 5, 4 and 3 were *terz* guitars, tuned a third above normal. Since the 1860s, the trend has been to larger guitars. Size 0, which was then Martin's largest model, is now the smallest.

The "27" in the guitar's designation refers to its decoration, Martin having introduced a system of numerical suffixes to indicate styles in the late 1850s. Like all late nineteenth-century Martins, this guitar has a spruce top with light X bracing, Brazilian rosewood sides and back, cedar neck, and ebony pin bridge with a small pyramid-shaped hump at each end. The special identifying features of style 27 included, at this date, ivory body bindings lined with a multicolored wood inlay on the top edge, abalone soundhole inlay, and ivory

fingerboard bindings. The bridge pins are also made of ivory, and are inlaid with mother-of-pearl dots. As on most nineteenth-century Martin guitars, tuning is by German-built machines mounted "upside down"—that is, so that the string spindle is above rather than below the shaft which carries the button.

The identifying mark on the front end-block, center back brace, and back of headstock reads "C. F. Martin, New York." This mark was adopted at some time in the 1830s and was retained through much of the nineteenth century despite the move to Nazareth in 1838.

This guitar was built to be played with gut strings, as were all nineteenth-century Martin guitars. Many fine old American flat-tops have been damaged by being played with steel strings, for which they were not designed. Anyone wishing to produce a "steely" sound on a guitar originally made for gut strings, without running the risk of damaging it, can do so by using the Austrian-made "Thomastik" strings. These combine low tension with a surprisingly loud, sharp sound similar to that produced by steel strings.

Martin model 0-28, 1889.
From the collection of John Pearse.

Martin's style 28 is believed to have been introduced in the late 1860s or early 1870s, and has continued to be built in various sizes, with slight modifications, right up to the present. Early examples, such as this, had plain ebony fingerboards, ebony pyramid bridges, ivory body binding, and herringbone inlay to the soundboard edge. The herringbone inlay, applied to all style 28s made before 1947, was imported from Germany and is a feature which makes style 28s particularly prized by Martin guitar enthusiasts.

Ivory tuning pegs were occasionally fitted by Martin as an alternative to machines. They

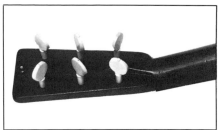

are not set directly into the cedar of the head, but are fitted with collars of some dark, resinous hardwood.

The identifying stamp on the back of the head reads "C. F. Martin, New York," while those on the endblock and center brace read "C. F. Martin & Co, New York." The "C. F. Martin & Co, New York" stamp was introduced in 1867, when C. F. Martin I took his son C. F. Martin II and C. F. Hartman into partnership. It appears on all Martin guitars made from 1867 to 1898, either by itself or together with the earlier "C. F. Martin, New York" stamp, which continued sometimes to be used on the headstock. There is usually no way of dating precisely a Martin guitar made before 1898, but in this case the figures "9/89" are penciled on the underside of the soundboard.

The sound of this 0-28 is very well balanced, with an even tonal change from string to string, and a surprising warmth and projection for so small a guitar. The number of nineteenth-century Martin guitars which survive as player's instruments rather than collector's pieces bears testimony to the high standards of their design and construction.

Howe-Orme guitar BOSTON, 1897.
From the collection of Kelvin Henderson.

Overall length: 96.4cm
Scale length: 64cm
Body length: 46.4cm
Body width: upper bout 22.7cm
     waist 18cm
     lower bout 31.7cm
Body depth: increasing from 8.7 to 10.5cm

The label reads "Pat: Nov 14 1893 Apr 28 1895 / HOWE-ORME / No... 1897 / Elias Howe Co Boston." It seems likely that this guitar was made for the Howe Company by Mr. Orme: many music stores and general trading companies had guitars made for them to which they affixed their own names in the late nineteenth and early twentieth century.

In size and shape this instrument is typical of American gut-strung guitars of the 1890s: the body dimensions are close to those of Martin's size 1, although the scale length is longer. It is very well built, with a fine spruce top, Brazilian rosewood sides and back, and ebony fingerboard. Its construction, however, shows several features which are definitely unusual. The most marked of these is the pronounced arching of the table in the lower bout, which is reinforced with three transverse braces. The pin bridge has been beautifully shaped to follow the curve of the table. The neck of the guitar is detachable, and its angle can be adjusted by turning two screw-mounted bearing spindles. Although Martin guitars of the 1830s and the first style 42s of the 1870s were built with adjustable neck angles (a feature deriving from Georg Staufer's guitars), it is surprising to find a guitar built in the late 1890s with an adjustable neck. The frets have a T section, which is also unusual for an American-built guitar of this period (this guitar's history is known, and it has not been re-fretted). Most American-made guitars of this date were built with rectangular-section frets, and T-section frets did not become general until the 1920s or 1930s.

Many makers of the late nineteenth century experimented with unusual aspects of guitar design and construction, and numerous patents were taken out. Although few of the patent "improvements" had any far-reaching effect on the guitar's design, they bear witness to the competition between luthiers, and to the shared aim of producing better instruments.

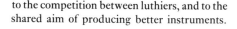

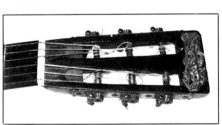

Martin model 1-21, *c.* 1898.
From the collection of the Wegner family.

Style 21 was introduced at the same period as style 28, and had a herringbone rosette inlay, multiple-wood body bindings, and a decorative wooden backstrip inlay. The bridge is fitted with ebony pins which have a mother-of-pearl dot inlay. The frets have a simple rectangular section; Martin did not start to use the modern type of T-section fret wire until 1934. The fretted silver scrollwork on the headstock, which incorporates the date 1898, and a set of undecipherable initials, is a custom addition.

The guitar carries both the "C. F. Martin & Co, New York" and the "C. F. Martin, New York" stamps. This suggests that the guitar was made late in 1897 and sold in 1898, when the scrollwork was added; the people at Martin finally recognized in 1898 that they had been in Nazareth and not New York for the past sixty years, and changed the brand to read "C. F. Martin & Co, Nazareth, Pa." Martin's confused sense of geography has resulted in all of its pre-1898 guitars being known as "New York Martins"—although nearly all of them were made in Nazareth.

At the same time that it changed its brand, Martin introduced a system of serial numbers, which were stamped on the forward endblock. The serial numbers start at 8000 (being a guess at the number of guitars the company had made by 1898) and run consecutively. They make it possible to date any Martin guitar built since 1898, and the table of numbers and dates may be found in Appendix 2.

Martin model 00-42, 1902 (left); **1-45 Ditson model,** 1919 (right).
From the collection of the Martin company.

Style 42 was the most lavish of Martin guitars from the days of its first listing in 1874 until the introduction of style 45 in 1904. This example is not a standard style 42, but one of three specials made in 1902 as prototypes for style 45. In addition to the usual abalone inlay to the soundhole and soundboard edge, it has abalone inlay to all body edges and to the front of the headstock in the manner of style 45. The 00 size was first introduced in 1877, and was Martin's largest guitar size until the introduction of the 000 size in 1902.

The 1-45 Ditson Model is one of a range of instruments manufactured by Martin between 1916 and 1921 for the Oliver Ditson Company, music publishers and instrument dealers. Three sizes were made, the largest of which was the prototype for Martin's famous Dreadnought design. The smaller sizes had a similar curvature, but narrower body.

Most of the Ditson guitars were simply decorated, but of the 473 instruments built for the company, 4 were built with Martin style-45 inlays.

Both the guitars shown here have spruce tops, Brazilian rosewood sides and back, and were built for gut strings. The bridge of the Ditson model is made of ivory.

239

Martin model 0-30, 1906.
From the collection of John Pearse.

Martin's style 30, which was last built in 1921, was very similar to style 27. Both had abalone soundhole inlay, and a multicolored wood inlay to the top edge inside an ivory binding, and an ivory-bound fingerboard. The only differences between the two styles were in the fingerboard inlay and in the tuning machines—which were silver on the more expensive style 30.

The pyramid bridge on this guitar is noticeably wider and heavier than those on earlier Martins.

John Pearse says of the guitar that "it has the finest neck of any Martin I have seen, and a very rich, resonant sound. I think that the size and shape are the optimum for the folk guitar."

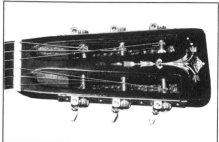

Martin model 0-45, 1907.
Photographed at Gruhn Guitars, Nashville.

Martin's style 45 was first issued in 1904 in 0 and 00 sizes, although prototypes were made in 1902 and 1903. They were only made in very small numbers: in the 27 years during which the 0-45 was in production, only 157 were built. This guitar would have cost $105 when it was new, over five times the price of Martin's cheapest guitar. Its present valuation is $4,000.

The 1907 0-45 shows the features of the style as it was first issued. Basic construction follows usual Martin practice of the time, and the finest available timbers are used throughout. The head is joined to the cedar neck with a V joint: one-piece necks were not introduced by Martin until the switch from cedar to mahogany around 1916. The body and fingerboard edges are bound in ivory, and all body edges, and the soundhole rosette, are abalone-inlaid. The headstock is also inlaid with abalone in what is known as the flowerpot or torch design. In early style 45s, the bulb at the top of the design was made of three separate pieces of abalone. This was simplified to a two-piece bulb in 1930.

The tuning machines are mounted on delicately engraved silver plates, and fitted

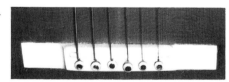

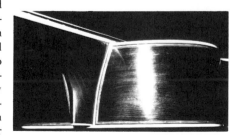

with ivory turn buttons. The bridge, saddle, and string pegs are also ivory.

The bridge has been damaged by the use of heavy steel strings, which have pulled the saddle forward and broken away the front edge of the bridge, necessitating repair.

Martin 00-45S "John Deichman" guitar, 1918.
Photographed at Gruhn Guitars, Nashville.

From time to time, unusual guitars are built in the Martin factory. This instrument carries no Martin brand or serial number, but was made in 1918 by John Deichman, a Martin employee. By tradition, Martin craftsmen are allowed to build themselves one guitar after a year's service with the company, using the facilities of the factory and the assistance of fellow employees. This is just such an instrument. It is modeled to the 00-45 pattern, but has additional abalone inlay to the soundhole and a double, instead of single, band of abalone to the body edges and fingerboard end. Also, the sides and back are made of walnut instead of rosewood.

Washburn guitar, *c.* 1920.
From the collection of Keith Johns.

Overall length: 95.4cm
Scale length: 62.6cm
Body length: 47.3cm
Body width: upper bout 24.1cm
           waist 19.4cm
           lower bout 33.3cm
Body depth: increasing from 8.3 to 9.4cm

The guitar is stamped on the center back brace: "1897 Style. George Washburn. New Model." Unfortunately, the label is missing — one of Washburn's label designs carried the charmingly immodest legend "Best in the World."

This guitar was built originally for gut strings. The fine spruce table was braced in the lower bout with only one transverse bar immediately below the soundhole, and one transverse bar set at a slight diagonal passing under the area of the bridge. This bracing proved insufficient to keep the table from distorting, and the guitar has been restored with X bracing. The sides, which are rosewood, have also been rebuilt.

The ebony fingerboard is bound with white plastic, as is the body, and the use of plastic for the bindings, along with gut strings, suggests a date of about 1920 for this instrument. The head is typical of Washburn, with sharply-cut square corners, and square corners to the tops of the string slots. The ebony pin bridge has a squared-off, flat-topped, pyramidal hump at each end.

Washburn guitars are often thought of as the American folk version of the Torres classical guitar. It is hard to see why. There is no similarity in shape, design or construction practice between Washburn and Torres instruments. Every feature of Washburn's instruments is typically American, with the exception of his soundhole inlay, which on this guitar is Spanish in inspiration. Neither can Washburn be said to stand in relation to the American folk guitar as Torres stands to the classical guitar: that is, as the founding father and greatest developer of the instrument. If the American guitar can be said to have such a founder figure (which is doubtful), then the honor must surely go to C. F. Martin I.

This does not, however, detract in any way from the quality of Washburn guitars. They show a delicacy of construction and a neatness of craftsmanship which assures their reputation as being among the finest guitars ever built in America.

241

Martin model 00-28K, 1921.
Photographed at Gruhn Guitars, Nashville.

Acoustic Hawaiian guitar by H. Weisseborn LOS ANGELES, *c.* 1925.
From the collection of Paul Godden.

Overall length 95.5cm
Scale length: 63cm
Body width: 39.2cm at the widest point.
Body depth: increasing from 3.5 to 8cm

Most acoustic Hawaiian guitars were built

exactly like ordinary guitars, with the exception of the nut and bridge setting, but this instrument has been specially built for Hawaiian playing in every respect.

The body cavity extends right up to the head, and the front, sides and back are all made of koa wood. The unconventional design gives an extraordinarily long sustain which is most appropriate for Hawaiian playing.

The top, sides and back of the guitar are all made of Hawaiian koa wood, indicated in the designation by the suffix K. Forty 00-28K guitars were built between the model's introduction in 1919 and discontinuation in 1933, and had the same decoration and fittings as the normal style 28s.

The 00-28K was originally made for Hawaiian playing, with a high saddle and nut, although it was fitted with an ordinary neck and fretted fingerboard (a few were made from 1926 with the frets ground flush). Most have been readjusted to make them suitable for conventional finger playing.

Koa-wood instruments were popularized by Hawaiian-style bands between the wars, and Martin made koa-wood guitars in various styles between 1917 and 1935. The use of koa was finally discontinued when its export was banned to prevent the decimation of Hawaiian forests. Koa-wood guitars have surprisingly good tonal properties: koa is quite similar to mahogany in its structure, but produces a guitar with a slightly fuller sound. Martin's all-koa models are characterized by a bright but rounded sound which is very well suited to fingerpicking styles. The clarity of their sound demands good playing, however, as it tends to spotlight any mistakes.

Martin 0-42 "Wurlitzer" guitar, *c.* 1924.
Photograph by courtesy of Robert Pliskin.

Between 1922 and 1924 the Martin company made a range of guitars for the Wurlitzer company: these instruments carried the Wurlitzer brand mark. The range was discontinued in 1924, after which date the Wurlitzer stores sold standard Martin guitars.

The decorative style of this guitar, which has the Wurlitzer stamp on the back brace, is identical to the Martin 0-42 of the period. Company records show that eleven 0-42-style guitars were made for Wurlitzer, but it is

thought this guitar was built separately, possibly for presentation to one of the Wurlitzer company officers. It is fitted with a cone-shaped metal box on the underside of the table in the upper bout, which may be a patent tone-suppressor.

At some stage in its life, this fine guitar was crudely converted for playing as a *tiple* and four extra strings were fitted, effectively destroying both head and bridge. The present head and bridge are modern replacements: originally, there would have been a "pyramid"-pattern bridge and a slotted, as opposed to solid, headstock.

Martin model 0-18, 1927.
From the collection of John Pearse.

Ever since its introduction in 1857, style 18 has been one of Martin's most popular designs. It has always been one of the least expensive of their styles, and in 1923 became the second regular style to be made with steel strings as standard issue.

The sides and back of this guitar are of mahogany (which replaced rosewood on the 0-18 in 1917); the top is spruce and the fingerboard ebony. Mahogany bodies give the guitar a freer, lighter sound than rosewood. The twelve-fret-neck 0-18 offered the player a very attractive combination of volume, brightness and balance at a low price. Though simply and plainly built, its fine proportions also made it a visually attractive guitar.

Gibson "Nick Lucas Special," *c.* 1927.
From the Country Music Hall of Fame, Nashville.

Overall length: 98cm
Scale length: 63cm
Body length: 49.3cm
Body width: upper bout 26cm
             waist 21.8cm
             lower bout 37.1cm
Body depth: increasing from 10.7 to 11.8cm

The "Nick Lucas Special" was one of the first flat-tops made by the Gibson company, and was built in small numbers for a period of approximately ten years from the late 1920s. The design was developed to meet the requirements of Nick Lucas, the popular crooner who is best remembered for writing "Tiptoe through the Tulips."

The guitar has a spruce top, strutted with Martin-type X bracing, rosewood sides and back with white plastic binding, and a sunburst finish. The fingerboard is made of rosewood, with narrow rectangular-section frets, and the neck-to-body junction occurs at the twelfth fret. The headstock is inlaid with "The Gibson" in mother-of-pearl.

The proportions of the Nick Lucas Special are noticeably different from those of most other guitars of the period. The body is unusually deep for its size and short for its width. It would seem that the aim of the design was to make a guitar with some added bass resonance for vocal accompaniment, without losing too much of the balance and clarity associated with smaller-bodied instruments.

Martin model 000-45, 1929.
Photographed at Gruhn Guitars, Nashville.

The 000 was Martin's largest guitar size from its introduction in 1902 until the first issue of the Dreadnought. The 000-45 was made between 1906 and 1942.

This guitar illustrates some of the changes that had occurred in style 45 since its introduction. The fingerboard has more pearl inlay, the head is bound, the bridge is of ebony instead of ivory, and ivory bindings have been replaced by white plastic.

Style 45 guitars were available for steel strings on special order in 1927, and steel strings became standard in 1928. The X bracing to the soundboard was consequently strengthened, and was heavier than on earlier models of the same size.

Martin model 0-45, 1929.
Photographed at Gruhn Guitars, Nashville.

Further changes occurred in style 45 in 1929, when the "belly bridge" with slanting saddle replaced the old pyramid bridge. The modification of the bridge design was directly caused by the change from gut to steel strings. The larger belly bridge provides a greater gluing area to resist the increased string pull, and a strongly slanted saddle was necessary to provide the differential compensation between bass and treble needed for steel strings. The characteristic Martin "teardrop" pickguard was not normally offered until 1931, but was sometimes fitted in earlier years in response to a customer's special request.

Comparison between this guitar and the 0-45 of 1907 reveals the extent to which slight changes of design accumulated to alter the visual character of the style. While the 1907 model still has essentially the looks and feel of a nineteenth-century guitar, the 1929 is immediately modern in appearance.

Style 45 models made between the introduction of steel strings and the discontinuation of the style in 1942 are the most highly sought after of all steel-string guitars. They

are prized equally for their acoustic and aesthetic qualities, and command fantastic prices.

Martin model OM-45, 1930.
From the collection of Stefan Grossman.

The OM Martin was essentially a 000 with a fourteen-fret neck and a slightly longer scale length. The first OMs were made in 1929, in response to a demand from banjoists who wished to change to the more popular guitar, and wanted a longer neck. The use of the longer neck produced a notable change in the shape of the guitar, giving it much squarer shoulders.

OM models were made alongside the twelve-fret-neck 000s until the end of 1933. By that time, the fourteen-fret neck had proved so popular that it was applied to almost all models of Martin guitars, and the separate OM designation was discarded.

The OM-45 was introduced in 1930 and 40 were built before the model went out of production in 1933. With the introduction of the OM came the adoption of a flat, unslotted headstock with individual machines, and the simplified version of the style 45 flowerpot inlay with a two-piece bulb.

Six-string Stella guitar, *c.* 1930.
From the collection of Stefan Grossman.

Overall length: 104cm
Scale length: 67.4cm
Body length: 53.2cm
Body width: upper bout 30.2cm
           waist 24.7cm
           lower bout 40.7cm
Body depth: increasing from 10 to 11cm

This guitar has a spruce top, mahogany body and neck, an ebony fingerboard joining the body at the twelfth fret, and a large ebony bridge. It is an exceptionally large instrument; although it has the normal curvature found on smaller steel-string guitars, the body has, as it were, been expanded outwards, and is actually wider in the bouts than the Martin Dreadnought. The combination of a large body with a twelve-fret neck suggests that this guitar was made in the opening years of the 1930s.

Externally it is a handsome instrument, with a good-quality spruce top and the broad wood-mosaic purflings typical of Stella. That Stella specialized in inexpensive guitars is revealed only by an examination of the interior, which shows crude construction and rough finish. The bracing on the lower bout consists simply of two cross bars, one below the soundhole and one under the bridge, and a broad flat plate of wood running across the instrument in the region of the bridge.

Stella guitars' popularity rested on the combination of impressive looks, good sound and low cost, all of which endeared them to bluesmen. They were lightly built for their size, however, and have proved fragile. Although they were built in large quantities, survivors are rare.

Gibson "Kalamazoo" KG-11, *c.* 1932.
From the collection of Paul Godden.

Overall length: 97cm
Scale length: 63cm
Body length: 44.3cm
Body width: upper bout 25.4cm
             waist 23cm
             lower bout 37.7cm
Body depth: increasing from 8.5 to 10cm

    The Kalamazoo range of instruments was introduced by Gibson in the early 1930s, and included both flat- and arch-top guitars, mandolins, banjos, mandolas, mando-cellos and mando-basses. They were specially designed at a time when the Depression created a demand for inexpensive but playable instruments.

    The Kalamazoo flat-top had a spruce top and mahogany sides and back. For reasons of economy, the top was not X-braced but supported by simple transverse bars. The neck had a rather deep triangular section and was not fitted with an adjustable truss rod.

    Gibson's Kalamazoo guitars met the company's aim of producing inexpensive guitars with accurate intonation, easy playing action and reasonable tone.

Martin model D-2, 1932.
From the Country Music Hall of Fame, Nashville.

    Although Martin had made some Dreadnought-type guitars for the Ditson company in the period from 1916 to 1921, the company did not introduce the design on its own account until 1931. The first experimental models were the D-1 (two made) and D-2 (seven made), which were the prototypes of the D-18 and D-28 respectively.

    This guitar was built for Luther Ossenbrink, a popular country singer of the 1920s and 30s, who was known professionally as "Arkie the Arkansas Woodchopper." The top is spruce, sides and back are rosewood, the neck joins the body at the twelfth fret, and the top edge has the same herringbone inlay as style 28.

    The Dreadnought design was introduced as a guitar for accompaniment. The large body cavity produces a heavily bass resonant instrument, with correspondingly less treble, which is better suited to vocal accompaniment than solo work. Although the Dreadnought was not very popular at first, it has become the most widely copied of all guitar shapes.

Martin model D-42S, 1934.
From the collection of the Martin company.

    This guitar (on the right of the photograph) is the only D-42 ever made. It was built for Tex Fletcher, a popular radio and movie performer in the 1930s.

    The top is inlaid in the standard 42 style, but the sides and back have a double black and white binding. The headstock carries a decal reading "C. F. Martin & Co. Est. 1833," which was first introduced in the 1930s.

    The guitar has one bizarre feature: the pickguard is placed for a left-handed player, but the bridge saddle and stringing are as for a right-handed player. The left-handed guitarist would be playing with his thumb over the treble instead of the bass string.

Gibson "Century" model, mid-1930s.
Photographed at Gruhn Guitars, Nashville.

Overall length: 101.2cm
Scale length: 63cm
Body length: 48.7cm
Body width: upper bout 26cm
             waist 21.5cm
             lower bout 37.4cm
Body depth: increasing from 8.7 to 11.1cm

The Gibson "Century" was introduced in 1933 for the Chicago "Century of Progress" exhibition. The spruce top has X bracing similar to that used by Martin, and a sunburst finish. The sides and back are maple. The top of the fingerboard and headstock are veneered in a mother-of-pearl imitation plastic.

When it was first introduced, the Century model was built with a twelve-fret neck-body junction. The design was modified shortly after to a fourteen-fret neck, which was fitted with an adjustable truss rod and had a somewhat V-shaped section much thicker than the current Gibson neck.

Prewar Gibson flat-tops are fairly uncommon, being something of a sideline for the company, which was more involved with its extraordinarily successful carved-top guitar production. Although Gibson flat-tops of the period lack the finesse of Martin in both design and construction, they are pleasantly built and have good playing characteristics.

Unfortunately, it is rarely possible to date prewar Gibson guitars exactly. The serial numbers do not follow a logical sequence, and company records that would make their interpretation possible have been lost.

Euphonon guitar, mid-1930s.
From the collection of Stefan Grossman.

Overall length: 104.5cm
Scale length: 64.6cm
Body length: 50.5cm
Body width: upper bout 29.7cm
             waist 25.5cm
             lower bout 40.4cm
Body depth: increasing from 9.2 to 11.6cm

The top is built of spruce, with a broad band of abalone inlay to the edge and soundhole, and the back and sides are maple. The ebony fingerboard, with mother-of-pearl inlay and white plastic binding, joins the body at the fourteenth fret.

This guitar has a very strange visual character, with a body shape like that of an OM Martin but larger, a head shaped like a Gibson, and a thoroughly idiosyncratic pickguard. Although it looks a little inelegant, it is nicely built. Both front and back have a pronounced arching, and the layout of the peaked X braces is unusual.

Euphonon and Prairie State guitars were made by the same company between the wars, and are now very rare. This example is in its original condition except for the bridge and tuning machines. At the time of writing, it is Stefan Grossman's first choice as a performance instrument.

Gibson SJ-200, 1938.
From the Country Music Hall of Fame, Nashville.

Overall length: 107.2cm
Scale length: 65.5cm
Body length: 53cm
Body width: upper bout 32cm
           waist 26.2cm
           lower bout 43cm
Body depth: increasing from 10 to 11.5cm

As the headstock inlay announces, this guitar was custom-built for Ray Whitley. It was the prototype for the Gibson J-200, which is still in production.

The sunburst-finish spruce top is fitted with X bracing, and the sides and back are made of rosewood. The multiple-bound ebony fingerboard is inlaid with engraved mother-of-pearl plaques.

Martin model D-45S, 1937.
From the collection of Charles Rosser.

The D-45 is the most famous, and expensive, of all Martin guitars. The style was introduced in 1933 with a guitar specially built for Gene Autry (see page 318). By 1942, when D-45 production was discontinued (as a result of the shortage of men and materials caused by the war), a total of 91 had been built. The D-45 design was reissued in 1968, and continues in production today.

Of the 91 prewar D-45s, only three are known to have been made with twelve-fret necks: the original Gene Autry prototype, a guitar built for Jackie "Kid" Moore, and this guitar.

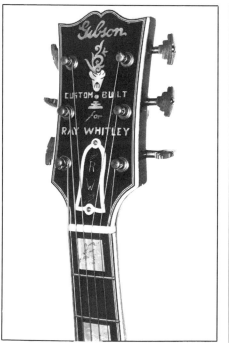

The current production model of the Gibson J-200 is built to essentially the same pattern, although there are numerous differences of detail. Rosewood was replaced by maple for the body immediately after the war, and the bracing pattern was changed to a symmetrical "double-X" in 1971. The current version also has a different bridge and pickguard, simpler bindings, different headstock and fingerboard inlays, and different tuning machines.

The tone of the twelve-fret-neck Dreadnought is slightly different from that of the more common fourteen-fret model. While all Dreadnoughts are to some extent tonally unbalanced by the weight of their bass response, the twelve-fret neck design seems to produce a more even response from string to string. This may be because a fourteen-fret neck results in the bridge being brought further up the table toward the soundhole, which has the effect of enhancing the *treble* frequencies. The combination of a large, bass-sympathetic body cavity and a comparatively treble-sympathetic table accentuates the difference in tone from string to string on the fourteen-fret model.

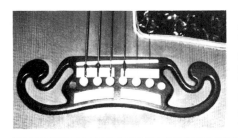

The J-200 is one of the largest flat-tops ever made. Its design originated because Ray Whitley wanted a guitar with a heavy bass to accompany his singing, but preferred Gibson necks to those of the Martin Dreadnoughts. The production model was intended specifically to compete with the Martin Dreadnought design, and its heavy bass and loud volume made it a favorite among country musicians. It remains a highly successful guitar and has been used in almost every field of popular music. Players as diverse as the Reverend Gary Davis, Elvis Presley and John McLaughlin have all been partial to the J-200, and McLaughlin once said that "A Gibson J-200 with a rosewood body was the best guitar I ever had."

Martin model D-45S, 1942.
From the Country Music Hall of Fame, Nashville.

Built for Austin Wood in the last year of production of the original issue of the D-45, this guitar has the familiar square-shouldered shape of the fourteen-fret-neck Dreadnought.

The "S" in the designation denotes non-standard features. In addition to the name inlay in the fingerboard, these include an oversize pickguard, and a plain D-28-style headstock in place of the normal "C. F. Martin" inlaid headstock applied to style 45s since 1934.

The body inlays are exactly as on the current D-45, with one exception. On prewar D-45s, the abalone inlay strips were surrounded by bands of wooden purfling. On the current D-45, these bands are made of plastic.

The American guitar makers' use of plastic bindings on even the most expensive and lavishly inlaid instruments is aesthetically incomprehensible. While the disappearance of ivory as a binding material is justifiable on conservationist, craft and economic grounds, the ready acceptance of plastic as a suitable complement to spruce, abalone, rosewood and ebony is quite astonishing.

Gibson Country Western Model, 1959.
From the collection of Derek Weskin.

Overall length: 103.3cm
Scale length: 62.5cm
Body length: 51.4cm
Body width: upper bout 29.7cm
         waist 28cm
         lower bout 41.5cm
Body depth: increasing from 10 to 12cm

The top of this guitar is of spruce, and is fitted with X bracing of a pattern similar to that used by the Martin company; the sides and back are made of mahogany. The bridge is "upside down," as on many Gibson flat-tops of the 1950s and 60s. The body shape is unusual for a fourteen-fret-neck Dreadnought, the shoulders being much rounder than on the Martins or modern Gibsons.

Gibson's fourteen-fret-neck Dreadnought guitars of this vintage were among the most successful ever made. With a decade and a half of aging behind them, the best have a delightful sound. Not only are the basses extremely rich, but the balance from string to string, and the carrying power of the treble, are exceptional for a Dreadnought.

Rickenbacker Jumbo, *c.* late 1960s.
Photographed at Orange, London.

Overall length: 107cm
Scale length: 62.5cm
Body length: 53.5cm
Body width: upper bout 33.8cm
        waist 29.6cm
        lower bout 44.3cm
Body depth: constant at 9.8cm over the upper
        bout, waist and part of the lower
        bout, then decreasing to 9.5cm at
        the base.

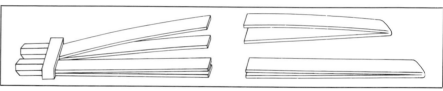

The Rickenbacker Company is not widely known for its acoustic instruments, which it has never produced in large quantities. This exceptionally large flat-top (one of 200 made) is not an instrument of great finesse, but has several unusual features.

The width of the body is even greater than that of the Gibson J-200, although the sides are quite shallow. The spruce top is built with the narrowest grain at the edge, an uncommon (but not unique) reversal of the normal procedure whereby the narrower, stiffer grain is placed at the center of the soundboard. The strutting is a heavy but simplified version of the standard X-bracing pattern. Maple has been used for the sides and back, and the body edges are bound with black and white plastic with a checker inlay pattern.

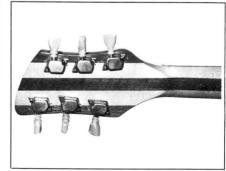

The neck is very slender for an acoustic guitar, with a width at the nut of only 4.1cm, and is built of a laminate of maple and mahogany. It is fitted with Rickenbacker's famous double truss rod, which allows the neck to be adjusted against both bow and twist. Essentially, the Rickenbacker truss rod consists of two pairs of linked rods, one pair for the bass side of the neck and one for the treble. When the nut is tightened, one of the rods of the pair is forced to arch in compression, and this effect counters the bowing pull of the strings on the neck.

Gallagher G-50, *c.* 1968.
From the Country Music Hall of Fame, Nashville.

Overall length: 104cm
Scale length: 64cm
Body length: 50cm
Body width: upper bout 31cm
        waist 28cm
        lower bout 39.7cm
Body depth: increasing from 9.6 to 10.2cm

The Gallagher G-50 has an X-braced spruce top, mahogany sides and back, rosewood fingerboard, and a mahogany neck joining the body at the fourteenth fret. It may be thought of as equivalent to the Martin D-18, although it has slightly different fittings.

The Gallagher Guitar company of Wartrace, Tennessee, founded in 1965, is one of a number of small American companies build-

ing high-class steel-string guitars. In recent years, Gallagher has received considerable publicity from the exposure given to their instruments by Doc Watson, to whom this guitar belonged.

Gallagher guitars are hand-built to order at a rate of approximately one hundred a year.

Martin model D-41, 1970.
From the collection of John Pearse.

The D-41 was added to the Martin range in 1969. It has white body bindings and abalone inlay to the top edge and soundhole. The bound ebony fingerboard is decorated with six hexagonal abalone position-markers, which are identical to the first six of the eight markers on the D-45. The headstock design is the same on both D-41 and 45, with "C. F. Martin" inlay and Grover Rotomatic tuning machines.

The soundboard is made of spruce, and the sides and back are Indian rosewood. Martin switched from Brazilian to Indian rosewood for all rosewood-bodied instruments in 1969. The internal construction is typical of modern Martin practice. The X bracing is heavier than on prewar models, the design having been strengthened in 1944 to take the heavier gauge strings then in use. In the modified design, the peaks to the braces, which had been such a feature of Martin construction, were eliminated.

Many players believe that the current Martin guitars are too heavily braced, and that pre-1944 models were superior in this respect. The company admits that the soundboards are slightly over-structured, but only to the degree necessary to make it possible to cover the guitars with a "lifetime" warranty against all defects for as long as they are in the possession of the original owner.

Guitar by Keith Johns BRIGHTON, 1975.
Owned by Jake Walton.

Overall length: 97.8cm
Scale length: 62.8cm
Body length: 49.9cm
Body width: upper bout 25cm
        waist 21.5cm
        lower bout 36.4cm
Body depth: increasing from 8.6 to 10.7cm.

Keith Johns has a well-deserved reputation as one of the finest guitar repairmen in Britain; unfortunately, his success in this field severely limits the time he can devote to guitar building.

This instrument was custom-made for its present owner. While it was obviously inspired by prewar Martins, it is by no means a slavish copy. It is slightly larger than the Martin 00 models and, in decoration, somewhere between their styles 40 and 42. The top is spruce, with abalone inlay to the top edge and around the soundhole; the sides and back are rosewood and the fingerboard ebony. The neck-to-body junction occurs at the twelfth fret, which is unusual on a modern steel-string guitar.

Other unusual features include the veneering of the back (as well as the front) of the headstock with rosewood, the design of the pyramid bridge, the delicate moon-and-stars inlay on the headstock, and the use of Schaller tuning machines mounted three to a plate.

It is a widely-held opinion that only Americans can build good steel-string guitars. However, this English-made instrument is finely crafted and sounds beautiful. The tone is very warm and full, and it has the balance from string to string which is associated with the best prewar Martin guitars.

"John Pearse Professional" guitar by Dieter Hopf, 1975.
From the collection of John Pearse.

Overall length: 104cm
Scale length: 65cm
Body length: 50.5cm
Body width: upper bout 29.5cm
waist 23.7cm
lower bout 40.5cm
Body depth: increasing from 9.8 to 10.6cm

Dieter Hopf is one of Germany's most successful classical guitar makers, and this instrument represents an interesting collaboration between a luthier and a player to develop an instrument for ragtime and general steel-string fingerpicking playing. The aim was to make a guitar which would help the player to extend his technique.

The top of the guitar is made of cedar, and the sides and back are built of a very pale Indian rosewood. The soundboard has seven fan struts which are disposed as on a classical guitar, but are much heavier to be able to resist the pull of steel strings. There is a strengthening plate of ramin under the area of the bridge. The bridge itself is designed to transfer the vibrations rapidly to the soundboard. It is fitted with removable saddle pieces, one for the treble and another for the bass strings, which come in a range of sizes to give the correct compensation for either nylon or light- or medium-gauge steel strings. The bridge also incorporates two Barcus Berry "Hot Dot" piezo-electric transducers for amplification of a natural acoustic sound; the output jack is concealed in the tail button.

Neck, head and fingerboard all show evidence of Dieter Hopf's experience as a classical luthier. The neck-to-body junction is made by a Spanish heel and slipper foot, which gives a stronger joint than a dovetail, but is only really possible on hand-made guitars. The fingerboard is 5cm wide at the nut, although the adjustable truss rod allows a shallow neck section.

The classical scale length, and wide fingerboard, might at first seem inappropriate on a steel-string guitar. They do, however, make complex left-hand fingering much simpler for the skilled guitarist. The tone of this guitar is more rounded and mellow than that of most modern steel-string instruments, and it possesses a very even balance from string to string.

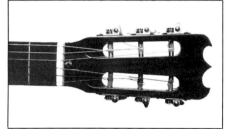

Gibson J-55, 1975.
Photograph by courtesy of Norlin Inc.

Overall length: 105cm
Scale length: 64.7cm
Body length: 50.7cm
Body width: upper bout 29.7cm
waist 27.8cm
lower bout 40.5cm
Body depth: sides increasing from 10 to 12.2cm

Since the war, Gibson has produced numerous flat-tops, almost all of which have been Jumbos or Dreadnoughts. The J-55 was introduced in 1975, at the same time as the maple-bodied Gospel. The current range also includes the J-200, the Dreadnought-shaped Dove, Hummingbird, Heritage, J-50, J-45, J-40, the J-160E Electric flat-top, and B-45-12 twelve-string.

Gibson's Dreadnought-type guitars are all built to the same size, although the body materials vary (either maple, rosewood or mahogany being used for sides and back), as does the styling of bridges, pickguards and inlays. All of them have spruce tops with the symmetrical double-X bracing introduced in 1971, and laminated maple necks with Gibson's adjustable truss rod.

The mahogany-bodied J-55 has a pronounced swell to the back, formed by laminating three sheets of veneer in a press. The aim is to increase still further the Dreadnought-shaped guitar's natural sympathy to the bass resonances.

Gibson's large-bodied flat-tops are sturdy and powerful guitars, without very much refinement but reliable and solidly made.

(a) **Guitar** by John Gréven, NASHVILLE, 1976.
Photographed at Gruhn Guitars, Nashville.
(b) **Custom inlay** by John Gréven to a
Martin D-28.
Photograph by courtesy of John Gréven.

Overall length: 105cm
Scale length: 64.5cm
Body length: 51.1cm
Body width: upper bout 29.4cm
            waist 25cm
            lower bout 40.6cm
Body depth: increasing from 8.3 to 10.5cm

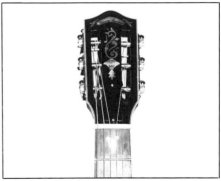

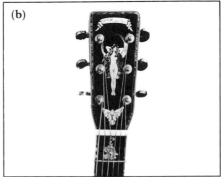

(b)

The increased affluence of musicians, both
professional and amateur, and the relative in-
flexibility of the large companies has brought
about a resurgence of the individual luthier
in America. John Gréven is just one of
a number of successful craftsmen who specialize in producing hand-built steel-string
guitars, and carrying out complex custom
inlay work in abalone and mother-of-pearl.

The guitar shown here has a German
spruce top with X bracing, Indian rosewood
sides and back, bound ebony fingerboard and
ebony "pyramid"-type bridge, and mother-
of-pearl inlays to the fingerboard and headstock. The neck is fitted with an adjustable
truss rod.

The guitar's design has been developed

(a)

from a consideration of the properties of
several Martin models, and the body shape is
that of Martin's F-size carved-top of the
1930s. John Gréven's aim is to produce an

instrument which combines the power of the
Martin Dreadnought with the balance of the
000.

Guild G-75, 1976.
Photographed at Top Gear Ltd, Shoreham.

Overall length: 102.9cm
Scale length: 65cm
Body length: 38.1cm
Body width: upper bout 25.7cm
            waist 25cm
            lower bout 37.6cm
Body depth: 12.7cm

Guild has succeeded in making considerable inroads on the market for quality factory-
built guitars over the last decade. The company
has concentrated on quality of materials and
workmanship, rather than on decoration and
ornament, and thereby produced instruments
which provide good value for money. There
have recently, however, been signs of a slight
sloppiness of finish that should not be present
on largely hand-made guitars.

Guild's present range includes both stand-

ard Dreadnoughts and more waisted folk
guitars. The G-75, which was originally
designed for Paul Simon, is unusual in having
a three-quarter-size Dreadnought-shaped
body. It has a spruce top with straightforward
X bracing, rosewood sides and back, mahogany neck, and ebony fingerboard and
bridge, and is fitted with Schaller tuning
machines. The shape of the headstock (common to all Guild acoustics and acoustic
electrics) is reminiscent of that applied to
many f-hole guitars in the 1930s, and although
in itself attractive, looks somewhat out of place
on a flat-top.

The three-quarter-size Dreadnought
body has many advantages besides being
easier to hold than the full-size version. While
retaining the fashionable square-shouldered
shape, it has a warmer, easier, less aggressive
and more balanced sound than the equivalent
full Dreadnought.

Gibson Mark 72 guitar, 1977.
Photographed at Norlin Music Ltd, London.

Overall length: 104.8cm
Scale length: 64.5cm
Body length: 51.4cm
Body width: upper bout 29.8cm
             waist 25.9cm
             lower bout 41.6cm
Body depth: increasing from 10.6 to 12.8cm

Competition for the upper end of the steel-string guitar market has become increasingly acute over the last ten years. Guild and Ovation, smaller companies such as Mossman, Rich, Gallagher and Gurian, and individual luthiers have all carved out shares of a market that was once largely the preserve of Martin and Gibson. The Mark guitar is the product of a major research and development program by Gibson, and is hoped to recapture areas of the market which have been lost to rival companies.

Gibson carried out its research program with the help of professors Adrian Houtsma of MIT and Eugene Watson of Pennsylvania State University (both experts on acoustics); Dr. Michael Kasha (who has been working on the scientific design of guitars for many years); and consultant luthier Richard Schneider. Essentially, the program aimed to determine what features of the sound of various guitars made them particularly popular, and then to combine these features in a single instrument. Numerous prototypes were evolved by Kasha and Schneider, tested for structural stability and sound output, and played to a panel of players, constructors and scientists for comparison with other guitars by Gibson, Martin, Ovation and Guild.

The design that evolved is very different from any other current steel-string guitar. It centers on a soundboard with an extremely complex system of strutting, developed according to Dr. Kasha's theories of the physics of the guitar (see pages 264, 272–4). The soundboard is designed to give a loud, steely sound rich in harmonics, with a very good tonal balance from string to string. The shape of the bridge also stems from Dr. Kasha's work, and was evolved to transfer both the low-frequency vibrations of the basses and the high frequencies of the trebles to the soundboard with greater efficiency than does the

conventional straight or belly bridge. There is a choice of three different heights of melamine saddle.

The curvature of the body was designed by Richard Schneider on aesthetic rather than acoustic principles. As the measurements show, the body is somewhat fuller and larger than it at first appears. The soundhole is not conventionally inlaid, but is fitted with a raised "purfling ring," to give it greater visual emphasis, and a pickguard is optional. The neck is essentially the same as on all Gibson flat-tops, although the head has been specially designed for the Mark series. Schneider says that he would have preferred to fit a twelve-fret junction neck, which would have given a prettier guitar and made it easier to obtain the desired tonal balance, but marketing considerations dictated a standard fourteen-fret neck.

Having produced the successful prototype, Gibson faced the problem of duplicating it in quantity. The company has had

difficulty achieving production models with the desired qualities, and the full launch of the Mark guitar has been somewhat delayed. However, in November 1976 Richard Schneider wrote to us that a breakthrough had been achieved, and ". . . two-hour-old guitars were out-sounding the best Martins we could find with two and three years aging on them."

The Mark design is made in several grades and timbers, from the mahogany-bodied 35, through the maple-bodied 53 and rosewood-bodied 72, to the top production model Mark 81, with rosewood body, ebony bridge and fingerboard, and abalone fingerboard inlay. At the time of writing, Gibson also plans to offer an entirely hand-made version on special order. Pre-production examples of both the Mark 35 and 72 have impressed us as being powerful guitars with which Gibson had achieved its stated aim of producing instruments with rich basses, incisive trebles, and exceptionally good balance of both tone and volume from note to note and string to string.

RESONATOR GUITARS

National "Duolian" resonator guitar, early 1930s.
From the Country Music Hall of Fame, Nashville.

Overall length: 98cm
Scale length: 63.4cm
Body length: 50cm
Body width: upper bout 25.9cm
          waist 23.6cm
          lower bout 35.9cm
Body depth: increasing from 7 to 8.2cm

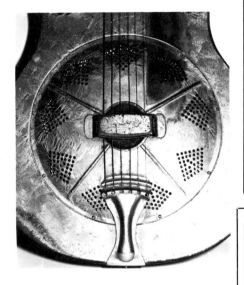

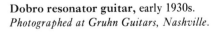

Dobro resonator guitar, early 1930s.
Photographed at Gruhn Guitars, Nashville.

Overall length: 97.5cm
Scale length: 63cm
Body length: 49cm
Body width: upper bout 27cm
          waist 22.5cm
          lower bout 36cm
Body depth: increasing from 7.3 to 8cm

The newly formed Dobro Company started out building wooden-body single-resonator guitars, while the National Company made metal-body instruments. Then in 1932 Dobro contracted the Regal Company to fabricate metal bodies for them and the National company also started to make wooden-body models in the early 1930s.

The National Guitar Company was founded to produce the triple-resonator guitar which the Dopera Brothers first started to develop in 1926. Initially it was a tiny firm, growing from a 3-man workshop in 1927 to one with 22 men in 1928.

Three of the five Dopera Brothers, John, Rudy and Ed, left National to form the Dobro company to produce guitars with a single large resonator, which came out first in 1929. From then until 1934 the two companies were competing rivals (although John, Rudy and Ed Dopera still kept 50 percent of the National stock!) and many of the instruments they produced were very similar.

The Duolian was the cheapest of National's resonator guitars, and sold originally for $32.50. The body was built entirely from metal, and had a dull gray galvanized finish. It was offered with either a conventional round-section neck, or a square-section neck for Hawaiian playing. Round-neck models had the advantage that they could be adapted to Hawaiian playing.

The resonator guitar has an exceptionally loud volume and a distinctive tone. It found immediate applications for playing Hawaiian-style in country music bands, and the round-neck model was widely played by blues musicians. The Duolian was particularly popular as a low-price model, and was often used for bottleneck playing.

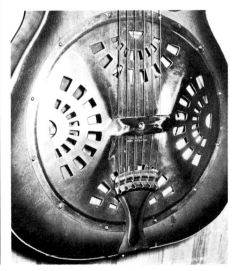

Also in 1932 the Dobro Company made a small number of electrically amplified resonator guitars. Although these were not a success, they gave the company the historical distinction of being among the first to market an electric guitar.

The instrument shown here has a mahogany body, and two round screened soundholes. It has the typical shape of the wooden-bodied Dobro; the upper bout is larger and the waist is more pronounced than on the metal-bodied models. It has a round-section neck, but has been set for Hawaiian playing with a high nut.

All National and Dobro company guitars of the 1920s and 30s have become collector's items, and the wooden-body Dobro model has become a very expensive instrument.

National Style O resonator guitar, mid-1930s.
Photographed at Gruhn Guitars, Nashville.

Overall length: 98cm
Scale length: 63.5cm
Body length: 49.5cm
Body width: upper bout 25.6cm
      waist 23.5cm
      lower bout 35.7cm
Body depth: sides increase from 7 to 8.6cm

After the merger of the National and Dobro companies to form the National Dobro Corporation in 1934, the company issued tri-plate resonator and single-plate resonator guitars, resonator tenor guitars, mandolins and ukuleles, and a range of electric instruments including Hawaiian, arch-top and tenor guitars, mandolin and violin. The Style O was the most expensive single-plate resonator model, and sold for $65.00 in 1935. It had a heavily chrome-plated brass alloy body, satin-etched with palm tree designs, and an ebony fingerboard bound in white plastic.

Despite its impressive range of instruments, the National Dobro Corporation was not a financial success, and the brothers started to split up and go their separate ways around 1937. Louis Dopera formed Valco with Al Frost and Vic Smith from National, but all resonator guitar production came to a halt in 1940. Although Valco started up again in 1948, it made no resonator instruments.

The resonator guitar did not make its reappearance until 1961, when Ed Dopera started to build them once more. The post-war history of the Dobro has not, however, been untroubled. Mosrite acquired the Dobro rights in the mid-1960s, and built a small number of instruments, and Gretsch has also produced some.

At present, resonator guitars are being built to Ed Dopera's designs by the OMI company of California. Perhaps with this venture the Dobro will at last become a financial success.

The aluminum resonator and spider assembly on a Regal resonator guitar.

TWELVE-STRING GUITARS

Stella twelve-string guitar, *c.* 1930.
From the collection of Stefan Grossman.

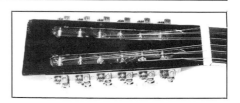

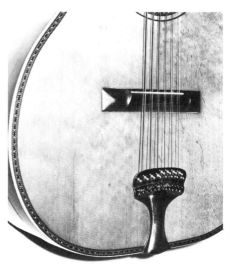

Overall length: 107.5cm
Scale length: 66.5cm
Body length: 53.6cm
Body width: upper bout 30.5cm
     waist 24.7cm
     lower bout 39.6cm
Body depth: increasing from 10 to 11cm

Stella made the most famous of all twelve-string, steel-strung guitars. In the 1920s through 40s, Stellas were the instruments preferred by most twelve-string blues players, including Leadbelly and Blind Willie McTell, and their sound can be heard on many records by these artists.

In design and construction this guitar is similar to the Stella six-string shown on page 245. It is similarly decorated, has a similar internal construction, and is similarly crude on the inside but handsome on the out. The two most important differences are the simulation of a rosewood finish on the mahogany body and the continuation of the strings over the bridge to fix at a tailpiece. This is a most sensible design for twelve-string guitars, which exert a tremendously high string pull. It reduces the stress on the table, and eliminates the risk of the bridge being pulled off. It does, however, change the modes of vibration of the soundboard and is a system not commonly used on flat-tops. The tailpiece on the Stella twelve-string is interestingly designed. It lies very flat on the soundboard, to pull the strings down hard on to the saddle, and can take strings with either ball or loop ends.

Guild F-412 twelve-string guitar, *c.* 1973.
From the collection of Sammy Vomáčka.

Overall length: 111.7cm
Scale length: 65cm
Body length: 52.8cm
Body width: upper bout 31.7cm
     waist 27cm
     lower bout 43.2cm
Body depth: sides increasing from 10 to 12.5cm

Guild's F-412 twelve-string has gone through several modifications. Early models, in the 1950s, had rosewood bodies and an arched swell back. This example has a maple body and swell back, and the current version is maple-bodied but flat-backed. The top is of high-grade spruce, and the ebony fingerboard has abalone-inlaid position markers.

Guild's twelve-strings are among its best-known and most successful guitars. The F-512 (very similar to the 412, save that it has a rosewood instead of a maple body) has been made famous by John Denver.

The F-412 illustrated here has the typical virtues of Guild's twelve-strings, being very loud and having a clarity and definition of sound not normally associated with twelve-string guitars. Sammy Vomáčka likes to play it bottleneck as well as finger style, and has accordingly had it fitted with a flat fingerboard, saddle and nut.

Bozo twelve-string guitar, 1975.
From the collection of John Pearse.

Overall length: 114cm
Scale length: 64cm
Body length: 52cm
Body width: upper bout 28cm
            waist 26.2cm
            lower bout 41.2cm
Body depth: increasing from 10.6 to 12.5cm

Bozo Podunavac was born in Yugoslavia, where he trained as a luthier. After working for several years in Belgrade, he left Yugoslavia in 1959 to settle in Chicago, where he worked as a repairman and maker for several companies. By 1965 he had built up a sufficient reputation to be able to set up on his own to hand-build guitars. In recent years, while continuing to produce hand-made guitars to special order, he has arranged for a Japanese company to build guitars to his exact designs and specifications.

This twelve-string guitar is one of the Japanese-built Bozos. It is constructed and finished to a very high standard. The spruce soundboard has a very heavy X bracing, and the sides and back are made of rosewood. Both fingerboard and bridge are ebony, and the tuning machines are gold-plated.

While Bozo (pronounced *bor-zho*) also produces conventionally-shaped Dreadnoughts, and some classical and arch-top guitars, he is best known for his "Bell"-shaped steel-string instruments. The twelve-string model has an extremely loud, gutsy sound and is regarded by many players as the finest twelve-string guitar currently in production.

Construction

Over the last fifty years the flat-top steel-string acoustic guitar has become the most popular acoustic form of the instrument. During this period, its design and the techniques by which it is built have become quite distinct from those of the classical guitar. This divergence is a result both of the physical nature of the instrument and of the way in which the guitar-building industry has come to be organized.

The guitar maker aims to make an instrument which is both sturdy and responsive, one which will use the power available from the strings but will not be distorted by the pull they exert. This aim is common both to the steel-string and the classical guitar builder. But steel strings have very different properties from the nylon strings of the classical guitar. They exert a much heavier pull on the neck and table, and have greater vibrational efficiency. As a result, they transfer correspondingly more energy to the top of the guitar and produce more volume.

The great tension of steel strings effectively reverses the nature of the guitar designer's problem: whereas in the classical guitar, volume is more difficult to achieve than structural stability, the need for strength in the steel-string guitar becomes a major factor in determining design. In the words of Richard Schneider, the Gibson company's consultant luthier:

> Nylon strings exert a pull of 75 to 105 pounds on the guitar, but with steel strings you have a pull of between 185 and 220 or even 240 pounds depending on the gauge. The design of the guitar has to incorporate something that resists that pull, and every time you put in structural bars you risk interfering with the tone bars. But with steel strings we have so much energy available that volume is hardly a consideration. This gives us more liberty, and in this way the steel-string guitar is easier to build than the classical.[1]

The steel-string guitar construction industry is dominated by a small number of large organizations, headed by the American firms of Martin, Gibson, Guild and Ovation. While the best classical guitars are hand-built by individual luthiers, the steel-string guitars which one sees on stage and hears on record are factory-built instruments made by the big companies. The reasons that steel-string guitar construction is so American-dominated and factory-based have to do with the history of the instrument (see page 222). Our point here is that any discussion of the building of the best steel-string guitars must concentrate on the procedures of the leading factories, and consider how the essential nature of factory production conditions construction techniques.

The individual luthier is geared to producing a small number of unique, very personal instruments. The factory aims to make a large number of standardized guitars which vary as little as possible from one another. To this end, the process of building a guitar is split up into its constituent operations. Each step—be it the fabrication of a particular part, the assembly of several parts, or the finishing of the assembled guitar—is a separate process carried out by a different craftsman. This system allows for rapid production on a large scale, and means that each worker need acquire only those skills relevant to one operation.

Factory production methods have both advantages and drawbacks. The scale of the business allows the companies to carry out programs of research, development and testing which are far beyond the scope of any one individual. Their size and buying power also allows them to dominate the market for high-quality timber. On the debit side, a factory-built guitar lacks the individual character of the luthier's hand-built instrument. Also, the mass-production system is inherently inflexible. If there is any deviation from the standard pattern the parts may not fit when they finally come together, in which case the whole operation is disrupted. The freedom of the individual luthier to adjust every part to take into account the exact properties of the individual piece of wood he is working has been lost.

The scale of factory production and the breaking down of the construction process into separate operations open the way to the widespread use of machinery. There is some disagreement among the leading companies as to what degree of mechanization is compatible with the production of high-quality guitars. At the C. F. Martin factory in Nazareth, Pennsylvania, most operations are still carried out by hand, with a very restricted use of machines. Company president Frank Martin says that "there is no mechanical way to build a good guitar."[2] Gibson, on the other hand, has moved much further down the road to

THE PARTS OF A STEEL-STRING FLAT-TOP GUITAR

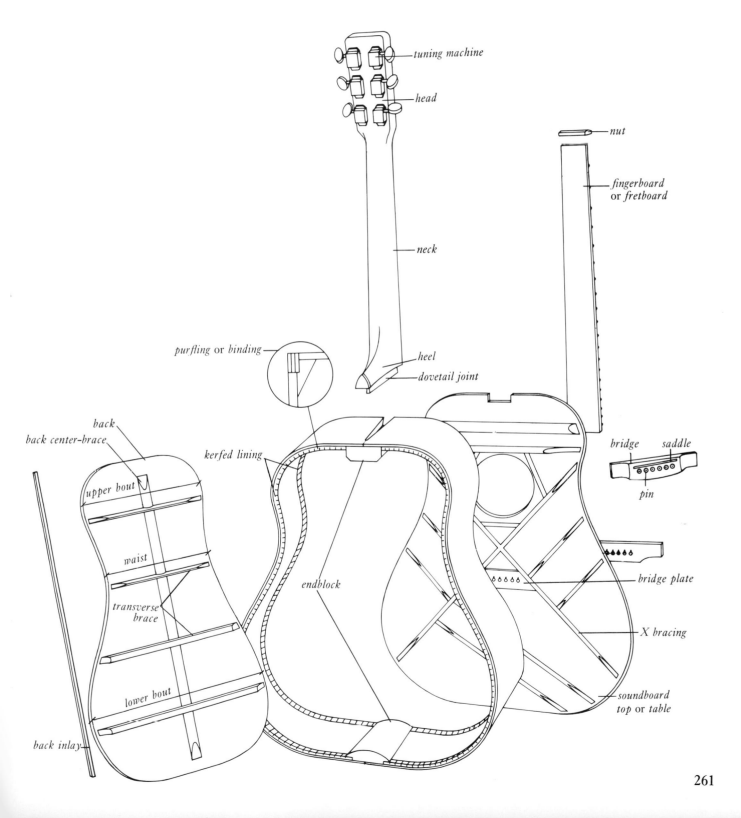

tuning machine

head

nut

fingerboard or *fretboard*

neck

purfling or *binding*

heel

dovetail joint

back

back center-brace

kerfed lining

bridge   saddle

upper bout

pin

waist

endblock

bridge plate

transverse brace

X bracing

lower bout

soundboard top or table

back inlay

mechanization and put great effort into the development of complex machinery and templates to assist its craftsmen. The company believes that well-designed machinery can do many tasks as well as they can be done by hand—and with greater speed and consistency. Nevertheless, the vital importance of hand work is still stressed, and Jim Beals, production manager at Gibson's Kalamazoo plant, points out that the use of sophisticated machine tools does not mean the elimination of skilled workmanship. A good craftsman working with machinery develops an understanding of its possibilities, and a kind of "machine craftsmanship" is born in which the machine's power and precision is allied with human skills. A high level of mechanization does, however, increase the need for strict quality control and checking. It can also inhibit the introduction of new design features, since any modification to the product may require expensive changes in tooling as well as a period of adjustment for the operatives to learn new procedures.

To give an idea of the essential nature of factory guitar production, and of the variations possible within factory production, the following section is based on the procedures of the C. F. Martin company's factory in Nazareth and the Gibson company's factories in Kalamazoo, Michigan and Nashville, Tennessee. Although the steps by which the companies make guitars are similar in principle, they are often quite different in their practical details—as are the instruments they produce.

The timbers used in steel-string guitar construction are much the same as those used for the classical instrument, and similar criteria apply to their selection.

Spruce is preferred for the soundboard. But whereas classical luthiers insist on European Alpine spruce, many of the best steel-string guitars use American Sitka spruce. Sitka spruce is readily available to the American guitar companies, while the best quality of European spruce is in limited supply. It has also been found that although Sitka spruce is inferior to European spruce for classical guitars, it is very well suited to the needs of the steel-string. The reason appears to be that Sitka spruce, because of its slightly different fiber structure, damps some of the extreme high harmonics associated with steel-string vibration. This makes for a slightly less jangling sound, and can be helpful in producing a well-balanced instrument.

None of the large steel-string guitar manufacturers use western red cedar—a timber which is now quite popular among classical luthiers for guitar soundboards. One suspects that the large companies are held back by market considerations: the guitar-buying public has come to expect spruce soundboards, and might be reluctant to accept anything else. Also, cedar is a very soft wood and therefore susceptible to marking and damage during the construction process. However, the German maker Dieter Hopf has recently shown that fine steel-string guitars can be made with cedar soundboards.

The timbers most favored for steel-string guitar bodies, both for appearance and for acoustic qualities, are East Indian and Brazilian rosewoods. But during the last decade, Brazilian rosewood—still the first choice of most classical luthiers—has almost completely disappeared from steel-string construction. In the mid-1960s, the Brazilian government placed an embargo on the export of unsawn rosewood logs, with the aim of diverting more work to their own sawmills. As a result, Brazilian rosewood became more expensive and the guitar makers could no longer control the cutting of their timber. In face of the Brazilian embargo, the guitar companies switched entirely to East Indian rosewood, which is less expensive and can be imported in the log. It also has the advantage of greater dimensional stability, being less affected by changes in temperature and humidity.

While rosewood is the most favored timber for guitar bodies, it is also the most expensive. Mahogany is widely used as a cheaper substitute, but has the disadvantage of producing a thinner and less resonant tone. Maple is also used by several companies. Maple's price and tonal qualities lie somewhere in between those of rosewood and mahogany. It helps give a bright, treble-accented tone, and its light color makes it a suitable choice for the sprayed "cherry" finish applied to some guitars.

As on the classical guitar, the timber for the neck must be strong and stable, so as to resist distortion by the pull of the strings and changes in temperature and humidity. Mahogany is the most common choice, followed by maple used either by itself or in lamination with mahogany.

Ebony is by far the best wood for the fingerboard, because of its exceptional hardness, strength and durability. Unfortunately, high-quality ebony is very expensive, and difficult to obtain in the quantities necessary for mass production. Rosewood is widely used as a less expensive substitute.

The large guitar-building companies buy their timber in bulk. Being big customers, they have considerable power and control over the supply and cutting of their wood. Also, the size of the stocks they hold ensures that they can always select pieces of the first quality for their most expensive instruments, and still use the lower grades for their cheaper models.

Martin's policy is to buy timber unsawn, in the log, and cut it in the specially designed sawmill built on the company's premises in 1975. This ensures that all timber is radially sawn to exact requirements, and the company maintains absolute control over the entire operation. Once it is cut, the timber has to be seasoned. This is done in two stages. First, it is kiln-dried to reduce the moisture content to a specified level. Then it is moved into the factory, where it will remain stored in racks for up to a year before use. Since the plant is completely air-conditioned, the timber is effectively seasoning under controlled conditions during the whole of this period. During the second stage of seasoning, the timber gradually matures as its chemical composition undergoes subtle changes which improve both the resilience and the tonal properties of the wood.

Martin is exceptional in having its own sawmill. The majority of manufacturers have their timber sawn and kiln-dried for them by specialist firms.

At first sight, a large guitar factory is a most confusing place. On every side, all the operations which go into the making of a guitar are being carried out simultaneously; it is difficult to form any idea of a logical sequence of events. In essence, though, the manufacturing process can be considered in three main stages: the making of the body, the making of the neck, and the assembly and finishing of the neck and body.

In the building of the guitar body, the operations can again be subdivided into those involving the top, the back, and the sides, and the joining of these components.

In any acoustic guitar, the selection, thicknessing and bracing of the timbers of the top determine the quality of the final instrument more than any other factors. Factory production does not allow each top to be worked individually, with modifications to thickness and bracing, to make best use of the individual properties of each piece of timber. Every top has to be treated identically. As a result, the initial timber selection assumes enormous significance, and the makers take great pains to ensure that the best tops will end up on the most expensive guitars. To date, however, no one has developed a test procedure to determine with absolute certainty which pieces of timber will produce the best sound.

To produce the blanks from which the tops are made, two thin sheets of spruce are joined together down what will be the centerline of the guitar. These sheets are cut from the same plank, and bookmatched to give a symmetrical grain pattern. Before the two halves are joined, the matching sheets are carefully inspected and graded for color, closeness and regularity of grain, and freedom from blemishes. After preliminary grading the sheets are glued together (usually with the narrowest grain to the center) to make a board large enough for a complete guitar top.

These boards are then put through a thicknessing sander, which reduces them to a uniform thickness of a little under 3mm ($\frac{7}{64}''$). After sanding, the spruce sheets are checked and graded again. The various manufacturers have different tests to help them assess the quality of the boards at this stage. Martin, for example, has a candling machine to reveal internal flaws. Gibson applies a deflection test, in which the bending of the board under a standard weight is measured, to give a guide to the stiffness of the timber. Stiffer boards are considered to be of higher quality, all other things being equal, and are used for the more expensive guitars

Once the top blanks have been thicknessed and graded, they are cut to profile on a bandsaw. They are usually left slightly oversize—final trimming will be done once the body is assembled. When the tops have been sawn, the soundhole decoration is inlaid. Steel-string guitar design traditionally eschews the complex wood-mosaic rosette of the classic guitar in favor of a few simple concentric circles of black and white plastic inlay. The slots for these are cut in one operation on a multiple-bladed drill saw. The inlays are glued in place, sanded down flush with the top, and the soundhole is cut. Alternatives to the basic pattern of black and white concentric rings are to be found in the abalone circle around the soundhole of Martin's 41 and 45 models,

Ovation's decorative soundhole pattern, and the raised "purfling ring" on Gibson's Mark guitars.

The guitar top is now ready to be strutted. The strutting serves two different purposes. One is to brace the thin wood of the top against the pull of the strings, to prevent it from being distorted or broken. The other is to control the way the top vibrates, to determine its response to different vibrational frequencies, and thus the guitar's volume, tone quality and acoustic balance.

Steel-string and classical guitar strutting have evolved along different lines. The most widely used type of bracing on steel-string guitars is the "X-bracing" pattern developed originally by C. F. Martin I in the middle of the nineteenth century. The Martin company has continued to use this design, in a slightly modified form, to the present, and it has been copied by many other manufacturers.

Ironically, the X-bracing pattern was originally designed for gut-strung guitars—for which it is less suitable than the classical Torres pattern of fan strutting. The Martin company did not start to offer steel-string guitars as standard models until the 1920s.

In the change from gut to steel strings the braces were made heavier, and the X bracing proved to be so successful that Martin did not alter it until 1944. Even then, the only modifications were to increase the weight of the struts to allow the use of heavy-gauge strings, and simplify their profiles for easier construction. The number and disposition of bars remained the same.

The Martin company carried out a series of scientific tests during the late 1960s and early 1970s to determine whether they could improve the X-bracing design, or if they should even change it altogether. The results of this program confirmed the company's faith in X-bracing, and resulted in no acoustic design modifications. Dr. Donald Thompson, Martin's head of research and development, has come to the conclusion that "The guitar is a very highly developed instrument. It is not easy to build a guitar significantly better than what is now being built."[3] Nevertheless, several other companies have introduced new bracing designs, with the aim of improving either the structural or the acoustic properties of the instrument, or both.

Until 1971, Gibson used an X-bracing pattern for its flat-tops which was closely modeled on the Martin design.

In 1971 the company switched to a "double-X" pattern. Gibson's aim was to improve the strength and stability of the top, and to produce a symmetrically strutted guitar which could be strung for either left- or right-handed players.

More recently, both Ovation and Gibson have introduced strutting patterns based on acoustic theories and tests to try to improve the tone, balance and projection of the guitar. While Ovation's researches have resulted in a wide range of different patterns for different guitars, Gibson's efforts have been devoted to producing one optimum design, which is incorporated in the Mark series. The soundboard design of these guitars is the product of two years of research and development into the application of the theories of physicist Dr. Michael Kasha, director of the Institute of Molecular Biophysics at Florida State University.

Dr. Kasha has been working on a scientific approach to classical guitar design since 1966: the Mark guitar represents an attempt to apply the principles he has evolved to the steel-string instrument. Gibson wanted to produce a good all-round guitar which could be used in either country, blues, jazz or folk playing. The designers' aims are summarized by Richard Schneider, who has worked with Dr. Kasha since 1969: "The main criteria we work to are balance and evenness of volume from string to string. The guitar must sound even all the way across."

The essential starting point for the Kasha design is the understanding that the bridge of the flat-top guitar transmits vibrations to the table by a rocking movement. Since the bridge rocks, it is possible to place a transverse bar directly beneath it as a pivot. This bar gives the instrument stability without reducing the table's vibration. The struts are then placed so that they radiate from the area of the bridge, to activate the table.

The disposition of the struts is determined with the scientific theory of vibrating plates in mind. The bars are asymmetrically placed so that only a small area of the top vibrates for high-frequency notes, a larger area for mid-range, and the whole top for bass frequencies. The guitar top is seen as analogous to a loudspeaker system which combines a tweeter, mid-range speaker, and woofer, each of which is designed to handle a specific range of frequencies with maximum efficiency.

The shaping of the struts themselves also owes much to scientific theory. The tone bars on Kasha-system guitars are heavier toward the "head" end under the bridge, and taper away toward the "tail." Dr. Kasha has found that the exact characteristics of the taper help to determine the attack and sustain of the guitar.

When applying Kasha's principles to the steel-string guitar, it was necessary to redesign the structural bracing so that it did not interfere with the acoustic function of the top. Schneider says of the final design, "We've got to the point where we have reduced the structural bars to a minimum. Then we have a bunch of bars that are there partly for mechanical and partly for acoustic reasons, and then some that are there purely for acoustic reasons."

Although the top is acoustically the most critical element of any guitar body, the back is also significant. As on the classical guitar, it is primarily a reflector of sound waves — which is why hard dense woods are preferred for its construction. The sheets of wood for the back are glued together along a long edge, and are bookmatched like the top. Any center inlay between the two halves is glued in at this stage. After gluing, the back is cut to profile on a bandsaw and the strengthening cross braces, which give a slight arch, are glued in place.

While it is chiefly a reflector, the back also vibrates, and many makers hold that tuning of the back in relation to the top has an effect on the tone of the guitar. However, in factory production it is not possible to tune the response characteristics of each back and front individually, and they will vary slightly with every piece of wood.

Ten years ago, Ovation developed a new technique of guitar body construction, in which sides and back are molded in one piece from a type of fiberglass laminate. The Ovation company believes that the parabolic arch back shape gives better projection, and the synthetic material is both a good sound reflector and more predictable in its behavior than timber.

Several makers, including Guild and Gibson, make some conventionally bodied models with a swell back, which has a quite pronounced arch. The purpose of this design is to produce a more heavily bass-resonant guitar, for accompanying singers, by increasing the size of the body cavity.

The sides are bent into shape after being sawn and thicknessed. Side bending in factory production is carried out on large power-operated presses. The sheets of timber are softened by immersion for a few minutes in a vat of very hot water before being transferred to the press. The press contains heated metal inside and outside molds which conform exactly to the curves of the finished guitar. Each side is placed between these molds, which are then brought firmly together. After only a few minutes of heat and pressure, the press is opened and the shaped sides can be removed.

Before the top and back can be glued in place, the sides must be joined together with the endblocks, and the linings added. As on the classical guitar, the linings increase the gluing area between the sides and top and back. They are made of triangular fillets of wood, with notches at regular intervals so that they can be easily bent to the contour of the sides, and may be fitted either before or after the sides are joined to the endblocks.

The forward endblock is a crucial element in the construction of any acoustic guitar. It connects the sides, front, back and neck at a point of stress. If the joint at this point is not accurately made and firmly fixed, the neck will lose its proper alignment. The classical guitar uses what is known as the Spanish heel and foot to make the junction between body and neck, and this provides the strongest joint for the purpose which has yet been discovered. Unfortunately, it is not easy to build, and not applicable in mass production.

Factory-built steel-string guitars make use of the weaker dovetail joint. A V-shaped slot, with tapered sides, is cut into the endblock to take an exactly matching tongue which protrudes from the back of the guitar heel. (Photographs of this can be seen on pages 279 and 283.) Although the dovetail joint has structural disadvantages, the two parts can be made accurately and rapidly under factory conditions. The dovetail also allows neck and body to be made separately, and brought together only when both are complete. The dovetail slot in the endblock may be cut either before the block is fitted, or after the body is assembled.

When the linings and endblocks are in place, the top and back of the guitar can be glued to the sides. Where the cross struts of top and back reach the sides, the linings are notched away. At this stage the top and back are still oversize. The excess is trimmed away after the body assembly is glued and the slots to take the body bindings are cut on a router.

The edge bindings along the junctions of side and top and side and back are practical as well as decorative, sealing the edge grain of the timbers against moisture. Where classical guitar bindings are made of strips of veneer, steel-string guitar bindings are most commonly made of black and white plastic. The binding strips are coated with glue and wrapped into the prepared slots, and the whole guitar body is cocooned with cloth tape to hold the bindings while the glue dries.

When the bindings are glued and the endblock dovetail-cut, the assembled guitar body is sanded down with progressively finer grades of sandpaper. It is now structurally complete and ready to be married with the neck, which will have been built simultaneously in a separate series of operations.

Steel-string and classical guitar necks differ in several important respects. Where the classical guitar neck is usually 5.3cm wide at the nut, most steel-string guitar necks have a width of either 4.75cm or 4.3cm. The narrow neck has evolved to suit generations of country, jazz, folk and blues players, who find it easier to handle and more appropriate to their fingering techniques. Naturally, the narrow neck is weaker; added reinforcement is necessary to resist the pull of steel strings.

Martin guitar necks are reinforced with a hollow square steel rod; most other companies fit adjustable truss rods, modeled on a design invented in the 1920s by Ted McHugh, an employee of the Gibson company.

The Gibson truss rod consists of a metal bar embedded in an arched groove running down the neck. One end is threaded to take a nut, which is concealed under a cover plate on the head. Tightening this nut exerts an opposing force to counteract the tendency of the pull of the strings to make the neck bow. For clean playing action, the truss rod is usually adjusted to give the neck a slight concave bow, which matches the envelope of the vibrating strings.

Almost all steel-string guitars are built with necks that join the body at the fourteenth fret. The fourteen-fret neck is popular with players, since it makes the higher positions more easily accessible, but many guitar builders prefer the twelve-fret neck commonly found on early steel-string

guitars, which allows for a better body shape.

Steel-string guitar necks are either made from one piece of wood or laminated longitudinally. Whichever the case, neck, head and heel are cut from the same piece of wood. The rough blank for the neck is cut on a bandsaw and given a preliminary shaping on a router before the groove for the truss rod is cut.

From this stage on, different companies adopt slightly different construction procedures for the neck and fingerboard. Martin's next step is to glue the headstock veneer, before inserting the neck rod. (The headstock veneer's chief function is decorative: the guitar would, one feels, look naked without it.) Martin continues by inserting the neck rod, and gluing on the fingerboard blank. Once the fingerboard is in place, the fret slots are cut and the holes for the position dots drilled. The neck receives its final shaping only after the fingerboard has been attached. When the neck and heel have been given their proper profile, the frets are installed and filed, and the neck sanded in preparation to receiving its lacquer finish.

At Martin, all the neck shaping and fret fitting operations are carried out by hand. Gibson, in contrast, makes considerable use of automatic and semi-automatic machinery, and follows a different sequence of operations, working the necks and fingerboards separately.

The adjustable truss rod is placed in a polythene sleeve (which prevents it from rattling) and installed in the rough-shaped neck blank. The slot over the rod is filled with a wooden plug, which is hammered into place and glued in a press. The headstock veneer, however, is not applied until later. Once the rod is installed, and before the fingerboard is glued, Gibson shapes the neck on an automatic copying machine. Meanwhile, the fingerboard blanks are cut on a bench saw and given their top curvature on a router. The fret slots are cut, and position markers inlaid. The frets themselves are then installed, trimmed and filed before the fingerboard is glued to the neck.

When the neck assemblies have been sanded clean, they are matched to the guitar bodies. Martin does not finally glue the two together at this stage, preferring to finish necks and bodies separately. This allows the application of a different finish to neck and body, and eliminates the problem of a buildup of lacquer in the angle where neck and body meet. Gibson, on the other hand, glues neck and body, and finishes both together.

Almost all steel-string guitars are sprayed with lacquer, but before this can be applied the body and neck grain must be sealed with filler and sanded smooth again. If the guitar is to have a sunburst finish, this too is applied before the lacquer is sprayed.

Martin and Gibson use a nitrocellulose lacquer, but some other companies (particularly the Japanese) have switched to acrylic. The lacquer finish is built up in a series of five or six coats. Between coats, the surface is sanded down with progressively finer grits to build up a deep-shine. After the final coat the guitar is polished to a high gloss with rouge on a large lambswool wheel. The effect of the finish on the guitar's tone is a subject of considerable controversy: the thickness of lacquer built up on steel-string guitars would be considered unacceptable on a classical instrument.

After the guitar has been polished, the bridge is glued in place. Wood-to-wood contact is essential for a strong joint and the effective transmission of vibrations from bridge to soundboard. Martin scrapes away the lacquer from the bridge area with a tool called a toothing iron; Gibson masks off the bridge location with tape before the lacquer is sprayed on.

When the bridge has been placed, the saddle is fitted. Some years ago there was a fashion for bridges with adjustable saddles to each string, after the manner of the electric guitar. All the leading makers have now returned to using conventional acoustic guitar saddles—now usually made of plastic instead of the traditional ivory—which give a better transference of string vibration to the guitar top.

In order that they should play in tune, steel-string guitars have what are known as compensated bridges, in which the saddle slopes toward the bass side of the guitar, making the bass strings longer than the treble. When a string is depressed, the act of depressing it increases the string tension slightly, raising the pitch of the note fractionally above its theoretical value. To correct for this, the saddle has to be set a little further back, giving a string length slightly longer than the theoretical scale length to which the fret intervals are calculated. The difference between these two lengths is known as the compensation. The bass strings of a steel-string flat-top guitar need more compensation than the trebles, so a slanted saddle is fitted.

The final step in construction is the fitting of the tuning machines. Most steel-string guitars have flat, unslotted headstocks, with individual machines mounted on the rear, their spindles simply poking through the front. This design greatly simplifies the head construction. The gears of the machines are housed in metal casings; the most expensive (such as the Grover Rotomatic, Schaller and Mk VI) have permanently sealed, self-lubricated casings which make the machines virtually everlasting.

When the gears are fitted the guitar is complete. It is now strung, tried and inspected before dispatch. Although no factory-built guitar can receive the degree of attention accorded to the individually hand-built instrument, the leading companies make honorable attempts at perfection within the disciplines of mass production. In the competitive state of the market, they have to. The established American manufacturers face serious competition from the Japanese, who have copied their designs extensively and have the advantage of lower labor costs. Also, while the aim of factory work is to increase production and lower costs, an exported American guitar can often be more expensive than a hand-built instrument in the country of its destination. These considerations provide a strong incentive for the American companies to maintain, and try to improve, their standards.

Inside the C. F. Martin company's sawmill.

Whole trunks of spruce, rosewood, ebony and mahogany are imported from their countries of origin and stacked to await cutting on the main saw, which can be seen in the background. When the time comes to cut them, these huge trunks are maneuvered on to the sawbed with the aid of an electric overhead hoist. The whole sawmill plant (which contains two smaller saws in addition to the main headrig) is operated by only four men.

Closeup of logs before sawing.

A rosewood trunk being reduced into the smaller baulks from which guitar backs and sides will be sliced.

The timber is firmly clamped to the hydraulically operated sawbed which feeds it through the blade. The baulks are cut from the trunk in such a way that they will yield perfectly radially cut slices for the sides and backs when they are resawn. The exact setting of the timber on the sawbed is critical: a slight error can ruin hundreds of dollars worth of timber.

Despite the saw's massive size, it is a very precise piece of machinery. It can cut slices of wood to an accuracy of the order of 0.1mm, and makes such a clean unwavering cut that the sawn timber needs only a light sanding.

Inspecting matched sheets of spruce, which will eventually become guitar tops, at the Martin factory.

The inspector is using a clear acrylic template to check if any visible blemishes or irregularities of grain will fall within the area of the top, or if they will be cut away as waste when it is sawn to shape.

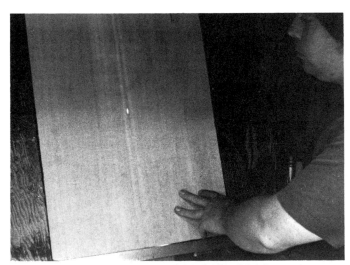

Checking a glued-up top blank for hidden blemishes, on Martin's candling machine.

The candling machine consists of a brilliant light table, which reveals flaws in the wood that are not normally visible. In this case, the flaw revealed in the center joint will not be significant if it falls in the area cut away to make the soundhole. After this inspection, the blanks are designated to a particular model according to their quality.

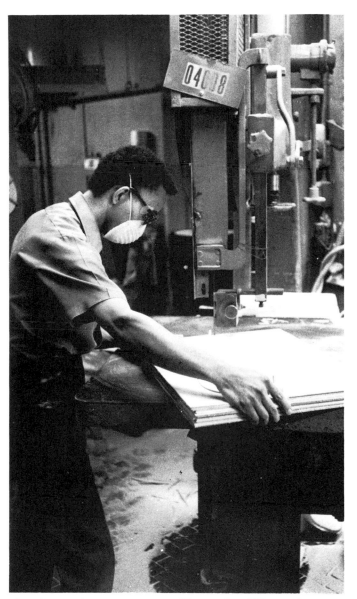

Cutting guitar tops to profile at the Gibson factory in Kalamazoo.

Gibson cuts fifteen tops at a time on a bandsaw. The boards are pegged together through locating holes, with a template on top to act as a cutting guide. The locating holes are used to position the tops on several subsequent pieces of machinery to ensure dimensional consistency. They are drilled through small stubs sticking out of the top at each end, which are trimmed off when the top is finally glued to the sides.

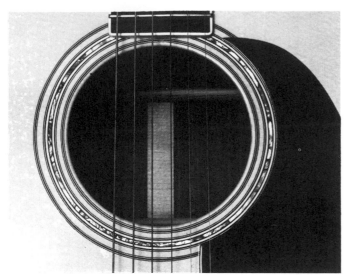

The soundhole inlay on a Martin D41.
(From the collection of John Pearse.)

Gluing braces to the undersides of guitar tops in the Martin factory. In the foreground, from left to right, are standard patterns for the normal X bracing, the heavier X bracing for a twelve-string guitar, and the bracing for Martin's N-series classical model.

The braces are made from the same type of spruce as the top of the guitar and prepared on a circular saw. The brace positions are marked on the top with the aid of a metal template, the braces glued on by hand, and the top assemblies placed in clamps while the glue dries.

The rosewood plate under the bridge provides greater strength and is not thought to have any significant effect on the guitar's sound.

The final shaping of braces for a Martin Dreadnought guitar.

The ends of the braces are carved to shape by hand and then receive a final sanding.

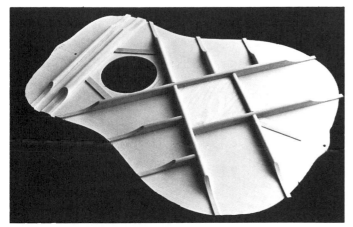

Gibson "double X" bracing.

(Photograph by courtesy of Richard Schneider.)

Bracing operations in the construction of a Gibson Dreadnought.

The braces are positioned and glued with the aid of power-operated presses.

The top is placed on the bed of the press and a metal template, slotted to take the braces, is fitted over it. Glue is applied to the braces, which are then located in the slots. The bed, with the top on, is then slid forward into the press, which descends to apply heat and pressure while the glue sets.

The use of the template and heated power press both speeds up the process of bracing the top and ensures absolute uniformity of construction from top to top.

The backs are braced at the same work station, on the press at the left.

The ends of the braces are trimmed on a machine which cuts a standard "scoop."

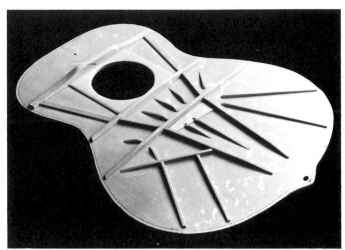

The two small braces which stop short of the edge of the top are fitted by hand, instead of on the machines. The braces have a quick sanding to remove any loose pieces left by the end-trimming machine, and the tops are ready to be fitted to the sides in the assembly process.

Gibson Mark guitar bracing.
(Photograph by courtesy of Richard Schneider.)

Bracing operations in the construction of Gibson's Mark series guitars at its factory in Nashville.[3]

The machinery and process by which the struts are fitted are the same in principle as those involved in the building of Gibson's standard models. But because of the complexity of the Mark design, the tops are strutted in two stages. Half the bars are glued in the press on the left. When these are set, the remainder are glued on the press in the center. The press on the right of the picture is used for gluing the back struts.

Some twenty different sizes and shapes of bar are used, all shaped by machine before being fitted on the gluing presses.

The top blank is placed on the press, the metal template located over it, and the struts glued by hand.

When the struts are in place, the press is closed and applies heat and pressure while the glue sets. The spring-loaded studs, which can be seen on this photograph taken through the press as it closes, bear down precisely on the struts and hold them firmly in place.

Once all the struts are glued in place, a dab of epoxy resin is applied to each end for extra strength.

Gluing rosewood back halves together on a "windmill" press in the Martin factory.

Sawing a back to profile at the Martin factory.

This three-piece back is for one of Martin's D–35 guitars. The D–35 is the only one of Martin's standard models to use a three- instead of a two-piece back; the design was introduced in 1965 due to a shortage of wide pieces of rosewood.

The power-operated press which is used to make the laminated swell on Gibson's J-55 and Gospel models, at the Kalamazoo factory.

Three thin sheets of veneer are bonded together to produce the deeply arched swell backs. The veneers are coated with glue and placed between formers in the press, which is then closed to apply heat and pressure for approximately half an hour. When the backs are taken out, the veneers will be bonded together and permanently formed to the arch.

Cutting sheets of maple for guitar sides at Gibson (Kalamazoo).

The plank is passed through the saw by a power-operated feed, which ensures operating safety and accuracy of cut.

A side-bending press at the Martin factory, with a timber softening tank in the foreground.

Mahogany sides take three and a half minutes to shape in the press, rosewood sides take four minutes. In this photograph, the press has just been opened so that two sets of mahogany sides may be taken out.

Gluing the linings (or "ribbons") to guitar sides at Gibson (Kalamazoo).

Gibson's usual procedure is to attach the sides to the endblocks before gluing the linings. Despite the extensive use of sophisticated machinery in the guitar factory, the linings are still applied by hand and held in place by clamps modeled on the domestic clothespin.

Side assembly of Mark series guitars at Gibson (Nashville).

On Mark guitars, Gibson workers attach the linings before fitting the sides to the endblocks. The design of the front endblock, into which the neck will be dovetailed, is unusual for a steel-string guitar. It is reminiscent of the Spanish slipper foot of the classical guitar, and is intended to increase the gluing area to top and back for greater strength.

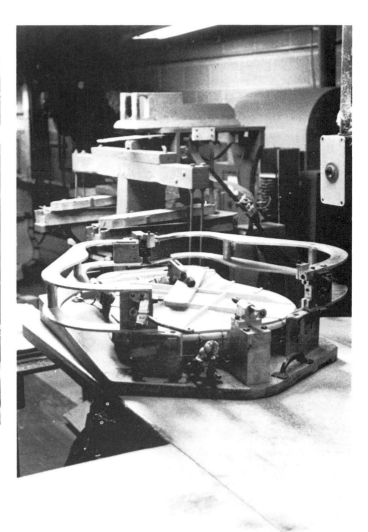

Body assembly at Gibson (Kalamazoo).

To cut away the linings where the cross braces fall, the sides are held in a clamp and a metal template is placed above them. A hand-held router is steered around the template, and the slots in the linings are automatically notched out in the correct places.

The guitar top is clamped to the baseboard of the collar in which the body is held during assembly.

Once the sides are placed on the top and glued, the collar is closed to hold them in shape. A temporary cross brace is inserted to press the guitar waist out against the collar.

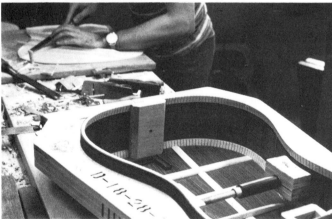

The back is fitted, and the assembly is ready to be slid into the power-operated press which will hold it while the glue sets.

Body assembly at the Martin factory.

Martin fits the sides to the back, and then cleans up the interior before fitting the tops. Here, the side-back assembly of a Dreadnought is fixed in its collar while the craftsman in the background finishes shaping the braces of the top. The dovetail in the endblock is cut before the guitar body is assembled.

The top is glued to the body in a hand-operated press designed to apply an even pressure all around the edge of the top, where it meets the sides.

Taping the binding in place at Gibson (Kalamazoo).

The bindings to the top and back edges are glued in separate operations.

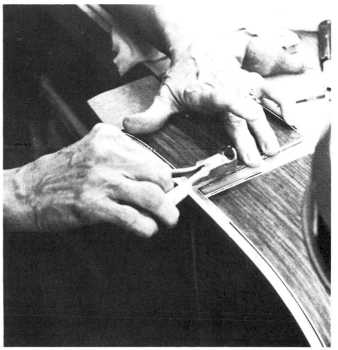

Inlaying a Martin D-45 with abalone.

45-series Martin guitars are inlaid on all body edges with abalone mother-of-pearl, as well as being bound in the normal fashion. Small slithers of abalone are fitted together in the slots which have been routed out to take them, and are set in a clear cement.

Abalone is a difficult material to work, being hard and brittle. Martin estimates that it takes fifty hours of hand work to fit the abalone inlays to the body edges, soundhole, and fingerboard surround of a D-45.

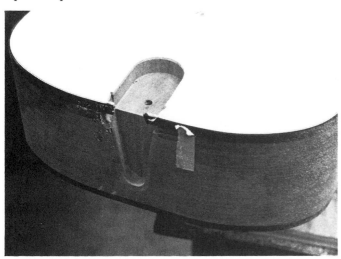

The dovetail in the endblock of a Mark guitar at Gibson (Nashville).

While most steel-string guitars have only the vertical dovetail slot, the design of the endblock on the Mark guitar allows an extra horizontal slot to be cut out of the top face of the guitar, into which a tongue on the neck is embedded. This strengthens the neck-body joint considerably.

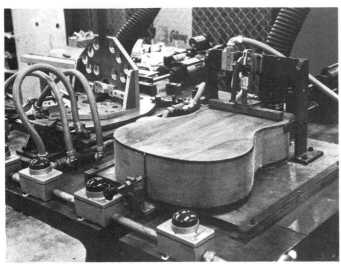

Dovetail cutting machinery at Gibson (Nashville).

To cut the dovetail on the Mark guitar, the body is firmly clamped in place and the entire clamp slid forward over the cutting blade of the router. Here, the slot on the top face of the guitar is being cut. When this is done, the guitar body is transferred to the machine on the left to cut the vertical dovetail slot in the end of the guitar.

Sanding down an assembled guitar body at Gibson (Nashville).

The guitar is being held on a vacuum clamp. This type

of clamp is very quick to apply, and can be swiveled in any direction.

Cross-section of a Martin guitar neck.

(From the collection of John Pearse.)

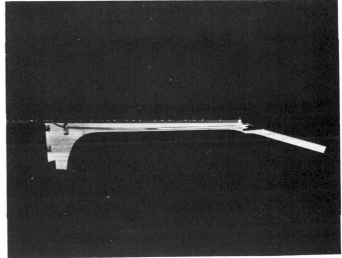

Longitudinal section of a Gibson guitar neck.

(Photograph by courtesy of Richard Schneider.)

Neck construction and fingerboard fretting at the Martin factory.

The neck reinforcing rod has just been fitted, and its cover strip is being glued in place. When the glue has dried, the fingerboard will be fitted and the neck finally shaped.

A rasp is then employed to smooth the neck down. Great skill is needed in these stages to make certain that consistent accuracy is achieved.

Final shaping of the neck is carried out entirely by hand. The main tool used is the drawknife, which the craftsman is here using to carve the heel.

Small lengths of fret wire are snipped off the roll and hammered home by hand.

Once the ends of the frets have been trimmed off and filed smooth, a dab of black sealing compound is applied to the end of each fret. This ensures a neat finish when the side of the fingerboard is sanded down. The neck assembly is now ready for sanding and varnishing.

The large manufacturers cut all the fret slots in one operation on a fingerboard with a multiple-bladed circular saw. The saw has a separate blade for each slot, with each blade ground to width so that the tang of the T-shaped fret wire will be firmly gripped by the sides of the slot. The blades are also set the correct distance one from another so that the guitar will be in tune at each position.

To take into account the curved surface on steel–string guitar fingerboards, the saw spindle rocks like a pendulum. Thus, the depth of the cuts into the fingerboard always remains constant.

Stages in neck and fingerboard construction at Gibson (Kalamazoo).

The necks are shaped on an automatic copying machine, which carves six at a time. The rough-shaped neck blanks are set up in pairs and a guide wheel traces the contours of a master pattern. The guide wheel's movements are followed by three "slave" cutters, which work around and down the neck blanks, carving them automatically to the shape of the master.

This is an extremely accurate piece of machinery. It can produce finished guitar necks which vary from one to another by less than 0.4mm ($\frac{15}{1000}''$) over any part of their section.

Each fret is located in its slot by hand, with two light taps of a hammer. The fingerboard is then transferred to a press which pushes all the frets home in one operation. (The fingerboards being fretted here are twenty-four-fret models for electric guitars; the process is the same for the twenty-fret fingerboards on acoustic instruments).

Neck operations at Gibson (Kalamazoo). Matching a neck and body.

Checking the alignment of neck and body for straightness and pitch.

In most cases, the guitar neck is set so that it is tilted slightly upward from the plane of the top, to help achieve a clean, buzz-free playing action. The exact angle is checked with a metal pitch gauge.

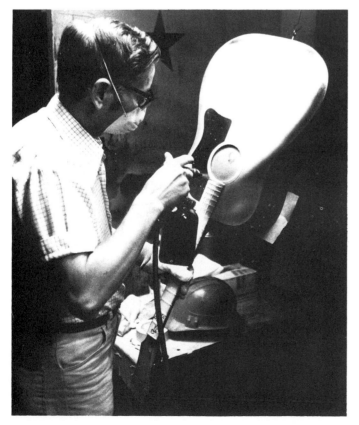

Clamping the neck in place while the glue sets.

Spray-finishing a sunburst-top guitar at Gibson (Kalamazoo).

To give the sunburst finish, the top is sprayed with a yellow undercoat. When this is dry, the dark finish is built up in layers, spraying from the edges toward the center to obtain a smooth gradation of color.

The fingerboard is covered by a protective masking, and the soundhole is blocked off to keep spray out of the interior of the guitar.

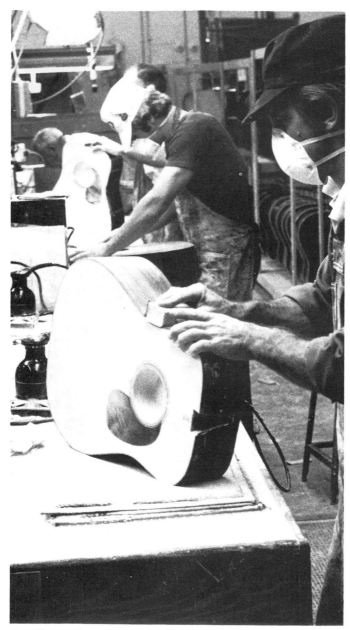

Gluing a bridge at Martin.

Scuff-sanding guitar bodies between lacquer coats at Martin.

Gluing a bridge at Gibson (Kalamazoo).
  A type of vacuum clamp holds the bridge in position while it is glued. When the air is exhausted from the clamp, the clamp's diaphragm top is pushed down on to the bridge by atmospheric pressure, holding it firmly in place.

Final inspection of completed Martin guitars.

All guitars are checked for playing action, intonation, and freedom from buzz at each fret. The finish is closely inspected, fingermarks polished off and—if it satisfies the inspectors—the guitar is passed for packing and shipment.

Fitting Schaller tuning machines at Gibson (Kalamazoo).

The spindle of each machine is slipped through a hole drilled in the headstock, and a retaining bush is screwed on from the front. The individual gear housings are then screwed to the back of the head. It takes only a few minutes to fit a complete set of machines.

Dave Roberts of Norlin (UK) trying out a brand-new Gibson Mark 35.

MUSIC AND PLAYERS

The Muses of Painting, Poetry and Music, *by William Edward West. The painting is American but the guitar is a Spanish-style instrument, with a flat peg head and large heel.*

[GIFT OF ELIZABETH H. E. MCNABB IN MEMORY OF
SARAH WEST NORVELL LEONARD, 1957.]

The birth of the American guitar

The known history of the American guitar begins with the gut-strung, classical instrument in Colonial and Revolutionary times. The instruments in the hands of rich and fashionable young ladies, and the music played on them, were similar to those that graced the drawing rooms of Europe. Benjamin Franklin is known to have played the guitar, so did rich Virginian planters.

> When we returned about Candle-light we found Mrs. Carter in the yard seeing to the Roasting of her Poultry; and the Colonel in the Parlour tuning his Guitar.[1]

Later Americans learned from tutors such as the *Complete Instructor for the Spanish and English Guitar, Harp, Lute and Lyre*, the first American manual (published in 1820 by J. Siegling of Charleston, South Carolina) or from classical guitar teachers in the Eastern cities. The demand for guitars encouraged many luthiers to emigrate from Europe, from Germany in particular, and these men laid the foundations for the American guitar industry.

The sweet-toned gut-strung guitar remained in the drawing rooms of the cities. For those who were moving westward, the sturdier steel-string guitar was more suitable. It was to become the instrument of America, and its music grew not from the mansions, but from the fields, trails and plantations. Little is known of the early history of the steel-string guitar, but there are scattered references to its use. Some of the earliest of these place the instrument in the hands of slaves.

The slaves who were shipped from the West coast of Africa brought with them a tradition of plucked stringed instruments. In 1781 a traveler had remarked on the *rabouquin*, an instrument that had been played on the coast for many years. This was

... a triangular piece of board with three strings made of intestines, supported by a bridge, which may be stretched at pleasure by means of pegs, like those of our instruments in Europe; it is indeed nothing else than a guitar with three strings.[2]

The slaves brought no possessions—and no instruments—with them, and when they arrived on the Southern plantations, drums and horns were denied them for fear that these would be used to send secret coded messages. Stringed instruments, on the other hand, were considered harmless. Mary Reynolds, a slave on a Louisiana plantation described how Saturday evenings were spent:

> the niggers which sold they goobers and 'taters brung fiddles and guitars and come out and play. The others claps they hands and stomp they feet and we young-uns cut a step round.[3]

The form of this guitar is not known, but we can assume that in the conditions of slavery it would be a home-made instrument.

The robust steel-string guitar began to make its official appearance from instrument makers' workshops in the late 1880s. Apart from its suitability as an accompanying instrument for the voice, the guitar was portable and very cheap. The Sears Roebuck catalogue of 1908 was advertising guitars by mail-order from $1.89 to $28.15. Otherwise the local country store sold a variety of guitars. For $1.95 you could purchase one of the "Spanish models with patent head, maple wood, red shaded, varnished soundboard, good quality in pasteboard box"; for $5 there was a wider choice.[4] But even these were often out of the reach of the poor country boy and many learned on home-made instruments:

> I made my first guitar. I made it out of a cigar box and a good stout long board, and it had five strings of baling wire. Hurt my fingers on it. That was when I was just a farm boy.[5]

Once introduced, the guitar appeared in all forms of American music. It was used in the maverick churches of the South, sometimes with drums and horns to accompany the rocking, noisy spirituals. Passengers on steamboats would be entertained between stops by a lone black singer

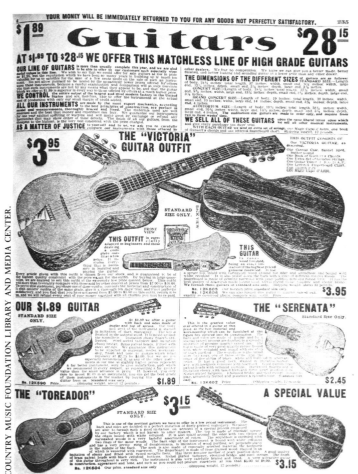

A page from the 1908 Sears Roebuck mail order catalogue.

with a guitar. Throughout the country string bands used fiddles, guitars and banjos to play popular tunes for guests at picnics and dances. By the turn of the century the guitar could be heard on back porches, in bars and brothels, and in the barbers shops of New Orleans:

> Uptown in New Orleans they had a lot of country guitar players used to come to town and sit around and in barber shops you know, and play. They hear [bands] playing and they sit around in the barber shops and if they catch the piece they pick it out on the guitar.[6]

In New Orleans the increasing popularity of the guitar coincided with the emergence of jazz as a separate musical form. One of the earliest known jazz bands was led by the guitarist Charlie Galloway in 1894, but the acoustic guitar was not really loud enough to compete with the main instruments of cornet, trumpet, trombone and clarinet. For years guitars were used in jazz solely as rhythm instruments, as six-string drums which provided a beat. Restricted to this role, it was another twenty years before jazz guitarists began to use the instrument in such a way as to destroy this rigid concept. Lonnie Johnson and Eddie Lang were the first to elevate the guitar in jazz.

The steel-string guitar found its first great expression in the blues. As the country blues developed in the early twentieth century, the guitar was the instrument adopted by almost all singers and was an important influence on the development of the music. One of the earliest datable references to the blues occurs in 1903, when W. C. Handy was traveling in Mississippi.

Then one night at Tutweiler, as I nodded in the railroad station while waiting for a train that had been delayed nine hours, life suddenly took me by the shoulder and wakened me with a start.

A lean, loose-jointed Negro had commenced plunking a guitar beside me while I slept. His clothes were rags; his feet peeped out of his shoes. His face had on it some of the sadness of the ages. As he played, he pressed a knife on the strings of the guitar in a manner popularized by Hawaiian guitarists who used steel bars. The effect was unforgettable. His song, too, struck me instantly.

"Goin' to where the Southern cross the Dog."

The singer repeated the line three times, accompanying himself on the guitar with the weirdest music I had ever heard.[7]

Black convicts, chained at night in mobile pens. One of the trusties was allowed to entertain fellow convicts and guards playing his guitar—a cheap mail-order guitar very like those of the 1908 Sears Roebuck catalogue.

"There's a lot of things that give you the blues . . ."

The history of the country blues as a distinctive and coherent style starts in the first decades of the twentieth century. But the music itself drew on an ancestry of ballads, work songs, field hollers and spirituals, elements of which came from African music. Confusion surrounds the formative years, for as with all true folk music there are no written records, and investigation of the origins began after the style had evolved. Only after the first recordings had been made in the 1920s was there any attempt at serious study and by then it was too late to untangle many of the older elements. Moreover, study and observation as well as recordings tended to standardize musical forms, and to bring a selfconscious approach to an art which was essentially spontaneous.

It was in the rural South and particularly in the countryside of the Mississippi Delta region that the early blues took on some of their most typical forms. In the eighteenth and early nineteenth centuries, slave gangs laboring to clear and work the land were led and encouraged by a crude type of song, itself part of a widespread African tradition. The leader shouted out a line, the rest of the gang joined in with the response. This leader-and-chorus pattern had a strong influence on the later blues, and the music, particularly in the Delta, retained its stamp in short vocal phrases, a limited melodic range and strongly marked rhythms. The song type outlived the end of slavery, persisting among work gangs on the Southern penitentiaries.

From the men working the lands of the Delta came one other distinctive form: the freely structured holler, modal in character, which a man would sing out to himself as he worked his way along the cotton rows, or cry in a falsetto voice to his animals. As a means of encouragement, or a spontaneous expression, the holler could still be heard long after its basic quality had become part of the blues song. In the 1960s there were still older bluesmen around who could remember their experiences in a farming community where traditions had hardly changed for generations. Muddy Waters recalled from his boyhood spent on his father's farm in Rolling Fork, Mississippi:

Every man would be hollerin', but you don't pay that no mind. Yeah, course I'd holler too. You might call

Convicts building roads near Atlanta, Georgia. Lightnin' Hopkins once told Paul Oliver: "Working out on the road gang—it ain't no easy thing, I tell you. Every evenin' when you come in they would chain you, they'd lock you with a chain aroun' your leg."

them blues but they was just made-up things.[1]

Howling Wolf, who lived on Boosey's plantation on the Quiver River, Merleville, had a similar musical background:

There was a lot of music around there. Work songs. . . . They'd just get out there and sing as they worked. Plowing songs, songs to call mules by. They'd get out there mornings and get to plowing, and get to hollering and singing. They'd make these songs up as they go along.[2]

Work songs and hollers are two of the most distinctive and traceable elements of the early Delta blues style, but by no means the only ones. The blues are entangled with many other forms of black music.

In towns and villages the early religious revival of the Methodist and Baptist Churches within the black communities had owed much of its success to the emotionalism of the music—the spirituals and revivalist hymns which

Day laborers carrying cotton from the fields to be weighed on Marcella Plantation, Mississippi, in 1939.

developed out of the more orthodox Wesleyan hymns. The connection between the church and the blues has always been a close one, though the relationship is often vehemently denied by those in the church. But many blues singers learned their early music in church choirs, or playing the accompaniment. This was often the only formal musical education available to a black person. The great bluesman Son House said of his early life:

> I wasn't playing guitar then. I was mostly a church man. Brought up in church and didn't believe in anything else but church, and it always made me mad to see a man with a guitar and singing these blues and things. Just wasn't brought up to it. Brought up to sing in choirs. That's all I believed in, then.[3]

The form of music known as "holy blues" was a rich and

popular one, heard at its best in the music of the Reverend Gary Davis.

Away from the complete isolation of the rural areas, contact was made with the white American—and with his music. In the 1870s and 80s the white ballad tradition was adopted by the blacks, who either took over established legends or created their own. This period saw the origin of some of the most famous: "John Henry," "Stackerlee" and "Frankie and Albert" (which later metamorphosed into "Frankie and Johnny"). These ballads became standard in the early blues repertoire. More importantly, the conventional twelve-bar, three-line pattern of the traditional ballad became the most common—though by no means the only—form in the blues.

The earliest black musicians were often "songsters," men with a local reputation and a wide repertoire to fit any occasion, and able to entertain with blues, ballads, religious songs or dance tunes. But the bluesman gave something more than just entertainment. In his music, the audience found the expression of a universal and common experience with which they could identify. When Ramblin' Thomas from Texas sang "Poor boy, poor boy, poor boy long ways from home," anyone who had been forced to migrate to find work felt an immediate personal response. John Lee Hooker explained to Paul Oliver:

> There's a lot of things that give you the blues, that give me the blues, that give any man the blues: it's somewhere down the line that you have been hurt some place.... and you get to playin' the blues that reaches. And so that's why when I sing the blues I sing it with the big feelin'. I really means it.... And so when you gets the feelin' it's not only what happened to you—it's what happened to your foreparents and other people. And that's what makes the blues.[4]

The blues flourished in the rural areas of Georgia, Louisiana, the Carolinas and Texas, and followed the migratory paths of black people. As the musicians moved from place to place, a wide variety of styles developed from the basic pattern of verses on a twelve-bar type, in $\frac{4}{4}$ time, divided into three call-and-response sections with the rhyme scheme of AAB. The blues were sung wherever there was a poor black community, from the levee camps of the Mississippi to the lumber camps of the Eastern states, from the slums of South Side Chicago to the red light district of Beale Street, Memphis.

During the first decades of the twentieth century, the music was developed by the country singers who went from community to community. The blues was first and foremost a vocal art—the singer's voice and his words were the most important elements, with the instrumental accompaniment in a subordinate role. They needed the most suitable instrument for accompanying the voice, and their choice unknowingly followed a centuries-old tradition. Like King Charles II of England and the gypsies of Spain, the bluesmen laid aside other instruments in favor of the guitar.

The guitar accompaniment had to have some of the flexibility of the human voice. The bending and flattening of notes, particularly the third and seventh and often fifth scale degrees, into "blue" notes, and the use of the droning sound of the guitar played with a bottleneck or slide could achieve the necessary interaction of sound. Of course, both techniques and skill of guitar playing varied enormously. To many of the older country players, for instance, departing from the conventional three-chord harmony of tonic, subdominant, and dominant removed the music too far from tradition.

Many of the early players knew no musical theory. They usually taught themselves, and then developed their playing by imitation or personal invention. Mance Lipscomb, born in 1896 in Navasota, Texas, and one of the older generation of "songsters" explained the rather casual process:

> I been playin' the git-tar now 'bout forty-nine years, and then I started out by myself, just heard it and learned it. Ear music. And nobody didn't learn me nothin'. Just pick it up myself; I didn't know any notes, just play by ear.... All my people can play some kind of music.[5]

Many techniques for achieving specific effects were unconsciously evolved among black guitarists in the early 1920s. Included here are examples of the most common of them, some of which have formed the basis of American playing techniques in fields beyond country blues.

CLAWHAMMER. See FINGERPICKING.

FINGERPICKING.
A pre-blues guitar technique in which the index finger—or the index and middle fingers—of the right hand picks out a melody against a rocking bass string accompaniment played by the thumb. Certain players have elevated it to great heights: Blind Blake, for example, and the Reverend Gary Davis. The fingerpicking technique was adopted by certain white country musicians in the late 1920s and early 30s—and, in the hands of players like Merle Travis, it has formed the basis for what is now called the "Nashville" guitar sound.

. . . see also CHOKING.

The HAMMER ON.
This is a device used by almost all American guitar players, black and white. A string is plucked, then, while it is still ringing out, a left-hand finger-tip is brought down onto it immediately behind a fret. This causes a second, higher note to be sounded. The hammer on is used either to facilitate the playing of a melody or just as a means of "texturing" a song accompaniment. Although hammering-on movements do occur in other cultures where the guitar is found—South America and Spain, for example—the unique emphasis given to the playing of the second note in the American form suggests that its origins in America lie probably in the five-string banjo techniques of Southern Appalachia rather than in any other established guitar tradition. Added weight is given to this theory by the many banjo terms—drop-thumb playing, clawhammer, etc.—to be found in the folk guitar player's vocabulary. (These are not necessarily applied to the same type of technique.)

. . . see also PULL OFF and TUNINGS.

The PULL OFF.
This is the reverse of a hammer on. A stopped string is plucked by a right-hand finger—then, while it is still sounding, the fretting finger is pulled slightly to one side and then raised fractionally, allowing the string to snap free. This has the effect of sounding a second, lower, note.

. . . see also HAMMER ON.

WHINE (also called BENDING, WHAMMING and—incorrectly—CHOKING)
A blues guitar invention which has been adopted by most rock guitarists. A stopped string is plucked and then either pushed or pulled in a sideways motion across the fingerboard, causing the pitch of the note to "whine" up in pitch—sometimes as much as two tones. A modern variation is the *reverse whine* in which a string is played "at strain" and then relaxed. Thanks to modern string technology and the low string actions typified by Fender electric guitars those techniques have been developed to a fine art both in electric rock music—by such players as Jimi Hendrix and Tim Renwick—and in country music where they are used for pedal steel mimicry by players like Roy Buchanan and Andrew Gold.

CHOKING (also called DAMPING)
In order to keep a string or strings from ringing out beyond their time value, a guitarist will "choke" or "damp" them. The choke is usually obtained by resting the edge of the right-hand palm—between the base of the little finger and the wrist—along the line of the bridge saddle. This technique is also used as an effect. Sometimes, for instance, only the bass strings will be choked. This provides a bass fiddle mimicry on the damped strings against which a melody is played by the fingers on the unchoked treble strings.

. . . see also FINGERPICKING.

A more primitive choke, much favored by Texas blues singers, is obtained by dropping the ball of the right-hand thumb down onto the bass strings.

. . . see also LEFT-HAND DAMPING.

LEFT-HAND DAMPING
Often it is necessary to terminate a sounding string note before it has had time to decay naturally. The left hand may be used to bring this about in one of two ways, depending on whether the string is fretted or open.
For a fretted string. If the holding finger is relaxed somewhat, the string will push it away from the fret and the note will be damped. This technique is used extensively in modern dance band guitar playing, where chords containing *open* (unfingered) strings are avoided because it is difficult to damp them.
For an open string. In order to damp an open string, a finger that is not being used in the chord is flicked down, allowing the fleshy pad of the fingertip lightly to graze the string and thereby muffle it.

. . . see also CHOKING.

BOTTLENECK PLAYING (also called SLIDE, RAZOR or KNIFE PLAYING)
Invented by the black urban street musicians early in the century in an attempt to imitate the Hawaiian guitar music in vogue at that time. The earliest attempts were made with the guitar resting across the knees, strings uppermost in Hawaiian style, and the strings being stopped by means of a beer glass or bottle held in the left hand. This soon became modified to just the neck of the bottle, which was slipped onto a left-hand finger (usually the third or fourth) and applied to the guitar held in the "normal" Spanish way. Cut-throat (straight) razors, pocket knives or empty metal cigar tubes are also seen from time to time, pressed into service to obtain this attractive "keening" sound. These are held lightly between the base of the third and fourth fingers and a measure of control is achieved by the same fingers curling over and gripping with the fingertips.

Nowadays, many of the younger bottleneck players prefer a lighter slide fashioned from a short length of highly polished metal tubing.

TUNINGS
Apart from the standard Spanish tuning (E-A-D-G-B-E), the most common "folk" tuning in North America is "Slack Key," D-G-D-G-B-D. This tuning has much in common with the standard G tuning on five-string banjo, and because of this, the theory has been advanced that it is a native American

invention. However, the same note sequence appears in the tuning of the German cittern — the Thuringer Waldzither. Since many of the early American guitar makers came from those areas in which the Waldzither was the most widely used plucked instrument — it is just as likely that "Slack Key" was brought to the U.S.A. by one of these European immigrants. Open tunings were frequently used by blues players so as to make a repetitive accompaniment easier. With the strings tuned to an open chord, the major or minor would be achieved by sharpening or flattening the third string. The open E tuning (E-B-E-G-B-E) was a minor tuning played raising the g to major g♯ (referred to by Skip James as "cross note"). Other widely used tunings were D-A-D-G-B-D and D-G-D-G-C-D.

"My home is in the Delta"

Early in the twentieth century there was a demand for entertainers in the communities of the deep South. Saturday night was the night out, the night for fish-fries, country breakdowns, suppers and dances. These occasions provided a living for many bluesmen. It was a lonely, often dangerous life, as Yank Rachel later recalled:

> They'd take down the beds to make room, put a table 'cross the kitchen door where they'd cook catfish and sell it, sell moonshine and shoot craps in the barn. Late at night it'd get rough. They'd shoot out the lights. One night I remember Sleepy John [Estes] and I had to run off; he got hung up on a barbed-wire fence.[1]

There were many singers and guitarists in the Mississippi Delta in the 1920s. The leading musicians formed a loose-knit, traveling community, drifting from town to town, playing together for a time and then going their separate ways. Songs, styles and techniques were passed around and adapted for personal use.

Charley Patton was the first known professional bluesman from the Mississippi Delta. One of twelve children, he was born in the late 1880s near Edwards, Mississippi but his family moved to Dockery's Plantation outside Cleveland, Sunflower County, where he remained until he was thirty-four. At weekends and sometimes for weeks at a stretch he sang around the countryside, a local figure well known and liked.

Patton was an all-round entertainer with a repertoire of religious songs, folk songs, dances and ballads as well as straight blues. His singing style was heavy, harsh, and direct. His accompanying guitar style had a particular rhythmic quality that no other blues artist managed to imitate. He used the bottleneck technique to bring out a sustained treble voice and to reach higher notes while still being able to play in the root position.

Charley Patton recorded forty-six songs which reflect the circle he moved in, and unlike many blues singers he often took local events, people and places as his subjects. A night in jail in 1934 led to "High Sheriff Blues" and he commemorated the disastrous 1927 floods on the Mississippi in "High Water Everywhere," an extended blues of six minutes in two parts, with spoken comments interspersed with the singing.

Many blues singers were taught or influenced by Charley Patton. Willie Brown, born in Robinsville around 1900, met him at Dockery's Plantation and the two of them traveled, sang and recorded together. Brown appears to have been a better guitarist than Patton, willing to explore a wider range of effects, and possessing a superb rhythmic control. But only four solos of his are known, of which two, "M & O Blues" and "Future Blues," have survived.

In 1930 Patton and Brown met Eddie "Son" House — one of the best of the older bluesmen whose first appearance at the 1964 Newport Folk Festival did much to help encourage a revival of interest in the blues. Son House was born in 1902 and had an early contact with music — both his father and his uncle played in a small band and he sang in the local church choir. Son learned the guitar in Mississippi in the late 1920s and began to make a living by his music.

Son House's story is often quoted because it gives such a good picture of the musicians of the period. He told it to Julius Lester in December 1965, the year after his rediscovery:

> I started playing in 1928, but I got the idea around about 1927. I came along to a little place they call Matson, a little below Clarksdale. It was on a Saturday and these guys were sitting out front of a place and they were playing. Well, I stopped, because the people were all crowded around. This boy, Willie Wilson, had a

Son House playing a National resonator guitar. After his recordings in the 1930s, Son House was not heard of until twelve years later, when Alan Lomax, setting up his recording equipment at a crossroads in Robinsville, Mississippi, found him again. In 1943 he took a job as a porter and gave up playing in 1948—one of the many older country singers whose music was no longer wanted, as the group-based urban blues became increasingly popular.

COURTESY OF BIOGRAPH RECORDS

thing on his finger like a small medicine bottle, and he was zinging it, you know. I said, "Jesus! Wonder what's that he's playing?" I knew that guitars hadn't usually been sounding like that. So I eases up close enough to look and I see what he has on his finger. "Sounds good!" I said. "Jesus! I like that!" And from there, I got the idea and said, "I believe I want to play one of them things." So I bought an old piece of guitar from a fella named Frank Hopkins. I gave him a dollar and a half for it. It was nearly all to pieces, but I didn't know the difference. The back was all broken in, but I got it from him and began to try to play. It didn't have but five strings on it, though. So I showed it to Willie Wilson and explained to him what I wanted to do. I wanted to learn to play. He said, "Well you'll never learn this way. You need another string. Takes six strings. It's all busted in the back, too. Tell you what I'll do. I'll see if I can fix it up for you." So he got some tape and stuff and taped it all up and got a string and put that on and then he tuned it. He tuned it in Spanish to make it easier for me to start. Then he showed me a couple of chords. I got me an old bottle. Cut my finger a couple of times trying to fix the thing like his, but finally I started to zinging, too. Finally, I got the idea about how to tune it myself. I used to be a leader in the choir and they were singing the old vocal music at that time, you know, like the "do-re-mi's," so I got the idea to make the guitar go like that, and in a couple of weeks time, I was able to play a little tune. It was a little tune I'd heard Willie Wilson play called, "Hold up Sally, Take Your Big Legs Offa Mine."

So the next time he came by, I showed him I could play it. He said, "Come on and play with me tonight." It was Saturday night. I said, "I ain't good enough for that." He said, "Oh yes, you is. You just play that. I'll back you up." So I started with him just like that. Finally he left from around there, but I kept on playing and got better and better, you know. I'd set up and concentrate on songs, and then went on to concentrating on me rhyming words, rhyming my own words. "I can make up my own songs," I said. And that's the way I started.[2]

When Charley Patton and Willie Brown met up with

House, Patton suggested to Paramount (his recording company) that Son should cut a disc. So in the summer of 1930, Son House went north to Grafton, Wisconsin with Willie Brown to make the famous "My Black Mama," "Preaching the Blues" and "Dry Spell Blues," each in an extended version in two parts.

Son House was a highly individual performer with an instantly recognizable style of singing and playing. Against the background of the guitar's driving rhythms in the bass and whining bottleneck on the upper strings, his harsh voice emphasizes the anguish of the words. Before beginning the vocal phrase, his voice often hesitates, a device which further heightens the feeling of tension, for this pausing contrasts strangely with a passionate vocal force. Son House was particularly important in developing the bottleneck style. He usually tuned his National resonator guitar to an open chord—G or E—and fretted the basses. His pieces were never set in a regular measure: he had trouble systematizing his verse lengths and often had to add here and there to fit the words. House's use of bottleneck was generally more sophisticated than Charley Patton's and paved the way for younger musicians such as Robert Johnson.

In his travels, Son House came to be heard by many other players. Muddy Waters was one of his admirers:

Yeah, I was influenced by Son House. I guess he made one or two records back then, but I knew him as a kid. He was all through the Delta back then, and I used to love to hear him play guitar. He had that bottleneck thing, and he could make the guitar real whiny.[3]

To many people, the greatest and most influential of all the Mississippi players was Robert Johnson. He only lived to be twenty-five or twenty-six, but his recorded songs have had an enormous influence on musicians of his own and succeeding generations.

Johnson was born around 1914, probably near Robinsville, Mississippi. One night he turned up at the juke joint where Son House and Willie Brown were playing. House described their first meetings.

He was just a little boy then. He blew a harmonica and he was pretty good with that, but he wanted to play a guitar. When we'd leave at night to go play for the

balls, he'd slip off and come over to where we were. His mother and stepfather didn't like for him to go out to those Saturday night balls because the guys were so rough. But he'd slip away anyway.[4]

Son House and Willie Brown moved on, and heard nothing of him for six months. When they met up again, Robert Johnson had taught himself how to play guitar and was already establishing a reputation. He learned fast from watching and listening to other singers or through their recordings. Henry Townsend said that "If you just went over something once Robert would get it and play it just as well as you did the next time, he was that kind of fellow."[5] Johnson grew up in the mid-1920s, when the blues was first being put on record, and he realized that through his music he could earn a good living. So he traveled—through the Delta, into Texas, up to Memphis and Chicago, sometimes alone, sometimes with others. While he was traveling he was heard by a local record salesman of the American Record Corporation and recommended to Don Law, who was recording local artists for the Vocalion label. Two sessions followed in San Antonio, Texas in November 1936 and June 1937.

The blues Johnson recorded at those sessions were spectacular. Much of his material was derivative: Son House, Willie Brown, Lonnie Johnson and Skip James have all left traces of their styles in his music. But his personality was such that whatever he played became uniquely individual. He had a passionate temperament and his most forceful songs were concerned with his own sexuality. Others reflected the urgency of pursuit, like the powerful "Hellhound on my Trail."

Johnson picked up all the Mississippi guitar techniques and used the typical open tunings, bottleneck and fingerpicking methods. But he advanced considerably beyond the simpler playing of many of the older bluesmen. "Terraplane Blues" for instance (in open G) is an exciting piece involving difficult rhythmic changes. In several pieces, his bottleneck guitar screams against the voice with a unique intensity. In "Love in Vain," the chords are vamped hard to make a cutting staccato effect within the standard $\frac{4}{4}$ time. The insistent hitting of the beat, followed by a damping with the open hand, gives a mean, thin sound with no sustain.

Robert Johnson is one of the vital links between the old country blues style and contemporary music. Muddy Waters took his early inspiration from him: "He was the kind of guy you wanted to listen to, get ideas from. . . ."[6] Sunnyland Slim remembered vividly the first time he heard him play:

> The first real fast blues I ever heard was from Robert Johnson—same thing that Elmore James made famous, "Dust My Broom"—and that was the first thing that had the beat; some kind of beat you could kinda get around a little fast on—walkin' the basses.[7]

Robert Johnson lived his live as fiercely as he played and sang, and died on August 16, 1938, killed, according to the latest research, by a man who had told him to lay off his wife. Son House was surprised he lived so long: ". . . he'd go up to a girl he saw at one of those dances and try to take her off, no matter who was around, her husband, or boyfriend or anybody."

Both Muddy Waters and Johnny Shines took material from him; through them and particularly Elmore James, who became one of the vital influences on post-war Chicago music, Robert Johnson's style persisted. Elmore James made "Dust My Broom" his theme tune and named his group the "Broomdusters." More recently Johnson's recordings have influenced the rock superstars of the 1960s: Cream recorded a version of "Crossroad Blues" and the Rolling Stones have recorded "Love in Vain" and "Dust My Broom."

The recording sessions of the 1920s and 30s were of the utmost importance for the blues and for the musical forms which were influenced by them. Though not always financially rewarding to the musicians involved, the records secured the survival of their names and at least some of their music.

The potential of the market for black singers was realized by the success of the "classic" female performers in the early 20s—such figures as Bessie Smith and Ma Rainey. The first black vocalist to record was Mamie Smith in 1920 for Okeh, a small independent label. Okeh made no special effort to advertise her, but the black newspapers took her up, and within the month she had a hit. Later recordings by black artists were sent out under "race" labels by companies aiming specifically at the black audience. But it was not until 1926 that the rural male blues singers were recorded in any numbers.

During the first great period of blues recordings (1927–30), there were seven main labels: Okeh, Columbia, Brunswick, Vocalion, Gennett, Victor and Paramount. The records were distributed in rural areas by traveling salesmen who followed the phonograph salesmen; in the cities records could be bought in music and furniture shops.

The early days of recording were fraught with difficulties. Victor found New Orleans so hot and humid that the microphones shorted. They tried changing to old-fashioned carbon microphones, but the heat made these hum so badly that they had to be packed in ice until the singers were ready. Often the singer's inexperience of recording led to disaster. Big Bill Broonzy described his first session in 1923 with his second guitarist, the otherwise obscure John Thomas:

> They had my head in a horn of some kind and I had to pull my head out of the horn to read the words and back in it to sing. And they had Thomas put on a pillar about two feet high and they kept on telling us to play like we would if we was at home or at a party, and they kept on telling us to relax and giving us moonshine whisky to drink—and I got drunk.[8]

Many singers were "collected" on field trips, a practice started in 1923 by Okeh, who sent talent scouts to Atlanta and St Louis. Alternatively, local scouts sent promising bluesmen to the recording studios in the large towns. In the 1920s Paramount was most assiduous in finding black singers, and recorded Charley Patton (1929), Son House and Willie Brown (1930) and Skip James (1931).

Skip James was born in Bentonia, Mississippi in 1902 into a religious family. He learned the guitar and piano and was one of the few singers with a high school education. As a young man he spent many years drifting around the South, laboring at menial jobs. Working in a sawmill, he met a pianist called Will Crabtree who helped him develop his musical talent. Later he met Little Brother Montgomery, from whom he learned "Special Rider Blues" and adapted it for the guitar. In Jackson in 1930 James came to the attention of Paramount's talent scout H. C. Spears, who in February 1931 sent him north to record some twenty-six sides in three days. But the session was not a success: none of the recordings were issued at the time, James was never fully paid, and the company went out of business. Angry and disappointed, and with his considerable pride hurt, he moved to Dallas and began a career in the church.

Much of Skip James's singing was typical of Mississippi in its closeness to the field holler, but by singing in a strong minor falsetto he could produce a strange, uniquely haunting sound. He also used a smoothly controlled vocal embellishment, which was in complete contrast to the harsh earthiness of other Mississippi singers. James's playing was, if anything, even more interesting than his vocal delivery. Many of his pieces, while using the major chord progression I–IV–V, had a strong minor bias. "Devil Got My Woman" is a good example with strange chord shadings. James's right-hand picking technique was fairly consistent throughout—a steady thumb and two-finger pick. He usually played the melodic line in unison with the voice (octave-spaced if in falsetto), but used subtle syncopation and complex rhythmic patterns in the breaks between voice parts. There was no vamping or in-filling, as in Big Bill Broonzy, or irregularities as in Charley Patton's playing. His style developed partly from his piano playing, but instead of the typical heavy walking basses, he used variations of tone color and gentle gapped scale runs to go with his light voice.

During the post-war revival, Skip was one of the major rediscoveries and has subsequently exerted great influence. Everyone who has heard the playing of Bert Jansch has heard echoes of Skip James's skipping guitar.[9]

Jackson, Mississippi was an important city for bluesmen in the 1920s. Many of the singers going to Memphis passed through there, and some, like Ishman Bracey and Tommy Johnson, stayed. Ishman Bracey, born in 1900, worked in his early years carrying water for the "gandy dancers" on the Illinois Central Line. He recorded in Memphis for Victor, but was not successful. His partner

Skip James in the 1960s.

on some of these recordings, Tommy Johnson, had a more powerful impact on the young bluesmen who came through Jackson. He was a polished performer, giving the impression of a fully integrated style with the guitar and voice perfectly matched. In his recording of "Big Road Blues," the most widely copied of his songs, he used the pianistic device of walking bass figures to evoke an image of walking down a road. He often used traditional verses, but reworked them with changes of rhythm and emphasis, even using the familiar "See See Rider" with great effect.

Inevitably, the early recordings distorted and affected the blues. Songs were altered according to where they were being played: a song played at a Saturday night dance or entertainment would probably be taken at a different tempo than in a recording. The lyrics of many of the songs were so explicitly sexual that they were never recorded, or, if recorded, were modified beyond recognition.

COURTESY OF YAZOO RECORDS

Leadbelly, "King of the Twelve-String Guitar Players," with his Stella twelve-string.

Walking the basses

"And I always sat on the bass side by the piano and that's the way I play. . . ."

Mississippi was not the only cradle of the blues. The music evolved differently in different states, giving rise to a number of regional variations of style which reflected the diverse backgrounds, experiences and circumstances of its creators.

Within five years of Texas gaining statehood in 1845, slaves were transported to work the cotton plantations. The slaves took with them their songs, elements of which persisted long after the abolition of slavery and could be heard in the prison farms that stretched along the Brazos River. Here the convicts continued the old tradition of leader-and-chorus work songs, but there was a specifically Texan variation in which the gang replied to the leader's call with a hummed chorus. The experiences of slavery and prison found their way into the blues. Leadbelly's version of the "Red River Blues" refers to this past:

Tell me which way/Do the Red River run,
Tell me which way/Do the Red River run,
Some folks all ready to say/It runs from town to town.
Red River/It's so deep and wide,
Red River/It's so deep and wide,
That I can't get a letter/From the other side.
Old folks all ready to tell me/Run from East to West,
Old folks all ready to tell me/ Run from East to West,
And I all ready to believe them/They didn't know the best.

The Red River marked the boundary between "slave" Texas and "free" Oklahoma. Its name lived on in the blues as a symbol of the barrier between freedom and oppression.

The development of the Texas blues was not a smooth and uniform process. The state's size and varied history, and the relatively low proportion of blacks to whites (one to three in 1880) discouraged the ready evolution of a distinctive blues style. Texas singers borrowed from the Delta style and used bottleneck guitar. However, they tuned the guitar higher, nearer to the concert pitch used by white players, and their playing was generally less complex and heavy than in Mississippi.

The diverse strains of the Texas style can be heard in

the repertoire of Huddie Leadbetter, better known as Leadbelly. In addition to the blues, he sang many blues-flavored ballads like "Frankie and Albert" and "The Grey Goose," cowboy songs like "Out on the Western Plains," and prison songs, of which the most famous is probably the "Midnight Special." This song came from one of the prison camps just outside Houston, beside the tracks of the Southern Pacific Railroad, where the legend ran that if the lights of the Midnight Special shone on an inmate it was a sign that he was soon to be released.

Leadbelly was born in 1885 and led a violent, rough life. From an early age he worked at Texas country breakdowns with a Colt revolver always close at hand. Such evenings, either in the country or the rougher parts of the cities, often ended in violence—usually over a woman:

> We like for women to be aroun' 'cause when women's aroun' that bring mens and that bring money. Cause when you get out there the women get to drinkin' . . . that thing fall over them, and that makes us feel good and we tear those guitars all to pieces.[1]

Leadbelly himself was particularly renowned for his sexual prowess, which was a theme in many of his songs.

It was in 1933, while he was serving a homicide sentence in Angola penitentiary (for shooting a man in a dispute over his girl) that the Lomaxes first heard him. John Lomax and his son Alan had begun to put together the huge and important collection of black folk music for the Library of Congress in 1933. They were so impressed by Leadbelly's tough arrogance and powerful singing that they interceded with the governor, and had him paroled into their custody a year later.

If Leadbelly's repertoire forms a link with earlier days, so does his unique vocal style. His voice was somber and grainy, his delivery harsh, direct and unadorned. Leadbelly's singing lacks the subtleties of some of his contemporaries in the Delta, or his fellow Texan Blind Lemon Jefferson, but replaces it sometimes with an uncompromising driving force, sometimes by a slow gravity with long-drawn notes that give a deep feeling of melancholy.

Because of his wide repertoire and his later success as a folk artist, Leadbelly was often denigrated as a bluesman. However, the best of his songs contain an aching sadness, as in "Goodnight Irene," or a terrifying menace, as in "Black Girl," which are unsurpassed by any other blues singer.

Leadbelly was not a modest man—he called himself "King of the Twelve-String Guitar Players of the World." The twelve-string guitar was less popular than the six-string guitar, but was favored by street singers for its volume—which was ideal for drawing crowds.

But there were drawbacks to the twelve-string guitar. Because of the difficulties in obtaining strings which could hold the high octave tuning (particularly on the third course) the guitars were normally tuned lower than standard pitch (usually two tones down). This lower pitch produced a looser action at the expense of a loss in tone and brilliance. The low tension could also result in a jangly imprecise tone against which it was necessary either to sing in a high voice or, by means of a capo, raise the pitch of the guitar to standard or higher. But using a capo on a twelve-string was not without its problems, for the arrangement of the strings—bass next to high octave—made it well-nigh impossible to use a capo without the uneven pressure causing the guitar to go out of tune. For this reason most players would keep a permanent capo on the third or fourth fret position. Although store-bought capos were used, more often than not a capo fashioned from a stick and heavy-duty rubber bands was the order of the day.

Leadbelly was able to cope effectively with all the problems inherent in using the twelve-string. Being a big man, he had immense power and could sustain the fast technique he developed. His voice was strong enough to compete with the big sound of the guitar even when he played with metal picks. The films of Leadbelly are interesting, for they show that he had a surprisingly good left-hand position, high above the fretboard like a classical guitarist. This was very useful for his particular technique of hammering on and pushing off the block chords.

Leadbelly developed the instrumental accompaniment of following the vocal melody in unison, and achieved his special style through a devastatingly fast thumb pick and boogie-woogie walking basses, developed from the barrelhouse piano playing that was popular in the brothels. Leadbelly had heard the juke-joint piano players in Shreveport's notorious Fannin Street. Introducing a song on *Leadbelly's Last Session*, recorded in 1948, he said:

Down in California we call this "Cry for Me." It's my mother crying for me not to go out on Fannin Street. . . .

Before the writers wrote this up, people didn't know what they was doing down home. That was way back. 1904, 1903, piano players were walking the basses. You walk up to a man and tell him "walk the basses for me," give him a drink or something. He started walking, it sounded good and the girls was jumping in the barrelhouse. The men didn't know what they was doing and I was walking too. I learned to play a guitar by the piano. I plays piano time, piano rhythms, that's me—and I like playing the bass sound in my music. And I always sat on the bass side by the piano and that's the way I play. There's old James P. John[son] and he used to walk the basses a long time. He didn't know what he'd done, but then they writers written it up and given it a name: boogie-woogie. Now everybody can boogie, but readin' boogie. We was speeding at that time, we didn't take time to read, which we couldn't. We wouldn't want to read, just speed.

Leadbelly's technique was peerless. Each note sounded dead on, with none of the fuzziness often present in twelve-string guitar playing. He stressed each note with equal deliberation, so there was no possibility of delicate shadings. His soaring bass was produced by a powerful thumb pick while the chord was flicked with a first-finger pick, producing a surprisingly complex cross rhythm. One other technique he used to give the rhythm a particular punch was the powerful left-hand hammering on and off the whole chord.

Leadbelly's most famous Texas contemporary was Blind Lemon Jefferson, who was born blind in 1897 on a farm near Wortham, Texas. As a young man he earned a living entertaining at country suppers and, from 1917, in Dallas bars and brothels. In 1925 he did a test recording for a local talent scout, and was sent to Chicago to record for J. Mayo Williams at Paramount in 1926.

Jefferson's style was varied and intricate and he influenced some great singers: Leadbelly, Lightnin' Hopkins, Big Bill Broonzy, Scrapper Blackwell and Muddy Waters, as well as the white country musicians who

Blind Lemon Jefferson in the late 1920s.

heard him in Dallas. His wide repertoire included blues like "Black Snake Moan" and "Oil Well Blues"; country numbers like "Texan, Lazy Rider" and "Jack O'Diamonds"; and gospel songs such as "He Rose from the Dead." He seldom kept strict time values, but interwove guitar and voice in a way that appeared closer to the field holler. The chromatic runs that he improvised between vocal breaks were highly individual and widely copied. In contrast, his light voice acted as a sustain over the intricate down-scale runs. Jefferson was willing to explore different effects and sometimes used boogie-woogie descents in octaves to imitate the walking basses of the barrelhouse pianists.

Jefferson was one of the most prolific bluesmen to be recorded—seventy-nine songs for Paramount and two for the Okeh label—and he made so much money that he was able to employ a chauffeur to drive his car. But most of the profits went on liquor and women. In 1929 he did a last recording session for Paramount and then apparently left the studios to go to a party. It was a bitterly cold night and for some reason his car wasn't there. He began to walk, and was found the next morning frozen to death by the road.

The recording companies were not so active in Texas. There were two main studios—in San Antonio and Dallas—but the talent scouts from New York did little field work outside these areas. The blues singers were often far from the large towns for they tended to follow the cotton plantation workers as they pushed further westwards.

The Okeh label did, however, find rural singers outside San Antonio. In 1929 they recorded the well-known Texas songster Texas Alexander. He was a singer only, but used some of the best guitarists around. One of these was Lonnie Johnson (born 1894) who came from New Orleans, a city that had absorbed the old field songs and dances into the mainstream of jazz rather than developing a blues style. In the 20s Johnson played with the guitarist Eddie Lang, who was the first to demonstrate the solo melodic potential of the guitar in jazz. Johnson's own playing reflected his jazz background and he played in a smoother and more regular style than the other country bluesmen. After the First World War he traveled through Texas, playing wherever he could find an audience. In 1925 he won a talent contest for bluesmen held at the Booker T. Washington Theater in St Louis, and on the strength of that was offered a profitable seven-year recording contract with Okeh. He had an immensely long career and was a major influence in the development of the blues after the Second World War.

Ragging the blues

The music of the Eastern states, and the Carolinas and Georgia in particular, was less gutsy than the rougher country blues style of Mississippi and Texas singers. The lush and fertile countryside of North and South Carolina brought less of the grinding poverty which the black from Mississippi or Texas suffered. The smallholder in the East grew tobacco, a crop that yielded more profit than cotton for less outlay of time and energy. From economic confidence came a greater emotional freedom, and this was reflected in the music. There was more emphasis on entertainment, both in the type of music played and in the style. Black people were less socially isolated; they came more into contact with white country music and many East coast singers show the influence of hillbilly songs. Both feeling and style were lighter, and there was a greater tendency to use dance and ragtime rhythms.

The main recording center for Georgia was Atlanta. The huge increase in Atlanta's population in the early years of the century provided a good market and an incentive for blues singers. Peg Leg Howell (born Joshua Barnes Howell in 1888) was a popular figure, who recorded for Columbia in nine sessions from November 1926 to April 1929, either solo or as "Peg Leg Howell and his Gang" with Henry Williams on second guitar and Eddy Anthony on violin. He picked up most of his music haphazardly: "I learned many of my songs around the country." And like most blues men, he was self-taught on the guitar: ". . . didn't take long to learn. I just stayed up one night and learned myself."[1] Howell formed a link with older music, for in his music there are strains of old songs, work songs, ballads and some white-influenced songs.

As in other cities with a strong blues tradition, the main figures knew each other and sometimes played together. The Georgia sound came from the diverse musical styles of figures like Peg Leg Howell, Robert and Charlie Hicks, Willie Baker (who, together with the slide player Fred McMullen, later formed the Georgia Browns), James "Kokomo" Arnold, Curley Weaver, Bumble Bee Slim, Blind Blake, Blind Willie McTell and Buddy Moss.

The early bluesmen coming into Atlanta from the surrounding countryside brought their rural styles with them and during the years after the end of the First World War formed a local style. The blues lyrics were simple, often loosely constructed, and sung with a particular nasal quality. Many of the Atlanta bluesmen, with the notable exceptions of Blake and Howell, played a twelve-string accompaniment based on a strummed approach (although fingerpicking techniques were occasionally used), and often made use of only one or two chords. One further feature of their style was an irregular rhythm produced by fractional pauses.

Both Charlie Hicks and his brother Robert (usually called "Barbecue Bob") were important figures, although not permanently influential. Bob was the better player and singer of the two, performing in typical early Georgia fashion. The two brothers were born at the turn of the century and raised on a farm in Walton County, coming to Atlanta early in their lives. In the mid-1920s they earned a living by washing windshields at a barbecue shack in Buckhead, a wealthy section of Atlanta. They were heard by a talent scout one day while playing for the customers after work, and Barbecue Bob recorded in Atlanta in 1927 before going to New York. Together they played only four sessions, and with Bob's death at twenty-nine from tuberculosis and the disappearance of Charlie, their music remains as a reminder of an earlier tradition.

But towards the end of the 1920s a more sophisticated style appeared in Atlanta. Complex fingerpicking and the tighter vocal style which predominated in Georgia in the late 20s and early 30s were mainly the result of influences from the Carolinas, where blues styles were more developed. Buddy Moss, born in 1914, was heavily affected by the Carolina players Blind Boy Fuller and Brownie McGhee. In Georgia the newer style could be heard in the blues of Fred McMullen and the better-known James "Kokomo" Arnold. Arnold was born in Lovejoy, Georgia in 1901 and spent his early years there, although he later moved north and recorded in New York between 1930 and 1938. In 1930 he was performing in Memphis as "Gitfidle Jim."

Of all the bluesmen of Georgia, Blind Blake and Blind Willie McTell stand out because of their superb musicianship and the new direction their ragtime-based guitar playing gave.

"Classic" ragtime, born of a fusion of plantation music and light white classics, was developed by turn-of-the-century composers and players like Scott Joplin, Scott

Blind Blake playing a rare koa-wood-topped Stella guitar, c. 1929. Blake was one of the first and most popular bluesmen to start "ragging the blues" and his style influenced both black and white musicians.

FROM THE COLLECTION OF PAUL OLIVER

Blind Willie McTell was one of the few players to continue recording throughout the Depression. He played an early Stella twelve-string guitar with the strings stopping at the bridge instead of passing over to a tailpiece.

COURTESY OF YAZOO RECORDS

Hayden and James Scott, and was played on the piano. The rag had a strict musical structure which was not followed by guitarists, banjoists and others who adopted ragtime for their own instruments. Ragtime guitar was played in quick time, with a syncopated melody and a developed counterpoint in the bass line. The music was often built around the key of C, as it raised the pitch to give a lighter tone, and made the typical four chord progression of C-A7-D-G-C easier. Also, in the key of C it was relatively easy to play an interesting counterpoint on the bass strings.

Blind Blake recorded about eighty sides between September 1926 and June 1932. His extraordinarily deft technique made him one of the fastest fingerpickers of all.

His technique included walking basses, boogie-woogie and cross rhythms while his extensive use of syncopated thumb rolls, as well as three-finger-picked rolls, made him one of the most exciting players of blues rags. Being immensely popular, he worked as a studio musician and influenced a large number of players, many of whom tried (usually without success) to imitate him.

The great twelve-string guitar player Blind Willie McTell was born in 1898 near Augusta. From the very beginning he traveled, playing in medicine shows and circuses. Although known of for many years he has emerged only recently from the obscurity which surrounds so many bluesmen. He recorded almost a hundred pieces, some of which are still being reissued. One of the problems of identifying his playing came from his extensive use of pseudonyms to get out of contract problems. Barrelhouse Sammy—The Country Boy, Blind Sammy, Blind Samuel, Hot Shot Willie, and Pig'n'Whistle Red were just some of his names.

The twelve-string was ideal for emulating the fast ragging piano style. The instrument could be either picked or strummed, and the rag style required an alternating and doubling of the bass line with the melody on the treble. When it came to sensitive chordal shading or complex gapped scale runs, however, the sound tended to get lost in a jangle of notes and odd harmonic resonances that resulted

from the octave tuning.

Blind Willie McTell produced both fast ragging numbers with walking basses and pieces with greater subtlety and sensitivity. He tended to vamp the chords which produced interesting percussive textures across the flow of the muffled rhythm. He sang easily in a light voice, playing bouncing runs taken out of the chord at the root position. Hammered off or on, these skipping triplets were the essence of the old piano style, producing the distinctive syncopated swing quality. McTell, of all the twelve-string players, displayed the most respect for his music—as music rather than the declamatory "message" of many of the Mississippi singers.

Daddy Stovepipe (Johnny Watson) in Chicago's Maxwell Street market, 1960. Born in Mobile, Alabama before 1900, he played for years in the street until the police cracked down on blues singers. He died in 1963.

"Train time"

During the first decades of the twentieth century, the rapidly growing towns acted as magnets to the poor blacks of the rural South. The black population of Dallas grew from about 10,000 in 1900 to double that in 1920, mainly in consequence of the boll weevil infestation that destroyed many of the Texas cotton plantations. Atlanta in the same period saw an influx that increased the numbers from 35,700 to 61,700, and a further growth to over 90,000 in the next 10 years. Migration tended to conform to a set pattern, often depending on the railroad network. The Illinois Central, which ran from New Orleans to Chicago, helped swell the black population there from 44,000 to over 100,000 between 1910 and 1920. This new urban population provided a ready audience for the blues style of the country singers who brought a taste of their rural background to the squalid city slums.

Memphis from early in the century had been important for the blues. As a rail and road network center, it was one of the main stopping places on the journey from the South to Chicago. And while the traveler was in the city, there was plenty of music to hear. The musical heart of Memphis, Beale Street, was one of the toughest slum areas of any American city:

> Beale Street, Memphis—there used to be a red light district, so forth like that. Used to be wide open houses in them days. You could used to walk down the street in 1900 and like that and you would find a man wit' throat cut from ear to ear . . . some thrown out of windows, no clothes on.[1]

Beale Street's growth was encouraged by an Italian immigrant called Pee Wee who moved there in the 1880s, and realized that to run his gambling saloon successfully and bring in the customers, he needed music. So he employed honky-tonk musicians to beat out music with a basic rhythm on guitar, fiddle, bass and drums. Soon Beale Street was a regular stop for traveling musicians. Many of the bluesmen played on the street outside the joints. In 1929 Sleepy John Estes was singing and playing on a street corner with his mandolinist partner Yank Rachel. A Victor talent scout heard them and they cut their first sides. Together with harmonica player Hammie Nixon, Estes was reasonably successful, recording in 1934 for the Decca label, which had just started up. His guitar work was never spectacular, but he sang with an intensity of feeling which caused Big Bill Broonzy to call his style "crying the blues."

The most popular musicians were the string bands that could make the most noise in the bars, and such groups as the Memphis Jug Band and Cannon's Jug Stompers, led by Banjo Jo, could be heard regularly up and down the street. The jug bands consisted of a variety of instruments— guitars, banjos, fiddles, harmonicas, washboard, and the gallon jugs which gave the bands their characteristic sound.

While there were many classic female blues singers during this period, female guitarists were rare. One of the few to emerge spent much of her early years in and around the bars of Beale Street. Minnie Douglas, known as Memphis Minnie, was born in Algiers, Louisiana in 1900. At the age of twenty she was heard by a Columbia talent scout and taken to Chicago. In 1933 Big Bill Broonzy met her when they were both taking part in a talent contest, which Memphis Minnie won. "Memphis Minnie," he recalled later, "can make a guitar speak words, she can make a guitar cry, moan, talk and whistle the blues."[2]

Other employment for Memphis musicians came from the traveling medicine shows. Musicians were employed to attract the crowds to the "doctor's" pitch, and when enough people had gathered to hear the music, the persuasive talk began. The shows traveled throughout the South: to Mississippi, Louisiana, and Alabama, taking bluesmen such as Walter "Furry" Lewis with them. Lewis was born in Greenswood, Mississippi in 1893 and traveled with the medicine shows for many years, picking up a variety of styles and guitar playing, using extensive bottleneck, and singing the ballads that were popular with the crowds.

The Depression and after

The early period of the blues had offered bluesmen a chance to earn some kind of a living by their music, but the Depression ended all that. The black man was often the first to be laid off from his job, there was no extra cash to spend on such luxuries as records and entertainment, and many blues singers suffered. With the shrinking market, the record companies became less adventurous until many of them closed their race lists to all but the most commercially successful singers. The older bluesmen drifted away from the towns, some trying any kind of work, others returning to their family farms to live out the worst of the early 1930s. Blues continued to be sung and played but the Depression had an effect on the music, with the content of many blues songs becoming more socially concerned than ever before.

On the other hand, the background of poverty and the all-pervading feeling of hopelessness led to a greater demand for escapist music. The names that continued to be popular through the Depression were the smoother-sounding Lonnie Johnson; the piano-guitar combinations of Tampa Red and Georgia Tom Dorsey, LeRoy Carr and Scrapper Blackwell; Memphis Minnie and the rising Big Bill Broonzy.

These artists were all city-based, and their music was different from that of their rural counterparts. What had been appropriate to the isolated communities in the Southern states was not suitable for the bars and brothels of large cities. A greater sophistication both of style and content was called for. Many of the bars had a resident pianist, and guitarists coming into the cities sought them out and began to play with them, the piano providing bass and rhythm, the guitar playing the melodic voice. Greater demand for entertainment was met by a lighter style, and an increasing emphasis on popular dance pieces.

Hudson Whittaker, born in Atlanta in 1900, had spent most of his childhood in Tampa, Florida, hence his name of "Tampa Red." Billed when a young man as "The Guitar Wizard," he had a flowing style, using a bottleneck technique probably unapproached by any other blues player to achieve a sustained drone against clear finger-picked melodies. This sounded good over a piano or in a small combo and much of his time was spent playing in groups, in bars, at parties, and for the Baptist Church. In

the 20s with Blind Blake, he had joined the great blues singer Ma Rainey, organizing her tours with a minstrel show throughout the South, and also recording with her and Georgia Tom Dorsey from 1928 onwards. After Ma Rainey's death in 1928 or 1929, he formed Tampa Red's Hokum Jug Band (also known as the Hokum Boys) to play the increasingly popular hokum music. This was an extension of the earlier string band style, a happy-sounding dance music with a swinging beat, and many of Tampa Red's pieces had relaxed rag and dance rhythms.

The other masterly piano-guitar combination was that of LeRoy Carr and Scrapper Blackwell. Blackwell was born in North Carolina in 1904, of Cherokee descent, but was brought up mainly in Indianapolis and began his musical life there. He met LeRoy Carr in the 1920s and together they performed in the cities linked by railroads to Indianapolis: St. Louis, Louisville, Nashville and Cincinnati. St. Louis in particular had a strong tradition of piano-guitar combinations. Blackwell and Carr were one of the most influential and successful duos of the late 20s and early 30s. Against Carr's rolling, rich, bass-oriented playing, Blackwell's guitar sang out with a distinctive quality. His usual keys were A, D, and occasionally E. His style was marked by a complex and skilful use of single-string finger-picked melodic lines and blues runs. The provision of the heavy bass on the piano allowed him to develop treble line playing to new heights of sophistication.

Blackwell and Carr's career together was short and ended sadly: in April, 1935, LeRoy Carr died suddenly after drinking bad whiskey. Blackwell was overwhelmed by the loss, turned to alcohol and stopped playing. He was rediscovered in 1958, but made only a small number of recordings and a few public appearances. He was murdered in an Indianapolis side street in 1962, too early to enjoy the real blues revival of the 60s.

But Blackwell and Carr's influence was tremendous. Both Eddie Durham and Charlie Christian, the pioneers of the electric guitar in jazz, were influenced by Blackwell's technique of single-string melody line playing.

In the mid-1930s a major reorganization of record companies took place. Through a series of mergers and takeovers, the main blues labels from 1934 to 1945 were Brunswick, Okeh and Vocalion (all owned by the American Record Company), and Victor and its subsidiary Bluebird label, owned by RCA. The economic recovery of 1934 led to English Decca's setting up of a race series, under the energetic guidance of J. Mayo Williams. In 1933 John Lomax and his son Alan began their priceless documentation of Southern bluesmen. Many of the older bluesmen had disappeared from sight during the 30s but the older-style rural blues did survive. The general lack of urban centers in the Southern states, and particularly Mississippi, ensured a continuing demand for Saturday-night entertainers. Some of these older rougher bluesmen were recorded in the late 30s. Arthur "Big Boy" Crudup was singing in a Chicago street in 1941 when he was approached by two men who offered him ten dollars for an appearance. Thinking it was for a house rent party, he followed them to a house where he was introduced to Lester Melrose, the man who did so much to influence the sound of Chicago blues through his extensive recordings for the Bluebird label. Crudup's records were a success and he became songwriter and race artist for RCA. He sang in the old country style—his voice was close to the field holler—while he played in a slow rhythmic guitar style, not particularly skilfully but with a rough force and intensity.

In 1938 Booker T. Washington "Bukka" White recorded two sides for Vocalion before being arrested and sent to Parchman Farm for shooting a man. In 1940 he was released and immediately recorded again. The experience of the harsh conditions at Parchman Farm left an indelible impression which found its way into his music. White had grown up in the same area as Charley Patton and was influenced by the man and his music. But his playing did not reflect Patton's variety. Playing with a bottleneck, he concentrated on open tunings, with vamped staccato rhythms (of the "boom-ching" variety). His singing style and lyrics reflected the desolation of prison life, yet his music has a tremendous vitality and strength. Although the musical structure of his pieces was limited, barely getting out of the I–IV relationship, the slide played over a repetitive bass line produced exciting effects.

Crudup, Bukka White, Big Joe Williams and Tommy McClennan were the last of the solo country bluesmen to be recorded for some years. On the other hand, the easier more relaxed style of the Southeastern states continued to be popular throughout the Depression and after. Blind Boy Fuller, born in South Carolina in 1903, recorded for

Bukka White playing a National Steel guitar with a bottleneck on his little finger.

various race labels between 1935 and 1940. He was an immediate success, partly because of his strong finger-picked melodic style, played on a National resonator guitar, and partly because of the content of many of his blues which were among the most suggestive ever. (He shrewdly covered all markets by recording religious tracks under the name of "Brother George.") Fuller had served his apprenticeship at country dances and suppers and the elements of dance and ragtime rhythms provided the basis of his playing. Blind Boy Fuller's early style was limited: he could only play in open tunings, and with a bottleneck. He learned new techniques of playing, and a number of songs, from the Reverend Gary Davis.

Reverend Gary Davis was born in Lawrence County, South Carolina in 1896. He learned the harmonica at the age of five, the banjo at six and the guitar at seven. At fourteen he organized his own string band to play around the streets of the tobacco towns of South Carolina, and for parties and dances. By 1933 he had joined the church, but this did not stop his musical activity. In July 1935 he was playing with Blind Boy Fuller, Sonny Terry and Bull City Red, an albino who played guitar and washboard and acted as their "eyes." The group was playing in Durham when they were heard by J. B. Long, a talent scout for Vocalion. They recorded later that year in New York, Gary Davis

307

Reverend Gary Davis with Sonny Terry and Brownie McGhee in the 1960s.

COURTESY OF BLUES UNLIMITED

Through his playing and later on his teaching the Reverend Gary Davis has become one of the strongest influences on both older and contemporary guitarists. His guitar technique was formidable, and his singing powerful. Davis has sometimes been compared unfavorably with Blind Blake, who was playing at the same time. But although their playing had a certain similarity, Gary Davis developed a far more sophisticated style by varying the basic syncopated or alternating bass against a complex treble melody. Moreover, using just the thumb and index finger of his right hand he developed an amazing facility. While some guitarists could play two or maybe three different styles, Gary Davis perfected many more, ranging from basic bottleneck to carnival-style banjo playing.

After Gary Davis had left them, Sonny Terry, Blind Boy Fuller and Bull City Red continued playing in North Carolina. In Burlington they met up and started playing with Walter "Brownie" McGhee, despite initial hostility between the two main guitarists. Brownie's honeyed voice contrasted strongly with Blind Boy Fuller's harsh tone, but their rocking rhythmic style, their backing of harmonica and washboard and their musical repertoire were similar enough to cause rivalry. The rivalry was ended by the death of Fuller in 1940. He had been immensely popular and influential and the record company was reluctant to let such a commercial opportunity pass. So McGhee was recorded playing Fuller's National guitar, and advertised as Blind Boy Fuller No 2. But McGhee's fortunes lay with Sonny Terry and the two spent the war years earning a living by their music in New York.

New York was the obvious focal point for singers from the Southeastern states. The extremely popular Josh White, born in 1908 in Greenville, South Carolina, made his home there in the late 1930s when he became a success in the night clubs. He had spent much of his early life acting as "eyes" for some of the many blind singers, including Blind Lemon Jefferson and Blind Blake. He developed a fluent guitar technique which he backed with his peculiar half-yodel style of singing.

In the 1930s and early 40s Chicago was the final stopoff for blacks from the South, and particularly from Mississippi. During the 20s the city had been controlled by corrupt mob rule and the South and West sides had become an area of speakeasies, bars and dives which

singing fifteen songs and playing guitar on several of Fuller's sides. But Gary Davis was angered by the treatment he received. Sacred music had always been his main interest, and the A-and-R man tried to persuade Davis to record blues. He was thoroughly disenchanted and went his own way earning a living as a roadside preacher and singer, first around the Carolinas and then, from 1940 onwards, in New York. The law forbade any form of begging at that time, but one way for a blues singer to earn money was to preach at the roadside and then sing, accompanying himself on the guitar. It was not an ideal life:

> I was glad to get away from it 'cause there's too many different kinds of people you meet up with in the street, and it's not recognized too. . . . They call it beggin', pan-handling'[1]

COURTESY OF BIOGRAPH RECORDS

Johnny Shines was born in Frazier, Tennessee in 1915, but is associated with the Mississippi Delta blues. He traveled with Robert Johnson in the mid-1930s before going to Chicago at the beginning of the Second World War. There he played with Memphis Slim, Walter Horton and Snooky Pryor. But working by day and playing at night finally proved too exhausting and he stopped playing in 1957. After his rediscovery in 1964 he became a popular figure.

Big Bill Broonzy.

FROM THE COLLECTION OF PAUL OLIVER

provided a constant source of income for musicians. One club might have Jelly Roll Morton rolling out his barrelhouse piano, while from next door came the smooth sound of Lonnie Johnson's guitar, backed by a small band.

In these clubs and on the recordings of Chicago's Bluebird label a new style was rapidly becoming popular. The new style came not from a lone singer with his guitar, but from combinations of musicians: guitarists, pianists, drums and sometimes reed and brass players. In the night clubs of the 1930s, clients were demanding the louder sound of such groups as Big Bill Broonzy's Memphis Five and Chicago Five, or Tampa Red's Hokum Jug Band. The restrictions placed on guitarists, who had for long been soloists, inevitably curbed their earlier style. An enormous adjustment had to be made, as Johnny Shines explained:

You take a man playing the country blues, he plays just what he feels because he's playing the country blues, he plays just what he feels because he's playing all by himself nine times out of ten, and he don't have to cooperate with nobody. But you take Chicago blues style, when you get up there with a band, you have to play together real tight just like it was any other arrangement. It was different, of course, with country blues, because there wasn't any arrangement. If your bluesman felt like holding a note for nine beats, he held it for nine. He didn't know nothin' about any one-two-three-four.[2]

One of the main bluesmen influencing the development of the new style was Big Bill Broonzy. William Lee Conteh Broonzy (1893–1958) was born in Scott, Mississippi and arrived in Chicago in the 1920s. He played at house rent parties and met many of the other bluesmen who were recording in Chicago or just drifting in and out of the city, men like Sleepy John Estes, Blind Lemon Jefferson, Blind

Blake and Lonnie Johnson. His eclectic style was formed by the playing of these bluesmen and by the need to entertain club audiences; he played dance tunes, ragtime and straight blues with equal ease. His first recording session in 1927 was not a great success and finally only one side, "House Rent Stomp," was issued. But in the 1930s he teamed up with the pianists Georgia Tom, Black Bob, Joshua Altheimer; the reed player Buster Bennett; banjoist Steel Smith and guitarists Louie Lasky and Bill Williams to play music in the happy hokum vein. He became immensely popular and recorded almost 200 sides between 1936 and 1942.

Broonzy owed much of his style to Blind Lemon Jefferson, and indeed on some of his recordings can sound uncannily like the Texas player, but with a greater swing. He used a number of Jefferson's blues runs, and the same technique of hammering to shape and color his pieces. Other echoes of Jefferson's playing appear in Broonzy's pushing of the third and first strings as well as pushing two notes together to make a major-minor dissonance. One characteristic of Broonzy's playing is the use of a continuous vamped bass instead of the usual alternating bass line. He used a choking technique to damp the bass strings to a percussive thump as an accompaniment to the treble-voice melody. Broonzy had a well-developed singing style. He would often cut completely free from the guitar accompaniment and let his voice soar, or sing a phrase and repeat it note-for-note on the guitar as an answering voice.

Big Bill Broonzy, together with other well-known musicians, dominated the Chicago music scene in the 30s. Many of the clubs employed resident bands, preferring to use musicians who had become popular through their recordings, and their styles predominated.

When America entered the war in 1941 shellac restrictions cut down the activities of the large recording companies. In the same year, general worry about the effects which jukeboxes would have on the livelihood of musicians led to the American Federation of Musicians banning its members from recording. The big record companies stopped issuing their race lists. But the gap left by this encouraged small independent labels known as "indies" to start up. These made only one or two thousand copies of records and so could use small amounts of shellac.

But the future of the blues after the war lay with the electric guitar. Many bluesmen had already made the change by 1945: T-Bone Walker, Arthur Crudup and Muddy Waters were just a few. Fashions, tastes and circumstances had changed, and the acoustic guitar player, traveling around the small Southern communities, had given way to the electrified sound in the clubs and bars of the large Northern cities.

Country music

The other major body of American music which has made extensive use of the steel-string guitar and helped popularize the instrument is country music. In the last few years there has been a tremendous revival of serious interest in the music. Its many forms have always had a devoted following, but the present explosion is an international one—and it is still growing. In its history, the music has gone through the changes which must mark any genuine folk music. It has served as dance music, encouraged the romantic image of the Wild West, been used as a means of social comment, inspired the popular bluegrass sound and given Elvis Presley, Carl Perkins and countless others a foundation on which to create a new musical style.

Some see the revival as an attempt to return to solid, worthwhile values which have become lost in the bewildering social changes of the last decades. Others view the return to traditional roots as a sentimental harking-back to a society whose morality was the result more of rigidity and narrowness of outlook than of any thought-out inner conviction. But whatever the reasons behind the revival, one of the main results has been to place once more an emphasis on live music and to bring the acoustic guitar into a central role.

The British settlers of America brought with them the ballads and folk songs of England, Scotland, Ireland and Wales, usually sung unaccompanied by a solo performer. These were sung for entertainment and for passing on the history of a society that had little time or energy for formal education. The ballad-making tradition has been an integral part of country music ever since.

In the Southern states where country music was developed, a rigid agrarian economy and rural environment encouraged an often inflexible traditionalism. Coupled with a defensive feeling toward slavery, which was being increasingly criticized during the first half of the nineteenth century, the South was determined to preserve its way of life and adopted an isolationist stance. Moreover, the communities were often remote from any agents of change. Physical conditions and emotional attitudes were equally important in helping preserve cultural traditions undisturbed.

Wherever the pioneers settled and formed a com-

COURTESY OF THE NEW BRITAIN MUSEUM OF AMERICAN ART (HARRIET RUSSELL STANLEY FUND)

Detail from Arts of the West *by Thomas Hart Benson, 1932.*

munity, they entertained themselves by the age-old tradition of music making. It was not only in the lonely Appalachian mountains that country music flourished, but also in the lands further to the Southwest—Arkansas, Louisiana and Texas. The original meandering solo style of the early ballads was modified by the practice of harmony singing and the introduction of instrumental accompaniment. A variety of instruments were adopted. The dulcimer, of German origin, remained popular in the remote mountain areas where other instruments took longer to appear; more widespread were the fiddle and banjo. The guitar made its appearance in the 1890s, at about the same period when black musicians were beginning to use it.

But the guitar was not so decisive in the development of country music as it was in the blues. In the blues, the guitar became a second voice; its qualities were exploited to produce sounds which in turn added an extra dimension to the music. Moreover, in the early history of the blues, the guitar was the principal solo instrument. The numbers of good black guitarists in the Southern states, the development of different styles and techniques in different areas, and the intermingling of musicians helped to build up a strong tradition of guitar playing among blacks.

In country music the story is rather different. Country music was usually played by groups of musicians and where there was a solo instrumentalist he was a fiddler. In white country music, the early guitarists usually played in a simple fashion—using three or four basic open chords to provide a rhythmic background which could be interspersed with the occasional run. Nonetheless, in the history of the music there are a number of notable guitarists, who invariably had learned from blacks a more intricate style of playing which came unfortunately to be known as "nigger pickin'." For wherever poor whites and blacks mixed—on railroads, down coal mines or along the rivers—there was an interchange of musical ideas. As traditional white ballad-making was taken over by black singers, so the white country musicians learned to pick a melody on the treble strings of their guitars while using the thumb to give a steady rhythm on the bass.

During the late nineteenth and early twentieth centuries the black influence on country music increased. The cities held just as much attraction for the poor white as

Dr. Humphrey Bates and his Possum Hunters, among the first performers on the Grand Ole Opry. Like so many old-time string bands, they played on the show only at weekends, and it was not until 1937, when Pee Wee King and his Golden West Cowboys joined the Grand Ole Opry, that there was a full-time professional band.

for the poor black. In Beale Street, Memphis; Deep Elm, Dallas; or Decatur Street, Atlanta, blues, ragtime and jazz could be heard by anybody for the price of a drink. In this way the styles and songs of such great bluesmen and guitarists as Blind Lemon Jefferson (based in Dallas from 1917) must have found their way into the music brought back to the white homesteads. For those who remained on their farms, the medicine and tent shows which traveled around the Southern states brought white and black musicians, performing a variety of styles: straight blues, dance tunes, religious songs and the latest Tin Pan Alley hits.

The great expansion of country music came, like the expansion of the blues, in the 1920s, when the recording companies discovered the potentially large audience. The first recordings were of solo fiddlers and string bands, which consisted of fiddle, banjo and guitar. At this period the music acquired its first name—"hillbilly." In 1925 a string band recorded for Okeh in New York, and when Ralph Peer asked them their name, the leader replied:

". . . call the band anything you want. We are nothing but a bunch of hillbillies from North Carolina and Virginia anyway."[1] The group became known as the "Hillbillies" and the name stuck to the music they played, though not without some misgiving on the part of many musicians who saw it as undignified.

The radio did far more to disseminate white country music than it did for the blues. Sales of radios increased nationally from $60,000 in 1922 to $548,000 in 1929 (mostly to whites). With such a large audience the program directors were eager for new ideas, and in the early 20s the radio barn dance concept was born with the start of the two longest-running and most popular programs. The World's Largest Station (WLS), owned by the World's Largest Store (Sears Roebuck), started its National Barn Dance in 1924, beaming the program to a Midwest and Great Plains audience. A year later the founder, George D. Hay, moved to WSM in Nashville and began the Grand Ole Opry. The first performer was a fiddle player, and the program was an instant success:

> . . . after three or four weeks of this fiddle solo business, we were besieged with other fiddlers, banjo pickers, guitar players and a lady who played an old zither.[2]

From 1925 to 1935 the Grand Ole Opry was dominated by string bands. Dr. Humphrey Bates and his Possum Hunters, the Crook Brothers, the Gully Jumpers and the Fruit Jar Drinkers were all regular contributors. It was in the Fruit Jar Drinkers that Sam McGee, one of the pioneers in country guitar playing, first started out as a professional entertainer.

Sam McGee was born on a farm in Franklin, Tennessee in 1894, and grew up surrounded by plenty of home-made music. His father was an old-time fiddler, his brother Kirk played the banjo and his uncle played both. Sam later said: "It seems it just fell my lot to play . . . accompaniment with them."[3] But the guitar was rare in the Tennessee hills before the First World War, and Sam McGee dated the instrument as "not much older than the radio."[4] The first guitarist the young Sam McGee heard was Tom Hood, who was fingerpicking the guitar in the way that Sam was trying to teach himself. Then the family moved into town and Sam had his first contact with black players.

My daddy ran a little store, and these section hands would come over from the railroad at noon . . . Well, after they finished their lunch, they would play guitars . . . that's where I learned to love the blues tunes. Black people were about the only people that played guitar then.[5]

From watching and listening, Sam McGee introduced a fingerpicking style into country music which was almost completely new at that period. When the professional entertainer and banjo player Uncle Dave Macon heard him, he took Sam with him. Then began Sam McGee's fifty-year association with the Grand Ole Opry and country music, an association that ended with his death in a tractor accident in August, 1975.

In 1925 Sam's brother Kirk joined him on the Grand Ole Opry. Together with Humphrey Bates they set out in the first touring program of the WSM, taking their music to small centers and large towns.

The guitar's role in country music was developed within the string-band. North Carolina in particular developed a flourishing tradition, centered around Charlie Poole and the North Carolina Ramblers. They began recording in 1925 and had such success that they gave up their regular jobs as mill hands to become professional musicians. At that time the group consisted of Charlie Poole on banjo and vocals, Posey Rorer, (a crippled coal miner who had played fiddle since he was twelve years old) and Norman Woodlieff on guitar, but in 1926 they replaced the guitarist with Roy Harvey, who also shared the singing. The group was one of the most disciplined and popular of the 1920s, with a following in Virginia, West Virginia and North Carolina. Their style of playing allowed each instrument to be heard properly: the complex bass runs of Harvey's guitar, blending perfectly with the melody line, made the guitar into more than just a steady backup instrument for the flashier fiddle and banjo players. In Atlanta, one of the most influential groups was Gid Tanner and his Skillet Lickers. Though continually changing, the group revolved around Gid Tanner, fiddler Clayton ("Pappy") McMichen, and Riley Puckett, guitar and vocals. Of all the early hillbilly singer-guitarists, Riley Puckett was the most popular. Born in 1894, he was blinded shortly after birth and turned to music for a living.

Gid Tanner and his Skillet Lickers with Riley Puckett and Clayton McMichen.

COURTESY OF THE JOHN EDWARDS MEMORIAL FOUNDATION, UCLA

COURTESY OF THE COUNTRY MUSIC FOUNDATION LIBRARY AND MEDIA CENTER

Riley Puckett, c. 1934.

His individual recording career began in 1924 with "Little Old Log Cabin in the Lane" and "Rock All Our Babies To Sleep" on which he yodeled (predating Jimmie Rodgers by three years). His repertoire was extremely wide, from songs of the minstrel era to humorous songs of the 1900s. He probably picked up many of these in his teens when he was playing at dances, parties and on street corners. Certainly his playing was influenced by black guitarists. He introduced the recording of his bottleneck version of "Darkey's Wail" (the ballad "John Henry") with the words:

> I'm going to play for you this time a little piece which an old southern darkey I heard play, coming down Decatur Street the other day, called "His Good Gal Done Throwed Him Down."[6]

Puckett's guitar playing consisted of complex single-note bass runs, non-chordal in structure and often syncopated, which made it difficult for fiddlers who were unused to

anything fancy. His playing was advanced for his time and he was one of the models later used by bluegrass bands.

The majority of country musicians in the 1920s were from the Southeastern states and their repertoire and style reflected the basically conservative and well-tried style of music. In 1927, however, the recordings of the Carter family and Jimmie Rodgers changed the direction of the music; they found a new audience and set a new style. Recorded for Victor by Ralph Peer, who had also recorded many blues singers, they represented two different strands: the Carter family performed traditional mountain material (although much of their instrumentation and arrangements were new), while Jimmie Rodgers turned country music westwards through his cowboy songs and popularized the musical style of the blues yodel which was then endlessly copied.

The Carter family group consisted of A. P. Carter, his wife Sarah, and his sister-in-law, Maybelle. A. P. Carter was born in 1891 into a devoutly religious family. Sarah,

COURTESY OF THE COUNTRY MUSIC FOUNDATION

The Carter Family. Maybelle Carter is playing one of the 1924-style Gibson L-5s, the first of the f-hole guitars, which she used throughout the group's musical career.

COURTESY OF RCA RECORDS

Jimmie Rodgers, the "Singing Brakeman."

born in 1898, absorbed much of the contemporary music of Wise County, Virginia, and had learned guitar, banjo and autoharp. Maybelle, who married into the family in 1926, also came from a musical background. Despite the later breakup of A. P.'s and Sarah's marriage, the group continued to record up to 1941 and finally disbanded two years later, although they continued separate musical careers.

During the time that they were the Carter family, they collected and recorded a rich selection of songs. Those they are credited with are often traditional; A. P. copyrighted them on the grounds that the Carters were the first people to put them on record. Certainly, many of A. P.'s arrangements were wholly original and presented well-known tunes in a different and fresh form.

The Carters' style revolved around Maybelle's strong guitar playing. In the songs they made famous, such as "Wildwood Flower" and "Engine 143," Maybelle played the melodic line on the bass string with a right-hand thumb pick, while the rhythm came from chords played on the treble strings, and she used an up-down brush stroke in place of the earlier down-brushing style. The Carter family blended their voices with that of the guitar rather than following the usual procedure of making the instrument,

whether guitar, banjo or fiddle, fit the voice. Many of the original melodies, often complex and irregular in rhythm, were thus made to fit the basic chord progression of tonic, dominant, subdominant played in steady $\frac{4}{4}$ time.

The Carter family's influence lasts to this day. Their early recordings were extensively rediscovered in the folk revival of the later 50s and early 60s and have provided both material and techniques for a new generation of musicians. Joan Baez has used such Carter songs as "Little Moses" and the classic instrumental "Wildwood Flower." Earlier, Woody Guthrie had used many of their melodies and adapted to his own use Maybelle's style of guitar playing. "When the World's on Fire" became one of the most famous folk songs of all time: "This Land is Your Land."

In 1927, the same year that the Carters first recorded, Jimmie Rodgers burst on the scene with "Blue Yodel No. 1 (T for Texas)." This was a standard blues type of song, but lifted by the falsetto blues yodel he uttered after every sixteen-bar verse. The public rushed to buy the record and from that moment to his early death from tuberculosis in 1933, Jimmie Rodgers was a star. In less than six years he recorded over a hundred songs, which ranged over popular sentimental ballads, hobo songs, vaudeville tunes, cowboy songs, railroad tunes and his famous blues and blue yodel songs. The accompaniments were as varied as the songs: on one session in Atlanta in October 1928, he had a backing of clarinet, cornet and bass, and his records often featured the dobro playing of Cliff Carlisle. Many of his songs were written by his sister-in-law, Elsie McWilliams; for others he dipped into traditional material.

Rodgers was born James Charles Rodgers near Meridian, Mississippi on September 8, 1897. His mother died when he was four and the young boy spent much of his early youth traveling around the South with his father, a gang foreman on the Mobile and Ohio Railroad. Jimmie himself joined the railroads when he left school at the age of fourteen to work as a water carrier for the railroad workers. In his early years he must have picked up many songs from musically rich Mississippi, but his main education came from the black section workers. His wife said that "During the noon dinner rests, they taught him to plunk melody from banjo and guitar. They taught him darkey songs; moaning chants and crooning lullabies."[7] He learned fast and was soon doing the entertaining himself.

Jimmie Rodgers worked for fourteen years on the railroads, making music his life only when his health became so bad that he could not continue doing manual labor. In 1925 he signed on as a blackface entertainer with a traveling medicine show and toured the South. A year later he formed the Jimmie Rodgers Entertainers, a small band which had little success. In July of 1927 the group was going to record for Ralph Peer, but on the eve of the recording deserted Rodgers, who cut two solo sides. The sound was good, and the record sold enough copies to justify another session. Then "T for Texas" hit the market, and Jimmie Rodgers never looked back.

Despite the lack of any major publicity, Rodgers became the first solo star and one of the most popular country musicians ever. His personal appearances were casual affairs, just Jimmie Rodgers and his guitar. He dressed in a white suit and a straw boater (although for publicity shots he occasionally wore a cowboy outfit or the uniform of a railroad brakeman). His foot rested on a chair and the guitar on his knee, and for just twenty minutes he captivated the audience. His gentle drawl and running commentary with a relaxed, simple guitar style made his performances enjoyable occasions.

Whatever the popularity of his repertoire in the 20s and 30s Rodgers is remembered today for his famous blue yodel. The yodel was a recognized performing trick but to combine it with a blues theme was new. Possibly influenced by the black singers' field holler, it was changed by Rodgers into a $\frac{4}{4}$ pattern.

Jimmie Rodgers spent much of his time in the Southwest and it was here, and above all in his adopted state of Texas, that his greatest popularity lay. He included many Texas songs in his performances and it is mainly due to his influence that the center of interest switched to the Southwest, with increasing attention focused on the romantic image of the "singing cowboy."

It is extremely unlikely that authentic cowboys could do anything other than croak out a song. As one commentator of the era remarked: "I never did know a cowboy with a real good voice. If he ever had one to start with, he lost it bawling at cattle."[8] Comments like this did not deter would-be stars, however, and the interest started by Jimmie Rodgers was continued by a whole new generation of singing cowboys. Many of these—such as Gene Autry, Montana Slim (an authentic cowboy who had actually ridden as a calf roper in the Calgary Stampede), the Canadian Hank Snow and Ernest Tubb—started off as straight copies of Jimmie Rodgers, although they developed their own styles later on. They rode to success on the wave of popularity for the highly romanticized Wild West. In 1934 Gene Autry got a part in a Ken Maynard film called *In Old Santa Fe* and in the next few years became a box-office winner. Other film companies were quick to cash in on the market and a host of booted and spurred guitar-playing cattlehands came to the public eye: Tex Ritter and Ray Whitley from the WHL Barn Dance in New York City, Eddie Dean and Jimmy Wakely from Gene Autry's old vocal group, and Roy Rogers. The love affair with the West was continued in the late 30s and early 40s with the many groups singing Western music: the Lone Star Cowboys, the Riders of the Purple Sage and the Girls of the Golden West.

Three genuine cowhands. The guitarist is probably playing a cheap Sears Roebuck guitar.

Gene Autry playing the first prototype of what was to become the Martin D-45, with a twelve-fret neck and slot head, built for him in 1933.

Nick Lucas, one of the most popular and successful crooners of the 1920s and 30s. He had an enormous effect on the sales of acoustic guitars.

The singing cowboy had an enormous effect on the popularity and sale of guitars in the 1930s. Gene Autry in particular made a huge impact through the sales of his "Roundup" guitar, priced at a modest $9.95 from the Sears catalogue. In 1931 Martin had introduced its Dreadnought range which became the most widely used country guitar. Manufacture of the Dreadnoughts increased from 130 in 1934 to 800 in 1941. But Martin was just one of the many guitar companies making guitars to suit all pockets. In 1938 the market was so good that Gibson introduced the J-200 in competition. But the cheaper ranges were more popular among young aspiring singers, and guitar manufacture increased in response. With the example of Roy Rogers and Gene Autry the guitar finally gained respectability in America. What had formerly been a folk instrument, confined largely to country musicians or to disreputable bluesmen, now became accepted in any family. The distribution of cowboy films and mail-order catalogues throughout America also helped spread the instrument's popularity.

During the period of expansion after the Depression, traditional material continued to be played in small family groups like Bill and Charlie Monroe, who performed dazzling up-tempo numbers on guitar and mandolin. Another group, the Delmore Brothers, had been strongly affected by blues. (This was strange as they came from Alabama, a state not particularly noted for its blues tradition.) Most of the groups of this period used guitar and string bass solely as rhythm instruments with the fiddle playing lead, but the Delmore Brothers featured the guitar as the main solo voice. Further black influence came in their use of ragtime and boogie-woogie rhythms, which were favored by the Eastern blues players (see page 302).

But as far as the guitar was concerned, the sound appearing more and more frequently at this period came from Hawaiian-style playing. The Hawaiian guitar had become immensely popular after the First World War when Hawaiian groups started to tour America extensively, producing their characteristic wailing tones by playing guitars flat and using a piece of bone or metal as slide. The bands traveled mainly in vaudeville and tent shows, but soon Hawaiian guitars began to appear in other forms of American music. Their popularity in the 1920s led many guitar companies to produce them. At this stage the majority were ordinary guitars, supplied with a nut adjustor to convert for Hawaiian-style playing (see page 242). The first recording of an Hawaiian-style guitar in country music was made in April, 1927 by a West Virginian singer, Frank Hutchison. In November of that year, Tom Darby and Jimmie Tarlton recorded the now famous "Birmingham Jail" and "Colombus Stockade Blues," but it took the records of Jimmie Rodgers with Cliff Carlisle to popularize the sound. Cliff Carlisle's dobro playing had more of a blues than an Hawaiian feeling to it, as his style was inspired by the famous bottleneck playing of the Mississippi guitarists. Another group featuring the dobro, which was widely played Hawaiian-style across the knees, was the Dixon Brothers from Darlington, South Carolina. Howard Dixon played the dobro against Dorsey's complex fingerpicking style. Together they recorded over sixty songs, some written by Dorsey, which have since become standard, such as "The Intoxicated Rat" and "Wreck on the Highway."

While interest in country music in Texas and Oklahoma led to "western swing," a dance music heavily influenced by jazz and performed in larger and larger groups, the older forms of country music survived in the Southeast. The Grand Ole Opry, that bastion of tradition, introduced the electric guitar in the early 1940s but it was not a success. Sam McGee, one of the first to use it, said:

I like the old country style of playing; I think that's

Bill Monroe and the Blue Grass Boys.

what the Grand Ole Opry started out to be. In fact, that's what Judge Hay told me when I came in with this electric guitar. I got by with it about two Saturday nights; about the third one, he came in and patted me on the shoulder, "Now, you wouldn't play that on the Grand Ole Opry. You know we're going to hold it down to earth."[9]

During the second half of the 1940s, a quiet revolution was taking place with the establishment of bluegrass as a popular country music form. In 1938 Charlie and Bill Monroe had split up and Bill formed his own group, the Blue Grass Boys, and in October of 1939 the group joined the Grand Ole Opry. The name passed into common use for the type of music Monroe's group played and does not come from the Bluegrass Region of Kentucky. Bill Monroe had learned as a child to play both mandolin and guitar, and learned much of his music from a black fiddler and guitarist, Arnold Schultz.

The first time I think I ever seen Arnold Schultz, this square dance was at Rosine, and Arnold and two colored fellows come up there and played for the dance.... People loved Arnold so well all through Kentucky there. If he was playing a guitar they'd go gang up around him till he would get tired.... There's things in my music that comes from Arnold Schultz, runs that I use a lot in my music.... I tried to keep in

Chet Atkins and Merle Travis.

mind a little of it, what I could salvage to use in my music. Then he could play blues, and I wanted some blues in my music too, you see.[10]

(Arnold Schultz also taught both Ike Everly, the father of the Everly Brothers, and Mose Rager, the man who was such an influence on Merle Travis.)

The vocal style of bluegrass is distinctive: a high-pitched, lonely, often strident sound, using two-, three-, or four-part harmony. The instrumentation was equally distinctive, consisting of five unamplified instruments. The sound really crystallized between 1945 and 1948 when Bill Monroe's groups (consisting of himself on mandolin, Lester Flatt on guitar, Chubby Wise on fiddle and Cedric Rainwater on bass) were joined by Earl Scruggs, who had

developed his complicated three-finger style of playing the five-string banjo. The banjo and fiddle were the main lead instruments, while the mandolin varied between playing lead and providing rhythm. Within this group, the guitarist played in the open chord manner, which provided the background rhythm, but he also picked spectacular bass runs that came at the end of the mandolin, fiddle or banjo sequences. These runs were not new—Riley Puckett, Roy Harvey and Charlie Monroe had all used them to great effect—but bluegrass featured them to a greater extent than before. The famous "Lester Flatt G-run" became one of the hallmarks of the bluegrass style. Lester Flatt had difficulty at first keeping up with Monroe's fast mandolin playing, so he caught up at the end of phrases by playing a guitar run in the key of G: from E to F♯ to G on the sixth string, B to C to C♯ on the fifth, D to E to F♯ on the fourth, to G on the third, with the last notes of the run often the only audible part. At this stage the guitar as a lead instrument was rare, although the example of "Mule Skinner Blues," with Bill Monroe himself playing the guitar part, is an outstanding exception. Later, however, the guitar took on a more prominent role in bluegrass.

Bill Monroe started the style and has rightly been called the father of bluegrass, but the groups who followed—the Foggy Mountain Boys, the Stanley Brothers and others—finally established bluegrass as one of the main forms of country music.

After the Second World War, country music lost some of its regional character and became nationally popular. The late 1940s saw a general eclipse of the acoustic guitar as it gave way in popularity to its louder electric counterpart. But many of the musicians who were to be such an influence on guitar styles, particularly Merle Travis and Chet Atkins, learned their basic technique on unamplified instruments.

Merle Travis was born in November 1917 at Rosewood, Kentucky, and brought up in the tough world of a coal mining community. While still at school he met Mose Rager and Ike Everly, who taught him the basis of their lively fingerpicking style. Life in the mines was difficult and dangerous; Travis' elder brother suffered when

An electric motor pulling coal on the 'lie-away' rolled him against the 'rib,' the bulkhead of the interior of the mine, and practically broke every rib in his body. . . . My older brother, John, just drifted away from the coal fields. . . . I left home with a guitar under my arm. . . .[11]

He made his first professional broadcast in 1935 and from then to the late 40s spent time playing with fiddler Clayton McMichen and the Georgia Wildcats, and with the Delmore Brothers. After the war he settled in Hollywood, becoming one of the brightest young musicians with the newly established Capitol label. He began writing in earnest and produced "Dark as a Dungeon" and "Sixteen Tons" and others which passed rapidly into the main body of folk music. With his complex and extremely fast fingerpicking style, he inspired many players including Chet Atkins and Doc Watson.

During the 40s the acoustic guitar became the sole accompanying instrument for a group of folk singers who has taken their songs into the bars and clubs of the cities: men like Burl Ives, Richard Dyer-Bennett, Woody Guthrie, Leadbelly and Josh White. It was these singers who were to provide continuity between older traditions and the folk and blues revival of the 50s and 60s.

Woody Guthrie c. *1943.*

PHOTOGRAPH BY ROBIN CARSON, COURTESY OF MARGORIE GUTHRIE

"Walking down the big road"

Walking down the big road, no money, no job, no home, no nothing, nights I slept in jails, and the cells were piled high with young boys, strong men and old men. They talked and they sung and they told the story of their lives—how it used to be, how it got to be, how the home went to pieces, how the young wife died or left, how Dad tried to kill himself, how the banks sent out tractors and tractored down the houses. So somehow I picked up an old rusty guitar and started to picking and playing the songs I heard and making up new ones about what folks said.[1]

Woodrow Wilson "Woody" Guthrie was born in Okemah, Oklahoma in 1914. He grew up to see the instant wealth brought by the oil boom of the Southwestern states, and then the instant poverty of the Depression and dust storms which ravaged the area. Like many fellow Southwesterners, he moved to California. Once there he began performing on radio in Los Angeles, writing songs which expressed the anger and sorrow he felt for the misery he had witnessed.

In 1938 Guthrie moved to New York, and became involved with a group of radical intellectuals who saw the potential of his music for their cause. Between 1932 and 1952 he wrote over 1000 songs which have come to epitomize the spirit of protest against injustice, hardship and dishonesty. Guthrie consciously extended the American tradition of balladeering by creating a body of songs of specifically propagandist content. Whereas blues singers did not expect their music to change the circumstances of their lives, Guthrie saw his playing as a political weapon.

Woody Guthrie marks the beginning of the romantic association of the lone musician with the quality of defiant honesty. The acoustic guitar became a symbol of the autonomous individual and the unsullied side of American life. The urban folk movement which grew in the 1950s saw its heroes—such as Guthrie, Cisco Houston, Pete Seeger and the Weavers—as the champions of the people's rights.

The guitar's importance in this movement was more symbolic than musical. It was required only to provide a basic accompaniment and give the rhythm. Indeed, any really good playing might get in the way, as Woody Guthrie had said earlier:

I learned that I could plunk along on "Birmingham Jail" in the key of, say, G and get by plumb and dandy with only one chord change in the whole song, up to D and back to greasy G. I've pounded out "Ida Red," "Old Judge Parker Take Your Shackles Offa Me" for as high as thirty or forty minutes with no more than two chords—D to A, D to A and D to A—ten blue jillion times through a square dance. Lots of the old full-blooded fiddlers will toss you off from his platform if you go to getting too fancy with your chording.[2]

The revival of interest in folk music rapidly gathered momentum in the late 1950s. From 1955 to 1958 the success of rock n' roll had preoccupied both the music industry and the young generation who claimed the music as their own. But the payola scandals in America accelerated a movement back to home-made music. Increasing numbers of young people took up the acoustic guitar as an expression of disenchantment with the commercially packaged product. The folk revival was popularized by the Kingston Trio and Peter, Paul and Mary. Their acoustic-based sound reflected the current ideal of simple, honest music, although they themselves were not without their commercial exploiters.

More importantly for the serious exploration of acoustic guitar music, a handful of enthusiasts traced, recorded and reissued the music of an older generation. The most impressive results of this activity were seen at the Newport Folk Festivals which began in 1959 and brought both white and black folk music to a new audience.

What had begun as a minority interest in the 1950s expanded rapidly. From 1960 onward the development of acoustic guitar music was furthered by the large and growing numbers of young enthusiasts. *Time* magazine in 1962 gave middle-class America's bewildered reaction to what it obviously considered a widespread phenomenon:

Anything called a hootenanny ought to be shot on sight, but the whole country is having one. A hootenanny is to folk singing what a jam session is to jazz, and all over the U.S. there is a great reverberate twang. Guitars and banjos akimbo, folk singers inhabit smoky metropolitan crawl space; they sprawl on the floors of college rooms; near the foot of ski trails, they keep time to the wheeze and splutter of burning logs; they sing homely lyrics to the combers of the Pacific.

They are everybody and anybody. A civil engineer performs in his off-hours in the folk bins of the Midwest. So do debutantes, university students, even a refugee from an Eastern girl's school choir. Everywhere, there are bearded fop singers and clean-cut dilettantes. There are gifted amateurs and serious musicians. New York, Boston, Chicago, Minneapolis, Denver and San Francisco all have shoals of tiny coffee shops, all loud with basic folk sound—a pinched and studied wail that is intended to suggest flinty hills or clumpy prairies.[3]

The guitar's association with protest movements, begun by Woody Guthrie, was continued by Ramblin' Jack Elliott, Tom Paxton, Phil Ochs, and others who were taken up in the 1960s by a new, politically conscious public.[4] Then the folk audience found a hero: Bob Dylan's record of "Blowin' in the Wind" appeared in April 1962 and made him the natural figurehead for radicals all over America. Dylan's widespread popularity was boosted by Peter, Paul and Mary, who sang his song across the country, introducing it: "Now we'd like to sing a song written by the most important folk artist in America today, Bob Dylan."

Bob Dylan had begun by modeling himself and his music on Woody Guthrie. When he went to New York in 1960 he learned from the other people around him, particularly Jack Elliott and Dave Van Ronk, and soon became an established part of the folk scene in the coffee houses and clubs of Greenwich Village.

As with many urban folk singers, it was Dylan's words which were most important. But Dylan was unique in his ability to catch an underlying mood and give it powerful expression. To Carl Oglesby, one of the founders of the Students for a Democratic Society in 1962, Dylan was a catalyst:

Dylan's early songs appeared so promptly as to seem absolutely contemporary with the civil rights movement. . . . He wasn't a song writer who came into an established political mood, he seemed to be a part of it and his songs seemed informative to the Movement as the Movement seemed informative to the song writer.[5]

Bob Dylan with Rick Danko and Robbie Robertson at the Isle of Wight Festival, 1969.

Dylan's guitar accompaniment at that time was basically simple: three-chord patterns and a rhythmic flat-picking style which pushed the song along. As he once remarked: "I could sing *Porgy and Bess* with two chords, G and D, and still get the story across."[6] But he made the acoustic guitar the essential instrument for an entire generation. Bob Dylan was the personification of the singer and poet who used the guitar as the most convenient vehicle to project his thoughts and help change the world.

The hostile reaction to Dylan's first appearances using electric instruments in 1965 clearly demonstrated the connection many of the audience made between the use of acoustic guitar and folk-song purity. Although Dylan turned away from the folk protest movement and the acoustic guitar, its other figurehead of the early 1960s, Joan Baez, for many years remained faithful both to the ideals and the instrument.

For those who were more interested in the musical than the political use of the acoustic guitar, the rediscovery of an earlier generation of musicians in the early 60s was inspirational. Suddenly, here were guitarists who had mastered their instruments and their playing came as a revelation. Both black and white traditions experienced a revival and many of the older musicians who had been

Doc Watson, one of the most important figures in the development of country music guitar playing. A Doc Watson concert or record encapsulates the history of American folk music: his repertoire includes everything from the oldest Appalachian songs to fiddle tunes.

Sonny Terry and Brownie McGhee.

forced to stop performing traditional material by changing popular tastes suddenly found that it paid them to return to their roots.

Arthel "Doc" Watson was one of the older players whose appearances at folk festivals enabled him to go back to the music of his country youth. Watson was born in 1923 and grew up in North Carolina surrounded by music: his father picked banjo and sang, his mother had a repertoire of hymns and some seventy songs which she sang to the boy from an early age. He learned to play first a home-made banjo and then turned to the guitar at the age of thirteen. He learned from the records and broadcasts of the Carter family, the Delmore Brothers, Charlie and Bill Monroe and the Skillet Lickers. But when Doc Watson turned professional in 1953, old-style country music was hardly a

profitable field and so he became a session musician, playing whatever was appropriate on either electric or acoustic guitar. In 1960 Ralph Rinzler and Eugene Earle began recording Clarence Ashley and his string band. They discovered Doc Watson and from 1962 featured him as a soloist. Doc Watson's virtuosity on the guitar—not to mention the autoharp, mandolin and banjo—caused an immediate sensation, and helped bring about a new interest in a music which many had thought of as simple and old-fashioned. Although Doc Watson sometimes seems to epitomize a traditional approach to American folk music, he is in many ways a radical and innovative guitarist. He often adapts melodies and techniques from various sources and uses them for his own purposes. He frequently transposes fiddle tunes to the guitar, and has developed a distinctive guitar-picking pattern from his experience with the mandolin.

The enthusiasm generated by the revival swept up in its wake both older players such as Doc Watson, and younger musicians like the New Lost City Ramblers who were playing authentic old-time country music with modern skill.

However, the body of music which had the greatest impact on acoustic guitar players in the early 1960s was the blues, when it was discovered that many of the best country bluesmen were still alive.

After the war, when the center of blues activity switched from the rural South to the northern towns of

325

Sam Lightnin' Hopkins, born in Texas in 1921, was one of the older generation of country bluesmen. Hopkins had a rough, unpolished singing style, and answered the vocal phrase with flashing arpeggios and bursts of single-note runs. He had a great gift for improvisation, both lyrically and musically. After the Second World War, Hopkins went to the West Coast to record with the pianist "Thunder" Smith, and it was during these sessions that he got his name "Lightnin'." Returning to Houston, he became the most important figure in the clubs for years, and imposed his own style on the blues scene there. By the mid-1950s, however, he was less popular and like so many older bluesmen was losing out to the new Chicago blues band sound. He disappeared in 1959, to be rediscovered in the early 1960s and introduced to a new audience.

Sleepy John Estes' Tennessee Jug Busters, with Hammie Nixon and Yank Rachel. Estes' ability as a songwriter (rather than as a musician) makes him a most important figure in the blues.

Chicago and Memphis, and changed in the process from an acoustic-based solo music to an electric group music, the country bluesmen seemed to be figures of the past. Leadbelly, Josh White and Sonny Terry and Brownie McGhee had continued to play in the Eastern cities, but the death of Leadbelly in 1949 to many marked the end of an era. In the 1950s, however, a handful of enthusiasts— record collectors, producers, musicians and musicologists—began to search out older bluesmen and persuade them, perhaps after a gap of ten or twenty years, to pick up a guitar and sing their old songs.

The search was often a haphazard affair. With very few clues to go on, the searchers sent off letters and scoured whole areas. Their results were often surprising. Sleepy John Estes was found after film-maker David Blumenthal mentioned to Bob Koester of Delmark Records that he had seen him living in an abandoned share-cropper's shack in Brownsville. Scarcely able to believe it (Estes was born in 1904), Koester traveled to Brownsville, found him and brought him back to Chicago to record. In 1963 Tom Hoskins went to Avalon, and found Mississippi John Hurt. The clue came from John's words "Avalon's my home town, always on my mind" on the prewar 78 of "Avalon Blues." In 1964 guitarists John Fahey and Henry Vestine, and record producer Bill Barth, found Skip James in a

Bukka White.

Fred McDowell (1905–72). McDowell was born in Rossville, Tennessee, went to Memphis in 1926, and from 1940 onwards lived in Como, Mississippi. He played guitar for Saturday night dances and house parties, but never full-time. He was discovered in the 1960s and acclaimed as the finest living bottleneck player.

Mance Lipscomb, Texas songster (1896–1976).
"I took up the guitar. That was about 1918, when everybody started getting guitars. They were getting these old pine guitars back then." Lipscomb had a wide repertoire of Texas blues, ballads, rags, spirituals and more. As he explained, "I learned myself to play in different keys. I change my music when I change my songs and you got somethin' new comin' up all the time. I get tired of one key." Lipscomb was one of the older men caught up in the 1960s revival, when he became a popular figure at many of the folk festivals.

John Jackson, born 1924 in Rappahannock County, Virginia. His relaxed style, concern with melody, and flowing rhythms present a sharp contrast to rougher country singers, and is typical of the "songster" tradition of the Eastern states.

PHOTO BY CHRIS STRACHWITZ, COURTESY ARHOOLIE RECORDS

Stefan Grossman.

COURTESY OF TRANSATLANTIC RECORDS

hospital in Tunica, Mississippi and in the same year Son House was found by Dick Waterman and Nick Perls. John Fahey wrote to "Booker T. Washington White (Old Blues Singer)" c/o General Delivery, Aberdeen. The letter was forwarded and contact made. Other bluesmen caught up in the revival included Reverend Gary Davis, Big Joe Williams, Fred McDowell, and Mance Lipscomb.

For many of the audience, rebelling comfortably against their middle-class backgrounds, the old bluesmen's way of life had a romantic appeal. The younger urban electric blues players were rejected by audiences and researchers alike. Muddy Waters, who had been playing electric guitar for years, produced it at a festival and was bewildered by the reaction: "They oughta' tol' me they didn't want electric guitar. I didn't know they want that ord'nary box, what they call 'coustic guitar.[7]

By the early 60s there were plenty of acoustic bluesmen to be heard playing in a variety of styles. One of the most important was Mississippi John Hurt. He had recorded a handful of 78s for Okeh in 1928 but with no great success. When rediscovered however, his appearance—he had a face like rubber—and his charming and self-effacing manner, combined with a superb guitar style and repertoire of songs, made him one of the most popular of singers. His playing was less rooted in the blues tradition than most, and in the older songster fashion he often adapted white ballads to his use. His style was not harsh, in the usual Mississippi manner, but warm and hypnotic. John Hurt's distinctive guitar sound was achieved by "tickling" the strings with the fleshy tips of his right-hand thumb and fingers, while his voice, dark and honeyed, matched the gentle tones of his guitar.

The interest in the blues in the early 60s took the music on to the concert platform and the bluesmen provided the musical foundation for a whole generation of young white guitar players. Those who were involved in the rediscovery feel a special involvement with their mentors. Stefan Grossman learned from the Reverend Gary Davis for two years and came to know most of the older bluesmen. To Stefan Grossman this was more than just a musical discovery. The emotional and psychological excitement of helping to bring together people who had previously been just names off scratched

78s is something for which he feels there is no substitute. Now that so many are dead, and can no longer hand on their knowledge direct, he feels that "The very best anyone could hope for would be that I would give them lessons."[8] Grossman's transmission of lessons learned from Mississippi John Hurt, Reverend Gary Davis and others in records, performances and books makes him the most direct link between older and contemporary styles.

The influence of the older blues players has helped many young white players to develop new versions of traditional music. Ragtime has assumed extraordinary importance on the modern steel-string guitar. "Ragging the blues" had become extremely popular in the 20s through the music of Blind Blake and Reverend Gary Davis. With the latter's rediscovery, this style of syncopated music with counter melodies on bass and treble, based on blues roots, underwent a revival. Then in New York in the 1960s Dave Van Ronk and Dave Laibman began striking out in a different direction by transcribing the classic rags of composers such as Scott Joplin for the guitar. The formal rules of ragtime were followed and this led to a complicated but highly exciting style of playing which has been adopted by many other guitarists. The rag-flavored styles that have subsequently appeared, using elements of older traditions, have produced a new repertoire of music for the steel-string guitar.

The increased exposure of young players to blues guitar, on record and in performance from the early 1960s onwards, has helped the development of the steel-string guitar as a major solo concert and recording instrument. The changeover from an accompanying to a solo role could only be achieved when there was a wide general interest in the guitar itself, and enough players who could produce consistently interesting music.

John Fahey has been one of the most important figures in developing the guitar as a solo virtuoso instrument. Fahey's music is strangely hypnotic. Although often based on traditional American motifs, his playing style and technical mastery of the guitar make his sound distinctive. He can play the guitar so that it sounds like an orchestra, capable of producing a wide variety of effects from angular bottleneck to a gentle swing. The extension of the acoustic guitar's sound heard on Fahey's dozen or so solo records — some of which use distortion — was one of the main reasons

COURTESY OF TAKOMA PRODUCTIONS

John Fahey.

for a feeling among a few musicians and enthusiasts during the late 60s that a "classical" tradition for the American steel-string guitar was being created.

Whereas American steel-string players are heavily blues-based both in original inspiration and style, English musicians are more eclectic. There is an important historical reason underlying this: while American folk music, whether black or white, has a long tradition of guitar accompaniment, there has been no equivalent use of the guitar in English or European music. Before the 1950s, the one way for a guitarist to make a living was in a dance band.

Thus when the revival of interest in the steel-string guitar began in Britain in the late 1950s, there was no ready-made audience with pre-formed musical tastes, and no one obvious tradition to draw on for inspiration. The English players therefore were not inhibited from using a wide range of sources in creating their own music. These sources included American blues and country music, and whatever other elements could be suitably adapted to the guitar from traditional British music, Indian music, Irish pipe and fiddle tunes.

The name of Davy Graham is not well known by the general public, but he is acknowledged by English guitarists and some American players like Paul Simon as one of the most influential steel-string players of the 1960s and the first to create an English style. He brought together an amazingly wide range of music, grafting Eastern music, jazz and folk styles on to the blues stock. His music had an authority which came from practical experience, for he traveled to hear in their native countries the styles he was adapting. But his influence did not come only from his ability to adapt unfamiliar musics to the guitar. Even more important, he had a jazz-like skill in chording and knowledge of the fingerboard, and his example inspired many other players to develop a virtuosity they had formerly thought either impossible or unnecessary.

The development of the folk guitar in Britain was hampered by the conflict between "traditional" and "modern" performers. One of the first to bridge the divide and so widen the scope for the guitar's use was Martin Carthy. He played complex and subtle music of a sort that offended the traditionalists, but gained acceptance after being taken up by A. L. Lloyd—doyen of the older generation of British folk musicians—in 1965.

The combination of virtuosity and diverse influences created a style popularly known as "folk baroque," whose two most famous exponents were the Scotsman Bert Jansch and the English player John Renbourn. The feeling was gentle and wistful: both the lyrics and delicately elaborate style of guitar playing (which earned the "baroque" tag) implied on almost fatalistic acceptance of life. Rarely do the English guitarists display the hard attack and brashness of American playing. Davy Graham himself used the word "spiritual" to describe the effect he aimed for.

Each of the leading English players developed a personal style within the confines of "folk baroque." Bert Jansch retained a fondness for early blues, and echoes of his Scottish background persisted. John Renbourn, on the other hand, became interested in early English music and modal styles. One of his later albums, *The Lady and the Unicorn*, was a collection of medieval pieces, English and

Pentangle.

Django Reinhardt (1910–53). Reinhardt learned his music as he roamed through the South of France, taking much of his inspiration from Arabic oud music. In November 1928 he lost the use of his third and fourth left-hand fingers as a result of a fire in his caravan. His brilliant single-string runs, often at high speed, were thereafter played with the first two fingers only. He was able to use the third and fourth fingers for chord work, but only in a limited fashion and on the first two strings only. His most famous work was with the Quintet of the Hot Club of France, made up of Reinhardt, violinist Stephan Grapelli, Django's brother Joseph on rhythm guitar, and Louis Vola on bass.

Reinhardt is here playing a guitar made by Selmer of Paris. A guitar owned by Reinhardt similar to this one is in the guitar gallery on page 232.

Italian dance tunes, and Elizabethan music, using guitar, sitar, violin, viola, concertina and flute.

The "folk baroque" movement reached its culmination in 1967 when the group Pentangle was formed, with Jansch and Renbourn on guitars, singer Jacqui McShee, Terry Cox on drums and Danny Thompson on bass. The band had considerable commercial success, but never lived up to its musical promise. It was widely hoped that the combination of Jansch's and Renbourn's guitar virtuosity within the format of a group would create a new direction for the acoustic guitar. In fact, Jansch and Renbourn seemed, instead of inspiring each other, to cancel each other out. The group developed an air of melancholy, and when they broke up, it seemed as if the British "folk baroque" movement had come to nothing.

In the mid- and late 1960s the acoustic guitar had players in every field of American music, and was even coming back into popularity among jazz guitarists. In jazz, the foundations laid by Eddie Lang and Lonnie Johnson in the 1920s had been extended, surprisingly, by the European gypsy Django Reinhardt. Born in Belgium in 1910, Reinhardt became the most important influence in European jazz up to 1945, and after the war inspired every major jazz guitarist in America. The richness of Reinhardt's playing has never been surpassed and his attack, superb chording and terrific passages of single notes have been an inspiration to players from Charlie Byrd and Barney Kessel to Julian Bream.

But to jazz players the acoustic guitar has remained a secondary instrument—even though the aim of many players is to achieve an unamplified and "natural" sound on the electric instrument.

As the 1960s drew to a close, the acoustic guitar lost its exclusive association with "purity" and became commercially popular. It remained before the public eye as the primary instrument of the singer-songwriter—regardless of whether he produced anything interesting. In England, American styles were closely copied, most successfully for a period by Donovan. He was promoted as the English answer to Dylan, but lacked Dylan's fire and originality and remained nothing more than a passing fad. In America, the entry of the acoustic guitar in a major way into popular music was symptomatic of the desire for a quieter style after the euphoric excesses of the late 1960s.

COURTESY OF A & M RECORDS.

Jazz guitarist Jim Hall with a custom-built carved-top guitar. This was hand-made by Jim D'Aquisto, the former apprentice and now successor to John D'Angelico, who builds exceptionally fine jazz guitars.

The acoustic guitar had become established earlier as part of the essential equipment of the latter-day balladeer and troubadour. But the music industry and public taste had changed by the late 1960s and now performers like James Taylor, Joni Mitchell and Neil Young with their introspective styles claimed the public's attention. The wave of singer-songwriters who sought inspiration for their music and words from their own experiences and view of life had begun with Gordon Lightfoot, Tom Paxton and Phil Ochs; Taylor, Mitchell and Young turned the self-examination of the times into a musical form in itself. James Taylor's album *Sweet Baby James* catapaulted him to stardom, a position he found at odds both with his music and his inspiration. As early as 1969 he was finding the status of guru hard to take and was protesting that "I'm a musician and songwriter, not a soothsayer."[9] But the music industry was relentless in its promotion of profitable soothsayers, with unfortunate results: after the success of *Sweet Baby James*, Taylor retreated both personally and musically.

Whereas the reaction of James Taylor and others to the disillusionment felt at the end of the 1960s was to turn

331

James Taylor.

PHOTOGRAPH BY COURTESY OF WEA RECORDS

José Feliciano

COURTESY OF RCA RECORDS

The Nitty Gritty Dirt Band with guests Doc Watson, Merle Travis, "Bashful Brother Oswald" Kirby, Earl Scruggs and Vassar Clements, recording "Will the Circle Be Unbroken."

COURTESY OF THE COUNTRY MUSIC FOUNDATION

inward, others sought a guide in a return to white American country roots. This rich heritage has provided the basis for the styles of younger players as diverse as John Prine, Jerry Jeff Walker and Kris Kristofferson.

The acoustic guitar spread to become part of the sound of some of the most successful groups, most importantly of Crosby, Stills, Nash and Young. Stephen Stills' powerful guitar playing gave the group a much needed impetus, adding an extra harmonizing element as well as complex melodic lines with some unexpected rhythmic accents. The group's concerts of 1969 and 1970 showed a new use of the acoustic guitar in rock. The first part of the concert was played on acoustic instruments, and sung by one or more of the group, while the second set was played on electric instruments with drums and bass. Following this pattern, the Byrds and the Flying Burrito Brothers were among other groups who divided their performances between an acoustic and electric sound. This increased use of the

Leo Kottke, playing a Bozo twelve-string.

Ry Cooder.

Martin Simpson, a young English player who reflects the eclectic approach of British musicians. He draws on music from traditional English material to Irish fiddle tunes, but refuses to identify with, or base his music on, one particular style. His technical sophistication allows him to achieve effects seldom attempted by steel-string players, such as shaping a phrase by controlled variations of dynamics.

333

David Bromberg.

COURTESY OF UNIVERSAL MUSIC SERVICE CORPORATION

acoustic guitar in rock, a music which relies heavily on live performance for its popularity, was enormously helped by the growing refinement of piezo-electric transducer pick-ups, which boost the volume of the guitar while keeping an essentially acoustic sound.

As the number of steel-string guitar players has increased, audiences have become more appreciative of technical skill on the part of performers. The conscious attempt to develop the American steel-string guitar as a virtuoso instrument, begun by John Fahey, has been continued in the 1970s by Leo Kottke. Although he plays six-string guitar, he is best known for his playing on a twelve-string, which seems at first an unlikely instrument for virtuoso performance. But Kottke's ability to play quietly hypnotic passages interrupted by startlingly rapid guitar riffs has made him very successful. While Kottke writes much of his own music and has a strong personal style, he, like most American players, is indebted to earlier blues traditions. Ry Cooder is another American guitarist to take the country blues as the basis for his virtuosity. He was initially influenced by John Fahey and for a time in the 60s worked with Taj Mahal in the Rising Sons, and with Captain Beefheart. He played extensively as a session man before embarking on his own career and has become known as one of the finest bottleneck players and interpreters of a range of American regional styles. Both Cooder and Kottke have won a degree of popularity which would have been impossible without the audience's growing sophistication and increased knowledge of the guitar over the last ten years.

As the steel-string guitar has moved on to the respectability of the concert platform, it has obscured one of the oldest traditions in music: that of the guitarist as entertainer. It is all too easy to forget that the bluesmen of the 1920s and 1930s, who provided music to drink and dance by, were also adept at the tricks that pleased their audiences. But in the 1970s there has been something of a resurgence of performers who are entertainers as well as skilled musicians and virtuoso guitarists. Such a one in America is David Bromberg, who began his musical career as a session and backing musician with Johnny Shines, Jerry Jeff Walker, Bob Dylan, John Prine and many others. Now he has become a performer who uses the guitar just as much to accompany the stories with which he amuses the audience, often half-sung and half-talked, as to demonstrate that he is perhaps the finest flat-picker in America. Similarly in Europe, John Pearse, who was among the founders of British steel-string guitar playing in the late 1950s and early 1960s, is an entertainer in a tradition (though not a style) that goes back to vaudeville. His stage act is deliberately casual: he jokes with the audience, amusing them with stories about his songs and instruments (which include the mouthbow and dulcimer), before playing a repertoire which includes rags, blues, country tunes and material drawn from British, European and American folk traditions.

The present-day popularity of the steel-string guitar is enormous, and while its most widespread use is still in America, the sound of the steel-string can be heard all over the world on concert platforms and in smoky coffee bars. From the limited three chords of the amateur to the technical skill of the virtuoso, its ability to please at all levels is a major factor in its success. But the steel-string guitar has proved its suitability in all forms of American popular music. Once heard mainly in accompaniment, the steel-string guitar has expanded its musical frontiers and now commands as much respect and attention as a solo instrument.

PHOTOGRAPH BY WOLFRAM GIMPLE

John Pearse.

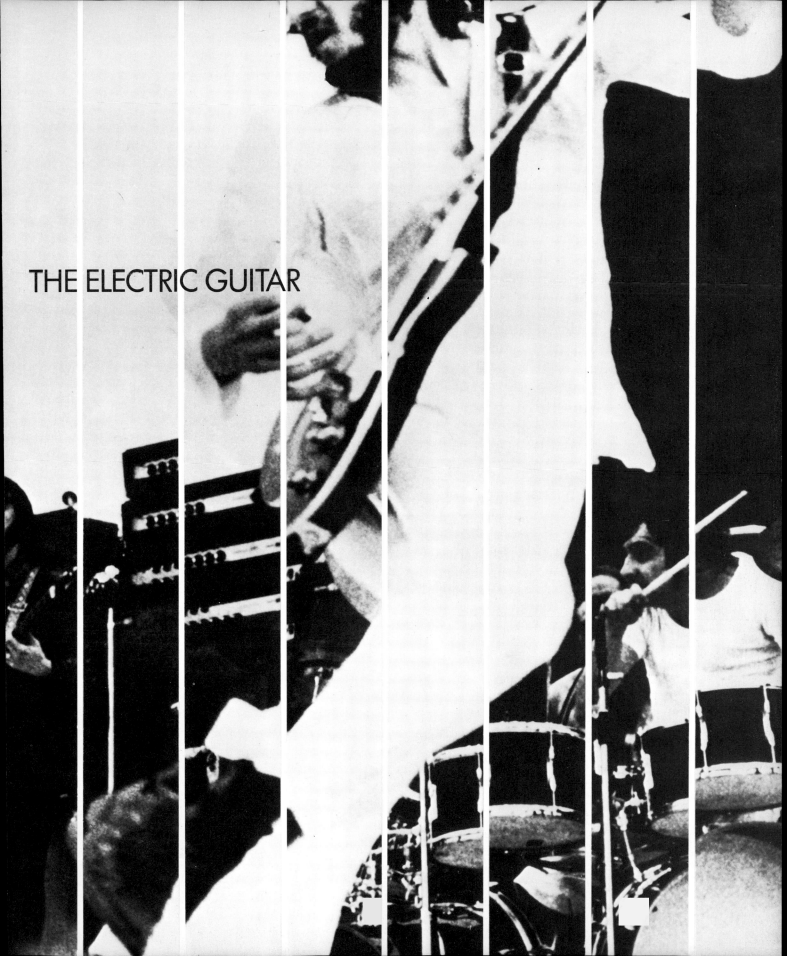

THE ELECTRIC GUITAR

THE INSTRUMENTS

Electric Guitar Gallery: Introduction

The electric guitar is the youngest member of the guitar family, yet it has gained an astonishing, worldwide popularity in the half-century of its existence. This popularity has very largely grown since the Second World War, with the introduction of the solid-body guitar and the application to it of advanced electronic and engineering techniques.

The solid-body differs from every other sort of guitar in being an almost purely electronic instrument; for this reason, some musicians are unwilling to accept it as a guitar. However, the solid-body guitar developed directly from the electric-acoustic guitar, which has much in common with purely acoustic instruments and was introduced with the simple aim of making a normal guitar sound louder. Although the solid-body guitar has unique properties of tone, volume and sustain, the closeness of its relationship to the electric-acoustic guitar ensures its legitimacy.

The differences in sound between the solid-body and electric-acoustic guitar stem directly from the essential differences in their design. On an electric-acoustic guitar (as on a purely acoustic instrument), energy is fed to the soundboard by the strings, making it vibrate as a diaphragm in order to amplify the sound. String vibration can only be sustained for a short time, as string energy is rapidly dissipated by the vibrating soundboard. When a pickup is attached, it moves up and down with the soundboard vibrations, and the amplified sound is a combination of string and body tones. Combining string and body vibrations cancels out some of the high harmonics, so giving the electric-acoustic guitar its characteristic mellow tone.

On a solid-body guitar, the body has considerable mass and inertia. It is designed not to respond to the vibrations of the strings, and absorbs little energy from them. Thus the string, after being plucked, continues to vibrate for a much longer time. So, when a pickup is fitted, the note of a solid-body guitar has a greater natural sustain than that of an electric-acoustic guitar. The stable mass of the solid body affects tone as well as sustain: since the body remains virtually motionless in relation to the strings, the pickup amplifies an almost pure string tone.

The date of the first application of a pickup to a guitar is uncertain, but the first proven use of pickups was by Lloyd Loar, who worked for Gibson from 1920 to 1924. During this period, Loar developed a pickup and the company produced a range of experimental electric instruments. These were not accepted by Gibson's agents, however, and were never put into production. Loar left Gibson with two colleagues to form the Vivi-Tone company, but Gibson's assessment of the market proved to be correct: there was no public demand for electrically amplified instruments, and the Vivi-Tone venture was short-lived.

None of Loar's original pickups is known to survive, but some information exists on them. Walter Fuller (formerly in charge of design and production of Gibson's electric instruments) recalls that, when he joined the company in 1933, he found some pickups at the factory which he believes to have been made ten years earlier under Loar's supervision. These units consisted of a container with one fixed anode and a charged, stretched diaphragm above. Vibrations of the diaphragm induced a fluctuating current which could be amplified. Unfortunately, the pickup had several drawbacks: though protected by a bakelite container it was susceptible to moisture, and would work only if the cable to the amplifier was kept short.

Despite the lack of public interest during the 1920s,

1976 Gibson "Les Paul Deluxe" solid-body electric guitar.

Loar was not the only man to turn his mind to the possibilities of amplifying the guitar electrically. Several players in the late 1920s tried to amplify their guitars by fixing a record player pickup to the underside of the soundboard.

The first truly successful electric guitars did not appear on the market until the early 1930s. In 1931 the Rickenbacher company (which spelled its name with an *h* in place of the second *k* in those early days) produced an electric Hawaiian guitar which was nicknamed the "Frying Pan" after the shape of its aluminum body. The success of the Frying Pan came from its use of an effective electromagnetic pickup: almost every electric guitar pickup since then has used a similar principle.

Electromagnetic pickups have two essential components: one or more permanent magnets and a coil of fine-gauge insulated copper wire. The coil is wound around either the magnet(s) or around iron pole piece(s) which are magnetized by contact with the magnet. The pickup is set so that a strong magnetic field is created in the region of the strings where they pass above it. The strings, which must have a magnetically sensitive ferrous base, cut the magnetic lines of force when they vibrate and thus induce an electric current in the coil.

The physical vibration of the string produces a low-voltage alternating current in the pickup coil; this current alternates at the frequency of the string's vibration. The electric signal from the pickup is modified by the tone and volume controls of the guitar before being amplified and,

ultimately, converted back into sound waves by the loudspeaker.

The guitar's volume control consists simply of a potentiometer, or variable resistor. Electrical resistors (made of coils of thin insulated wire) cause a drop in the voltage in the circuit, since it takes energy to force the current through them. A potentiometer consists of a resistor which can be tapped at continuously varying values by turning a knob connected to a moving contact. The knob determines the value of the resistance in the circuit; the value of the resistance in turn determines the amount by which the voltage generated by the pickup is reduced, and so controls the eventual volume.

The tone control is a separate unit which combines a potentiometer with a capacitor. A capacitor consists of two metal plates separated by a layer of insulation,

the plates being charged by the current in the circuit. Capacitors have the property of allowing alternating currents to pass through them and become better and better conductors as the frequency of the current increases. Thus, in a guitar circuit, a capacitor can be used to filter out high frequencies from the signal and short them to earth. To give a variable control, the capacitor is wired together with a potentiometer; when the potentiometer is set to its maximum value, the capacitor is effectively isolated from the main circuit and is completely bypassed by the signal from the pickup. As the value of the potentiometer's resistance is reduced, however, so more and more high frequencies are filtered off through the capacitor.

The combination of a pickup, tone and volume controls gives the simple circuit shown in the diagram below.

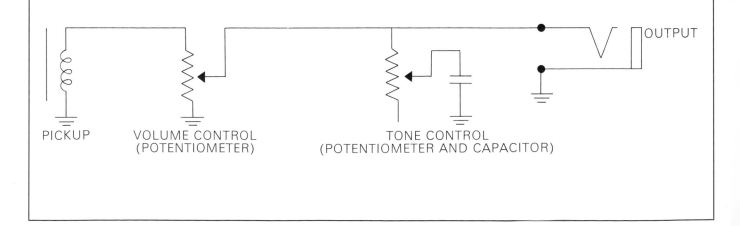

PICKUP   VOLUME CONTROL (POTENTIOMETER)   TONE CONTROL (POTENTIOMETER AND CAPACITOR)   OUTPUT

Rickenbacher was not the only firm to pioneer electric guitars in the early 1930s. The Rowe-De Armond company was formed early in the decade to market electromagnetic pickups, and the Dobro company made a small number of amplified resonator guitars in 1932. By the mid-1930s, Gibson and National had also joined in, and were building both electric Hawaiian and "electric Spanish" guitars, as electric-acoustic guitars were then called.

The electric Hawaiian guitars of the 1930s were built with small solid bodies of wood, bakelite or metal, the solid body giving the sustain necessary for Hawaiian playing. The electric Spanish guitars of the same period were simply standard f-hole arch-top guitars modified by the addition of a pickup and tone and volume controls.

Although the electric Hawaiian guitars were solid-bodied from the start, the modern type of solid-body standard electric guitar was not produced until after the Second World War. The aim in the 1930s was to produce an electric guitar which sounded like an acoustic guitar, but louder, so it was natural to approach the problem simply by putting a pickup on an f-hole guitar. Certainly, the resulting tone approached the unamplified sound of the orchestra guitar much more closely than did that of the solid-body electric Hawaiian. The feedback problems sometimes encountered when electric-acoustic guitars are played at loud volume, and the top is sent into forced vibration by the sound from the speakers, hardly existed in those days of modest amplification.

Electric Spanish guitars were surprisingly slow to catch on, and during the mid-1930s many musicians were unaware of their existence, let alone their capabilities. The real growth of interest did not start until the late 1930s and early 1940s, when Charlie Christian's records and broadcasts with the Benny Goodman band carried the sound of the electric guitar across America and made the Gibson ES-150 famous (see page 344).

The further development of the electric guitar was hampered by the war; the largest companies stopped making guitars, turning the resources of their factories to making products more directly helpful to the war effort. But experiments continued in the home workshops and backyards of dedicated enthusiasts.

Some of the most important development work was being carried out by Les Paul (born 1916), who had experimented with home-made pickups as early as 1929. He became convinced that the electric guitar pickup should remain still while the strings moved, and was working toward the solid-body guitar. In the mid-1930s he fitted a cheap Gibson with a soundpost to keep the top still, and in 1937 commissioned a guitar with a heavy solid top and no soundholes from the Larsen brothers of Chicago. A little later, he made an experimental rig from a railroad tie fitted with strings and a pickup and found that

> You could go out and eat and come back and the note would still be sounding. It didn't sound like a banjo or a mandolin, but like a guitar, an electric guitar. That was the sound I was after.[1]

To make a guitar with the same properties, Les Paul borrowed the facilities of Epiphone's New York factory for several weekends in 1941 and built an instrument he calls "the Log," in which the two pickups were mounted on a central solid baulk of timber (see page 345).

Shortly after building "the Log," Les Paul moved to the West Coast, where he continued to work on the solid-body guitar concept. When guitar production resumed after the war, he tried to persuade Gibson to market a twin-pickup solid-body model, but without success.

Although the large companies were interested only in making ever more sophisticated electric-acoustic guitars, Les Paul was not alone in his belief in the solid-body concept. Two of his friends and neighbors in California, Paul Bigsby and Leo Fender, were also working on solid-body guitars. Paul Bigsby (the inventor of the famous Bigsby vibrola unit) made a single-pickup solid-body guitar for Merle Travis in 1947. At about the same time, Leo Fender formed the Fender Electrical Instrument Company, and in 1948 started to market the "Broadcaster," the name of which was changed to the "Telecaster" in 1950. With the Broadcaster, the modern solid-body, two-pickup electric guitar had finally come into production.

The solid-body guitar was not the only new amplified instrument to emerge in the 1940s. At the beginning of the decade, a machinist named John Moore approached Gibson with his design for a mechanism for changing the pitch of one or more strings of a console-mounted Hawaiian guitar by means of pedals. Gibson named the instrument the "Electraharp"; this was the first pedal steel guitar—although, as Gibson's name suggested, it could hardly be considered a guitar at all.

The electric "bass guitar," first marketed by Fender in 1951, is another hybrid instrument. Although it borrows the shape, and usually the frets, of the electric guitar, in range and function it is an electric bass.

The popularity of the electric guitar became firmly established in the 1950s, and as the decade progressed, the solid-body version began to oust the electric Spanish. Gibson built its first solid-body guitars in 1952, designed with the help of Les Paul and bearing his name, and Fender introduced the three-pickup solid-body Stratocaster in 1953.

The next breakthrough in electric guitar design came with Gibson's introduction of the "humbucking" pickup (see page 380). The increasing use of electric guitars in broadcasting and recording studios created a need for a quieter pickup. Players liked to keep their amplifiers close to them for easy adjustment, but the single-coil pickups of the day were sensitive to radio frequency hum from the power source, and hum was critical in the quiet atmosphere of the studio.

The principle of the humbucking pickup was suggested by existing hum-canceling transformers. In the pickup, two coils were connected out of phase, wound around cores with reverse magnetic polarities. Various dates are quoted for the invention of the humbucking unit, but Walter Fuller (who worked on the design with Seth Lover) recalls that the first was produced in 1954.[2]

The humbucking pickup was fitted first to Gibson's ES (Electric Spanish) 135 and entered regular production with the solid-body Les Paul guitars in late 1957. Early humbuckers, which carried the stamp "patent applied for," have entered the mythology of the electric guitar as the most desirable pickups ever made, and change hands for outlandish prices. In fact, they were no different in sound or specification from the standard full-size humbuckers Gibson has been making ever since; while Gibson has developed many different pickups on the humbucking principle, the standard model has remained unchanged.* The humbucking pickup gave a marvelously gutsy sound which was ideal for the solid-body guitar, and Gibson's design has been widely copied since the expiry of the original patent.

Other new electric guitar concepts developed in the 1950s included stereo wiring (which either separated the front and rear pickups or split a pickup to separate bass and treble strings), twin-neck guitars, semi-solid guitars, and three-pickup guitars. More versatile control circuitry was introduced, although the main elements continued to be simple switches, capacitors and potentiometers.

The solid-body guitar's potential for sustain and controlled feedback was increasingly realized through the 1960s, and harnessed to the service of high-energy rock music. The earlier search for a pure, clean sound was replaced by a drive toward controlled distortion. Devices such as the fuzz-box, wah-wah pedal, univibe and octave divider became standard issue for many players. While this trend has great significance for amplifier and accessory designers, guitars themselves were little affected.

In the 1970s there have been signs of a move back toward a less modified sound, and of a greater interest in the resources of the electric guitar rather than its amplification systems. Accordingly, there has been a crop of new pickups in humbucking, superhumbucking* and single-coil configurations, each designed for particular tonal characteristics, and a growing interest in the possibilities of low-impedance units. New pickup designs have gone hand in hand with ever more ingenious circuitry. The Alembic company (formed in 1968 to supply the Grateful Dead's sound systems) has pioneered the use of transistorized preamplifiers built into the guitar, which allow tone control by frequency filters with pre-selected roll-off points. Ovation's solidy-body guitars now use a simpler version of the same concept (see page 359). Gibson has rejected the use of built-in preamplifiers and transistorized circuits which need their own power source: the company believes that musicians will not buy guitars containing batteries, which may embarrass them by going flat during a performance. Instead, Gibson has shown great inventiveness in the design of systems that produce extraordinary tonal variations through conventional components.

Throughout the entire history of the electric guitar, musicians have been searching for a pickup that could be fitted to an acoustic guitar to allow it to be played at "electric" volume without losing the acoustic tone. Microphones restrict the performer's movement, and can pick up unwanted noise; conventional electromagnetic pickups attached to the top or suspended in the soundhole are susceptible to feedback and produce too electric a sound.

The development of piezo-electric transducers since the mid-1960s has pointed the way to a possible solution of this problem. Piezo-electric transducers use materials (some natural, some synthetic) which produce an electric current when subjected to a physical stress. Some work under bending loads, others under direct pressure. The output of piezo-electric pickups is usually small, and often needs boosting by a preamplifier mounted either in the guitar or on the lead.

Since piezo-electric transducers work in response to physical force, they can be used with either steel or nylon strings, and either fitted to the soundboard of the guitar or built in to the bridge. The latter has proved to be the more satisfactory; transducers in the bridge respond to a combination of string and table vibration and cut down external noises of fingering, bumps and taps.

Ovation's acoustic-electric guitars are fitted with a separate piezo-electric element for each string, mounted beneath the saddle. Other piezo-electric pickups of proved effectiveness are the Barcus Berry Hot Dot and the FRAP (Flat Response Audio Pickup, invented by Arnie Lazarus in 1969), which are marketed for fitting to any acoustic guitar.

While electric guitars are now made throughout the world, the American companies remain almost unchallenged as producers of high-quality instruments. Their most serious rivals for export sales have been the Japanese, who have usually concentrated on producing cheap copies of the most successful American designs. But the Americans continue to be the innovators, and the Gibson company, above all others, steadily produces guitars that combine fresh ideas with quality craftsmanship.

The guitar gallery which follows contains a selection of electric guitars which has been made to illustrate general trends in instrument design as well as individually outstanding guitars.

---

* The only difference between batches of the standard Gibson humbucker has been that some have had coils wound on black cores and others wound on white. The color difference was caused only by the availability of pigment!

* The superhumbucking pickup, designed for Gibson by Bill Lawrence in 1971, uses three ceramic magnets in place of the single alnico magnet of the standard humbucker, producing a different type of output (see page 381).

Rickenbacher A-22 seven-string electric Hawaiian guitar, *c.* 1931.
Owned by Stephen Frankau, photographed at Cass Music, Mitcham.

Overall length: 73.5cm
Scale length: 57cm
Body diameter: 17.7cm
Body depth: 4cm

The Rickenbacher A-22 and A-25 "Frying Pan" electric Hawaiian guitars, in-

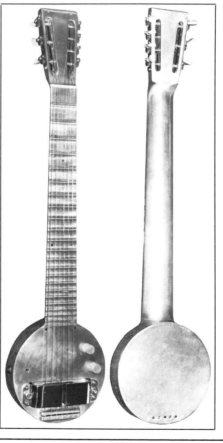

troduced in 1931, have gone down in history as the first commercially marketed electric guitars. The 22 and 25 in the designations referred to the scale lengths (in inches), and versions with six, seven and eight strings were made. The first Frying Pans were made of aluminum, the head, body and neck being produced in a single casting; shortly after, a bakelite-bodied version was introduced.

The Frying Pan was designed by George Beauchamp and Paul Barth, both of whom had worked for the National Guitar Corporation. The pickup has individual iron pole pieces activated by two large, chrome-plated tungsten steel horseshoe magnets. Two magnets were used instead of one to produce a higher output from the pickup: the amplifiers of the day were weak and inefficient. The magnets were mounted on a non-ferrous baseplate, which is attached to the body at each end by a spring-loaded height adjustment screw. As on most single-pickup guitars, there is one tone and one volume control.

Between 1931 and 1937, some 2,700 guitars and amplifiers were sold. The Frying Pan was eventually superseded by the bakelite BD-6 and Electro models, and by the latter half of the 1930s several makers (including Gibson and National) were in competition with Rickenbacher for the electric Hawaiian guitar market.

Gibson ES-150 electric-acoustic guitar, from the 1936 Gibson catalogue.
Reproduced by permission of Julius Bellson and the Gibson company.
ES-150 pickup from the collection of Gibson, Kalamazoo.

The ES-150 was Gibson's first electric-acoustic guitar. The neck, body and tailpiece were very similar to those of the L-50, the least expensive of Gibson's L series arch-top instruments.

Walter Fuller, who joined the company in 1933, started work on the development of Gibson's pickups in 1935. Gibson's first electric guitar, the EH-150 electric Hawaiian, was produced the same year and was followed shortly by the ES-150. The pickup unit on the ES-150 had a straight bar pole piece, activated by two powerful bar magnets. Walter Fuller remembers that these were made of a 36 percent cobalt steel. The pickup coil originally

had 4,000 turns of no. 38 wire, but was modified in 1937 or 1938 to 10,000 turns of no. 42 wire, giving a much higher impedance.

The main body of the unit was mounted beneath the soundboard of the guitar and attached to it by three spring-loaded screws giving full adjustability for pickup height. Notches were filed in the top of the pole piece as necessary, to balance the response characteristics of the different strings. Gibson preferred a bar pole piece in place of individually adjustable poles for each string, to avoid the possibility of dead spots which can occur between individual pole pieces. (Dead spots cause problems if the string is "bent" from its median position during playing.)

The ES-150 was popularized by Oscar Moore and Charlie Christian. Indeed, Gibson's single-bar pickup is often referred to as the "Charlie Christian" pickup. The ES-150 had the mellow tone and relatively short sustain characteristic of single-pickup acoustic-electric guitars. The amplifier supplied for use with both the ES-150 and EH-150 was manufactured for Gibson by the Lyon and Healy company (founded in the 1890s by George Washburn Lyon). At $75.00 the amplifier cost just $2.50 less than the guitar.

"The Log," two-pickup electric guitar by Les Paul, 1941.
From the collection of Les Paul.

This guitar, which Les Paul built for himself over several weekends at the Epiphone factory in Long Island, marks the transition from the hollow-bodied electric-acoustic guitar of the 1930s to the post-war solid-body guitar.

The Log is assembled from a Gibson guitar neck, a 10cm square (4″ × 4″) baulk of timber, and the two halves of an Epiphone guitar body. The pickup coils are wound around straight bar magnets, which Les Paul preferred to individual pole pieces because of their greater power and evenness of response. The bridge consists of a straight metal bar with adjustment screws at each end, and the guitar is fitted with a home-made vibrola attachment. Les Paul has told us that he was experimenting with vibrola arms as pitch-changing devices as early as the 1930s, although they did not become generally available commercially before 1950.

Despite its appearance, this instrument

operates and sounds like a solid-body guitar. The pickups are held stationary by the central baulk, which provides sustain. The hollow

"wings" do not affect the guitar's sound but are simply bolted on to make the instrument convenient to hold and play.

Solid-body electric guitar, built by Paul Bigsby for Merle Travis, 1947.
From the collection of the Country Music Hall of Fame, Nashville.

Overall length: 103cm
Scale length: 63cm
Pickup center: 58.2cm from nut

Paul Bigsby, Leo Fender and Les Paul were all working independently on the development of solid-body guitars in California in the mid-1940s. They were familiar with each

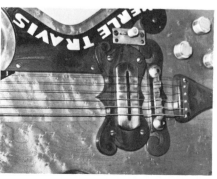

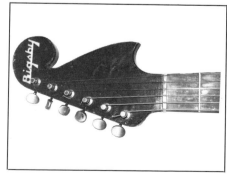

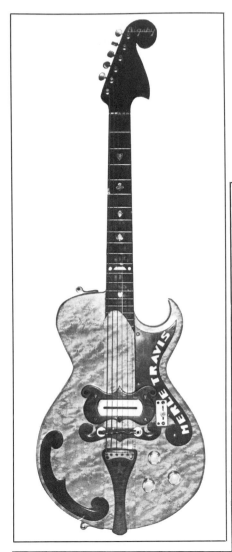

Gibson ES-5, 1949.
Photographed at Gruhn Guitars, Nashville.

Overall length: 109cm
Scale length: 64cm
Body length: 53.5cm
Body width: upper bout 32.4cm
           waist 27cm
           lower bout 43.5cm
Depth of sides: 8.4cm
Pickup centers: 49, 54.7 and 60.5cm from nut

When Gibson started production again after the Second World War, it found an enormous demand for amplified instruments

other's work, and there are some notable similarities between this guitar and the Fender Broadcaster (as the Telecaster was originally known) which was first issued the following year.

As on the Broadcaster, all the tuning machines are mounted on one side of the head, and the strings pass through holes drilled through the body.

Both body and neck are made of curly bird's-eye maple, the neck member continuing through to form the center section of the

which had not existed before the war. While electric Hawaiian guitars remained popular, the real growth was in the demand for electric-acoustic guitars, which rapidly superseded the unamplified arch-top guitars of the 30s.

In the years immediately after the war, Gibson produced a range of single-pickup (the ES-125 and 150) and double-pickup (ES-300 and 350) electric guitars with body and neck designs closely similar to their f-hole arch-top acoustic models. The three-pickup ES-5 was introduced in 1949 as an electric counterpart to the famous acoustic L-5. The body had a carved spruce top with sunburst finish, and maple sides and back. The two-footed bridge was fitted with individually adjustable saddle pieces for each string, after the manner of the current Gibson small tune-o-matic bridge, to allow individual adjustment of intonation of each string.

The pickups were designed by Walter Fuller. They had two magnets each, set beneath the coil and lying parallel to it but separated by a soft iron core into which individual pole pieces were screwed. The controls consisted of a master tone control and individual volume controls for each pickup, allowing a wide variety of tonal possibilities. The ES-5 shown here has been modified by the addition of a master volume control, and a different headstock veneer. The Bigsby tailpiece could be original. Paul Bigsby made his first vibrato arm in 1939, and patented some of his ideas in the 1940s. Gibson was the first company to offer them as a catalogued option and developed the swing-back handle.

In 1955 the ES-5 was replaced by the ES-5 Switchmaster, which was fitted with a toggle switch in addition to the ES-5's tone and volume controls. This allowed the pickups to be played either separately or together.

body. This type of construction is very strong, and adds marginally to the instrument's sustain. The control circuitry for the single bar-type pickup is unusual. Instead of the single tone and volume controls, there are three knobs and a three-way toggle switch. This suggests that the body contains several tone control circuits of different values, probably for mid-range and treble roll-off.

Paul Bigsby also made some twin-pickup solid-body guitars of very similar design.

Epiphone Zephyr Emperor Regent,
c. 1950.
Photographed at Gruhn Guitars, Nashville.

Overall length: 111.5cm
Scale length: 65cm
Body length: 55cm
Body width: upper bout 33cm
    waist 26.5cm
    lower bout 47.7cm
Depth of sides: 8.6cm
Pickup centers: 48, 54.2 and 60.2cm from nut

After the war, the Epiphone company was Gibson's greatest rival as a producer of high-quality electric-acoustic guitars. The arch-top maple-bodied Zephyr Emperor Regent with its laminated neck, adjustable truss rod, and three single-coil individual pole piece pickups was in direct competition with Gibson's ES-5. There is one tone and one volume control, and the pickup combinations are controlled by six push-button switches mounted on the lower bout. Epiphone made a similar model, the Zephyr Deluxe Regent, with only two pickups operated by a three-way switch.

The Epiphone company was bought out by Gibson in 1957, and Gibson produced Epiphone guitars at its Kalamazoo factory

from 1958 to 1969. Gibson continued to produce the Epiphone Emperor as the top model of the line, but modified the design by a change to humbucking pickups, with different control circuitry and switching, and a change of bridge. Many former Epiphone craftsmen moved to the Guild company, and their influence was apparent in the design of many of Guild's early electric guitars. In design, circuitry and switching, Guild's X-350 was closely modeled on the Epiphone Emperor shown here.

The Epiphone name has survived since 1969 on inexpensive Japanese-made guitars which have nothing in common with the finely crafted instruments of the original Epiphone company.

Gibson Super 400CES, 1952.
Photographed at Orange, London.

Overall length: 125cm
Scale length: 64cm
Body length: 55.5cm
Body width: upper bout 34.8cm
    waist 29.6cm
    lower bout 46cm
Body depth: approximately 11.5cm overall
Pickup centers: 47.5 and 60.8cm from nut

The Gibson Super 400CES has been made on special order since it was first catalogued in 1951 and first sold in 1952 as the electric version of Gibson's most expensive arch-top f-hole guitar.

It has the largest body of any of Gibson's electric-acoustic guitars, with a carved spruce top, maple back and maple sides. The neck is laminated from strips of maple with a center strip of dark timber, and fitted with the usual

347

Gibson adjustable truss rod. The head carries gold-plated Kluson tuning machines. There are two single-coil pickups controlled by a three-way toggle switch on the shoulder, allowing the pickups to be played singly or together. Each pickup has its own tone and volume control.

The bridge of this Super 400 is unusual, being the type of combination bridge-tailpiece normally associated with the less expensive ES-295 of the same period and the first Les Paul solid-body guitars made by Gibson in 1952. There is no doubt that it is original, however, since it carries a plaque engraved with the original owner's name and the model designation. Subsequently, the Super 400CES was normally fitted with separate bridge and tailpiece units.

The Super 400CES has always been extremely costly, and has only been built in small numbers. Early examples are very rare: records show that this was the only one made in 1952. The current version of the Super 400CES is virtually identical, save that the single-coil pickups have been replaced by humbuckers.

Gibson "Les Paul Model," 1952.
Photographed at Top Gear, London, by courtesy of I. C. Bishop.

Overall length: 98cm
Scale length: 63cm
Body length: 43.8cm
Body width (maximum): 32.3cm
Depth of sides: 5.2cm
Pickup centers: 48 and 58.5cm from nut

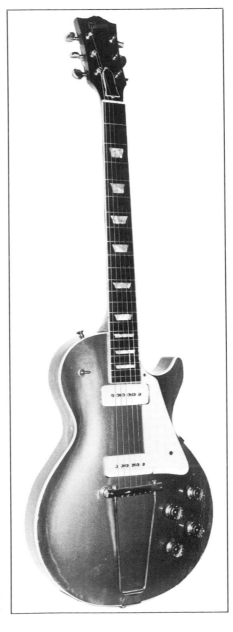

Gibson was wary at first of the concept of the solid-body guitar, so much so that the company originally agreed with Les Paul that any solid-body instruments it built should carry his name—but not that of the company! In the course of the development work it undertook with Les Paul, the company gradually gained confidence, and when its first solid-body guitars appeared in 1952 they bore the Gibson logo as well as a "Les Paul" decal on the headstock.

This example is one of the first twenty or so ever made. It has the feeling of weight and solidity that was so much a part of Les Paul's original concept, and which gives Les Paul guitars their great sustain properties. The weight comes from a thick mahogany body capped with a solid carved maple top, cut from a half-inch slab. The maple top does much to give Les Paul guitars their distinctive sound. Les Paul says, "A half-inch maple top on a mahogany backing is as effective as an all-maple body."

The pickups are high-output, single-coil units with alnico magnets and individually adjustable pole pieces. Their location was worked out by Les Paul with the aid of a test rig which allowed a pickup to be slid along beneath the string and tried in various positions. Depending on the pickup positions, different harmonics are emphasized and those with node points above the pole pieces are eliminated. Now, as the left hand moves on the fingerboard, so the positions of the nodes alter. In Les Paul's words, "At no point can you pick up the whole sound, the whole thing is a compromise. It can only be trial-and-error and personal judgment." The control circuitry, as on most subsequent Les Paul models, is straightforward, and consists of a three-way selector switch (front, rear, or both pickups together) and individual tone and volume controls for each pickup.

The trapeze tailpiece fitted to the 1952 Les Paul was a source of disagreement between him and the company. Paul wanted to use the bridge-tailpiece combination (developed for electric-acoustic guitars) with the strings wrapping *over* it, so he could rest his hand on it and damp the strings. From the company's point of view this was awkward; it made it difficult to bring the strings down low over the solid-body guitar's fingerboard, which is aligned differently from that of the electric-acoustic instruments. Gibson realized that if the strings were wrapped *under* the tailpiece, they could be brought low over the neck and the pickups could be sunk deep into the body, which helped the sound. Unfortunately, this made the guitar awkward to pick, and the trapeze tailpiece was unpopular with players. It was changed in 1954 in favor of a stop tailpiece (which still combined bridge and

tailpiece in one unit).

The Les Paul Guitar was originally offered in a gold-top finish, with a natural mahogany side and back, because Les Paul felt "It's a rich color, and it wasn't on any other guitar in the world."

This example of the 1952 Les Paul—now a very rare guitar—is in its original condition save that the Kluson tuning machines have been replaced with gold-plated Schallers. It is

one of the first of the line of instruments bearing Les Paul's name which have become the most famous electric guitars ever built. From slow beginnings, when just a handful were sold each month, Les Paul guitars with their "big, round shiny sound" have become so popular that the man himself says "nobody anticipated this thing was going to be so big."

Fender Stratocaster, 1953 and 1976 models.
1953 model photographed at Gruhn Guitars, Nashville.
1976 model photographed at CBS/Arbiter, London.

Overall length: 98.5cm
Scale length: 64.5cm
Pickup centers: front 49cm, center 55cm,
              rear slanting 60 to 61cm from nut

The Stratocaster was designed in 1953 by Leo Fender and his chief engineer Leo Tavares, and was first manufactured the same year. It has remained in production ever since, with only the slightest modifications, and has proved itself to be a true thoroughbred among electric guitars.

The neck and head of the Stratocaster are made from one piece of maple. The head is designed to carry the tuning machines on one side so that the strings pass straight over the nut, and carries straight on from the line of the neck without a backward inclination. This allows for a continuity of wood grain between neck and head, and partially overcomes the problem (inherent in all one-piece necks) of a weak spot at the point the head begins. The lack of an angle between head and neck is compensated for on all but the earliest models by metal clips that hold the top four strings firmly down on the nut. The heads on post-1966 Stratocasters are slightly larger than on early models.

The Stratocaster was designed to be built without a separate fingerboard, the frets being set directly on to the top of the neck. In 1960 a separate rosewood fingerboard became standard, but since 1970 the original type of maple neck-fingerboard has been available once again. The fingerboard surface is slightly arched in cross-section, and is well matched to

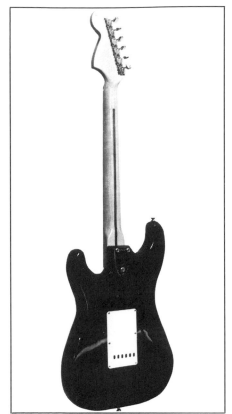

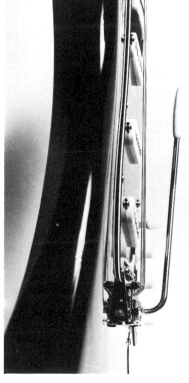

the envelope of the vibrating strings, being cut away further on the bass side. The combination of contour, narrow width (4cm at the nut) and maple surface gives the Stratocaster fingerboard a distinctive feel, and the all-maple neck contributes just a little to the guitar's sound.

The truss rod is fitted through a slot routed from the back of the neck. Originally, the truss rod was fixed at the head and adjusted by a turn screw at the base of the neck. The adjustment was awkward to perform: it was often necessary to loosen the bolts securing the neck to the body and tilt the neck back to gain access to the truss rod screw. The current Fender bullet truss rod was introduced in 1972, and eliminated the difficulty by being adjusted from the head end with an Allen key. The actual neck-to-body attachment has also been modified. Since 1972 the simple bolt attachment, in which the neck angle could only be adjusted by inserting shims, has been replaced by a micro-tilt neck adjustment. The neck is held to the body by one screw only, and its angle can be adjusted by a second small bearing screw. Although this system offers greater adjustability, it does not provide such a rigid neck-to-body junction, and the neck can go out of alignment if knocked or roughly handled.

The Stratocaster body is made of ash in blond-finish models, and poplar in lacquered models. The back is contoured at the waist to fit the player's body snugly. All electrical components are fitted in slots routed in the front of the body behind the plastic pickguard.

One of the most successful features of the Stratocaster is the combination of the bridge, tailpiece and vibrola in a single unit. Each string has its own individual bridgepiece which is adjustable for both height and string length. These are attached to a plate, which can pivot slightly about the screws at its front which fix it to the body. Attached to the rear of the bridge plate is a metal block (originally steel, now die-cast zinc), which acts as the string anchor. This whole unit can be pivoted by the vibrola arm to change the pitch of a note. To counterbalance the string pull on the unit, and return the strings to pitch when the vibrola is used, there are tension springs in a cavity in the body. These are fixed at one end to the string anchor block, and at the other to the body itself. Five springs are used with

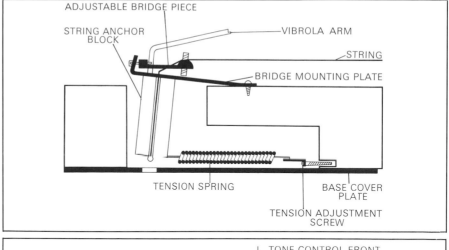

ADJUSTABLE BRIDGE PIECE

STRING ANCHOR BLOCK

VIBROLA ARM

STRING

BRIDGE MOUNTING PLATE

TENSION SPRING

BASE COVER PLATE

TENSION ADJUSTMENT SCREW

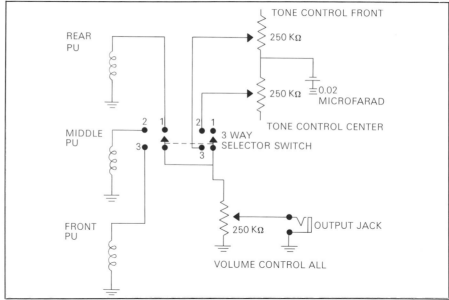

REAR PU

MIDDLE PU

FRONT PU

TONE CONTROL FRONT

250 KΩ

250 KΩ

0.02 MICROFARAD

TONE CONTROL CENTER

3 WAY SELECTOR SWITCH

250 KΩ

OUTPUT JACK

VOLUME CONTROL ALL

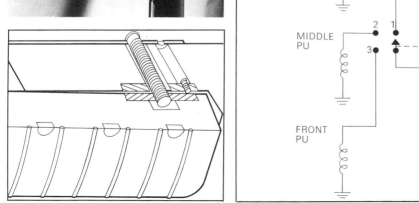

standard-gauge strings, three with light-gauge. Adjustment screws allow the spring tension to be re-adjusted for perfect balance of the string pull if the guitar is tuned at a higher or lower pitch than normal. The Stratocaster vibrola is one of the most reliable vibrolas in returning the strings to true pitch.

The Stratocaster's electric system is characterized by an elegant simplicity. Although the Stratocaster was the first commercially marketed three-pickup solid-body guitar, and many electronic innovations in guitar design have been made since its introduction, its pickups and circuitry remain unchanged. The pickups are single-coil type,

with non-adjustable individual pole pieces pre-set at the factory for height. The pole pieces are individual alnico magnets, attached to a common baseplate, wound with a coil of 7,600 turns of no. 42 wire. The coils are dipped in wax to stop any tendency to microphonic vibration in the coil itself. The circuitry is designed to allow any of the three pickups to be played singly, although it has proved possible to play front and center or rear and center pickups together by balancing the toggle switch in intermediate positions. There is one master volume control on the output. The two tone controls operate on the front and center pickups: the bridge pickup has no tone

control. Switching from pickup to pickup produces marked changes in tone.

The Stratocaster, which is still comparatively inexpensive for an American-made guitar, has been played by many of the leading rock musicians, and was particularly associated with Jimi Hendrix. The Fender company was bought by CBS in early 1965, and many guitarists believe that the quality of the instruments dropped after the takeover. In recent years, however, this trend has been reversed and the current Stratocaster is a finely made guitar.

351

Maccaferri pickup, *c.* 1953.
Owned by Mario Maccaferri.

Mario Maccaferri, despite his successful career as a concert guitarist, says that he has always been frustrated by the lack of power of the nylon-string guitar. In the early 1950s, after his concert days were over, he evolved a method of amplifying nylon strings without using a microphone and with which, he says, "You could play to an audience of any size without feedback and with a natural tone."[3]

Naturally, the principle of the magnetic pickup is inapplicable to nylon strings; the Maccaferri pickup is essentially a capacitance pickup. The strings are metallized for a small length beyond the bridge, which is covered with metal foil to act as a contact. A charged metal plate or sheet of foil is placed between the metallized area of the strings and the

soundboard, and the whole area is surrounded with a metal shield. The charged plate is connected to a preamplifier inside the guitar, and the changes in the electric field caused by vibrations of the metallized string are amplified.

Wide variations of tone can be produced with this pickup, which is shown here with the protective cover removed and attached to one of Maccaferri's plastic guitars. Maccaferri remembers playing a nylon-stringed amplified guitar to Segovia, who was greatly impressed. Unfortunately, the example Maccaferri demonstrated had a plastic body and a spruce top with f-holes, and Segovia objected to the shape. Maccaferri says, a little wistfully, "If I had listened to Segovia and made the classic model, maybe he would have played it." As it is, this unique pickup design has never been developed commercially.

Gibson "Les Paul Custom," 1974 limited edition reissue of 1954 design.
Photograph by courtesy of Norlin Inc.

The "Les Paul Custom" was built to the same dimensions as the 1952 model save that it was 3cm longer and, like subsequent models, it had a slightly thinner body. Like so many of Gibson's earlier solid-body guitars, the originals became collectors' items after discontinuation of the line.

The 1954 Les Paul Custom differed from the basic Les Paul model in that it was built with a solid one-piece mahogany body, was fitted with a front pickup with gold-plated staple-shaped poles, and had a separate tune-o-matic adjustable bridge and stop tailpiece. The "ebony" finish and low, fine frets earned it the nicknames "Black Beauty" and "Fretless Wonder." The black finish was used because Les Paul thought it would draw attention to the guitarist's hands.

In 1957 the design was changed to incorporate three humbucking pickups, and this model was produced until 1960. The Les Paul Custom was finally reintroduced in 1968, with a maple top for a sharper sound and better sustain, two standard humbucking pickups, black finish and "fretless" action. The three-pickup version was made again in 1976. Although fine wire frets made the Les Paul Custom famous (and were also, in-cidentally, fitted to the 1952 model), they are not liked by all guitarists. Many rock players prefer a larger fret, which they find helps them to bend notes, and re-fret jobs on Les Paul Customs are not uncommon.

"Joe Maphis" double-neck guitar by Semie Moseley, 1954.
Photographed at the Country Music Hall of Fame, Nashville.

Overall length: 106cm
Scale lengths: 63cm and 36cm

Gibson is often credited with the first introduction of twin-neck guitars, but this instrument pre-dates Gibson's first double-necks by four years. It was hand-built for Joe Maphis by Semie Moseley, formerly of Rickenbacker and founder of the Mosrite company, and combines a standard guitar neck with a short scale neck designed to be tuned one octave higher.

The construction of this guitar has two interesting features, which have both been used in various succeeding twin-neck guitars. The two necks are set at an angle, which brings the bridges closer together to allow for a similar picking position while leaving enough space between the necks for left-hand fingering. To reduce weight—a serious problem on twin-neck instruments—the maple body is largely hollowed out.

The electrical design is straightforward, with single-coil pickups, one tone and one volume control, and a pickup selector switch for the standard neck.

Gibson Explorer, 1958.
Photographed at Gruhn Guitars, Nashville.

1958 was a vintage year for Gibson, with the introduction of the Flying V and Explorer, the semi-solid series, and the first production of the double-neck series.

The Explorer and Flying V had similar electric components, with two standard-size humbucking pickups, a three-way selector switch, separate tone controls for each pickup and one overall volume control. The Explorer was fitted with a tune-o-matic bridge and stop tailpiece, while the strings on the Flying V passed through to the rear of the guitar. Both Explorer and Flying V had bodies made of korina wood [4]

The shapes of both Explorer and Flying V were far ahead of the fashions of the time, and very few were made. Since then, tastes have changed. Explorer and Flying V have been widely copied by Japanese manufacturers, and Gibson has reissued both in limited editions. Despite this, the rarity of the original issue models makes them highly sought by collectors. Original 1958 Explorers, of which under a hundred were built, are now the rarest and most expensive of all solid-body electric guitars.

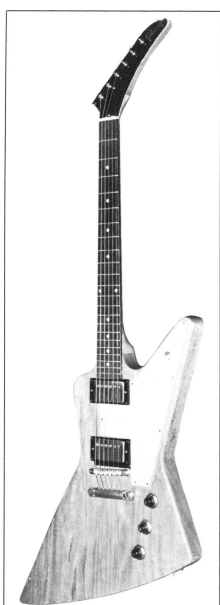

Gibson "Les Paul" Model, 1958.
Photographed at Orange, London.

The Les Paul model was modified for the second time late in 1957, when humbucking pickups were used instead of single-pole pickups, and separate stop tailpieces and adjustable tune-o-matic bridges were fitted (as on the Les Paul Custom). In 1958 the gold top finish was replaced by a cherry sunburst finish (as on this guitar) which shows the extremely high quality of the maple used for the tops. Although produced in 1958, this guitar has a 1957 serial number. The serial numbers of Gibson guitars are put on the neck at a very early stage of construction—which can cause confusion! In 1961 the shape was changed to that of the SG, with a thinner all-mahogany body and double cutaway.

Les Paul was never happy with the relatively lightweight SG type body and his name was taken off the guitars late in 1961. At that time he was preoccupied with the breakup of his marriage to Mary Ford and retired from the connection with Gibson: from 1961 until 1968, none of the typical carved-maple-top, mahogany-backed, solid-body, single-cutaway Les Paul-design guitars were made.

Production eventually started again as a result of a telephone call from Les Paul to company president Maurice Berlin. The call was prompted by the discovery that professional musicians were paying two or three thousand dollars for old Les Paul guitars. Ironically, Maurice Berlin was, at the time, thinking of phasing out solid-body guitar production altogether. Fortunately for the company and musicians alike, he changed his mind and production of the Les Paul design guitars was resumed in 1968.

There is a mythology in the music business about the varying quality of Les Paul guitars made in different years. Les Paul himself is scornful of the idea that "the older the better," and feels that the best guitars have, in general, been those made between 1957 and 1959 and from 1968 to the present. Indeed, he has told us that he considers the present Les Paul Custom, and the Les Paul De

luxe (which is fitted with Gibson's small humbucking pickups) to be as good as any that have been produced. Of the enormous popularity of the 1957 design, and the increasingly high prices it fetches, he says: "That's all nonsense. The pickups are exactly the same as what's made now. Like any year, there are good and not so good—no two 57s are alike. In fact, no two guitars of *any* year are the same." The current generation of Les Paul models have one hidden design advantage over their predecessors, in that they are the first Gibson guitars to make use of the concept of total shielding—which will eventually be applied to all the company's electric guitars. Every component is grounded except for the strings, which gives a studio-quiet guitar and eliminates the possibility of a shock through the strings should the polarity switch on the amplifier fail.

Gretsch "Chet Atkins Country Gentleman," c. 1959.
Photographed at Gruhn Guitars, Nashville.

Overall length: 110cm
Scale length: 62cm
Body length: 54cm
Body width: upper bout 30.6cm
　　　　　　 waist 26.3cm
　　　　　　 lower bout 43.5cm
Body depth: 4.8cm at sides, 6.5cm overall

The Gretsch company has been in existence since 1883. Its best-known guitars were those produced from the mid-1950s through the 1960s, many of which were designed with the assistance of Chet Atkins. The distinctive sound of these guitars was particularly favored by country musicians.

The "Country Gentleman" shown here is a thin-bodied electric-acoustic. The f-holes are not real, however, but painted on. (For a time, in the late 1950s, Gretsch made guitars with painted f-holes to reduce feedback.) There are two twin-coil pickups, controlled by a system that includes an on-off switch, three-way pickup selector switch, three-way tone selector switch to change the value of tone control capacitances, as well as tone and volume controls. Like many Gretsch guitars of this period, the Country Gentleman was fitted with string dampers just forward of the

bridge, one for the bass and one for the treble strings. In most cases these were operated by levers near each f-hole; here they are controlled by screw knobs. The use of a metal string-separator and a zero fret, in place of a simple nut, is typical Gretsch practice, and is designed both as an aid to correct intonation and to reduce the difference in tone between the open and the fretted string.

One of the most interesting features of Gretsch's top models, including the Projectasonic and White Falcon, was an innovative use of stereo, produced by splitting the wiring of each pickup so that the bass and treble strings fed separate channels.

Gibson ES-175D, 1958.
Photograph by courtesy of Norlin Inc.

Despite the predominance of solid- and semi-solid-body guitars, a large range of electric-acoustic instruments continues to be built: Gibson's current catalogue alone includes eight models.

The ES-175 is the least expensive of Gibson's electric-acoustic guitars, and is built with a press-formed maple arch top, maple sides and arched maple back. Gibson's factory records show that the ES-175D was first introduced in 1949, the original version being fitted with one single-coil pickup. A second pickup was added in 1953, and the pickups were changed to humbuckers in 1958. Since then, the specification has remained unchanged, although a thin-bodied version (the ES-175T) was also introduced in 1976.

Deep-bodied electric-acoustic guitars are particularly popular among jazz musicians; the ES-175D is used by Joe Pass, Herb Ellis and Jim Hall. Although deep-bodied guitars are not normally popular among rock guitarists, because of the feedback problems they can cause when played at high sound levels,

Steve Howe has a particular liking for the ES-175.

Unwanted feedback can be caused in guitars of this type by sound from the amplifier sending the top of the guitar—and therefore the pickups—into sympathetic vibration. There are various ways of curing this defect. The crudest and most widely used solution is to stuff the guitar body with plastic foam or rags, and tape off the f-holes. A better method is to clamp a metal bar around the bridge, to damp the acoustic movement of the top. Both of these operations inhibit the natural performance of the guitar. Feedback can also be cured, without modifying the guitar, by including in the circuit a selective notch filter equalizer, which can be used to filter out the natural resonant frequencies of the guitar body which cause feedback. This, however, involves considerable expense. The cheapest and easiest answer is for the guitarist to place the amplifier some six to eight feet behind him and pointing away from the direction he is facing by an angle of about 40°. With such a setup, it is possible to play an electric-acoustic guitar at very considerable volume, but without feedback.

Gibson ES-355TD-SV, 1959
Photograph by courtesy of Norlin Inc.
Circuit diagram by courtesy of the Gibson company.

Gibson first issued double-cutaway, thin-bodied, semi-solid electric-acoustic guitars in 1958. The ES-355T, as it was first designated, was the top model of the range, and its successors have remained so since.

The ES-355TD-SV has a thin hollow body made of laminated maple, with a spruce center block for sustain and elimination of unwanted feedback, and a twenty-two-fret neck on which the double cutaway allows easy access to all frets. The guitar is available with either Bigsby or Gibson vibrola, and every metal part in sight is gold plated.

The ES-355TD-SV has some interesting electrical features. From the very first issue in 1958, the ES-355 has been wired for stereo by connecting each pickup to a different channel of a stereo output jack. To get the full benefit of the system, it is necessary to use a stereo lead and put the front and rear pickups through separate amplifiers. Although this

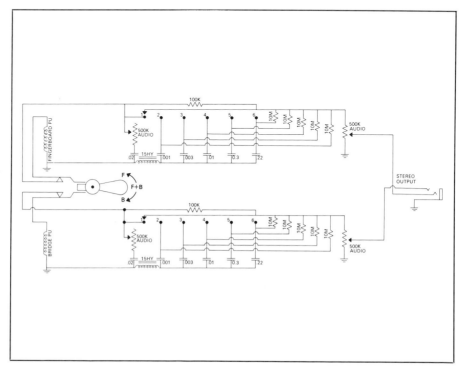

type of stereo separation of pickups is now quite common, it was not used on commercially made guitars before the introduction of the ES-355.

The ES-355 was modified in 1959 by the addition of what Gibson terms "varitone" circuitry. Varitone circuitry routes the signals from the pickups through a system of resistances and capacitors, which acts as a treble filter. Changing the position of the varitone control switch from one through to six brings in a larger capacitance at each step, and so increases the amount of treble cut-off. In addition to the varitone switch there is a three-way pickup selector and two standard tone and volume controls.

Gibson has made numerous other models in its semi-solid-body range. Among these, the ES-335TD is fitted with a coil tap which makes it possible to short out one coil of each of the humbucking pickups, effectively turning them back into single-coil pickups at the flick of a switch. This version of the ES-335 was not introduced until 1976, although the design drawing for the coil-tap circuitry is dated 1965.

Since their first introduction, slim-line semi-solid guitars have become standard instruments for black urban blues, and the ES-355TD-SV is particularly associated with B. B. King.

Gibson Melody Maker, 1961.
Photographed at Orange, London.

Overall length: 98cm
Scale length: 62.3cm
Pick-up center: 58.5cm from nut

While Gibson has always specialized in producing electric guitars for the upper end of the market, it produced a number of simple and inexpensive models in the 1950s and 1960s. The Melody Maker was introduced in 1959, and was offered with either one or two single-coil pickups. The original design had a flat body with single cutaway; the double

cutaway was introduced in 1960. In 1966 the body shape was changed again to an SG-type contour, and the Melody Maker was eventually merged into the SG range.

Although the single-pickup Melody Maker was designed as a very basic guitar in every part, from its simple tuning machines to combination bridge-tailpiece, it was a highly successful instrument. It had a particularly good neck, and proved throughout that a simple guitar well made by the leading manufacturer is better than a complicated instrument cheaply built by a less experienced firm.

Mosrite "Joe Maphis" model double-neck guitar, late 1960s.
Photographed at Rhodes Music, London.

Overall length: 107cm
Scale lengths: 62.3cm on both necks
Pickup centers: 48.5 and 58.5cm from the nut on twelve-string. 48.6 and 58.8cm from nut on six-string.

Mosrite's production twin-neck models differed considerably from the hand-built prototype made for Joe Maphis. The Double 12 had a solid, white lacquered body and two maple necks set at a slight angle. The control system utilized three three-way selector switches—one for neck selection, two for pickup selection—and master tone and volume controls.

The small details of construction and fittings are typical of guitars made by Semie Moseley's California-based company. Like Gretsch, Mosrite fits metal "nuts"—which act only as string separators—and zero frets. Mosrite's adjustable bridges have a slightly crazy ingenuity, the strings resting on small pulley wheels, carried on metal bobbins, which can be moved backward and forward on threaded bolts. The bulbous covers to the single-coil pickups, and the bowler hat-

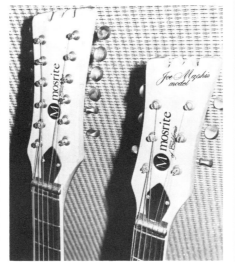

Gibson "Double Bass" twin-neck guitar, *c.* 1965.
Photographed at Gruhn Guitars, Nashville.

Overall length: 110.5cm
Scale length: 62cm on six string neck, 76cm on bass
Pickup centers: 44.8 and 58cm from nut on six-string neck. 56.5 and 72cm from nut on bass neck

Gibson produced its first twin-neck guitars, the "Double 12" and "Double Mandolin" models, on special order in 1958. These had semi-solid bodies and combined a standard six-string neck with either a twelve-string or a short-scale six-string neck, tuned an octave higher than normal.

In the early 1960s, the twin-neck models (still produced on special order only) were redesigned with smaller solid bodies in the shape of the SG series, and a "Double Bass"

was added to the range. The Double Bass is essentially a combination of Gibson's EB3 bass with a straightforward SG, with the same pickups and the same narrow fingerboard (4cm at the nut). Usually (though not on this example) the Double Bass had a built-in Gibson "Fuzztone" unit, fitted at the center of the body between the two tailpieces.

Gibson's SG-type twin-neck instruments were the most successful and famous of all double-neck guitars. Their production was discontinued in the late 1960s but Gibson has recently produced a limited edition of the Double 12.

shaped control knobs, have something of the same air of amiable eccentricity.

Double 12s are probably the most interesting twin-neck guitars for the player, allowing some strange resonances if the necks are switched on together. For all their versatility, the appeal of twin-neck guitars is limited by their physical size and clumsiness, and by their cost.

Gibson "Les Paul Recording," 1971.
Photograph by courtesy of Norlin Inc.
Circuit diagram by courtesy of the Gibson company, Kalamazoo.

Gibson has, since 1969, been the only major American guitar company to produce a range of instruments designed for low-impedance pickups. This range has been produced at the instigation of Les Paul, who told us that "I've been into low impedance since 1941, but it didn't really start to come in until 1968. With low impedance you can plug straight into the recording board, and you can have a high-impedance output into an amp so you can hear what you're doing. You can eliminate interference and radio frequency cable hum problems, and it allows you to use a hundred-foot cable on stage."

Low-impedance pickups have less output, but in Paul's view "The pickup is one of the most barbaric parts of the guitar. You can either have power or distortion. If you put on a more powerful pickup you change the response characteristics, and you have plenty of output already."

The Recording model was introduced in 1971. It is fitted with two center-weighted humbucking pickups, with alnico magnets and low-impedance windings. The pickups can be played singly or together, in or out of phase, and either low- or high-impedance output is available.

The tone and volume control circuitry reflects Gibson's ingenuity in constructing versatile and sophisticated systems without resorting to transistorized circuitry. A tone selector switch is linked to a decade control and to a range of capacitors, which can be used when the guitar is being operated on low-impedance output as a type of frequency filter. There are also separate bass and treble range tone controls, and both pickups are linked to a single master volume control on the output.

The physical construction, unlike the electrical construction, is quite straightforward. The body and neck are made of mahogany. The bound rosewood fingerboard is 4.3cm wide, as on other Les Paul models, and joins the body at the sixteenth of its twenty-two frets. There is a stop tailpiece, and a wide-throw tune-o-matic bridge of the type made for Gibson by Schaller.

The other low-impedance models made by Gibson at present are the semi-solid Les Paul Signature, which has two output sockets (one for low and one for high impedance, both of which can be used at once), and two electric basses. Past models in the series were the Les Paul Personal and Professional, which were built from 1969–71.

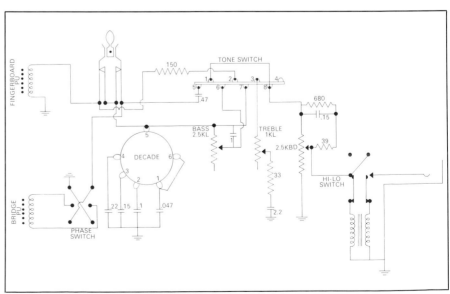

Ovation "Electric Country Artist" acoustic-electric guitar, 1971.
Photograph by courtesy of Rose-Morris Ltd, London.

Piezo-electric transducers work equally well on nylon- and steel-string guitars. This is the amplified version of Ovation's "Country Artist," a guitar designed for steel-string players who wish to play nylon strings but feel uncomfortable on a classical guitar.

The "Electric Country Artist" uses Ovation's system of individual piezo-electric pickups for each string. The plastic saddle is divided into six sections, under each of which is a separate piezo-electric transducer, the whole assembly being contained in a black plastic trough pegged to the table. The output from the pickup unit is fed to a miniature battery-powered preamplifier by the forward endblock, which has a volume control and incorporates two filters to help give a balanced sound across the tonal range.

Ovation "Breadwinner," 1972.
Photograph by courtesy of Rose-Morris Ltd, London.

Overall length: 100.3cm
Scale length: 62.8cm
Fingerboard at nut: 4.3cm

Ovation entered the solid-body electric field in 1972 with the Breadwinner and Deacon (which is identical to the Breadwinner except that it has more expensive inlays and hardware). Both have an unconventional,

asymmetric mahogany body and bolt-on twenty-four-fret neck. The bridge design is also out of the ordinary, bridge and tailpiece being combined in a single brass unit fitted with individually adjustable plastic saddles.

The electrics of the Breadwinner combine two hum-canceling pickups with a three-way selector switch, phase switch, master tone and volume controls, and a built-in transistorized preamplifier powered by a nine-volt battery. The preamplifier is designed to provide a constant output level whether the pickups are used singly or together, in or out of phase,

whatever the position of the tone control.

Ovation solid-body guitars are surprisingly comfortable to play and are reasonably priced in view of their technical sophistication, but they have not as yet caught on widely among musicians. On past evidence, guitarists are quite conservative about the shape of their instruments (witness the lack of success of Gibson's Explorer and Flying V when they first appeared). It is also possible that they are wary of the built-in preamplifier.

Gibson L-6S, 1973.
Photograph by courtesy of Norlin Inc.

Overall length: 100.5cm
Scale length: 62.8cm
Body length: 41.8cm
Pickup centers: 50 and 59cm from nut
Fingerboard at nut: 4cm

The Gibson L-6S, introduced at the end of 1973, was designed by Bill Lawrence, who is widely regarded as one of the few genuinely outstanding designers of electric guitars.

The L-6S has interesting features in both its physical and electrical construction. It was designed to have twenty-four frets, two more

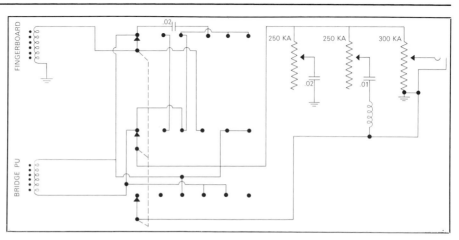

than usual, but still to be physically well balanced. This has been achieved by joining the neck at the eighteenth fret to a dense maple body with a single deep cutaway. The maple body also helps to provide excellent sustain qualities.

The electrical design of the L-6S is ingenious. The initial aim was to build a guitar that would give rock players the widest possible tonal variety without using complex varitone circuitry (see page 355). Two superhumbucking pickups are wired into a circuit which has a master volume control, standard tone control, additional mid-range tone control, and six-way selector switch. This allows the pickups to be used singly or together, in phase or out of phase, wired in series or in parallel. The resultant variation in tone, gained simply by switching the pickups, is enormous. Carlos Santana said of the L-6S (in an interview in *Guitar Player*, November 1974), "With the controls, I can make it sound like a Stratocaster, a Telecaster, an SG or a Les Paul—I get them all."

Gibson SG Standard, 1974.
Photograph by courtesy of Norlin Inc.

The SG series is Gibson's "other" long-running solid-body electric guitar series, alongside the even more famous Les Paul models. The immediately recognizable double-cutaway SG body shape was first introduced on the Les Paul Standard and Custom models manufactured in 1961, the designation of which was officially changed to

SG later the same year.

The SG Standard has been produced continuously from 1961 to the present, except for a break in the period 1971 to 72. There have been numerous small modifications. The current design, which came in in 1974–5, has the familiar lightweight mahogany SG body, mahogany neck and rosewood fingerboard. The SG Standard is fitted with two superhumbucking pickups, with a straightforward wiring circuit. The other current SG

models are the three-pickup Custom and the Special, which has two superhumbucking pickups encapsulated into plastic pickup covers.

In the past, numerous other guitars have been made by Gibson with the SG designation and twin-cutaway mahogany body. These include the SGI, II and III, SG Professional and Deluxe.

Veleno guitar, *c.* 1974.
Photographed at Top Gear, London.

Overall length: 98.5cm
Scale length: 63.5cm
Body length: 39.5cm
Body width 32.3cm max.
Body depth: 3.7cm
Pickup centers: 48.5 and 61.5cm from nut to
active poles

John Veleno's company in St. Petersburg, Florida, specializes in all-aluminum guitars, which have some very strange features.

The body of the guitar is machined out of two solid pieces of aluminum, a front and a back, which are screwed together. The chan-

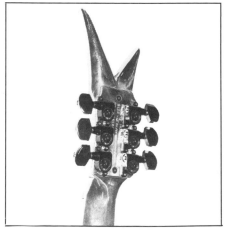

nels for wiring and controls are routed out of one of the halves. The bolt-on neck and head are machined together from a single piece of aluminum, and there is no separate fingerboard, frets being fitted straight into the upper surface of the neck. Schaller tuning machines are mounted on an aluminum plate which, in turn, screws on to the back of the head.

The guitar is fitted with two standard humbucking pickups, with individual tone and volume controls, three-way pickup selector switch, and pickup phase switch.

The standard finish is a highly polished natural aluminum to the body, semi-matt natural to neck and head, and black anodized for bridge and tailpiece. A gold-plated body finish is offered for those who can afford it.

The all-aluminum construction makes it possible to build a very slim neck, and offers unusual properties of sustain and shielding for the electrical components. Aluminum, however, is not a particularly pleasant material to handle, and in climates colder than Florida's, this guitar can be positively numbing to the fingers.

Guild S100, 1975.
Photographed at Top Gear, Shoreham.

Overall length: 102.5cm
Scale length: 62.8cm
Body length: 41.9cm
Fingerboard at nut: 4.1cm

The basic concept of the Guild S100 is quite similar to that of the better-known Gibson SG. The Guild has a one-piece mahogany body, and a slim, glued-on mahogany neck. It is fitted with two high-output humbucking-type pickups with ceramic magnets, three-way selector switch and two tone and volume controls. One of the attractive features of all Guild solid-bodies is the fitting of a pickup phase switch: two pickups out of phase produce a snarling tone in which the high harmonics predominate, fundamental, first and second harmonics being effectively canceled out by the phase difference of the pickups.

The solid-body range is offered in either mono or stereo versions, the stereo being achieved by putting each pickup through a separate channel. This example of the S100 is unusual in that it is fitted with a mono-stereo switch; this is no longer a standard feature.

Custom-built guitar by John Gréven.
Photographs by courtesy of John Gréven.

John Gréven of Nashville made this instrument for Jeff Hanna of the Nitty Gritty Dirt Band. It is remarkable for the quality of the engraved abalone inlays to the headstock, fingerboard and scratch plate. Ironically, the rest of the guitar is modeled on the 1954 Les Paul TV—one of the simplest and least expensive electric guitars ever made by Gibson.

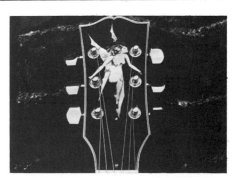

Rickenbacker 360/12, 1975.
Photographed at CBS/Arbiter, London.

Overall length: 101cm
Scale length: 62.5cm
Body depth: 3.7cm
Pickup centers: 49.5 and 59cm from nut
Fingerboard width at nut: 4cm

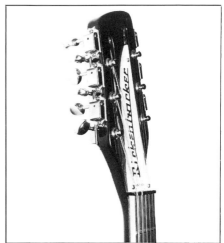

This guitar is the twelve-string equivalent of the Rickenbacker 360 six-string electric. The slim body is hollow right through, and has no center block (although the top is thickened up in the center, beneath the pickups). The neck carries twenty-four frets, and is incredibly thin for a twelve-string guitar. The slender neck section is largely made possible by Rickenbacker's ingenious double truss rods, which allow the bass and treble sides of the neck to be corrected separately, and will straighten out almost any twist, bow or warp.

One of the most delightful features of the guitar is the ingenious head design. Rickenbacker has "double banked" the Kluson machines, so that the spindles of six poke through from the back while the other six are mounted as on a slot head. This design eliminates the need for an enormously long, cumbersome head, which looks so out of place on twelve-string electrics.

The two pickups are single-coil units. They have a relatively low output, but give an unusually clear sound for an electric twelve. The controls—pickup selector, two standard tone and volume controls, and overall master volume control—are not mounted direct on the guitar body but on a "floating" plastic plate. A second plastic plate, raised above the first, acts as a pickguard, and there are separate outputs for stereo and mono.

Electric twelve-string guitars are uncommon, although electric twelve-string necks are quite popular as part of a twin-neck combination. Roger McGuinn (a Rickenbacker user) is one of the few guitarists to make a reputation as an electric twelve-string player.

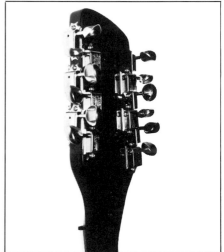

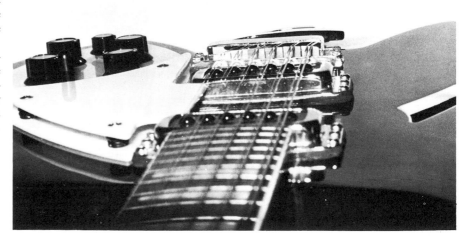

Gibson S-1, 1975.
Photograph by courtesy of Norlin Inc.

Overall length: 100.5cm
Scale length: 62.8cm
Pickup centers: 48.7, 55.1 and 58.7cm from
        nut
Fingerboard width at nut: 4.3cm

The Gibson S-1 continues the theme set by the L-6S of gaining striking tonal variations with simple electrical components and essentially simple circuitry. It is fitted with three epoxy-encapsulated single-coil pickups, with alnico magnets. These are wired via a four-way selector switch, which allows them to be combined front and center, rear and center, front and rear out of phase, or all three together. Though single-coil pickups, they are wired so that any two together are hum-canceling, and all three together are 66 percent hum-canceling. As a fifth alternative, a toggle switch can be used to short out the front and center pickups, leaving the rear (treble) pickup to give the typical piercing attack of a single-coil pickup in the bridge position. There is one volume and one tone control.

The S-1 was designed as an inexpensive guitar by Gibson's standards, and was intended with the Marauder to capture some of the middle ground of the market. The tonal combinations gained by the device of wiring single-coil pickups in humbucking configuration have, however, proved attractive to players such as Ronnie Wood of the Stones, to whom price is scarcely a consideration.

Gibson Marauder, 1975.
Overall photograph by courtesy of Norlin Inc. Detail photographed at F. D. & H. Music, London.

The physical construction of the Marauder is almost exactly the same as that of the S-1. Both guitars have similarly shaped alder bodies and the same type of bolt-on maple neck. The difference between the two lies in their electrical specification.

The interesting feature of the Marauder is its use of a combination of a superhumbucking pickup in the front ("rhythm") position, to produce a gutsy sound with some filtering-off of high frequencies, and a single-coil pickup in the rear ("lead") position.

The design of the single-coil pickup is in itself a little unusual. The unit, which is encapsulated in epoxy, has two Indox-7 ceramic magnets and *three* bar pole pieces, one in the center and one on each edge of the coil. The Marauder pickup coil, which has fewer turns and a somewhat heavier-gauge wire than normal, produces a good high-frequency response. The return pole pieces, however, cut some of the extreme high frequencies to produce a rougher sound, with a little more harmonic distortion, than would be produced by a normal single-coil unit. A further effect of the Marauder's magnet pole piece structure is to create a strong magnetic field just above the surface of the unit, which is therefore set as close to the strings as possible.

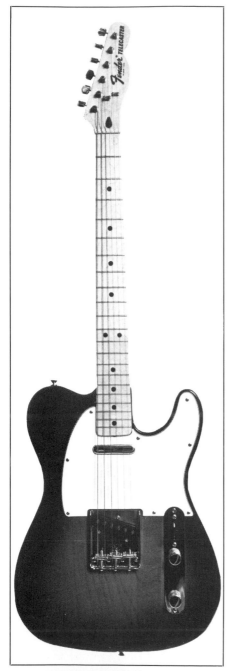

Fender Telecaster, 1975.
Photographed at CBS/Arbiter, London.

Overall length: 97cm
Scale length: 64.5cm
Fingerboard width at nut: 4cm

The Fender Telecaster has been in continuous production for longer than any other solid-body electric guitar. The design of the current model has changed but little from that of the original Broadcaster, introduced in 1948, whose name was soon changed to Telecaster.

The first Telecasters were fitted with two single-coil pickups, with one tone and volume control, and a three-way selector switch which gave either front or rear pickup, or front pickup played through a large value capacitance. This acted as a heavy treble filter, and was incorporated in the days before the introduction of the electric bass to give the guitar a suitable sound for heavy bass lines. The electrical circuitry was changed in the mid-1950s to give the present setup of one tone and volume control, and a selector which allows either front or rear pickup or both together.

One of the most notable features of the Telecaster, which has never changed, is the design of the bridge assembly. The strings pass in pairs over three short metal rods, the height of which can be adjusted at each end and which can move forward and back on spring-loaded screws. There is no tailpiece as such, the strings being passed through the body from the rear.

The clear, twangy sound of the Telecaster's single-coil pickups gained it early success with country players. Since then it has been used in almost every type of popular music; although somewhat primitive by modern standards, its phenomenal popularity still continues. Indeed, the Telecaster is used by some of the finest electric guitarists playing at present, including James Burton and Roy Buchanan.

The Telecaster has been made in several variants in the course of its long career. These include the Esquire (a Telecaster minus one pickup, made from 1954 to 1969); Thin Line (hollowed on the bass side, with a single f-hole, introduced in 1969 and given humbucking pickups in 1972); Custom (one single coil and one humbucking pickup, introduced 1970) and Deluxe (two humbucking pickups, carved body, new bridge, new controls, neck and head, introduced 1973). However, the basic Tele continues to be the most popular.

Although Fender has made ranges of f-hole and semi-solid-body electrics, and other solid-body guitars including the Jaguar and Mustang, the Telecaster and Stratocaster are their only models to have been lastingly successful. These two, alongside the electric basses, continue to dominate the company's output as they did twenty years ago.

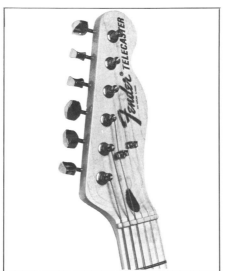

Yamaha SG 2000, 1976.
Photographed at F. D. & H. Music Ltd, London.

Overall length: 100.5cm
Scale length: 62.8cm
Fingerboard width at nut: 4.3cm
Pickup centers: 48.5 and 58.5cm from nut

Japanese instrument manufacturers have not, in the past, been noted for their originality. At last, however, the better Japanese firms are showing signs of trying to make guitars with some original qualities.

Yamaha's SG2000, introduced in 1976, has no specific design features of either physical or electrical construction which are particularly new in themselves, but is unusual in the combination of details. The body is built of mahogany, with a carved top plate laminated from five pieces of maple to help give sustain. The back of the guitar is contoured similarly to that of the Stratocaster, and the neck is laminated from strips of maple and mahogany. Instead of being bolted or glued on, the neck laminate runs right through the center of the body, as in the Gibson Firebird and all Alembic guitars. There are two humbucking-type pickups, encapsulated in plastic covers, with a standard wiring link of three-way selector switch, two tone and two volume controls. The bridge and tailpiece are derived from the common Gibson design, except that the bridge is mounted on a brass block to help sustain (as are Alembic bridges).

The tuning machines are similar to Grovers.

The SG2000 appears to be aimed to compete with Gibson's Les Paul Deluxe and Custom, and is in a similar price range. Yamaha has an aggressive sales and publicity policy, and it will be interesting to see what headway the company's expensive guitar makes. It must be said that, for all its qualities, the SG2000 lacks the classical looks of the Les Paul, and the example we examined suffered from a poorly finished fingerboard.

Guild "Artist Award," 1976
Photographed at Top Gear, Shoreham.

Overall length: 112.4cm
Scale length: 65cm
Body length: 43.1cm
Body width: upper bout 32.3cm
　　　　　 waist 27.2cm
　　　　　 lower bout 43.2cm
Body depth: sides 8.5cm, overall depth *c.* 11.5cm.

Guild, like Gibson, continues the tradition of the deep-bodied f-hole jazz guitar, and its instruments of this type have gained by the presence in the company of craftsmen who formerly worked for Epiphone. The Artist Award is the most expensive guitar built by Guild and has been in production since the early years of the company's existence.

The Artist Award has a carved spruce top,

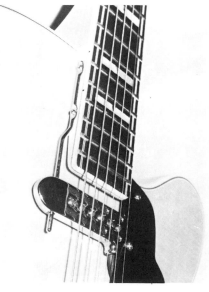

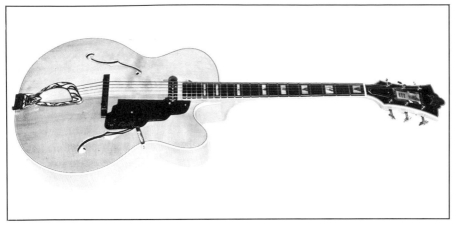

and sides and back of high-quality flame maple. It is fitted with a Rowe-De Armond pickup, fixed to the fingerboard and pickguard, which floats above the table on felt pads so as not to interfere with acoustic performance. As on Gibson's top electric-acoustic (the Citation), there is a single volume control, and no tone control. In guitars of this type, which have carefully graduated carved tops, the acoustic tone is as important as the electric.

Demand for luxury electric-acoustic guitars is small, but even so the companies who make them often have difficulty in obtaining timber of sufficient quality. Guild produces the Artist Award on custom order in quantities of twenty to thirty a year.

Gibson "The Les Paul" guitar, 1976.
Front photograph by courtesy of Norlin Inc.
Front detail photographed at Gibson, Kalamazoo.

The Les Paul guitar is a luxury instrument. It is the most expensive solid-body guitar that Gibson builds at present.

Electrically and dimensionally, this instrument is essentially the same as the Les Paul Custom. The difference lies in the materials. The Les Paul has a body of two solid pieces of the very highest quality flame maple, bookmatched around the center joint. All body edges are multiple-bound in hardwood, with a broad outer layer of rosewood, and the control knobs, pickguard, pickup surrounds and headstock veneer are also made of natural rosewood. The headstock, pickguard and ebony fingerboard have edge inlays of twin strips of red-dyed hardwood, and every single exposed metal part is gold-plated —except for the frets.

Gibson electric-acoustic guitar with sympathetic strings, custom-made for John McLaughlin, 1976.
Photographs by courtesy of Patrick Aldworth, Gibson.

Overall length: 100.2cm
Scale length: main strings 64.8cm
           sympathetic strings 29.2cm
Body length: 53.5cm
Body width: upper bout 31.2cm
          waist 25.5cm
          lower bout 42.5cm

Body depth: increasing from 10.2 to 12.4cm
Fingerboard width at nut: 4.6cm

The major guitar companies frequently make special modifications to guitars for famous musicians, and occasionally build them "one-off" instruments. This is the second guitar with resonating strings which Gibson has produced for John McLaughlin, and was custom-built under the supervision of luthier Abraham Wechter.

The idea of sympathetic strings was suggested to McLaughlin by the sitar. Their

presence makes the luthier's task all the more difficult, since they place considerable extra stress on the top of the guitar. To restrain the forces involved without impairing the guitar's acoustic performance demanded a complex strutting pattern. In designing this, Wechter drew on Gibson's experience with the Mark guitar, and on the acoustic theories of Dr. Michael Kasha.

The guitar's body shape is based on that of the J-200, with the addition of a deep cutaway, and the fingerboard is deeply scalloped. McLaughlin wanted the scalloped finger-

board to assist fast fingering. He plays the guitar with ultra-light-gauge strings and frets it by very light finger pressure, without depressing the strings into the fingerboard's hollows. The combination of scalloped fingerboard and light strings also allows tremendous note bending.

The guitar is fitted with three FRAP FS200 piezo-electric stereo pickups. Two of these are incorporated into the saddles of the sympathetic strings, and the third is set under the table on the treble side of the main bridge. All three are wired to a switch box on the inside of the tailblock, which allows different combinations to be wired in stereo. When the guitar left the factory, the switch was set to mix the sympathetic strings on one channel and give the main strings on the other.

The concept of placing sympathetic strings diagonally beneath the main strings of the guitar is not new—José Porcel built a guitar with this feature in 1867. The combination of sympathetic strings, scalloped fingerboard, Kasha strutting and piezo-electric transducers is, however, unique!

Hoyer Foldaxe, 1977.
Photographs by John Pearse.

Folded length: 51cm
Scale length: 63.5cm

The Hoyer Foldaxe was designed by Roger Field and Thomas Stenger so that it can be folded in half for easy transport (it can be fitted beneath an aircraft seat, for example) without having to take off the strings. To make this possible, the neck folds about a roller pivot, which is linked to an identical roller which forms the string anchorage. The two rollers rotate together as the neck is folded, so that a constant string tension is maintained. The guitar body has a built-in carrying handle.

The Hoyer Foldaxe would seem like nothing more than an expensive gimmick were it not for the quality of its electrics, and the sound they produce. There are two hum-canceling pickups with one tone and one volume control, five-way tone selector switch, and pickup phase switch.

Les Paul guitar bodies under construction at Gibson's Nashville factory.

Construction

Although there are a few individual makers who build electric guitars by hand, the electric guitar is ideally suited to factory production with a high degree of mechanization. Indeed some operations, such as the winding of pickups, can be carried out rapidly and consistently only with the use of machinery. The purely practical arguments for the factory construction of amplified instruments are reinforced by the circumstances of history. The electric guitar was invented and popularized in America at a period when the guitar industry had already become organized into large, factory-based units. Accordingly, the trend from the

THE PARTS OF AN ELECTRIC GUITAR: Exploded view of a Fender Stratocaster

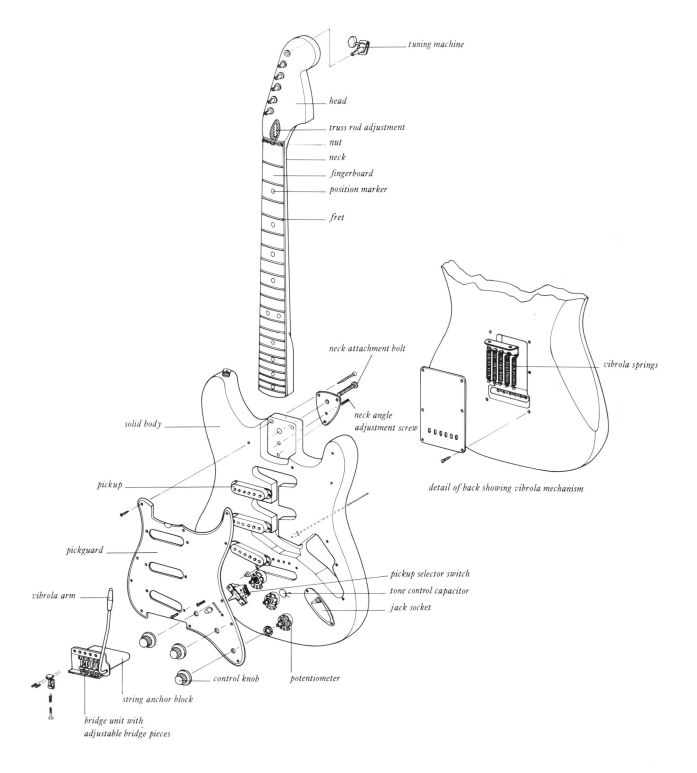

tuning machine

head

truss rod adjustment

nut

neck

fingerboard

position marker

fret

neck attachment bolt

vibrola springs

solid body

neck angle
adjustment screw

detail of back showing vibrola mechanism

pickup

pickguard

pickup selector switch

tone control capacitor

vibrola arm

jack socket

control knob

potentiometer

string anchor block

bridge unit with
adjustable bridge pieces

Selecting and grading planks of seasoned mahogany.

first has been for electric guitars to be factory-built. The photographs which accompany the following discussion of current electric guitar construction practice were taken at the Kalamazoo factory of the Gibson company, which is widely regarded as the world's leading manufacturer of electric guitars.

The factory production of electric guitars, like that of steel-string guitars, is organized so that many of the processes are carried out simultaneously in different parts of the plant. However, the various processes may be grouped under the headings of body construction; neck construction; neck and body assembly and finishing; electronics assembly; and hardware fitting.

Body construction procedures are quite different for each of the three main types of electric guitar: solid-body, thin-body semi-solid, and deep-body electric-acoustic.

Gluing together sections of mahogany on a windmill press to make body blanks.

Although the sound of the solid-body guitar is produced entirely electrically, the choice of wood is important. First, since the guitar must not warp, well seasoned, straight-grain, quarter-sawn timber is nearly as necessary for electric guitar bodies as it is for the sides, back and top of an acoustic guitar. The type of timber used will also have a slight but important effect on the sound of the guitar. While the pickups only amplify string vibration, the density and elasticity of the body material will affect the exact way the string vibrates. As a general rule, denser timber gives greater sustain, and more elastic timber gives a brighter sound. Hardwood is almost always chosen for solid-body guitars, the most widely used timbers being mahogany, maple, ash and poplar. Other hardwoods have been used from time to time—the original 1958 models of Gibson's Explorer and Flying V had korina-wood bodies— and some guitar bodies use a combination of timbers. Almost all Les Paul guitars are built with a 1.2cm maple top on two layers of mahogany, the maple top making an important contribution to the sound of the instrument. A few guitars use materials other than timber for the body— Ampeg's "Dan Armstrong" had an acrylic body, and Veleno uses aluminum—but these are rare exceptions.

The body construction is fairly straightforward. Sawn planks are glued together to make a sufficiently wide baulk of wood for the whole body and are sanded on both sides on a thicknessing sander, which reduces them to slightly oversize. The sanded baulks can then be cut to shape on a bandsaw, and the holes for controls drilled on a bench press. The shape of a solid-body electric guitar has almost no effect on the instrument's sound except insofar as the shape determines the amount of timber used and therefore the final body weight. Body shape is, however, important in determining the instrument's physical balance, feel, and visual appeal, and all of these factors have a major effect on its commercial success. As in all factory production, strict tolerances have to be precisely met at every stage of the body construction. The design of the manufacturing machinery and tooling setups is critical and good production engineering is as important as skilled craftsmanship.

Once the body has been sawn approximately to outline, it must be given its final profile, after which the slots for the neck housing and for the electrical components can be cut. These operations are usually carried out with the aid of

Smoothing down body blanks on a thicknessing sander before cutting them to shape. The economic resources of the large companies allow them to invest in massive machinery to carry out basic woodworking operations at high speed and with great accuracy.

Cutting a body blank to profile on a bandsaw. The body under construction in this sequence of photographs is for Gibson's limited edition reissue of the Explorer. At Gibson, the holes for controls are usually drilled at an early stage. The holes are then used to locate the body on the various formers and templates to which it is attached during machining.

371

Shaping the rough-sawn body blank on a router bench. The body is pegged to a guide template which ensures consistent accuracy of shape.

The body edges are beveled on a second router spindle, mounted on the same bench. The template used in shaping the body can be seen on the left.

high-speed routers, which cut the wood rapidly and leave a smooth finish. The location of the body cavities for the electrical components can affect the sound of the guitar, as well as the ease of component installation. Cavities in the wrong place, particularly if they are in the region of the bridge, can cause unwanted resonances and feedback.

The shaping of guitar bodies that have a contoured top (such as Gibson's Les Paul models) or back (such as the Fender Stratocaster) involves an additional process. Gibson carves the top surfaces of Les Paul guitars on an automatic machine in which a router is guided by a wheel that traces over a metal pattern. The pattern is shaped to the exact contour of the guitar top; the rise and fall of the guide wheel, as the pattern is passed back and forth beneath it on a moving table, is copied by the router which cuts the wood of the guitar body.

Most solid-body guitars are built without any edge binding. When bindings are used (purely for decoration) they are applied exactly as on an acoustic guitar. A narrow slot is cut round the top edge of the body on a router. White glue is applied to the slot, and plastic binding material is wrapped around. The body is then swathed in a cocoon of white cotton tape to hold the binding as the glue dries.

Finally, the guitar body is ready for fine sanding. At this stage it receives its final contour, and is smoothed off ready for finishing.

The construction of a thin-body semi-solid guitar is a

Cutting the slot for the controls.

Applying the body binding to a Les Paul guitar.

The automatic carving machine which shapes the top surfaces of Les Paul guitars two at a time. Gibson installed this machine to rough-carve the tops of its mandolins and f-hole guitars. The Les Paul solid-bodies were originally made with carved tops to make them more difficult for other manufacturers to copy.

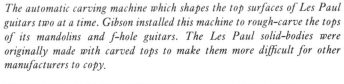

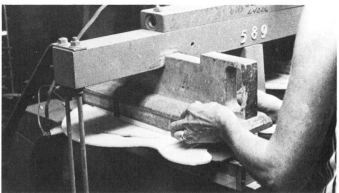

Smoothing down the body for a Gibson Explorer on a belt sander.

Gluing the center spruce brace to the underside of a thin-body semi-solid guitar top.

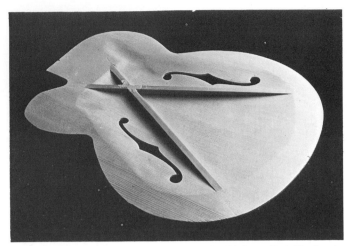

The underside of the carved top of Gibson's "Johnny Smith" electric-acoustic guitar. (Photograph by courtesy of Richard Schneider)

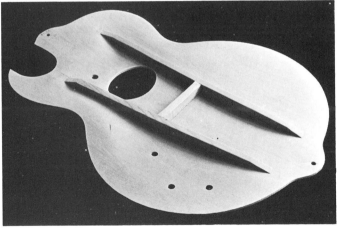

The underside of the laminated, arched maple top of Gibson's "Howard Roberts" electric-acoustic model. (Photograph by courtesy of Richard Schneider)

little more complicated than that of a solid-body. The aim of the thin-body guitar is to produce a sustain approaching that of the solid-body guitar, but with a slightly mellower sound.

The arched top and back are built of laminated maple, usually with three layers of veneer: it has been found that laminated tops and backs give as good a result as solid timbers for this type of guitar. The veneers are coated with glue, and placed over a former in a power-operated, heated press. Under heat and pressure, they take up the desired conformation.

When the glue has set, the top and back are taken out of the press, and a broad shallow spruce brace is glued down the center of each. The sides are immersed in a tank of very hot water until they are pliable, and then clamped to a heated former which molds them to the desired shape. The tight curves of the cutaways of semi-solid guitars make the side shaping a delicate operation which demands skill and care. Once the sides are shaped, they can be glued to the top and back, with linings to increase the gluing area and endblocks at neck and base.

During the body assembly, a solid core of maple is glued down the length of the center of the body, joining the spruce braces of top and back. It is this central core of hard, dense wood which gives the thin-body guitar its sustain. The mellowness comes from the presence of the air cavities in the wings, and from the spruce braces connecting top and back to the maple core.

The deep-body f-hole electric-acoustic guitar (or electric Spanish, as it is sometimes known) is now built only in small numbers. The body is constructed and assembled in essentially the same manner as that of the steel-string flat-top, with the exception of the front and back. On the most expensive f-hole electric-acoustics, the top is cut from a solid block of spruce. Both the outer and inner surfaces are carved to give the top a pronounced arch, and to graduate the thickness of the timber. Carved tops are normally thickest at the center, and thinned down toward the edge to combine strength with efficient vibrational characteristics. Gibson carries out the rough carving on its automatic machine, and finally shapes each top individually by hand. The bracing of arch-top guitars is much simpler than that of flat-top acoustic guitars, often consisting of no more than a simple X, or two parallel bars running lengthwise. The back is carved from a block of maple in the same way as the top, and strengthened with transverse braces.

An alternative method of constructing the front and back of an electric-acoustic guitar is to press-form both, usually from maple, as for a semi-solid-body guitar. This is a cheaper process but produces an instrument with a less sensitive acoustic response.

The pickups of an electric-acoustic guitar are traditionally mounted direct on to the top, with slots cut beneath them, and the tone and volume potentiometers and capacitances are mounted beneath the soundboard. However, any attachments to the guitar's top, or holes cut into it, will affect its acoustic performance. To overcome this, some models (such as Gibson's "Johnny Smith" and Guild's "Artist Award") are built with the pickup mounted on the end of the fingerboard, and the controls attached to the pickguard, so that there is no interference with the top's vibrational pattern. The f-holes of spruce-top models are normally bound, to prevent the penetration of moisture into the end grain of the timber.

The construction of the neck is one of the most sensitive areas of electric guitar manufacture. Neck material, profile, length, and method of attachment to the body, all affect the playability, physical balance, tone and sustain of the instrument. There are numerous combinations of neck material and design in current use, each of which has been developed to meet a particular musical requirement, and each of which demands slightly different constructional procedures.

Perhaps the single most important consideration in neck design is that the neck should not twist, warp or distort under the pull of the strings. Maple and mahogany are the two woods most commonly chosen for neck construction, and are preferred for their strength and stability. Sometimes a combination of the two is used, as in the Yamaha SG2000, whose neck consists of a sandwich with a maple center section and mahogany on each side. When the neck is made from one type of timber only, it can either be cut from a single piece or laminated from several. The problem of neck distortion on electric guitars has been increased in recent years by the tendency toward necks with thinner sections for faster playing action, which commonly join the body at around the eighteenth fret, and

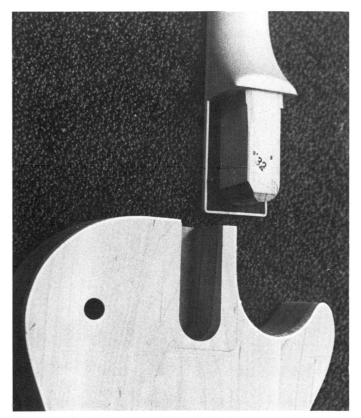

The neck-to-body junction on a Gibson Les Paul.

sometimes at the twentieth or beyond. To counteract the tendency of the strings to bow the neck, all modern electric guitar necks are fitted with an adjustable truss rod, running in a groove down the center.

There are three main methods of attaching the neck to the guitar body. The simplest procedure is to glue the neck directly into a corresponding slot in the body to form a strong, permanent joint. An alternative (used on all Fenders) is to bolt the neck in place, allowing adjustment of the neck angle. Finally, the neck pieces of some guitars (including the Yamaha SG2000, Gibson Firebird, and all Alembics) continue the whole length of the instrument, forming the center section of the body. The vibrational characteristics of the neck affect tone and sustain in the same way as do the characteristics of the body. Gibson, which has used all three methods, finds that each system has a different effect on the sound of the guitar.

The order in which the neck construction procedures are carried out varies from manufacturer to manufacturer, and to some extent is determined by the particular neck design. The essential steps, however, are common to all.

The process starts with rough neck blanks of maple or mahogany, which are sawn to their approximate shape on a bandsaw. The front surface of the neck and headstock is smoothed flat, and the slot for the truss rod is cut on a router. This is a precise operation, which is complicated by the design of many truss rods. Most, like the Gibson rod, require an arched rather than a straight groove. Normally, the slot for the truss rod is cut from the front face of the neck, and concealed by the fingerboard. On those Fender guitars that have no separate fingerboard, the frets being set straight into the top of the maple neck, the truss rod slot is routed from the back.

While many manufacturers wait until the neck has been brought closer to its final shape, Gibson inserts the truss rod as soon as the slot is cut. The rod is hammered down so that it fits tightly along the curve of the groove in the neck. A cover fillet is hammered into the slot on top of the rod, and glued in place. It is essential that the rod fit tightly and cause no buzzes or rattles.

The neck is now ready to receive its detailed shaping, and to have the fingerboard fitted. Some manufacturers fit the fingerboard blank while the neck is still in a very rough state. Others, such as Gibson, shape the neck and

Rough neck blanks for Gibson's reissue of the Explorer. It would be wasteful of timber to cut the exaggeratedly asymmetrical head of the Explorer from one piece of wood with the neck, so extra pieces of mahogany are laminated on for the head before the neck is shaped.

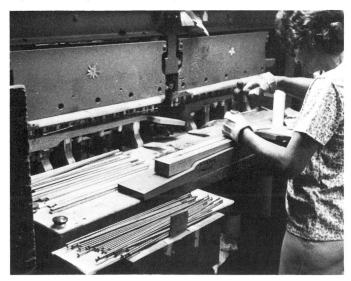

Fitting the truss rod.

fingerboard separately. The neck blank is usually shaped on a series of routers, which first trim it to width and then, using specially curved blades, shape the curve of the back of the neck. Gibson also uses an automatic copying machine to carve some heads and necks in a single operation.

Electric guitar fingerboards are most commonly rosewood, although the harder and more costly ebony is preferred for the most expensive models. Fender popularized the maple fingerboard, and several other manufacturers now use maple—often to complement the appearance of a natural-finish body.

The first step in building the fingerboard is to cut the blank to size, and to shape the arch of its top. The shaped blank can then either be glued to the neck or worked up on its own. If it is to be fitted with multiple edge bindings, the slots for the inner layers of binding will be cut before fretting operations are started.

The fret positions for an electric guitar are worked out on exactly the same principle, with the same formula, as is used for classical, flamenco and steel-string guitars. The large companies carry out the calculation by computer, printing out the intervals to perhaps six places of decimals.

The fret slots are cut in one operation on a multiple-bladed power-operated circular saw which has a separate blade for each fret position. The blades are positioned on the spindle in accordance with the computer printout, and ground to precisely the right width so that the tang of the fret wire will be firmly gripped by the slot.

Before the frets themselves are fitted, the fingerboard is drilled or routed to take the position markers. These are made of natural or synthetic mother-of-pearl, or of abalone on the most expensive guitars, and are cemented into place. Once the position markers are installed the fingerboard is ready for fretting. Pieces of fret wire are tapped into place in the slots, snipped to length, smoothed level, and beveled at each end. In keeping with the company's approach to automization, Gibson uses a machine to push all the frets home at once, and another to apply an absolutely uniform bevel.

Many electric guitar fingerboards are finished with a single edge binding of white plastic. This is applied after the frets have been installed and their ends filed to an even

Shaping the neck for a Gibson Firebird on a router. The Firebird's neck piece will be laminated into the body, and form its center section.

Routing out the fingerboard to take position markers.

Setting pearl inlay blocks into the fingerboard. The cement used is dark brown, to match the color of the rosewood.

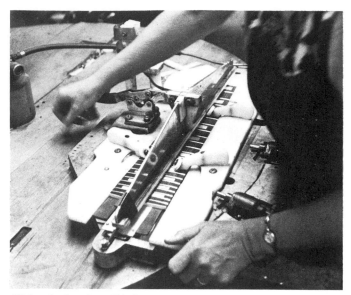

Gluing the fingerboard bindings.

Sanding down a neck assembly on a power sander.

bevel. The bindings are glued and clamped in place while the glue sets. They are aligned so that the plastic lips slightly over the end of each fret, to help keep the frets from lifting. When the glue is set, the fingerboard can be removed from the clamp and the binding filed and sanded flush with the fingerboard edges.

If fingerboard and neck have been constructed separately, the two may now be joined together, and the assembly prepared for finishing. The headstock veneer is glued in place, and the whole assembly smoothed and sanded. Both neck and body are now essentially ready for finishing. In the case of guitars with a permanent glue joint between neck and body, the joint is usually made before application of the finish. Guitars with detachable necks are finished in two parts.

On solid and semi-solid-body electrics, the finish is purely decorative and protective. On electric-acoustic guitars the finish can in theory have a marginal effect on the sound quality. Nitrocellulose lacquer, the most widely used finish, is suitable on all counts; acrylic lacquers (which are faster drying) are also becoming popular. Both types are applied with a spray gun.

Before any lacquer is applied, the fingerboard is masked off. The first coat to be applied is a sealer coat, after which the main finish, either clear, sunburst or solid color, is sprayed on layer by layer. Sunburst finishes are achieved by first spraying the body with a base color (usually a transparent yellow) and then building up the second sunburst shade over it. The sunburst shade is worked from the center toward the edge, giving a smooth gradation from the faintest tint to the full strength of the color. Once a

Gluing bound and fretted fingerboards to guitar necks.

sunburst has been applied, body spraying continues as for a clear-finish guitar with the application of six or seven coats of transparent lacquer. To speed up drying times, the guitars are dried in ovens between coats. To build up the gloss and ensure freedom from blemishes, the finish is given a light sanding between alternate coats.

The application of a solid-color finish is very similar, except in so far as the majority of the coats are of a colored rather than a clear lacquer. The final layers are clear, however, to give a depth to the shine.

When all the lacquer coats have been sprayed and are dry, the guitar is given its final polish on a power-operated machine fitted with a lambswool pad. This looks easy but is in fact a highly skilled operation. After polishing, the guitar is inspected for any blemishes, unevenness in the polish or ripples on the surface. It is now ready for the installation of the pickups and control circuitry, and the hardware of bridge, tailpiece and tuning machines.

The design and construction of the pickups, and the design of the control circuitry, is the most critical part of electric guitar manufacture. The electric components determine directly the output, distortion, tone quality and range of tones available on the guitar. Accordingly, great attention is now paid to the design and manufacture of pickups and controls, and the electronic engineer is one of the most important members of the guitar-building team. The design of pickups is a complex problem with a large number of variables. The configuration of the pickup, the shape of the coil, the gauge and number of turns of the winding, the type, size and degree of magnetization of the magnet will all affect the properties of the finished pickup. A good designer will be able to dream up a pickup to meet any one of a wide range of performance specifications. Indeed, modern electric guitar design has reached a point of sophistication where the problem is not so much to build a guitar to meet a particular performance specification as to determine what that specification should be. The ability to assess the market and players' requirements at a particular moment (which are largely swayed by musical fashions) has come to be as vital to the guitar manufacturer as skilled craftsmen and engineers. The variety of musicians' requirements has led to a great variety of design: the Gibson company currently produces about seventeen different pickup designs.

Buffing a lacquered guitar on a polishing machine fitted with a large lambswool pad.

The great variety of electromagnetic pickups built at present can be divided into two basic categories: single coil, and humbucking.

Single-coil pickups consist of a coil of lacquered copper wire wound on a bobbin, through which pass the pole piece(s), which may be either a single bar magnet, individual magnets one to a string, or one or more iron load pieces powered by a magnet beneath the coil. Pickups with individual pole pieces to each string are usually constructed in such a way that the pole pieces may be screwed up and down, either through the magnet or through the pickup's baseplate, to allow individual height adjustment in relation to the string.

SINGLE COIL PICKUPS

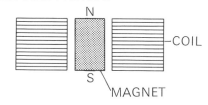

WITH DIRECT MAGNETS

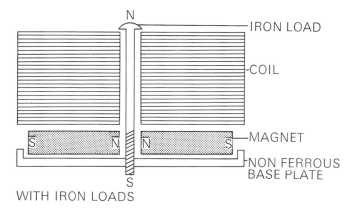

WITH IRON LOADS

Diagrammatic cross-section

Pickup magnets are made either of alnico (an alloy of iron, aluminum, nickel, copper and cobalt) or ceramic. There are sixteen types of alnico magnet and eight of ceramic, each with different properties. There is no single, simple reason for preferring one type of magnet to another:

each different sort of magnet has qualities which the designer can use to produce a pickup with a particular type of sound. In general, though, the two magnet properties in which the designer is most interested are the flux and the demagnetizing force. Alnico magnets offer higher flux ratings than their ceramic equivalents, but correspondingly lower demagnetizing force values.

The type, shape and size of the magnet, and the degree to which it has been magnetized will determine the field it produces; the coil must also be designed to match the characteristics of the magnet field.

In essence, the greater the number of turns on the coil, and the finer the wire, the easier it is to obtain a high output. However, the number of turns and gauge of the wire will affect the tone as well as the volume which the pickup can produce. Increasing the number of turns and decreasing the wire gauge both increase the impedance of the pickup, and the higher the impedance, the less the sensitivity to high-frequency signals. Additionally, increasing the power of the pickup beyond a certain point usually results in some tonal distortion.

Humbucking pickups come in many configurations, but they all have two coils and two sets of pole pieces. The coils are wired in series but out of phase, so that any radio frequency hum is canceled out between the two coils. The pole pieces have opposite magnetic polarities, so that the signals from the strings are not canceled.

BASIC HUMBUCKING CONFIGURATION

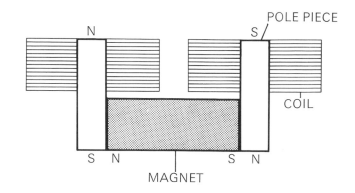

Whereas single-coil pickups detect the vibrations of the strings at just one point, standard humbuckers respond to the strings at two points. As a result, those very high harmonics which have a wave form with opposite phasing above the two pole pieces of the pickup are canceled out. Humbucking pickups which eliminate some of the high-frequency components of every note thus have a mellower tone than single-coil pickups. The tendency of humbuckers to mellowness is further increased by their high impedance, which results from the linking of two coils.

Numerous variations have been produced on the humbucking theme, most of them designed to produce a hum-canceling pickup with a single-coil pickup's high-frequency response.

Gibson's "superhumbucking" pickup has individual pole pieces and three high-power ceramic magnets (in place of the single magnet of the standard humbucker). The increased strength of the magnetic field makes it possible to construct a pickup with high output but fewer turns of wire than would be needed on a standard humbucker. This allows a lower impedance for a given output (and thus a better high-frequency response), or alternatively a larger output.

CENTER-WEIGHTED HUMBUCKING CONFIGURATIONS

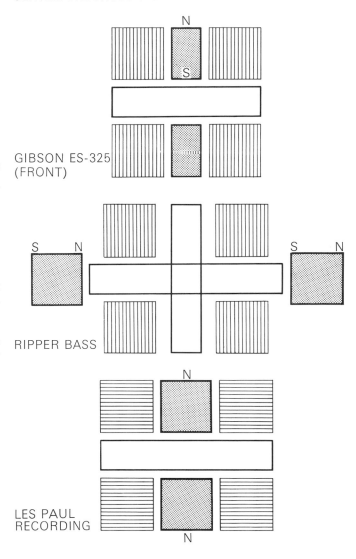

GIBSON ES-325 (FRONT)

RIPPER BASS

LES PAUL RECORDING

SUPERHUMBUCKING CONFIGURATION

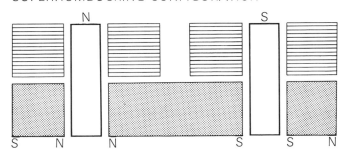

There are other humbucking configurations in which the pickup is "center-weighted," so that it is sensitive to the string vibrations at only one point. This can be achieved by turning the coils on their side, or by placing one coil above the other.

The center-weighted humbuckers on the Les Paul Recording and Signature guitars, which effectively pick up string vibration at a single point, are unusual in having a much lower impedance than most other pickups. Low-impedance pickups have a reduced output, but they have the advantage of being directly compatible with the modern recording studio console. The output from a low-impedance pickup can be plugged in directly to the console without going through an amplifier. Some amplifiers, indeed, cannot handle a low-impedance input.

Just as it is possible to build center-weighted humbuckers, it is possible to wire single-coil pickups

Winding pickups. Both of the two machines seen here can wind six pickup coils at a time. The plastic bobbins on which the coils are wound are held by the machine and rotated at high speed, the fine insulated copper wire being drawn out from the reels contained in the clear plastic drums. For a humbucking pickup to be effectively hum-canceling, the coils must be perfectly matched with exactly the same number of turns, wound at the same tension and distributed in the same way on the bobbins.

Assembling pickup components.

together in pairs so that they are hum-canceling. Gibson uses this technique on the S-1 model, and Alembic wires its single-coil low-impedance pickups to a dummy hum-canceling pickup mounted in the guitar body. The result in both cases is a combination of the humbucker's quietness with the single-coil pickup's brightness.

The actual construction of a pickup is a more straight-forward procedure than its design. The coil is wound by an automatic machine, which applies the desired number of turns at controlled tension. The tightness of the winding is important, since it determines how closely the wire packs to the pole pieces and thus how it lies in relation to the magnetic field, which affects output.

What happens after the coil is wound depends very much on the design of the pickup, but in all cases the magnets, pole pieces (if they are separate) and coil are married together; humbucking pickups are made essentially as two separate pickups, which are then wired together and placed in a single cover. Many pickups are assembled on a non-magnetic metal baseplate, which helps to shield the pickup against hum and provides convenient soldering points for connections to the pickup.

In the last few years, several of the leading manufacturers, including Gibson and Rickenbacker, have taken to encapsulating some of their pickups in epoxy resin. The resin used is extremely long-lasting, electrically non-conductive, and highly resistant to chemicals and moisture. The greatest advantage of encapsulating pickups is that the resin holds the coil, magnet and pole pieces rigidly together, so that none of the pickup components can vibrate. This eliminates any microphonic tendencies in the pickup, whereby vibrating components cause unwanted distortions in the sound. Other methods of counteracting microphonic pickup behavior are available: Fender pickup coils are dipped in wax, and Alembic uses pickup wire with an alcohol-soluble covering which allows the turns to be solvent-welded together.

Most pickups are protected by a metal or plastic cover (on some epoxy-encapsulated pickups, the encapsulation itself acts as the cover). Pickup covers are designed simply to protect the unit from damage and, in the case of metal covers, to provide some shielding. They have, however, entered into the myth and folklore of the electric guitar, and some players insist on removing pickup covers.

Plastic covers can, of course, have no effect on the electrical performance of the unit. The material used for metal pickup covers must be non-magnetic so as not to interfere with the pickup's field, and should be as thin as possible. In theory metal pickup covers cut off some high-frequency signals, but the loss is too slight to be noticeable with standard amplification. The sound difference caused by the removal of metal pickup covers can only be detected if the guitarist is using special high-frequency cabinets and amplifiers.

While the pickups are normally made by the guitar company itself, the other components of the circuitry are standard capacitors and potentiometers, and are bought off the shelf. All the guitar builder has to do is to wire them up and install them in the body.

Most capacitors used in tone controls have a value of 0.02 microfarads, except for those in bass guitars which have much higher values. The potentiometers used for regulating tone and volume are normally either "linear-taper" or "audio-taper." A linear-taper potentiometer changes resistance at the same rate over the whole range of values through which it operates. This means that when a linear-taper potentiometer is used as the volume control,

Connecting switches, pickups and control components into preassembled units ready for installation into guitar bodies.

Pickguards for Gibson S-1s, with the pickups and all control circuitry preassembled, ready for screwing down to the guitar body.

Rear view of a Les Paul guitar with the cover plates removed to show the pickup selector switch, and the tone and volume controls.

Fitting the rear pickup of a Gibson ES-335 thin-body guitar. Like most semi-solid guitars, the ES-335 is fitted with a trapeze tailpiece.

the power output varies evenly as the knob is turned. However, our perception of loudness does not follow a simple straight line graph, and the volume does not appear to change smoothly. On many guitars with linear-taper controls, the whole change obtainable in tone or volume sounds as if it happens over only a third of the available rotation of the control. Audio-taper potentiometers are designed to overcome this problem, and to give an output which *sounds* as if it varies evenly over the whole range of the control.

The values of the potentiometers, and their taper, are determined largely by the pickup—although the range of values which will work satisfactorily is very wide. Gibson, for example, used to fit 500K ohm potentiometers as tone and volume controls for use with humbucking and superhumbucking pickups, but has now decided that 300K linear volume controls and 100K extreme audio taper tone controls actually give the best possible result.

The installation procedure for the electrics depends very much on the individual guitar design. Sometimes, when connecting leads have to be threaded through holes drilled in the guitar body, components have to be installed and connected individually. Other times, they can be preassembled into a self-contained unit, and some electric guitars (such as Gibson's S-1) are designed so that the pickups and controls, switches and jack socket can all be mounted on the pickguard which is screwed on to the body.

The actual method of mounting the pickup is important: movement can result in a distortion of the guitar's sound. Most designs allow the height, and sometimes the tilt, of the whole unit to be altered via the adjustable screws with which the pickup is attached. Height adjustment can be particularly useful on humbucking pickups: by lowering the pickup down into the body, and raising one set of pole pieces, it is possible to produce a sound closer to that of a single-point pickup, as one set of pole pieces becomes less effective.

The bridge, tailpiece and tuning machines are usually attached after the electrics are fitted. Deep-body electric-acoustic guitars have bridges like those on any arch-top guitar, with two adjustable feet to set the height and a non-adjustable saddle. The traditional design has been kept because, although the guitar is amplified, its acoustic performance is still important, and the bridge must be designed according to acoustic principles. On solid and semi-solid-body guitars, the bridge does not have to be designed faithfully to transfer vibration to the body and a different set of design criteria operates. Indeed, a heavy bridge is often a positive advantage: the heavier the bridge, the less string vibration energy is transferred to it, and the longer the sustain. Many electric guitars are therefore fitted with complex metal bridges, with individual adjustable saddles for each string. The most important adjustment on the saddle is for compensation, to allow correct intonation whatever type of string is fitted. The many different types of electric guitar string have widely varying tensions and weights, and require correspondingly different compensation at the bridge. Accurate compensation is particularly important to rock guitarists, who frequently play at positions around the twentieth fret; errors in the saddle placing become increasingly noticeable in the higher positions.

The adjustment of each saddle for intonation is achieved by mounting it on a screw, so that it can be screwed back and forth in relation to the bridge. On some guitars each saddle is individually adjustable for height. More commonly, the whole bridge unit itself is adjustable by screws at each end.

It has become standard practice in electric guitar construction to restrict the bridge's function solely to defining the vibrating length of the strings and the height of the action. The strings are actually stopped separately, either by a tailpiece or by passing them through the guitar body from the back, where eyelets restrain the toggles on the string ends.

Most solid-body guitars are fitted with a stop tailpiece, which consists essentially of a solid metal bar drilled out to take the strings and is attached to the guitar body by heavy screws at each end. Many stop tailpieces are adjustable for height, since the angle formed by the strings as they pass over the bridge to the tailpiece controls the tension of the strings between the bridge and tailpiece. This tension in turn affects the guitar's playing action and tone.

An alternative to the stop-type tailpiece is the trapeze tailpiece, which is attached to the base of the guitar. Trapeze tailpieces are usually only fitted to arch-top and semi-solid-body electrics. In general, trapeze tailpieces do not give as long a sustain as stop tailpieces. This is because

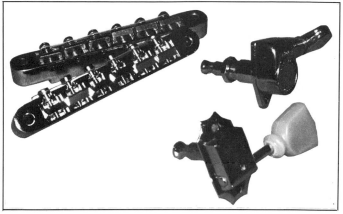

Gibson tune-o-matic adjustable bridges, Gibson and Grover Rotomatic machine heads. The Gibson machines are made for the company by Kluson.

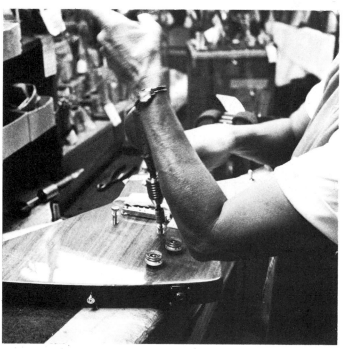

Installing the fixing screws for a stop tailpiece.

385

Setting up a Gibson Explorer and checking the level of the frets before final inspection and despatch.

of their slight flexibility, which allows them to absorb some string energy, and because they do not pull the strings down so hard on top of the bridge.

The hardware components are not usually made by the guitar manufacturing companies themselves, but are produced to their specifications by specialist metalwork sub-contractors. Bridges and tailpieces are designed so that they can be supplied as self-contained sub-assemblies which can be simply and quickly screwed into place on the almost completed guitar.

Electric guitars are fitted, like most steel-string acoustic guitars, with individual tuning machines for each string. These too are designed for easy installation. Two of the most highly regarded machine heads, renowned for their smoothness, are the Grover Rotomatic and the Schaller. The cases of each of these are completely sealed, and filled with lubricant. The lubricated inner face of the case serves as a bearing surface for the main gear, carried on the spindle which takes the string. The units are installed by slipping the spindle through a hole drilled in the headstock, and screwing down a retaining bush on to it from the front. There is a single small retaining screw at the rear of the unit, which prevents it from slipping.

Simpler and more conventional individual machines are also widely used. On these, the metal cover is there for no more than protection, and does not contain a permanent reservoir of lubricant. Units are usually fixed to the rear of the headstock with two screws, and a press-fitting bush is fitted to the hole in the headstock to provide a permanent bearing surface for the spindle.

Once all the electric components and hardware have been fitted, the guitar is ready to be set up, adjusted and inspected. The frets receive their final filing, to make sure there are no high or low spots, the bridge saddles are adjusted, and the guitar is thoroughly tested for intonation, buzzes or rattles at every fret. After a final polish to remove any dust or fingermarks, it is now ready for packing and despatch.

Les Paul guitars on the production line at Gibson's new Nashville factory.

MUSIC AND PLAYERS

Pee Wee King and his Golden West Cowboys with singer San Antonio Rose in the early 1940s. As leader of the first full-time professional band on the Grand Ole Opry, Pee Wee King was one of the men responsible for spreading the dance music known as western swing.
The guitar in the center foreground is a Rickenbacker double-neck steel guitar; to the right is a Gibson Super 400 (acoustic) from the second half of the 1930s, fitted with a Rowe-De Armond pickup.

The birth of a new sound

Experiments in the electric amplification of guitars have been carried out from the early 1920s, since when it has become the dominant instrument in popular music. However, neither musicians nor the general public were ready for the electric instruments when they first appeared; their musical origins were humble, and the initial spread of their popularity slow. It was not until the early 1930s that the first electric guitars were put on the market. These were Hawaiian guitars, which in their natural state had become tremendously popular during the 1920s in American dance bands. To amplify them was a logical development, for the instrument had been considerably restricted by its small voice. Nonetheless, the first electric guitars were not manufactured in large quantities and many professional musicians made their own. The first "electric guitar" recording was made on a converted acoustic in January of 1935 when Bob Dunn of the "western swing" band Milton Brown and his Musical Brownies adapted his Martin for Hawaiian playing, fitted ferrous-based strings and attached a pickup connected to an amplifier. Once amplified, the instrument became the central voice for jazz-influenced solo breaks featured by such popular bands as Milton Brown's, Bob Wills and His Texas Playboys, and Pee Wee King and his Golden West Cowboys.

In the mid-1930s the electric-acoustic guitar (essentially an amplified f-hole guitar) began to come on the market. Initially its spread was slow, limited by lack of demand. There seemed little call for an amplified instrument either in white country music or in the blues. In both these musics, the acoustic guitar was the ideal accompaniment to the human voice, and was not called on to compete with any particularly loud instruments. But the craze for dance music created a proper setting for the use of the electric guitar. The new dance music was played not at rural hoedowns or country suppers but in the bars and taverns of rapidly growing towns, where the raucous atmosphere of voices, laughter and the chink of glasses effectively drowned out acoustic instruments. One of the most popular brands of dance music which had developed from an older tradition was "honky tonk," which relied for much of its rollicking effect on the use of the electric guitar. But "honky tonk" remained relatively unsophisticated, and it was among jazz musicians that the electric guitar found its first great role.

The potential of the acoustic guitar as a solo jazz instrument had been demonstrated by a handful of players as early as the 1920s, but again its relatively low volume restricted it to small groups. To compete in the larger bands popular in the 1930s the guitar had to be amplified, and one of the first known players was Eddie Durham, trombonist, arranger and guitarist with Count Basie's band. But it was the young Charlie Christian who, playing with the enormously popular Benny Goodman band, first brought the instrument to a mass audience.

Charlie Christian was born in Dallas in 1919 and brought up in Oklahoma City, a place where many jazz bands had started. He learned the guitar very young, and by his late teens was playing around the Southwest, starting as a bass player with Alphonso Trent in 1934 and then playing bass and guitar in his brother Eddie's band. In 1939 John Hammond Sr. tried to persuade Benny Goodman to give Christian an audition. Though horrified by the sight of him in pointed yellow shoes, bright green suit with purple shirt and string bow tie, the whole topped off with a ten-gallon hat, Goodman finally agreed to listen. Christian's genius was immediately apparent and he was hired at once. For the next few years his arrangements for the band and his own guitar playing within the group helped produce the successful Benny Goodman sound.

In 1940 and 1941 the band played in the East, and while in New York, Charlie Christian got into the habit of dropping into Minton's club in Harlem. He would jam for hours after the club was shut to customers with any other musician who was there at the time. At these sessions, Christian's improvisations were an inspiration to the other young jazz musicians who joined him, including Dizzy Gillespie, Thelonious Monk, and Charley Parker, creators

Charlie Christian with Benny Goodman, 1940.

of the bebop and modern jazz sound of the 1940s.

Fortunately Charlie Christian was well recorded, for in the summer of 1941 a severe attack of tuberculosis put him into hospital, and he died on March 2, 1942 at the age of 23.

Christian displayed an inventiveness of melody and harmony unique among electric guitarists. He used the sustain and tonal properties of the instrument to produce clear ringing lines perfectly set off by the big band backing. The single-note runs which he played came as a revelation to guitarists brought up on the chordal sound of the big band rhythm section. His approach has been imitated on countless occasions since then, but never surpassed. Having played an electric guitar throughout his professional career, he had a complete understanding of the amplified instrument, and had the delicacy of touch necessary to bring out its qualities.

Christian's playing was of enormous importance to both his own contemporaries and succeeding generations of guitarists. The reaction of Tal Farlow was a typical one: "As soon as I heard Charlie Christian I knew there was more to music than I thought."[1] In the early 1940s guitarists such as George Barnes, Billy Bauer, Herb Ellis and Les Paul were all helping to consolidate the electric guitar's position as an essential jazz instrument, building on the foundations Christian had laid.

Electrification increased the guitar's effectiveness in its supporting as well as its solo role within an ensemble. In the jazz guitar's function of feeding chords for other soloists to improvise on, a single electric guitar was more subtle and flexible than a multi-instrument rhythm section. This flexibility became increasingly important with the development in the 1940s of bebop. The complex improvisatory music played in small groups placed different demands on the guitarist. He had to display a new inventiveness in the free-form exchange of musical ideas. At the same time, the small group format gave the guitarist new opportunities to develop an individual style. The trio pattern of bass, guitar and piano was first set by the popular Nat King Cole. Then groups led by George Shearing and Red Norvo pushed the electric guitarist into the spotlight as a soloist.

Tal Farlow, who "came on the scene poppin' and burnin,'"[2] as Wes Montgomery put it, joined the vibes player Red Norvo in 1949. He found that he had to speed up his playing to keep pace with Norvo's lightning-fast swing and bebop lines. The facility that Farlow developed astounded other guitarists, and enabled him to execute his famous solos in artificial harmonics at fantastic speed. As Howard Roberts remarked, "Tal represents an epoch milestone in improvising on the electric guitar. He set a new pace for what became a style that now permeates the entire field of electric guitar playing."[3] The Oscar Peterson Trio provided another testing ground for young players. Starting with Irving Ashby, then with Barney Kessel and later Herb Ellis, Oscar Peterson's demands on the guitar player to keep up with his pianistic pyrotechnics was very important in expanding their rhythmic and harmonic horizons.

In the company of other superb jazz players who were masters of their own instruments, many guitarists concentrated mainly on the development of technical skill at the expense of musical ideas. One player, however, who progressed beyond thinking solely of technique was Barney Kessel. After leaving Oscar Peterson he made a number of records within the trio format. He explained at the time his concept of the guitarist's function:

Tal Farlow.

PHOTOGRAPH BY PHIL LINDSAY, COURTESY OF CONCORD JAZZ INC

In small groups today, the amplified guitar is hardly ever used as a rhythm instrument. It's used either to supplement the function of the piano, or to work sometimes instead of the piano, serving as the harmonic basis. Or it's used as an improvised voice in solos. With some guitarists there is a tendency to identify themselves, as far as improvising goes, mainly with what has been created on their own instrument. But I think once you are improvising, being the prominent solo voice, then it's a matter of having a particular idea, or something to say which is within you, and then whatever instrument you play becomes your vehicle for expression. All such things as basic techniques, what picking you use, what fingering you use, these are all means to an end. . . .[4]

During the 1950s several other innovative jazz guitarists were taking the instrument in new directions and finding new audiences. In 1952 Johnny Smith had a hit with his record of "Moonlight in Vermont," made while he was working as resident guitarist for NBC in New York. This brought a wide popular following for his cool and clear style in which chordal and melodic passages were fluently interwoven with the greatest skill. Billy Bauer was striking out in a different direction, playing free-form music first with the avant-garde pianist Lennie Tristano and then with alto sax player Lee Konitz. Later in the decade Wes Montgomery became immensely popular. When his records first appeared, his ability for using octaves to round out lines, contrasting them with single-note runs and mellow chords, had an amazing impact on musicians, critics and the public alike.

In the first epoch of the electric guitar, it was jazz musicians who were the real virtuosi on the instrument and who produced its most interesting music. Moreover they were playing to a large audience who appreciated the skilled technique and complex music of the players. As pioneers of a new sound, jazz guitarists had some of their best years in the 1940s and early 50s.

The social and economic changes brought about by the Second World War had an enormous effect on the blues and on white country music. Before the war both had been largely regional, developing different styles in different areas and reaching mainly local audiences. But huge shifts of population, brought about first by the demands that war made on heavy industry and second by conscription, destroyed this isolation. The move from a rural to an urban environment exposed music to new and diverse influences, and musical styles were modified accordingly.

The urban blues that developed after the war drew its inspiration from a variety of musical strands. From the popular prewar Kansas City jazz bands came a shouting, confident vocal style and a widespread use of the tenor saxophone as solo instrument. The boogie-woogie rhythms of the Texas bluesmen, derived from the barrelhouse piano players, were adopted to give a heavy pumping dance beat. And the electric guitar was almost universally adopted. From the beginning the instrument had essentially been an urban one, well suited to the clubs, dance halls and bars of the big cities. The urban audience wanted a music whose style suited the more sophisticated, faster moving life of the cities. In place of the solo singer, accompanying himself on an acoustic guitar, came small groups consisting of tenor saxophone, electric guitars, and the occasional harmonica and drums. The demands of playing with other instruments, and adapting to the styles of other players, brought about an evolution of the music.

The first notable electric blues guitarist was T-Bone Walker. Born in Texas in 1913, he went to the West coast in 1934, recording under the name Oak-Cliff T-Bone and

T-Bone Walker.

accompanying the classic female blues singers Ma Rainey and Ida Cox. By the early 1940s he was leading his own group of piano, bass and drums, to which he later added tenor sax and occasionally a trumpet. His guitar playing was exciting and fluent, using the instrument in a way that made the most of its strong clear sound and powers of sustain. He had much the same effect on bluesmen that Charlie Christian had on jazz players, although his technique of using the volume control extensively with the bending and finger vibrato of the country blues player gave his music an earthy feel quite different from the clear horn-like sound of the jazz players.

Walker's influence was enormous, as Little Milton later described:

> T-Bone, now there's a cat. T-Bone Walker inspired me and a lot more guitar players and singers because that cat always played clean. He would like pick one string at a time and most of the other guitar players in those days would like frail it and make chords.[5]

391

King Biscuit Time—a radio show from Helena, Arkansas—broadcast the blues to a black audience in the late 1940s. Two of the original contributors, Sonny Boy Williamson and James Peck Curtis, were still playing on the show thirty years later. With them here is Houston Stackhouse, one of the older musicians from Jackson, Mississippi.

Walker was a showman too, one of a long line which stretches from the older bluesmen to Buddy Guy, Hendrix and others: he would often play the guitar between his legs, and over his head.

Memphis and Chicago remained the most important centers for urban blues players after the war. The migration of blacks to the Northern cities intensified during the 1940s due to the demands of war and the increased mechanization of cotton farming which took the jobs of many farmworkers. This was a different type of migration from that of earlier decades, when the Northern cities were looked on as places to make a little money to take back home. Now whole families were moving, leaving no ties, and many of the younger blacks were changing their pattern of life for good.

After the war, the larger population and prosperity of the cities made them attractive for musicians who could find work in the clubs, and sometimes as disc jockeys on radio programs which were beaming music almost continuously to their vast audiences. The demand for new records led to the establishment of small independent labels on the lookout for new talent in the cities. In Memphis, which had one of the most active radio stations, WDIA, Ike Turner was employed to find new bluesmen for the Bihari Brothers' labels RPM and Modern (based on the West coast) and for the Chess brothers, who had the strongest hold over the recording industry in Chicago.

Many of the older generation of bluesmen who came to the cities to earn a living by their music began in Chicago. In the black areas clubs such as Key Largo, Sylvio's, Smitty's Corner and Pepper's Lounge offered different blues groups. Their audiences came mainly from Mississippi and appreciated rougher "down-home" blues. The young Muddy Waters arrived in the city in the late 1940s with the sounds of the older Mississippi bluesmen in his ears. He had been brought up on the music of Son House, Charley Patton and Robert Johnson and had molded his style on theirs. But he had to modify this in the new environment, for "I was playing in the clubs then. And you can't hear an acoustic in a liquor club. There's just too much noise."[6] By the early 1950s Waters' band—consisting of himself on electric slide with Pat Hare playing second guitar, bass, drums, harmonica and piano—dominated the Chicago blues scene. He played a

COURTESY OF PAUL OLIVER

Muddy Waters with Pat Hare as second guitarist and James Cotton broadcasting from a club on Chicago's WOPA radio station. Waters is playing a Telecaster, Hare has a 1952 Style Les Paul (Gold Top).

Elmore James.

Arthur "Big Boy" Crudup. His rougher style of country blues became less popular in the 1950s and despite having been on the King Biscuit Time show and tours with Elmore James and Sonny Boy Williamson, he retired from singing and playing in the 1960s. His rediscovery in 1967 led to several recordings and appearances at festivals.

COURTESY OF BLUES UNLIMITED

COURTESY OF PAUL OLIVER

heavily, rhythmic music as a backing for his harsh Mississippi style of singing. At around this time, Waters' great rival Howlin' Wolf arrived in Chicago. Wolf was probably the most primitive of all the older bluesmen: he had an unsophisticated guitar style and a fierce voice, and an incredible stage presence. Elmore James and his Broomdusters were another of the bands who offered an older blues style. James, born in Durant, Mississippi in 1918, was a tremendously exciting guitar player. His dashing technique was based on whining bottleneck and strong walking basses taken from Robert Johnson, who also provided James with some of his material. When applied to the electric guitar, the bottleneck technique gave a tremendous punch and drive to the music.

Memphis, being the first important stop out of Mississippi, had experienced a wider variety of musical styles before the war. Tastes had been formed by the jug bands and the medicine shows which had brought both black and white musicians with them. Post-war Memphis blues shared some of this diversity. It achieved a synthesis between the agressive sound of Chicago blues and a more sophisticated style exemplified in the playing of T-Bone Walker.

Of the Memphis electric guitarists, the most influential player immediately after the war was B. B. King. Born in Itta Bena, Mississippi in September 1925, he had begun playing three-chord accompaniment to spirituals, and it was only later when he met Robert Jr. Lockwood and Sonny Boy Williamson, that he began to consider playing blues. He had listened to the great players like Blind Lemon Jefferson and Bukka White (King's cousin), but also had high admiration for T-Bone Walker, Elmore James, Lonnie Johnson and Django Reinhardt. The single-note runs of the jazz guitar and the emphasis he placed on melody and harmony gave him a cleaner style than most blues players which in the early 1950s earned him a large following in the black audience.

King went to Memphis in 1947, met Bukka White and got a job as a disc jockey on the radio station WDIA. At first he was named the Beale Street Boy, but this was changed to Blues Boy King and the name has stuck ever since. He began recording in 1949 and a year later his "Three O'Clock Blues" got to the top of the national rhythm and blues charts. But even so, for some years his life was the life of most black artists of that period: one long round of touring, often to small towns and crummy joints.

The electric guitar became established in white country music in the same period as it came to dominate the blues. In the late 1940s, the music was changing: it seemed that the days of old-time string bands and family groups, singing traditional songs and accompanying themselves on unamplified instruments, had gone forever. Now the radio shows and stage acts were presenting more and more music from the Southwest which had a greater jazz influence. After the constraints of the war years, people wanted to hear the danceable rhythms of the honky tonk singers and western swing bands with their electric instruments. The style was spread by singers such as Ernest Tubb, Al Dexter, Rex Griffin, Floyd Tillman and Merle Travis. Travis, the most popular singer, developed from traditional country sources a complex finger-picking

FROM THE COLLECTION OF JULIUS BELLSON

A page from an early 1950s Gibson catalogue.

style which he transferred to the electric guitar. In 1947 he and Paul Bigsby designed a solid-body guitar (see page 345), and the seal of approval was finally set on the use of electric instruments in white country music. Soon even "Little" Jimmy Dickens, proclaiming himself a simple mountain boy and wearing wildly flamboyant cowboy dress, could sing with a loud electric backing.

By the early 1950s the electric guitar sounded as if it belonged naturally in all forms of American popular music. Indeed, for most of the decade, the acoustic guitar seemed an anachronism, part of a tradition of music making which had become lost in the increasing commercialism of the entertainment industry.

Many people were involved in developing the electric guitar, but one man, Les Paul, is particularly important in its history. He developed new instruments (see page 348)

Les Paul and Mary Ford, with the SG-shaped Gibson Les Paul guitar of 1960–61.

COURTESY OF NORLIN INC.

and was one of the first to see the potential of electric sound and the natural association of the electric guitar with electric recording methods.

As early as 1937 Les Paul had begun experimenting with multiple recording techniques. Unable to find a bass or rhythm guitar player willing to record with him at odd hours of the day or night, he devised a system of setting down each part himself on a single-track tape. But it was not until 1946 that he began to think about the commercial possibilities of multiple recording. Together with a friend he built a studio in his garage, using a Cadillac flywheel as a recording lathe. There the Andrews Sisters, Pee Wee Hunt, Kay Starr, Jo Stafford and W. C. Fields—with Paul playing guitar in the background—were recorded. He continued his experiments in the late 1940s and early 1950s. In 1951 he and his wife Mary Ford—who, as Coleen Summers, had been singing with Gene Autry—recorded their first huge hit: "How High the Moon." Les Paul later described the setup:

. . . we had eleven parts down and Mary is singing her last part and I'm playing my last guitar part, and a plane goes over, back to number one. The second time a guy knocks at the door, bringing a wire. . . . Anyway, here we are recording, and we've got to get a tight sound with Mary's vocal. So I've got the mike very close because you didn't want the noise of the machine, plus the people upstairs complained. So Mary's doing an oddball part that only sells in Arabia, singing ooh, aah, and I'm clanking on a piece of wood, they think I'm killing her. So I put a blanket over Mary and she's got earphones on under this blanket and this is how we made "How High the Moon" and others.[7]

The record hit the charts and in March 1951 became number one. It finally sold over one and a half million copies. From 1952 to the end of the decade, Les Paul and Mary Ford were hugely popular. They sold millions of records and had their own television show. On many of his records, Paul tried new techniques: using tape speeded up and slowed down, repeat echo and any trick he could dream up. One of the most important of his ideas was for an eight-track tape machine, and he persuaded Ampex to make one, a project which took them two years.

A Capitol engineer said of Les Paul in 1954: "He gets

an impossible musical idea, and then invents the mechanical means for carrying it out."[8] The kind of manipulated sound which he was exploring, which depended so much on the electric guitar, was not fully exploited until the rock era and then it was taken, less consciously, in other directions. But this was not to happen for another decade.

Les Paul and Mary Ford, c. 1951.

Bill Haley.

Rock 'n' roll—"Hey! That's our music. . . ."
Around the early fifties the musical world was starved for something new . . . the days of the solo vocalist and the big bands had gone. About the only thing in fact that was making any noise was progressive jazz, but this was just above the heads of the average listener. . . . I felt then that if I could take, say, a Dixieland tune and drop the first and third beats, and accentuate the second and fourth, and add a beat the listeners could clap to as well as dance, this would be what they were after.[1]

The rock 'n' roll boom created a revolution in the structure of the music industry. Up to 1954 the industry was divided into three main sections, each aimed at a specific audience and with a distinctive style and character: popular, country and western and rhythm and blues. Musical taste was changing however, and listening habits were not as rigidly fixed as the music industry imagined. Crossovers, the process whereby a record made for one market does well in another, had become increasingly common. This had happened with country music after the war and up to the early 1950s, and then, as everyone went boogie-mad, black music took on a new popularity. More and more young people were tuning in to the black stations and a few astute people in the music business began to realize the commercial potential of a new kind of music. One of these was Sam Phillips, a young recording engineer in Memphis who started the Sun label. His secretary said later that "Over and over again I remember Sam saying 'If I could find a white man who had the Negro sound, the Negro feel, I could make a billion dollars.'"[2]

Rock 'n' roll was intimately tied up with the emergence of a youth culture after the Second World War. The loosening of social attitudes and increasing prosperity had helped create a young audience who cared little for the goals and aspirations of their parents; they were looking for their own social and cultural expressions, and had sufficient economic independence to pay for them. Rock 'n' roll epitomized to many the feelings and attitudes of this restless generation: it was noisy, often aggressive and brash, and appeared vulgar to those brought up on the romantic songs of Perry Como or Nat King Cole. The success with a young audience of Bill Haley's "Rock Around the Clock," used as the music for *The Blackboard Jungle* confirmed the connection. Bob Dylan shouted on first hearing it: "Hey! that's our music. . . . That was written for us."[3]

Rock 'n' roll borrowed its instrumental lineup from urban blues. As its popularity grew, so the instrument most associated with it, the electric guitar, became a symbol of youth. From now on the fortunes of the electric guitar were intermingled with those of popular music and the music industry as a whole.

It was the astute Bill Haley and his Comets who initially defined the new sound. Originally a country group calling themselves the Saddlemen, they took their new title in 1953 and began recording such early successes as "Crazy, Man, Crazy," "Shake, Rattle and Roll" and "Rock Around the Clock." Bill Haley's music was exciting: his shouting vocal style, heavy four-to-the-bar dance beat, and distinctive guitar breaks were a skillful combination of familiar elements, but the style appeared fresh and new.

Haley and his sidemen were professional musicians who had a shrewd idea of what would be popular. His lead guitarist for many years, Frank Beecher, came from a jazz background, having played with Buddy Greco and Benny Goodman. But he found himself in difficulties when faced with the peculiar demands of rock 'n' roll:

> At the first recording session we came to an ad lib guitar solo, and I started playing with a jazz feel. I played the first four bars, and everything came to a halt. Haley said he'd never sell any records if I played like that. I had to stick to major scales. No flatted fifths or anything like that.[4]

Bill Haley set the style, but it was Elvis Presley who captured the greatest audience. Presley came from a background of white country music, but had had contact with gospel and blues:

> I'd play [guitar] along with the radio or phonograph, and taught myself the chord positions. We were a religious family, going round together to sing at camp meetings and revivals, and I'd take my guitar with us when I could. I also dug the real low-down Mississippi singers, mostly Big Bill Broonzy and Big Boy Crudup, although they would scold me at home for listening to them.
>
> "Sinful music" the townsfolk in Memphis said it was. Which never bothered me, I guess.[5]

Presley produced the magic combination which Sam Phillips wanted: the driving power of black rhythm and blues with the straightforward emotional appeal of white country music. He had the added advantage over Bill Haley of being young and good looking. Dressed in black leather, with a sulky pout and greasy black hair, he was the musical incarnation of the film image projected by James Dean and Marlon Brando.

399

Elvis Presley playing a Martin D-18 with a pickup attached.

COURTESY OF RCA RECORDS

Presley's early successes with Sam Phillips' Sun label were purely local Southern ones, and he only became a national success when RCA began to record him after purchasing his contract from Sun (for $40,000) in 1955. Under the supervision of Chet Atkins—who was recording and organizing sessions for RCA/Victor in Nashville—Elvis made a series of smash hits that earned him the name "King of Rock and Roll." Atkins arranged a heavy backing sound with electric guitars, vocal group and drums. Presley's own guitar playing, despite his assertion of early influences, was basic in the extreme. But his fans cared little that Scotty Moore, not Elvis, produced the forceful guitar sound in "Heartbreak Hotel" and "Hound Dog." Elvis above all others confirmed that the guitar was a youth instrument. Before him the electric guitar had been regarded as an instrument played by jazz musicians, blues, country and sessionmen who had made a career of being serious players. Elvis proved that it was not necessary to

have played for years to be a success. The idea that given the right circumstances, three chords and a bash could make you a millionaire and a professional musician took firm hold in the late 1950s.

The vitality of the electric guitar could produce exciting music without the need for a great deal of technical skill. Sheer noise could, and often did, cover mediocre playing. Moreover, the three- or four-chord guitar music and unsophisticated single-note solos perfectly suited the simple lyrics and feelings of the songs. Countless small groups started to play at local clubs and dances in both America and Europe. In this way the electric guitar became the new urban folk instrument, and inspired a whole generation to create its own music.

From 1955 onward the music industry expanded enormously and the electric guitar manufacturers benefited accordingly. Fender, for example, had introduced the Telecaster (originally called the Broadcaster) in 1948. Up to 1955 they had manufactured ten thousand of them; from 1955 to the mid-70s they produced over a quarter of a million. One other change was the early rock 'n' rollers' orientation to recording rather than performing live. (Notable exceptions to this were Fats Domino, Elvis Presley, Bo Diddley and Chuck Berry.) Between 1954 and 1956 the 45–rpm disc took over from the 78 and helped the expansion of the record companies, for it was light, durable, easy to make and easy to distribute. And there was more demand than ever before, for apart from the popular juke boxes, radio programs were devoting more time to rock music. Competition inevitably increased among disc jockeys eager to reach the growing audience. The audience's demand for novelty meant that record producers were continually on the lookout for new talent: many unknown performers made a record or two, enjoyed a brief success, and then disappeared.

Of the many singer-guitarists of the 1950s, two stand out as having lasting influence and producing records of consistent quality: Chuck Berry and Bo Diddley. Chuck Berry was not only a competent guitarist, he had a genius for simple but effective lyrics. He was at his best between 1955 and 1959 with such songs as "Maybelline," "Roll Over Beethoven," "School Days," "Johnny B. Goode" and others. On these records he created a style of guitar playing that became classic. Berry's style was based on boogie-woogie rhythms, achieved by alternating guitar chords, embellished with distinctive off-the-beat lead lines. He reinforced the element of insistent repetition by the use of standardized guitar phrases as introductions to the vocal. Even with the increasing sophistication of rock since the late 1950s, this has remained one of its basic elements.

In the same year that Chuck Berry came to fame, 1955, Bo Diddley produced his first record—named "Bo Diddley." His guitar style was simple but he played with an idiosyncratic syncopated rhythm. Diddley was famous for his customized guitars. Of the rectangular-bodied instruments made for him by Gretsch, which he saw as an extension of his personality, he said:

> I had always wanted a guitar that was different, that would be *me*. I wanted something that would be just mine and no one else's. . . . There are four altogether and I have them all . . . .[6]

Bo Diddley used the guitar as part of a flashy strutting performance of flamboyance and obvious sexual suggestion.

Toward the end of the 1950s guitar-based instrumental numbers became extraordinarily popular. While instrumentals had been played by many rhythm and blues dance bands, they had mainly featured pianos or saxophones in solo breaks. The first electric guitar group instrumentals therefore had considerable novelty value. Lead, rhythm and bass guitars were used to provide a spectrum of related tone color: the lead guitar line was usually melodically simple with little tonal subtlety and few pyrotechnics. Beginning the fashion was Link Wray's "Rumble" of 1958, which rapidly sold over a million copies. Link Wray was an inventive guitarist, whose use of dynamics and distinctive loud and rough rhythm guitar had a lasting impact on Pete Townshend of The Who.

Most successful of all, however, was Duane Eddy with his twangy guitar and easy attractive rhythms. Eddy's trademark came from swinging bluesy figures played on the bass strings, alternating with aggressive saxophone breaks, and the use in the studio of techniques such as harmonized clapping and whoops from the backing band. He produced twenty relaxed, easy-listening hits to a formula that used the guitar's popularity but discarded the

COURTESY OF JOHN COOK

Bo Diddley.

brashness of rock 'n' roll, which would have alienated the older record buyers.

The instrumental remained a major force in the music industry until the mid-1960s: hits ranged from the Ventures' "Walk Don't Run" to Johnny and the Hurricanes with their harder rocking versions of well-tried tunes. In England, the most successful group was the Shadows. They backed Cliff Richard as well as making instrumental records on their own, built around Hank Marvin's lead guitar.

The instrumental marked the beginning of a more serious attitude among young rock 'n' roll musicians to the electric guitar as an instrument in its own right, with its own particular properties. Whereas before it had been seen mainly as a backup instrument for a singer, its new prominent position drew attention to the sound of the instrument, and limited attempts were made to exploit its

Muddy Waters.

COURTESY OF BILL GREENSMITH

properties: both Duane Eddy and Hank Marvin, for instance, made new imaginative use of the vibrola arm.

Rock 'n' roll was both lyrically and musically limited: the songs reduced teenagers' emotional problems to a few stock situations, simplified the rhythm and blues beat to 2/4 time with an accent on the back beat, and concentrated on straightforward, catchy melodies. One of the consequences of the dictates of youth was to bring hard times to the real virtuosi of the electric guitar: jazz players and urban bluesmen.

In the late 1950s most urban blues styles could still be traced to early country styles. Men like Muddy Waters, Elmore James, John Lee Hooker and Howlin' Wolf had an ensured but limited audience, mainly composed of older people who had migrated from the South and who found comforting echoes of their early lives in the music. The younger bluesmen, however, led by B. B. King, who had incorporated a more sophisticated jazz feel into their music, found themselves stranded between two audiences. They were not close enough to the down-home style to appeal to the transplanted country man. Nor were they smooth enough to capture the young audience who scented the possibility of success on their own terms and who were impatient of the hardships and struggles of their forefathers. B. B. King found that he

> . . . really began to fight for the blues. I refused to go as rock 'n' roll as some people did. The things people used to say about those I thought of as the greats in the business, the blues singers, used to hurt me. They spoke of them as though they were all illiterate and dirty. The blues had made me a better living than any I had ever had, so this was when I really put my fight on. A few whites gave me the blah-blah about blues singers, but mostly it was Negro people, and that was why it hurt. To be honest, I believe they felt they were trying to lift the standards of the Negro, and that they just didn't want to be associated with the blues, because it was something still back *there*.[7]

Jazz guitarists were suffering for a different reason: the rock 'n' roll audience was accustomed to a guitar style that had none of the musical and technical complexities displayed by jazz musicians. Jazz by this period had become a minority taste, and guitarists in particular felt the pinch. Whereas in the 40s and early 50s they were pioneers both of jazz and of the guitar, by the late 50s and early 60s they were on the sidelines. There was little recording or broadcasting work left in jazz and many of the players were tired of the endless, often unrewarding dates which involved continuous traveling. In 1958 Tal Farlow gave up playing because

> . . . the music business—the backstage parts, the non-musical parts—is terrible. It's just a crummy way to make a living. And it seemed that jazz was becoming too self-limiting; you had to be an expert to tell if what you were hearing was good or bad.[8]

In the same year Johnny Smith went into semi-retirement as a music dealer, and in 1961 Herb Ellis, also tired of the road, became a studio musician in Los Angeles. Jazz guitarists were seeing amateur players with little skill earning fame and fortune in rock 'n' roll. To add insult to injury, many of the most successful rock 'n' roll records were studio productions which relied on jazz musicians to make and play the arrangements. Bucky Pizzarelli, a fine jazzman famous for his seven-string guitar and his six-string Danelectro bass guitar, said that from 1957:

> For almost every rock and pop date four or five guitars were used. . . . I made zillions of rock dates with Al Caiola, Mundell Lowe, George Barnes, Kenny Burrell and Tony Mottola. Truthfully, I was on almost every hit rock and popular song recorded in New York City up through the mid-60s: Dion and the Belmonts, Frankie Avalon, Fabian—I could go on for hours naming them.[9]

Many of the best jazz guitarists went into session work: to some the variety was a challenge, to others it was just a job of work. Herb Ellis said in an interview later:

> I do it the best I can and I do it with a smile, but I get nothing from it. After playing with Oscar Peterson all those years of playing creative music, I find it quite boring.[10]

One of the few guitarists to succeed on his own terms was Chet Atkins, who worked as a performer and also became one of the moguls of the recording industry. Through his twin careers he has been a powerful influence on the music industry's use of the guitar.

Chet Atkins' musical career began when he played on various radio shows before going to Nashville in the late 1940s to work for RCA. At this time, the studios in Nashville were regarded as little more than field stations. But as the recording industry in Nashville grew, so did Atkins' importance. His recording and producing of Elvis Presley in 1955 helped put Nashville on the musical map.

In the late 1950s a small circle of able musicians, who played together first in small jazz clubs and then on record, produced what became known as the "Nashville sound," a loose, jazzy, easy-listening music. The central figures were pianist Floyd Cramer with his "slipnote" style, drummer Buddy Harmon, bassist Bob Moore, guitarists Grady Martin and Hank Garland (who died before reaching his full maturity as a jazz guitarist), and Chet Atkins himself. With vocal backing (such as the Jordanaires, who backed Elvis Presley) the music moved from the old-style country

Chet Atkins.

tradition. Its popularity helped keep Nashville going commercially during the years when rock 'n' roll had taken up a large part of the popular record market.

From the early 1950s Chet Atkins played electric guitar in the Merle Travis tradition. He had an unusually complex picking style for a popular guitarist, using the thumb and three fingers. Since the early 1960s he has also been playing the nylon-string instrument and applied classical guitar to jazz and popular material. Chet Atkins' output is enormous and therefore necessarily uneven. However, his impressive technical skill and his playing of relaxed melodic numbers has made him a household name among music fans and guitar enthusiasts.

As a popularizer of the electric guitar, Atkins' influence has been considerable. His commercial success is based on a thorough knowledge of what he likes to play, and what people want to hear:

> I'm strictly a melody man. One reason jazz has never been a great success is because it is improvisational, and the public loses the melody. It takes a well-trained ear to enjoy jazz. Music, to be commercial, should have a melodic line somewhere that is appealing, and I try to keep this in mind in all my recordings.[11]

The Beatles onstage, 1965.

Scream Power

In the early 1960s popular music found a new direction in the music of the Beatles and the Rolling Stones. They were the first groups with an international following that verged on the hysterical, and were greeted with an enthusiasm which horrified parents, amazed the authorities and delighted record companies.

In January 1964 the Beatles released "I Want to Hold Your Hand" in America. Sales reached one million in ten days and it became one of the fastest selling records in the history of the business. Between January and March of that year twelve Beatles records were estimated to account for sixty percent of all singles sold. Their success came from the ability to produce consistently high quality music. Witty, evocative lyrics and a cohesive musical style were combined with an inventiveness that gave each piece a freshness and spontaneity unmatched by any other group.

The Beatles, followed by the Rolling Stones, spear-headed the British takeover of the popular music industry and provided the foundations for the 1960s rock boom. Together they helped create an audience that was sophisticated, discriminating in taste and conscious of its role as creator of a new culture. They opened audiences' ears, both in Britain and America, to a new spectrum of sounds. Where the Beatles were harmonious, the Stones were raucous; where the Beatles faintly mocking, the Stones were vicious and aggressive. The Stones' violent, virile music, along with the heady sensuality of Mick Jagger, drove their audiences wild; it even frightened the group:

> We'd walk into some of those places and it was like they had the Battle of the Crimea going on, people gasping, tits hanging out, chicks choking, nurses running around. . . . "Scream power" was the thing everything was judged by, as far as gigs were concerned. . . . You know that weird sound that thousands of chicks make when they're really lettin' it go. They couldn't hear the music. We couldn't hear ourselves, for years. Monitors were unheard of. It was impossible to play as a band on stage, and we forgot all about it.[1]

The Stones' music was directly inspired by American blues. They were the first supergroup to take the Chicago blues and present it in a form that excited a mass white audience. For the guitar, the great musical significance of the Stones and many of the British groups who followed them was to redirect electric playing back to the blues.

Ironically, young British guitarists were much more familiar with blues playing than their American counterparts. Keith Richard's early influences were the mixture most young British players had been weaned on:

> . . . then I started to get into where it had come from. Broonzy first. He and Josh White were considered to be the only living black bluesmen still playing. So let's get that together, I thought, that can't be right. Then I started to discover Robert Johnson and those cats. . . . The other half of me was listenin' to all that rock and roll, Chuck Berry, and saying yeah, yeah.[2]

The foundations of the British interest in black American music had been laid as early as the mid-1950s when the English clarinetist Chris Barber, leader of a popular jazz band, brought a wide range of styles to the notice of British audiences. In addition to his activities as a jazz player, he was one of the pioneers of skiffle, a popular

mixture of elements of traditional jazz, blues and American folk. Lonnie Donegan's skiffle group, formed in 1957 with Donegan on guitar, Barber on bass and singer Beryl Bryden on washboard, had a series of smash hits starting with their version of "Rock Island Line" and "John Henry."

Skiffle's one importance was that it inspired some of the audience to explore the sources of the material, and discover the original music of Leadbelly and Woody Guthrie. This interest led Chris Barber to bring to Britain American performers of the caliber of Big Bill Broonzy, Sonny Terry and Brownie McGee, Muddy Waters, and Sister Rosetta Tharpe. Skiffle inspired an interest in acoustic blues, but in the small clubs in London the blues rapidly went electric—just as it had on the south side of Chicago.

In the early 1960s when white American audiences were completely unfamiliar with electric blues, Alexis Korner's Blues Incorporated was playing post-war rhythm and blues. Korner was inspired by the heavy electric sound of Howlin' Wolf, Muddy Waters, Jimmy Reed, John Lee Hooker and Sonny Boy Williamson, and he educated his young audience in black American music. And many of them not only went to hear, they also went to play. Brian Jones, Charlie Watts, Mick Jagger, and Graham Bond were among those who furthered their blues education with Alexis Korner's band. The clubs were small, noisy and crowded; the music loud and exciting; often the neighbors complained. Altogether, it was an inauspicious beginning for the British players who were to bring a new fusion of musical styles, another restructuring of the music industry, and a revolution in the sound of the electric guitar.

The exploration of solid-body electric guitar sound properties started with the accidental discovery of the controlled use of feedback. The English music scene was decidedly amateur and sophisticated equipment was beyond the reach of most groups. Jeff Beck recalls his early days with the Yardbirds, in which group he succeeded Eric Clapton in 1965:

> . . . playing in small clubs you always get feedback because of bad systems, and really the electrical thing hadn't been sewn up. All the amps were underpowered and screwed up full volume and always

whistling. My amp was always whistling! And I'd kick it and bash it and a couple of tubes would break, and I was playing largely on an amp with just one output valve still working. It would feed back, so I decided to use it rather than fight it. It was hopeless to try and play a chord, because it would just *rrr*, so when I progressed on to a bigger amp and I didn't get it, I kind of missed it. I went to hit a note and there wasn't any distortion; too clean. It was horrible. So the ideal thing was to get the beauty of the feedback, but *controllable* feedback.[3]

Feedback could be controlled and directed in several ways: by moving around the speakers to change the intensity, by damping some strings while allowing others to vibrate, using finger vibrato, throwing the guitar or throwing things at the guitar, or using the vibrola arm.

During the 1960s there was a greater emphasis on live performance than during the previous decade, and this was to have a lasting impact on the development of rock music. No longer could an aspiring singer or group rely on records to achieve success. The spectacular expansion of rock's popularity and its consequent spread to large halls and open-air concerts encouraged the further exploration of guitar showmanship, high volume and distortion. There was a new open attitude toward the discovery and manipulation of electric guitar sounds which then by definition became "natural" to the instrument. Once the principle had been established, fuzz boxes, wah-wah pedals and a whole array of modifying devices could be exploited as a valid part of the music.

The grand master of manipulated sound was James Marshall Hendrix (1942–1970). In a short period from 1965 to 1970 Hendrix was the man most responsible for redefining the possibilities of the electric guitar.

From 1963 Hendrix toured the South as a sideman to various different acts. Three years later he had formed his own band and was playing around the clubs of Greenwich Village. For a time he played lead guitar with John Hammond Jr. before Chas Chandler, formerly bassist with the Animals, found him and took him to England. Together with Mitch Mitchell on drums and Noel Redding on bass, he formed the Jimi Hendrix Experience. Hendrix's musical skill astonished fans, fellow musicians

Jimi Hendrix restringing his Stratocaster.

and roadies. Eric Clapton, one of the first to hear him in London in September 1966, said later:

> What we were stretching to do then, Pete [Townshend] in his way and I in mine, and then to walk into a club and see someone that you'd never seen before who'd got it covered. . .! You see, we thought that we must be ahead of everyone else, so that if anyone's trying to do what we're doing they're nowhere as good as we are at doing it. And then to have Jimi lay all that down was quite heavy.[4]

Hendrix was a great guitarist. He could play fine blues or jazz as well as rock, produce delicate chord work or play melodies in octaves. But these aspects of his skill were often overlooked in the excitement and fury of the new sounds he created, which could seem incoherent, but which he carefully controlled.

Hendrix had three main aids for producing distortion: the Univibe (a device to simulate a rotating speaker especially adapted for him from its use with electric organs), fuzz box, and wah-wah pedal. Other players had used the last two before, but no one as well as Hendrix. The wah-wah pedal in particular found a new role in his playing, giving force and precision to a riff or stressing certain notes within a run. He also made extensive use of the vibrola arm to control feedback, altering the pitch and intensity of the noise, and for a host of other effects such as imitating the whine of a bottleneck. His control of feedback was extraordinary: he could orchestrate it so that he played undistorted lead on some strings while getting feedback on others, a trick which made guitarists listening to his records at the time speculate on the identity of the second and third guitarists. No one fully understood his technique, and no one since has been able to reproduce his mixture of sounds. Eric Barrett, his road manager, later explained his setup:

> Jimi started out with 75 watts and ended up with six 4 × 12 Marshall cabinets, a 4 × 12 monitor, and four 100–watt Marshall tops, all souped-up and coupled-up through fuzz, wah-wah pedals and a Univibe! He had a special box of gadgets and the fuzz and wah-wah pedals acted as preamps. If I tried to test his equipment, all I got was feedback. Jimi could control it all with his fingers, and I still don't understand to this day how he did it.[5]

Hendrix developed further the concept of rock music as a show, and his showmanship, coupled with the volume and aggression of his sound, alienated many outside the rock circle and public. But the audio-visual feast he provided, with smashed and burning guitars, fulfilled his audience's demand for a cathartic Experience.

Sound manipulation, distortion and physically violent performances pointed to a new concept of the electric guitar. From being a conventional musical instrument on the one hand or a stage prop on the other, the electric guitar became the heart of a sound system, in which artificially induced noise was as legitimate as a musical note. The Who was the first group consciously to realize this possibility.

Pete Townshend with The Who.

Jerry Garcia of the Grateful Dead, one of the most popular and long-lasting groups to have come out of the San Francisco sound in the late 1960s. Their style developed in the long jamming sessions of their concerts.

Pete Townshend's famous guitar smashing was not just a visual spectacle, but had a musical purpose: he was selfconscious in his assertion of rock as a legitimate art form.

> I think the most important musical development we've made in pop music is in free-form music which does exactly what it wants. We don't allow our instruments to stop us doing what we want. . . . We smash our instruments, tear our clothes and wreck everything. The expense doesn't worry us because that would be something which would get between us and our music. . . . So I don't have a love affair with a guitar, I don't polish it after every performance; I *play* the fucking thing.[6]

Despite its violence, Townshend's act relied on a perfect understanding of his guitar's role within the group, and his playing combined lead and rhythm roles in a heavy chordal style that has influenced many others.

Marty Balin of the Jefferson Airplane reacted in 1967 to English developments:

Eric Clapton at the Rainbow Concert held in London in January, 1973, with Pete Townshend.

We really believe that electronics play a very big part. . . . Take the Yardbirds. They've done some fantastic things with feedback. The Who from England. Why, they're . . . they're taking the guitar and smashing it into the amplifier. Or they're taking the guitar and they're rubbing it against the microphone stand. Creating different sounds.[7]

In the end, though, the most popular guitarist of the 1960s turned out to be Eric Clapton. He played the guitar in a different way from either Hendrix or Townshend, but to his fans he was more than just a fine musician: he was "God." Clapton's music was rooted in the blues, and one of his most important periods was spent in John Mayall's Bluesbreakers, which he joined in 1965. Although playing within a strict blues format, his sense of timing enabled him to phrase around a beat, giving a new kick to the basic rhythm. His mastery of dynamics created a tension and subtlety which was new to the electric guitar.

In 1967 Clapton, together with Ginger Baker on drums and Jack Bruce on bass, formed the Cream. Although the group stayed together for only a year and a half from 1967 to the end of 1968, as a group they were unique in rock for their virtuosity and musicianship, and their example encouraged greater technical skill among rock musicians. According to Eric Clapton, Cream was supposed to be a blues trio on the lines of Buddy Guy's group, playing straight blues to small audiences. But at their first gig (the 1967 Windsor Jazz and Blues Festival) they ran out of numbers and were forced to improvise: "So we just made up twelve-bar blues and that became Cream."[8] From then on, they were typecast as an improvisatory blues-based supergroup.

During his time with Cream, Clapton developed a style of soaring fluidity which depended on the electric guitar's properties of sustain. He made great use of the finger vibrato he had learned from B. B. King and Buddy Guy, moving the fingers of the left hand from side to side while keeping pressure on the fret, with the speed of movement depending on the effect wanted. The clean sound thus produced became the hallmark of his playing. Although Clapton also used a wah-wah pedal at times, he never shared Hendrix's interest in distortion:

I always attempted to get a lot of volume but to take as

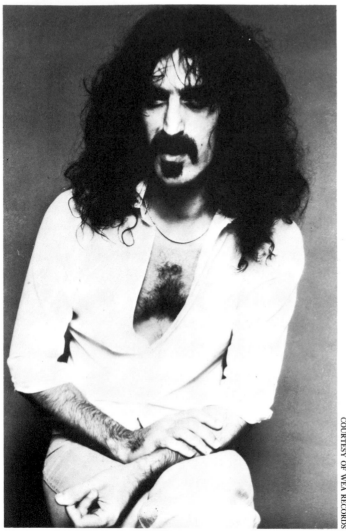

Frank Zappa of the Mothers of Invention. Zappa was playing organized, tightly arranged music at a time when other musicians were developing looser styles. His social message and satiric approach at first disguised his considerable musicianship and inventive guitar playing.

COURTESY OF WEA RECORDS

much edge off it as I could so that it was round and not harsh. You could then still listen to it without it hurting your ears. That was the birth of a sound in a way, which I then carried on using over and over again because I liked it.[9]

Groups in the late 1960s developed their styles in live performances where they could play long improvisatory breaks. The style would have been severely restricted had not the recording industry changed. The LP took over from the 45-rpm single as the main recording format for rock music, and once free of the three-minute limitation, live performances could be directly recorded. Guitarists were encouraged further to play extended solos which demanded greater musical knowledge and fluency. The LP also made possible the creation of ambitious records that were musically and thematically integrated. The first such "concept album," *Absolutely Free* by the Mothers of Invention, was composed, arranged and conducted by Frank Zappa and appeared in 1967.

The success of the English groups inspired the American electric blues revival of 1968. The first white American group to try to spread electric blues to a wider audience had been Paul Butterfield's Blues Band. Butterfield took the music he had heard in Chicago bars for years, and in 1965 formed a band with Mike Bloomfield and Elvin Bishop on guitars, Jerome Arnold on bass, Sam Lay on drums, and Mark Naftalin on keyboard. But he never achieved a large following and in 1966 Mike Bloomfield left to start his own band.

But it was not until the coming of Cream in 1968 that electric blues found a mass audience in America. Clapton consistently acknowledged the sources of his music and playing, and directed American listeners to B. B. King, Freddie King, Buddy Guy and the like.

In the late 1960s, B. B. King suddenly became widely known. The mixture of influences on him and his lack of attachment to any one traditional blues style helped his popularity with a new generation of young whites. He is a superb guitar player, as concerned in his own way with exploiting the potentialities of the instrument as Hendrix was: "Sounds are more important to me than trying to play a lot of notes. . . . I practice scales, but then I go right back to trying to get certain sounds." His clear single-string runs

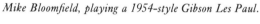

Mike Bloomfield, playing a 1954-style Gibson Les Paul.

B. B. King playing a Gibson ES-355 TD SV semi-solid-body stereo guitar.

Freddie King.

and full chord playing, often around the ninth chord, are shaped by masterful phrasing. This was influenced by saxophone players, whose phrasing comes naturally from the need to draw breath. Like many urban blues players, B. B. King uses a semi-solid-body guitar which combines sustain with fullness of tone. He has a remarkable ability to hit a note, bend and sustain it, using the finger vibrato technique which influenced Eric Clapton. King evolved the technique in an attempt to simulate the sound of bottleneck playing:

> Bukka (White, B.B's cousin) . . . had a steel bar he'd put on his finger and the sound he'd get from the string

Albert King with an original Flying V, issued in 1958 and one of the rarest Gibson solid-body guitars.

Otis Rush.

with it would go all through me. I never could do that, but I learned to trill my hand, and with the help of the amplifier I could sustain a note.[10]

B. B. King and his contemporaries have remained faithful to basic blues concepts: their borrowings from outside sources have been relatively limited, and tend to give each bluesman a personal stamp rather than change the fundamental nature of the music. The Texan Freddie King (1934–1976) remained one of the most consistent blues players, varying his exuberant style very little from his first success in the early 60s with instrumental numbers like "Hideaway." Clapton did a version of this song, and has acknowledged King's importance for his own playing. Many other younger white players have taken basic licks and phrases from Freddie King.

Albert King, born in St. Louis in 1924, has a calm unhurried guitar style and a smooth baritone voice. He has taken the sharp edges off a basic blues technique, and says of his music:

I play a kind of modern blues and I wanta keep up with what's happenin' now. I still wanta keep the old feeling of the blues, but I want it modern. So I have to mix it up, and I guess you could call that brightening up the blues.[11]

The younger guitarists following B. B. King began by playing in the long shadow he has cast. Even in Chicago, the home of harsh electric blues, King has popularized a smooth style of playing backed by more sophisticated bands. During the 1960s the older style could still be heard in the cruder electric slide playing and shouting vocals of Homesick James and his Dusters. But more popular were figures like Jimmy Dawkins, Buddy Guy, Magic Sam, Otis Rush and Fenton Robinson.

Buddy Guy, who went to Chicago in 1957 (a tough time for young blues players), was directly influenced by B. B. King. His first success came when he won a competition, and Magic Sam took him to the Cobra/Aristocratic label. When that folded, Otis Rush helped introduce him to the influential Chess brothers. After recording and club dates, he came to be billed as Chicago's answer to B. B. King. Certainly in the mid-60s Guy was consciously copying B. B. King's jazz-influenced licks. However, a successful

Jimmy Dawkins.

Magic Sam.

career cannot be maintained by imitation, and Guy, like his contemporaries, was forced to develop his own style. His mature style uses fewer notes in aiming for a gutsier, bluesier, less jazzy sound, and his stage act, in which he plays the guitar against the ceiling and between his legs, is more flamboyant than King's.

Both Otis Rush and Magic Sam, sponsors of Buddy Guy's success, have forged their own "post-B. B. King" styles. Otis Rush's style is busier, with less consistent use of long sustained notes and string bending but with a great inventiveness in playing riffs. Set against a powerful trembling voice, the jumping licks he repeats with variations in tone color, give a disjointed feeling to the music which is quite different from the fluency of his mentor. On slower numbers, his intense vocal delivery alternates with concise ringing guitar and sax breaks.

Magic Sam's band of guitars, tenor sax, piano, bass and drums pumps out a hard driving rhythm for his often brash, confident guitar style and light voice. His eclectic, inventive approach is typical of the present urban bluesmen:

> I play the blues. I am a bluesman, but not the dated blues—the modern type of blues, I'm the modern type of bluesman. But I can play the regular stuff, and I'm also a variety guy. I can play the soul stuff, too.[12]

Jimmy Dawkins is another of the younger Chicago blues players who have revitalized and redirected electric blues. These guitarists have taken B. B. King's style as a basis and adapted it to their own brands of music. The sustain is chopped to give a greater tension, the answering guitar riffs played often with a greater force.

Although the younger bluesmen are willing to look outside the older blues songs for their material, they are nonetheless aware of the tradition to which they belong. The music remains rooted in older country blues, but their

Keith Richard of the Rolling Stones.

Ronnie Wood, who replaced Mick Taylor in the Stones.

willingness to experiment has created a new urban blues style.

The discovery in the late 1960s that the white electric blues bands were largely derivative caused some of the more discerning audiences to cool a little towards their idols. The extraordinarily high quality of black electric guitarists helped kill the "Clapton is God" type of adulation. As far as popularity and commercial success went, white blues-based rock groups were still way ahead, but the persistent presentation of black urban guitarists — *Rolling Stone* ran numerous articles on new players and their bands between 1969 and 1971 — made audiences less easily roused than before by music based on blues guitar licks. And although many of the best groups continued to interpret the blues as they had been doing for years — the Stones being the most consistent and successful example — others found it necessary to reassess their playing and look elsewhere for inspiration.

By the late 1960s rock had grown into a huge business; enormous rewards were to be had for the successful. Hendrix at his height in 1968 and 69 was earning anything from $18,000 to $60,000 per performance and was offered $100,000 on one occasion for a 45-minute gig. In 1969 Johnny Winter signed with Columbia for $300,000. "The dollar dictates what music is written,"[13] Chuck Berry commented in 1969.

By the late 1960s guitarists were the superstars of rock. Guitar companies relied heavily on them to help sell their instruments: Hendrix probably turned more people to buying Fender Stratocasters than anyone else. Jeff Beck in 1968 was remarking: ". . . this instrument thing is out of hand. If Eric Clapton sold his guitar and bought a ten-dollar guitar, the kids would do the same."[14]

Unfortunately the brilliance of a few players had often led the audience to exaggerate the importance of guitarists within groups, and the public's expectations influenced musicians. More and more groups such as Led Zeppelin and Ten Years After were formed as little more than vehicles for lead guitarists.

For those who had achieved superstardom, the pressures were enormous. It was necessary continually to be before the public eye, to produce new music. These pressures were exacerbated by the fact that the music industry is geared to speed. Recording companies, rock journalists, and the public were always waiting to see what their heroes would produce next — but were unwilling to give them time to work it out. And whereas a less popular artist could get away with a mediocre performance or even series of performances there was no such leniency allowed to the major heroes. Jimi Hendrix summed up the pressures placed on the performer:

> People see a fast buck and have you up there being a slave to the public. They keep you at it until you are exhausted and so is the public, and then they move off to other things. That's why groups break up — they just get worn out. Musicians want to pull away after a time, or they get lost in the whirlpool.[15]

To the industry's pressure were added those associated with traveling for long periods in the same company for rounds of one-night stands, taking a vast amount of equipment which had to be set up and taken down rapidly, tested and looked after by an army of helpers. And all for what Pete Townshend called the "Circus" of the rock show.

Many of the former superstars found themselves unable to continue. The expectations they had aroused were impossible to fulfil and a wish developed to remove the guitar and the guitarist from their dominant position. Eric Clapton had a brief career as backup guitarist to Delaney and Bonnie. Jeff Beck was claiming in 1969:

> I don't want to hog it all the time. . . . I want it there when I want it. I don't have enough confidence to be a solo artist — I want to be in a group and if they're playing the sort of stuff that I like to hear, it may just be that I can be a soloist.[16]

And Hendrix died before he could fulfil his wish of playing with a big band and vocal backing.

There was a definite feeling that the end of an era had been reached for both rock music and for the electric guitar. The prevailing feelings were of exhaustion and confusion. In retrospect, the 1969 Woodstock Festival was one of the most inspiring and one of the most saddening occasions of the 1960s. It was inspiring for the feeling of love and solidarity among the audience, but instead of marking a new dawn for humanity (as its participants hoped), Woodstock proved to be the monument to a passing age of rock music. At the Festival, Jimi Hendrix's

OPPOSITE: *Johnny Winter.*

solo "Star Spangled Banner" was in many ways a symbolic summary of a decade of confusion, violence, traumas, excitement and lyricism.

Taking the American national anthem as the basis for a violent free-ranging improvisation produced mixed reactions. To some it was the act of a disillusioned cynic, to others the act of a disillusioned lover, compounded of love and frustration, hope and despair. In "Star Spangled Banner" Hendrix used all the devices he had mastered. Within the simple format of the theme he wove an intricate tapestry of sounds, sometimes playing the theme straight as single notes, sometimes surrounding every note with a distortion which could be almost painful. Whether he intended the piece to carry in it the sounds of war or not, the echoes of sirens, bugle calls, the references to fire and destruction are unmistakable. But despite the barrage of sound, it is one of Hendrix's most subtle and inventive solos and conveys an intense feeling of sadness. As he hit a top note and bent it to its limits, or suddenly forced a clear bell-like phrase out of the welter of feedback, he seemed to be defying the world to follow his playing.

Hendrix appeared to have taken the electric guitar to its ultimate limits: his successors would have to find different directions, for the avenue which he had explored was closed. "Star Spangled Banner" was Hendrix's farewell to the 1960s. In September 1970 he was dead. Even to those who were shocked and grief stricken, there seemed a certain inevitability in his death. Guitarist Roy Buchanan said:

I wasn't surprised at all when Hendrix died. You knew he was going to die by just listening to his music. It was all there, he had done it and he almost had to die to finalize it.[17]

A recording studio in Nashville.

BELOW: *Jimmy Page of Led Zeppelin.*

"There's one in every crowd . . ."

At the end of the 1960s electric guitarists appeared to have mapped out their areas of interest. The instrument was regarded and played differently by jazz and rock guitarists. But during the 1970s the barriers between guitarists in the different fields of music began to break down. The growing sophistication and wider awareness among both the audience—who are now open to listening and accepting experimentation—and among musicians, has encouraged an interchange of ideas. The exploration of new sounds, the greater integration of the electric guitar with other instruments, and the attempts to merge jazz and rock are indications of a willingness to look outside previously established bounds.

Although creativity in distortion and violence had to a large extent died with Hendrix, the formula proved commercially successful, and lived on to spawn a new breed of heavy metal guitarists. The forerunners were The Who, Hendrix, Beck and Jimmy Page of Led Zeppelin. Those who took the concept over—Deep Purple, Grand Funk Railroad, Black Sabbath, Alice Cooper, Queen, Kiss and the like—specialized in stage acts that frequently included specific violence. Their sound is that of heavy, simplistic, often-repeated guitar riffs distorted through the usual devices, and while the connection between distorted sound and extreme violence is an obvious one, the groups have done little to advance the electric guitar either technically or musically.

For many other rock guitarists, disillusionment with the broken promises of the 1960s caused a turning away from the distortion which had characterized the decade. But the exploration and exploitation of sound had brought about a far greater understanding of the electric guitar's sonic possibilities and made a return to a clear, round, shiny sound easier.

This move to a quieter style was part of a general trend within rock. The rising popularity of acoustic-based music, and of figures such as Stephen Stills and James Taylor who used both acoustic and electric instruments, necessarily changed the emphasis, and affected popular taste. The Band, who had become popular in the late 1960s with *Music from Big Pink*, characterized the new concern for integration. Robbie Robertson was immediately hailed as one of rock's best guitarists, but never occupied the

COURTESY OF CBS RECORDS

COURTESY OF WEA RECORDS

ABOVE: *Steve Howe, the success of whose complex and technically refined playing is a reflection of the sophistication of rock audiences of the 1970s. Howe is one of the few rock stars to use a deep-body electric-acoustic guitar, and has a particular fondness for the Gibson ES-175 (seen here) and ES-5.*

Jeff Beck.

limelight in the way of the 1960s superstars. Perhaps the finest guitarist of all to emerge with the clear bell-like sound of the 1970s was Roy Buchanan. His first solo album was a revelation of his genius: where Hendrix had made his guitar scream and rage, Buchanan made his sing and cry. But though musicians as well-known as Jeff Beck have paid tribute to Buchanan's skill on their own records, he has largely remained a guitarist's guitarist.

During the 1970s the realization grew that behind the big names there are countless guitarists working as back-up or session musicians who have a high degree of technical and musical skill. And the numbers are steadily increasing, as Eric Clapton remarked in 1975:

> I did more session work when I was younger because there was less competition around. Now when I go into a studio and cut a session I've really got to work hard to

OPPOSITE: *Kiss.*

425

The J. Geils Band.

keep my head above water when there's so many other good young players about.[1]

The fact that some of these, such as James Burton and Danny Kortchmar, have emerged from obscurity is a sign of the audience's growing awareness that excellence of playing does not always lie with the superstars. Others have formed groups to record in their own right. Area Code 611 was made up of a number of the finest Nashville session men; more recently a group of first-rate soul and rhythm and blues session players have formed Stuff.

The greater popularity of electric slide guitar in the late 1960s and early 1970s was another indication of the move away from distortion. By the end of the 1960s electric slide was an established sound in several rock bands. Moving on from slavish imitations of Muddy Waters and Elmore James, the technique achieved a new impetus in the playing of Duane Allman. Before he was killed in 1971 he was the force which lifted the Allman Brothers Band to its artistic success, as well as contributing to others—the most notable being Derek and the Dominoes' album *Layla*. Ry Cooder (though at his best on acoustic guitar) achieved much of his popular success through his seductively impressive electric guitar slide playing.

But it was Carlos Santana who proved that a large part of the mass audience cared just as much for the melodic qualities and round shiny sound of the electric guitar as they did for its power and force. At its best, Santana's controlled playing with its clear flow of ideas makes his music one of the most satisfying musical and emotional experiences of the last few years. Santana also typifies the direction among rock guitarists of assimilating their instruments with others. He plays as rhythm guitarist as well as being the outstanding up-front soloist of the band. Seeing such groups as Santana's and David Bromberg's, where the players exchange instruments with the ease born of great skill, is to witness a true interaction of ideas.

A self-conscious attempt at assimilation of musical forms was made in the music referred to as "jazz-rock." In the late 1960s the idea was established among rock musicians through groups like Blood, Sweat and Tears, and Electric Flag who made extensive use of horns and improvisation. But the improvisatory lead was usually taken by the guitarist who was a rock rather than a jazz

Roy Buchanan.

428

ABOVE: *John McLaughlin playing a custom-built twin-neck guitar.*

LEFT: *David Bromberg.*

OPPOSITE: *Carlos Santana.*

musician. When the idea came from jazz musicians, it often had a greater success. Miles Davis began to incorporate electric rock instrumentation and rhythms and proved that the fusion was a viable one. John McLaughlin, who played in Tony Williams' Lifetime and on two of Davis's albums, also realized that this particular brand of music could not be made just by grafting certain ideas on to a basic jazz or rock structure, or by adding certain instruments, but needed a new approach. Playing at a volume no traditional jazz guitarist would consider, he achieved a satisfactory interaction, reinterpreting traditional jazz rhythms and balancing the sound between electric instruments which had the capacity to cancel each other out.

With the Mahavishnu Orchestra, formed in 1971 and disbanded after four years, he blended jazz and rock elements in a way which helped shake many listeners out of their preconceived notions of music. McLaughlin

has been equally influential as a guitarist: his machine-gun style and lyrical single-note runs are instantly impressive, but it is never possible to overlook the knowledge and subtlety of his chording. Other guitarists, notably Bill Connors of Chick Corea's Return to Forever and Larry Coryell, later followed McLaughlin's lead in fusing elements from jazz and rock techniques. These players acknowledge a wider range of influences than many rock guitarists. As their mentors they cite musicians from Django Reinhardt to Jimi Hendrix and Ornette Coleman, to name a few.

The aim of players like McLaughlin is to combine the musical expertise of the jazz guitarist with the sound qualities and effects of the rock guitar. Whether jazz-rock guitarists succeed in making the fusion or not, one important consequence of their efforts will remain to their credit. They have focused audiences' increasing discontent with simplistic, standard rock licks, and have brought to public notice some outstanding jazz guitarists who had been shockingly neglected for a decade.

From the 1960s the popularity of rock guitarists had driven their jazz rivals further to the periphery. Mundell Lowe was just one of the many guitarists who had found it difficult and depressing to be a jazz player:

> The record companies killed us all. They stopped promoting jazz guitarists, letting the LPs die. . . . Now there's almost nowhere for jazz guitarists to work. There are only a few clubs you can play, and records are out.[2]

In the cacophony of sounds produced through fuzz boxes and wah-wah pedals, the jazz guitarist's concentration on technical excellence and the harmonic and melodic qualities of the instrument seemed eccentric. Even to those interested in jazz, electric guitarists had never completely established themselves as essential to the music. Like all jazz players, the guitarist needs to be able to think inventively, fast, and above all, compositionally. But there is a feeling in jazz circles that the technical difficulties of the guitar have impeded its musical development, and the guitarist has become overly concerned with fingerings, picking techniques and how best to get a "natural" (i.e. unamplified) sound from the instrument. The guitar has thus remained rather an outcast in jazz, and many players feel that the level of musicianship is higher among pianists and saxophonists.

One further difficulty which has impeded the jazz guitar's popularity (and which applies to all jazz players) is the need to perform live. While many rock guitarists can produce better sounds in the studio, because of their dependence on electronic aids, jazz musicians need contact to inspire them to improvise creatively. Jazz guitarists in particular, the most technically correct of electric players, find it difficult to produce the lyrical grace and inventiveness on which their music depends in the impersonal atmosphere of the studio.

When jazz guitarists have achieved commercial success, they have invariably lost part of their mainstream audience and been criticized for bastardizing their music. It is difficult for guitarists who have spent a lifetime formulating their music to make a successful and musically

PHOTOGRAPH BY PHIL LINDSAY, COURTESY OF CONCORD JAZZ INC.

Barney Kessel.

satisfying change to a more popular style. The jazz guitarist is often a beleaguered purist, his horizons limited by his unwillingness to exploit the electric qualities of the instrument. In the fight for survival, he is all too often reduced to producing "easy listening" arrangements of popular tunes. Wes Montgomery, one of the most innovative and brilliant of jazz players, fell into this trap in the last years of his life, although he is now remembered for his great jazz playing.

George Benson, an excellent jazz guitarist, shot to general fame with his 1975 golden album *Breezin!* Having been forced to earn an early living by playing rhythm and blues and rock music, he was in a better position than most jazz musicians to adapt himself to different demands.

The general encouragement of the jazz-rock musicians has turned more people to listening to jazz guitarists than at any time since the early 50s. Many of the older players find that the number of clubs where they can perform is growing and record companies are showing interest in recording them again. The music of George Barnes, Herb Ellis, Joe Pass, Barney Kessel and many others is becoming increasingly available to and appreciated by a young audience. Younger guitarists are once more being drawn to jazz, and many of them (such as Lenny Breau and Bill Connors) find it as natural to use a solid-body as an electric-acoustic guitar. They show an

Joe Pass.

ABOVE: *Howard Roberts playing a Gibson "Howard Roberts." This is an electric acoustic, with a pressed maple top and oval soundhole. It was originally issued by Gibson as an Epiphone, and retains the Epi style headstock.*

RIGHT: *Kenny Burrell.*

interest in exploiting more of the possibilities of electric sound, and incorporating techniques from rock and blues playing.

After decades of being regarded solely as an instrument for popular music, the electric guitar is now beginning to attract the attention of conservatory-trained composers. Some classical composers, most notably Sir Michael Tippett and Hans Werner Henze, have written electric guitar parts, but of a conventional nature, using amplification chiefly to make the guitar heard through the ensemble. More ambitious in exploiting the electric guitar's properties is the Englishman David Bedford, who studied at London's Royal Academy of Music before working in Italy with electronic music composer Luigi Nono.

Bedford's "Eighteen Bricks left on April 21st," was written for two electric guitars. Though warmly received at its London premiere in 1967 Eric Clapton was prompted to point out deficiencies in the composer's understanding of the possibilities of amplification. Subsequently, from 1970 to 1972, Bedford toured with Kevin Ayers' group The Whole World (which included Mike Oldfield on guitar), working as keyboard player and arranger. The fruits of this education can be heard in Bedford's arrangement of Mike Oldfield's *Tubular Bells* (1974), and in *Star's End* (1974), *The Rime of the Ancient Mariner* (1975) and *Odyssey* (1977), all of which contain electric guitar parts written with Mike Oldfield in mind. *Star's End*, commissioned by the Royal Philharmonic Orchestra, is a massive work scored for two electric guitars (lead and bass, to be played by the same musician), and rock percussion.

Star's End differs from most other attempts to incorporate rock instruments with symphony orchestra in that it was written by a composer used to handling the musical demands of a forty-minute piece. It was not an attempt to gain "status" for rock music, but aimed to use rock instruments as a concertante group within the orchestra. The performance of this piece illuminates the physical and conceptual barriers to the acceptance of the electric guitar in the world of "serious" music.

The guitar part in *Star's End* had to be performed by a rock musician—no classical player could as yet produce the sound effects demanded—but there were few rock guitarists who could follow a conductor's beat. And many orchestras (though not the Royal Philharmonic) found it impossible to take the presence of a rock guitarist seriously: at one performance, members of the brass section were seen to cover their ears every time the guitarist played a note, however softly.

The great development of electric guitar sound through the 1960s was achieved largely by rock musicians in unconscious and unplanned experiments. But the possibilities they uncovered are now being consciously extended by several avant-garde guitarists who cannot be categorized as either rock, jazz or classical, but are conversant with developments in all three forms. The music of such players as Derek Bailey, Hans Reichel and Fred Frith is unlikely ever to be widely popular, but is nevertheless significant for the amplified guitar.

Fred Frith (who plays both solo and with the radical, improvisatory rock group Henry Cow) has applied to the electric guitar John Cage's dictum that any noise can be the basis of music. He plays complex improvisations on a specially modified Gibson stereo guitar, which is fitted

PHOTOGRAPH BY BRIAN COOKE, COURTESY OF VIRGIN RECORDS

Mike Oldfield with a 1966-style Gibson SG Junior.

433

COURTESY OF VIRGIN RECORDS

David Bedford conducting the Royal Philharmonic orchestra in a performance of Star's End.

with a third (removable) pickup at the nut end of the neck. A capo is placed on the fingerboard (effectively cutting the strings in two lengths) and crocodile clips at harmonic points on the strings between the two normal pickups; the three pickups are individually controlled through volume and "effects" pedals. With this setup, Frith can effectively play two or three separate voices simultaneously and he sometimes uses a violin bow and glass prism to obtain sound effects beyond the normal range of the instrument.

The electric guitar has now reached a point where it can produce rich chordal textures, unique tonal colorations, the sustain and melodic fluency of a wind instrument, and (if desired) a shattering volume which in itself adds a new dimension to music. In its short history, it has made its mark throughout the musical world, changed popular music, and prompted attempts at fusions between apparently incompatible styles. Perhaps what is most exciting about the electric guitar is that every new development in the instrument suggests still further advances, which open the door to unexpected sounds and undreamed-of musics. Whether the chances are taken or not, the electric guitar has become an instrument which can challenge our preconceptions about the very nature and functions of music.

OPPOSITE: *Jimi Hendrix.*

APPENDIX

APPENDIX 1
Standard Martin Guitar Measurements
(in cm)

(a) full-size flat-tops, twelve-fret necks.

	2	1	0	00	000	D
Overall length	94	95.9	95.9	95.9	100.5	100.5
Scale length	62.2	63.2	63.2	63.2	63.2	64.5
Body length	46.4	48	48.6	49.8	51.9	53.2
Body width:						
upper bout	21.6	23.5	24.1	24.8	27.3	29.2
waist	17.2	18.5	19.6	21.6	22.8	27.2
lower bout	30.5	32.9	34.2	35.9	38.1	39.7
Body depth:						
upper bout	9.5	8.6	8.6	8.3	8.3	10
lower bout	10.2	10.6	10.6	10.3	10.3	12.4
Fingerboard at						
nut	4.7	4.8	4.8	4.8	4.8	4.8

(b) flat-tops, fourteen-fret necks.

	0	00	0M	000	D
Overall length	97.5	98.1	101.3	100	102.2
Scale length	63.2	63.2	64.5	63.2	64.5
Body length	46.7	48	49.3	49.3	50.8
Body width:					
upper bout	25.4	27.6	28.6	28.6	29.2
waist	19.6	21.6	23.9	23.9	27.2
lower bout	34.2	36.3	38.1	38.1	39.7
Body depth:					
upper bout	8.6	8.5	8.5	8.5	10
lower bout	10.8	10.5	10.5	10.5	12.4
Fingerboard at					
nut	4.3	4.3	4.3	4.3	4.3

(c) arch-tops

	F	C	R
Overall length	101.3	99.4	97.5
Scale length	63.2	63.2	63.2
Body length	51.1	49.3	48
Body width:			
upper bout	29.4	28.6	27.5
waist	25	23.9	
lower bout	40.6	38.1	37.2
Body depth:			
upper bout	8.3	8.6	8.5
lower bout	10.5	10.6	10.8
Fingerboard at			
nut	4.3	4.3	4.3

APPENDIX 2
Martin Guitar Serial Numbers

The number next to each year indicates the serial number of the last guitar made in that year.

YEAR	No.	YEAR	No.
1898	8348	1936	65176
1899	8716	1937	68865
1900	9128	1938	71866
1901	9310	1939	74061
1902	9528	1940	76734
1903	9810	1941	80013
1904	9988	1942	83107
1905	10120	1943	86724
1906	10329	1944	90149
1907	10727	1945	93623
1908	10883	1946	98158
1909	11018	1947	103468
1910	11203	1948	108269
1911	11413	1949	112961
1912	11565	1950	117961
1913	11821	1951	122799
1914	12047	1952	128436
1915	12209	1953	134501
1916	12390	1954	141345
1917	12988	1955	147328
1918	13450	1956	152775
1919	14512	1957	159061
1920	15848	1958	165576
1921	16758	1959	171047
1922	17839	1960	175869
1923	19891	1961	181297
1924	22008	1962	187384
1925	24116	1963	193327
1926	28689	1964	199626
1927	34435	1965	207030
1928	37568	1966	217215
1929	40843	1967	230095
1930	45317	1968	241955
1931	49589	1969	256003
1932	52590	1970	271633
1933	55084	1971	294270
1934	58679	1972	313302
1935	61947	1973	333873

GLOSSARY

Those words given in small capital letters have a separate glossary entry of their own.

Aficionado An enthusiast, particularly of flamenco.

Aire The Spanish for "air," "atmosphere" or "manner." This term is widely used in flamenco in describing the character of a piece or a particular performance.

Alnico A magnet material, widely used in guitar pickups, the constituents of which are iron, aluminum, nickel, cobalt and copper. There are sixteen different types of alnico alloy available, each with different properties.

Alphabeto A method of denoting a standard chord in strummed music by a single letter of the alphabet so that it is unnecessary to write out the individual notes of the chord. *Alphabeto* systems were popularized by Italian composers for the guitar in the early seventeenth century.

Alzapua A right-hand technique in flamenco guitar whereby the thumb is used as a plectrum and plucks the string with both up-strokes and down-strokes.

Apoyando A plucking method whereby the finger is pushed through the string, coming to rest on the string below.

Appoggiatura A musical ornament or grace note linked to a second note, above or below, which is either harmonized or whose harmonization is implied.

Arch-top guitar A steel-string acoustic guitar whose top and back have a noticeable arch and whose strings pass over the bridge to a separate tailpiece. Arch-top guitars are particularly associated with jazz, and are sometimes referred to as f-hole, plectrum, orchestra or cello guitars. Those that have a top carved from a thick block of wood (rather than press-formed from a thin sheet) are also called carved-top guitars.

Arpeggio A chord played so that the notes are sounded individually in sequence instead of simultaneously.

Autoharp A type of keyed zither, with each key connected to dampers so that, when it is depressed, only the notes of a particular chord are sounded.

Baile Spanish for "dance": one of the three main elements of flamenco.

Bandurria A small Spanish folk "lute" somewhat like a CITTERN, with a flat, pear-shaped body.

Belly bridge A common type of steel-string guitar bridge, the center section (or "belly") of which is deeper and thicker than the ends.

Binding The border or edging inlaid to the guitar body and sometimes to the fingerboard. The terms "binding" and "PURFLING" are often used synonymously.

Bookmatch To split a piece of timber into two thin sheets with exactly matched grain.

Bourdon A heavy bass string, often used together with a light string (tuned an octave higher) on the lower courses of early guitars.

Bouts, upper and lower The convex portions of the guitar body respectively above and below the waist.

Braces see **Struts**

Café cantante A type of café which flourished in late nineteenth-century Spain, whose raison d'être was the performance of flamenco.

Cante Spanish for "song": one of the three main elements of flamenco.

Cante andaluz Spanish for "Andalucian song": one of the main constituents of flamenco.

Cante gitano Spanish for "gypsy song": one of the main constituents of flamenco, considered by many to be the most important and profound element of the art.

Capacitor An electrical component consisting of two charged metal plates separated by an insulating layer. Capacitors are capable of conducting alternating currents, their efficiency as conductors increasing with the current's frequency, and are used in electric guitar tone controls.

Capo or **capotasto** A bar that can be clamped across a guitar's fingerboard behind any fret to raise the pitch of all the strings. Capos are widely used in steel-string and flamenco playing. (The flamenco name for a capo is *cejilla*.)

Chitarra battente A type of early guitar that had five double- or treble-strung courses of wire strings passing over the bridge, fixed frets, and a vaulted back.

Chitarrone A bass lute with a very long neck which supports open bass strings in addition to the normal strings stopped against the fingerboard.

Chordophone Any musical instrument sounded by vibrating strings.

Cittern An instrument with a small, flat, pear-shaped body and wire strings, which was popular in Europe from the early sixteenth to the late eighteenth century.

Compás Spanish for "rhythm," "beat" or "tempo": in flamenco, *compás* is the pattern of accented beats in a *cante*, *baile* or *toque con compás*.

Compensation The difference between the theoretical SCALE LENGTH and the actual length of an open string on the guitar. Compensation must be taken into account in the guitar's construction if it is to play in tune.

Dreadnought guitar A steel-string guitar with a very large body, square shoulders and very little indentation at the waist.

Duende A Spanish word meaning, literally, "elf" or "spirit." A term used figuratively in flamenco to describe the performer's state of creative inspiration.

Dulcimer A musical instrument related to the zither. The best-known type today is the Appalachian dulcimer, which usually has three strings and a fretboard mounted along nearly the entire length of a slender body.

Electromagnetic pickup A pickup made of a coil of copper wire wound around magnetic pole pieces. When ferrous-based strings vibrate in the magnetic field, an alternating current is induced in the coil.

Endblock A substantial block of wood inside the guitar body where the two sides, top and back are joined. There are two endblocks, one at the front and one at the rear end of the body; on most classical and flamenco guitars the front endblock takes the form of a SLIPPER FOOT.

Equal or **Even temperament** The division of the octave into a scale with precisely equal semitones. The twelve semitones of the modern equal-tempered scale, as used on the guitar and piano, give intervals and pitches slightly different from those of the "natural" scales based on whole-number frequency ratios between notes.

Falseta A passage of melodic variations played on the guitar in flamenco.

Fan strutting A fan-shaped system of bars glued beneath the guitar soundboard in the lower bout to give it strength and control its vibration. Fan strutting is used on most classical and flamenco guitars. The number of bars can be anything from three to nine, but seven is most common.

Floreo A Spanish word meaning, literally, "idle talk" or "chatter." The flamenco term for decorative playing which adds nothing substantial to the music.

Fundamental see **Harmonic**

Fuzz-box A distortion-producing device, normally operated by a footswitch, which modifies the signal from an electric guitar pickup to give a rasping tone.

Glissando Sliding up or down the scale, running one note into the next.

Golpeador The tap-plate which protects the soundboard of a flamenco guitar from the drumming of the guitarist's fingers. *Golpeadores* used to be made of wood; now they are made of either clear or white plastic.

Harmonic A tone of the harmonic series. The harmonic series consists of the fundamental and upper partials (the second, third, fourth and higher harmonics) of any note. For a vibrating string, the fundamental corresponds to the natural frequency of the entire vibrating length, the second harmonic to the frequency of half the string length, the third to one third, and so on. The pitch of the note is perceived as that of the fundamental; the tone color is determined by the proportions in which the partials are present, and this depends on the way the string is plucked and the properties of the particular instrument. When playing "in harmonics" by touching the string lightly at a NODAL POINT without fretting it, all harmonics not having a node at that point are eliminated. Thus, when the harmonic at the twelfth fret is played, the fundamental,

third and fifth harmonics of the open string are eliminated, but the second, fourth and sixth harmonics sound.

Hawaiian guitar A guitar made for Hawaiian-style playing. The strings are raised high above the fingerboard (which does not have to be fretted) and pitch is changed by sliding a metal bar across the strings.

Heel That part of the neck of the guitar which extends down the sides at the junction between neck and body.

Hitch pins Pins at the base of the body on a CHITARRA BATTENTE or similar instrument. The strings are attached to them after passing over the bridge.

Humbucking pickup An electromagnetic pickup containing two single-coil pickups in the same housing. The two are connnected so the coils are out of phase and the pole pieces have opposite magnetic polarities. This cancels out radio frequency hum between the two coils; a side-effect is to reduce the pickup's high-frequency response.

Indox A ceramic material used for making permanent magnets, now frequently used in guitar pickups. There are eight different grades, with different magnetic properties. Other commercial names for the same material are Diox and Arnox.

Intabulation (1) The art of transcribing music into tablature. (2) A piece of music so transcribed.

Juerga A spontaneous party for the performance of flamenco.

Just intonation Literally, correctness of pitch. A scale system which uses the exact whole-number frequency ratios of the harmonic series, wherever possible, to determine the intervals between notes.

Ligado A technique in flamenco whereby passages of notes are played with the left hand alone.

Linings Strips of wood used in an acoustic guitar to strengthen the junction of sides and back and sides and top. They may either be continuous or kerfed: kerfed linings are notched at regular intervals so that they can easily be bent to the shape of the guitar.

Lutherie The art of making lutes, guitars, violins and related instruments.

Luthier A practitioner of lutherie.

Mastic A slow-drying paste or gum. Mastic with a black filler was used as a decorative inlay on many guitars until the early part of the nineteenth century.

"Moustaches" The decorative fretwork curlicues at each end of the bridge on the soundboard of an early guitar.

Nodal point A stationary point on a vibrating string (or diaphragm). A string's vibration is compounded from several wave forms corresponding to the fundamental and higher HARMONICS. The fundamental of an open string has nodal points at the nut and saddle; the second harmonic's nodal points are at the nut, saddle and twelfth fret; the third harmonic's at the nut, saddle and third points, and so on.

Nut A bar (usually of ivory, bone or plastic) at the point where the fingerboard joins the head. The nut provides a bearing surface for the strings, and holds them at the correct height above the fingerboard and the correct distance from one another.

Octave divider A sound-modifying device which splits a note from an electric guitar to give either the octave above or the octave below, in addition to the original note.

Phrygian mode One of the scales used in early church music, now used in flamenco, giving the sequence of notes E, F, G, A, B, C, D, E.

Picado A fast run or passage of repeated notes in flamenco, plucked with two fingers of the right hand.

Pickguard A protective plastic plate attached to the top of a steel-string or electric guitar to protect it against marking or damage from fingerpicks or a plectrum.

Piezo-electric transducer A pickup that uses a piezo-electric crystal to convert physical stresses in the guitar top or bridge into electrical impulses.

Pin bridge A type of bridge on which the strings are attached by means of ivory, wooden or plastic pins. The string ends are inserted in holes drilled through the bridge into the body cavity of the guitar and wedged into place by the pins, which are pushed tightly into the holes. Pin bridges were common on nineteenth-century gut-strung guitars and are now used on most steel-string guitars.

Polyphony Music in several parts played together, each with an independent melodic line.

Potentiometer A variable electrical resistor. Both linear- and audio-taper potentiometers are used in electric guitar controls; a linear-taper potentiometer's value varies evenly over its whole operating range, while the variation of an audio-taper potentiometer is matched to the non-linear perception of the human ear.

Punteado A style of playing in which the strings are plucked rather than strummed.

Purfling A decorative inlay strip around the edges of a guitar or other musical instrument. The terms "purfling" and "BINDING" are often used synonymously.

Pyramid bridge A type of bridge, found on many American guitars made between 1850 and 1930, which has a decorative pyramid-shaped hump at each end.

Pythagorean scale The earliest known systematic division of the octave, based on simple whole-number ratios between notes and the rule that fifths must be perfect. On the Pythagorean scale not all semitones are of equal size and there is a real difference in pitch between, for example, E♭ and D♯.

Quarter-sawing The sawing of a log so that the cuts are effectively radial to the log, and the annular rings of the wood are perpendicular to the face of the resulting planks.

Rasgueado Strumming with the right hand, a term now used chiefly with respect to flamenco guitar.

Resonator guitar A steel-string guitar fitted with a spun metal resonator inside the body to increase the volume. Resonator guitars are often called "Dobros" after their inventors, the Dopera Brothers.

Ritornello A recurring instrumental passage, often between the verses of a song.

Rose; rosette (1) The fretted wood or parchment decoration filling the soundhole of early guitars and kindred instruments. (2) The marquetry decoration around the soundhole of classical and flamenco guitars.

Saddle A thin strip, usually of ivory, bone or white plastic, set into the bridge of a guitar to provide a bearing surface for the strings.

Scale length The theoretical length of the open string, from which the location of the frets is calculated. The scale length is twice the distance from the nut to the twelfth fret, and in practice this is normally a little less than the actual STRING LENGTH.

Scordatura A tuning in which the pitch of one or more of the strings is changed from normal.

Single-coil pickup An electromagnetic pickup with one coil wound around a single pole piece or set of pole pieces.

Slipper foot The forward endblock of a classical or flamenco guitar which connects the neck, sides, top and back, and extends down the inside of the back in a shape like a foot.

Soundboard or **table** The top of the guitar body.

Stop tailpiece A type of tailpiece, separate from the bridge, used to anchor the strings on most solid-body electric guitars. Stop tailpieces usually consist of a heavy metal bar attached to the guitar body by two large screws which can be adjusted for height.

String length The length of a string from the SADDLE to the NUT.

Struts or **braces** The strengthening bars fitted within the guitar to give it stability and control the way it vibrates. The size and disposition of the struts on the soundboard play a vital role in determining the guitar's tone, volume and balance.

Sunburst finish A decorative finish applied to some steel-string and electric guitars, achieved by spraying a dark lacquer over a pale undercoat. The dark lacquer is graduated, being applied most heavily at the edges. Sunburst finishes were originally used to mimic the appearance of the varnish on old violins.

Superhumbucking pickup A HUMBUCKING PICKUP with additional magnets. Superhumbucking pickups can be made either to give a greater output than normal humbucking pickups or to give the same output with a better high-frequency response.

Syncopation The displacement of an accent to a beat which is not usually accented.

Tablature A system of writing music which shows the location of the player's fingers on the fingerboard, rather than the pitch of the note.

Table see **Soundboard**

441

Theorbo A bass lute, generally similar to a CHITARRONE but with a shorter neck.

Tied bridge A guitar bridge to which the strings are directly tied.

Tone projector or *tornavoz* A device designed to modify the guitar's sound, consisting of a metal cylinder or conoid fitted below the soundhole.

Tone wood Any timber suitable for making the soundboard of a musical instrument.

Toque (1) A general flamenco term for guitar playing. (2) A piece of music played on the guitar (particularly in flamenco).

Toque con compás A flamenco guitar piece with a set rhythmic pattern.

Toque libre A flamenco guitar piece without a strictly fixed rhythm.

Trapeze tailpiece A type of tailpiece, separate from the bridge, used on some arch-top and electric guitars. The strings are anchored to a metal bar fixed to the base of the body by two stays, the whole unit looking something like a trapeze.

Tremolo (1) A rapid, regular variation in the loudness of a note. (2) The rapid repetition of the same note to simulate this effect.

Truss rod A metal bar set in to the neck of a steel-string or electric guitar to counteract the tendency of the strings to bow the neck. Most truss rods are adjustable.

Tune-o-matic bridge A type of adjustable electric guitar bridge, developed by the Gibson company, which has a separate saddle for each string. All six saddles are mounted on the same metal block, whose height can be adjusted by a screw at each end, and can be screwed back and forth for accurate compensation.

Two-footed bridge A type of bridge on arch-top guitars, developed in principle from the violin bridge and standing on two feet.

Univibe A transistorized device used with an electric guitar to mimic the sound of a rotating speaker.

Vibrola or **vibrato arm** A device (often misnamed "Tremolo arm") used on some electric guitars to alter the pitch of the strings and then return it to normal.

Vihuela *de mano* A guitar-like instrument which normally had six courses of strings tuned to the intervals of the lute. The vihuela *de mano* was popular among the Spanish aristocracy in the sixteenth century and was also played in Italy, where it was called the *viola da mano*.

Wah-wah pedal A transistorized tone-modifying device, operated by a foot pedal, used to give a wide range of special effects with an electric guitar.

Wolf note A "rogue" note on a stringed instrument which has a different tone color and volume from those around it, and whose volume oscillates wildly after it has been sounded. A wolf note can occur when the frequency of a note coincides with a natural resonant frequency of the instrument's body.

FOOTNOTES

THE CLASSICAL GUITAR

THE VIHUELA AND FOUR-COURSE GUITAR

1. A Spanish document of 1360 mentions one Nicholous Vecherii as a "sonator de viula." Quoted in *Anuario Musical* no. 5, 1950, p. 199.

2. See José Subirá, *Historia de la música española e hispanoamericana*, Barcelona, 1953, p. 219.
   John Ward's thesis on *The Vihuela de Mano and its Music* also gives sources for information on similar guild regulations in Seville in 1527 and Granada in 1528 and 1552.

3. Juan Bermudo, *Declaración de Instrumentos Musicales*, Book II, Chapter XXXVI, states that "Ten frets is a good mean, and on well-proportioned vihuelas there can sometimes be room for more than eleven."

4. Bermudo, ibid., Book IV, Chapters LXXVII and LXXV respectively.

5. Bermudo, ibid., Book IV, Chapter LXXV.

6. Bermudo's description of the basic method of fretting the six-course *vihuela común*, given in Book IV Chapter LXXV, corresponds exactly with one given in a French source of 1556. Bermudo also gives more complex procedures, including one in Book IV Chapter LXXXXVI for fretting a seven-course vihuela "to play all the semitones," but it is not clear whether the method he describes was ever used.

7. Bermudo, ibid., Book IV, Chapter LXXXIII.

8. Bermudo, ibid., Book IV, Chapter LXXXVI.

9. The method used for calculating equal temperament fret positions was the "rule of eighteen," according to which the string length was divided into eighteen and the first fret placed on the first division. The second fret was placed one eighteenth of the way along the remaining string length, and so on. For truly accurate fretting, the dividing figure should be 17.817, but the "rule of eighteen" gave a reasonably true approximation, and with movable tied frets final adjustments could be made by ear. The "rule of eighteen" was published in several sixteenth–century lute books.

10. Bermudo, op. cit., Book IV, Chapter LXXVII.

11. Don Sebastián de Covarrubias Orozco, *Tesoro de la Lengua Castellana*, 1611, p. 670.

THE FIVE-COURSE GUITAR

1. Juan Bermudo, op. cit., Book II, Chapter XXXII.

2. Bermudo, ibid., Book IV, Chapter LXV.

3. A fuller discussion of Bermudo's and Fuenllana's tunings can be found in James Tyler's "The Renaissance Guitar 1500–1650," *Early Music*, October 1975.

4. Gaspar Sanz, *Instrucción de Música sobre la Guitarra Española*, 1964, "Regla Primera" p. 1.

THE TRANSITIONAL GUITAR

1. George Hogarth, "Musical Instruments: The Harp and Guitar," *The Musical World*, Volume III, no. XXXII, 1836, p. 85.

THE MODERN CLASSICAL GUITAR

1. See the article by José Romanillos, "Antonio de Torres Jurado, Un Genio en el Olvido," *La Voz de Almería*, December 7, 1974.
   Señor Romanillos quotes a letter of 1931 from Juan Martínez Sirvent to Canon Rodríguez Torres which mentions Torres' skill in playing the *citara*, which is thought to refer to a pear-shaped guitar. Such an instrument, attributed to Torres, survives in a private collection in Japan.

2. We are indebted for this information to José Romanillos, who discovered the document.

3. A classical guitar by Torres, dated 1854, has a label with an address in the calle de la Ballestilla, Seville.

4. A clear account of this theory is given by Terence Usher in "The Spanish Guitar in the Nineteenth and Twentieth Centuries," *Galpin Society Journal*, no. XI, 1956, p. 5 & ff.

5. Discussion of the acoustics of concert halls can be found in P. H. Parkin and H. R. Humphreys *Acoustics, Noise and*

Buildings, London, 1958. The absorption coefficients for different materials at different frequencies, as measured by the National Physics Laboratory, show that a member of an audience is acoustically two-and-a-half times as absorbent at a frequency of 400cps as at 125cps. The absorption coefficient of air is negligible up to a frequency of 1000cps, but rises with frequency thereafter. Both these factors suggest that guitars for playing in large halls should be made treble-resonant (to overcome the absorption of high frequencies), a point reinforced by Parkin and Humphreys' statement that it is increasingly difficult to attain sufficient high-frequency response as the size of hall increases.

6. Andrés Segovia, *Guitar Review* no. 16, 1954.

CONSTRUCTION

1. Quoted by David George, *The Flamenco Guitar*, Madrid, 1969, p. 54

2. From an interview with Tom Evans, Madrid, 1976.

3. All quotations from David Rubio are taken from "David Rubio, Master Craftsman" by George Clinton, *Guitar*, October, 1972.

4. From an interview with Tom Evans, Kalamazoo, 1976.

MUSIC FOR THE VIHUELA

1. Juan Bermudo, *Declaración de Instrumentos Musicales*, Osuna, 1555, f. 30r.

2. Miguel de Fuenllana, *Orphenica Lyra*, Seville, 1554, f. 5r.

3. Ibid., f. 6v and r.

4. Ibid., f. 5r and 6v.

5. Quoted in Emilio Pujol, *El Dilema del Sonido en la Guitarra*, Buenos Aires, 1960, p. 41.

6. Bermudo, op. cit., f. 99v.

7. Ibid., f. 30.

8. The manner of playing this piece today is the subject of some controversy. When played on the modern guitar with standard guitar tuning, it is possible to finger it so that consecutive notes are played on different strings. In this way, the sounds of the notes can be made to sustain and overlap, as they do on the harp. This effect, however, is a possibility arising from the transcription to the modern guitar, and it seems certain that Mudarra was inspired solely by the dissonances which Luduvico obtained by his sophisticated use of artificial semitones on the old diatonic harp. (Harp players in South America still use this technique.)

9. Venegas de Henestrosa included vihuela pices in his *Libro de cifra nueva para tecla, arpa y vihuela*, Alcalá de Henares, 1557. See also Antonio de Cabeçon, *Obras de Música para Tecla, Arpa y Vihuela*, Madrid, 1578, and Tomás de Santa María, *Libro llamado Arte de tañer fantasia, assí para tecla como vihuela*, Valladolid, 1565.

FOUR-COURSE GUITAR MUSIC

1. Melchiore de Barberiis, *Opera Intitolato Contina . . . Libro Decimo*, Venice, 1549.

2. Juan Bermudo, op. cit., f. 96v.

3. Thomas Morley, *A Plaine and Easie Introduction to Practicall Musick,* 1597. Quoted in O. Strunk, *Source Readings in Music History*, London, 1952, p. 277.

4. Thoinot Arbeau, *Orchesography*, 1588, trans. Cyril W. Beaumont, 1925, p. 33.

5. The discovery was made by François Lesure in the Vadianbibliothek, St. Gall, Switzerland. See F. Lesure, "La Guitare en France au XVIe. Siècle," *Musica Disciplina*, vol. IV, 1950.

6. Daniel Heartz, "An Elizabethan Tutor for the Guitar," *Galpin Society Journal*, vol. XVII, 1964.
   There was an English edition and a further French edition of 1578—which together would have amounted to 3,600 copies. There are no known surviving copies, but one Pierre Phalèse, a music publisher in Louvain, borrowed the *Instructions* wholesale for *Selectissima elegantissimaque, Gallica, Italica, et Latinain Guiterne Ludenda Carmina* (Louvain and Antwerp, 1570). The music in this book consists of 106 pieces, eighty of which are certainly lifted from the known guitar books of LeRoy and Ballard, and the remainder presumably borrowed from the missing *Instructions*.

7. For four-course guitar books see Howard M. Brown's *Instrumental Music Printed Before 1600*, Harvard University Press, 1965, and James Tyler, "The Renaissance Guitar 1500–1650," *Early Music*, October, 1975.

FIVE-COURSE GUITAR MUSIC.

1. For dating this work, see Emilio Pujol, "Significación de Juan Carlos y Amat (1572–1642) en la historia de la guitarra," *Anuario Musical*, Barcelona, vol. V, 1950.

2. Dr. Juan Carlos y Amat, *Guitarra Española y Vándola*, Gerona, 1639, p. 23–4.

3. Treatise against public amusements of Juan de Mariana

(1536–1624), quoted in "Saraband" entry in Willi Apel, *Harvard Dictionary of Music*, London, 1969.

4. Giovanni Paolo Foscarini, *Il Primo, Secundo, e Terzo Libro della Chitarra Spagnuola, c.* 1629, introduction.

5. For further music see "Bibliography of Guitar Tablatures, 1546–1764," *Journal of the Lute Society of America*, vol. V, 1972 and vol. VI, 1973.

6. The Bibliothèque Nationale in Paris holds collections containing 54 guitar pieces and 118 theorbo pieces, and there is also a large collection of 137 pieces for lute and theorbo in the Bibliothèque Municipale of Besançon, France. Some of these works do appear in the published books and many of the pieces for guitar are, in fact, versions of theorbo music adapted and transcribed by de Visée.

7. Rafael Mitjana, "La Musique en Espagne," *Encyclopédie de la Musique et Dictionnaire du Conservatoire*, eds. A. Lavignac and L. de la Laurencie, Paris, 1927. Part 1, Vol. 2, p. 2080.

8. Gaspar Sanz, *Instrucción de Música sobre la Guitarra Española*, 1674, f. 6r.

9. Francisco Guerau, *Poema Harmonica compuesto de Varias Cifras por el Temple de la Guitarra Española*, Madrid, 1694. Quoted in Alexander Bellow, *The Illustrated History of the Guitar*, New York, 1970, p. 102.

10. There is a copy of this in the Euing Library, Glasgow University.

11. Jean-Jacques Rousseau, *Dictionnaire de Musique*, Paris, 1768, quoted in T. F. Heck, *The Birth of the Classic Guitar and its Cultivation in Vienna*, Ph.D. dissertation, Yale University, 1970, p. 149–50.

MUSIC FOR THE TRANSITIONAL GUITAR

1. Fernando Sor, ed. Napoleon Coste, *Méthode complète pour la Guitare*, Paris, n.d., p. 1.

2. Emilio Pujol, *El Dilema del Sonido en la Guitarra*, Buenos Aires, 1960, p. 46.

3. F. Sor, *Méthode, c.* 1845, transl. A. Merrick, n.d., p. 43.

4. Quoted in P. J. Bone, *The Guitar and Mandolin*, London, 1954, P. 256.

5. Hector Berlioz, *A Treatise on Modern Instrumentation and Orchestration*, trans. Mary Cowden Clarke, London, 1856, p. 67.

6. Frank Mott Harrison, *Reminiscences of Madame Sidney Pratten*, London, 1899, p. 22–23.

7. George Henry Derwort, *New Method of Learning the Spanish Guitar*, London, 1825, p. 7.

8. Dionisio Aguado, *Nuevo Método*, Paris, 1820.

9. N. Jauralde, *The Complete Preceptor for the Spanish Guitar*, London, *c.* 1827, p. 5.

10. Derwort, op. cit., p. 8.

11. Ibid., p. 8.

12. See Emilio Pujol, op. cit., p. 44.

13. F. M. Harrison, op. cit., p. 85.

MODERN GUITAR MUSIC.

1. V. Bobri, *The Segovia Technique*, New York, 1972, p. 44.

2. Jaime Pahissa, *Manuel de Falla, his Life and Works*, transl. Jean Wagstaff, London, 1954, p. 112–113.

3. Martin Bookspan, "The Basic Repertoire," *Stereo Review*, New York, May 1974.

4. Sleeve notes to Rodrigo's *Fantasia para un Gentilhombre*, with John Williams, CBS 72661.

5. George Clinton, "Segovia," *Guitar*, December, 1974.

6. Article on Segovia, *Guitar*, December, 1972.

7. Sleeve notes, CBS 72661.

8. Interview with Tim Walker, October 13, 1975.

9. Sleeve notes to Timothy Walker, *Guitar Recital*, L'Oiseau Lyre, OSCO 3.

10. Interview with David Bedford, October 28, 1975.

PRINCE AND PEASANT

1. From a manuscript in the Barbieri collection, Biblioteca Nacional, Madrid, quoted in Emilio Pujol, *Monumentos de la Música Española*, VII 13, n.7. Barcelona, 1949.

2. Bermudo, quoted in F. V. Grunfeld, *The Art and Times of the Guitar*, New York, 1969, p. 81.

3. Letter of October 13, 1550, quoted by John Roberts, "Some Notes on the music of the vihuelists," *Lute Society Journal*, vol. VII, 1965.

4. Rafael Mitjana, "La Musique en Espagne," *Encyclopédie de la Musique et Dictionnaire du Conservatoire*, ed. A. Lavignac and L. de la Laurencie, Paris, 1913. Part 1, Vol. 2, p. 2083.

5. Anthony Baines, "Fifteenth-century instruments in Tinctoris's De Inventione et Usu Musicae 1487," *Galpin Society Journal*, vol. III, 1950.

6. A. Salazar, "Music in the Primitive Spanish Theatre Before Lope de Vega," *Papers read by the Members of the American Musicological Society*, 1938, p. 104.

7. Lope de Vega, *Dorotea*, 1632, quoted in J. B. Trend, *Luis Milán and the vihuelists*, London, 1925, p. 30.

8. Juan Bermudo, *Declaración de Instrumentos Musicales*, Osuna, 1555, f. 99v.

9. Vicente Espinel, *The history of the life of the Squire Marcos de Obregón*, translated from the edition of 1618 by A. Langton, London, 1816.

10. Miguel de Cervantes, *Don Quixote*, part 2, chapter 34.

11. From an anonymous treatise, *La manière de bien et justement entoucher les lucs et guiternes*, Poitiers, 1556, quoted in Jean Baptiste Theodore Weckerlin, *Nouveau Musicana*, Paris, 1890, p. 105.

12. Quoted in Pierre Trichet, *Traité des instruments*, *c*. 1630, edited and published for the first time by François Lesure, *Annales Musicologiques*, vols. III and IV, Paris, 1955–56, vol. IV, p. 217.

13. Thomas Morley, *A Plaine and Easie Introduction to Practicall Music*, quoted in Oliver Strunk, *Source Readings in Music History*, London, 1952, p. 277.

14. Shakespeare, *Love's Labours Lost*, Act III, scene 1.

15. Thoinot Arbeau, *Orchesography*, 1588, translated by Cyril W. Beaumont, 1925, p. 66.

16. Ibid., p. 86.

17. François Lesure, "La Guitare en France au XVI Siècle," *Musica Disciplina*, vol. IV, 1950, p. 188.

18. Thomas Whytehorne, *Autobiography*, *c*. 1576, ed. J. M. Osborn, London, 1962, p. 11.
When talking about the guitar in England, confusion arises from the continuing use of the word "gittern," which was applied to types of medieval gut-strung plucked instruments. Though these instruments had disappeared by the time the guitar emerged, the name persisted and was often applied to the guitar.

19. Ibid., p. 21.

20. Gerald Hayes, *The King's Music*, London, 1937, p. 87.

21. Robert Laneham, *Captain Cox, his ballads and Books, or Robert Laneham's Letter (1548–49)*, ed. F. J. Furnivall, London, 1871, p. 59–60.

22. Walter Woodfill, *Musicians in English Society*, Princeton, 1953, p. 276.

BAROQUE GLORY

1. Don Sebastián de Covarrubias Orozco, *Tesoro de la Lengua Castellana o Española*, 1611, see "vihuela" entry.

2. Pierre Trichet, op. cit.

3. Luis de Briceño, *Método mui facilissimo para aprender a tañer la guitarra a lo Español*, Paris, 1626.

4. Vicenzio Giustiniani, *Discorse sopra la Musica de suoi tempi*, 1628, see Nigel Fortune, "Giustiniani on instruments," *Galpin Society Journal*, vol. V, March 1952.

5. Michael Praetorius, *Syntagma musicum*, vol. II of *De Organographia*, 1615–20, p. 53.

6. The instrument's popularity in Paris was not always matched in the provinces. A mathematician of Aix-en-Provence invented a method of making a guitar play automatically when placed in the hands of a skeleton. His ingenuity was sadly rewarded. Accused of witchcraft, he and his skeleton were burnt at the stake in 1664 in the market place at Aix.

7. Lady Frances P. Verney and Lady Margaret M. Verney, *Memoirs of the Verney Family during the Seventeenth Century*, London, 1904. Letter of October 10, 1647, vol. 1, p. 367–8.

8. Ibid., March 17, 1647, vol. 1. p. 496.

9. Ibid., 1657, vol. 2, p. 94.

10. Quoted in Sir F. Bridge, *Samuel Pepys Lover of Musique*, London 1903, p. 78–9.

11. Ibid., p. 79.

12. Anthony Hamilton, *Memoirs of the Count of Grammont*, ed. Sir Walter Scott, London, 1905, p. 204–5.

13. Roger North, *Memoirs of Musick*, London, 1846, p. 126.

14. One of Sanz's biographers states that he studied there under Cristoval Carisani, although this has been questioned as Carisani was born later than Sanz (in 1655) and became organist in Naples in 1680, sometime *after* Sanz had occupied the post. However, in the introduction to his guitar book—one of the few firm sources of information about his life—Sanz refers to Carisani as "mi maestro." This implies that Carisani, if not his direct teacher, was at least a very strong influence on him.

FASHION AND SENTIMENT

1. Denis Diderot and Jean LeRond d'Alembert, *Encyclopédie, ou Dictionnaire raisonné des sciences, des arts et des métiers*, Paris 1751–1765, vol. 7, p. 1011.

2. John Brown, *An estimate of the Measures and Principles of the Times*, vol. II, 1758, quoted in Frederic Grunfeld, *The Art and Times of the Guitar*, New York, 1969, p. 130.

3. Dr. Charles Burney, *The Present State of Music in France and Italy*, London, 1771, p. 6.

4. Ibid., p. 143–4.

5. Ralph Kirkpatrick, *Domenico Scarlatti*, Princeton, 1953, p. 205.

6. Johann Mattheson, *Neu eröffnetes Orchester*, Hamburg, 1713, para. 17.

7. Sir John Hawkins, *A General History of the Science and Practise of Music*, edition of 1875, vol. II, p. 834.

8. Richard Twiss, *Travels through Portugal and Spain in 1772 and 1773*, London, 1775, p. 17.

9. William Beckford, *The Travel Diaries of William Beckford*, ed. Guy Chapman, 2 vols., Cambridge, England, 1928, vol. 2, p. 218–9.

10. Richard Ford, *Gatherings from Spain*, London, 1846, p. 356.

11. François Lesure, *Music and Art in Society*, trans. D. and S. Stevens, Pennsylvania, 1968.

12. Antonio Bartolommeo Bruni, *Un inventaire sous la terreur*, ed. J. Gallay, Paris, 1890, passim.

VIRTUOSI AND ENTHUSIASTS

1. *The Giulianiad, or Guitarist's Magazine*, London 1833, no. 1, p. 27.

2. Hector Berlioz, *Memoirs*, trans. R. and E. Holmes, New York, 1932, vol. 1, p. 187–8.

3. Ibid., p. 199–200.

4. Fritz Buek, *Die Gitarre und ihr Meister*, Berlin, 1926, p. 8.

5. H. C. Kock, *Musikalisches Lexicon*, Frankfurt, 1802. Quoted in T. F. Heck, *The Birth of the Classic Guitar and its Cultivation in Vienna*, Ph.D. dissertation, Yale University, 1970, p. 61.

6. *The Harmonicon*, 1929, part 1, p. 30.

7. See T. F. Heck, "The role of Italy in the early history of the classic guitar," *Guitar Review*, 34, 1971.

8. Sir Charles Burney, *The Present State of Music in France and Italy*, London, 1771, p. 189.

9. *The Harmonicon*, no. 1, January 1823, p. 22.

10. *The Giulianiad*, no. 1, introduction, p. 1.

11. T. F. Heck, *The Birth of the Classic Guitar* . . . p. 127.

12. Ibid., p. 129.

13. Ibid., p. 145.

14. *The Giulianiad*, no. 1, p. 9–11.

15. Flamini Duvernay, *A Complete Instruction Book for the Guitar*, London, 1827, p. 4.

16. *The Giulianiad*, no. 1, p. 38.

17. See José Romanillos, "Julián Arcas (1832–1882)," *La Voz de Almería*, April 21, 1976.

18. Frank Mott Harrison, *Reminiscences of Madame Sidney Pratten*, London, 1899, p. 27.

19. Ibid., p. 71.

THE WIDENING AUDIENCE

1. Emilio Pujol, *Tárrega*, Lisbon, 1960, p. 156–7.

2. Miguel Llobet, *Revista Musical Catalan*, Paris, January 20, 1910, quoted in "Notes on Tárrega," trans. John Roberts, *Guitar*, December 1975.

3. Pujol, op. cit., quoted in John Roberts, "Historical Notes, Tárrega," *Guitar*, October, 1972.

4. Article on Segovia, *Guitar*, December, 1972.

5. Pujol, op. cit., quoted in John Roberts, "Historical Notes, Miguel Llobet," *Guitar*, December, 1972.

6. Bernard Gavoty, *Andrés Segovia, Great Concert Artists series*, Geneva, 1955, p. 12.

7. George Clinton, "Segovia," *Guitar*, December, 1974.

8. Ibid.

9. Lance Bosman, "Oscar Ghiglia," *Guitar*, August, 1974.

10. Press handout from Deutsche Grammophon Gesellschaft.

11. Julian Bream talking to Peter Sensier on BBC 3's scrics, "The Classical Guitar," December 22, 1973.

12. George Clinton and R. Brown, "Julian Bream," *Guitar*, April, 1974.

13. Interview with Peter Sensier, op. cit.

14. Sleeve notes to John Williams' recording of Rodrigo and Dodgson, CBS 72661.

15. John Williams talking to Peter Sensier on the BBC 3 series, "The Classical Guitar," December 6, 1972.

16. George Clinton, "John Williams," *Guitar*, July, 1972.

THE FLAMENCO GUITAR

ORIGINS AND DEVELOPMENT

1. David George, op. cit., p. 110.

2. "Paco de Lucia," *Guitar*, April, 1976, p. 22.

3. George Borrow, *The Zincali; or, An Account of the Gypsies of Spain*, London, 1841, p. 341.

4. Mikhail Ivanovich Glinka, *Memoirs*, translated by Richard B. Mudge, Oklahoma, 1963, p. 206.

5. Richard Ford, *Gatherings from Spain*, London, 1846, p. 355.

6. Donald Pohren, *Lives and Legends of Flamenco*, Seville, 1964, p. 77.

7. Ibid., p. 293.

9. From an interview with Tom Evans, London, 1975.

THE GUITAR IN FLAMENCO

1. All quotations from Paco Peña are from an interview with Tom Evans, London, 1976.

2. All quotations from Juan Martín are from an interview with Tom Evans, London, 1975.

3. All quotations from Sabicas are from an interview conducted for Tom Evans by Kati Boland in New York, 1977.

4. All quotations from Paco de Lucia are from "Paco de Lucia," *Guitar*, April, 1976.

THE GUITAR IN LATIN AMERICA

1. Gilbert Chase, *The Music of Spain*, New York, 1941, p. 258.

2. Irving A. Leonard, "Romances of Chivalry in the Spanish Indies," *University of California Publications*, vol. 16, no. 3, 1933.

3. R. M. Stevenson, *The Music of Peru*, Washington, 1960, p. 57.

4. Nicolas Slonimsky, *Music of Latin America*, New York, 1972, p. 79.

5. Thomas Gage, *The English American, A New Survey of the West Indies* (1648), ed. A. P. Newton, London, 1928, p. 53.

6. Although the name "vihuela" is used, the tablature calls for a five-course instrument. In fact the term "vihuela" has remained in continuous use and is still heard today in the Pampas of Argentina to refer to the guitar.

7. R. M. Stevenson, *Music in Mexico*, New York, 1952, p. 162.

8. Segundo N. Contreras, *La guitarra argentina*, Buenos Aires, 1950, p. 10.

9. From Arturo Torres-Rioseco, *The Epic of Latin American Literature*, New York, 1942, quoted in Slonimsky, op. cit., pp. 73–4.

THE STEEL-STRING ACOUSTIC GUITAR

INSTRUMENTS

1. Julius Bellson states in *The Gibson Story*, Kalamazoo 1973, that Orville Gibson was originally paid a lump sum and a monthly fee for a period of two years to allow the newly-formed company to use his name and draw on his skills as designer and constructor. Further agreements were made until in 1915 it was finally arranged that Gibson (who was in failing health) should receive a lifetime royalty for the use of his name.

    The Gibson company became a subsidiary of Chicago Musical Instruments in 1944, and in 1974 the name of the parent company was changed to Norlin Music Inc.

2. Details of this, and the subsequent history of the Martin company, can be found in *Martin Guitars, A History* by Mike Longworth, Cedar Knolls, 1975. The Martin company is unusual in that it has remained in the control of the Martin family from its foundation.

3. From an interview with Tom Evans, New York, 1976.

4. From an interview in *Guitar Player*, February, 1975.

CONSTRUCTION

1. All quotations from Richard Schneider are from interviews with Tom Evans, Kalamazoo, 1976.

2. From an interview with Tom Evans, Nazareth, 1976.

3. At the time when this series of photographs was taken, Gibson was building the Mark guitars at Nashville. Since then, Mark production has been switched to Kalamazoo.

THE BIRTH OF THE AMERICAN GUITAR

1. Clinton Simpson, "Some Early American Guitarists," *Guitar Review*, No. 23, 1959.

2. Le Vaillant, 1781, quoted in Percival Kirby, *The Musical Instruments of the Native Races of South Africa*, London, 1934, p. 250.

3. Quoted in Paul Oliver, *The Story of the Blues*, London, 1969, p. 13.

4. Thomas D. Clark, *Pills, Petticoats and Plows, A History of the Country Store from 1865–1915*, New York, 1944, p. 299.

5. Robert Pete Williams, quoted in Bruce Cook, *Listen to the Blues*, London, 1975, p. 35.

6. Charles Love talking to Paul Oliver, *Conversation with the Blues*, London, 1965, p. 77.

7. W. C. Handy, *Father of the Blues*, London, 1957, p. 74.

THERE'S A LOT OF THINGS THAT GIVE YOU THE BLUES . . ."

1. Paul Oliver, *Conversation with the Blues*, p. 30.

2. Howling Wolf, interview with Pete Welding, published in *Downbeat*, Dec. 14, 1967, and *Blues Unlimited*, no. 60, March, 1969.

3. Interview with Julius Lester, *Sing Out!* Vol. 15, no. 3, July 1965.

4. Paul Oliver, *Conversation with the Blues*, p. 25.

5. Ibid., p. 27.

"MY HOME IS IN THE DELTA"

1. Yank Rachel talking to Bob Koester, quoted in Paul Oliver, *The Story of the Blues*, p. 133.

2. *Sing Out!* op. cit.

3. Bruce Cook, op. cit., p. 184.

4. *Sing Out!* op. cit.

5. Samuel Charters, *The Bluesmen*, New York, 1967, p. 95.

6. Paul Oliver, *Conversation with the Blues*, p. 66.

7. Ibid., p. 68.

8. Big Bill Broonzy and Yannick Bruynoghe, *Big Bill Blues*, 1955, Oak reprint, 1964, p. 21.

9. Nehemiah James was given the nickname Skippy because of his habit, as a boy, of skipping around at parties.

WALKING THE BASSES

1. Paul Oliver, *The Story of the Blues*, p. 37.

RAGGING THE BLUES

1. Paul Oliver, *The Story of the Blues*, p. 43.

"TRAIN TIME"

1. Interview with Will Shade, quoted in Paul Oliver, *Conversation with the Blues*, p. 85.

2. Bruce Cook, op. cit., p. 122.

THE DEPRESSION AND AFTER

1. Rev. Gary Davis, *Blues and Gospel*, vol. 1, Biograph, BLP-12020.

2. Bruce Cook, op. cit., p. 133.

COUNTRY MUSIC

1. Bill C. Malone, *Country Music USA*, University of Texas, 1968, p. 43.

2. George D. Hay, *A Story of the Grand Ole Opry*, 1953, p. 1, quoted in Bill C. Malone, op. cit., p. 72.

3. Bob Krueger, "Sam McGee," *Guitar Player*, June, 1976, p. 17.

4. *The McGee Brothers*, Folkways FA 2379, sleeve notes by Jon Pankake.

5. *Guitar Player*, op. cit., p. 38.

6. Douglas B. Green, *Country Roots, The Origins of Country Music*, New York, 1976, p. 57.

7. Carrie Rodgers, *My Husband, Jimmie Rodgers*, Nashville, 1935, p. 7.

8. Fred G. Hoeptner, liner notes to "Authentic Cowboys and Their Western Songs," quoted D. Green, op. cit., p. 92.

9. *Guitar Player*, op. cit., p. 38.

10. Ralph Rinzler, "Bill Monroe," ed. Bill C. Malone and Judith McCulloh, *Stars of Country music*, University of Illinois Press, 1975, p. 208.

11. Archie Green, *Only a Miner*, Illinois, 1972, p. 306.

"WALKING DOWN THE BIG ROAD"

1. Alan Lomax, *Folk Songs of North America*, New York, 1960, pp. 426–7.

2. Quoted in Jerry Silverman, *The Folksinger's Guitar Guide*, New York, 1962, p. 6.

3. *Time*, Nov. 23, 1962.

4. Numerous assertions of the subversive effects of folk singing were made in the 1960s. In 1963 for instance, a resolution was passed by the Fire and Police Research Association of Los Angeles which stated that:

> ... there is increasing and cumulative evidence indicating a deep interest in, and much activity by the Communist Party, USA, in the field of Folk Music. ...

and:

> ... certain of the "Hootenannies" and other similar youth gatherings and festivals, both in this country and in Europe, have been used to brainwash and subvert, in a seemingly innocuous but actually covert and deceptive manner, vast segments of young people's groups ....

Nicolas Slonimsky, *Music since 1900*, New York, 1971, pp. 406–7.

5. Anthony Scaduto, *Bob Dylan*, London, 1972, p. 137.

6. Gil Turner, "Bob Dylan—A New Voice Singing New Songs," *Sing Out!* Vol. 12, no. 4, October–November 1962.

7. Paul Oliver, *Conversation with the Blues*, p. 6.

8. Interview with Stefan Grossman, December 14, 1976.

9. *Rolling Stone*, July 23, 1969.

THE ELECTRIC GUITAR

INSTRUMENTS

1. All quotations from Les Paul in this chapter are from an interview with Tom Evans, New York, 1976.

2. This information, along with details of early Gibson pickups, was given in the course of an interview between Walter Fuller and Tom Evans, Kalamazoo, 1976.

3. From an interview with Tom Evans, New York, 1976.

4. Gibson's reissue of the Explorer, in limited edition, was planned to be identical to the original in every respect, but was eventually produced with a mahogany body. The company was disappointed with the sound of the korina-wood prototypes made for the reissue, and switched to mahogany for better results.

THE BIRTH OF A NEW SOUND

1. Sleeve notes by Jim Crockett on *Tal Farlow Guitar Player*, Prestige P-24042.

2. Ibid.

3. Ibid.

4. M. J. Summerfield, *Barney Kessel ... a living legend*, London, 1973.

5. Michael Haralambos: *Right On: From Blues to Soul in Black America*, Cambridge, 1974, p. 24.

6. Bruce Cook, *Listen to the Blues*, London, 1975, p. 185.

7. "Les Paul," in *Jazz Guitarists*, Saratoga, California, 1975, p. 81.

8. Sleeve notes from Les Paul and Mary Ford's *The World is Still Waiting for the Sunrise*, Capitol SM-11308.

ROCK 'N' ROLL

1. Haley News 1966, quoted in Charlie Gillett, *The Sound of the City*, London, 1970, p. 30–31.

2. Peter Guralnik, *Feel Like Going Home*, New York, 1971, p. 140.

3. Anthony Scaduto, *Bob Dylan*, London, 1972, p. 6.

4. Bob Berman, "Frank Beecher and the Bill Haley Years," *Rock Guitarists*, Saratoga, California, 1974, p. 13.

5. Charlie Gillett, op. cit., p. 36.

6. "Bo Diddley," *Guitar Notables*, Saratoga, California, 1975, p. 18.

7. *B. B. King*, Amsco Music Publishing Company, 1970. Interview by Stanley Dance from *Jazz*, p. 7.

8. *Tal Farlow Guitar Player*, Prestige P-24042.

9. Robert Yelin, "Bucky Pizzarelli," *Jazz Guitarists*, op. cit., p. 86.

10. Ibid., p. 38.

11. William Ivey, "Chet Atkins," in *Stars of Country Music*, ed. Bill C. Malone and Judith McCulloh, Chicago, 1975, p. 282.

SCREAM POWER

1. Interview with Keith Richard by Robert Greenfield, *Rolling Stone*, August 1971.

2. Ibid.

3. Steve Rosen, "Jeff Beck," *Rock Guitarists*, op. cit., p. 11.

4. Steve Turner, *Conversations with Eric Clapton*, London, 1972, p. 47.

5. Chris Welch, *Hendrix, A Biography*, New York, 1972, p. 72.

6. Tony Palmer, *Born Under a Bad Sign*, London, 1970, p. 131.

7. Ralph Gleason, *The Jefferson Airplane*, New York, 1969, p. 93.

8. Steve Turner, op. cit., p. 58.

9. Ibid., p. 45.

10. Sleeve notes by Stanley Dance to B. B. King *Blues is King*, HMV CLP 3608.

11. Interview by Chuck Berg with Albert King, *Downbeat*, November, 1976.

12. Sleeve notes by Jim O'Neal to Magic Sam's Blues Band *Black Magic*, Delmark, DS-620.

13. Interview with Chuck Berry, *Rolling Stone*, January, 1972.

14. John Sharkey: "Beck is Back," *Rock Guitarists*, op. cit., p. 8.

15. Chris Welch, op. cit., p. 32.

16. Article on Jeff Beck in *Rolling Stone*, August, 1969.

17. Article on Roy Buchanan in *Rolling Stone*, February 1971.

THERE'S ONE IN EVERY CROWD

1. Steve Turner, op. cit., p. 50.

2. Jim Crockett, "Mundell Lowe," *Jazz Guitarists*, op. cit., p. 63.

BIBLIOGRAPHY

CLASSICAL

INSTRUMENTS

Agricola, Martin: *Musica Instrumentalis Deudsch.* Wittemberg, 1528 and 1545, reprinted Leipzig, 1896.

Baines, Anthony: *Musical Instruments through the Ages.* Harmondsworth, 1961.
European and American Musical Instruments. London, 1966.
Victoria and Albert Museum Catalogue of Musical Instruments. London, 1968.

Barber, J. Murray: *Tuning and Temperament, a Historical Survey.* Michigan, 1953.

Bermudo, Juan: *Declaración de Instrumentos Musicales.* Osuna, 1555.

Bessaraboff, Nicholas: *Ancient European Instruments in the Leslie Lindsey Mason Collection of the Museum of Fine Arts, Boston.* New York, 1941.

Bierdimpfl, K. A.: *Die Sammlung der Musikinstrumente des baierischen National museums.* Munich, 1883.

Bonanni, Filippo: *Gabinetto Armonico.* Rome, 1722.

Boyden, David: *Catalogue of the Hill Collection of Instruments in the Ashmolean Museum, Oxford.* Oxford, 1969.

Bragard, Roger and Ferdinand J. De Hen: *Musikinstrumente aus zwei Jahrtausenden.* Stuttgart, 1967.

Brown, M. Elizabeth: *Catalogue of the Crosby Brown Collection of Musical Instruments in the Metropolitan Museum.* New York, 1902–5.

Buchner, Alexander: *Musical Instruments through the Ages.* London, 1957.

Charnassé, Hélène: "Sur l'Accorde de la Guitare." *Recherches sur la Musique Française Classique,* no. VII, 1967.
"La Guitare." *Connaissance des Arts,* November, 1965.

Chouquet, Gustave: *Le Musée du Conservatoire Nationale de Musique, Catalogue raisonné des instruments de cette Collection.* Paris, 1894–1903.

Clemencic, René: *Old Musical Instruments.* London, 1968.

Clinton, George: "David Rubio, Master Craftsman." *Guitar,* October, 1972.
"José Romanillos, Luthier." *Guitar,* December, 1972.
"Robert Bouchet: Luthier." *Guitar,* February, 1973.

Dart, Thurston: "Instruments in the Ashmolean Museum." *Galpin Society Journal,* vol. Vii, 1948.

Devoto, Daniel: "Métamorphoses d'une cithare." *Revue de Musicologie,* vol. XLI, July, 1958.

Diagram Group: *Musical Instruments of the World.* London, 1976.

Donington, Robert: *The Instruments of Music.* London, 1962.

Engel, Carl: *A Descriptive Catalogue of the Musical Instruments in the South Kensington Museum.* 2nd, ed., London, 1874.

Fissore, Robert: *Les Maîtres Luthiers.* 4th. ed., Paris, *c.* 1890.
La Lutherie. Parts I & II, Paris, 1900.

Gabry, Gyorgy: *Old Musical Instruments.* Budapest, 1969.

Gallini, N.: *Mostra di Antichi Strumenti Musicali.* Milan, 1958.
Museo degli Strumenti Musicali. Milan, 1963.

Galpin, F. W.: *Old English Instruments of Music.* 4th. ed., London, 1965.
A Textbook of European Musical Instruments. London, 1937.

Garnault, Paul: *Le Temperament, son histoire, son application aux violes de gambe et guitares.* Paris, 1924.

Geiringer, K.: *Musical Instruments.* New York, 1943.
Alte Musikinstrumente im Museum Carolina Augusteum, Salzburg, 1932.

Gill, Donald: "The Stringing of the five-course Baroque Guitar." *Early Music,* October, 1975.

GLEICH, C. C. J. von: *Catalogues of the Music Library and Music Instruments of the Hague Municipal Museum.* The Hague, 1969, 1970.

HAMMERLICH, A.: *Das musikhistorische Museum.* Copenhagen, 1909.

HAMMOND, F. R., and N. J. ERICSSON: *The Belle Skinner Collection of Old Musical Instruments.* Holyoke, 1933.

Handbuch den Europäischen Volkmusikinstrumente. Stockholm Musik-historiska Museet, Stockholm, 1967.

HARRISON, Frank, and Joan RIMMER: *European Musical Instruments.* London, 1964.

HELLWIG, Günther: "Joachim Tielke." *Galpin Society Journal,* vol. XVII, 1964.

HIPKINS, A. J., and W. GIBB: *Musical Instruments, Historic, Rare and Unique,* Edinburgh, 1888.

HUTTIG, H. E.: "The Guitar Maker and his Techniques." *Guitar Review,* no. 28, 1965.

JACQUOT, A.: *La lutherie lorraine et française.* Paris, 1912.

JAHNEL, Franz: *Die Guitarre und ihr Bau.* Frankfurt am Main, 1963.

JEANS, James: *Science and Music.* Cambridge, 1937.

KASHA, Michael: "A New Look at the History of the Classic Guitar." *Guitar Review,* no. 30, 1968. *Scientific Development of a New Classical Guitar.* Tallahassee, 1971.

KINSKY, Georg: *Musikhistorisches Museum von Wilhelm Heyer in Köln.* Cologne, 1910.

KIRBY, P. R.: *The Musical Instruments of the Native Races of South Africa,* London, 1934.

KIRCHER, Athanasius: *Musurgia Universalis.* Rome, 1650.

LESURE, François: "La facture instrumentale à Paris au dix-septième siècle." *Galpin Society Journal,* no. VIII, 1954.

LICHTENWANGER, W.: *Survey of Musical Instrument Collections in the USA and Canada.* Ann Arbor, 1974.

LLOYD, Ll. S.: *Music and Sound.* London, 1937.

LUTGENDORFF, W. L. von: *Die Geigen- und Lautenmacher von Mittelalter bis zur Gegenwart.* Frankfurt am Main, 1922.

MAHILLON, V. C.: *Catalogue descriptif et analytique du Musée Instrumental du Conservatoire Royal de Musique de Bruxelles.* Ghent, 1893–1912.

MAIRANTS, Ivor: "The Ramírez Dynasty." *Guitar,* October, 1974.

MARCUSE, Sibyl: *Musical Instruments: A Comprehensive Dictionary.* New York, 1966.

MERSENNE, Marin: *Harmonie Universelle.* Paris, 1636. The books on instruments translated by R. E. Chapman, The Hague, 1957.

MURPHY, Sylvia: "The Tuning of the five-course Guitar." *Galpin Society Journal,* no. XXIII, 1970.

Musical Instruments. Horniman Museum, London, 1958.

NASSARE, Pablo: *Escuela música.* Zaragoza, 1724.

NEF, C.: *Katalog der Musikinstrumente.* Basel, 1906.

PANUM, Hortense: *Stringed Instruments of the Middle Ages.* Revised and edited by Jeffrey Pulver, London, 1940.

PATTERSON, John: "Richard Schneider, Luthier." *Guitar Player,* June, 1971.

PIERRE, Constant: *Les Facteurs d'Instruments de Musique.* Paris, 1893.

POST, C. N.: "The Origin and Growth of the Guitar, Mandolin and Banjo Industry in America." *Music Trades,* vol. 26, no. 24, 1903.

PRAETORIUS, Michael: *Syntagma Musicum II De Organographia.* Wolfenbüttel, 1619. Facsimile edition: Kassel, 1929.

PRYNNE, Michael: "A Surviving Vihuela de Mano." *Galpin Society Journal,* no. XVI, 1963.

PERLMETER, Alan: "Redesigning the Guitar." *Science news,* 98, 180, 1970.

ROMANILLOS, José: "Antonio de Torres Jurado, un Genio en el Olvido." *La Voz de Almería,* December 7, 1974.

ROOLEY, Anthony: "Orpheus with his Vihuela de Mano and Gittern." *Guitar,* May, 1975.

SACHS, Curt: *The History of Musical Instruments.* London, 1942. *Sammlung alter Musikinstrumente.* Berlin, 1922. *Real-Lexicon der Musikinstrumente.* Berlin, 1913.

SCHLOSSER, Julius Ritter von: *Die Sammlung alter Musikinstrumente. Kunsthistorisches Museum in Wien.* Vienna, 1920.

SEGOVIA, Andrés: "Guitar Strings before and after Albert Augustine." *Guitar Review*, no. 17, 1955.

SENSIER, Peter: "Torres and the First Generation." *Guitar*, October, 1973.
"Louis Panormo." *Guitar*, June, 1975.
"When a Vihuela is not a Vihuela," *Guitar*, November, 1975.

SHARPE, Albert Percy: *Make your own Spanish Guitar*. London, 1957.

STRUTT, J. W. (Lord Rayleigh): *The Theory of Sound*. London, 1894–6.

STANLEY, A. A.: *Catalogue of the Stearns Collection*. Ann Arbor, 1918.

TAYLOR, C. A.: *The Physics of Musical Sounds*. London 1965.

THOMPSON, Thomas Perronet: *Instructions to my Daughter for Playing on the Enharmonic Guitar*. London, 1829.

TYLER, James: "The Renaissance Guitar 1500–1650." *Early Music*, October, 1975.

USHER, Terence: "The Spanish Guitar in the Nineteenth and Twentieth Centuries." *Galpin Society Journal*, vol. XI,

VANNES, René: *Dictionnaire Universel des Luthiers*. Revised edition, Brussels, 1951, 1959.

VIRDUNG, Sebastian: *Musica getuscht*. Basel, 1511. Facsimile edition edited by Leo Schrade, Kassel, 1931.

MUSIC AND SOCIAL HISTORY

ALVER, Alfred W.: "The Golden Age of the Guitar." *The Chesterian*, vol. II, 1929.

ANGLÉS, Higinio: *Gloriosa contribución de España a la historia de la música universal*. Madrid, 1948.
La música de las Cantigas de Santa María del rey Alfonso el Sabio. Barcelona, 1943.
La música en la corte de Carlos V. Barcelona, 1944.
La música española desde la edad media hasta nuestros días. Barcelona, 1941.
"Latin Church Music on the Continent 3-Spain and Portugal." *The New Oxford History of Music*, vol. IV, Oxford, 1968.

ANGLÉS, Higinio and José SUBIRÁ: *Catálogo musical de la Biblioteca Nacional de Madrid*. Barcelona, 1943–51.

APEL, Willi: "Early Spanish Music for Lute and Keyboard Instruments." *Musical Quarterly*, XX, 1934.
The Notation of Polyphonic Music 900–1600. Cambridge, Mass., 1953.
"Solo Instrumental Music." *The New Oxford History of Music*, vol. IV, Oxford, 1968.

ARBEAU, Thoinot: *Orchesography*, 1588. Trans. Cyril W. Beaumont, London, 1925.

AZPIAZU, J. de: *The Guitar and Guitarists from the Beginning to the Present Day*. London, 1960.

BAL Y GAY, Jesús: "Fuenllana and the Transcription of Spanish Lute (Vihuela) Music." *Acta Musicologica* XI, 1939.

BARZUN, Jacques: *Berlioz and the Romantic Century*. New York, 1950.

BECK, Sydney and Elizabeth E. ROTH: *Music in Prints*. New York, 1965.

BELLOW, Alexander: *The Illustrated History of the Guitar*. New York, 1970.

BERLIOZ, Hector: *Memoirs*. Trans. Rachel and Eleanor Holmes, New York, 1932.
Treatise on Modern Instrumentation and Orchestration. Trans. Mary Cowden Clarke, London, 1856.

BIERNATH, Ernst: *Die Guitarre seit dem III Jahrtausend vor Christus*. Berlin, 1907.

BLANCHARD, Henri: "Les Guitaristes." *Revue et Gazette Musicale de Paris*, Paris, 1842.

BOBRI, Vladimir: *The Segovia Technique*. New York, 1972.

BOETTICHER Wolfgang, and Hans HICKMANN: "Gitarre." *Die Music in Geschichte und Gegenwart*, ed. F. Blume, Kassel and Basel, 1949.

BONE, Philip James: *The Guitar and Mandolin*. London, 1954.
"Paganini and the Guitar." *Hinrichsen's Musical Year Book*, vol. VII, London, 1952.

BONNER, Stephen: *The Classic Image*. Harlow, 1972.

BREAM, Julian: "How to write for the guitar." *The Score*, No. 19, March, 1957.

BRENAN, Gerald: *The Literature of the Spanish People*. Harmondsworth, 1963.

BRIDGE, Sir John Frederick: *Samuel Pepys, Lover of Musique*. London, 1903.

BRONDI, Maria Rita: "Il liuto e la chitarra." *Rivista Musicale Italiana*, vol. XXXII, 1925, and vol. XXXIII, 1926. *Il liuto e la chitarra*. Torino, 1926.

BROWN, Howard Mayer: *Instrumental Music Printed Before 1600. A Bibliography*. Cambridge, Mass., 1965.

BRUNI, Antonio B.: *Un Inventaire sous la Terreur. Etat des instruments de musique relevés chez les emigrés et condamnés*. Ed. J. Gallay, Paris, 1890.

BUEK, Fritz: *Die Gitarre und ihre Meister*. Berlin, 1926.

CARFAGNA, Carlo and Alberto CAPRANI: *Profilo Storico della Chitarra*. Ancona and Milan, 1966.

CHARNASSÉ, Hélène: "A propos d'un récent article sur la méthode pour la guitare de Luis Briceño" *Revue de Musicologie*, vol. LII, No 2, 1966.

CHASE, Gilbert: *The Music of Spain*. New York, 1959.

CHILESOTTI, Oscar: "Intavolature di chitarra, appunti." *Le Chronache Musicali*, I, Rome, 1900. "Francesco Corbetta guitarrista." *Gazetta Musicale de Milano*, XLIV, 1888. "Notes sur le guitariste Robert de Visée." *Sammelbände der Internationalen Musikgesellschaft*, IX, 1907–8. "La Musique en Italie," *Encyclopédie de la Musique et Dictionnaire du Conservatoire*. Ed. A Lavignac and L. de la Laurencie, Part 1, Vol. 1, Paris, 1920

CLINTON, George: "Segovia." *Guitar*, December 1974.

COHEN, Albert: "A Study of Instrumental Ensemble practice in Seventeenth-Century France." *Galpin Society Journal*, vol. XV, 1962.

COUTAGNE, Henri: *Gaspard Duiffoproucart et les Luthiers lyonnais du XVIe. siècle*. Paris, 1893.

DEUTSCH, Otto Erich: "W. Matiegkas Gittarren-Trio und Schubert." *Zeitschrift für Musikwissenschaft*, XIV, 1932–33.

DEVOTO, Daniel, "Poésie et musique dans l'oeuvre des Vihuelistes." *Annales Musicologiques*, IV, 1956.

DIDEROT, Denis and Jean le Rond D'ALEMBERT: *Encyclopédie, ou Dictionnaire raisonné des sciences, des arts et des métiers*. Paris, 1751–65.

EMMERSON, F. G.: *Tudor Secretary: Sir William Petre at Court and Home*. Cambridge, Mass., 1961.

ESCUDERO, José Castro: "La Méthode pour la guitare de Luis Briceño." *Revue de Musicologie*, vol. LI, No 2, 1965.

ESPINEL, Vicente: *The history of the life of the Squire Marcos de Obregón*. Trans. A. Langton, London, 1816, from the Madrid edition of 1618.

FEDERHOFER, Hellmut: "Eine Angelica- und Gitarrentabulatur aus der zweiten Hälfte des 17 Jahrhunderts." *Festschrift für Walter Wiora, Kassel, 1967*.

FORTUNE, Nigel: "Giustiniani on Instruments." *Galpin Society Journal*, vol. V, 1952. *Italian Secular Song from 1600 to 1635*. Unpublished Ph.D thesis, Cambridge University, 1953. "Solo Song and Cantata." *The New Oxford History of Music*, vol. IV, Oxford, 1968.

GARCÍA MARCELLAN, José: *Catálogo del Archivo de Música*. Madrid, *c*. 1945.

GAVALDÁ, Miguel Querol: *La música en las obras de Cervantes*. Barcelona, 1948.

GAVALL, John: "The Guitar—an Evaluation." *The Musical Times*, vol. XCV, November, 1954.

GAVOTY, Bernard: *Andrés Segovia—an Evaluation*. Geneva, 1955.

GÉRARD, Yves: *Thematic, Bibliographical and Critical Catalogue of the Works of Luigi Boccherini*. Trans. Andreas Mayor, London, 1969.

GIORDANO, Mario: *Contributo allo studio della chitarra*. Milan, 1936.

GRUNFELD, Frederic V.: *The Art and Times of the Guitar*. New York, 1969.

HAMILTON, Mary Neal: *Music in Eighteenth-Century Spain*. Illinois, 1937.

HAMILTON, Anthony: *Memoirs of the Count of Grammont*. London, 1905.

HARRISON, Frank Mott: *Reminiscences of Madame Sidney Pratten, Guitariste and Composer*. London, 1899.

HAYES, Gerald: "Instruments and Instrumental Notation." *The New Oxford History of Music*, vol. IV, Oxford, 1968.

HEARTZ, Daniel: "Les styles instrumentaux dans la musique de la Renaissance." *La Musique Instrumentale de la Renaissance*. Ed. Jean Jacquot, Paris, 1955. "Parisian Music Publishing under Henry II a propos of four recently discovered guitar books." *The Musical Quarterly*, vol. XLVI, No. 4, 1960. "An Elizabethan Tutor for the Guitar." *Galpin Society Journal*, vol. XVII, 1964.

HECK, Thomas Fitzsimmons: *The Birth of the Classic Guitar and its Cultivation in Vienna, reflected in the Career and Compositions of Mauro Giuliani (d. 1829)*, and *vol. II: Thematic Catalogue of the Complete Works of Mauro Giuliani.* Ph.D. dissertation, Yale University, 1970.
"The role of Italy in the early history of the classic guitar." *Guitar Review*, 34, 1971.
"Giuliani, birth and death dates confirmed." *Guitar Review*, 37, 1972.

HOGARTH, George: "Musical Instruments—The Harp and Guitar." *The Musical World*, vol. III, No. 32, October 1836.

HUDSON, Richard: "The Concept of Mode in Italian Guitar Music during the First Half of the Seventeenth Century." *Acta Musicologica*, vol. XLII, 1970.
"The *Zarabanda* and *Zarabanda Francese* in Italian Guitar Music of the Early 17th Century." *Musica Disciplina*, vol. XXIV, 1970.
"The *Folia* Dance and the *Folia* formula in 17th-Century Guitar Music." *Musica Disciplina*, vol. XXV, 1971.
"Further Remarks on the Passacaglia and Ciaconna." *Journal of the American Musicological Society*, vol. XXIII, No. 2, 1970.

JACQUOT, Jean, ed., *La Musique Instrumentale de la Renaissance.* Paris, 1955.

JAFFEE Michael: "Harmony in the Solo Guitar Music of Heitor Villa-Lobos." *Guitar Review*, 29, 1966.

JOHNSON, L. G.: *General T. Perronet Thompson.* London, 1957.

KEITH, Richard: "The Guitar Cult in the Courts of Louis XIV and Charles II." *Guitar Review*, 26, 1962.
"'La Guitarre Royale': A study of the career and compositions of Francesco Corbetta." *Recherches sur la Musique Française Classique* vol. VI, 1966.

KINSKY, George: *A History of Music in Pictures.* London, 1930.

KIRKPATRICK, Ralph: *Domenico Scarlatti.* Princeton, 1953.

KOCZIRZ, Adolf: "Die Gitarren Kompositionen in Miguel de Fuenllanas Orphenica Lyra." *Archiv für Musikwissenschaft*, IV, 1922.
"Die Fantasien des Melchior de Barberis für die Siebensaitige Gitarre." *Zeitschrift für Musikwissenschaft*, IV, 1921–22.
"Über die Fingernageltechnik bei Saiteninstrumente."

Festschrift für Guido Adler, Vienna, 1930.
"Zur Geschichte der Gitarre in Wien." *Musikbuch aus Oesterreich*, Vienna, 1907.

KOCZIRZ, Adolf and Josef ZUTH: *Beiträge zur Geschichte der Gitarre und des Gitarrenspiels.* Vienna, 1919.

LESURE, François: "La Guitare en France au XVIe. Siècle." *Musica Disciplina* vol. IV, 1950.
Music and Art in Society, Pennsylvania, 1968.

LESURE, François and G. THIBAULT: *Biographie des Editions d'Adrien le Roy et Robert Ballard, 1551–1598.* Paris, 1955.

MARESCOT, Charles de: *La guitaromanie*, Paris, c. 1850.

MENDEL, A.: "Pitch in the 16th and early 17th Century." Parts I–IV, *Musical Quarterly* XXXIV, January, April, July, October, 1948.

MITJANA, Rafael: "La Musique en Espagne." *Encyclopédie de la Musique et Dictionnaire du Conservatoire.* Ed. A. Lavignac and L. de la Laurencie, Part I, Vol. I, Paris, 1920.

MORECK, Kurt: *Die Musik in der Malerei.* Munich, 1924.

MORLEY, Thomas: *A Plaine and Easie Introduction to Practicall Musick.* 1597.

MORPHY, Guillermo: *Les luthistes espagnols du XVIe. siècle.* Leipzig, 1902.

MUÑOZ, Ricardo: *Historia de la guitarra.* Buenos Aires, 1930.

MURPHY, Sylvia: "Seventeenth-Century Guitar Music: Notes on Rasgueado Performance." *Galpin Society Journal*, vol. XXI, 1968.

NELSON, Martha: "Canarios." *Guitar Review*, 25, 1961.

NICOLA, Isaac: "Notas históricas de la guitarra." *Conservatorio*, Madrid, 1948.

NORTH, Roger: *Roger North on Music, being a selection from his essays written during the years c. 1695–1728.* Ed. John Wilson, London 1959.
Memoires of musick. Ed. E. F. Rimbault, London 1846.

OSBORNE, James M.: *The Autobiography of Thomas Whytehorne.* Oxford, 1967.

PAHISSA, Jaime: *Manuel de Falla, his Life and Works.* Trans. Jean Wagstaff, London, 1954.

PARKER, K. T. and J. MATHEY: *Antoine Watteau: Catalogue complet de son oeuvre dessiné.* Paris, 1957.

PEDRELL, Felipe: *Cancionero musical popular español.* Barcelona, 1958.
"La Musique indigène dans le théâtre espagnol du dix-septième siècle." *Sammelbände der Internal Musikgesellschaft*, 1903–4.

PIRROTTA, Nino: "Music and Cultural Tendencies in fifteenth-century Italy." *Journal of the American Musicological Society*, vol. XIX, No. 2, 1966.

POPE, Isabel: "La vihuela y su Música en el Ambiente Humanístico." *Nueva Revista de Filología Hispanica*, vol. XV, 1961.
"Vicente Espinel as a Musician." *Studies in the Renaissance*, vol. V, 1958.

POULTON, Diana: "Notes on some Differences between the Lute and the Vihuela and their Music." *The Consort*, No. 16, July, 1959.
"Notes on the Spanish Pavan." *The Lute Society Journal*, vol. III, 1961.

PRAT, Domingo: *Diccionario biográfico, bibliográfico, histórico, crítico, de Guitarras, Guitarristas y Guitarreros.* Buenos Aires, 1934.

PUJOL, Emilio: "La Guitarre." *Encyclopédie de la Musique et Dictionnaire du Conservatoire*, ed. A. Lavignac and L. de la Laurencie, Part II, vol. III, Paris, 1927.
La Guitarra y su Historia, Conferencia. Buenos Aires, 1932.
"Significación de Juan Carlos y Amat (1572–1642) en la historia de la guitarra." *Anuario Musical*, vol. V, 1950.
"The Guitar in Portugal." *Guitar Review*, 5, 1948.
"Les ressources instrumentales et leur rôle dans la musique pour vihuela et pour guitare au XVIe siècle et au XVIIe." *La Musique instrumentale de la Renaissance.* Ed. Jean Jacquot, Paris, 1958.
Escuela Razonada de la Guitarra. Buenos Aires, 1934.
El Dilema del Sonida en la Guitarra. (In Spanish, English and French.) Buenos Aires, 1960.
Tárrega, Ensayo Biográfico. Lisbon, 1960.

REVUELTA, B. V.: *La guitarra.* Madrid, 1962.

RIAÑO, Juan F.: *Critical and Bibliographical Notes on Early Spanish Music.* London, 1887.

RIBERA, Julián: *Music in Ancient Arabia and Spain.* Trans. E. Hague and M. Leffingwell, Stanford, 1929.

RICART Matas, J.: *Refranero internacional de la música y de la danza.* Barcelona, 1950.

RIEMANN, Hugo: "Das Lautenwerk des Miguel de Fuenllana 1554." *Monatshefte für Musikgeschichte*, vol. XXVII, No. 6, 1895.

RIERA, Juan: *Emilio Pujol.* Lerida, 1974.

ROBERTS, John: "Some Notes on the Music of the Vihuelists." *The Lute Society Journal*, vol. VII, 1965.
"The Death of Guzmán." *The Lute Society Journal*, vol. X, 1968
"Miguel Llobet." *Guitar*, December, 1972.
"Notes on Tárrega." *Guitar*, December, 1975.
"Historical Notes: Tárrega." *Guitar*, October, 1972.

ROCAMORA, Manuel: *Fernando Sor (1778–1839), Ensayo Biográfico.* Barcelona, 1957.

ROMANILLOS, José: "Julián Arcas, 1832–1882." *La Voz de Almería*, 21 April, 1976.

ROTHSCHILD, Germaine de: *Luigi Boccherini, his Life and Work.* Trans. Andreas Mayor, London, 1965.

RUTH-SOMMER, Hermann: *Alte Musikinstrumente.* Berlin, 1920.
Laute und Gitarre. Stuttgart, 1922.

SAINZ DE LA MAZA, R.: *La guitarra y su historia.* Madrid, 1955.

SALAZAR, Adolfo: *La música en Cervantes y otros ensayos.* Madrid, 1961.
Música, instrumentos y danzas en las obras de Cervantes. Mexico City, 1948.
"El laud, la vihuela y la guitarra." *Nuestra Música*, 1946.

SASSER, William: *The Guitar Works of Fernando Sor.* Unpublished Ph.D. dissertation, University of North Carolina, 1960.
"In search of Sor," *Guitar Review*, 26, 1962.

SAUSSINE, Renée de: *Paganini.* Trans. Majorie Laurie, New York, 1954.

SAUERLAND, Max: *Die Musik in Fünf Jahrhunderten der Europäischen Malerei.* Königstein and Leipzig, 1922.

SCHEIT, Karl: "Von der Gitarre." *Musikerziehung*, September, 1951.

SCHMITZ, Eugen: "Uber Guitarrentabulaturen." *Monatshefte für Musikgeschichte*, XXXV No. 9, 1903.

SEGOVIA, Andrés: "The Guitar and Myself." Trans. Eithne Golden, *Guitar Review*, 4, 1947.
An Autobiography of the Years 1893–1920. New York, 1976.

SHARPE, A. P.: *The Story of the Spanish Guitar.* London, 1954.

SHERRINGTON, Unity and Guy OLDHAM (eds.): *Music, Libraries and Instruments.* Hinrichsens's 11th Music Book, London, 1961.

STEVENS, Denis: *The Mulliner Book. A Commentary.* London, 1952.

STEVENS, John: *Music and Poetry in the Early Tudor Court.* London, 1961.

STEVENSON, Robert M.: *Music before the Classic Era.* London, 1952.
Juan Bermudo. The Hague, 1960.

STRAETEN, Edmund van der: *La Musique aux Pays Bas avant le XIXe siècle.* 8 vols., Brussels, 1867–1888.

SUBIRÁ, José: *Historia de la música española e hispanoamericana.* Barcelona, 1953.
Historia de la música teatral en España. Madrid, 1945.

TAPPERT, Wilhelm: "Zur Geschichte der Guitarre." *Monatshefte für Musikgeschichte,* vol. XIV, No. 5, 1882.

TERZI, Benvenuto: *Dizionario dei chitarristi e liutai italiani.* Bologna, 1937.

THOMAS, Juan M.: "The Guitar and its Renaissance." *The Chesterian,* October, 1955.

TILMOUTH, Michael: "Some Improvements in Music noted by William Turner in 1697." *Galpin Society Journal,* vol. X, 1957.

TONAZZI, Bruno: *Miguel Llobet, Chitarrista dell' Impressionismo.* Ancona and Milan, 1966.

TREND, J. B.: *Luis Milán and the Vihuelistas.* London, 1925.
The Music of Spanish History to 1600. London, 1926.
Manuel de Falla and Spanish Music. New York, 1929.

TRICHET, Pierre: *Traité des instruments de musique* c. *1640.* Ed. F. Lesure, *Annales Musicologiques,* vol. III, 1955 and IV, 1956.

TURNBULL, Harvey: *The Guitar from the Renaissance to the Present Day.* London 1974.

TWISS, Richard: *Travels through Portugal and Spain in 1772 and 1773.* London, 1775.

TYLER, James: *The Early Guitar.* Oxford, 1977.

VIDAL, Robert J.: "Quelques grands guitaristes." *Musica,* No. 31, Paris, October, 1956.

VERNEY, Lady F. P. and Lady Margaret M.: *Memoirs of the Verney Family during the Seventeenth Century,* London, 1904.

WALKER, Thomas: "Ciaconna and Passacaglia: Remarks on their Origins and Early History." *Journal of the American Musicological Society,* vol. XXI, 1968.

WARD, John M.: "The Editorial Methods of Venegas de Henestrosa." *Musica Disciplina,* vol. VI, 1952.
The Vihuela de Mano and its Music 1536–1576. Unpublished Ph.D. dissertation, New York University, 1953.
"Le problème des hauteurs dans la musique pour luth et vihuela au XVIe siècle." *Le Luth et sa Musique,* ed. Jean Jacquot, Paris, 1968.
"Spanish Musicians in Sixteenth-Century England." *Essays in Musicology in Honour of Dragan Plamenac on his 70th Birthday,* eds. Gustave Reese and Robert J. Snow, Pittsburgh, 1969.

WECKERLIN, Jean Baptiste Theodore: *Nouveau Musiciana: extraits d'ouvrages rares et bizarres.* Paris, 1890.

WOLF, Johannes: *Handbuch der Notationskunde.* Leipzig, 1919.

WOODFILL, Walter L.: *Musicians in English Society from Elizabeth to Charles I.* Princeton, 1953.

ZUTH, Josef: *Handbuch der laute und gitarre.* Vienna, 1926.
Simon Molitor und die Wiener Gitarristik. Vienna, 1920.

FLAMENCO

BARETTI, Joseph: *A Journey from London to Genoa through England, Portugal, Spain and France.* London, 1770.

BORROW, George: *The Zincali.* London, 1841.
The Bible in Spain. London, 1904.

BOURGOING, Jean François: *Nouveau Voyage en Espagne.* Paris, 1788.

BUTLER, Augusto: *Javier Molina, jerezano y tocaor.* Jerez, 1964.

CARRERAS Y CANDI, Francisco, ed.: *Folklore y costumbres de España.* Barcelona, 1931.

CHASE, Gilbert: *The Music of Spain.* New York, 1941.

DEMBOWSKI, Charles: *Deux Ans en Espagne et en Portugal pendant la Guerre Civile 1838–40.* Paris, 1841.

DURAN MUNOZ, García: *Andalucia y su cante.* Madrid, 1962.

FALLA, Manuel de: *El cante jondo (cante primitivo andaluz).* Granada, 1922.

GEORGE, David: *The Flamenco Guitar*. Madrid, 1966.

GLINKA, Mikhail Ivanovich: *Memoirs*. Trans. R. B. Rudge, Oklahoma, 1963.

GONZÁLEZ CLIMENT, Anselmo: *Antología de poesía flamenco*. Madrid, 1961.
Flamencología. Madrid, 1964.
Bibliografía flamenca. Madrid, 1965.
Segundo bibliografía flamenca. Madrid, 1966.

Guitar Review, no. 19, 1956.

LAFUENTE, R.: *Los gitanos*. Barcelona, 1955.

LORCA, Federico García: *Obras completas*. Madrid, 1965.

MAIRANTS, Ivor: *The Flamenco Guitar*. London, 1958.

MOLINA, Ricardo: *Cante flamenco*. Madrid, 1965.

MOLINA, Ricardo and Antonio MAIRENA: *Mundo y formas del cante flamenco*. Madrid, 1963.

MORALES, Rafael: "Ramón Montoya." *Guitare et Musique*, nos. 32, 33.

PEMARTÍN, Julián: *El cante flamenco*. Madrid, 1966.

POHREN, Donald: *The Art of Flamenco*. Jerez, 1962.
Lives and Legends of Flamenco. Seville, 1964.

QUIÉVREUX, Louis: *Art Flamenco*. Brussels, 1959.

QUINONES, FERNANDO: *El flamenco, vida y muerte*. Madrid, 1971.

RODRÍGUEZ, Fernando (Fernando el de Triana): *Arte y artistos flamencos*. Madrid, 1952.

STARKIE, Walter: "*Cante jondo*, Flamenco and the Guitar." *Guitar Review*, no. 20, 1956.

THE GUITAR IN LATIN AMERICA

There are many books on Latin American music. For detailed bibliographies, see the two books listed by Gilbert Chase. The following list is intended as a basic introduction.

ALVARENGA, Oneyda: *Música popular brasilena*. Buenos Aires, 1947.

ARETZ-THIELE, Isabel: *Música tradicional argentina, historia y folklore*. Tucuman, 1946.

CHASE, Gilbert: *Guide to the Music of Latin America*. Washington, 1962.
The Music of Spain. New York, 1941.

COELHO, Olga: "The guitar in Brazil . . . and some reminiscences." *Guitar Review*, 21, 1957.

CONTRERAS, Segundo N.: *La guitarra argentina*. Buenos Aires, 1950.

CORRÊA DE AZEVEDO, Luis-Heitor: "La guitare archaïque au Brésil." *Studia Memoriae Belae Bartok Sacra*, Budapest, 1956.

HAGUE, Eleanor: *Latin American Music, Past and Present*. California, 1934.

MUÑOZ, Ricardo: *Tecnología de la guitarra argentina*. Buenos Aires, 1952.

SLONIMSKY, Nicholas: *Music of Latin America*. New York, 1972.

STEVENSON R. M.: *Music in Mexico*. New York, 1952.
The Music of Peru. Washington, 1960.

SUBIRÁ, José: *Historia de la música española e hispanomericana*. Barcelona, 1953.

VEGA, Carlos: *Música sudamericana*. Buenos Aires, 1946.
"The Classical Guitar in Early Buenos Aires." *Guitar Review*, 10, 1949.
Panorama de la Música Popular Argentina. Buenos Aires, 1944.
Bailes Tradicionales Argentinos. Buenos Aires, 1948.

WEINSTOCK, Herbert: *Mexican Music*. New York, 1940.

STEEL-STRING AND ELECTRIC

Because the same sources are often usable for both steel-string and electric guitars, we have combined their bibliographies. Where a set of books applies to both types of guitar we have given them in a single, undifferentiated list. Those sources applying only to one type of guitar are given separately.

INSTRUMENTS: COMBINED
BISHOP, I. C.: *The Gibson Guitar from 1950*. London, 1977.

BELLSON, JULIUS: *The Gibson Story*. Kalamazoo, 1973.

KAMIMOTO, Hideo: *Complete Guitar Repair*. New York, 1975.

LONGWORTH, Mike: *Martin Guitars, A History*. Cedar Knolls, 1975.

WHEELER, Tom: *The Guitar Book: A Handbook for Electric and Acoustic Guitarists*. New York, 1975.

INSTRUMENTS: STEEL-STRING
BAILEY, John: *Making a Folk Guitar*. London, 1965.

BROSNAC, Donald: *The Steel-String Guitar, its Construction, Origin and Design*. San Francisco, 1975.

TEETER, D. E.: *The Acoustic Guitar (Adjustment, Care, Maintenance and Repair)*. Oklahoma, 1975.

INSTRUMENTS: ELECTRIC

Brosnac, Donald: *The Electric Guitar, its History and Construction*. San Francisco, 1975.

TAYLOR, Rupert: *Electricity*. Harmondsworth, 1975.

International Musician

MUSIC AND PLAYERS: COMBINED

ATKINS, Chet, and Bill NEELY: *Country Gentleman*. Chicago, 1974.

BMG (Banjo, Mandolin, Guitar). London, 1903–

Billboard. Los Angeles, 1894–

BELZ, Carl: *The Story of Rock*. New York, 1969.

Blues Unlimited. London, 1973–

COHN, Nik: *Pop from the Beginning*. London, 1969.

BARZUN, Jacques: *Music in American Life*. New York, 1956.

BRADFORD, Perry: *Born with the Blues*. New York, 1965.

COOK, Bruce: *Listen to the Blues*. London, 1975.

Crawdaddy. New York, 1966–

Downbeat. Chicago, 1934–

ESCOTT, Colin and Martin HAWKINS: *Catalyst: The Sun Records Story*. London, 1975.

FEATHER, Leonard: *Encyclopedia of Jazz*. New York, 1960.
"A History of Jazz Guitar." *Downbeat*, July, 1958.

GENTRY, Linnell, ed.: *A History and Encyclopedia of Country, Western and Gospel Music*. Nashville, 1969.

GREEN, Archie: *Only a Miner: Studies in Recorded Coal-Mining Songs*. University of Illinois, 1972.

GREEN, Douglas B.: *Country Roots, The Origins of Country Music*. New York, 1976.

GUITAR PLAYER MAGAZINE PUBLICATIONS: *Jazz Guitarists*. Saratoga, California, 1975.

Guitar Player. Los Angeles, 1967–

GILLETT, Charlie: *The Sound of the City*. New York, 1970.

HARALAMBOS, Michael: *Right On: From Blues to Soul in Black America*. Cambridge, England, 1974.

HEMPHILL, Paul: *The Nashville Sound*. New York, 1970.

HENTOFF, Nat and Albert McCARTHY: *Jazz*. New York, 1959.

JONES, Leroi: *Blues People*. New York, 1963.
Black Music. London 1969.

LAING, Dave, Karl DALLAS, Robin DENSELOW, and Robert SHELTON: *The Electric Muse. The Story of Folk into Rock*. London 1975.

LEADBITTER, Mike, and Neil SLAVEN: *Blues Records 1943–1966, A discography*. London, 1969.

LEADBITTER, Mike: *Nothing but the Blues*. London, 1971.

MALONE, Bill C.: *Country Music USA: A Fifty-Year History*. American Folklore Society (University of Texas Press), 1968.

MALONE, Bill C., and Judith McCULLOH: *Stars of Country Music*. University of Illinois, 1975.

McCARTHY, Albert, ed.: *Jazz on Record*. London, 1968.

Melody Maker. London, 1926–

New Musical Express. London, 1952–

OLIVER, Paul: *Blues Fell This Morning*. London, 1960.
Conversation with the Blues. London, 1965.
Screening the Blues. London, 1968.
The Story of the Blues. London, 1969.

RAMSEY, Frederic, Jr.: *Been Here and Gone*. Rutgers, 1960.

Rolling Stone. San Francisco, 1967–

ROONEY, Jim: *Bossmen, Bill Monroe and Muddy Waters*. New York, 1971.

ROXON, Lillian: *Rock Encyclopedia*. New York, 1969.

SCADUTO, Anthony: *Bob Dylan*. London, 1972.

SHELTON, Robert, and Burt GOLDBLATT: *The Country Music Story*. New York, 1966.

STAMBLER, Irwin and Grelun LANDON: *Encyclopedia of Folk, Country, and Western Music*. New York, 1969.
Golden Guitars. New York, 1971.

SHAPIRO, Nat and Nat HENTOFF: *Hear me Talkin' To Ya*. Gloucester, 1955.

MUSIC AND PLAYERS: STEEL-STRING

BADEAUX, Ed: "The Carters of Rye Cove." *Sing Out!* XI. no. 2 (April–May, 1961).

BROONZY, Big Bill and Yannick BRUYNOGHE: *Big Bill Blues.* Reprinted New York, 1964.

CHARTERS, Samuel: *The Bluesmen.* New York, 1967.
The Poetry of the Blues. New York, 1959.
The Country Blues. New York, 1955.

CHASE, Gilbert: *America's Music,* New York, 1955.

COHN, Lawrence: "Mississippi John Hurt." *Sing out!* XIV. no. 5 (Nov. 1964).

COHEN, Norman, "The Skillet Lickers: A Study of a Hillbilly String Band and its Repertoire." *Journal of American Folkore,* LXXVIII. no. 309 (July–September, 1965).

COURLANDER, Harold: *Negro Folk Music U.S.A.* New York, 1963.

DIXON, Robert M. W. and John GODRICH: *Blues and Gospel Records, 1902–42.* London, 1964.

DELAUNAY, C.: *Django Reinhardt,* 1961.

EVANS, David, and Tommy JOHNSON: *A Study of a Tradition.* London, 1971.

GREENWAY, John: "Jimmie Rodgers— a Folksong Catalyst." *Journal of American Folklore,* LXX, no. 277 (July-Sept., 1957).

GUTHRIE, Woody: *American Folksong.* New York, 1961.
Bound for Glory. New York, 1943.

HANDY, W. C.: *Father of the Blues.* London, 1957.

LAWLESS, Ray M.: *Folksingers and Folksongs in America.* New York, 1960.

LEADBETTER, Huddie: *The Leadbelly Songbook.* Eds. Moses Asch and Alan Lomax. New York, 1962.

LOMAX, Alan: *The Folk Songs of North America.* New York, 1960.
American Folk Guitar. New York, 1957.

LOMAX, John A.: *Negro Folk Songs as Sung by Leadbelly.* New York, 1937.
Cowboy Songs and other Frontier Ballads. New York, 1910.

LOMAX, John and Alan: *American Ballads and Folk Songs.* New York, 1934.
Folk Song: U.S.A. New York, 1947.

ODUM, Howard and Guy B. JOHNSON: *Negro Workaday Songs.* University of North Carolina Press, 1926.
The Negro and His Songs. Folklore Associates, 1964.

RODGERS, Mrs Jimmie (Carrie): *My Husband, Jimmie Rodgers.* Nashville, 1935.

SANDBURG, Carl: *The American Songbag.* New York, 1927.

Sing Out! New York, 1950–

SIMPSON, Clinton: "Some Early American Guitarists." *Guitar Review,* no. 23 (June, 1959).

SILVERMAN, Jerry: *The Folksinger's Guitar Guide.* New York, 1962.

WHITE, Newman I.: *American Negro Folk Songs* (1928). Folklore Associates reprint, 1965.

WORK, John W. ed.: *American Negro Songs and Spirituals.* New York, 1940.
Folk Song of the American Negro. New York. 1915.

MUSIC AND PLAYERS: ELECTRIC

DALTON, David, ed.: *Rolling Stones: An unauthorized biography.* New York, 1972.

DAVIES, Hunter: *The Beatles.* New York, 1968.

EISEN, Jonathon: *The Age of Rock.* New York, 1969, 1970.

GUITAR PLAYER MAGAZINE PUBLICATIONS: *Rock Guitarists.* Saratoga, California, 1974.
Guitar Notables. Saratoga, California, 1975.

GILLETT, Charlie: *Rock File 1, 2* and *3.* London, 1973, annually.

GLEASON, Ralph: *Jefferson Airplane and the San Francisco Sound.* New York, 1969.

KEIL, Charles: *Urban Blues.* Chicago, 1966.

PIGEON, John: *Eric Clapton.* London, 1976.

MILLER, Jim, ed.: *The Rolling Stone Illustrated History of Rock and Roll.* New York, 1976.

SIMON, Bill: "Charlie Christian." In *The Jazz Makers,* ed. Nat Shapiro and Nat Hentoff, New York 1957.

TURNER, Steve: *Conversations with Clapton.* London 1976.

INDEX

Sub-headings under the entries for Gibson company, guitar, and Martin company are arranged in alphabetical order. All other sub-headings are arranged in page number order. Page numbers in *italic* type indicate illustrations or their captions.

Abondance, Pierre, *29*
Absolutely Free, 414
acoustic-electric guitars, *see* electric-acoustic guitars
acoustics: in concert halls, 58; and guitar shape, 79, 81–3, 264; and guitar volume, 57–8, 66, 69, 79, 118, 158, 254
Adame, Rafael, 215
Aguado, Dionisio, 41, 117, 120, 121, 152, 154, 215
Aguado, Victoriano, *68*
Albéniz, Isaac, 122, 166
Alcañiz, Josef, *46*
alegrías, 170
Alembert, d', Diderot and, 144, *147*
Alembic company, 342, 365, 376, 382
Alice Cooper, 423
allemande, 108, 113, 133
Allman, Duane, 427
Almeida, Laurindo, 217
alphabeto, 112, 114, 115; *see also* tablature
Altheimer, Joshua, 310
Altimira, *52*
aluminum-bodied guitars, 360, 371
alzapua, 196, 199
Amat, Dr. Juan Carlos y, 23, 110, 131, 148
Amaya, Carmen, 178
America, *see* United States
amplifiers and amplification, 222, 338, 342–3, 379–85; *see also* electric guitars
Andrews Sisters, 396
Anthology of Cante Flamenco (Perico el del Lunar), 178
Anthony, Eddie, 302
apoyando, 10, 120, 122
Arbeau, Thoinot, 108, 134
Arcas, Julián, 56, 122, 158
arch-top guitar, 220–4, 225–35 *passim*; *see also* steel-string acoustic guitar, forms of
Area Code 611, 427
"Argentina, La," 177–8
Arias, Vincente, 57, *63*, 182–3, *184*, *185*
Arkie the Arkansas Woodchopper, *see* Ossenbrink, Luther
Arnold, James "Kokomo," 302
Arnold, Malcolm, 127

Artaria, Domenico, 157
Arte de tocar la guitarra española (Ferrandière), 40, 117
Arte y Artistos Flamencos (Triana), 195
Arts of the West (Benson), *311*
Artzt, Alice, 164
Asencio, Vicente, 164
Ashby, Irving, 233
Atkins, Chet, *320*, 321, *354*, 400, 403–5, *404*
Attaignant, Pierre, 108, 130
Augustine, Albert, 59
Augustus, Jacob, 153
Austria, guitar in, 42, 118, 154, 156
Autrey, Gene, 248, 316, *318*, 318, 396
Ayers, Kevin, 433

Bach, J. S., 122, 162, 165–6
back: diagram, 76; construction, 80–1, 84, 95 (classical), 221, 263–5, *274*, *278* (steel string), 374 (electric)
Baez, Joan, 315, 324
baile, 170, 172–3, 179, 182, 200–1
Bailey, Derek, 433
Baker, Ginger, 412
Baker, Willie, 302
Baker tuning machines, *see* tuning machines
Balin, Marty, 411–12
ballads, 112, 291; 16th century, 104–5, 131; blues, 289, 299, 302; country, 311–12; folk, 322–3, 331
Ballard, Robert, 108–9
Ballesteros, Antonio, 40, 117
Balli di Sfessania, *133*
Band, The, 423
banjos, *221*, 231, 287, 312, 320
Barber, Chris, 407
Barberiis, Melchiore de, 109
Barbero, Marcelo, 57, *65*, 68, 183, *187*, 188
Barcelona, luthiers in, 57
Barcus Berry "Hot Dot" piezo-electric transducers, 252, 334, 343
Barenboim, Daniel, 167
Barnes, George, 389, 403, 430
baroque music, 25, 111, 123, 134–6

Barroso, Torres, 130
barrelhouse piano, 299–300
Barrett, Eric, 409
Barrios, Augustine Pio, 10, 123, 215
Barrios, Don Angel, 162
Barth, Paul, *344*
Bartok, Belâ, 124
Basie, Count, 233
Basilio, Father, *see* García, Miguel
bass guitar, 44; electric, 342, 364
Bates, Dr. Humphrey (and his Possum Hunters), *312*, 313
Bauer, Billy, 389–90
Bayeu, Ramón, *148*
Beale Street, *see* Memphis
Beatles, 406–7
Beau, *52*
Beauchamp, George, *344*
bebop, 389–90
Beck, Jeff, 407–8, 421, 423, *425*, 425
Beckford, William, 149
Bedford, David, 126, 432–3, *434*
Beecher, Frank, 399
Beethoven, Ludwig van, 122, 156
Benavente-Osuna family, 149, 153
Benedit, Josef, 41, *43*, 44–5, 51
Bennett, Buster, 310
Bennett, Richard Rodney, 127
Benson, George, 430
Benson, Thomas Hart, 311
Berg, Alban, 124
Berkeley, Lennox, 127
Berlioz, Hector, 48, 148, 153
Bermudo, Juan, 17–18, 21, 24, 44, 102–7, 131
Bernabe, Paulino, 57, *73*, 78, 83, *189*
Berry, Chuck, 400, 407, 421
Biberian, Gilbert, 167
"Big Road Blues," 297
Bigsby, Paul, 341, 345–6, 355, 395
biguela, *see* vihuela
binding (purfling), *32*, 46; diagram, 76; plastic, 249; steel-string, 266, *279*; electric, 372–3, 377–8
"Birmingham Jail," 319, 323
Bishop, Elvin, 414
Black Sabbath, 423
Blake, Blind, 302–3, *303*, 306–10, 329
Blackwell, Scrapper, 300, 306
Blood, Sweat and Tears, 427
Bloomfield, Mike, 414, *415*
"Blowin' in the Wind," 323
bluegrass music, 311, 319–21
Blue Guitar and Vase (Léger), *160*
blues, 222–3, 266, 312, 318; country blues, 288–91; Chicago

blues, 291, 295–6, 304–10, 326, 393–4, 395; Memphis blues, 293–8, 305–12, 326; Texas blues, 298–301; ragtime, 302–5, 312, 319, 329; yodels, 314–16; rediscovered, 325–30; electric guitar in, 388, 391–5, 402–3, 414–22; influence on rock, 407–8, 412
"Blue Yodel No. 1 (T for Texas)," 315–6
Boccherini, Luigi, 149
body (electric guitar, 338–40; construction, 368–74; *see also* soundboard
Boilly, L. L., *159*
Boldini, Giovanni, *154*
bolero, 149
Bond, Graham, 407
Bonfa, Luis, 211
Bonnart, H., *138*
Bonnart, Nicholas (I), *137*
Bonnart, Robert, *138*
boogie-woogie (walking basses), 297–301, 319, 391, 401
Book of New Lessons . . . (Playford), 109
Borreguero, Modesto, 68
Borrow, George, 173–4, 191
Borrull, Miguel (sr), 192
bossa nova, 10, 217
bottleneck playing, 255, 258, 291–2, 295, 298, 306, 314, 394, 415; *see also* technique
Boucher, François, *144*
Bouchet, Robert, 57, 62, 66–7, 72, *74*, 83
Boulez, Pierre, 126
Bourbon, Mlle de Nantes, Duchesse de, 34, 139
bourdons, 25–6
bourrée, 111
bouts, 16; diagram, 76
bow, musical, *10*, 11, *12*
Bozo guitars, *259*, *333*
Bracey, Ishman, 297
bracing, back: diagram, 76; construction of, 83, *93; see also* strutting
brackets: diagram, 76
branle, 108–9, 133
Braye, Lord (manuscript), 135
Brayssing, Grégoire, 108–9, 132
Brazil, music from, 124; *see also* Latin America
breakdowns, country, 293, 299
Bream, Julian, 66–7, 88, 124, *125*, *165*, 165–6, 331
Breezin!, 430
Briceño, Luis de, 112, 136
bridges: on early instruments, 24–5; tied, 40, 42, 57; pin, 42, 221, 238; pegged, 47; unusual, 71; on classical guitars, 84, 86, *98*; on steel-string guitars, 220–1, 224, 264, 267, *284*; pyramid, 236, 244; belly, 244; on electric guitars, 348, 350, 364, 384–6
Britten, Benjamin, 125, 165

Bromberg, David, *334*, 334–5, 427, *429*
Brondi, Rita, 122
Broonzy, Big Bill, 226, 296–7, 300, 305–6, 309–10, 407
Brouwer, Leo, 167
Brown, Milton (and his Musical Brownies), 388
Brown, Rev. Dr. John, 144
Brown, Willie, 293, 295–6
Bruce, Jack, 412
Buchanan, Roy, 364, 422, 425, *427*
bulerías, 199, 204–6
"Bull City Red," 307, 308
Bumble Bee Slim, 302
Burney, Dr. Charles, 144, 148, 156
Burton, James, 364, 427
Butterfield, Paul, 414
Buxtehude, Dietrich, 36, 139
Byrd, Charlie, 331
Byrds, The, 332

Cabeçón, Antonio de, 17
Cadiz, lutherie in, 40–1, 43, 45
Cadiz, Las Calles de, 177
café cantante, 174, *175*, 176, 181, 181–2
Cage, John, 433
Calderón, Maria, 143
Callot, Jacques, *133*
campanellas, 26
Campi, Gironimo, 30
Campion, François, 114
caña (flamenco song), 173, 176
canarios, 112, 114, 133
Canessière, Philippe de la, 134
Cano, Manuel, 193
cantaor, 191
cante, 170, 173, 179, 182, 192, 199–201
cante andaluz, 173–4, 176
cante gitano, 172–4, 176
cante jondo, 174, 174fn., 176–9, 202, 206
Cantigas de Santa Maria, *19*
capacitor, 340, 356, 375, 383–4
capos, 299, 434
Captain Beefheart, 334
Carcassi, Matteo, 121, 154, 156
Carlisle, Cliff, 316, 319
Carlos y Amat, Dr. Juan, *see* Amat, Dr. Juan Carlos y
Carmontelle, (Louis Carrogis), *150*
Carr, LeRoy, 306
Carter family, 314–15, *315*, 325
Carthy, Martin, 330
Carulli, Ferdinando, 119, 121, 154, 156
Castellón, Agustin, *see* "Sabicas"
Castelnuovo-Tedesco, Mario, 122–3

Cavatina Suite (Tansman), 123
cedar: of Lebanon, 17; Western Red, 68, 70, 77, 262; Honduras, 78, 92; *see also* woods
Cerone, Pedro, 131–2
Cervantes, Miguel de, 132
Chabran, F., 116
Chacón, Antonio, 176, 178, 183, 192
chaconne, 111
Chaconne (Bach), 122, 162, 165
chansons, 108–9
charango, *214*
Charles II, 113, 139–40, 291
Charles V, Emperor, 104, 171
Chartres, Mlle de (Elizabeth-Charlotte d' Orleans), 139
Chicago, *see* blues
chitarra battente, 22–5, *27–33*, *37*
chitarrino, 22
chitarrone, 28
choking (damping), 292, 310; *see also* technique
Chopin, Frederick, 122, 124, 215
chordophones, 11–12, 16
Choros Number One (Villa-Lobos), 124
Christian, Charlie, 165, 306, 341, 344, 389, 389–91
cifra (tablature), 171
Cimmaron, El (Henze), 126
Cinq Préludes (Villa-Lobos), 124
Clapton, Eric, 407–8, 412–16, *413*, 421, 425, 432
Clare, John, 125
classical guitar: development of, 10–13, 40–2, 54, 56–7, 286; concert models, 58; experimental design, 58; examples of, 60–73 *passim*; music for, 122–8, 432
classical guitar construction: choosing wood, 75–8, 89–90; preparing sides, 79, *90–1*; neck, 80, *91*; strutting, 80–4, *93*; neck, 80, *91*; strutting, 80–4, *93*; assembly, 84–5, *95*; fretting, 85–6; fixing bridge, 86; polishing, 86–7; illustrations of, *88–101*
clawhammer, *see* fingerpicking
Cocko, Christopho, *28*
Coffe-Goguette, 51
Cole, Nat "King," 233, 390, 399
Coleman, Ornette, 429
Colin, *39*, 46
colombianas, 178
"Colombus Stockade Blues," 319
Colonna, Ambrosio, 136
Como, Perry, 399
compás, 102
Complete Instructor for the Spanish and English Guitar . . . (Siegling), 286
concert flamenco guitars, 183, *190*
concert halls, design of, 58; flamenco in, 199–200
Concerto for Guitar and Chamber Ensemble (Bennett), 127

Concerto for Guitar and Chamber Orchestra (Dodgson), 124
Concerto for Guitar and Orchestra (Adame), 215
Concerto in D (Castelnuovo-Tedesco), 123
Concert sous le Consulat, Un (Taunay), *152*
Concierto de Aranjuez (Rodrigo), 123
Conde brothers, 57, 183, *188, 190*
Conde Claros, 106, 109
Connors, Bill, 429
consonances (chords), 102
consort music, 106, 129
Contreras, Manuel, 57
Conversation Galante (Lancret), *147*
Cooder, Ry, 333–4, 427
Cooper, Alice, 423
Corbetta, Francesco, 26, 112–15, *113*, 137, 139–41, 143
Cordoba, lutherie in, 57
Corea, Chick, 429
Corrette, Michel, 31, *115*, 115
Coryell, Larry, 429
Costa, Diego, *38*
Coste, Napoleon, 117
country music, 222–3, 266, 311–29 *passim*; electric guitar in, 388, 395–7, 399
Coupa, John, *235–6*
courante, 108, 111, 113
Covarde Cavallera (Vásquez), 108
Covarrubias Orozco, Don Sebastián de, 18, 105, 136
cowboy music, 315–18, *317*
Cox, Ida, 391
Crabtree, Will, 296
Cream, 296, 412–14
Créquillon, Thomas, 105
Crespo, Gómez, 215
Crook Brothers, 313
Crosby, Stills, Nash and Young, 332
"Crossroad Blues," 296
Crucifixus est, 108
Crudup, Arthur, "Big Boy," 307, 310, *394*
Cuatro, 213
Curtis, James Peck, 392
cypress: Spanish, 21, 37, 40, 43, 45; in flamenco guitars, 61, 80, 181–2

"Daddy Stovepipe" (Johnny Watson), *304*
dance bands, 221, 388–9, 391, 398
dance forms: Andalucian, 41; and vihuela, 101, 105, 131; and guitar music, 108, 111–14, 115, 133–4, 149; flamenco, *173*, 177; Latin American, 212
Dance on the banks of the Manzaneros (Bayeu), *148*
D'Angelico, John, 222, *231*, 231, 331
Danko, Rick, *324*
D'Aquisto, Jim, 231, 331

Darby, Tom, 319
Davis, Mary, *140*
Davis, Miles, 429
Davis, Rev. Gary, 249, 291, 307–8, *308*, 328–9
Dawkins, Jimmy, 416–17, *417*
Daza, Esteban, 102, *104*, 105, 211
Dead Mouse, The (Boilly), *159*
Dean, Eddie, 316
Dean, James, 399
Debussy, Claude, 122
Declaración de Instrumentos Musicales (Bermudo), 17–18, 24, 102
Deep Purple, 423
Deichman, John, *241*
Delaney and Bonnie, 421
Delmore Brothers, 318–19, 321, 325
Delphin de Música (Narváez), 105
Denis, Robert and Claude, 134
Denver, John, 258
Derek and the Dominoes, 427
Dexter, Al, 395
Diabelli, Anton, 157
Dias, Belchior, *27*
Diaz, Alirio, *69*, 164
Díaz, Francisco *see* Paco de Lucena, 192
Dickens, "Little" Jimmy, 395
Dictionnaire de Musique (Rousseau), 115
Dictionnaire Universel des Luthiers (Vannes), 51
Diddley, Bo, 400, *401*, 401
Diderot, d'Alembert and, 144, *147*
Diego del Gastor, (Diego Amaya Flores), 193, 204
diferencia (variation), 106
distortion, controlled, 342, 358, 408–9, 423, 427
Ditson, Oliver, 239, 246
Dixon Brothers (Howard and Dorsey), 319
Dobro guitars, 255–7, 316, 319; electric, 341; *see also* resonator guitars
Dodgson, Stephen, 124–5, 166
Doisy, Charles, 41
Domino, Fats, 400
Donegan, Lonnie, 407
Donovan, 331
Don Quixote (Cervantes), 132
Dons d'Apollon, Les (Corrette), *31, 115*, 115
Dopera Brothers, 224, 255; *see also* Dobro guitars
Doré, Gustave, *171, 174*
Dorotea (de Vega), 131
Dorsey, Georgia Tom, 306, 310
Dos Amigos, Los (Sor), 154
Douze Etudes (Villa-Lobos), 124
Dowland, John, 125, 130
Dreadnought models, *see* Gibson guitar models, Martin guitar models

Dronge, Alfred, 223
"Dry Spell Blues," 295
Dudley, Robert, *see* Leicester, Earl of
duende, 170, 179, 204
Dukas, Paul, 162
dulcimer, 312, 335
DuMesnil, *32*
Dunn, Bob, 388
Duo Concertante (Dodgson), 124
Durham, Eddie, 306, 389
"Dust My Broom," 296
Duvernay, Flamini, 157
Duyffoprucgar, Gaspard (also called Tieffenbrucker), 30, 134
Dyer-Bennett, Richard, 321
Dylan, Bob, 323–4, *324*, 334, 399

ebony: as decoration, 17, 24, 32–4, 38; for fingerboards, 78, 377; in steel-string guitars, 262, *268*
Eddy, Duane, 401–2
electraharp, *see* pedal steel guitar
electric-acoustic guitars (electric-Spanish), 13, 254, 338, 342–3, *355*, *366*; construction of, 373–5; music for, 388
Electric Flag, 427
electric guitars, 10, 13, 52; and classical musicians, 166–7; resonator, 256; in jazz, 306, 388; in blues, 310, 328; in country, 319; in folk, 324; development of, 338–43; examples of, *344–67 passim*; construction of, 368–87 *passim*; f-hole, 374–5; social history, 388–97; music for, 398–434 *passim*; composers for, 432; avant garde music for, 432–4
Elegy (Rawsthorne), 127
Elliot, Ramblin' Jack, 323
Ellis, Herb, 355, 389–90, 403, 430
Encyclopédie (Diderot and d'Alembert), 144, *147*
endblock: diagram, 76; construction, *95* (classical); 265, 266, 276 (steel-string)
England: lutherie in, 38, 42, *52*, 57; dance forms in, 105; guitar music in, 114–16, 119, 127, 134–5; history of guitar in, 131, 139–41, 153, 157–8; folk music in, 329–35
English Tea Party at a Salon (Ollivier), *150*
engraving, on guitars, 24, *30*
Enharmonic guitar, *50*
Epiphone Guitar Company, 221, 224, 341, 431; acoustic models, *230*; electric models, *347*
Escalada, Gustavo Sosa, 215
Escudero, Mario, 196
Escuela de Música (Aguado), *68*
Escuela Música (Nassare), 18
Escuela Razonada de la Guitarra (Pujol), 122, 161–2
españoletas, 114
Espinel, Vicente, 131–2
Estel, Joseph, 42
Estes, Sleepy John, 293, 305, 309

Esteso, Domingo, 57, *65*, 68; and flamenco, 183, 186, 187, 188
Euphonon guitar, 247, *247*
Everly, Ike, 320–1
Examen de Violeros, 16, 18

f-hole guitar, *see* steel-string guitar, forms of; electric guitar, construction
Fahey, John, 326, 328, *329*, 329, 334
Falla, Manuel de, 122, 162, 176
False consonances of musick . . . The (Matteis), 114, 141
falsetas, 114, 191–3, 194, 196, 199, 204
fandango, 149, 170–3, 206, 211
Fandanguillo (Turina), 122
fandanguillos, 176
fan strutting, see strutting, fan
Fantasia para un gentilhombre (Rodrigo), 123
fantasias, 104, 107–9, 123
Fantasy-Divisions (Dodgson), 124
Farandouri, Maria, 166
Fardino, Lorenzo, 114
fandangos, 115
Farfan, Miguel, *55*
Farlow, Tal, 389, *390*, 390, 403
feedback, 341, 355, 372; controlled, 342, 407–8, 409; *see also* distortion
felag mengu, 171
Feliciano, José, *332*
Fender, Leo, 341, 345, 349
Fender Electrical Instrument Company, 341, 342, 376, 382; Broadcaster, 341, 346, 400; Stratocaster, 342, *349–51*, 360, 365, 372, 421; Telecaster, 341, 360, *364*, 393, 400
Fernández, Arcángel, 57, *68*
Fernández, Gerundino, 183, *190*
Ferrandière, Fernando, 40, 117, 152
Ferranti, Zani de, 118, 155
Fezandat, Michel, 108
fiberglass-bodied guitars, 223, 265
Fields, W. C., 396
Figaro, 162
fingerboards: on early instruments, 12, 17, 24; on six-course guitar, 40, on six-string guitar, 42, 49, 54; on enharmonic guitar, 50; scalloped, *52*; standardized, 57; diagram, 76; construction, 78, 84–6 (classical), 182–3 (flamenco), 262, 266–7, *281–2* (steel-string), *376–8* (electric)
fingerpicking (clawhammer), 242, 292, 302; in country music, 313, 395
Fires of London, *69*, 126, 167
Fitzgerald, Ella, 206
Five Bagatelles (Walton), 127
Five Pieces for Chamber Group (Webern), 167
Flac, Philippe, 134

flamenco, 10, 13, 122, *168–9*, 170–219 *passim*; guitars, 40, 54, 57, 61, 64, 70, 73, 80, 176, 178 (mentioned), 181–3 (construction), *184–91* (examples; aficionados, 170, 174–6, 178, 197, 199–200; history and traditions, 170–80; artists, 191–201

"Flamenco Ballet," 176, 179

Flamenco Puro: record, 195; group *198*

Flat Response Audio Pickup (FRAP), 343, 367

flat-top guitar, 220–4, *235–54 passim*; *see also* steel-string acoustic guitar

Flatt, Lester, 320

Fleischer, Hans Christoph, *35*, 36, 139

Flemish musicians, 104, 171

Fleta, Ignacio, 57, 64, *67*, 68, 77, 83

Flores, Diego Amaya, *see* Diego del Gastor

Flying Burrito Brothers, 332

Foggy Mountain Boys, 321

folias (later *Folies d'Espagne*), 105, 111, 115, 149, 211

folk music, 114, 266; 16th-century, 106, 109; in flamenco, 172, 174; in Latin America, 212; in United States, 222–3, 299, 311, 321; revival, 322–9; in Britain, 329–35

foot, diagram, 76; construction of, 79, 84, *95*

Ford, Mary, 353, *396–7*, 396–7

Ford, Richard, 149

Fortea, Daniel, 122

Foscarini, Giovanni Paolo, 112–15, 143

Four Poems of John Clare (Dodgson), 125

France: guitar fashionable in, 18, 24, 108–9, 133–4, 136; luthiers in, 23, 25, 32–3, 50, 57, 137; guitar styles in, *38*, 40, 42, 46; 16th-century music in, 105, 108–9, 111–16; 133

Franconetti, Silverio, 174, 176, 192

"Frankie and Johnny (Albert)," 291, 299

Freeman, Eddie, 232

frets: early methods of placing, 17–18, 24, 40; types of, 17–18, 21, 25, 42, 238–9; on enharmonic guitar, 50; adjustable, 54; unusual, 63; diagram, 76; formula for placing, 85; construction, 85–6, 96–7 (classical), 266–7, *281–3* (steel-string), 375, 377–8 (electric)

Friedrich, Daniel, *70*

Frith, Fred, 433, 434

Frontera, Jerez de la, 172, 204

Fuenllana, Miguel de, 24, 102, 105, 106, *107*, 108, 110, 131, 211

Fuller, Blind Boy, 302, 307–8

Fuller, Walter, 338, 342, 344, 346

Fruit Jar Drinkers, 313

fuzz-box, 342, 357, 408, 409

Gage, Thomas, 211

Gagliano, 41

Gallagher guitars, *250*, 254

galliard, 108, 114, 133–4

Galloway, Charlie, 287

Gamme D'Amour, La (Watteau), *145*

García, Enrique, 57, 64

Garcia, Jerry, *411*

García, Miguel (Father Basilio), 117, 149, 152

Garland, Hank, 403

gavotte, 111

Gavoty, Bernard, 162

Geils, J. Band, *426*

Germany: lutherie in, 24, *30*, *31*, *35*, 36, 42, 57, 139; tuning machines from, 87; guitar music in, 108, 115, 153–4

Gerolamo dai Libri, *20*, *21*

Gherardi, Giovanni Everisto, 137

Ghiglia, Oscar, 164

Gibson, Orville, 220–1, *225*

Gibson Guitar Company: history, 70, 220–4, 347, company records, 247, 338; factory operations, 260–85 *passim* (acoustic guitars), 368–87 *passim* (electric guitars)

Gibson guitars, acoustic models: B–45– 12 twelve string, 252; country western, 249; Century, 247; Dreadnought, 249, 252, *271*; Gospel, 252, *274*; J-55, *252*, *274*; J-200, 248–9, 250, 252, 318, 366; J-160 E, 252; L model, 201; L-4, *226*; L-5, 201, 229, *234*, *315*, 346; L-7, 229; L-10, 229; L-12, 229; L-50, *229*; Mark series, 254, 264, *272*, *276*, *279*, *285*, 366; Nick Lucas Special, *244*; O model, 201, 225; O-style artist model, *225*; O-style Deluxe, *225*; SJ200, 55, *248*; Super 400, 234

Gibson guitars, electric models: Double Bass, *357*; ES-5, 346–7; ES-135, 342; ES-150, 341, *344*; ES-175D, *355*; ES-355 TD-SV, *355*, *415*; Explorer, 353, 359, 371–6, 386; Firebird, 376–7; Flying V, 353, 359, 371, *416*; Howard Roberts, 374, *431*; Johnny Smith, 374, 375; L-6S, *359*; Les Paul models, 339, *348*, *352*, *353–4*, *358*, 360, 365, *366*, *368*, *386*, 381–2, 393, *396*, 397, 415; Marauder, *363*; Melody Maker, *356*; SG Standard, *360*; Super 400 CES, 347, *388*

gigue, 111

Gilberto, Joao, 217

Gilles and his Family (Watteau), *147*

Gillespie, Dizzy, 389

Girls of the Golden West, 316

gittern, 16

Giuliani, Mauro, 118–19, 121, 154, 156–7, 215

Giulianiad, The, 157–8

Glinka, Mikhail Ivanovich, 173, 191

Goemuette, Norbert, *155*

golpeador, 60, 65, 182–3, 190, 204

Gombert, Nicolas, 104–5

Gómez, Francisco Sánchez, *see* Lucia, Paco de

González, Francisco, *62*, 63

Goodman, Benny, 165, 341, *389*, 389, 399

Gorlier, Simon, 108, 132, 134

gospels, *see* spirituals
Goya, Francisco, 173
Graham, Davy, 330
Granada, lutherie in, 56–7
granadinas, 204, 206–7
Granados, Enrique, 122
Granaino, Roman el, 178
Granata, Giovanni Battista, 112, 114
Grand Funk Railroad, 423
Grand Ole Opry, *312*, 313, 319, *319*, 388
Granjon, Robert, 108
Grapelli, Stephan, 330
Grateful Dead, 342, *411*
Greco, José, 196
Green, Freddie, 233
Gretsch Guitar Company, *354*, 357, 401
Greuze, Jean Baptiste, *151*
Gréven, John, *253*, *361*
Griffin, Rex, 395
Grobert, *47–8*
Grossman, Stefan, 247, 328–9
Guárdame las vacas, 106, 107
Guerau, Don Francisco, 114
Guercino, *132*
Guerra, Dionisio, *43*
Guild company: acoustic models, 223, *253*, 254, *258*, 260;
  electric models, 347, *361*, *365*, 375
guitar:
  acoustics of, 56–8, 66, 69, 79, 81–3, 118, 158, 254, 264
  construction;
      early methods, 40–2, 45, 48–9, 51, 134
      see also classical, electric, flamenco, and steel string
      guitar, construction of
  decoration, 57, 60; *see also* types of decoration, i.e. inlay,
      marquetry, etc., and materials used in decoration, i.e.
      ebony, ivory, mother-of-pearl etc.
  double-backed, *53*
  evolution of,
      early, 10–15; 13th–16th century, 16–17, 129–35, 138;
      17th–18th century, 24–6, 40–1, 136–43; 19th century,
      (transitional), 40–2, 152–60; modern, 40–4, 54, 56–7,
      161–7; flamenco, 168–80; steel string, 220–5; Latin
      American, 210–17; electric, 338–43
  music for,
      four-course, *103*, *107*, 107–09; five course, 110–16;
      transitional, 117–21; modern, 122–8; *see also* blues,
      country, folk, jazz, rock
  papier mâché bodied, 58, *61*
  shapes of, 16, *20*, 25, 40, 42, 45–6, 52, 56, 66
  social status of, 18, 24, 107, 111, 116, 127–8, 129, 134–5
  stringing, evolution of methods,
      four courses, 18–19, *19*, 22–3, 132, 212; five courses, 18,

22–6, *27–39*, 40, 131, *134*; six courses, 36, 40–1, *43–6*,
50–1, 152; seven courses, *43*; five single strings, 41; six
single strings, 40–2, *46–56*, ten strings, *165*; *see also*
strings, types of
  unusual (experimental), 42, *43–4*, 58, 66, 70
  see also bass, classical, electric, enharmonic, f-hole,
      flamenco, flat-top, Latin American, steel-string
Guitar Player, The (van Schuppen), 138
Guitar Player, The (Vermeer), *142*
Guitarre Royalle, La (Corbetta), *113*, 140
guitarra, 16, 24
Guitarra Española y Vándola (Carlos y Amat), *110*, 110
guitarra latina, 16, *19*
guitarra moresca, 16, *19*
guitarrón, 212
Gully Jumpers, 313
Gurian guitars, 254
gut strings, *see* strings, gut
Guthrie, Woodie, 315, 321, *322*, 322–3, 407
Guy, Buddy, 393, 412, 414, 416–17
Guzmán, Luis de, 102, 130
gypsies, 171–2, *171*, 174, 178, 192, 219

hacer garganta, 105
Hachas, Las, 114
Haley, Bill, *398*, 399
Hall, Jim, *331*, 355
Hamburg, lutherie in, 25, 35, 36, 139
Hamilton, Anthony, 140
hammer on, 292, 299, 300, 304
Hammond, John (Sr), 389
Handel, George Frederick, 122
Handy, W. C., 288
Hanna, Jeff, 361
Hare, Pat, *393*, 393
Harker, Roland, 167
Harmonicon, The, 154, 156
Harmonie appliquée à la Guitare (Carulli), 119
Harmony guitars, 223
harps, *11*, 16, 104, 114, 131
harpsichords, 115, 141, 144, 148
Harrison, Frank Mott, 158
Hartmann, C. F., 237
Harvey, Roy, 313, 320
Hauser, Hermann, 57, 58, *65*, 88, 93
Hawaiian guitar, 226–7, *242*, 255, 319; electric, 340, 341, *344*,
388
Hawkins, Sir John, 148
Hay, George D., 313, 319
Hayden, Scott, 303
Haydn, Franz Joseph, 117–8, 215
head, *22*, *29*, *36*, *42*; construction, 36, 80–1, *96* (classical), 182,

(flamenco), 266–7 (steel string), 378 (electric); diagram, 76;
heel: design, 64; diagram, 76; construction, 79–80, 84, 86, 92, 98
Hendrix, Jimi, 351, 393, *408*, 408–9, 412, 421–2, 423, 425, 429, *434*
Henze, Hans Werner, 126, 165, 432
Heredia, Andrés, 204
Hernández, Manuel, *68*, 183
Hernández, Santos, 57, *64*, 65, 68; and flamenco, *186–7*, 193
Hicks, Charlie and Robert "Barbecue Bob," 302
hillbilly music, 302, 312–13; *see also* country music
hokum music, 306, 310
hollers, field, 289, 297, 300, 316
"Homesick James and his Dusters," 416
Hommage à Tárrega (Turina), 122
Hommage pour le Tombeau de Debussy (Falla), 122
honky-tonk music, 305, 389, 395
Hood, Tom, 313
Hooker, John Lee, 291, 402, 407
Hopf, Dieter, *252*, 262
Hopkins, Lightnin' Sam, 289, 300, 326
Horetzky, Felix, 118
Hornepipe d'Angleterre, 109
House, Eddie "Son," 290, 293, *294*, 294–6, 393; rediscovered, 328
Houston, Cisco, 322
Houtsma, Adrian, 254
"How High the Moon", 396
Howe-Orme, guitar, *238*
Howe, Steve, 355, 425
Howell, Peg Leg, 302
Howlin' Wolf, 289, 394, 402, 407
Hoyer Foldaxe Erlangen, *367*
Huelva, Manolo de, 170, *177*, 193–4, 195, 204
Huerta y Caturla, Don Trinidad, 118, 155
Hulinzky, Thomas, 42
humbucking pickup, 342, 343fn., 356, 380–2, 384; *see also* superhumbucking
Hunt, Pee Wee, 396
Hurt, Mississippi John, 326, 328–9
Hutchinson, Frank, 319
hymns, *see* sacred music

inlay, 24, *30*, 40, 222, 263, *279*; *see also* descriptions of individual guitars
inlay, back, 76, 80
Instrucción de Música sobre la Guitarra Española (Sanz), 25–6, 35, *114*, 143
Instructions . . . for Playing on the Enharmonic Guitar (Thompson), 50
intabulation, 103, 108–9; *see also* tablature
Intavolatura Facile (Sanseverino), *111*

Islam (Moors), 12, 172; expelled from Spain, 106, 130; and flamenco, 171, 173, 180, 199, 204
"Intoxicated Rat, The," 319
Italy: history of guitar in, 16, 40–2, 136; guitar styles in, 22, 24–5, *28*, *30–1*, *47*; music for guitar in, 104–8, 111–16
Ives, Burl, 321
ivory, as guitar decoration, 23–35 *passim*, *see* descriptions of individual guitars

jácaras, 112, 114
Jackson, John, *328*
Jacquemart André Museum, 21, 161
Jagger, Mick, 407
James, Elmore, 296, *394*, 394–5, 402, 427
James, Skip, 293, 295–7, *297*, 326, 328
Jansch, Bert, 297, 330–1
Japan, 12; lutherie in, 57, 72; steel string guitars from, 223–4, 228, 259, 267; electric guitars from, 343, 347, 353, 365
jarana jarocha, *213*
jazz, 165, 166, 222, 301, 319, 398, 405; influence on flamenco, 179, 199, 206; bands, 221; guitars for, 228, 231–2, 266, 306, 331; history of, 287–8, 312, 402–3; musicians, 389–93, 395; influence on rock, 423, 427–8; contemporary, 430
Jefferson, Blind Lemon, 299, *300*, 300–1, 308–10, 395
Jefferson Airplane, 411–12
Jeroma, Curro de la, *177*, 204–5
Jobim, Antonio Carlos, 217
"John Henry," 291, 314, 407
Johnny and the Hurricanes, 401
Johns, Keith, *251*
Johnson, Lonnie, 288, 295, 301, 306, 309–10, 331, 395
Johnson, Robert, 295–6, 309, 393, 407
Johnson, Tommy, 297
joints used in guitar construction: head-to-neck, 51, 80, *96*; neck-to-body, 42, 85, 265–6; slipper foot, 39–40, 43, 48, *276*, *279*; pivot, 49; V-joint, 45, 48, 66, 71, 80, 95–8; bell-shaped end block, 67; dovetail, *279–80*; on electric guitars, 375–6
jondo, 174, 174fn., 176, *177*–9, 202, 206
Jones, Brian, 407
Joplin, Scott, 302, 329
Josquin des Pres, 104, 105, 129
jota aragonesa. 115, 149, 211
Jourdan de la Salle, L., 141
Jug Bands, 305–6, 309

Kaman, Charles, 223
Kammermusik (Henze), 126
Kapsberger, Johan, 114
Kasha, Dr. Michael, 58, 70–1, 83–4, 254, 264, 265, 366
Kessel, Barney, 166, 331, 390, *430*, 430
King, Albert, *416*, 416

King, B. B., 356, 395, 402–3, 412, 414–15, *415*, 416–17
King, Freddie, 414, *415*, 416
King, Pee Wee (and his Golden West Cowboys), *312*, *388*, 388
"King Biscuit Time," 392, 394
Kingston Trio, 323
Kiss, *423*, 424
Kithara, *11*, 11–12
Kneller, Andreas, 139
Koa wood, 242
Koch, Christopho, *see* Cocko, Christopho
Koester, Bob, 326
Kohno, Masaru, *72*
Konitz, Lee, 390
korina wood, 353
Korner, Alexis, 407
Kortchmar, Danny, 427
Kottke, Leo, *333*, 334
Kristofferson, Kris, 332

Lacôte, René, *49*, 52, *53*, 54
lacquer, 69, 87, 267, 378–9; *see also* polish
Lady and the Unicorn, The, 330
Lafon, Jean, 62
Lagoya, Alexandre, 67, 123, 167
Laibman, Dave, 329
lamination, 80
Lancret, Nicolas, 144, *147*
Laneham, Robert, 134
Lang, Eddie, 226, 288, 301, 331
Lasky, Louie, 310
Latin America: stringed instruments in, 10, 18; guitar styles in, 55, 210–17 *passim*; influence on European music, 111, 123, 130, 162, 166, 224; flamenco in, 177–9
Lauro, Antonio, 123, 215
Law, Don, 295
Lawrence, Bill, 343*n*, 359
Layla, 427
Lazarus, Arnie, 343
Leadbelly (Huddie Leadbetter), 224, 258, 298–301, 321, 326, 407
Leadbelly's Last Session, 299
Léandre, Charles, 157, 161
Leçon de Musique, La (Boucher), *144*
LeCoq, François, 115
Led Zeppelin, 421, 423
Léger, Fernand, *160*
Legnani, Luigi Rinoldo, 49, 51, 119, 155
Leicester, Robert Dudley, Earl of, 134
Lely, Sir Peter, *140*
LeRoy, Adrian, 108, *109*, 109, 130, 132–4
Lester, Julius, 293
Levin Company (Sweden), 224

Lewis, Walter "Furry," 305
Libro del Buen Amor (Ruiz), 16
Libro de Música de Vihuela (Pisador), 105, *106*
Lightfoot, Gordon, 331
linings: diagram 76; construction, 95 (classical), 265 (steel-string)
Lipscombe Mance, 291, *327*, 328
Livre de Guitarre (LeRoy), 107, 108
Liszt, Franz, 156
Llobet, Miguel, 61, 122, *161*, 162, 193, 215
Lloyd, A. L., 330
Loar, Lloyd, *221*, 221, 226, 338–40
Lockwood, Robert, 395
Lomax, John and Alan, 299
London Sinfonietta, 126
Lone Star Cowboys, 316
López Nieto, Marcelino, 57, *72*, 83
Lorca, García, 170, 176
Louis XIV, 26, 34, 111, 113, 137
Louis XIV's Musicians (Puget), *141*
"Love in Vain," 295, 296
Lowe, Mundell, 430
Lucas, Nick, 244, *318*
Lucena, Paco de (Francisco Díaz), 192
Lucia, Paco de (Francisco Sánchez Gómez), 170, *180*, 183, 190, 196–8, 200, 204
Luduvico (harpist), 104
Luis el de la Juliana, El Tio, 172
Lullaby for Ilian Rainbow (Maxwell-Davies), *127*, 127
Lully, Jean Baptiste, 111, 137
Lunar, Perico el del (Pedro del Valle), 177–8, 183, 187, 193
Lupot, François, 41–2, *46*
lute, 12, *19*, 26, 72, 165; popularity of, 16, 115, 129–30, 132; tone of, 30; music for, 101, 105, 108–13, *163*, 164
Luz y norte musical (Ruiz de Ribayez), 114
Lyon, Lutherie in, 134
Lyon, George Washburn, 223, 345
lyre, *11*, 11–12

"Macarrona, La," *177*
Maccaferri, Mario, *163*, 222, 227–8; 232, *330*; G-40 style, *234–5*; pickup design, *352*
McClennan, Tommy, 307
McDowell, Fred, *327*, 328
McGee, Kirk, 313
McGee, Sam, 313, 319
McGhee, Brownie, 302, *308*, 308, *325*, 325, 405, 407
McGuinn, Roger, 362
McHugh, Ted, 229, 266
McLaughlin, John, 249, *366*, *429*, 429
McMichen, Clayton "Pappy," 313, *314*, 321
McMullen, Fred, 302

Macon, Uncle Dave, 313
McShee, Jacqui, 331
McTell, Blind Willie, 224, 258, 302, *303*, 303–4
McWilliams, Elsie, 316
Madonna and Child with St. Anne (Gerolamo dai Libri), 20
Madrid, lutherie in, 57, 62, 64, 149
madrigals, 104, 136
Maestro, El (Milán), 17, *20*, 21, *101*, 101–2, 129
"Maestro Malagueño," 192
"Maestro Patino, El," 191
Magic Flute, The (Mozart), 118
Magic Sam, 416, *417*, 417
Mahavishnu Orchestra, 429
Mahler, Gustav, 167
mahogany, 78, 80, 262, 268, 370, 375; *see also* woods
Mairena, Antonio, 178
malagueñas, 170, 173, 204, 206–7
mandolins, 12, 220–1, 226
Manet, Edouard, *155*
Manzanero, Felix, 57, 83
Maphis, Joe, *352–3*, *357*
maple, 35, 38, 48, 62, 78; for flamenco guitars, 182; for steel-string, 262; for electric, 375, 377; *see also* sycamore
Marchena, Melchor de, *194*, 194, 204
mariachi bands, 212
Maria Theresa, Empress, 156
Marín Montero, Antonio, 57, *73*
Marín, Don José, 114
marizápolos, 112, 114
marquetry, 17, 24, 25; examples, *21*, *30*, *33*; *see also* descriptions of individual guitars
Marteau sans Maître, Le (Boulez), 126
Martin, C. F. I, 42, *55*, 222, 235, 241
Martin, C. F. II, 237
Martin, Frank, 124
Martin, Grady, 403
Martin Guitar Company: history of, 222–24; partnership with Coupa, *235*; sizes defined, 224, 237, 238, 253; dating of guitars, 239; factory operations, 260–85 *passim*; sawmill, *268*; steel string acoustic models,
    2-27, *55*, *237*, 240
    1-21, *239*
    1-45 Ditson, *239*
    0-18, *243*
    0-28, *237*, 239
    0-30, *240*
    0-41 "Wurlitzer," *243*
    0-45, *240*, *244*
    0-45S "John Deichman," *241*
    00-18S, *229*
    00-28K, *242*
    00-42, *239*
    000-45, *244*
    OM-45, *245*, 247
    Dreadnought styles, 239, 245–6, 248–9, 253, *270*, 318
    D-2, *246*
    D-28, 249
    D-35, *274*
    D-41, *251*, 263, *270*
    D-42S, 246
    D-45S, *248*, *249*, 251, *279*
    C-style, 229, 253
    F-7, *233*
    R-style, 229, 253
  electric models, *400*
Martín, Juan, 178–9, 187, 190, 194, 198–9, *201*, *202*; on *toques*, 202–3
martinetes, 174, 176
Martínez, Pepe, 187, 193
Marvin, Hank, 401–2
mastic, black, 22, 24, 28, 35, 40; *see also* descriptions of individual guitars
Matiegka, Wenzel Thomas, 118
Matteis, Nicola, 114, 143
Maxwell-Davies, Peter, 126, *127*, 127
Maya, Juan, 204
Mayall, John, 412
"Maybelline," 400
Mayo Williams, J., 307
Mazarin, Cardinal, 137
Mazot, François, 136
medicine shows, 305, 312
Medina-Celi, Duke of, 153
medullary rays, 65, 77
Melopeo y Maestro, El (Cerone), 131
Melrose, Lester, 307
Memoirs of the Count of Grammont (Hamilton), 140
Memphis (Beale Street), 295, 297, 305, 312, 326; blues, 393, 394–5
"Memphis" Minnie, 305–6
Mendelssohn, Felix, 122, 153, 215
mesura, 102
Méthode pour Guitare (Sor), *120*
Método mui facilissimo . . . (de Briçeño), 112
"Midnight Special," 299
Milán, Luis, 17, *20*, 21, *101*, 101–5, *129*, 131
Milano, Francesco da, 130
Minguet y Yrol, Pablo, 115, 148
Mirecourt, luthiers of, 50–2
Mitchell, Joni, 331
Molina, Javier, 177–8, 192, 194
Molitor, Simon, 118
Monge, Victor, *see* "Serranito"
Monk, Thelonious, 389

Monroe, Bill (and Charlie), 318, *319*, 320–1, 325
Montana Slim, 316
Montesardo, Girolamo, 111
Monteverdi, Claudio, 129
Montgomery, Little Brother, 296
Montgomery, Wes, 390–1, 430
Montoya, Carlos, 195
Montoya, Ramón, 176, 177–8, 183, 187, *192*, 192–3, 195
Moore, Jackie "Kid," 248
Moore, John, 341
Moore, Oscar, 345
Moore, Scotty, 400
Moors, *see* Islam
Morales, Cristóbal de, 103–4, 129
Moretti, Federico, 41, 117, 152, 155
Morlaye, Guillaume, 108–9, 132
Morley, Thomas, 133
Morlot, Nicholas, *50*
Moseley, Semie, *352–3*, 357
Mosrite Company, 353, *357*
Moss, Buddy, 302
Mossman guitars, 254
mother-of-pearl, 28, 31, 35, 36, 40; *see also* descriptions of
    individual guitars
"moustaches," *33, 36, 38*, 40, 46
Mozart, Wolfgang Amadeus, 117, 118, 149, *150*, 151
Mozzani, Luigi, 163, 227
Mudarra, Alonso, 104, *107*, 107, 131
Muddy Waters, 289, 295–6, 300, 310, 328, *393*, 393–4, *402*,
    402, 407, 427
"Mule Skinner Blues," 321
Mulliner book, 134–5
Munting, Simon, 71, 167
Murcia, Santiago de, 115, 149
"Murciano, El," (Francisco Rodríguez), 191
Muses of Painting, Poetry and Music (West), *286*
Music from Big Pink, 423
music, *see* types of music i.e. baroque, blues, classical, country,
    folk, jazz, Renaissance, rock, etc.
Música de Vihuela (Santa Cruz), *114*
Musick's Delight on the Cittern (Playford), 141
Musikalischen Gemüths-Ergotzung (Kremberg), 115
"My Black Mama," 295

Narváez, Luis de, 105–6, 131, 211
Nashville sounds, 403, 405
Nassare, Pablo, 18
National Barn Dance, 313
National Guitar Company (National Dobro), 255–6, *294, 307*,
    308, 341
neck: diagram, 76; construction, 78, 80, 84–6, 92, *95–6, 98*
    (classical), 221, 262, 266–7, *280–3* (steel string), 375–7

(electric)
nefer, 12, *13*
Netscher, Caspar, *140*
New Instructions for the Spanish Guitar (Chabron), 116
New Lost City Ramblers, 325
Newport Folk Festivals, 293, 323
Newseidler, Hans, 130
Night, The (Mazot), 136
Niña de los Peines La, (Pastora Pavón), 176, 178
Niño de Almaden, El, 178
Niño Ricardo, El (Manuel Serrapí), 176, *177*, 178
Nitty Gritty Dirt Band, *332*, 361
Nixon, Hammie, 305
Nocturnal (Britten), 125
Nono, Luigi, 432
Norvo, Red, 390
notation, modern, 111–12, 115–17, 171; *see also* tablature
Nouvelles Découvertes sur la Guitarre (Campion), 114
Nuevo Metodo para Guitarra (Aguado), *120*, 120
Nuova Inventione . . . sopra la Chitarra Spagnuola
    (Montesardo), 111
Nüske, J. A., 119
nut: diagram, 76; construction, 86

Obra para Guitarra de seis órdenes (Ballesteros), 40, 117
Obras de Música para Tecla Arpa y Vihuela (Cabeçón), 17
Obregón, Alberto, 122
Ochs, Phil, 323, 331
octave divider, 342
Odyssey (Bedford), 433
Oglesby, Carl, 323
Oiseleur accordant sa guitarre, Un (Greuze), 151
Oldfield, Mike, *433*, 433
Oliveira, Pedro Ferreiro, *44*
Oliver, Paul, 289, 291
Ollivier, M. Barth, *150*
Omega Quartet, 167
opera, 144, 148, 153
"Opera Flamenca," 176, 179
Orleans, Elizabeth-Charlotte d', *see* Chartres, Mlle de
Orleans, Henrietta, Duchess of, 140
Orphenica Lyra (Fuenllana), 24, 102, *107*, 108, 110
Ortego, Señor, *154*
Ossenbrink, Luther (Arkie the Arkansas Woodchopper), 246
Ott, Andreas, 25
Ovation guitars, 223, 254, 260, 264, 265; electric, 342–3, 359

Paco de Lucena (Francisco Díaz), *192*
Paco de Berbero (Francisco Sanchez), 191–2
Paganini, Niccolò, 48, 118, 153, 156, 157, 215
Page, Jimmy, *423*, 423
Pagés family, 56; José, 41, *45*, 51; Juan, 41, *44*, 45, 48, 51

palmas, 179
Palmero, Alfredo, 175
Panormo, George and Joseph, 52
Panormo, Louis, *39*, 42, 45, *48*, *50*, *52*, 56
Panormo, Vicenzo, 48
Pantomimes (Cole), 167
Papier-mâché bodied guitar, 56, *61*
Paquera, La, 204
Paris: lutherie in, 25, 32, 39, 49, 134, 137, 222; music
    publishing in, 130, 154–5
Parkening, Christopher, 164
Parker, Charley, 389
Parnaso, El (Daza), *104*, 105
Pass, Joe, 355, 430, 432
passacalle, 111, 114
passamezzo, 108
Passeavase el rey moro, 108
Patton, Charley, 293–4, 295–7, 307, 393
Paul, Les, *339*, 341–2, *345*, *348*, 358, 390, 395–7, *397*
pavanas, 105, 107–8, 114
Pavón, Pastora, *see* La Niña de los Peines, 176, 178
Paxton, Tom, 323, 331
Pears, Peter, 125, 165
Pearse, John, 55, 240, 252, *335*, 335
pear wood, 78, 189
pedal steel guitar, 341–2
Peer, Ralph, 313, 314, 316
Pellegrini, Domenico, 112
Pelzer, Catherine, *see* Pratten, Madame Sidney
Peña, Paco, 180, 190, 191, 196–8, *198*, 200
Pentangle, *330*, 331
Pepys, Samuel, 139–40
Perea, Maestro, *20*
Perez, Francisco, *39*
Perkins, Carl, 311
Pernas, José, 56
Peru, guitar in, *55*
peteneras, 173
Peter, Paul and Mary, 323
Peterson, Oscar, 233, 390, 403
Philip II, 131
Philip III, 111
Philip IV, 131, 143
Philip V, 115, 148
Phillips, Sam, 399–400
Phrygian mode, 171, 204
pianoforte, 115, 117, 144, 148, 157, 390
picado, 191–3, 196–7, 199
Picasso, Pablo, *167*
pickguard, 221, 246, 383
pickup units, 13, 221, 232; Rowe-DeArmond, 234, 341, 366,
    388; development of, 338–43; low-impedance, 358; design

of, 379–85
Pièces Characteristiques (Torroba), 122
piezo-electric transducers, 252, 334, 343, 359, 367
Pimentel, Juan, 70
pine, 17, 28, 41, 47, 49; *see also* woods
p'i p'a, 12
Pisador, Diego, 105, *106*, 106, 130
pitos, 173
Pizzarelli, Bucky, 403
Plaine and Easie Introduction to Practicall Music, A. (Morley),
    133
Plainte Moresque, La (Manet), *155*
Planeta, El, 173
plastic guitar, 234
Plata, Manitas de, 197
Playford, John, 109, 141
plectrum, 16, *19*
Podunavac, Bozo, 259
Poema harmonica (Guerau), 114
Poitiers, Diane de, 132
Polifemo de Oro, El (Smith-Brindle), 127
polish: effect on guitar, 67, 86, 99, 266–7; types of, 86–7, 247,
    262, *283–4*, 378–9
polo, 173, 176
Ponce, Manuel, 10, 122, 123, 124, *164*, 215
Pont Neuf, *137*, 137
Poole, Charlie (and the North Carolina Ramblers), 313
Porcel, José, 367
Portugal: guitar styles in, *27*, 41, 44–5; dance in, 105
potentiometer, 340, 375, 383–4
Powell, Baden, *216*, 217
Praetorius, Michael, 111, 137
Prairie State guitars, 247
Prat, Domingo, 61, 162, 215
Pratten, Madame Sidney (Catherine Pelzer), 119, *158*, 158–9,
    161
"Preaching the Blues," 295
Premier Livre de Tabulature de Guiterne (LeRoy), 108, 109
Pres, Josquin des, 104, 105, 129
Presley, Elvis, 249, 311, 399–400, *400*, 403
Presti, Ida, 123, 167
Preston, *38*
Primo, secondo e terzo libro della Chitarra Spagnola (Foscarini),
    112
Principes Généraux de la Guitarre à cinq et à six Cordes (Doisy),
    41
Principios para tocar la guitarra de seis órdenes (Moretti), 41,
    117
Prine, John, 332, 334
Prunières, Henri, 122
Puckett, Riley, 313, *314*, 314, 320
Puget, François, *141*

Pujol, Emilio, 21, 56, 67, *117*, *122*, *161–2*
pull off, 292, 299
punteado, 112, 114, 115, 117, 152
purflings (bindings), *32*, 46; diagram, 76; construction of, 85, *96*
Puyana, Rafael, 124
Pythagorean scale, 17

Quart Livre de Tablature de Guiterre (Brayssing), 109
Quatre Pièces Brèves (Martin), 124
Quatrième Livre (Morlaye), 109
Queen, 423
Quine, Hector, 125
quintern, 22; *see also* guitar, four-course
Quintet for Guitar and Strings (Castelnuevo-Tedesco), 123

rabouquin, 286–7
Rachel, Yank, 293, 305
Rager, Mose, 320–1
Ragossnig, Konrad, 164
ragtime, 302–5, 312, 319, 329
Raimondi, Marcantonio, 24
Rainey, Ma, 296, 306, 391
Ramírez, José I, 57, 62–4, 66, 186
Ramírez, José II, 57, 65, 183, 186–7
Ramírez, José III, 57, 58, 64, *68*, 77, 80, 83, 87, *189*
Ramírez, Julián Gómez, 66
Ramírez, Manuel, 57, 62, *63*, 65, 69, 162, 183, 186
Ramos, Manuel López, 67
Raponi, O., *69*
rasgueado style, 26, 110–11, 125, 136, 217; in flamenco, 191–2, 193–4
Rawsthorne, Alan, 127
Recio, José, *50–1*
recording companies: blues, 296–7, 300–1, 306–7, 393; ragtime, 302–5; restrictions on, 310; rock'n'roll, 399–400; rock, 414
Recueil de pièces de guitare (LeCoq), 115
Recuerdos de la Alhambra (Tárrega), 122
redobles, 102
"Red River Blues," 298
Reed, Jimmy, 407
Regondi, Jules, 158
Reichel, Hans, 433
Reinhardt, Django, 127, 165, 222, 228, 232, 330, 331, 395, 429
religious music *see* sacred music
Renaissance music, 25, 129–35
Renbourn, John, 330, 331
requinto Vera Cruzana, 213
resonator guitar, (dobro), 224, *255–7*, *294*, *307*
restoration of early instruments, *27*, *29*
Resumen de acompañar la parte con la Guitara (Murcia), 115

Revue Musicale, 122
Reyes, Manuel, 57, 75, 183, *188*
Ricardo, Niño (Manuel Serrapí), *177*, 187, 192, *194*, 194–6, 200, 203–4
Richard, Cliff, 401
Richard, Keith, 407, *418*
Rich guitars, 254
Rickenbacher (Rickenbacker) Company, *250*, 340–1, *344*, 353, 362, 382, 388
Ricordi, House of, 156
Riders of the Purple Sage, 316
Rime of the Ancient Mariner (Bedford), 433
ritornello, 111
Ritter, Tex, 316
"Rizzio guitar," *26*
Roberts, Dave, *285*
Roberts, Howard, 390, *431*
Robertson, Robbie, *324*, 423, 425
Robinson, Fention, 416
"Rock Around the Clock," 399
rock music, 10, 406–14, 423, 427–30
Rock 'n' roll, 398–402
Rodgers, Jimmie, 314, *315*, 315–16, 319
Rodrigo, Joaquín, 123
Rodríguez, Francisco, *see* "El Murciano"
Rodríguez, Manuel, 57
Rogers, Roy, 316, 318
Rolling Stone, 421
Rolling Stones, 296, 406–7, *418*, *419*
romance, 105–6, *105*, *106*, 108
romanesca (Guárdame las Vacas), 106–7, 134
Romanillos, José, 57, 58, 71, 78; construction methods of, 88–101 *passim*
Romero, Rafael, 178, *201*, 204
Roncalli, Ludovico, 112
rondeña, 170, 173, 193, 206
Ronsard, 133
Rorer, Posey, 313
Rosas, Don Manuel de, 52
rosettes, 21, *29*, 40, 57; construction of, 80–1, *92*
rosewood, *28*, 37, 43, 49, 54; on classical guitars, 40, 61–2; Brazilian, 71, 73, 78, 90, 262; Indian, 71, 73, 78, 89, 262–3; on flamenco guitars, 181–3; in steel-string guitars, 228, 262–3, 268; in electric guitars, 377
Rossini, Gioacchino, 153
Rousseau, Jean-Jacques, 115
Roussel, Albert, 162
Rowbotham, James, 134
Rowe-DeArmond company, 234, 341, 366, 388
Rubio, David, 57–8, 78–9, 83–4
Rueda, Lope de, 131
Ruiz, Juan, 16

Ruiz de Ribayez, Don Lucas, 114
Rush, Otis, *416*, 416–17
Russia (Soviet Union, guitar in), 154–5, 162

"Sabicas" (Agustin Castellón), 178, *195*, 195–6, 198, 200, 204–5
sacred music, 101, 103–7, 129, 171–2, 308; *see also* spirituals
saddles: on early instruments, 42; diagram, 76; construction, 84–6, 96 (classical), 267 (steel string), 384, 386 (electric)
Sainz de la Maza, Regino, 123
samba, 10, 217
samisen, 12
Sánchez, Antón, *19*
Sanchez, Francisco, *see* Paco el Barbero
Sanguino, Francisco, 43
Sanlúcar, Manolo, 183, 196, 204
Sanseverino, Benedetto, *111*, 136
Santa Cruz, Don Antonio de, 113, *114*
Santana, Carlos, 360, 427, *428*
Santos, Ignacio de los, *45*
Santos, Turibio, 67
Sanz, Gaspar, 25, 35, *114*, 114–15, 123, 143, 166
saraband (zarabanda), 111, 114, 140, 212
scales: Pythagorean, 17; even-tempered, 17, 85–6; diatonic, 171
scale lengths: vihuela, 21; five-course guitar, 35; standardized, 57, 60, 85; in flamenco, 171–2, on steel string guitars, 267
Scarlatti, Domenico, 124, 148, 166
Schaller tuning machines, *see* tuning machines
Schatz, Henry, 51
Scheit, Karl, 164
Schneider, Richard, 58, *70–1*, 84, 254, 264, 265
Schoenberg, Arnold, 124
Schubert, Franz, 123, 157
Schultz, Arnold, 319–20
Schulz, Leonard, 119
Schumann, Robert, 122, 161
Schuppen, Jacob van, 138
scordatura, 25, 112
Scott, James, 313
Scruggs, Earl, 320, *332*
Sears Roebuck catalogue, *287*, 287, 288, 313, 317
Second Livre (LeRoy), 109
Second Livre (Morlaye), 109
Second Partita in D Minor (Bach), 122
Seeger, Pete, 322
"See See Rider," 297
Segovia, Andrés, 64, 66, 69, 122, *123*, 124, 162–6, *163*; and flamenco, 170; and electric guitars, 352
Segovia (Roussel), 162
Seguidillas, 149, 174, 214
seguiriyas, 170, 174, 176, 194, 204–5

Sellas, Giorgio, *31*, 33, 143
Sellas, Giovanni, *33*
Sellas, Matteo, *30*, *31*, 33
Sellas, Michael, *33*
Selmer Company, 163, 222, *227*, *232*, *330*; Eddie Freeman Special, *232*
Sensier, Peter, 21, *39*
"Serranito" (Victor Monge), 196, *197*, 197–8
Serrano, José, *54*
Serrano, Juan, 197–8, *198*
Serrapí, Manuel, *see* Ricardo, Niño
session musicians, 167, 403, 427
Seventh Symphony (Mahler), 167
Seville, lutherie at, 40, 43, 45, 54, 56
sevillanas, *179*
Shadows, 401
Shakespeare, William, 131, 133
Shearing, George, 390
Shepherd Carillo his Song (romanesca), 106
Shines, Johnny, 296, *309*, 309–10, 334
sides: diagram, 76; construction, 77–80 (classical), 263, 265, *275–6* (steel string)
Sigma Company (Japan), 224
Silva de Sirenas (Valderrábano), *103*, 105
Simon, Paul, 253, 330
Simplicio, Francisco, 57, *64*
Simpson, Martin, *333*
sitar, 12, 366
"Sixteen Tons," 321
skiffle, 407
slaves and slavery, 211–12, 286–7, *288*, 289, *290*, 298, 311
slide playing, 291
slipper foot, 39, 40, 43, 48
Smit, Giovanni, 22, *31*
Smith-Brindle, Reginald, 127
Smith, Bessie, 296
Smith, Johnny, 390, 403
Smith, Mamie, 296
Snow, Hank, 316
Sojo, Vicente Emilio, 123, 215
soleares, 170, 174, 176, 194, 204–5
Sombrero de Tres Picos, El (Falla), 122
Somerset, Lady John, 158
Sonata Romantica (Ponce), 123
Sonatina (Berkeley), 127
Sonatina (Turina), 122
Sonatina Meriodional (Ponce), 124, 164
Songs from the Chinese (Britten), 125
Sor, Fernando, 51, 117–18, *119*, 119–21, 152–3, 155–6, 215
Sotos, Andrés de, 148
soundboard (top, table): on early instruments, 24, 41–2; diagram, 76; construction, 77, 79–84, *92*, *94* (classical),

220–1, 263–6, *269–75* (steel string), 373–4 (electric)
soundhole, 42, 49, 228; decoration, 40, 263, *270*; diagram, 76; construction, 93 (classical), 263–4, *270* (steel string)
South America, *see* Latin America
Spain: history of guitar in, 12, 16, 24, 39, 40–1, 45, 130–1, 136, 143, 147, 154; guitar styles in, *37, 39*; luthiers in, 57, 79; music from 101–7, 108, 111–16; *see also* flamenco
"Special Rider Blues," 296
spirituals, 289–90, 300
spruce, 17, 28, 32, 34, 38, 46, 48, 52, 64–5, 70, 228; Alpine, 77, *89, 92*, 262; Sitka, 77, 262; sawing of, 268
"Stackerlee," 291
Stackhouse, Houston, 392
Stadler, Jacob, *31, 39*
Stadlman, Michael, 42
Stafford, Jo, 396
Stanley Brothers, 321
Starr, Kay, 396
Star's End (Bedford), 433–4
"Star Spangled Banner," 422
Stathopoulo, Epi, 224; *see also* Epiphone
Staufer, Johan Georg, 42, 49, 51, 156, 222, 235, 238
steel-bodied guitars, *255*, 307
steel string acoustic guitar, 10, 13, 42, 55; development of, 220–4; examples of, 225–60 *passim*; construction of 222–4, 260–85 *passim*; 263–5, *268–80* (body construction), 266–7, 280–3 (neck construction), 267, 283–5 (assembly and finishing); music for, *see* blues, country, folk, etc.
Stella guitars, 223, *245, 258, 298, 303*
stereo, wiring on guitars, 342, 354, 355, 361, 367
Stills, Stephen, 332, 423
Stimmer, Tobias, 22
Stradivari, Antonio, *34–5*, 56, 77, 100
Stravinsky, Igor, 124
stringed instruments: primitive, *10*, 11; Egyptian, *11*, 12; Greek, *11*, 11; Roman, 12
strings, types of: wire, 25; gut, 41–2, 55, 58–9, 220, 221; steel, 10, 42, 55, 220, 260, 359; nylon, 10, 58–9, 220, 359; silk floss and metal, 58–9, 221; strength of, 78, 102; loop and ball ended, 228; Thomastik, 237; on electric guitars, 338; sympathetic, 366–7, 385; ferrous-based, 388
Stromberg, Charles, 222, *233–4*
strutting (bracing): fan, 21–2, 39, 40–5, 48, 55, 73, 236; Torres and, 56–7, 60–2, *81*; transverse, 37, 40–1, 48, 53, 76; X-pattern, 55, 222, 236, 264; Double-X, 264, *271*; unusual variations, 64, 66–7, 70–1, *82–3*; diagram, 76; construction, 79, 81–3, *93* (classical), 181–3 (flamenco), 220, 263–5, *270–4* (steel string), 373–4 (electric); scientific methods of, 83–4
Students for a Democratic Society (SDS), 323
Stuff, 427
style: finger or nail controversy, 102, 120; strummed (*rasgueado*), 26, 110–12, 114–15, 131, 143; *punteado*, 112,

114–15
Suite Antique (Ponce), 123
Suite Castellano (Torroba), 122
suite form, 108, 111–12, 113
Summerfield, Maurice, 228
Sunnyland Slim, 296
superhumbucking, 342, 343fn., 381–2, 384; *see also* humbucking
Sweet Baby James, 331
sycamore, 35; *see also* maple

tablaos flamencos, 178–9
Tablatura de Vihuela, 211
tablature, 17, 102–3, 108, 112, 114–15, 171; *see also* notation
table, *see* soundboard
tailpieces, 220–1 (steel string), 348, 350, 384–5, 386 (electric)
Taj Mahal, 334
Tallis, Thomas, 129
"Tampa Red," 306, 309
Tanner, Gid (and his Skillet Lickers), 313, *314*, 325
Tansman, Alexander, 123
tarantas, 204, 206–7
Tarlton, Jimmie, 319
Tárrega Eixea, Francisco, 56, 61, 122, 158, *161*, 161, 162, 193
Taunay, Nicolas Antoine, *152*
Tavares, Leo, 349
Taylor, James, 331, *332*, 423
Taylor, Mick, 419
technique, 102, 114, 117, 120; playing position, *119*, 119, *120*, 120; modern, 122; in flamenco, 191–2, 193, 199; in blues, 292, 299–300, 310; for electric guitar, 415; *see also* distortion, style
Telemaco on the Island of Calipso (Sor), 153
Ten Years After, 421
"Terraplane Blues," 295
Terry, Sonny, 307, *308, 325*, 325, 407
Tessler, Giovanni, *28*
"Texas Alexander," 301
Texas blues, 298–301
theaters: music for, 114–15, 137, 149; strolling players, 136–7; flamenco in, 176–8; in Latin America, 212
Thème Varié et finale (Ponce), 124
Theodorakis, Mikis, 166
theorbo, 113, 144
"This land is Your Land," 315
Thomas, John, 296
Thomas, Ramblin', 291
"Thomastik" strings, 237
Thompson, Dr. Donald. 264
Thompson, T. Perronet, 50
Three Musicians (Picasso), *167*
Tielke, Joachim, *36, 37*, 139, 143

tientos, 104, 199
Tieffenbrucker, *see* Duyffoprucgar, Gaspard
Tillman, Floyd, 395
timber, *see* wood
Tinctoris, Johannes, 131
tiple, *214*, 243
Tippett, Sir Michael, 432
tone projector, 61, 83
tonos, 114
Tony Williams' Lifetime, 429
top, *see* soundboard
toque, 170, 179, 191, 193, 196–7, 202–7
Torre, Manuel, 176, 178
Torres Jurado, Antonio de, 42, 44, 54, 55, 83, 122, 241;
    biography, 56–7, 85; guitars by, *60–2*; compared to other
    luthiers, 62, 63, 65–6, 88, 93, 99; and flamenco guitars,
    181–2, 183, *184*, 185
Torroba, Federico Moreno, 122
tortoiseshell, *23, 32, 35; see also* descriptions of individual
    guitars.
Townsend, Henry, 295
Townshend, Pete, 401, 408–11, 412, *413*, 421
Travis, Merle, *320*, 320–1, *332*, 341, 345, 395, 405
Treatise on Modern Instrumentation and Orchestration (Berlioz),
    118
Trent, Alphonso, 389
tres, 212
Tres Libros de Música en cifra para vihuela (Mudarra), 104,
    107
Triana, Fernando el de, 195
Triana, Gordito de, *194*
Trichet, Pierre, 136
tripodion, 120
Tristano, Lennie, 390
Trotto, Gioacchino, *47*
Troysieme Livre . . . mis en tablature de Guiterne (Gorlier), 108
truss rod, adjustable, 226, 229, 233, 250, 266; on electric
    models, 348, 376
Tubb, Ernest, 316, 395
Tubular Bells, 433
tuning, methods of, 24–6, 31, 40, 136; vihuela, 102; four-
    course guitar, 107–8; of enharmonic guitar, 50; flamenco,
    63; of five-course guitar, 110, 112; *scordatura*, 112; in the
    blues, 292–3
tuning machines, 41–2, 49, 52, 54; Baker, 48; unusual, 66;
    Schaller, 71, 228, 251, 267, *285*, 349; diagram, 76;
    construction of, 85, 87, *99*; for flamenco guitars, 182;
    for steel string guitars, 222, 228; Grover Rotomatic, 228,
    251, 267, 385, 386; Kluson, 234, 348, 349, 362, 385;
    planetary gear, 235; on electric guitars, 384–5
Turina, Joaquin, 122
Turner, Ike, 393

Twelve Preludes (Ponce), 124
twelve-string guitars, 224, 252, *258–9*, *298*, 299, 302–4;
    electric, 362

United States (America), 155, 162; guitar styles in, 42, 51, 55;
    classical luthiers in, 57; flamenco in, 177–8, 195, 198; steel
    string guitar manufacture, 220, 260–85 *passim*; electric
    guitar manufacture, 343, 368–87 *passim; see also* types of
    American music, i.e., blues, country, folk
univibe, 342, 409
ukuleles, plastic, 235

Valderrábano, Enriquez de, *103*, 105–6, 131
Valle, Pedro de, *see* Perico el de Lunar
van der Staak, Pieter, 62
Vannes (!luthier), 51
Van Ronk, Dave, 323, 329
Variations (Fisher), 149
Variations (opus 71, Castelnuovo-Tedesco), 123
Variations on a Theme by Mozart (Sor), 118, 122
Variations sur Folia de Espana et Fugue (Ponce), 122
Vásquez, Juan, 105, 108
Vega, Lope de, 131
Vega company, *231*
Velásquez, Manuel, 57
Veleno, John, *360*, 371
veneer, 25, 28, *32, 35, 36, 38; see also* descriptions of
    individual guitars
Ventures, 401
Verdelot, Philippe, 105
Vergara, Juan Nicolas de, 130
Vermeer, Jan, *142*
Verney, Sir Ralph and family, 139
vibrola arms, 345, 350–1, 355, 402, 408–9
Vida del escudero Marcos de Obregon, La (Espinel), 132
Vienna, guitars in, 42, 118, 154–5, 157, 164
vihuela: history of, 16–17, 24, *130*, 130–1, 134, 136, 161, 210;
    shapes of, 16–17; types of, 18, *20, 21*; obsolete, 18; replicas,
    21, 72; music for, 101–7, 111, *114*; social status of, 102
Vihuelita, 212
Villa-Lobos, Heitor, 10, 123, 124, 166, 215
villancico (villanesca), 105, 108, 131
Vinaccia: Antonio I, 47; Antonio II, 47; Vicenzo, 47
viola, 16, *20*
violao, 212
violins, 12, 131, 221; *see also* Stradivari
Visée, Robert de, 26, 112–13, 115, 141, 143, 166
Vivi-Tone company, 338
Voboam: Alexandre, 32, *33*, 137; Jean, *26*, 31, 33, *34*, 137;
    René, *32*, 137; family, 137, 138, 143
Voices (Henze), 126
Vomáčka, Sammy, 258

von Call, Leonard, 118
vuelta, la, 105
Vuillaume, J. B., 48

wah-wah pedal, 342, 408, 409
waist, 16; diagram, 76
Wakeley, Jimmy, 316
Walker, Jerry Jeff, 332, 334
Walker, T-Bone, *391*, 391, 393, 395
Walker, Tim, 69, 124, 126, 167
walking basses, 297–301, 304, 394; *see also* boogie-woogie
Walton, William, 127, 165
Washburn Company, 223, *241*
Watson, Arthel "Doc," 250, 321, *325*, 325, 332
Watson, Eugene, 254
Watson, Johnny, *see* "Daddy Stovepipe"
Watteau, Antoine, 33, 144, *145*
Watts, Charlie, 407
Weaver, Curly, 302
Webern, Anton von, 124, 167
We Come to the River (Henze), 126
Wechter, Abraham, 366
Weiss, Leopold, 123–4
Weisseborn, H., *242*
Wellington, Duke of, 158
West, William Edward, 286
"western swing," 319, 388–9, 395
whine (bending, whamming), 292
White, "Bukka," *307*, 307, *327*, 328, 395, 415
White, Josh, 308, 321, 326, 407
Whiteman, Paul, 233
Whitley, Ray, 248, 249, 316
Whittaker, Hudson, *see* "Tampa Red"
Who, The, 401, *409*, 409, *410*, 411–12, 423
Whytehorne, Thomas, 134
"Wildwood Flower," 315

Willaert, Adriaan, 105
Williams, Big Joe, 307, 328
Williams, Bill, 310
Williams, Henry, 302
Williams, John, 67, 124, *125*, *165*, 165, 166, 199, 215
Williams, Tony, 429
Williamson, Sonny Boy, 392, 394–5, 407
Wills, Bob (and his Texas Playboys), 388
Wilson, Willie, 293–4
Winter, Johnny, *420*, 421
Wood, Austin, 249
Wood, Ronnie, *419*
Woodlieff, Norman, 313
woods used in guitar making, 17, 46, 73, 75, 181–2, 187, 242; qualities of various types, 77–8, 89–90, 242, 254, 262–3; in electric guitars, 368–71; *see also* types of wood, ebony, rosewood, spruce, etc.
Woodstock Festival, 421
work songs, 289, 298, 302
Wray, Link, 401
"Wreck on the Highway," 319
Wurlitzer company, 243

Yamaha guitars, *365*, 375, 376
Yardbirds, 407, 412
Yepes, Narciso, 164, *165*
yodeling, 314
You Asked for it (Bedford), 126
Young, Neil, 331–2

zapateado, 170
Zappa, Frank, *414*, 414
zarabanda, see saraband
Zincali, The (Borrow), 173
Ziryab of Baghdad, 172
Zuloaga, Ignacio, 176

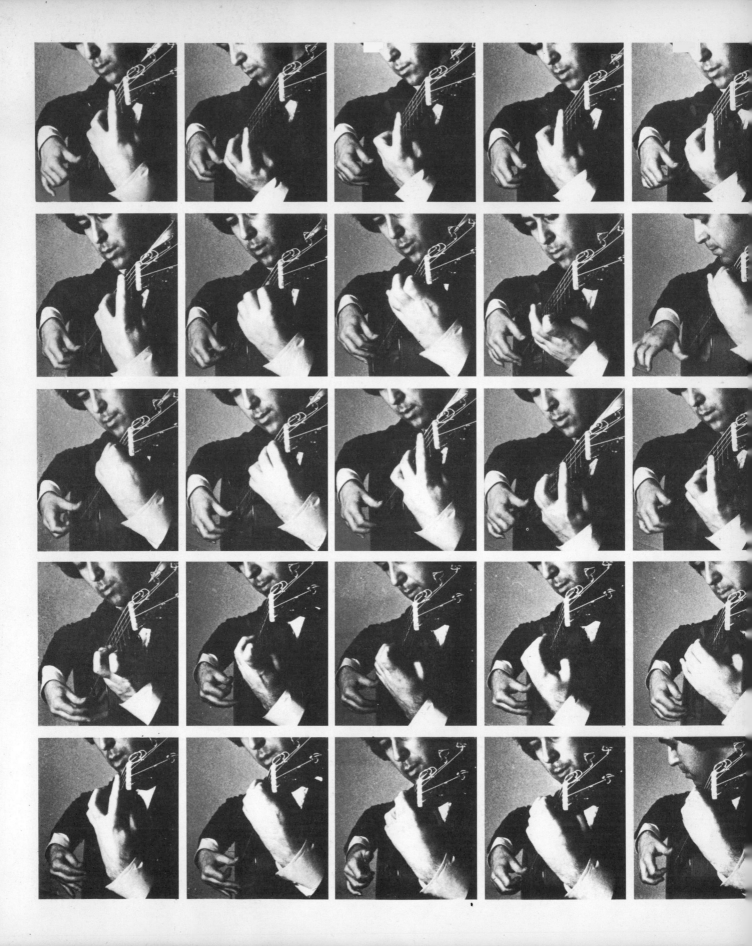